Lecture Notes in Computer Science 4017

Commenced Publication in 1973
Founding and Former Series Editors:
Gerhard Goos, Juris Hartmanis, and Jan van Leeuwen

Stamatis Vassiliadis   Stephan Wong
Timo D. Hämäläinen (Eds.)

Embedded Computer Systems: Architectures, Modeling, and Simulation

6th International Workshop, SAMOS 2006
Samos, Greece, July 17-20, 2006
Proceedings

 Springer

Volume Editors

Stamatis Vassiliadis
Stephan Wong
Delft University of Technology
Mekelweg 4, 2628 CD Delft, The Netherlands
E-mail: {s.vassiliadis, j.s.s.m.wong}@ewi.tudelft.nl

Timo D. Hämäläinen
Tampere University of Technology
P.O. Box 553, 33101 Tampere, Finland
E-mail: timo.d.hamalainen@tut.fi

Library of Congress Control Number: 2006928741

CR Subject Classification (1998): C, B

LNCS Sublibrary: SL 1 – Theoretical Computer Science and General Issues

ISSN	0302-9743
ISBN-10	3-540-36410-2 Springer Berlin Heidelberg New York
ISBN-13	978-3-540-36410-8 Springer Berlin Heidelberg New York

Springer is a part of Springer Science+Business Media

springer.com

© Springer-Verlag Berlin Heidelberg 2006

Typesetting: Camera-ready by author, data conversion by Scientific Publishing Services, Chennai, India
Printed on acid-free paper   SPIN: 11796435   06/3142   5 4 3 2 1 0

Preface

The SAMOS workshop is an international gathering of highly qualified researchers from academia and industry, sharing ideas in a 3-day lively discussion on the quiet and inspiring northern mountainside of the Mediterranean island of Samos. The workshop meeting is one of two colocated events (the other event being the IC-SAMOS). As a tradition, the workshop features presentations in the morning, while after lunch all kinds of informal discussions and nut-cracking gatherings take place. The workshop is unique in the sense that not only solved research problems are presented and discussed but also (partly) unsolved problems and in-depth topical reviews can be unleashed in the scientific arena. Consequently, the workshop provides the participants with an environment where collaboration rather than competition is fostered.

SAMOS VI follows the series of workshops started in 2001 in a new expanded program. This year there were also two parallel sessions for current and foreseen topics. The SAMOS VI workshop and IC-SAMOS attracted a total of 130 papers and 12 invited papers on special topics. We are grateful to all authors who submitted papers. The papers came from 27 countries and regions: Austria(3), Bangladesh(1), Belgium(4), Brazil(4), Canada(4), China(6), Taiwan(1), Czech Republic(6), Finland(17), France(3), Germany(14), Greece(8), Hong Kong(1), India(6), Iran(3), Italy(4), Japan(1), Mexico(1), Republic of Korea(13), Republic of Singapore(1), Romania(1), Spain(11), Sweden(1), The Netherlands(15), Tunisia(1), UK(3), and USA(9).

The papers went through a rigorous reviewing process and each paper received at least three individual reviews, with an average of four reviews. Due to time constraints in the workshop program and the high quality of the submitted papers, the selection process was very competitive and many qualified papers could not be accepted. The program also included two keynote speeches by Jinsung Choi from LG Electronics and by Panagiotis Tsarchopoulos from the European Commission.

A workshop like this cannot be organized without the help of many other people. Therefore, we thank the members of the Steering and Program Committees and the external referees for their dedication and diligence in selecting the technical presentations. The investment of their time and insight is very much appreciated. We would like to express our sincere gratitude to Carlo Galuzzi for maintaining the website and paper submission system and preparing the workshop proceedings. We thank Lidwina Tromp for her support in organizing the workshop.

We hope that the attendees enjoyed the SAMOS VI workshop in all its aspects, including many informal discussions and gatherings.

June 2006

Stamatis Vassiliadis
Stephan Wong
Timo D. Hämäläinen

Organization

The SAMOS VI workshop took place during July 17 − 20, 2006 at the Research and Teaching Institute of East Aegean (INEAG) in Agios Konstantinos on the island of Samos, Greece.

Workshop Chairs

Stamatis Vassiliadis   Delft University of Technology, The Netherlands
Stephan Wong   Delft University of Technology, The Netherlands

Program Chair

Timo D. Hämäläinen   Tampere University of Technology, Finland

Proceedings Chair

Carlo Galuzzi   Delft University of Technology, The Netherlands

Publicity and Financial Chair

Stephan Wong   Delft University of Technology, The Netherlands

Steering Committee

Shuvra Bhattacharyya   University of Maryland, USA
Ed Deprettere   Leiden University, The Netherlands
Andy Pimentel   University of Amsterdam, The Netherlands
Patrice Quinton   IRISA, France
Jarmo Takala   Tampere University of Technology, Finland
Jürgen Teich   University of Erlangen-Nuremberg, Germany
Stamatis Vassiliadis   Delft University of Technology, The Netherlands

Program Committee

Piergiovanni Bazzana   ATMEL, Italy
Koen Bertels   Delft University of Technology, The Netherlands
Holger Blume   RWTH Aachen University, Germany

Geoffrey Brown	Indiana University, USA
João M. P. Cardoso	University of Algarve, Portugal
Luigi Carro	Universidade Federal do Rio Grande do Sul, Brazil
Vassilios V. Dimakopoulos	University of Ioannia, Greece
Nikitas Dimopoulos	University of Victoria, Canada
Pedro Diniz	University of Southern California, USA
Nikil Dutt	University of California Irvine, USA
Paraskevas Evripidou	University of Cyprus, Cyprus
Fabrizio Ferrandi	Politecnico di Milano, Italy
Gerhard Fettweis	Technische Universität Dresden, Germany
Manfred Glesner	Technische Universität Darmstadt, Germany
David Guevorkian	Nokia Research Center, Finland
Timo D. Hämäläinen	Tampere University of Technology, Finland
Fadi J. Kurdahi	University of California Irvine, USA
Johan Lilius	Ado Akademi University, Finland
Wayne Luk	Imperial College London, UK
Walid Najjar	University of California Riverside, USA
Sule Ozev	Duke University, USA
Dionisios N. Pnevmatikatos	Technical University of Crete, Greece
Bernard Pottier	Université de Bretagne Occidentale, France
Tanguy Risset	IRISA/INRIA, France
Suleyman Sair	North Carolina State University, USA
Michael Schulte	University of Wisconsin-Madison, USA
Olli Silven	University of Oulu, Finland
Leonel Sousa	TU Lisbon, Portugal
Dirk Stroobandt	Ghent University, Belgium
Sriram Sundararajan	Moxair, USA
Won Yong Sung	Seoul National University, Korea
Serge Vernalde	IMEC, Belgium
Jens Peter Wittenburg	Thomson Corporate Research, Germany

Local Organizers

Lidwina Tromp	Delft University of Technology, The Netherlands
Karin Vassiliadis	Delft University of Technology, The Netherlands
Yiasmin Kioulafa	Research and Training Institute of East Aegean, Greece

Referees

Aho, E.
Al-Ars, Z.
Bazzana, P.
Bertels, K.
Betul Buyukkurt, A.
Blume, H.
Brown, A.
Brown, G.
Calderon, H.
Cardoso, J.
Carro, L.
Chang, Z.
Chaves, R.
Christiaens, M.
Cope, B.
de Andrés, D.
de Langen, P.
Deprettere, E.
Devos, H.
D'Haene, M.
Dias, T.
Dimakopoulos, V.
Dimopoulos, N.
Diniz, P.
Duarte, F.
Dutt, N.
Eeckhout, L.
Erbas, C.
Evripidou, P.
Faes, P.
Falk, J.
Ferrandi, F.
Fettweis, G.
Flich, J.
Gädke, K.
Galuzzi, C.
Gaydadjiev, G
Germano, J.
Glesner, M.
Glossner, J.
Gordon-Ross, A.
Guevorkian, D.
Guntoro, A.

Guo, Z.
Hamalainen, T.
Haubelt, C.
Heikkinen, J.
Heirman, W.
Hinkelmann, H.
Hounta, A. E.
Jääskeläinen, P.
Jachalsky, J.
Janes, D.
Jenkins, C.
Kachris, C.
Kangas, T.
Kaxiras, S.
Keinert, J.
Koch, D.
Kohvakka, M.
Kropp, H.
Kulmala, A.
Kuorilehto, M.
Kurdahi, F.
Kuzmanov, G.
Kyriacou, C.
Lafond, S.
Lahtinen, V.
Langerwerf, J. M.
Lappalainen, V.
Lilius, J.
Lopez, P.
Lotfi Mhamdi
Luk, W.
Majer, M.
Mak, T.
Mäkelä, R.
Manzoni, P.
Matus, E.
Meenderinck, C.
Mladen, B.
Momcilovic, S.
Morel, L.
Moscu Panainte, E.
Najjar, W.
Oliver, J.

Orsila, H.
Ozev, S.
Palermo, G.
Papaefstathiou, I.
Paya Vaya, G.
Petit, S.
Petoumenos, P.
Pieper, S.
Pimentel, A.
Pitkänen, T.
Plosila, J.
Pnevmatikatos, D.
Polstra, S.
Porres, I.
Pottier, B.
Pourebrahimi, B.
Quinton, P.
Risset, T.
Rodas, A.
Sahuquillo, J.
Sair, S.
Salminen, E.
Snchez, M.
Santambrogio, M. D.
Santonja, V.
Schlichter, T.
Sculte, M.
Sedcole, P.
Shahbahrami, A
Silla, F.
Silven, O.
Smailbegovic, F.
Soares Indrusiak, l.
Soffke, O.
Sourdis, I.
Sousa, L.
Stitt, G.
Stoyanova, T.
Streichert, T.
Streubhr, M.
Stroobandt, D.
Strydis, C.
Sundararajan, S.

Table of Contents

Wireless Sensor Networks

Processor Design

Dependable Computing

Architectures and Implementations

Embedded Sensor Systems

Reconfigurable Platform for Digital Convergence Terminals

Jinsung Choi

Senior Vice President and Head of Mobile Communication Technology
Research Lab LG Electronics

Abstract. It is apparent that future IT terminals including handsets
will be multi-mode convergence devices. Therefore it becomes more and
more important to be able to devise a low-power platform which is
flexible enough to implement multiple different basebands on top of it.
Moreover, real time reconfigurability is crucial considering the fact that
technologies keep evolving and over the air software/firmware upgrade
is being required. In this paper, a new type of reconfigurable platform
will be discussed and we see how it help end user device manufacturer
deliver better multi-mode terminals with better maintenance scheme.

S. Vassiliadis et al. (Eds.): SAMOS 2006, LNCS 4017, p. 1, 2006.
© Springer-Verlag Berlin Heidelberg 2006

European Research in Embedded Systems*

Panagiotis Tsarchopoulos

Embedded Systems Unit, European Commission

Digital information technology has revolutionized the world within less than four decades. It has taken the step from mainframe computers, mainly operated as hosts in computing centres, to desktops and laptops, connected by networks and found nearly on all office desks and tables today. Computers have become every day tools deeply integrated into all kinds of activities of our life.

More remarkable, however, is the less visible revolution where digital technology is increasingly embedded in all kinds of equipment and systems to provide new functionalities and improved operation at low cost. Embedded computers are now found in nearly all technical devices: in simple everyday home appliances; in facilities and facility management such as heating, air conditioning, elevators and escalators; in production units from robotics to production automation and control systems; in medicine where equipment for diagnostics and medical support is enhanced by computers and in the increasing variety of intelligent devices that are implanted into the human body. Remarkable is also the rapid proliferation of embedded systems in transportation, be it cars, trucks, ships, trains or airplanes.

Already 90% of all computing devices are in embedded and not desktop systems. The growth rate exceeds 10% per annum in all application sectors and there are forecast to be over 40 billion embedded chips worldwide by 2020. In terms of market value, for example, the Semiconductor Industry Association estimates that in 2006 the automotive sector alone will account for almost 8% of the world semiconductor market (the world semiconductor market is forecasted at approximately 200 billion in 2006). Even more striking is the growing share of the value of the final product that is due to embedded systems: 20% of the value of each car today is due to embedded electronics and this is expected to increase to 36% in 2009. In the same year, 22% of the value of industrial automation systems, 41% of consumer electronics and 33% of medical equipment will be due to embedded electronics and software.

Embedded systems have evolved from the simple stand-alone and single-processor computers of the eighties and early nineties, to the sophisticated multi-processor systems with increasing communication capacities of today. This evolution is driven by the constant need to bring to the users innovative products and services with increasing functionality at ever diminishing price. It alsoresults in significant technological, research and educational challenges. To face these challenges, European industry alone is expected to invest more than 22 billion

---

* The views expressed are those of the author and do not necessarily represent the official view of the European Commission on the subject.

S. Vassiliadis et al. (Eds.): SAMOS 2006, LNCS 4017, pp. 2–4, 2006.

euro in embedded systems research and development in 2009[1], a large increase from the 12 billion it invested in 2003.

These challenges, combined with the importance of the field for key sectors of European industry, from industrial automation and medical equipment to automotive and avionics, led the European Commission to devote a specific part of its IST Programme to embedded systems research. In the last three years that this programme is in operation, it has invested €140 million in collaborative projects between industry, academia and research centres, largely in the areas of systems design, safety-critical systems, embedded computing, middleware platforms, wireless sensor networks and distributed and hybrid control systems. Embedded systems are also one of the six *pillars* of ICT research in the European Commission's proposals for the 7th Framework Programme that is due to start in 2007.

Another important development is the set up of the Technology Platform ARTEMIS - *Advanced Research & Technology for Embedded Intelligence and Systems* in 2004. ARTEMIS is an industry-led initiative to reinforce the position of the EU as a leading worldwide player in the design, integration and supply of embedded systems. After it produced a 2004 manifesto called *Building ARTEMIS* that was signed by 20 executives of EU companies, it set out to establish and implement a coherent and integrated European strategy for Embedded Systems that covers all aspects - from research and development priorities to the research infrastructures needed, the standardisation policy, the educational curricula etc. In March 2006, this strategy was published as the ARTEMIS *Strategic Research Agenda*. While ARTEMIS seeks maximum commonality across application sectors, it is recognised that different application domains impose differing demands on the technology to be developed. ARTEMIS has therefore identified a number of representative *Application Contexts* in which: sets of applications can share common domain expertise, design characteristics and requirements so that they can, in turn, share methods, tools, technologies and skills; the domains have a large market value and are of sufficient strategic importance to Europe to justify the investment in a shared research agenda. These Application Contexts are:

- *Industrial systems* - large, complex and safety critical systems, that embraces Automotive, Aerospace, Manufacturing, and growth areas such as biomedical.
- *Nomadic Environments* - enabling portable devices and on-body systems to offer users access to information and services while on the move.
- *Private Spaces,* - such as homes, cars and offices, that offers systems and solutions for improved enjoyment, comfort, well-being and safety.
- *Public Infrastructure* - major infrastructure such as airports, cities and highways that embrace large scale deployment of systems and services.

---

[1] FAST Study on *Worldwide Trends and R&D Programmes in Embedded Systems in view of maximising the impact of a Technology Platform in the area*, 2005.

The ARTEMIS strategy is to establish common technology to support the development of high value-added Embedded Systems across these application contexts. The common technology will include:

- Reference designs that offer standard architectural approaches for a range of applications to address the complexity challenge and build synergies between market sectors.
- Middleware that enables seamless connectivity and wide-scale interoperability to support novel functionality, new services and build the ambient intelligent environment.
- Systems design methodologies and associated tools for rapid design and development.
- Generic enabling technologies derived from foundational science.

The overall target of European research in this area is to create an environment that favours and supports innovation in embedded systems and to focus the $R\&D$ resources on common and ambitious objectives. Rapid progress in that direction over the last years provides a lot of confidence that this will indeed be the case and that this collective effort will be successful.

Interface Overheads in Embedded Multimedia Software

Tero Rintaluoma[1], Olli Silven[2], and Juuso Raekallio[1]

[1] Hantro Products Oy, Oulu, Finland
{Tero.Rintaluoma, Juuso.Raekallio}@hantro.com
[2] Department of Electrical and Information Engineering, University of Oulu, Finland
Olli.Silven@ee.oulu.fi

Abstract. The multimedia capabilities in battery powered mobile communication devices should be provided at high energy efficiency. Consequently, the hardware is usually implemented using low-power technology and the hardware architectures are optimized for embedded computing. Software architectures, on the other hand, are not embedded system specific, but closely resemble each other for any computing device. The popular architectural principle, software layering, is responsible for much of the overheads, and explains the stagnation of active usage times of mobile devices. In this paper, we consider the observed developments against the needs of multimedia applications in mobile communication devices and quantify the overheads in reference implementations.

1 Introduction

Current high-end mobile communication devices integrate wireless wide band data modems, video cameras, net browsers, and phones into small software controlled packages. The small size of the devices is a design constraint as the sustained heat dissipation should be kept low, and long untethered active usage times should be provided [1]. Their software systems must satisfy a multitude of requirements, resulting in a complex software solution that can only be implemented via concerted action of experts.

To facilitate this task most mobile communication device manufacturers have created common platforms for their product families and define application programming interfaces that remain the same across products, regardless of system enhancements and changes in hardware/software partitioning, including the number of processors used. Obviously, the software architectures and the components used need to be generic and reusable, but it is at the cost of efficiency. Consequently, middleware is widely applied in these systems as a key challenge is to enable uncomplicated integration of hardware and software components to the defined platform.

An exhibit of the undesired side-effects of this development is the stagnation of the talk-times of the mobile phones to around the 3h level, although the basic application has not changed in an essential manner [2]. The reasons have been traced to increased software architecture and interface overheads. In multimedia applications the overheads can be expected to be even more significant due to the need to support numerous standards, such as JPEG, H.264, MPEG-4 and VC-1, in the same execution environment. To provide control over these alternatives, more software layers are needed on top of them, adding to the number of instructions to be executed. The number of instructions executed matters, because the relative energy per instruction of embedded processor

S. Vassiliadis et al. (Eds.): SAMOS 2006, LNCS 4017, pp. 5–14, 2006.

Table 1. Energy efficiencies and silicon areas of ARM processors [3]

Processor	Max. clock frequency (MHz)	Power consumption (mW/MHz)	Silicon area (mm2)
ARM7 (720T)	100	0.2	2.4
ARM9 (926EJ-S)	266	0.45	4.5
ARM10 (1022E)	325	0.6	6.9
ARM11 (1136J-S)	550	0.8	5.55

Table 2. Cycle and instruction counts of software based MPEG-4 decoders end encoders (VGA 30frames/s, 512kbit/s)

Processor	Core/Bus CLK	decoder		encoder	
		MIPS	Mcycles/s	MIPS	Mcycles/s
ARM7 (720T)	2/1	129,7	303.9	646,8	1446,3
ARM9 (926EJ-S)	2/1	129,2	211,9	638,2	948,5
ARM10 (1022E)	3/1	129,2	151,5	638,2	722,9
ARM11 (1136J-S)	3/1	99,2	147,3	570,6	740,1

architectures has grown during the last few years. Table 1 shows the characteristics of ARM processors implemented using a 130nm CMOS process. Obviously, the advances at silicon level have been swallowed by the solutions that enable higher clock rates.

In Table 2 we illuminate the impact of architectural improvements at application level by comparing the instruction and cycle counts of software based MPEG-4 decoders. The results come from simulations made using the RVDS 2.2 tool [4] and assuming 0-wait-state memory accesses. The results for ARM11 are not completely cycle accurate. We notice that the number of instructions to be fetched and executed is slightly reduced between ARM7 and ARM10, indicating moderate instruction set improvements. Clearly, the real performance increases have come from higher clock rates.

Consequently, a multiprocessor based on lower performance processors could be more energy efficient than a single processor solution. However, larger silicon area adds to the cost, and the accompanied increasing leakage currents add to static energy consumption. We may also ask, whether a multiprocessor solution with middleware is really more energy efficient than a conceptually simpler single processor system.

Multitasking, APIs and middleware have big impacts on system performance due to cache effects and the execution of instructions needed by the interface mechanisms. Based on overhead measurements by Mogul and Borg [5] in 1991 and Sebek [6] in 2002 the context switch latencies appear to have remained the same for more than a decade despite processors becoming much faster. This is explained by the low cache hit ratios during the context switches.

Park et al (2004) measured the operating system effects on the performance of a MPEG-4 codec run as a single task on an ARM926 processor with embedded Linux. With this operating system the encoder run 20% and the decoder 27% slower [7]. Again, the cache effects were pinpointed as the key reason for the slowdown. Using a Linux platform, Verhoeven et al (2001) found that the performance of different middleware solutions varied between 260 and 7500 calls per second [8].

Based on our findings presented in the following, middleware layers in embedded system software may increase the overheads in a very significant manner. A contributing factor is the constantly increasing number of abstraction layers between software platform generations. As a result, monolithic hardware accelerators even in computing intensive multimedia processing are very attractive due to their low internal overheads.

2   Mobile Video Codecs and System Platforms

Typical mobile video codecs are currently built to adhere to MPEG-4 and H.264 standards. Both encoders and decoders consist of 10-20 algorithms that are in total invoked around 1-2 million times each second for a VGA sequence, making the overheads of the invocation mechanisms important, regardless of whether the implementation is in the software or hardware.

Table 3 shows the typical overheads of interface mechanisms as ARM11 processor cycles on a Symbian operating system. Due to the interrupt latency it is obvious, why the commercially available implementations are either pure software or monolithic hardware accelerators, that interrupt the control processor, for example, once for each frame. Fine grained hardware accelerators would be an inefficient approach due to the high software overheads from interrupt based hardware/software interfacing. Middleware as an interfacing mechanism must be exploited sparingly, limiting its use to rare long latency services. In general, the total architectural overhead costs are unknown and hidden in the application performance.

Table 3. Typical software interface costs in an embedded system environment (Symbian 9)

Mechanism	Overhead/cycles
Procedure call	3-7
System call (user-kernel)	1000-2500
Interrupt latency	300-600
Context switch	400
Middleware	60000

2.1   MPEG-4 Software Decoder

Figure 1 shows the rough organization of a software based MPEG-4 decoder [9] that consists of layers that each provide decoding functions for the upper layer. This is the structure designed already into the standards. The sequence layer is executed once for each frame or video packet, and extracts information on the employed coding tools and parameters from the input stream. The macro-block layer in turn controls the block layer decoding functions that have been designed to ensure the locality of addressing. For a VGA bit stream, the macro-block layer is invoked at most 1200 times per frame, while the block layer is run at most 7200 times.

Table 4 demonstrates the costs of software interfaces, when the APIs enabling reusability of functionalities are placed on the sequence, macroblock and block layers, and the assumed call overhead is 7 cycles. The figures do not contain the costs of

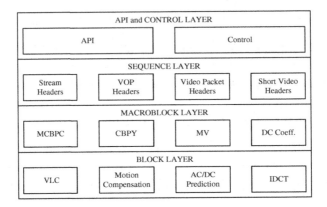

Fig. 1. Layered software architecture of a MPEG-4 video decoder

Table 4. The internal overhead share and energy costs of an MPEG-4 decoder with three API layer options (VGA 30 frames/s, 512kb/s, ARM926EJ-S implemented at 130nm CMOS)

APIs	Overhead (cycles/s / $\sim$ MHz)	Energy consumption (mW)
Sequence layer only	1806 / $\sim$ 0	0
Sequence and macroblock layers	2671599 / $\sim$ 2.7	1.2
Sequence, macroblock, and block layers	11376267 / $\sim$ 11.4	5.1

any functionality in the layers, and the experiments have been run without an operating system for maximum efficiency.

Based on the above, the internal overheads of the decoder on the ARM926 are about 5.4% of the total decoder cycles given in Table 2. Energywise they cost about the same as a hardware implementation of the MPEG-4 decoder using the same silicon technology. The control code in the sequence layer consumes additionally about 1.5 MHz, while the share of control load elsewhere in the code is difficult to quantify.

The MPEG-4 software encoder and decoder codes do not fit in typical 16-32 kbyte instruction caches. With an operating system, based on Park et al. [7], we should reserve at least 20% of the processor cycles to cache related overheads alone.

2.2 MPEG-4 Hardware Decoder

The monolithic hardware decoder API is almost identical to the above software decoder implementation [10]. Internally only a part of the sequence layer is implemented in the software and already the bit-oriented stream parsing is in the hardware for the sake of efficiency. The hardware interrupts the CPU after decoding each frame, on average 30 times per second. The sequence layer control software requires about 1 MHz, which is somewhat less than with the software implementation (1.5MHz). The internal organization of the accelerator is again as instructed by the MPEG-4 standard.

2.3   Multimedia Software Frameworks

Mobile multimedia software frameworks are defined software architectures, including APIs and middleware, intended to standardize the integration of software and hardware based video coding solutions into embedded devices. In addition, the goal is to provide mechanisms that enable building multimedia applications that are portable between platform generations.

The Symbian Multimedia Framework (MMF, Figure 2) is a multithreaded approach for handling multimedia data, and provides audio and video streaming functionalities. Regardless of whether the codecs are implemented in software or hardware, they are interfaced as plugins to the Multimedia Device Framework (MDF). With actual hardware codecs the plugins hide the vendor specific device drivers.

MDF with plugins is middleware that can be used to hide the underlying possible distributed implementation, for example, a decoder plugin may hide a decoder running on a Texas Instruments DSP processor behind an XDAIS interface. The codec vendors implement the MDF plugins with specified interfaces, and the MMF controller plugins that take care of synchronization between audio and video [11], for example. The application builders use the Client API that handles requests such as *record*, *play*, *pause*. At minimum, these activations of requests go through five software interface layers before reaching the codec. The performance depends greatly on the vendor provided controller plugins.

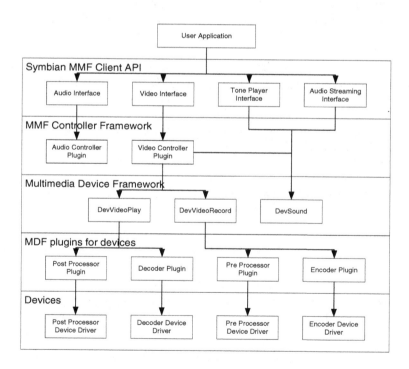

Fig. 2. Symbian Multimedia Framework

Table 5. The costs of multimedia APIs

	Decoder software interfaces		
	Proprietary API	Symbian MMF	Difference
Total cycles	220890240	225165845	2.14 MHz
D-cache misses	1599992	1633425	33433
I-cache misses	250821	322635	71813
D-cache hit ratio	94.7%	94.6%	0.1%
I-cache hit ratio	99.7%	99.6%	0.1%

In the Symbian operating system version 7 of 2003 the MDF was the whole framework, and that increased with two new abstraction layers, Client API and Controller Framework, in version 9 released in 2005. We are probably safe assuming additional layers in the future to support more versatile multimedia applications, based, for example, on the emerging MPEG-21 standard.

The proprietary solutions from mobile video codec manufacturers approach the portability issue from a different angle. For instance, in [10] thin software wrapper layers are used to facilitate porting the hardware and software codecs to the *multimedia engines* that provides, for example, video recording and playback functionalities in a tightly integrated manner. Table 5 compares the costs of accessing the video decoder functionality directly via a proprietary API, and through the Symbian MDF level. These costs are approximately the same for both software and hardware decoders. In power consumption the difference between the multimedia frameworks would be around 1mW on the ARM926 processor of Table 1.

The above measurements were made by running an MPEG-4 software decoder without display post-processing and audio for a QVGA sequence (320x240 pixels, 30 frames/s). The experiments were made on an actual ARM11 platform without SIMD optimizations and with a system supporting a single video coding standard. With more codecs the overheads of using any of them are slightly higher, especially when middleware interfaces are employed.

The results also provide a ballpark estimate on operating system and memory related overheads. The decoding of a QVGA stream requires around 110MHz, while 0-wait-state simulations predict half of that.

3   Energy Efficiency

To understand the role of the software interfaces in the energy efficiency of multimedia, it is necessary to consider the characteristics of whole implementations. For this purpose we use commercial hardware and software implementations of MPEG-4 and H.264 VGA video codecs [12]. Table 6 shows the estimated power consumptions of hardware based codecs with their necessary control software (1MHz in all cases) on a proprietary API. The applications were run on an ARM9 processor, and a 130 nm low power 1V CMOS process is used for all hardware.

Due to the disparity between the algorithmic and computational complexities of H.264 and MPEG-4 codecs, their monolithic accelerators differ significantly by gate

Table 6. Gate counts and estimated power needs of 30 frames/s hardware codecs

	MPEG-4		H.264	
	kGates	Power (mW)	kGates	Power (mW)
Decoder	161	5.6	373	24.2
Encoder	170	9.6	491	33.4

Table 7. Power consumption estimates (mW) for software based MPEG-4 and H.264 decoders

	MPEG-4	H.264
ARM7 (720T)	64	140
ARM9 (926EJ-S)	96	232
ARM10 (1022E)	92	232
ARM11 (1136J-S)	118	348

counts and required silicon area. The above H.264 codec also supports MPEG-4 as that adds only a few percentage points to the total gate count. The hardware shares of the power consumption are almost independent of the bit rate that is an essential difference to software implementations.

Table 7 shows the approximate power consumptions for architecture optimized software implementations of MPEG-4 and H.264 decoders. The figures have been determined for 30 frames/s VGA 512kbit/s stream and the decoders are the only tasks being run on ARM processors implemented using a 1V low power 130nm CMOS process. The costs of system software interfaces and post-processing the video for display are not included. Based on these results, multiprocessor solutions can indeed provide energy efficiency benefits.

The Symbian MDF supports multiprocessing and adds approximately 1mW to the decoder power consumptions. This is not significant except with the MPEG-4 hardware decoder (18%). We also observe that the power consumption of the ARM11 implementation of the software decoder is roughly 20% more than with the ARM9, which may not justify the added complexity of a multiprocessor system.

Figure 3 compares the findings for both software and hardware decoders in terms of normalized silicon areas (Mpixels/s/mm2) and power efficiencies (Mpixels/s/W) of the

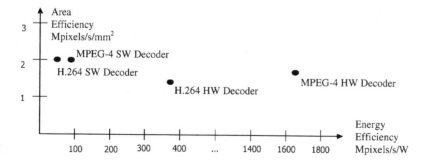

Fig. 3. Area and energy efficiencies of video decoder implementations

MPEG-4 and H.264 implementations. The gap between respective software and hardware implementations is striking, and there are no implementation options in between.

Returning to Table 4 that itemized the software function interface costs, we can estimate that an interrupt driven macroblock accelerator implementation would need around 50mW for software interfacing alone with an ARM926 (130nm CMOS). This eliminates most of the potential energy gains from hardware acceleration, and is not an attractive option.

4   Directions for Development

With an efficient software/hardware interfacing mechanism the energy overhead of fine grained hardware acceleration should not exceed that of a pure software implementation. We estimate that the lower bound power consumption (again 130nm CMOS and ARM926) for such a decoder would consist of 5.1mW from software interfaces and 5.6 mW from hardware accelerators and control software, totalling 10.7mW. Software implementation defines a 96mW upper bound, so the energy efficiency should fall midway between hardware and software implementations in Figure 3.

A model for the energy efficient approach can be obtained from periodically scheduled embedded real-time systems that run their tasks in a fixed order, and use hardware accelerators without interrupts relying on their deterministic latencies. Even some early GSM mobile phones employed this principle that in essence results in a multithreaded system [13]. In those implementations fixed hand made schedules could be used. However, video coding has data dependent control flows, so the scheduling of the threads and the allocation of hardware resources must be done dynamically. This can be performed, for instance, by using a Just-In-Time (JIT) compiler. Figure 4 below illustrates decoding an inter-macroblock using fine grained short latency hardware accelerators with a schedule created from the contents of the video bit stream.

The accelerators, color conversion for display, inverse quantizer (IQ)+IDCT, and bilinear interpolator, have deterministic latencies, and the software uses the results when they become available. Color conversion to display executes in hardware simultaneously with sequence and macro-block layer decoding. The threads alternate between software and hardware execution without an interrupt based synchronization overhead.

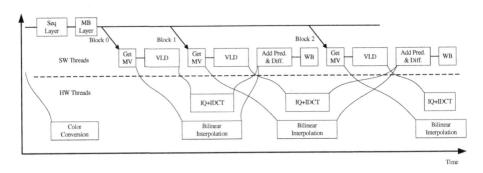

Fig. 4. Multithreaded decoding of an inter-macroblock from a coded video bit stream

To implement the hardware/software multithreading applications, efficient means for generating the schedules are needed. One option is to employ a set of fixed schedules to choose from based on the task at hand, while JIT compilers provide for more flexibility, although at the cost of higher overheads. Such compilation techniques could perhaps reduce the number of defined layers in software architectures, in turn providing compensationary savings. From the system developer's point of view fine grained accelerators cut the design verification time and provide faster time-to-market capability. The enabling missing elements appear to be on the side of software technology.

5   Summary

In computing intensive software applications, such as video coding, the interface overheads are in principle only a small portion of the total processor cycles. Much of the overheads originate from the layered software architecture style, and are amplified by cache related phenomena due to the decreased locality of code execution and data accesses. The operating systems have similar effects on the performance. In total, the overheads can exceed the number of cycles needed by the actual application.

When improved energy efficiency is targeted by the utilization of hardware accelerators, the software overheads may play a very significant role. Based on our experience, even the multimedia framework software interfaces may demand more processor cycles than the actual control of a hardware accelerator.

The efficiency of software/hardware interfaces is becoming a critical issue, because of the increasing leakage currents of silicon implementations. This makes run-time silicon re-use, for example, via fine grained acceleration very attractive. The conventional interrupt driven approach for hardware/software interfacing results in high overheads, in fact, much higher than in pure software implementations. If fine grained hardware accelerators could be interfaced to software at the cost of software functions, flexible energy efficient solutions could be implemented.

Current comparable MPEG-4 decoder implementations in hardware and software (ARM11) need 5.6mW and 118mW of power, respectively, without operating system and cache overheads that range between 20% and 100%. Solutions that fall between these figures are needed. The proposed simultaneous hardware/software multithreading is a possible option that is under investigation.

Multiprocessor implementations offer 20-50% improved energy efficiency in video coding when older processor architectures are used instead of the most recent ones. However, for the same performance, twice the silicon area is needed, resulting in higher static power consumption due to leakage currents. Furthermore, interprocessor communications can add significant overhead that falls in to the range of middleware costs.

Acknowledgements

Numerous people have contributed to this paper by providing their comments, questions and technical expertise. In particular, we wish to thank Mr. Jani Huoponen and Mr. Jarkko Nisula from Hantro Products, and Mr. Kari Jyrkkä from the Nokia Corporation.

References

1. Neuvo, Y.: Cellular phones as embedded systems. In: Solid-State Circuits Conference. Volume 1. (2004) 32–37
2. Silven, O., Jyrkkä, K.: Observations on power-efficiency trends in mobile communication devices. In: Proc. $5^t h$ Int. Workshop on Embedded Computer Systems: Architectures, Modeling, and Simulation, LNCS 3553 (2005) 142–151
3. ARM: Processor core overview. In: www.arm.com/products/CPUs. (2005)
4. ARM: RealView Developer Suite. In: www.arm.com/. (2005)
5. Mogul, J., Borg, A.: The effect of context switches on cache performance. In: ASPLOS-IV, Santa Clara, ACM (1991) 75–84
6. Sebek, F.: Instruction cache memory issues in real-time systems. Master's thesis, Department of Computer Science and Engineering, Mälardalen University, Västerås, Sweden (2002)
7. S. Park, Y.L., Shin, H.: An experimental analysis of the effect of the operating system on memory performance in embedded multimedia computing. In: EMSOFT-04. (2004) 26–33
8. P.H.F.M. Verhoeven, J.H., Lukkien, J.: Network middleware and mobility. In: PROGRESS workshop. (2001)
9. Hantro: 4100 MPEG-4 / H.263 Software Decoder. In: www.hantro.com. (2006)
10. Hantro: 8300 Multimedia Application Development Platform. In: www.hantro.com. (2006)
11. Symbian: Introduction to the ECOM Architecture. In: http://www.symbian.com/. (2006)
12. Hantro: Hardware and Software Video Codec IP. In: www.hantro.com. (2006)
13. Jyrkkä, K., Silven, O., Ali-Yrkkö, O., Heidari, R., Berg, H.: Component-based development of DSP software for mobile communication terminals. Microprocessors and Microsystems **26** (2002) 463–474

A UML Profile for
Asynchronous Hardware Design

Kim Sandström and Ian Oliver

Nokia Research Center, Finland
{kim.g.sandstrom, ian.oliver}@nokia.com

Abstract. In this work we present UML for Hardware Design (UML-HD), a UML profile suitable for Asynchronous Hardware Design and an approach for automatically generating a Hardware Description Language (HDL) model from UML-HD models. A UML-HD model comprises solely class diagrams and an action language. We use stereotypes in two categories - structure and activity - to categorise classes. Structure type stereotypes signify state and activity type signify transitions. The approach is largely inspired by Petri nets. Several model transformations are suggested in this paper, but only code generation to Haste was implemented.

1 Introduction

As the size and complexity of silicon designs have increased, demands on systems productivity and design time have largely stayed the same. Generating synthesisable HDL from abstract models both decreases design time and increases the designers ability to manage complexity. A more abstract definition of a design offers advantages for both reuse and understandability.

Asynchronous design requires less implementation detail in the HDL model than synchronous design, because no hardware (HW) needs to be designed for synchronisation beyond a simple handshaking protocol. Asynchronous design is done on a higher abstraction level, since it needs no functional elements dedicated to synchronisation such as PLLs, clock divisors, clock domain synchronisation or path synchronisation; even FIFO buffering can sometimes be neglected.

The level of abstraction is also raised by a modeling language that allows behavioural modeling. Compilation and netlist synthesis is done by behavioural compilers or synthesisers. A behavioural HDL model lets a compiler do a larger part of the design decisions than a Register Transfer Level (RTL) synthesiser would do. Behavioural modeling often implies new HDL languages and sometimes specific design tools.

UML [13] has long been the favoured approach for formal design in many fields of engineering. It provides a formal, extensible, easy to understand syntax for a high level design language and many possibilities to abstract used design structures for an abstract modeling paradigm.

UML's widely known syntax helps in training and understanding of a language based on it. UML is understood and used in a large part of the engineering world and thus suitable for documentation and re-use. UML is used in many ways for specification or abstraction, Use for HW design is less common, though

S. Vassiliadis et al. (Eds.): SAMOS 2006, LNCS 4017, pp. 15–26, 2006.

particular work has focused on VHDL mappings, as can be seen in [1], which produced VHDL suitable for simulation but not synthesising; other similar work but using SpecC can be seen in [8] and a more generic approach in [7]. Otherwise work has focused on methodology for this domain [9, 11, 10].

2   UML

2.1   UML-HD

UML for Hardware Design (UML-HD) uses three approaches for an easily understandable methodology of high level synthesisable descriptions of digital designs: asynchronous design, behavioural design and mapping to UML.

UML-HD is a UML profile with a model transformation to Haste [2], a high level, behavioural, asynchronous hardware description language. Since Haste is a character based language, the transformation is actually a code generation. Code generation was implemented as scripts in Coral [12]. Coral's transformation generation engine uses extended Python as a scripting language.

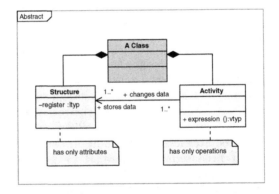

Fig. 1. Activity/structure paradigm

The semantics of the model is directly inspired by Petri nets [6] and based on a semantic interpretation of structure and activity much in the sense of a Petri net's state and transition. The paradigm's basis is that state and transitions are stored in respective identifiable model elements. Activity is represented by a category of UML classes and structure respectively by another.

2.2   Comparison to Petri Nets

In Petri nets the state primitive stores the system's state by tokens residing in an active state. Transition primitive allows a transition of tokens from one state to another. Tokens indicate both which states are active and which transitions can be triggered. UML-HD class diagrams express a Petri net like structure. Activity classes trigger operations, structure classes access attributes. The semantics of an activity class map onto transition, the semantics of a structure class onto state.

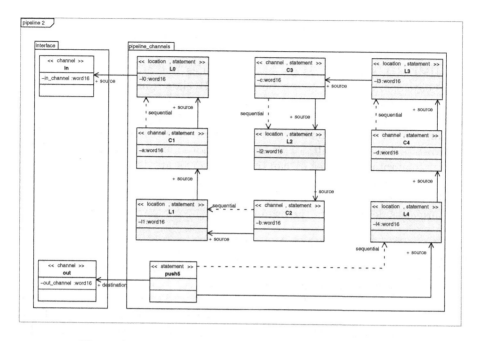

Fig. 2. An example of a UML-HD design. A simple pipeline.

Mapping Petri net tokens is less obvious. They signify attribute data and may trigger an activity class. Activity classes may guard each other, but are implicitly assumed to trigger once during an execution cycle. Thus in structure classes; tokens are provided and consumed by locations but passed on by channels.

An example can be seen in figure 2 and Haste code generated from it in quote 3.3. Data is read from input channel 'in' and pipelined to the output channel 'out'. Note that a class may have several stereotypes and thus have a role both as activity class and structure class. In this example, the destination role is omitted as the destination locations are merged with the statements in such a way.

2.3   Comparison to Generic OO UML

The UML-HD approach is quite different from generic UML. A detailed analysis of refinement to UML-HD from an OO model - that comprises class and state diagrams and an action language - is not in the scope of this paper, but we will shortly propose a transformation here.

Figure 1 describes a quite obvious approach to transform a generic UML to the UML-HD activity/structure paradigm, but it's not implemented within this work. As we propose it we put forward the argument that UML-HD is indeed a useful UML profile. A transformation from generic UML was a strong argument of implementation in UML rather than another syntax.

In UML-HD behaviour and structure become two aspects of the same diagram, represented by activity and structure classes respectively. Separation of structure and activity into separate modeling elements is as such not Object Oriented (OO) and atypical to UML and OO design, but there are also similarities. Classes in UML-HD are descriptive of physical elements of an asynchronous HW implementation and represents an OO approach in that design domain.

In UML-HD, structure classes have attributes but no operations, activity classes have operations but no attributes. A UML class transformed to UML-HD may be mapped to two classes, one structure and one activity class connected by an association.

Transforming from UML state diagrams is not equally simple since UML-HD uses no state diagrams at all. States and transitions must be mapped onto UML-HD class diagrams. However we can transform any state diagram to a Petri net, and map transitions onto activity classes and states onto structure classes. We would add associations from the resulting set of structure classes to the UML-HD structure class derived from the owning class.

2.4   Meta-model and UML Modeling Elements

To create a UML profile tha's easily mapped onto the HDL, the activity/structure paradigm was implemented using UML stereotypes and structures in a more hardware specific way than explained earlier. The meta-model shown in figure 3 and figure 4, defines the syntactic rules of a UML-HD model and the meta-meta-model in figure 1 ditto of the meta-model. They define allowed UML modeling structures, such as what stereotypes and associations maybe used. The meta-model's classes represent the usable stereotypes, associations define legal associations in the corresponding model.

Some meta-model classes are stereotyped activity or structure, as defined in the meta-meta-model. From the meta-model, we can see that some UML-HD stereotypes are in turn stereotyped according to rules set in the meta-meta-model. Some are in the structure category some in the activity category. The meta-model

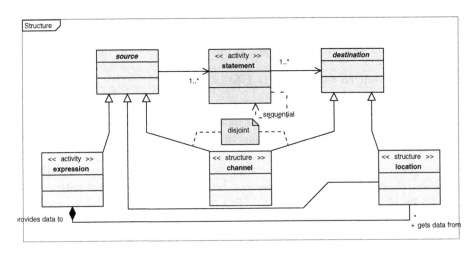

Fig. 3. Part of the meta-model of UML-HD, the most important stereotypes

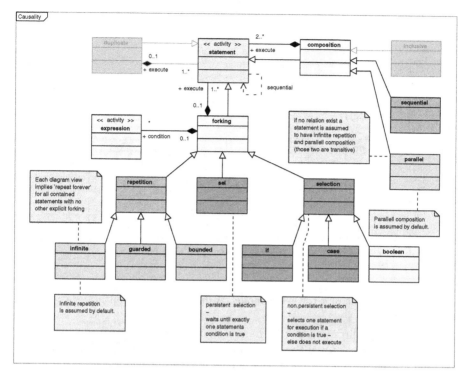

Fig. 4. Suggested stereotypes for extension of UML-HD

in figure 3 shows the most important stereotypes: Statement, Expression, Location and Channel. A less central part of the meta-model is shown in figure 4 on page 19.

All UML-HD classes are stereotyped. The activity category's key stereotype is 'statement'. A statement defines a concurrent process to be mapped onto a CSP based language; such as Haste. Statements act as parallel processes that communicate a value from a source to a destination. Both are defined by roles from the statement over navigable associations, but if such roles can't be found the statement class itself is tested for suitability for either role. Only a non-ambiguous class with appropriate structure category stereotype is accepted.

As shown in figure 3, a destination may be a channel or a location. A source may be a channel or an expression or an expression implied by a location. If the source is a location, then an expression solely referring to that expression is implicitly assumed. Channels may be used only disjointly so that not both source and destination are channels.

Locations define data structures that store data values. They map onto HDL structures that define the static storage on silicon: registers, latches and flip-flops. Features to control the physical representation exists in Haste. A mechanism for it in UML-HD could be added as stereotypes or tags.

Channels do not store data. They act as a means to exchange information between statements in a reliable way. During communication, sender and receiver

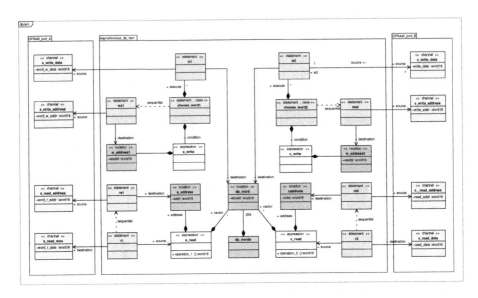

Fig. 5. An example of a UML-HD model. A dual port ram arbitration scheme.

statements are synchronised by the channel that schedules the execution. A channel can be; written to only if the previous data in it has been read, and read from only if it has been written to. This is known as asynchronous non-buffered communication. Haste has some extended features of this synchronisation and a mechanisms to use them can be added to UML-HD as stereotypes or tags.

An expression acts as a source or guard to a statement. It composes locations to be used by an action script. Only locations with a composition from the expression can be referenced. The location's name or role name is used as the reference. Location attributes may not be referenced. The expression stereotype is in the activity category because of its strong association with statement.

An action script – written in the action language – operate on location data and constitute the method of an expression class' operation.

A more extensive UML support for the HDL's higher level features, allow the generated code to be more readable and better suitable for the HDL compiler's advanced capabilities. Repetition, conditional statements and explicit composition allow a hierarchical structure of statements. It also raises the level of abstraction of the UML model.

To further enhance code generation from the HDL in such a way, composite statements were added. These specialised or extended statements have their own stereotypes, but the 'statement' stereotype must always be explicitly defined, even if it could be implied. Stating it explicitly makes code generation easier.

The diagram in figure 4 describes this larger set of stereotypes but they were not fully implemented. An example of implemented higher level constructs can be found in figure 6 and figure 5.

The implemented higher level constructs map onto the conditional statements 'if', 'case' and 'sel'. A guard – defined by an expression class – selects a statement

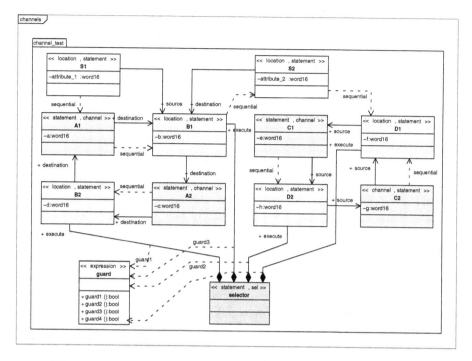

Fig. 6. An example of UML-HD. Using channels triggered by guards.

to be executed. If the guard's values do not fit, no statement is executed; the conditional statement is terminated if it's non-persistent, but if persistent it waits until the value fits. An 'if' or a 'case' is non-persistent, but the 'sel' clause is persistent. 'sel' and 'case' have the same semantics except for persistance.

Since all features of the Haste language need not have a direct high level mapping in UML-HD, support for constructs not mentioned earlier was dropped from the code generator. Thus, not all extensions in figure 4 were implemented, for example: the composite statements for repetition. Haste supports three types of repetition; infinite, guarded and bounded. They are syntactically expressed in Haste by 'forever do', 'for' and 'do'. Implementation would comprise no technological challenge beyond already implemented features, thus support could easily be added.

UML-HD can support the dependency primitive. The semantics of a UML-HD dependency depends on its name. Currently two types of dependencies are supported: 'if' and 'sequential'. Dependencies named 'sequential' offer an additional way to control the scheduling of statements. Dependencies named 'if' implement the if-conditional and are drawn between a statement and a boolean expression. It can be mapped onto a statement class with the 'if' stereotype.

A UML-HD package is mapped onto a container structure in the HDL. The container holds a set of CSP like processes mapped from UML-HD statements. Any package that does not contain statements, are not mapped onto a container. A

Haste process acts as the container. All statements in a package will be statements of the Haste process.

The statements are executed infinitely in a 'forever do' loop, with parallel execution as default. Alternatively a dependency (named 'sequential') between two statements makes the execution sequential. Execution order is also affected by composite statements Any associations to classes not in the package are mapped onto the process' I/O parameters.

2.5   Behaviour

UML-HD's Action Language is identical to what Haste's authors define as "an expression". It is used only in action scripts of expression classes. It can reference location classes that have a composition from the expression class. These classes map onto Haste locations and the scripts are in fact Haste expressions. If the expression class has an empty method and a single composite location, a direct reference of it is implicitly used as the action script.

Scheduling is controlled by four overlapping mechanisms. By an execution cycle, by channel handshaking, by sequential type dependencies and by composite statement. A considerable effort was put into a code generation that transparently respects the scheduling constraints defined within each mechanism.

An example of using all four scheduling structures can be seen in figure 6. Every execution cycle, data is toggled between locations B1 and B2 via the channels A1 and A2. As well, data is toggled between locations D1 and D2 via the channels C1 and C2. The location B1 outputs data to location S1 and inputs data from location S2. Data transfers are guarded by the execution cycle, by four channels, by seven sequential dependencies and one 'sel' statement with four guards. Code generated from the example can be seen here:

```
&  channel_test : proc().
begin
     A2 : chan word16 & A1 : chan word16 & C1 : chan word16
   & C2 : chan word16
   & B2 : var word16 & D1 : var word16 & S2 : var word16
   & D2 : var word16 & B1 : var word16& S1 : var word16
   & t_nonput_D2 : chan ~ & t_nonput_D1 : chan ~
   & s_nonput_B1 : chan ~ & t_nonput_B1 : chan ~
   & t_nonput_B2 : chan ~
 | forever do
 ( (     t_nonput_D2?~ ; C1!D2 )
   || ( t_nonput_D1?~ ; (  B1:=S2 || C2!D1 )
     ; s_nonput_B1!~ ; t_nonput_B1?~ ;  A1?B1 ; S1:=B1 )
   || ( t_nonput_B2?~ ;  A2?B2 )
   || sel D2[0] then C2?D2 ; t_nonput_D2!~
    or D1[0] then C1?D1 ; t_nonput_D1!~
    or B1[0] then s_nonput_B1?~ ; A2!B1 ; t_nonput_B1!~
    or B2[0] then A1!B2 ; t_nonput_B2!~
   les
 ) od
 end
```

3   Code Generation

3.1   MDE Platform

Code generation was implemented as transformation script on the Coral platform developed at Åbo Akademi. It is a general purpose Model Driven Engineering (MDE) platform[1], that can traverse a model and output another. Coral's MDE engine can read any language that has been defined using Object Management Group's (OMG) Meta Object Facility (MOF).

Coral reads and stores models conforming to MOF definitions. The scripting language is Python extended with the Coral library. Models can be transformed to other models by execution of a Coral script. A Coral script can alter, create and delete models, traverse a model and create modeling elements in the same or another model. Output can be generated using another or the same MOF definition. The script can also use any other facility of Python to execute any Python instructions, such as string manipulations and file access to generate a character based language.

The UML-HD language conforms to the UML 1.4 MOF model in Coral but it is also a proper subset of UML 2.0. Code generation output from UML-HD is based on Pythons standard libraries. The output is character based and conforms to the Haste language's syntax and semantics.

3.2   Haste HDL Language

Haste [2] – a language for asynchronous HW design developed by Handshake Technologies – was chosen as the target of code generation, because it offers a high model abstraction and yet a very straight semantic mapping to physical silicon. Much due to asynchronous design methodology. It's originally inspired by Hoare's CSP [3] and Dijkstra's GCL [4], but it now has a more verbose syntax. A Haste model can be compiled to a netlist targeting a VLSI implementation. Haste does not generate any scheduling logic except the explicitly defined channel handshakes, sequential dependencies and composite statements. Synchronisation is done as asynchronous single-rail handshaking and no clock is needed.

Haste declares either procedures (denoted by proc), or functions (denoted by func). A procedure communicates their input and output values via a parameter list, whereas functions terminate, have input parameters and return values. Haste programs can define either a main procedure, or a main function. A meta-language syntax template for a process or function:

```
<process name> : [main] {proc,func} ( <param1>,<param2>,... ).
  begin <declarations> | <process body> end
```

Process bodies consist of parallel statements separated by the '||' operator. Each parallel statement may consist out of several sequential statements sepa-

---
[1] cf. OMG's MDA, www.omg.org/mda

rated by the ';' operator. A location represents a register. Each statement performs an assignment to a location. An expression which terms may consist of locations determines the assigned value. The asynchronous handshaking is implemented as channels with with non-buffered asynchronous locking on input and output. A channel may be; written to iff it is empty or has been read from, read from once iff it has been written to. Thus the channel propagates a data token. Input from a channel in Haste is expressed with the '?' operator and output to a channel with the '!' operator.

A meta-language syntax templates for a statement, for channel input and channel output followed by an example of a channel input and output in a process (the expressions 'E' and 'F' are not shown explicitly) and a tiny increment program that uses a channel.:

```
<location>:=<expression>
<channel>!<expression> || <channel>?<location>


& channel_assign : proc().
begin a:chan bool | (a!<E> ; a!<F>) || (a?x ; a?y) end

Top:increment proc(a!chan [0..255]).
  begin
    x:var [0..255] ff := 0
  | a!x ; do (x<255) then  x := x+1 ; a!x od
  end
```

3.3   Code Generation

The model in the repository is traversed for key modeling elements. Global type declarations are found and generated into Haste. Packages are generated into Haste processes while traversed for statements and possible type declarations. Dependencies are parsed before output of the process, its parameters, declarations and statements. At all times the code generator respects the scheduling.

A stereotype on a class is parsed in such a way that statement classes and their sources and destinations are found. Classes joined by associations may have been merged to one class with the stereotypes of both original classes. The only restriction is that such joining of classes may not cause ambiguity of which stereotyped class should be parsed by the code generator. Some wellformedness checking is implied by this described ambiguity parsing.

The code generation was implemented in 2414 lines of Coral script in 6 files. The Python based code reads a UML-HD model stored in an XMI file and parses it into the Coral model repository. Small examples of design structures in such a model are shown in figure 2, figure 6 and figure 5. The generated Haste code is written into a file from which the Haste compiler can generate a netlist. As an example we show here generated code from the model in figure 2:

```
&  pipeline_channels : proc(out!chan word16 & in?chan word16).
 begin
      C1 : chan word16 & C4 : chan word16
   &  C3 : chan word16 & C2 : chan word16
   &  L3 : var word16 & L0 : var word16
   &  L2 : var word16 & L4 : var word16 & L1 : var word16
   |
 forever do
 (     ( C4?L4 ; out!L4 ) || ( in?L0 ; C1!L0 )
    || ( C1?L1 ; C2!L1 ) || ( C2?L2 ; C3!L2 )
    || ( C3?L3 ; C4!L3 ) )
 od
 end
```

4   Conclusions

A fully functional subset of Haste's semantic features was implemented. An even more minimal subset would have been sufficient for UML design, but we wanted to demonstrate that advanced features of the target HDL can be supported.

Implementing a model transformation to HDL was more complex than anticipated. Even if the semantics of UML-HD seemed very close to the CSP based target HDL there were some semantic differences as well as differences in the expressibility of the languages. The biggest differences were in type declarations, process parameters and dependencies. Dependency parsing became quite complex, comprising almost half of the code.

The UML-HD profile is oriented towards asynchronous parallel processes with non-buffered synchronisation. Particular care was taken to adapt the profile to code generation of a CSP like language like Haste. Little observance to HW design was needed beyond that, because the Haste language and an asynchronous design methodology offers a high level abstraction of HW design.

UML-HD's way of using class diagrams and no state diagrams is unusual. The basis for this solution comes both from CSP like languages and Petri Nets. Describing more than usual of the model's behaviour in the class diagram and giving it state chart like semantics might be considered unorthodox by UML purists, but the possibility of model transformation from generic OO UML suggests benefits of an UML approach. UML-HD objects have a direct mapping to physical silicon and thus it's OO in its own domain.

References

1. William E. McUmber, Betty HC Cheng. *UML-Based Analysis of Embedded Systems using a Mapping to VHDL*, In: "High Assurance Software Engineering.", IEEE. 1999
2. Ad Peeters, Mark de Wit, Handshake Solutions, High Tech Campus Eindhoven, The Netherlands: *Haste Manual*, 1st of September 2005
3. C. A. R. Hoare: *Communicating Sequential Processes*, 1985-2004
4. E W Dijkstra. *A Discipline of Programming*, Prentice-Hall, Englewood Cliffs, N.J. 1976

5. Ulrich Becker, Daniel Moldt, University of Hamburg Fachbereich Informatik: *Object-Oriented Concepts for Coloured Petri Nets*, In: "Conference Proceedings, IEEE International Conference on Systems, Man and Cybernetics.", October 1993
6. Lars M. Christensen, Søren Christensen, Kurt Jensen, University of Aarhus, Denmark: *The practitioner's guide to coloured Petri nets*, In: "International Journal on Software Tools for Technology Transfer.", 1998, pp. 98–132
7. Michele Marchetti, Ian Oliver. *Towards a Conceptual Framework for UML to Hardware Description Language Mappings*, In: "UML-B Specification for Proven Embedded Systems Design.", Kluwer. 1-4020-2866-0. 2003
8. Jorge Diaz-Herrera. *An isomorphic mapping to SpecC in UML*, In: "Proceedings of OMER-2: Workshop on Object-oriented Modeling of Embedded Real-Time Systems.", May 2001
9. Luciano Lavagno, Grant Martin, Bran Selic. *UML for Real - Design of Embedded Real-Time Systems*, Kluwer Academic Publishers. 1-4020-7501-4. 2003
10. Maher Awad, Juha Kuusela, Jurgen Ziegler. *Object-Oriented Technology for Real-Time Systems. A Practical Approach Using OMT and Fusion*, Prentice-Hall. 1996
11. Bran Selic, Garth Gullekson and Paul T. Ward. *Real-Time Object Oriented Modelling*, Wiley. 1994
12. Johan Lilius, Tomas Lillqvist, Torbjorn Lundkvist, Ian Oliver, Ivan Porres, Kim Sandstrom, Glenn Sveholm and Asim Pervez Zaka1. An Architecture Exploration Environment for System on Chip Design. In: Nordic Journal of Computing. 2006
13. Object Management Group, *UML 2.0 Super Structure Specification*, OMG ptc/03-08-02. 2002

Automated Distribution of UML 2.0 Designed Applications to a Configurable Multiprocessor Platform

Mikko Setälä, Petri Kukkala, Tero Arpinen,
Marko Hännikäinen, and Timo D. Hämäläinen

Tampere University of Technology, Institute of Digital and Computer Systems
P.O. Box 553, FI-33101 Tampere, Finland
mikko.setala@tut.fi

Abstract. This paper presents automated distribution of embedded real-time applications modeled in Unified Modeling Language version 2.0 (UML 2.0). The automated distribution requires methods and tools for design automation, as well as the run-time environment for the distributed execution on the target platform. Executable application code is generated from UML models, and UML with a custom profile is used to abstract hardware architecture and configure application mapping. For experimenting, a full featured WLAN terminal was designed in UML and implemented as a distributed multiprocessor system-on-chip (SoC) on an FPGA prototype platform. Measurements show that a 50-70% reduction in protocol delays is achived with distribution, and delay variations are reduced 45-85%.

1   Introduction

To fulfill the real-time constraints of complex embedded real-time systems, parallelism and heterogeneous multiprocessor architectures are exploited. With complex hardware, distribution of the application functionality onto the different processing elements is a challenging task. To enable the development of hardware independent, reusable software, the hardware implementation should be invisible for the software designer. At the same time, mapping different application tasks to the architecture should be straightforward.

In this paper we present automated distribution of applications described in Unified Modeling Language 2.0 (UML 2.0). The automated distribution consists of methods and tools for design automation, as well as the run-time environment for the distributed execution. The applications are executed on a configurable multiprocessor platform with a Real-Time Operating System (RTOS). The run-time environment enables the communication of processes of the same application executed on different CPUs, while remaining invisible for the application level, as shown in Fig. 1.

Traditionally UML has been used in designing large software systems, but recently it has been emerging also in embedded system design. The publication of the UML 2.0 standard [1] brought several important extensions to the language. Consequently, modern UML modeling tools automatically generate executable code from UML models, making it possible to use a single language for modeling, verification and even implementation of applications. In our approach, UML is also used to create an abstract

S. Vassiliadis et al. (Eds.): SAMOS 2006, LNCS 4017, pp. 27–38, 2006.

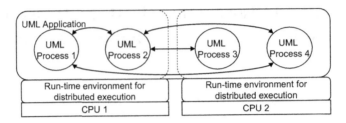

Fig. 1. Communicating processes of a UML application executed on different CPUs

model of hardware architecture and configure application mapping. The implementation of a full featured Medium Access Control (MAC) protocol for Wireless Local Area Networks (WLAN) is presented as a case study to evaluate the feasibility and performance of the approach.

The paper is organized as follows. Chapter 2 presents the related work. The automated implementation flow is presented in Chapter 3. Chapter 4 presents the WLAN protocol case study and the related UML models. The run-time environment is presented in Chapter 5. In Chapter 6 the performance of the implementation is studied. Chapter 7 concludes the work.

2   Related Research

Studies in microprocessor design have shown that a multiprocessor architecture consisting of several simple CPUs can outperform a single CPU using the same area [2], if the application has a large degree of parallelism. Kaiserswerth has analyzed parallelism in communication protocols [3], stating that they are suitable for distributed execution, since they can be parallelized efficiently and also allow for pipelined execution.

A common approach in designing distributed systems is the utilization of *middleware*, such as the Common Object Request Broker Architecture (CORBA) [4], to abstract the underlying hardware implementation from the application level. However, the general middleware implementations are too complex for embedded systems. Thus, several middleware approaches have been developed especially for real-time embedded systems [5] [6] [7].

UML has potential to be used as a design environment for distributed embedded systems, due to its powerful and extensible notations. However, the absence of a standard UML profile for modeling hardware and mapping has slowed down the development of supporting methods and tools. The UML Platform profile proposed in [8] as well as the Embedded UML profile proposed in [9] support the modeling of hardware resources and services, as well as application mapping. Object Management Group (OMG) has specified a UML profile for CORBA, which allows the presentation of CORBA semantics in UML [10].

Born *et al.* have presented a method for the design and development of distributed applications using UML [11]. It uses automatic code generation to create code skeletons for component implementations on a middleware platform. However, direct executable code generation from UML models or modeling of hardware in UML are not utilized.

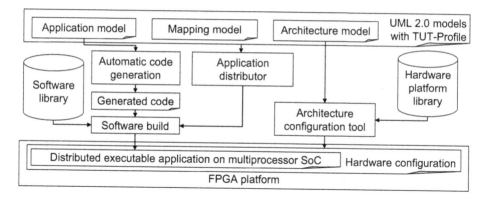

Fig. 2. Implementation flow for UML based multiprocessor systems

3   Automated Implementation Flow from UML to FPGA

The automated implementation flow for UML based multiprocessor systems is presented in Fig. 2. First, UML models for the system are developed. To model hardware and mapping, a UML extension for embedded system design is utilized [12]. The structure and behavior of the application is described in the application model. The application consists of processes described as state-machines. The architecture model defines the processing elements in the hardware, as well as the communication architecture. Applications described in UML are platform independent, and thus application and architecture models can be designed independently. In the mapping model, the application processes are mapped onto the processing elements.

The application model is transformed into executable code using automatic code generation. In the software build the generated code is compiled and linked together with components from a software library, as well as code generated by the application distributor tool. The application distributor is discussed in detail in Chapter 5. As a result, an individual application image for each processor is generated.

Based on the architecture model the hardware configuration is generated automatically by an architecture configuration tool. It generates a model for the top-level architecture where the RTL models from the hardware platform library are instantiated, and performs hardware synthesis.

The application distributor and architecture configuration tool are custom made tools. Telelogic Tau G2 is used for the UML modeling and automatic code generation, and the architecture configuration tool uses Altera Quartus II for the hardware synthesis. For the software build, Nios II GCC toolset is utilized.

4   Case Study: WLAN Terminal

To evaluate the feasibility of our distribution approach in practice, a full featured WLAN terminal was designed in UML and implemented on a prototype platform. TUTWLAN is a proprietary WLAN designed at the Tampere University of Technology (TUT) [13].

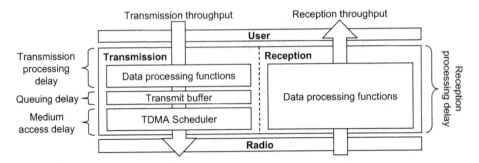

Fig. 3. Key performance parameters of TUTMAC protocol

The central part of TUTWLAN is the TUTMAC protocol, which is a dynamic reservation Time Division Multiple Access (TDMA) based MAC protocol. Several configurations of the TUTMAC protocol have been developed, one of which is presented in this paper. The features of TUTMAC include Quality of Service (QoS) support, data fragmentation, 8-bit CRC for packet headers, and 32-bit CRC and encryption with Advanced Encryption Standard (AES) algorithm for payload data.

The computationally intensive parts of TUTMAC, such as AES encryption, place substantial requirements to the computational capabilities of the hardware platform. Further, the TDMA scheduler has real-time requirements to maintain accurate frame synchronization. Due to its high amount of parallel processing, TUTMAC is capable of reaching its real-time requirements better as a distributed multiprocessor implementation than as a single CPU implementation.

In Fig. 3 the key performance parameters of TUTMAC are illustrated. Processing delay is the time consumed in processing data in transmission or reception. Queuing delay is the time between the arrival of a packet into the transmit buffer and the time the packet is fetched from the buffer. Medium access delay is the time between fetching a packet from the transmit buffer and sending it to the radio. In addition to the actual delays, minimum variation of the delays is a key real-time requirement. Variation of the medium access delay is of special interest, since it affects the accuracy of the frame synchronization.

4.1 TUTWLAN Terminal Configurable Platform

The multiprocessor prototype TUTWLAN terminal is implemented on Altera's Nios II Development Kit, Stratix II Edition. The development board has a Stratix II ES2S60 FPGA and several peripherals such as external memories, serial ports, and an Ethernet controller. An Intersil MACless Prism HW1151-EVAL radio is connected to the prototype expansion headers on the board. The radio is physically IEEE 802.11b compatible but does not implement the standard MAC layer.

The configurable platform consists of multiple Nios II CPUs and custom hardware accelerators, and is presented in detail in [14]. An instance of the platform is shown in Fig. 4. It consists of five CPUs, a radio interface module, and custom hardware accelerators for 32-bit CRC calculation and AES encryption. One of the Nios II CPUs is an I/O CPU, which connects to a wired network via Ethernet.

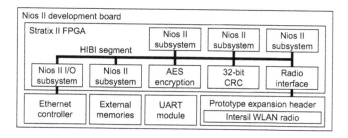

Fig. 4. Platform implementation on the development board

The platform components are connected with a Heterogeneous IP Block Interconnection (HIBI) segment [15], a communication architecture targeted for complex SoC designs. Communication is handled by an Application Programming Interface (API) for HIBI. It offers data transfer services to device drivers for components connected to HIBI, in this case AES, CRC, and WLAN radio.

Each Nios II subsystem is an independent module with local instruction and data memories, and is running a local copy of the eCos RTOS [16]. Using a local copy of an RTOS provides easy scalability, and different operating systems and CPUs can be used in the same architecture. The main benefit of eCos is the real-time kernel providing interrupt and exception handling, multithreading, thread synchronization, and timing mechanisms.

4.2 Protocol UML Model with TUT-Profile

The TUTMAC protocol as well as the hardware architecture and application mapping are modeled in UML 2.0. TUT-Profile defines a set of design practices and stereotypes for embedded system design. The purpose is to enable automated system design using only UML description.

The application components are modeled as classes, and their behavior as statechart diagrams combined with action language. The structure of the application is described with composite structure diagrams, which specify the component instances and their interconnections. The composite structure can be hierarchical, i.e. components can have an internal structure.

Parts of the UML application, e.g. complex algorithms, can be implemented as functions calls. The functions can be implemented either in UML or as external C functions. Further, the C functions can perform the calculation on a hardware accelerator or as a software implementation. If both are available, the decision is based on the process mapping. It is also possible to embed C code directly into the statechart diagrams.

The architecture model is a highly abstracted representation of the actual architecture, described as a composite structure diagram that instantiates the processing elements taken from a platform library. The components in the library have parameterizable UML models, i.e. it is possible to set e.g. different cache sizes for CPUs or different buffer sizes for communication wrappers. Each library component has also an RTL model for the hardware synthesis, and an API for the UML application.

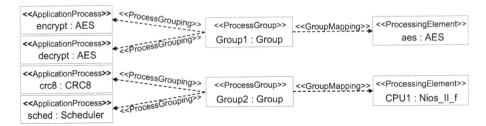

Fig. 5. Mapping of some application processes onto processing elements

Mapping of some application processes onto processing elements is shown in Fig. 5. The mapping is done in two phases: process grouping and group mapping. First, processes are divided into process groups. The grouping can be based on several different criteria, but it is guided by dependencies between processes, such as amount of interaction, different priorities or shared resources. In the second phase, process groups are mapped onto processing elements.

The hardware architecture and mapping in this case have been selected by the designer, but we have developed a sophisticated method for automated architecture exploration for UML based applications [17].

5   Automated Distribution

The automated distribution flow is presented in Fig. 6. The application software consist of code generated by automatic code generation and the application distributor, and software components from a library. The library components contain the platform software, as well as the run-time environment for the distributed execution, consisting of an RTOS API, Inter-Processor Communication (IPC) support, state-machine scheduler, and signal passing functions.

To enable the distributed execution, information about the process mapping needs to be included in the software. The information needed in the distribution is parsed from the UML models with the UML parser tool, which stores the distribution information in a compact XML format. Using this information, the application distributor creates code including a mapping table, defining on which processing element each process group is to be executed, as well as the processes in each group. Information about the signal

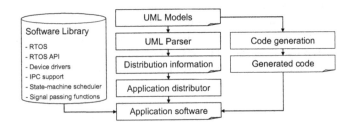

Fig. 6. Automated distribution flow

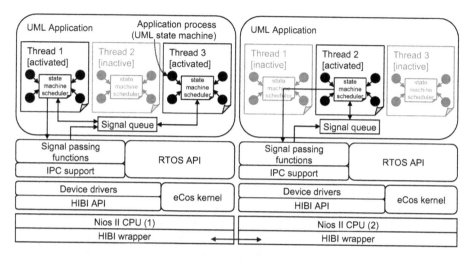

Fig. 7. Run-time environment of a distributed UML application

parameters is also extracted from the generated code to implement the inter-processor signal passing.

Fig. 7 presents the run-time environment for a distributed UML application. In an RTOS, a process group corresponds to a thread, as processes in a group are executed in the same thread. The priority of the groups can be specified in the mapping model, and processes with real-time requirements can be placed in higher priority threads. The execution of processes within a thread is governed by the state machine scheduler. The internal and external signal passing are handled by signal passing functions, which take care that the signal is transmitted to the correct receiver, independent of which CPU the receiver is executed on.

5.1   Scheduling of Application Processes

The same generated code is used for all CPUs in the system, so that each CPU is able to execute all processes of the application. When a CPU starts execution, it checks the mapping table to decide which process groups (threads) it should activate. The signal passing functions take care that signals are delivered to the correct receiver, and the state-machine scheduler does not need the mapping information. All signals are handled in the the order they are received. Inside threads, the state-machine scheduling is non-preemptive, meaning that state transitions cannot be interrupted by other transitions.

The state-machine scheduler is integrated with an underlying operating system by defining an RTOS API, which offers thread creation and synchronization services through a standard interface. Consequently, different operating systems can be used on different CPUs.

5.2   Inter-processor Signal Passing for UML Processes

The signal passing functions need services to transfer the UML signals between different CPUs. The IPC support provides these services by negotiating the data transfers and handling possible data fragmentation. On the TUTWLAN platform, it uses the HIBI API for the data transmissions.

State transitions occur when a UML process sends a signal which triggers a transition in another process, or when a timer expires. Signals are comprised of a standard header and payload data. Header includes information about the signal sender, receiver and priority. Payload consists of zero or more parameters, which may have different data types including integer values, strings, and arrays.

The signal passing at run-time is performed using two signal queues: one for signals passed inside the same thread and other for signals from other threads. Processes within a thread share common signal queues. When a signal is received, it is placed to the corresponding queue.

Our run-time environment extends this basic functionality by enabling the communication between CPUs. When the state-machine scheduler detects that a signal is sent to a process which resides on a different CPU, the signal passing functions transmit the signal to the signal queue on the receiving CPU. The mapping table is used to determine the target CPU. The signal passing functions use the code generated by the application distributor to find information about the parameters of the signal. Based on this information, the signal header and parameters are copied and sent to the receiver using the IPC support.

When a signal is received, the IPC support passes the signal to the signal passing functions. A UML signal is reassembled and added to the external signal queue. The state-machine scheduler fetches the signal from the queue and passes it to the receiving process. From the point of view of a UML process, IPC is transparent; the reception of a signal is exactly the same for signals from all processes in the system, regardless of which CPU or thread the sending process is executed on.

5.3   Dynamic Mapping

The context of a UML state machine is completely defined by its current state and the values of its internal variables. Since threads have a common memory space, and the variables are stored as global data structures, it is possible to change the mapping of application processes between threads at run-time by updating the mapping table and moving existing signals to correct queues.

Further, since all CPUs use the same generated code, it is possible to re-map processes between processing elements at run-time. This operation is somewhat more complicated, since it involves transferring the state-machine variables and signals between CPUs. This issue is beyond the scope of this paper and will be considered in detail in future publications.

6   Performance Measurements

A distributed multiprocessor implementation of an application is expected to affect the performance in terms of reduced execution time and variance. However, the distribution itself causes overhead both in memory requirements and in execution time. The experimental measurements were performed to evaluate the absolute amount of overhead as well as the total effect on performance.

Table 1. TUTMAC static memory requirements for a single CPU

Software component	Code (bytes)	Data (bytes)	Total (bytes)
Generated code	21 748	1 916	23 664
State-machine scheduler	26 064	13 137	39 201
External functions	22 600	33 889	56 489
Signal passing functions	7 064	10 764	17 828
HIBI API	3 552	36 100	39 652
IPC support	3 304	14 084	17 388
Device drivers	2 940	212	3 152
eCos	49 576	5 818	55 394
Total software	136 848	115 920	252 768

6.1   Resource Usage

The static memory requirements for a single CPU are given in Table 1. For each software component the code and data memory requirements are shown. The total memory requirements for a complete multiprocessor system can be evaluated by multiplying the requirement of a single CPU with the number of CPUs in the system.

In addition to the static requirements, TUTMAC uses dynamic memory for signaling between UML processes, and to buffer outgoing packets. The signaling requires approximately 4-5 kilobytes of memory, and depending on the size of the transmit buffer, the total dynamic memory usage is 50-100 kilobytes. Dynamic memory usage is independent on the number of CPUs. Altogether, a TUTWLAN terminal with four CPU's requires approximately 1.1 megabytes of memory.

The Stratix II FPGA used in the prototype implementation has 60,440 equivalent 4-input look-up tables and 2,544,192 bits of on-chip RAM memory. A TUTWLAN terminal configuration consisting of five Nios II CPUs and AES, CRC, and radio interface modules requires 69% of the logic elements and 36% of the on-chip memory.

6.2   Performance Evaluation

To evaluate the performance overhead caused by distribution, delays for signals passed between processes were measured in three different scenarios: two communicating processes on the same thread, on different threads on the same CPU, and on different CPUs. The measured delays are shown in in Fig. 8. In each case the size of the signal payload affects the delay, since the data is copied. On different CPUs, the delay is also increased because of the IPC. If a data type passed as a pointer is used, then the delay would be independent of the payload size between processes on the same CPU, but between CPUs the data is always copied because of local memories.

The delay between different CPUs is 2.5-3 times larger compared to the delay between different threads, depending on the payload size. However, measurements with the TUTMAC protocol show an increase in the total performance of an application by distribution.

The measurements were performed on an architecture configuration consisting of four CPUs and the AES hardware accelerator. Protocol functionality was divided to

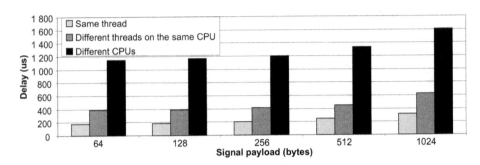

Fig. 8. Delays for UML signal passing in three different scenarios

Table 2. Mappings used in the performance measurements

Process group	Mapping 1 CPU #	Mapping 2 CPU #	Mapping 3 CPU #	Mapping 4 CPU #	Mapping 5 CPU #
Control	1	1	1	1	1
Data processing (reception)	1	2	2	2	2
Data processing (transmission)	1	1	3	3	3
AES decryption	1	2	2	4	Hardware acc.
AES encryption	1	1	3	4	Hardware acc.

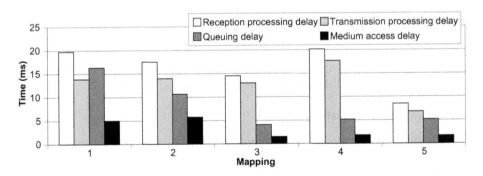

Fig. 9. Measured delays for TUTMAC protocol with different mappings

five process groups, and TUTMAC was executed using different mappings which distributed the groups to different processing elements according to Table 2. The control group includes the TDMA scheduler, 8-bit CRC, radio interface, frame buffering and protocol management. The data processing groups include 32-bit CRC, fragmentation and user interface processes for transmission and reception, respectively. The last two groups include the AES encryption and decryption.

The measured protocol delays are presented in Fig. 9. The results show that the distribution has a significant effect on the execution times. The most notable effect is

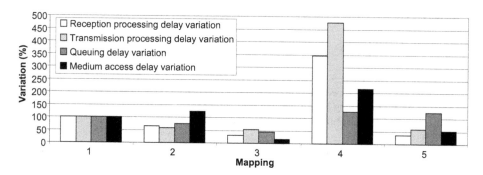

Fig. 10. Measured delay variations for TUTMAC protocol with different mappings

the reduction of the queuing delay, which with three CPUs is reduced to just 25.4% of the original delay with a single CPU. In the first two mappings, the TDMA scheduler is unable to meet all of its real-time requirements and some TDMA data slots are missed. Thus, frames cannot be transmitted at full speed, which increases the queuing delay.

With three CPUs and the AES encryption module, the real-time requirements are fulfilled and a 50-70% speed-up is achieved for all delays when compared to the single CPU mapping. Using a fourth CPU for the AES calculation proved to be inefficient in terms of reducing the delays, since the AES calculation is the most time consuming function of the protocol and thus it is not efficient for transmission and reception to share a common CPU for it. However, in the fifth mapping the hardware accelerator can perform the AES calculation fast enough to reduce both processing delays.

Changes in the delay variations compared to the single CPU mapping are shown in Fig. 10. With three CPUs, the medium access delay variation is reduced by 84.0%. Further, all other delay variations are also reduced 45-70%. These improve the accuracy of TDMA scheduling and the robustness of the system.

7 Conclusions

This paper presented automated distribution of applications modeled in UML to a multiprocessor SoC. With the aid of design automation and modeling of hardware and mapping in UML, the distribution is fully automated and straightforward.

The case study showed that the approach is feasible, and the measurements performed on the prototype platform showed significant improvement in the protocol performance. The future work will include measuring the efficiency overhead incurred by high-level UML design compared to other implementation approaches. The state-machine scheduler and IPC should be optimized to reduce the distribution overhead. Further, possibilities of the dynamic process re-mapping in power management will be studied.

38   M. Setälä et al.

References

1. Object Management Group (OMG): UML 2.0 Superstructure Specification (Version 2.0). (2004)
2. Olukotun, K., Nayfeh, B.A., Hammond, L., Wilson, K., Chang, K.: The case for a single-chip multiprocessor. In: Proceedings of the Seventh International Symposium on Architectural Support for Programming Languages and Operating Systems. (1996)
3. Kaiserswerth, M.: The Parallel Protocol Engine. IEEE/ACM Transactions on Networking **1** (1993) 650–663
4. Object Management Group (OMG): The Common Object Request Broker Specification (Version 3.0). (2004)
5. Schmidt, D.C., Kuhns, F.: An overview of the real-time corba specification. Computer **33** (2000) 56–63
6. Brinkschulte, U., Ungerer, T., Bechina, A., Picioroaga, F., Schneider, E., Kreuzinger, J., Pfeffer, M.: A microkernel middleware architecture for distributed embedded real-time systems. In: Proceedings of the 20th IEEE Symposium on Reliable Distributed Systems. (2001) 218–226
7. Gill, C., Subramonian, V., Parsons, J., Huang, H.M., Torri, S., Niehaus, D., Stuart, D.: ORB middleware evolution for networked embedded systems. In: Proceedings of the 8th International Workshop on Object Oriented Real-time Dependable Systems. (2003) 169–176
8. Chen, R., Sgroi, M., Lavagno, L., Martin, G., Sangiovanni-Vincentelli, A., Rabaey, J.: UML and platform-based design. In: UML for Real: Design of embedded Real-time Systems. Kluwer Academic Publishers (2003) 107–126
9. Martin, G., Lavagno, L., Louis-Guerin, J.: Embedded UML: A merger of real-time UML and co-design. In: Proceedings of the Ninth International Symposium on Hardware/Software Codesign. (2001) 23–28
10. Object Management Group (OMG): UML Profile for CORBA Specification (Version 1.0). (2002)
11. Born, M., Holz, E., Kath, O.: A method for the design and development of distributed applications using UML. In: Proceedings of the 37th International Conference on Technology of Object-Oriented Languages and Systems. (2000) 253–264
12. Kukkala, P., Riihimäki, J., Hännikäinen, M., Hämäläinen, T.D., Kronlöf, K.: UML 2.0 profile for embedded system design. In: Proceedings of the Design, Automation and Test in Europe. Volume 2. (2005) 710–715
13. Hännikäinen, M., Lavikko, T., Kukkala, P., Hämäläinen, T.D.: TUTWLAN - QoS supporting wireless network. Telecommunication Systems - Modelling, Analysis, Design and Management **23** (2003) 297–333
14. Arpinen, T., Kukkala, P., Salminen, E., Hännikäinen, M., Hämäläinen, T.D.: Configurable multiprocessor platform with RTOS for distributed execution of UML 2.0 designed applications. In: Proceedings of the Design, Automation and Test in Europe. (2006)
15. Salminen, E., Lahtinen, V., Kangas, T., Riihimäki, J., Kuusilinna, K., Hämäläinen, T.D.: HIBI v.2 communication network for system-on-chip. In: Proceedings of the International Workshop on Systems, Architectures, Modeling and Simulation. (2004) 413–422
16. Massa, A.J.: Embedded Software Development with eCos. Prentice Hall PTR (2002)
17. Kangas, T., Kukkala, P., Orsila, H., Salminen, E., Hännikäinen, M., Hämäläinen, T.D., Riihimäki, J., Kuusilinna, K.: UML-based multi-processor SoC design framework. Accepted on ACM Transactions on Embedded Computing Systems (2006)

Towards a Transformation Chain Modeling Language*

Bert Vanhooff, Stefan Van Baelen, Aram Hovsepyan,
Wouter Joosen, and Yolande Berbers

Department of Computer Science, K.U. Leuven, Celestijnenlaan 200A, 3001 Leuven, Belgium
{bert.vanhooff, Stefan.VanBaelen, Aram.Hovsepyan, Wouter.Joosen,
Yolande.Berbers}@cs.kuleuven.be

Abstract. The Model Driven Development (MDD) paradigm stimulates the use of models as the main artifacts for software development. These models can be situated at high levels of abstraction, close to the application's business domain. Many consecutive automatic transformations (a transformation chain) can be applied to these models to add the necessary details in order to generate a concrete implementation. This means that a large part of the total development effort is relocated to the development of transformations and hence we should have the necessary tooling support for designing transformation chains. In this paper we propose a metamodel for a transformation chain modeling language that enables implementation independent composition of transformations. We also propose a concrete syntax for this language that is based on UML activity diagrams.

1 Introduction

Model Driven Development (MDD) is an approach to developing software that proposes using machine-readable models as its main artifacts. These models can be constructed with domain specific modeling languages (DSMLs), which are tailored to a specific type of applications and often have a rich visual syntax that hides implementation-level details. These highly abstract models can then be (semi-)automatically transformed to lower-level models by filling in missing details, which eventually makes its straightforward to generate a concrete implementation.

The Object Management Group (OMG) is one of the major endorsers of MDD. Their specific approach is well-known as the Model Driven Architecture (MDA), which is both a specific vision on MDD as well as a collection of technology specifications that support this vision. These specifications include a metamodeling language (MOF) [1], a generic software modeling language (UML) [2], a (not yet fully standardized) transformation specification language (QVT) [3] and many more.

Because the MDD philosophy relocates much of the development effort to transformations it is important to take up the transformation development task with care. In this paper we argue for the need of multiple transformations to get from the highest level models (possibly DSMLs) to the lowest level models (section 2). This requires configuring many transformations in a certain sequence in order to address the concerns of

---

* The described work is part of the EUREKA-ITEA MARTES project, and partly funded by the Flemish government institution IWT (Institute for the Promotion of Innovation by Science and Technology in Flanders).

S. Vassiliadis et al. (Eds.): SAMOS 2006, LNCS 4017, pp. 39–48, 2006.

a specific type of application. Such a transformation sequence is referred to as a transformation chain. We propose a first step towards a modeling language for specifying transformation chains that is based on UML Activity Diagrams. To accomplish this, we provide a metamodel for this language in section 3 and map this to a UML profile in section 4. We wrap up this paper by drawing conclusions and indicating future work in section 5. Related work will be discussed throughout the paper when appropriate.

2   Multiple Transformations

Many papers concerning MDD use the notions of PIM (Platform Independent Model) and PSM (Platform Specific Model), which were introduced by MDA. A PIM is a model of a system that contains no technical details while a PSM is a representation of the same system containing all technical details that are needed to realize it on a concrete technology platform. The mapping between PIM and PSM is realized using an automatic transformation. Such a single-level transformation process allows us to capitalize on the stable platform independent matters and generate PSMs for a range of different technology platforms (figure 1). The platform specific knowledge is moved to the transformations, effectively separating those concerns from the main application model.

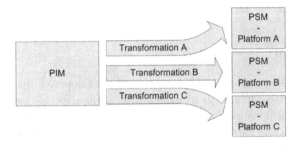

Fig. 1. Single-level transformation (PIM to PSM)

We believe that single-level transformations are not the best way to fully exploit the MDD opportunities. The use of transformations can provide a more elaborate sense of separation of concerns than just pure technical concerns (as in the single PIM/PSM case). Other concerns can be functional, non-functional or just convenience-related such as preventing manual modeling inconsistencies or offering rich domain specific modeling environments. It would be hard and impractical to integrate all these concerns into one big do-it-all transformation. Therefore we argue that it is better to feed a model to a chain of many (small) transformations that each manipulate the model with regard to one specific concern. This would allow us to better modularize the transformations themselves and as a consequence make individual transformations easier to implement and reuse.

Transformation reuse will be most clear in product-line oriented development, as is the case for many embedded applications. Product-lines share a common set of concerns that have to be included or excluded depending on the specific product. If we can encode each of those concerns in a separate transformation, we can more easily leave out unwanted stuff and incorporate new things without having to redo the whole application.

Figure 2 shows an abstract example of composing transformations into a transformation chain. This chain could be the replacement of one of the paths in figure 1.

If multiple transformations are in place, each intermediate model can be seen as being specific to a virtual intermediate platform while being independent of platforms further up the transformation chain. The notion of such a platform is introduced in [4] as abstract platform and is defined as "an acceptable or, to some extent, ideal platform from an application developer's point of view". Abstract platforms not only allow the developer to model an application using appropriate concepts but also allow intermediate transformation developers to create mappings between models using concepts that make sense at their particular level. We could for example treat distribution at one level and timing constraints at another. We consider abstract platforms an integral part of a transformation chain and consequently they are also represented in the model (figure 2).

If we use multiple transformations, the design of their composition (the transformation chain) becomes important next to their implementation. A transformation chain model specifies the composition of many transformations by describing their sequence, input and output model types, dependencies among transformations (such as traceability), platforms etc. Such a model can serve as a construction plan for implementation or as an execution plan after implementation.

Mind that we should very carefully consider how we distribute concerns over transformations. Even though a specific concern can be tackled during one transformation step, it is not always that obvious how all these concerns can be integrated in the overall system. This is especially true for non-functional concerns since they often have subtle effects on one another. A same type of problem arises in the Aspect Oriented Programming (AOP) community, where the application of several aspects on top of each other can produce undesired effects. Our approach to transformation chain modeling does not specifically address these problems.

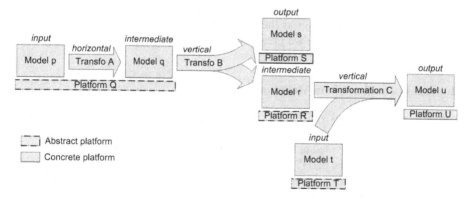

Fig. 2. Multi-level transformation showing intermediate platforms, multi-in/output transformations and vertical/horizontal transformations (respectively between platforms or within a single platform)

In the next section we provide a metamodel that contains the necessary concepts to model transformation chains.

3   Transformation Chain Modeling

In this section we identify the basic requirements of a transformation chain specification language and we present the metamodel that we have conceived to answer to these requirements.

3.1   Requirements

We did not start from scratch in defining a transformation chain specification language. The ORMSC proposal for an MDA Foundation Model [5] gives a good starting point. It consists of a metamodel that defines and relates basic transformation concepts, but does not include concepts specific to composing transformations in transformation chains. We identified the following shortcomings:

1. No specific support for connecting several transformations together.
2. No notion of (abstract) platform; the only typing of models is done through meta-models.
3. No notion of composite transformations, which are reusable transformations that are defined as a chain of lower level transformations themselves.
4. No support for input/output model constraints (pre/post conditions) other than those enforced by the metamodel.
5. No technical considerations – each transformation is assumed to produce models in compatible formats. In real life, even compatible metamodels can be expressed in incompatible formats.

At the same time the MDA Foundation Model proposal contains some concepts that are not that important for defining transformation chains or that are too MDA specific. We consider the listed shortcomings as the additional requirements that our model has to address. In the next subsection we present a metamodel that specifically addresses the shortcomings.

3.2   Transformation Chain Metamodel

In order to adhere to good MDD practice, we define the abstract syntax of the transformation chain by using a metamodel (figure 3).

The model can be divided in two parts: a specification part (*TransformationSpecification*) and an executional part (*TransformationExecution*). The *TransformationSpecification* has two orthogonal specializations: *Atomic* or *Composite* and *Directed* and contains one or more *TransformationFormalParameters*. Such parameters are typed by an abstract *Platform*, which is in turn characterized by a *Metamodel*, optional *ModelConstraints* on that metamodel and possibly additional functionality offered by a *ModelLibrary*. A *TransformationFormalParameter* can also have specific *ParameterConstraints* with which we can enforce additional pre- and postconditions.

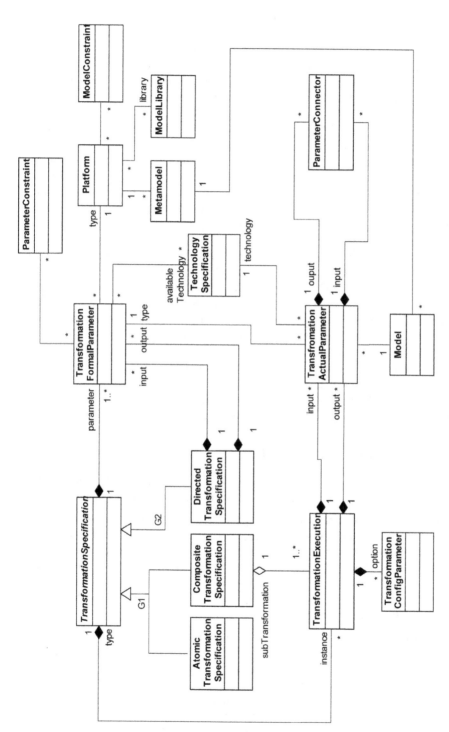

Fig. 3. The metamodel to specify transformation chains

A *TransformationExecution* is always directed (an undirected *TransformationSpecification* becomes directed when it is executed) and has a number of *TransformationActualParameters*, typed by the *TransformationFormalParameters* of the related *TransformationSpecification*. The *Model*, referred to by the actual parameter must adhere to platform of the formal parameter. Each *TransformationActualParameter* in the role of *output* can be connected to one or more other *TransformationActualParameters* in the role of input through a *ParameterConnector*.

The *TechnologySpecification* element is in place to be able to define technical specifications of transformation in- and outputs besides their types of metamodels. This is needed because even if two models adhere to the same metamodel, they can be expressed using a number of different technologies (e.g. XMI v1.x, HUTN – Human Useable Textual Notation, JMI – Java Metadata Interface). Each *TransformationActualParameter* belongs to a concrete implemented transformation so it has to specify a technology for its model. In case of a *CompositeTransformationSpecification* the *TechnologySpecifications* of the containing *TransformationActualParameters* will be propagated to the *TransformationFormalParameters* (hence the association between *TransformationFormalParameter* and *TechnologySpecification*).

The issue of specifying type (*Platform* and *ParameterConstraint*) and technology (*Technology*) of transformation parameters is related to interoperability between transformations. This subject is extensively addressed in [6], where a distinction is made between functional (types) and protocol (technology) connectivity.

To make the metamodel complete we need to add some additional constraints, for example to ensure that a *Model* bound to a *TransformationActualParameter* is compliant with the *Metamodel* that can be reached though the associated *TransformationFromalParameter*. We do not show these constraints due to space restrictions.

In the following section we attach a concrete syntax to our conceptual metamodel.

4 Transformation Chain Profile

A metamodel is worth little without an accompanying concrete modeling language to specify its models. There are roughly two options to specify a concrete syntax:

- A heavyweight approach: define a completely new language with its own symbols (DSML) or extend an existing language (e.g. UML) at the meta level. This approach allows the most freedom in tailoring the language to your own taste.
- A lightweight approach: adapt an existing language to your needs. In this case the base language needs to support a kind of extension mechanism. The UML is probably the most well-known language that allows such adaption in the form of UML profiles (stereotypes, tagged values and constraints).

The first approach is conceptually the best but it has some practical drawbacks. Having to precisely define semantics besides abstract and concrete syntax from the ground up together with the need for custom tool support kept us from applying this approach. The UML on the contrary contains the *Activity package* that is used to model actions executed against a flow of objects, which is similar to transformations and models flowing between them. Therefore we chose to define a UML profile that tailors the standard activity diagrams to our specific needs. Also, both the MEDAL [7] and VMT

[8] approaches to MDD make use of activity diagrams to specify transformations but they operate at the transformation implementation level instead of at the transformation chaining level.

In figure 4, we show a mapping of the transformation concepts from the metamodel of figure 3 to stereotypes and tagged values. The figure is only shown as an illustration and does certainly not contain the complete mapping, which would take too much space. We also do not show constraints to prevent the use of unwanted activity elements such as *ControlFlow* and *CentralBufferNode*.

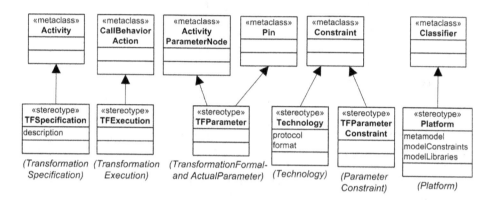

Fig. 4. Partial mapping of the metamodel elements (in italic) to a UML profile; only the most important stereotypes and tagged values are shown, constraints are omitted

The figure shows the UML metaclasses that are specialized using stereotypes and refers to the original metamodel element. The mapping specializes the *Activity* meta-class with the *TFSpecification* stereotype. A *TFSpecification* is *atomic*, if it does not contain any *TFExecutions* (a specialization of *CallBehaviorAction*) or is *composite* when it does. *ActivityParameterNodes* as well as *Pins* must be stereotyped with *TFParameter*, respectively indicating a formal or an actual parameter. Two types of *Constraints* are introduced: *Technology* and *TFParameterConstraint*. Finally a *Platform* is a specialization of the *Classifier* element. Besides these, many other UML Activity elements need to be specialized or excluded from the model in order to make the mapping complete.

Because the metamodel-profile mapping still leaves much to the imagination, we give some examples using the concrete activity diagram notation in the next subsection.

4.1   Example of a Transformation Chain Model

Comprehending a modeling language is the easiest when looking at examples of its concrete syntax. We therefore provide two examples.

Our first example is shown in figure 5. It specifies a transformation component that transforms between domain specific models of cellphone applications and UML component models.

We can see that the Phone2UML *TFSpecification* contains two parameters and has a description, which should be more detailed in a real situation. The *TFParameters* are

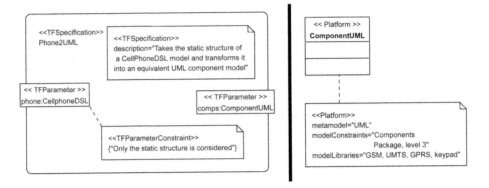

Fig. 5. Example of an atomic transformation specification (on the left) and an accompanying platform specification (on the right)

typed by a platform, specified by the *Platform* classifier. The *ComponentUML* platform on the right is given as an example. It is based on the UML *metamodel*, constrained to use component package at compliance level 3 (*modelConstraints*) and includes some cellphone specific *modelLibraries*. The input parameter has an additional *TFParameterConstraint* saying that only the static structure of our cellphone model will be taken into account.

The second example (figure 6) shows a composite transformation that has two inputs and one output and is specified by an internal structure of two *TFExecution*s. The top one (*Phone2UML*) is reused from figure 5. The *TFExecution* at the bottom

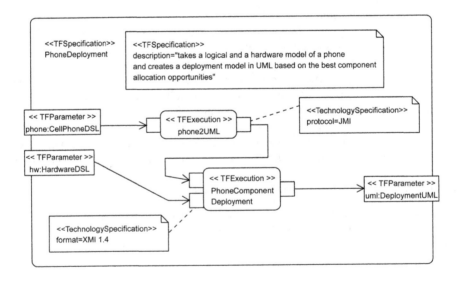

Fig. 6. Example of a composite TransformationSpecification

(*PhoneComponentDeployment*) takes the UML component model (output from *Phone2UML*) together with a hardware model for a specific type of phone and generates the most optimal UML deployment model. We can further see that two *TechnologySpecifications* are given: the output of *Phone2UML* is accessible through a Java Metadata Interface (JMI), while the second input of the *PhoneComponentDeployment* is required to be given in XMI format.

The given examples just give a flavor of what can be specified in a transformation chain model. Real world models will need to be more detailed in many ways, for example in the specification of metamodel and parameter technology. More formal specification of constraints on input/output parameters can be done using the OCL-based approach of [9].

5   Conclusions and Future Work

An important part of the effort in an MDD-based project lies in the development of an appropriate transformation chain, which in turn eases the construction of the application(s) described in the project. Having multiple levels of transformations facilitates transformation reuse, especially in product-line oriented development, which is often the case for embedded systems.

Being faithful to the MDD philosophy, transformation chains also have to be designed and modeled before implementation. We have proposed a transformation chain modeling language of which we defined the abstract syntax using a metamodel. This metamodel is an elaboration of the MDA Foundation Model proposal. We then mapped the metamodel's elements onto UML's Activity Diagrams, which are well-suited, though not ideal, to model transformation chains.

The design of a transformation chain is only part of a project-specific MDD infrastructure. In order to support the concrete realization of transformation chains we will design and implement a transformation chaining framework that uses the proposed language to allow easy concatenation of transformation components that may be implemented in different transformation languages. The results of experimenting with this infrastructure will be used to refine the proposed transformation language. We are also developing a design process to guide the development of transformation chains [10]. This process should help MDD developers in identifying the correct transformation components, platforms, etc.

References

1. Object Management Group: Meta object facility 2.0 core specification. Misc (2004)
2. Object Management Group: Uml 2.0 superstructure conv. document. Misc (2004)
3. Object Management Group: Qvt-merge group submission for mof 2.0 query/view/transformation. Misc (2005)
4. Almeida, J.P., Dijkman, R.M., van Sinderen, M., Pires, L.F.: On the notion of abstract platform in mda development. In: EDOC. (2004) 253–263
5. Object Management Group ORMSC: A proposal for an mda foundation model, white paper (2005)

6. Blanc, X., Gervais, M.P., Sriplakich, P.: Model bus: Towards the interoperability of modelling tools. In: MDAFA. (2004) 17–32
7. Guelfi, N., Ries, B., Sterges, P.: MEDAL: A CASE Tool Extension for Model-Driven Software Engineering. In: SWSTE '03: Proceedings of the IEEE International Conference on Software-Science, Technology & Engineering, Washington, DC, USA, IEEE Computer Society (2003) 33
8. Sendall, S., Perrouin, G., Guelfi, N., Biberstein, O.: Supporting model-to-model transformations: The vmt approach. Technical report (2003)
9. Cariou, E., Marvie, R., Seinturier, L., Duchien, L.: Ocl for the specification of model transformation contracts. In Patrascoiu, O., ed.: OCL and Model Driven Engineering, UML 2004 Conference Workshop, October 12, 2004, Lisbon, Portugal, University of Kent (2004) 69–83
10. Vanhooff, B., Ayed, D., Berbers, Y.: Towards a Transformation Chain Design Process. (2006)

Key Research Challenges for Successfully Applying MDD Within Real-Time Embedded Software Development*

Aram Hovsepyan, Stefan Van Baelen, Bert Vanhooff,
Wouter Joosen, and Yolande Berbers

Katholieke Universiteit Leuven, Departement Computerwetenschappen, Celestijnenlaan 200A,
B-3001 Leuven, Belgium
{Aram.Hovsepyan, Stefan.VanBaelen, Bert.Vanhooff, Wouter.Joosen,
Yolande.Berbers}@cs.kuleuven.be

Abstract. Model-Driven Development (MDD) is a software development paradigm that promotes the use of models at different levels of abstraction and perform transformations between them to derive one or more concrete application implementations. In this paper we analyze the current status of MDD regarding its applicability for the development of Real-Time Embedded Software. We discuss different modeling framework approaches used to specify the various models, and compare OMG/MDA-based approaches (MOF, UML Profiles and executable UML) with a generic MDD-based approach (GME). Finally, we identify the key challenges for future MDD research in order to successfully apply MDD within RTES Development. These challenges are mainly situated in the field of modeling and standardization of abstraction levels, model transformations and code generation, traceability, and integration of existing software within the MDD development process

1 Introduction

Model-Driven Development (MDD) is a software development paradigm that promotes the use of models at different levels of abstraction and performs transformations between them in order to derive a concrete application implementation. MDD promotes the construction of high-level models which can be (semi-) automatically transformed to lower-level models and ultimately into optimal code for the selected target implementation platform. A model is a coherent set of formal elements built for some purpose that is amenable to a particular form of analysis. A model is expressed in a modeling language at some abstraction level which in itself can be defined by metamodels. MDD captures expert knowledge as mapping functions that transform between one model and another.

In the same manner as compilers raised the programming abstraction level from assembler code towards higher-level programming languages, thereby automatically transforming the language constructs into machine-level instructions, MDD tries to upgrade the software development process artifacts from code towards models. Models

---

* The described work is part of the EUREKA-ITEA MARTES project, and is partly funded by the Flemish government institution IWT (Institute for the Promotion of Innovation by Science and Technology in Flanders).

S. Vassiliadis et al. (Eds.): SAMOS 2006, LNCS 4017, pp. 49–58, 2006.

will as such become the key development assets within software development. Such approach will allow to design an application once and target it towards distinct software and/or hardware platforms, even towards future platforms that are still unknown during the initial development. MDD will enable better integration and interoperability on top of the target platform and supports system evolution as platform technologies evolve.

Even though research on several aspects of MDD (modeling abstractions, transformations, processes, ...) has been going on for several years, there are still a number of issues to be solved in order to successfully apply MDD for software development in general and for Real-Time Embedded Software in particular.

In section 2, we compare the distinct approaches towards an MDD modeling framework and application model specifications at different levels of abstraction. On the one hand, a meta-metamodel approach could be used in order to create a DSML, using OMG's MOF or another meta-metamodel. The newly specified DSML can then be used in turn to specify dedicated application models. On the other hand a general purpose modeling language such as UML could be used, profiling it to simulate the required DSML. As a third approach, executable UML could be used as a high-level platform abstraction on top of which applications could be simulated or executed.

In section 3, we identify the key challenges for future MDD research in order to successfully apply MDD within Real-Time Embedded Software Development. These challenges are mainly situated in the field of modeling and standardization of abstraction levels, model transformations and code generation, traceability, and integration of existing software within an MDD development process.

2   MDD Approaches

This section compares the different approaches towards an MDD modeling framework and application model specifications at different levels of abstraction.

2.1   MDD Versus MDA

MDD is a generic software development paradigm that can be applied in different manners. The Object Management Group (OMG) has defined a variant of MDD called Model-Driven Architecture (MDA). MDA aims to represent systems using OMG's general-purpose Unified Modeling Language (UML) along with specific profiles, or using a Domain-Specific Modeling Language (DSML) expressed in OMG's MOF (Meta-Object Facility). The key idea behind MDA is to start with the specification of an Platform-Independent Model (PIM), extracting the common concepts of an application targeted towards a number of platforms and as such allowing a higher level of application specification. Starting from this PIM, a PSM is generated which defines an application model targeted towards a specific platform. A PSM is an elaboration of a PIM that includes platform specific details. For many parts of the application model, the process of obtaining a PSM from a PIM can be automated and the transformation knowledge captured into platform-specific transformation rules. From this PSM, code can be (semi-)automatically generated for the target platform to a certain extent (skeleton, partial or full code generation).

Model-Integrated Computing (MIC) [1] is another variant of MDD, introduced by the Institute for Software Integrated Systems (ISIS) at Vanderbilt University. MIC uses DSMLs to represent system elements and their relationships as well as their transformations to platform-specific artifacts. We discuss in the next section how the meta-metamodel approach can support MIC.

2.2   Modeling Frameworks

Models and transformations are key concepts in MDD. Currently several different approaches exist for specifying application models at different abstraction levels within MDD software development. Although we do not aim to be exhaustive, we will discuss the main distinctive approaches.

2.2.1   Meta-metamodel Approach

A rather formal approach consists of firstly creating a generic modeling infrastructure in order to describe different kinds of metamodels. This meta-metamodel can then be used to create DSMLs which in turn are used to specify dedicated application models. The meta-metamodel should be able to describe what exactly should exist in the DSML in terms of concepts, how they relate to one another and which rules govern their existence and behavior.

MDA-based MOF. Probably the most known instance of a meta-modeling framework is the MOF. The MOF architecture conceives of four "meta-levels". The highest level (M3) is the MOF meta-metamodel which is an instance of itself. The MOF can be used to create a DSML (M2). This newly created DSML can be used to model an application (M1), which in turn contains a run-time instantiation model (M0).

Currently there are very limited number of tools that support a DSML definition based on the complete MOF 2.0 metamodel. Several shortcomings of MOF and its implementation are outlined by [2] and [3]:

- As any standard, the MOF standard prescribes no choice for implementation.
- The standard API for browsing through models in a MOF repository is too low-level to be really efficient.
- MOF lacks any standard mechanisms for specifying DSML concrete syntax. There is no standard way to declare a particular graphical notation.
- MOF's lack of support for associations incorporating state makes the definition of some DSMLs awkward.
- Interoperability between "MOF-compliant" tools is a huge issue (see the discussion on XMI in section 3).

Generic Modeling Environment. Even though MDD is mostly associated with MDA and OMG standards there are modeling frameworks other than MOF. The Generic Modeling Environment (GME) [4] is an alternative implementation of the meta-metamodel approach, and supporting the MIC approach.

GME is a configurable toolkit for creating DSML and program synthesis environments. The configuration is accomplished through metamodels specifying the modeling language of the application domain. The metamodel contains all the syntactic, semantic, and presentation information regarding the domain and the concepts to be used for constructing models. The modeling framework also specifies what relationships may exist among those concepts, how the concepts may be organized and viewed by the modeler, and rules governing the construction of models. The metamodels specifying the DSML are used to automatically generate a target domain-specific modeling environment. This environment can then support the specification of dedicated domain models that are stored in a model database. From these models, applications can automatically be generated. GME has full-featured universal predicate expression language (based on OCL), which can represent very complex relational constraints.

2.2.2 "Lightweight" Approach Using UML Profiles

OMG advocates the more pragmatic approach for a modeling framework based on the idea of developing a DSML using UML Profiles. UML has been improved with modeling language extension features which can raise UML's abstraction level. Stereotypes and tagged values are the extension mechanisms that can be grouped in a profile. The profiling information is used by modeling tools, model transformators and code generators in order to perform domain-specific actions. An example of such an extension is the UML profile for Modeling and Analysis of Real-Time and Embedded systems (MARTE) [5], which is discussed in section 3.

Even though extending UML is considered to be easy, UML as well as its extension mechanisms are quite complex. It is also not clear how well tools will be able to manipulate and exchange these UML Profile extensions.

2.2.3 xUML Approach

Executable UML (xUML) [6] is a third approach to MDD, whereby compilers for the UML modeling language (or a specific subset) are built, treating UML as a programming language on its own. Developing applications using xUML offers several advantages, such as precise and complete semantics, and model visualization and simulation at early stages. However an executable UML model does not have the expressive power of programming languages at the current moment. For example, an executable UML model does not specify issues regarding distribution, the number and allocation of separate threads, or the organization of data. In addition, xUML does not have the power of domain specific modeling languages and supports only a small subset of UML.

2.2.4 Discussion

There are two OMG visions on MDA, supporting respectively MOF and UML extensions (UML Profiles and xUML). Non-OMG MDD approaches mostly rely on meta-metamodel approaches in order to define dedicated DSMLs. GME is an example of such generic MDD modeling framework. GME as most of other non-OMG approaches introduces proprietary standards which inhibit the interchange capabilities. This is precisely one of the strongest points of MOF, which introduces unique means of model interchange and storage. However from a modeling framework perspective, MOF still misses generic editor and generator definitions for DSML creation, and proper tool support. On the other hand, GME and other similar non-OMG modeling frameworks do offer tools to support their modeling frameworks, although they are rather specific for the underlying approach.

There is no reason why UML cannot be used as a base for the development of a domain specific modeling framework, although it is questionable whether using such approach is a good way to build modeling frameworks. Since UML Profiles are defined on top of the whole UML standard, any DSML that is defined as a UML Profile carries the whole UML metamodel within (if not specifically excluded from the profile). The profile approach also restricts the DSML from using the full semantic power of object-oriented class modeling that a true meta-metamodel approach could offer. In addition, within a UML Profile one cannot declare new associations among UML metamodel elements or among stereotypes.

2.3   MDD Promises

The MDD and MDA approach promise a number of important benefits to significantly improve the software development process once a full MDD software development process is in operation.

Time savings. A full MDD development process supported by adequate tool support can provide significant time savings by generating dedicated code for a specific execution platform from the high-level models. Advanced tools will generate code from dynamic models and even provide suitable code for the realization of constraints expressed in e.g. OCL (Object Constraint Language). In addition, reuse of architectures and designs will be actively supported.

Quality improvement. A well-defined architecture incorporates adequate solutions for the realization of the system quality attributes, such as performance, availability, security, modifiability, scalability, reliability etc. In traditional software approaches the system architecture is well-designed during the first iteration, but tends to get diluted by subsequent iterations and new upcoming requirements. Because models and automatic transformations are central in an MDD approach, the system architecture can always be enforced and updated as new requirements arise. The transformation and code generation mechanisms will be created and extensively tested by experts. This raises the quality of every step in an MDD-based development process.

Cross-platform development and enhanced platform migration. As platforms change over time, software applications must continuously be re-implemented. Typically software developers either start everything from scratch or try to port the application to the new platform. In the first case the previous solution gets (partially) lost, while in the second case developers often invent low-level hacks in order to get the application running on the new platform. MDA offers support for cross-platform development and enhanced platform migration by introducing a PIM representation of a software system. When the platform changes, the application can be preserved by reusing the PIM in order to generate a PSM and code of an application targeted towards this new platform.

3   Key Research Challenges

This section presents a number of key issues that currently obstruct the application of MDD for the development of Real-Time Embedded Software.

3.1   Modeling Levels

Even though models are a central concept in MDD, it is not yet obvious which abstraction levels and notations are the most suitable.

3.1.1   Models for Embedded Platforms

Although MDD has already been successfully applied in a number of embedded pilot projects, it is not yet very clear how to integrate the variations of the software platforms, hardware platforms, and available services and devices of a system. There is no simple notion of a "platform" as in the case of more general software development (e.g. J2EE, .NET). Moreover, the gap between an embedded platform and an application model abstraction is usually larger. A number of UML profiles have been designed to assist modeling for embedded systems.

SysML [7] is a domain-specific visual modeling language for System Engineering. SysML supports the specification, analysis, design, verification and validation of a broad range of systems and systems-of-systems. These systems may include hardware, software, information, processes, personnel and facilities.

UML profiles for System on Chip (SoC) and SystemC are designed in order to assist integrating UML modeling into the current SoC design process. The UML 2.0 profile for SystemC captures both the structural and the behavioral features of SystemC language. It makes translation from a high-level platform independent to a lower-level platform dependent SystemC model straightforward.

The MARTE profile intends to provide a common way of modeling both hardware and software aspects of Real-Time and Embedded Systems. As a result, interoperability between development tools used for specification, design, code generation etc. will be possible. Quantitative and partitioning predictions regarding hardware and software characteristics will be fostered. The profile is intended to provide a foundation for applying transformations from UML models into a wide variety of analysis models. The MARTE profile defines precise semantics for time and resource modeling. These precise semantics allows to automatically transform models to lower abstraction level models such as UML for SoC for hardware/software simulation or into C++ for implementation purposes.

However all the profiles are still under development and not yet officially standardized. Moreover they tend to overlap and their interrelationships are still unclear.

3.1.2   Concepts to Model

While static class and component diagrams describe the software structure, dynamic models describe its behavior. Clearly we cannot expect a generator to produce more than just skeleton code if we do not provide information about the behavior.

The MDD community has progressed very little concerning the code generation from dynamic models. Even though most of the modeling frameworks allow users to create dynamic models, the lack of uniform methodology to generate code from models decreases the added value of creating and maintaining dynamic models. It is also not clear how far we should go using dynamic models. Different mathematical algorithms (e.g. Fast Fourier Transforms) could be modeled using UML collaboration diagrams.

But it is unclear whether the benefits still outweigh the complexity of creating complete models. Very often, such algorithms are easier and shorter to write directly in code.

3.2   Model Transformations

Even though model transformations and code generation are central concepts in MDD, it is not yet obvious how to define and apply the model transformations in order to establish an adequate MDD transformation chain.

3.2.1   Transformation Implementation

One of the biggest limitations of the MDA approach is the lack of a unique standard for specifying transformations between models, as well as between models and code. Many custom solutions have been introduced such as Atlas Transformation Language (ATL)[8], usage of OCL to generate code, and Velocity Templates[9]. However these solutions are not standardized and work only with specific tools.

OMG has issued two Requests for Proposals (RFP) for MOF 2.0 QVT[10] and for MOF Model to Text Transformation (MOF2T) [11]. MOF2T is still in its early development stage. QVT describes the needs for a new standard that should be able to manipulate any model based on the Meta-Object Facility (MOF) meta-model. Since the RFP issue, there have been several submissions which were ultimately merged into one [12].

3.2.2   Transformation Composition

We expect that transformations should be able to incorporate functional, non-functional (e.g. memory management) and technical (e.g. J2ME specifics) concerns. Obviously, such transformations could become very cumbersome and complex. Ideally, there should be a chain of transformations each addressing only one concern so that it becomes easy to implement and to reuse. However most of the current MDD practices imply MDA's monolithic forward PIM-to-PSM and PSM-to-code transformations.

We believe that it is better to feed a model to a chain of several transformations that each manipulate the model with regard to one specific functional, non-functional or technical concern. Multiple transformations would allow us to better modularize the transformations themselves. As a consequence the individual transformations would be easier to implement and reuse. When introducing a transformation chain we should not only identify the transformations, but also pay attention to their interdependencies in order to obtain composable, loosely coupled transformations.

3.2.3   Model Interchange and Storage

In order to use MDD for software development, a wide range of model transformations need to be applied and different tools need to be connected for performing all required operations. This creates the need for linking the output of a process step to the input of another process step. Due to the heterogeneity of tools in both functionality and the way users interact with them, connecting tools is very difficult.

OMG tries to solve this problem by introducing XMI, an XML standard for interchanging MOF-compliant models. However XMI versions 1.x are known to lack strong semantics which has forced each tool provider to interpret the standard differently. Versions 2.x are said to fix the issues from previous versions however no implementation results are available yet.

An alternative to the OMG solution is to admit the heterogeneity of model representation and storage and try to implement a "model bus" [13] which realizes model interchange. The idea behind a model bus is to ensure functional and protocol connectivity. Functional connectivity means that the input and output of each transformation should have compatible metamodels in order to be connected. Protocol connectivity should ensure that transformation connections can be realized. In particular, the connected transformations must agree in a model representation form and interaction styles.

3.3   Traceability

Traceability is often associated with the tracking of requirements across all artifacts throughout the software development process. However, it can also refer to the logging of transformation operations and their source/target model element mappings. We define traceability as the ability to extract transformation history out of a transformed model. A specific model element can then be traced back to their originating artifact, which can be another model element, a use case, a requirement, etc.

We can distinguish between generic/full traceability and specific traceability. Full traceability could be automatically accomplished by the transformation engine by linking every changed element in the output model to its counterpart in the source model. This makes traceability complete but not necessary very usable in subsequent transformations since the created links are tightly coupled with the particular implementation of the previous transformation. Specific traceability does not aim to link every source/target tuple but rather aims to form tuples that have a more semantically rich meaning without overcrowding that traceability model. Such specific links can be used more easily across transformations, but may require the developer to insert them manually. It is also not very clear how to determine which kinds of specific links could be useful for subsequent transformations.

Related to the levels of traceability is the issue of standardization of traceability models. It is important to think about what information exactly will be stored in the traceability model. For example, do we want to link as far as textual requirements, do we want traceability across different types of models, do we want to record responsible developers, etc. The advantage of having a single standardized traceability metamodel is that every transformation can always understand the included information, while the disadvantage probably would be its genericity. A possible solution is to have a basic but extensible traceability metamodel that can be adapted to specific needs while still allowing interoperability and interchange between tools and people.

Finally there is the issue of representation of traceability links and integration of traceability in models. Should we store traceability information inside our models themselves (intra-model) or rather externally in a separate traceability model that refers to the elements of the former model (extra-model)? One could argue that the intra-model approach, which can for example be realized with profiles in the UML case, leads to a certain pollution of the model. In the extra-model approach, we need a mechanism to refer to model elements from within our traceability model, for example unique identifiers. In this case a problem would be keeping both models synchronized. Using two separate models can potentially make transformations more complicated since they need to take an extra input if they want to use traceability information.

3.4 Integration of Existing Software

Programming languages usually provide a rich set of libraries which contain implementations of complex mathematical functions, different algorithms, text manipulation, etc. These libraries of existing functionality can save developers a huge amount of time. It is however not always very clear how to make these functions available to the modeler. Two possible approaches that are taken by tool manufacturers are the following:

- Provide a domain abstraction layer that captures all knowledge on these API calls. This approach does not scale and each time a new programming language or API version arises the tool should be modified to include the new mappings.
- Reverse engineer the whole language API into a model. This results into a rather huge and unstructured API model. Moreover we can reverse engineer only to the lowest level of abstraction, and thus cannot easily use higher-level API-related design patterns in the PIMs.

Besides integration of standard libraries it is also important to consider the integration of COTS software and legacy applications into new MDD efforts. Existing systems often serve as a starting point for new developments since they have proven their strength and are considered to be "trustworthy". Therefore it is unrealistic for an MDD project to assume starting from scratch. COTS and legacy system integration is often a matter of representing existing interfaces in our modeling environment using adequate wrappers. However, it is not always clear how to do this. Should we just take the raw interfaces (e.g. by capturing them in UML interfaces) or should we hide the interfaces behind a domain concept? Many problems in this field are worked on by OMG's ADM (Architecture Driven Modernization) task force.

4 Conclusion

MDD is based on the idea to describe the software using a model and apply an automated transformation which creates the source code from the model. MDD is a generic paradigm which does not aim to specify how and which models and transformations should be specified. MDA and MIC are specific visions of MDD which present different modeling frameworks and guidelines. It is still unclear at this moment whether to favor a Meta-metamodel based MDD approach above a UML Profile-based MDD approach.

Projects that have successfully applied MDD do exist, but they tend to fill the gaps in an ad-hoc way. In order to obtain the benefits from a full MDD Software Development Process for Real-Time Embedded System Development, there are a number of research challenges that still have to be addressed adequately, including proper standardization and tool support, in the field of modeling levels, model transformations, traceability and existing software integration.

References

1. ISIS: (Model integrated computing)
2. X. Blanc, S.B., Gervais, M.P.: (A critical analysis of mda standards through an implementation: the modfact tool)
3. Emerson, M.: (Gme-mof: A mda metamodeling environment for gme)
4. ISIS: (Generic modeling environment)
5. ProMARTE: (Uml profile for modeling and analysis of real-time and embedded systems)
6. S. Mellor, M.B.: Executable UML. (2002)
7. SysMLPartners: (Sysml)
8. authors-not specified: Atl : Atlas transformation language (2002)
9. authors-not specified: (Velocity templates)
10. Group, O.M.: Omg/rfp/qvt mof 2.0 query/views/transformations rfp (2001)
11. Group, O.M.: (Omg rfp: Mof model to text transformation rfp)
12. Group, O.M.: Qvt-merge group submission for mof 2.0 query/view/transformation (2005)
13. Blanc, X., Gervais, M.P., Sriplakich, P.: Model bus: Towards the interoperability of modelling tools. In: MDAFA. (2004) 17–32

Domain-Specific Modeling of Power Aware Distributed Real-Time Embedded Systems

Gabor Madl and Nikil Dutt

Center for Embedded Computer Systems
University of California, Irvine, CA 92697, USA*
{gabe, dutt}@ics.uci.edu

Abstract. This paper provides two contributions to the research on applying domain-specific modeling languages to distributed real-time embedded (DRE) systems. First, we present the ALDERIS platform-independent visual language for component-based system development. Second, we demonstrate the use of the ALDERIS language on a helicopter autopilot DRE design. The ALDERIS language is based on the concept of platform-based design, and explicitly captures asynchronous event-driven component interactions as well as the underlying platform for the computation. Unlike most modeling languages, ALDERIS has formally defined semantics providing a way for the formal verification of dense real-time properties and energy consumption.

1 Introduction

Component-based design is an emerging principle for the engineering of complex high-availability distributed real-time embedded (DRE) systems. It has been successfully applied in the domains of hardware design [1], QoS-aware middleware [2], and intellectual property (IP) reuse [3], among others. Components provide an intuitive way to reuse proven designs and implementation, shifting the focus from development by construction to development by *composition*.

Despite recent advances in component-based system design, several key challenges remain that make it hard to develop complex DRE systems with hard QoS-support. Mission-critical system design requires a paradigm shift from conventional methods; the worst case behavior of components have to be considered instead of the average behavior. QoS-support has to be an integral part of the design process providing a way for the rapid evaluation of system designs on a formal basis. To provide a practical modeling language for embedded systems one has to consider how to express *multiple QoS properties* using the same language. Designers have to provide a method that allows to find a balance between various properties such that the system as a whole satisfies all major design constraints.

Domain-specific modeling languages (DSMLs) are languages targeting a well-defined application domain. This approach is rather different from mainstream modeling efforts that focus on creating a language for a wide range of applications, such as *UML*. DSMLs in our approach are defined using *meta-modeling* [4] therefore the designer has the option of creating languages that have well defined semantics and are a good

---

* This research was partially supported by the NSF Grant ACI-0204028.

S. Vassiliadis et al. (Eds.): SAMOS 2006, LNCS 4017, pp. 59–68, 2006.

fit for a problem domain. Large-scale systems that involve several application domains are modeled as a *composition* of DSMLs. We believe that defining semantics to smaller modeling languages and their composition is more likely to succeed than to define it for a large generic modeling language.

This paper presents the *Analysis Language for Distributed, Embedded and Real-time Systems* (ALDERIS) DSML. ALDERIS is a specification language for power aware distributed real-time embedded systems. The language captures dense (continuous-scale) real-time properties on a distributed platform, and energy savings methods based on frequency- and voltage-scaling. ALDERIS provides a way for the design-time formal verification of system models as well as automated simulation. We also present an equivalent compact XML representation that is the input language of the open-source *Distributed Real-time Embedded Analysis* (DREAM) tool. DREAM implements several analysis and optimization algorithms [5] and also supports formal verification based on the UPPAAL [6] and IF toolsets [7].

The remainder of the paper is organized as follows: Section 2 describes the ALDERIS language its design by meta-modeling, Section 3 describes a case study that demonstrates the use of the ALDERIS modeling language, Section 4 compares the results with related work on the field, and Section 5 presents concluding remarks.

2   The ALDERIS **Domain-Specific Modeling Language**

This section describes the ALDERIS DSML and its role in our model-based analysis framework. The formal semantics of ALDERIS is described in [5]. We formalize an abstract model of computation that can express dense real-time properties and power consumption in a common semantic domain. We propose a platform-based analysis of DRE systems consisting of two major aspects: *dependency*, which describes various relations and dependencies between tasks, and *platform*, which specifies the platform

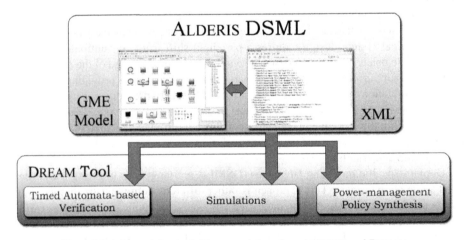

Fig. 1. Model-based Analysis Framework based on ALDERIS and DREAM

that executes the tasks. We capture both these aspects in ALDERIS by specifying the event flow between tasks and their mappings to platform processors.

The ALDERIS language has both visual and textual concrete syntax. Subsection 2.2 describes how we used the meta-modeling to specify the visual syntax of ALDERIS using the *Generic Modeling Environment* (GME) [8] tool by specifying elements and associations between them. Associations can express various relations such as containment, inheritance etc. The textual syntax of ALDERIS is based on XML *schemas* that provides an easy way to exchange the models between various tools. The XML representation has the same abstract syntax as the visual models.

Figure 1 shows an overview of the model-based analysis framework based on ALDERIS and DREAM. ALDERIS models can directly be analyzed using the DREAM tool. The DREAM tool is based on the timed automata [9] model of computation and implements algorithms for (1) real-time verification using the UPPAAL [6] and Verimag IF [7] tools, (2) simulation-based verification of non-preemptive systems based on a discrete event scheduler [5], and (3) power management policy synthesis using the UP-PAAL tool [5]. The timed automata models are automatically generated from ALDERIS models as described in [10]. This paper describes the format of the visual and textual ALDERIS models in a simple helicopter autopilot case study. We illustrate the use of the timed automata-based analysis in Section 3. However, the ALDERIS DSML does not assume the timed automata formalism and allows the use of other models of computation such as data-flow or Petri-nets. For the detailed discussion of analysis methods already implemented in DREAM please see [10, 5].

2.1 Syntax

The ALDERIS model of computation is a tuple $M = \{T, C, TR, TH, PR\}$ where T is a set of *tasks*, C is a set of *event channels*, TR is a set of *timers* which are special tasks that publish events at a given rate, TH is a set of *threads* that represent tasks that are scheduled non-preemptively, and PR is a set of *platform processors*. Tasks and timers are assigned to execute on a specific thread and processor. The thread associated with a given task or timer is specified by the map $\mathsf{Thread} : T \cup TR \rightarrow TH$, and the processor associated with a given thread is specified by the map $\mathsf{Processor} : TH \rightarrow PR$. Timers generate periodic events as specified by the map $\mathsf{Period} : TR \rightarrow \mathbb{N}^+$. Tasks are attributed by the properties *priority, sub-priority, deadline, worst case execution time, best case execution time* specified by the mappings $\mathsf{p}(t) : T \rightarrow \mathbb{N}^+$, $\mathsf{sp}(t) : T \rightarrow \mathbb{N}^+$, $\mathsf{deadline}(t) : T \rightarrow \mathbb{N}^+$, $\mathsf{wcet}(t) : T \rightarrow \mathbb{N}^+$, $\mathsf{bcet}(t) : T \rightarrow \mathbb{N}^+$. We write $\mathsf{State}(t, x)$ to denote the state of t at (global) time x_g: $(\forall t \in T)(\forall x \in \mathbb{N})\ \mathsf{State}(t, x) \in \{\mathtt{init}, \mathtt{wait}, \mathtt{run}, \mathtt{pass}\}$.

2.2 Specifying the ALDERIS DSML Using Meta-modeling

The ALDERIS language is expressive enough to capture a wide range of DRE systems [5]. This section demonstrates how the concepts of *model-integrated computing (MIC)* [4] can be utilized to define the ALDERIS DSML. MIC promotes a metamodel-based approach for powerful domain-specific abstractions that capture key concepts and concerns of DRE systems, such as their structure, behavior, and environment, as well as the QoS properties they must satisfy.

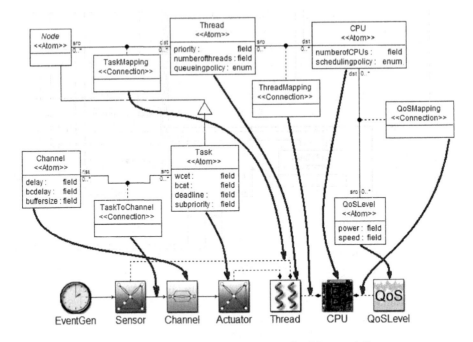

Fig. 2. Specifying the ALDERIS DSML using Meta-modeling

GME [8] is an MIC toolsuite that provides a visual interface to simplify the development of domain-specific modeling languages (DSMLs). GME contains a metamodeling environment that supports the definition of paradigms, which are type systems that describe the roles and relationships in particular domains. GME has a flexible object-oriented type system that supports inheritance and instantiation of elements of DSMLs.

Figure 2 illustrates the specification of the ALDERIS language using the GME meta-model, which is a variation of UML class diagrams. The figure shows a part of the ALDERIS meta-model with its corresponding visual representation in GME. The curvy arrows show how individual modeling elements and their relations are defined by different parts of the meta-model. The ALDERIS modeling language is automatically synthesized from the meta-model by the GME tool. The next section describes how the synthesized ALDERIS DSML is used to model power aware DRE systems.

3   Applying ALDERIS to Helicopter Autopilot Design

This section describes a small-scale helicopter autopilot case study to illustrate the use of the ALDERIS modeling language. Please see our technical report [5] for more detailed discussion, performance analysis and large-scale examples, and the underlying analysis methods based on timed automata model checking methods and simulations.

Helicopter controllers are well-known real-time mission-critical systems, since helicopters inherently have unstable flight modes that have to be avoided, otherwise the safety of the helicopter can be at risk. Although energy consumption is not a traditional

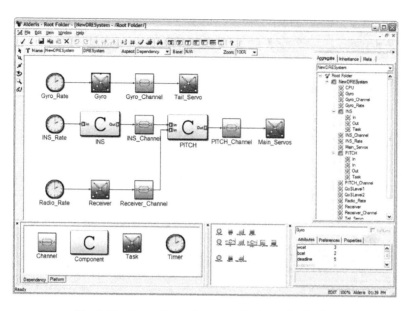

Fig. 3. The Dependency Aspect of the Autopilot Design

problem domain for autopilot design, the wider adoption of *unmanned aerial vehicles (UAVs)* will require cheaper and smaller DRE systems where power consumption is an essential design constraint. Traditional engineering practices used in airplane and helicopter design involve extensive testing and validation that is too costly for UAV design. ALDERIS provides a simple modeling language to experiment, evaluate, and formally verify power aware DRE systems.

Figure 3 shows the dependency aspect of the autopilot application. Dependencies are captured using generic (not synchronous) dataflow semantics, following the *publisher/subscriber* communication pattern [11]. The event channels serve two major purposes in the design: (1) they can model delays in the communication between tasks and components. The event channel captures delays as intervals similarly to the tasks' execution intervals. (2) Event channels provide simple FIFO buffering between tasks and components alleviating the need to synchronize communication between the event sources (publishers) and the event sinks (subscribers).

The dependency aspect focuses mainly on the software components and their interactions. The autopilot consists of 3 major components and a few tasks that represent simple sensors and actuators. There are 3 timers in the system (Gyro_Rate, INS_Rate, and Radio_Rate) that drive the computations with different rates. The top part of Figure 3 shows the tail rotor controller. The Gyro component reads the gyroscope sensor values and is connected directly to the tail servo that controls the tail rotor speed. This setup provides fast response times resulting in stable tail movement, and is therefore commonly used in helicopters.

The INS component represents the internal navigation system of the helicopter, and is based on several sensors such as the inertial measurement unit, compass, and/or GPS devices. The INS component implements computationally more expensive

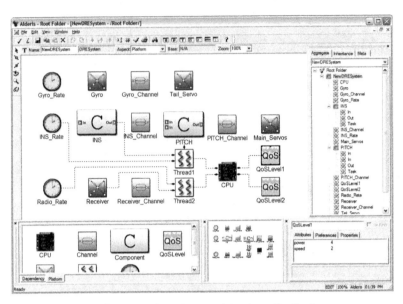

Fig. 4. The Platform Aspect of the Autopilot Design

functionalities than the Gyro component. Instructions for the autopilot may be transmitted over the radio that is handled by the receiver. The received message together with the INS data is fed into the Pitch component that controls the cyclic and collective pitch of the main rotor. The control signal is sent to the servos/actuators "steering" the aircraft as necessary.

Figure 4 shows the platform aspect of the autopilot case study. There is one main CPU in the system that schedules the Control_Thread and Radio_Thread preemptively based on their priorities. The assignment of tasks and timers to the two threads is shown with dashed lines. The event channels and some of the simple tasks representing sensors and actuators are not mapped to the main CPU as these components are scheduled non-concurrently. The reason for this in the case of sensors/actuators is that they have their own hardware and their execution depends solely on their own states. The event channels model delays and the buffering of the network layer which does not require further scheduling. Priorities for the threads and sub-priorities for the tasks are represented in the model as simple attributes that can be updated using the visual GUI.

Table 1. Timing Information for the Autopilot Case Study

Task	WCET	BCET	DL	P
Gyro	3	2	5	-
Tail_Servo	1	1	2	-
INS_Task	4	2	5	high
Pitch_Task	2	1	7	high
Main_Servos	2	2	3	-
Receiver	3	3	20	low

Channel	WCDelay	BCDelay
Gyro_Channel	2	1
INS_Channel	3	2
Pitch_Channel	3	1
Receiver_Channel	4	2

```
<?xml version="1.0" encoding="UTF-8"?>
<DRESystem xmlns:xsi="http://www.w3.org/2001/XMLSchema-instance"
xsi:noNamespaceSchemaLocation="alderis.xsd" name="helicopter_autopilot" version="1.0">
    <DependencyAspect>
      <Node>
        <Task name="Gyro" deadline="2" subpriority="1" wcet="1"/>
        ...<Channel name="Gyro_Channel" buffersize="2"/>
        ...<Timer name="Gyro_Rate" period="5"/>
      <Hierarchy>
        <Component name="INS">
          <TaskContainment task="INS_Task"/>
        </Component>
        ...</Hierarchy>
      <Dependency>
        <TimerToTask timer="Gyro_Rate" task="Gyro"/>
        ...<TaskToChannel task="Gyro" channel="Gyro_Channel"/>
        ...<ChannelToTask channel="Gyro_Channel" task="Tail_Servo"/>
        ...</Dependency>
    </DependencyAspect>
    <PlatformAspect>
      <Thread name="Control_Thread" priority="1" queueingpolicy="FixedPriority">
        <TimerMapping timer="INS_Rate"/>
        <ComponentMapping component="INS"/>
        ...</Thread>
      <CPU name="Main_CPU" schedulingpolicy="FixedPriority">
        <QoSLevel speed="2" power="4"/>
        ...<ThreadMapping thread="Control_Thread"/>
        ...</CPU>
      <CPU name="NonConcurrentManager" schedulingpolicy="NonConcurrent">
        <ThreadMapping thread="NonConcurrent"/></CPU>
    </PlatformAspect>
</DRESystem>
```

Fig. 5. Partial ALDERIS XML Representation for the Helicopter Autopilot

The possible execution speeds and their corresponding power levels can be specified as QoS-level attributes of the Main_CPU. In the helicopter autopilot case study we assume that Main_CPU has a full speed and a half-speed mode, and that tasks that execute in the full speed mode consume 4 times as much energy.

Figure 4 shows how we modeled these two QoS-levels by introducing two QoSLevel atoms and associating them with the CPU. Any number of QoS-levels can be modeled this way, however ALDERIS cannot capture voltage scaling on a continuous scale. This method provides a way to capture dynamic voltage scaling as well as frequency scaling by specifying the relation between execution speed and its corresponding power level for each QoS-level. Algorithmic methods can utilize this information to obtain a power management policy that respects real-time guarantees. Please see [5] for the thorough discussion of the timed automata-based method for power management policy synthesis, and the timed automata models generated from ALDERIS. Figure 5 shows the XML representation of the helicopter autopilot case study shown in Figure 3 and Figure 4. The XML format is specified using *schemas* and provides a simple method to exchange ALDERIS models between tools.

Table 1 shows the parameters assigned to the case study. We have analyzed the helicopter autopilot case study using these parameters using the DREAM tool, and found that it is unschedulable because the INS component misses its deadline. At first this seems strange as the INS component is deployed on the high-priority Control_Thread, and depends only on the INS_Rate timer, therefore it should not wait for low-priority tasks.

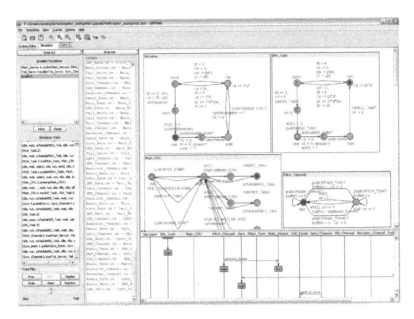

Fig. 6. Unschedulable Execution Trace Detected using Timed Automata Models

A great advantage of the model checking method is that whenever a property is violated a counter-example can be automatically obtained. Figure 6 illustrates the execution trace of the counter-example generated by the UPPAAL model checker. The reason behind the missed deadline is that the Pitch component may already been executing when the INS component becomes enabled. Since non-preemptive scheduling is used between tasks deployed on the same thread the INS component has to wait for the Pitch component to finish its execution. To compensate for this hidden dependency between the INS and Pitch component we have increased the deadline of the INS component to 7 units which turns the system schedulable. Moreover, our analysis shows that if we specify 10 units deadline for the INS and Pitch components the processor can save 24% energy by switching to the half speed mode during the execution of these tasks.

The performance of the timed automata-based verification scales exponentially with respect to the number of tasks. Verifying the example shown in Figure 3 and 4 takes around 2 seconds on a 1.6GHz Pentium 4-M processor with 768 MB memory running the Windows XP OS. Please see [10, 5] for the detailed discussion on the verification method.

4 Related Work

The SAE AADL is an international standard avionics architecture description language. AADL is a successor of the *Honeywell MetaH* toolset [12], a commercially available domain-specific architecture description language (ADL) for developing reliable, real-time multiprocessor avionics system architectures. AADL, however, does not consider energy savings as an objective. In contrast, ALDERIS targets power aware DRE systems.

Ptolemy II [13] is a complex modeling framework that composes heterogeneous models of computation to simulate and evaluate embedded systems. Although the MoCs and their composition is formally defined the focus in Ptolemy II is simulation, not verification. In contrast, ALDERIS and the DREAM tool provide a way for formal verification of dense timed systems using several model checkers.

The SYSWEAVER [14] toolset is a component-based framework that supports the reusability of components across systems with different requirements. It supports code generation, as well as automated analysis based on Matlab/Simulink and real-time rate-monotonic analysis tools, such as the TIMEWIZ model-checker. In contrast, ALDERIS focuses on dense time formal verification using the asynchronous event-driven paradigm.

The CADENA [15] framework is an integrated environment for building and analyzing CORBA Component Model (CCM) based systems. Its main functionality includes CCM code generation in Java, dependency analysis, and model-checking. The emphasis of verification in Cadena is on software logical properties. In contrast, ALDERIS represents time and power levels explicitly and allows dense time verification.

The Component Synthesis using Model Integrated Computing (CoSMIC) [16] toolkit is an integrated collection of DSMLs that support the development, configuration, deployment, and evaluation of DRE systems based on CIAO, which is an implementation of the CORBA Component Model that is integrated with Real-time CORBA. The major focus of CoSMIC is software development, and does not support formal verification.

The Virginia Embedded Systems Toolkit (VEST) [17] is a framework designed for the reliable and configurable composition and analysis of component-based embedded systems from COTS libraries. VEST applies key checks and analysis but - unlike ALDERIS and the DREAM tool - does not support formal proof of correctness.

5   Concluding Remarks

This paper presents the ALDERIS domain-specific modeling language for component-based power aware distributed real-time embedded systems with both visual and XML textual syntaxes. ALDERIS explicitly captures component interactions as well as the platform for computations providing an abstract framework for formal verification and analysis. The ALDERIS meta-model is available for download at http://alderis.ics.uci.edu. Models developed using ALDERIS can be verified and analyzed using the open-source DREAM tool available for download at http://dre.sourceforge.net.

References

1. Alberto Sangiovanni-Vincentelli: Defining Platform-based Design. EEDesign of EETimes (2002)
2. Schmidt, D.C.: Model-driven engineering. IEEE Computer **39**(2) (2006)
3. Daniel D. Gajski and Allen C.-H. Wu and Viraphol Chaiyakul and Shojiro Mori and Tom Nukiyama and Pierre Bricaud: Essential Issues for IP Reuse. In: Asia and South Pacific Design Automation Conference (ASP-DAC 2000). (2000) 37 – 46

4. Sztipanovits, J., Karsai, G.: Model-Integrated Computing. IEEE Computer (1997) 110–112
5. Madl, G., Dutt, N.: Tutorial for the Open-source DREAM Tool. In: CECS Technical Report. (2006)
6. Pettersson, P., Larsen., K.G.: UPPAAL2k. Bulletin of the European Association for Theoretical Computer Science **70** (2000) 40–44
7. Bozga, M., Graf, S., Ober, I., Ober, I., Sifakis, J.: The IF Toolset. Formal Methods for the Design of Real-Time Systems, LNCS 3185 (2004) 237–267
8. Ledeczi, A., Bakay, A., Maroti, M., Volgyesi, P., Nordstrom, G., Sprinkle, J.: Composing Domain-Specific Design Environments. Computer (2001) 44–51
9. Alur, R., Dill, D.L.: A theory of timed automata. Theoretical Computer Science **126**(2) (1994) 183–235
10. Madl, G., Abdelwahed, S., Schmidt, D.C.: Verifying Distributed Real-time Properties of Embedded Systems via Graph Transformations and Model Checking (accepted). The International Journal of Time-Critical Computing (2006)
11. Schmidt, D.C., Stal, M., Rohnert, H., Buschmann, F.: Pattern-Oriented Software Architecture: Patterns for Concurrent and Networked Objects, Volume 2. Wiley & Sons, New York (2000)
12. Vestal, S.: Formal Verification of the MetaH Executive Using Linear Hybrid Automata. In: RTAS '00: Proceedings of the Sixth IEEE Real Time Technology and Applications Symposium (RTAS 2000), Washington, DC, USA, IEEE Computer Society (2000) 134
13. Lee, E.A., Hylands, C., Janneck, J., II, J.D., Liu, J., Liu, X., Neuendorffer, S., Stewart, S.S.M., Vissers, K., Whitaker, P.: Overview of the ptolemy project. Technical Report UCB/ERL M01/11, EECS Department, University of California, Berkeley (2001)
14. de Niz, D., Bhatia, G., Rajkumar, R.: Model-Based Development of Embedded Systems: The SysWeaver Approach. In: Proceedings of the 12th IEEE Real-Time and Embedded Technology and Applications Symposium (RTAS'06). (2006) 231–242
15. Hatcliff, J., Deng, X., Dwyer, M.B., Jung, G., Ranganath, V.P.: Cadena: An Integrated Development, Analysis, and Verification Environment for Component-based Systems. In: Proceedings of International Conference on Software Engineering. (2003)
16. Gokhale, A., Balasubramanian, K., Balasubramanian, J., Krishna, A.S., Edwards, G.T., Deng, G., Turkay, E., Parsons, J., Schmidt, D.C.: Model Driven Middleware: A New Paradigm for Deploying and Provisioning Distributed Real-time and Embedded Applications. The Journal of Science of Computer Programming: Special Issue on Model Driven Architecture (2005 (to appear))
17. Stankovic, J., Zhu, R., Poornalingham, R., Lu, C., Yu, Z., Humphrey, M., Ellis, B.: VEST: An Aspect-based Composition Tool for Real-time Systems. In: Proceedings of the IEEE Real-time Applications Symposium. (2003)

Mining Dynamic Document Spaces with Massively Parallel Embedded Processors

Jan W.M. Jacobs[1], Rui Dai[2], and Gerard J.M. Smit[3]

[1] Océ Technologies BV, PO Box 101,
5900MA Venlo, The Netherlands
jan.wm.jacobs@oce.com
[2] National University of Singapore, Design Technology Institute Faculty of Engineering,
10 Kent Ridge Crescent, Singapore 119260
[3] University of Twente, PO Box 217,
7500AE Enschede, The Netherlands

Abstract. Currently Océ investigates future document management services. One of these services is accessing dynamic document spaces, i.e. improving the access to document spaces which are frequently updated (like newsgroups). This process is rather computational intensive.

This paper describes the research conducted on software development for massively parallel processors. A prototype has been built which processes streams of information from specified newsgroups and transforms them into personal information maps.

Although this technology does speed up the training part compared to a general purpose processor implementation its real benefits emerges with larger problem dimensions because of the scalable approach.

1 Introduction

We are living in a society that is flooded with information. People need tools to structure this information and/or inform users on new trends or remarkable events. One way of visualising the unknown structure of the targeted information sources is by using the Self Organising Map (SOM) neural network [1][2][3]. This network can be visualised by a rectangular map, see Fig. 1. In the map similarity between newsgroup articles, indicated by the labelled dots, is expressed as proximity[1]. The colour of the neurons indicates whether neighbouring neurons are similar or different. Clusters of similar articles are grouped into a "country", which has been given a name and is bordered by red lines.

For recurring visualisations the map is only useful if its global structure does not change that much when new articles are incorporated. Only then will the user be able to quickly reorientate so he/she can see the new changes (cognitive spatial memory effect).

The generation of these maps, however, is very demanding in compute power. Earlier implementations based on Intel's Pentium lack the required responsiveness but do show a straightforward development process, a property of programmable systems. Fortunately, many datamining tasks show simple massively parallel processing.

---

[1] The shown partial example map covers the newsgroup BBC News and BBC Sports in June 2005. It is built up by a grid of 16 by 32 squared tiles (neurons) and each tile can accommodate one or more samples (newsgroup articles).

S. Vassiliadis et al. (Eds.): SAMOS 2006, LNCS 4017, pp. 69–78, 2006.

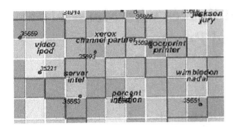

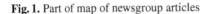

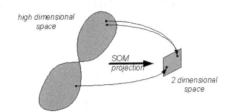

Fig. 1. Part of map of newsgroup articles

Fig. 2. SOM reduces dimensions with good preservation of structure. The original space $doc \in \mathbb{R}^N = (f_0, f_1, \ldots, f_{N-1})$ is mapped on a better comprihensible space $doc \in \mathbb{N}^2 = (i, j)$.

This research is inspired by the potential advantages of massively parallel embedded processors, namely flexibility and shorter design cycles compared to an FPGA approach, while attaining better performance (by scalable design) than a general purpose processor. An important departure point, and in our eyes a novelty, is the reuse of the same hardware for other demanding tasks like colour image processing [4] in Océ's problem domain. This research has been conducted in co-operation with Aspex Semiconductor, a fabless semiconductor company specialising in high performance, software programmable, parallel processors based on associative technology [5].

The problem addressed in this paper is the implementation of the performance demanding SOM neural network training on a massively parallel processor in both an effective and efficient way.

In chapter 2 the reader is introduced to some for this paper relevant concepts such as: SOM, data mining and hardware architectures used for SOM. In chapter 3 we will elaborate on the particular application and in subsequent chapters on implementation issues (chapter 4) and results (chapter 5). Finally, in chapter 6 some conclusions will be drawn.

2   Related Work

Data mining is an application that tries to find hidden patterns and relationships in data that can be used for various purposes such as data analyses, observing trends, prediction etc. One nice way to visualise the hidden relationships is by using the SOM neural network. The network reduces the data volume of the original space while preserving its original structure as faithfully as possible, see Fig. 2. The SOM network projects the data in the N-dimensional space to a two-dimensional space. The original space is encoded by sparse vectors, typically having over 10^4 dimensions, containing the relative frequency of occurrence of significant words in the whole collection. After training, the network exhibits a topological ordering, i.e. data samples (or newsgroup articles) which are similar to each other are positioned in their proximity. Successful applications of SOM networks can be found in visualising document spaces such as newsgroup articles [2] and conference abstracts [3].

The reasons why SOM is taken as a clustering and visualisation tool are: it is better suitable for human interpretation (2D graphic presentation versus 1D list as in Google), it maintains the original structure as closely as possible, it allows for associativity (topological ordering) and it is less computational intensive and more robust than its competitor Multi Dimensional Scaling (MDS) [6].

SOM training is in general a relative computational intensive step in data mining applications [7][6]. That is the reason why many hardware mappings for SOM have been described since its conception in 1982. Because of its inherent parallel structure also parallel implementations have been made. The most advanced ones have been written for SIMD architectures such as CNAPS, Hypercube, Connection Machine and MasPar, which, however, are expensive, bulky and have extremely high power consumption [8][7][9]. Also other, more embedded parallel solutions have been devised like Transputer [10] or FPGA [11]. The latter, however, exhibits rather long development cycles. Fast development is supported by a general purpose processor with special SIMD extensions [12], but is too costly to be a serious contender for embedded applications.

Traditional computers, rely upon a memory that stores and retrieves data by its address rather than its content. In such an organisation (von Neumann architecture), every accessed data word must travel individually between the processing unit and the memory. The simplicity of this retrieval-by-address approach has ensured its success, but has also produced some inherent disadvantages. One is the von Neumann bottleneck, where the memory-access path becomes the limiting factor for system performance. A related disadvantage is the inability to proportionally increase the performance of a unit transfer between the memory and the processor as the size of the memory scales up. Associative memory, in contrast, provides a naturally parallel and scalable form of data retrieval for both structured data (e.g. sets, arrays, tables, trees and graphs) and unstructured data (raw text and digitised signals). An associative memory can be easily extended to process the retrieved data in place, thus becoming an associative processor. This extension is merely the capability of writing a value in parallel into selected cells [5]. Applications range from handheld gaming, multi-media, base transceiver stations (BTSs), on-line transaction processing to heavy image processing, pattern recognition and data mining [13][5].

Aspex's Linedancer is an implementation of a parallel associative processor. The approach taken by Aspex Semiconductor is to use many simple associative processors in a SIMD arrangement. Each of the 4096 processing elements on the Linedancer device has about 200 bits of memory (of which 64 bits are full associative) and a single bit ALU, which can perform a 1 bit operation in 1 clock cycle. Operations on larger data types take multiple clock cycles. The aggregate processing power of Linedancer depends entirely on parallel processing. For example: a 32-bit add will take many times the number of clock cycles taken by a high-end scalar processor, but due to the parallelism 4096 additions can be performed in parallel. Multiple Linedancer devices can be easily connected together to create an even wider SIMD array.

The Linedancer device (shown in Fig. 3) includes an intelligent DMA controller, to ensure that data is moved in and out of the ASProCore concurrently with data processing, and a RISC processor, to issue high level commands to the ASProCore and to set-up the DMA controller. All parts of the device run at the same clock frequency, which can be up to 400MHz.

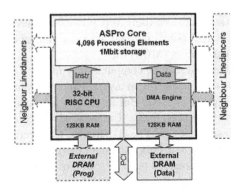

Fig. 3. Aspex Semiconductor's Linedancer

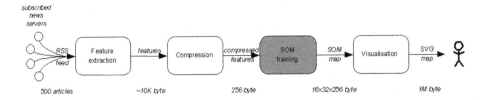

Fig. 4. Processing pipeline, the amount of data communicated between the modules is indicated

A Linedancer is programmed in an extended version of C, with additional syntax for controlling the ASProCore.

3   Specification of the Application

The purpose of the system presented in this paper is to transform the personal news-group feeds into a personal 2D map. In this way the user will have a quicker overview of the changes in his area of interest. The whole pipeline is described in Fig. 4. In order to cluster newsgroups all articles have to be expressed in a common notation. As in [2] we use multi-word terms extracted from the corpus (a collection of documents) of newsgroup articles. Currently a tool named Sigmund is used, a Prolog project developed at the University of Amsterdam [14].

The number of features in a newsgroup collection can become very large, even with a modest number of articles. Since these document spaces are very sparse simple com-pression methods suffice and good results have been reported [2].

One of the most time consuming tasks in the pipeline is the training of the SOM neural network. The purpose of a neural network is to generalise from its training input so that new and not trained samples can be clustered or classified correctly. The process simply boils down to a controlled annealing of a set of neurons arranged in a rectangular grid as will be described in section 3.1. The SOM exhibits spatial ordering, that is neighbouring neurons have similar content.

The spatial order in the SOM is now exploited: similar newsgroup articles are positioned near each other. This allows for associativity since related articles are positioned in each other vicinity. The final module prepares a Scalable Vector Graphics [15](SVG) file for a light weight client. This SVG format allows for operations like zooming, panning and selection for viewing the article itself.

3.1 SOM Training

In this section we will go into some of the details of SOM training. First some definitions are given, then followed by a mathematical framework and finally an example is included. The most important concepts are:

- a neuron $m_{ij}(t) \in \mathbb{R}^N$ with dimension N on a fixed position in a grid $r = (i, j)$,
- an input sample $x_s \in \mathbb{R}^N$ with the same dimension N as the neurons,
- a learning rate $\alpha(t) \in \mathbb{R}$ to control the amount of learning,
- a neighbourhood matrix $\Lambda_{ij}(t) \in \mathbb{R}^2$, defined on the same grid $r = (i, j)$ to provide for spatial ordering and finally
- a scalar $\sigma(t) \in \mathbb{R}$ to control the effective size of the neighbourhood matrix.

In the annealing process all samples x_s are repeatedly offered (in so called epochs) to all neurons $m_{ij}(t)$ in the grid. The neurons will be tuned towards a particular sample x_s by a certain fraction, see (1) below. This fraction is determined by the difference between the sample x_s and the neuron $m_{ij}(t)$, the learning rate $\alpha(t)$ and the neighbourhood matrix $\Lambda_{ij}(t)$. The learning rate is relatively large in the early epochs to allow for large changes and is small towards the end. In order to realise spatial ordering the neighbourhood matrix $\Lambda_{ij}(t)$ is controlled by the neighbourhood parameter $\sigma(t)$. The neighbourhood is as large as the network in the beginning and small in the end, see (2). The function exp refers to the standard exponential function with base Euler's number e. The norm or length of a vector x can in general be defined by $L_p(x = \sqrt[p]{\Sigma_i^N |x_i|^p}$, where $p \in \mathbb{R}, p \geq 1$. For $p = 1, 2, \infty$ the norm represents respectively Manhattan distance (1-norm), Euclidian (2-norm) and the max-norm, which is equivalent to $\max_i(x_i)$. The neighbourhood function, often a Gaussian function, is positioned in the 2D grid at the location $r_{win} \in \mathbb{N}^2$ of the best matching neuron, i.e. the neuron which is most similar to the sample x_s, see (3).

$$m_{ij}(t+1) = m_{ij}(t) + \alpha(t) \cdot \Lambda_{ij}(t) \cdot (x_s - m_{ij}(t)) \qquad \text{update rule (1)}$$

$$\Lambda_{ij}(t) = \exp\left(\frac{\|r - r_{win}(t)\|^2}{2\sigma^2(t)}\right) \qquad \text{neighbourhood (2)}$$

$$r_{win}(t) = (r, (i, j) \in \mathbb{N}^2 \mid \forall_{ij} \min(x_s - m_{ij}(t)) \qquad \text{winning neuron (3)}$$

The following 5 steps will compute the update for a single neuron for a given sample within an epoch:

Step 1. determine the high dimensional distance: $\forall_{ij}(x_s - m_{ij}(t))$
Step 2. determine winning neuron location: $r_{win}(t) = \forall_{ij} \min(x_s - m_{ij}(t))$
Step 3. 2D distance computation: $\forall_{ij}(r_{ij} - r_{win}(t))$
Step 4. neighbourhood computation: see equation (2)
Step 5. compute the update for the neurons: see equation (1)

3.2   Complexity Analysis for SOM Training

For this research we restricted ourselves to the SOM training. The algorithm of the training process is given below, see program in Table 1. The training consists of a sequence of epochs, training sessions, in which 2 parameters are decreased in a controlled way: the learning rate (α) and the neighbourhood (σ). Typical values for epochs is 250, number of samples is 500 and map sizes $W = 32$, $H = 16$ and $N = 256$. The following

Table 1. SOM training program

for all epochs **do**
   decrease α; decrease σ;
   for each sample **do**
      $dist\_N\_D = compute\_N\_D\_distance(sample, all\_neurons);$ (1)
      $winning\_neuron = determine\_winner(dist\_N\_D);$ (2)
      $dist\_2D = compute\_2D\_distance(winning\_neuron, all\_neurons);$ (3)
      $neighbourhood = compute\_neighbourhood(dist\_2D, \sigma);$ (4)
      $all\_neurons = all\_neurons + \alpha \cdot neighbourhood \cdot (sample - all\_neurons);$ (5)
   end
end

table not only summarises the sequential complexity but also includes concrete operation counts for the herefore mentioned values (in cycles per epoch per sample). In the

Table 2. Base complexity, for comparison purposes and projected gain by parallelisation

training step	sequential complexity order of operations	# sequential operations	projected order of parallel operations
1. Distance in highD	$O(W \cdot H \cdot N)$	393216	$O(H + log_2 N)$
2. Winner selection	$O(W \cdot H)$	768	constant
3. Distance in 2D	$O(W \cdot H)$	2560	constant
4. Determine neighbourhood	$O(W \cdot H)$	512	$O(H)$
5. Update neurons	$O(W \cdot H \cdot N)$	393216	$O(H)$

second column cycles are expressed in (big O) order notation. Conversion to concrete numbers of operations is straightforward; the distance computations (steps 1 and 3), however have to account for the subtraction, taking absolute value (for the 1-norm) and finally adding all component values together. The 3rd column contains an estimate of number of operations for a sequential processor. The last column shows the projected parallel complexity for a particular parallel architecture, which is parallel in $W \times N$ but sequential in H. The additional $O(log_2 N)$ accounts for the time to compute a binary adding tree in parallel.

4   Implementation Restrictions and Choices

In order to map the SOM algorithm on the Linedancer in a performance optimal way the following observations are important. It is shown in [11][7] that SOM is flexible in the sense that it is somewhat robust to 1) lower precision (e.g. to 8 bit), 2) using a simple distance metric (e.g. 1-norm or Manhattan distance) and 3) approximating the neighbouring function as a box function.

With a 2 Linedancer system we have an 8K PE budget. Every PE is equipped with 128 bit Extended Memory (EM) and 64 bit Content Addressable Memory (CAM). We have chosen to store the neurons in the array and the input samples in off-chip DRAM. For the choice of dimension N, [16] has shown that for newsgroup articles $N = 315$ is adequate. For our application we used $N = 256$. Reference [11] reports a precision of 8 to 16 bit; we used 8 bit. Although not tested extensively we, however, have the impression that these values are sufficient for our purposes. The same applies to the box function [7], our choice for the neighbouring function.

This leaves us with the following choice for map dimensions: $W \times H \times N = 32 \times 16 \times 256$. The EM is used to store the neurons, the CAM is used to host the temporary work registers. Each set of 256 PEs covers a row of $H = 16$ neurons with dimension $N = 256$ and precision 8 bits, which fits in EM (i.e. 16 neurons $\times$ 8 bit=128 bits), see Fig. 5. The DMA engine will copy the current input sample into I/O memory in a fast way and in parallel to the computations.

The algorithm above is mapped in the following way, see also Fig. 6:

Step 1. The distance between the current sample and all neurons allows for parallel computation of steps (1) and (5). For the current neuron column these absolute differences is stored in the middle column of CAM (Fig. 6). The max-norm is used to compute the length of these 32 differences in parallel instead of a time consuming parallel adding tree. These results are stored in location 0 at the bottom of each 256-segment. Subsequently the 15 other neuron columns have their distances with this sample computed and stored at locations 1..15.

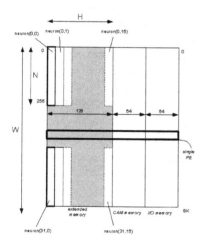

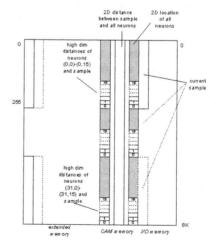

Fig. 5. Vertical arrangement of neurons over PEs in extended memory

Fig. 6. Selecting the winning neuron and computation of the neighbourhood in CAM memory

The end result is a single byte wide column (left column in CAM), covering all $32 \times 16 = 512$ distances between the current input sample and the neurons.

Step 2. The winner selection is performed by a global minimum operation on these 512 distances, which can be done in a relatively fast way by using the associative property of the array. The winning neuron is indicated by one exclusively tagged PE.

Step 3. From now on steps 3, 4 and 5 are performed per neuron column (so H times in sequence). The (x,y) location of each neuron is conveniently stored in an adjacent, rightmost, 16 bit column in the CAM. Hence the winning location is selected to be broadcasted to each neuron, after which the 2D distance is determined.

Step 4. The neighbourhood matrix is computed by a parallel comparison of locally computed 2D distance from the previous step with the current global neighbourhood parameter (2).

Step 5. The final update step is computed in parallel by multiplying the global learning rate with the recomputed difference between neurons and input sample, only for those neurons which were selected in the previous step (1).

5 Results

The performance measurements are now compared with two Pentium implementations, one with SSE instructions and one without SSE instructions. See Table 3 for a detailed comparison. Since the SSE can operate on 4 single precision floats at a time step 1 and 5 can speed up the sequential computation with this factor at maximum. Both Pentium versions use the 1-norm for computing the length of a vector. The SSE version is derived by compiling the algorithm Table 1 with the Intel C++ compiler (version 8.0). The Linedancer results are measured cycles; the Pentium results are estimates derived from assembly code. The Linedancers do speed up step 5 significantly beyond the clock frequency ratio (2 GHz / 300 MHz). However, the performance of step 1 is disappointing for the 1-norm as well as for the max-norm. Especially for the max-norm, which was expected to take fewer cycles because there is no need to sum up all components as in 1-norm. In comparison with a Pentium a speed up of a factor 7 is achieved by a 2 Linedancer system, see Fig. 7. Using the 1-norm distance metric a speedup of 3.5 is

Table 3. Comparison

Training step	Pentium		Aspex Linedancers	
	sequential version estimate [cycles]	SSE estimate [cycles]	1-norm [cycles]	max-norm [cycles]
1. Distance in highD	393216	65024	43384	18028
2. Winner selection	768	768	2158	2158
3. Distance in 2D	2560	2560	100	100
4. Determine neighbourhood	512	512	38	38
5. Update neurons	393216	98304	5590	5536

achieved. The expected speed up is somewhat disappointing because the inherent parallel nature of the SOM training process should map efficiently on the massively parallel Linedancer.

The main reason for that is the relative high communication overhead in the time spent in the inner loop. We collected for the most dominant part, the high dimensional distance (step 1), how many cycles were spend in communication and how many in computation. See Fig. 8. This figure shows that the communication overhead dominates the computation cost.

If inter PE communication would be improved then for this step the performance could match $O(H+log_2N)$ for 1-norm and $O(H)$ for max-norm. When processing and communication were perfectly balanced then this would result in a $3\times$ performance improvement for 1-norm and $5\times$ for max-norm.

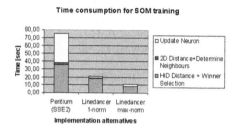

Fig. 7. Comparison of implementation alternatives

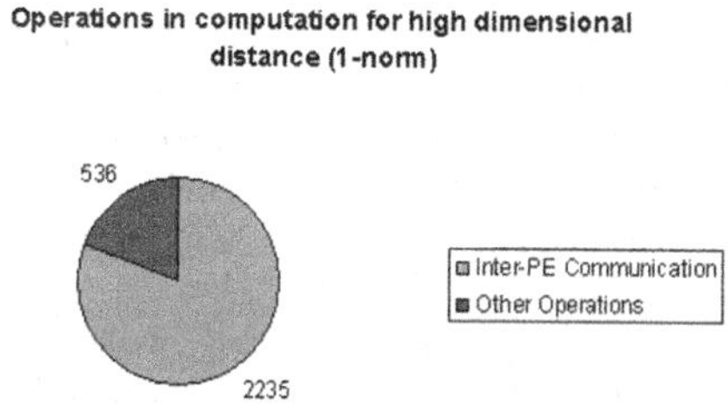

Fig. 8. Distribution of communication and computation in High Dimensional Distance computation

6 Conclusions

A single Linedancer is 3.5 times faster than a Pentium implementation in training a SOM neural network.

Improving on inter PE communication such that computation and communication are better balanced would not only increase the performance significantly (factor of 3 for 1-norm and 5 for max-norm) but would also improve the scalability to larger network dimensions using multiple Linedancers.

It is recommended to improve the performance of the inter PE communication. A solution could be to introduce a chordal ring communication structure [17] or wired-OR functionality.

References

1. Meij, J., ed.: Introduction to Multidimensional Scaling. In: Dealing with the data flood. Mining data, text and multimedia. STT/Beweton, The Hague, The Netherlands (2002)
2. Perelomov, I., Azcarraga, A.P., Tan, J., Chua, T.S.: Using structured self-organizing maps in news integration websites (2002) http://citeseer.ist.psu.edu/perelomov02using.html.
3. Skupin, A.: A cartographic approach to visualizing conference abstracts. In: IEEE Computer Graphics and Applications. (2002) 50–58

4. Jacobs, J., Bond, W., Pouls, R., Smit, G.: Colour image processing with massively parallel embedded processors. To appear in Parallel Computing (2005)
5. Aspex Semiconductor Ltd: Linedancer - overview (2005) http://www.aspex-semi.com/pages/products/products_linedancer_overview.shtml.
6. Duda, R., Hart, P., Stork, D.: Pattern Classification. Wiley-Interscience (2000)
7. Kohonen, T.: Self-Organizing Maps. Springer (1997)
8. Nordstrom, T.: Designing parallel computers for self-organizing maps (1992) http://citeseer.ist.psu.edu/nordstrom92designing.html.
9. Schikuta, E., Weidmann, C.: Data parallel simulation of self-organizing maps on hypercube architectures. In: Proceedings of WSOM'97, Workshop on Self-Organizing Maps, Espoo, Finland, June 4-6. Helsinki University of Technology, Neural Networks Research Centre, Espoo, Finland (1997) 142–147 http://citeseer.ist.psu.edu/72587.html.
10. Wu, C.H., Hodges, R.E., Wang, C.J.: Parallelizing the self-organizing feature map on multiprocessor systems. Parallel Computing **17** (1991) 821–832
11. Pohl, C., Franzmeier, M., Porrmann, M., Rückert, U.: gnbx reconfigurable hardware acceleration of self-organizing maps. In: Proceedings of the IEEE International Conference on Field Programmable Technology (FPT'04), Brisbane, Australia (2004) 97–104
12. Garcia, C., Prieto, M., Pascual-Montano, A.: A speculative parallel algorithm for self-organizing maps. To appear in Parallel Computing (2005)
13. Krikelis, A., Weems, C.: Associative Processing and Processors. IEEE Computer Society (1997)
14. Anjewierden, A., de Hoog, R., Brussee, R., Efimova, L.: Knowledge flows in weblogs. In: Proceedings of the 13th International Conference on Conceptual Structures (ICCS 2005), Kassel, Germany (2005)
15. W3Schools: Introduction into svg (2006) http://www.w3schools.com/svg/svg_intro.asp [Online, accessed 12/04/2006].
16. Azcarraga, A.P., Teddy N. Yap, J.: Extracting meaningful labels for websom text archives. In: CIKM '01: Proceedings of the tenth international conference on Information and knowledge management, New York, NY, USA, ACM Press (2001) 41–48
17. NeoMagic Corporation: The technology of associative processor array (2002) http://www.neomagic.com/product/apa_version3_1.pdf.

Efficient Automated Clock Gating Using CoDeL

Nainesh Agarwal and Nikitas J. Dimopoulos

Department of Electrical and Computer Engineering
University of Victoria
Victoria, B.C., Canada
{nagarwal, nikitas}@ece.uvic.ca

Abstract. We present a highly efficient automated clock gating platform for rapidly developing power efficient hardware architectures. Our language, called CoDeL, allows hardware description at the algorithm level, and thus dramatically reduces design time. We have extended CoDeL to automatically insert clock gating at the behavioral level to reduce dynamic power dissipation in the resulting architecture. This is, to our knowledge, the first hardware design environment that allows an algorithmic description of a component and yet produces a power aware design. To estimate the power savings, we have developed an estimation framework, which is shown to be consistent with the power savings obtained using statistical power analysis using Synopsys tools. To evaluate our platform we use the CoDeL implementation of a counter and various integer transforms used in the realm of DSP (Digital Signal Processing): discrete wavelet transform, discrete cosine transform and an integer transform used in the H.264 (MPEG4 Part 10) video compression standard. These designs are then clock gated using CoDeL and Synopsys. A simulation based power analysis on the designed circuits shows that CoDeL's clock gating performs better than Synopsys' automated clock gating. CoDeL reduces the power dissipation by 83% on average, while Synopsys gives 81% savings.

1 Introduction

For rapidly prototyping hardware architectures, we have developed a system level design language, called CoDeL (Controller Description Language) [1,2,3], which allows system description at the algorithmic level. CoDeL allows rapid design and implementation of hardware modules without understanding the intricacies of hardware description languages such as VHDL and Verilog. In fact, CoDeL compiles to create synthesizable VHDL code that can be simulated and synthesized using standard VHDL tools. CoDeL is a procedural language in which the order of the statements implicitly represents the sequence of activities. It extracts the data and control flow from the program automatically, assigns the necessary hardware blocks and exploits inherent parallelism. It is similar to the C programming language and is therefore easy to learn. Details of the language can be found in [1,4].

We have now developed extensions to the CoDeL compiler which implement clock gating to dramatically lower dynamic power dissipation in CMOS VLSI

S. Vassiliadis et al. (Eds.): SAMOS 2006, LNCS 4017, pp. 79–88, 2006.

circuits. To estimate these power savings from automated clock gating, we have developed an analysis framework, which allows quick and accurate power savings estimation based on the description at the behavioral level. This estimation framework is built into the CoDeL compiler and the estimates are output upon compilation of a design. To test this CoDeL platform we have built and analyzed four architectures: a simple counter, a discrete wavelet transform, a discrete cosine transform and an integer transform used in the H.264 (MPEG4 Part 10) standard [5].

Section 2 provides a brief description of CoDeL's clock gating extension. In section 3 we present an analysis framework for estimating the power savings from CoDeL's clock gating extension. In section 4, four architectures are presented and implemented to test the CoDeL platform. Results are presented in section 5, while section 6 concludes.

2   CoDeL Clock Gating

In synchronous circuits, it is well known that the continuously switching clock signal can account for as much as 45% of the system power [6]. Thus, reduction in the power used by the clock signal is key in reducing total power dissipation. *Gated clocks* can be used to reduce the clock switching in the clock tree and to the leaf registers and flip-flops, where feasible. Clock gating has been explored by several researchers [6, 7, 8, 9, 10].

CoDeL uses a sequential machine to determine the sequence of operations and data transfers in and out of registers. Because of this sequential machine, we know the exact time of the events, and we can anticipate them.

The compiler gathers information on register reads and writes in each state of the finite state machine. We express reads as r_i^s, where a read is performed for register i in state s. Similarly, writes to register i in state s are referred to as w_i^s. The set of all registers written in state s is w^s, while the set of all registers read in state s is r^s. Let the total number of registers be N and the total number of states be M, $i \in [1, N]$, and $s \in [1, M]$.

Using state transition information and the set of reads and writes in each state we can determine the register writes which are necessary and which are useless. The following rules determine that a particular write (w_i^s) is useless.

- Multiple writes without any read in between means all but the last write are useless.
- All writes after the last read of a further-unused register are useless.

Using these rules the set of writes w^s is minimized to include only those register writes that are necessary. We call this minimized set $\tilde{w}^s$.

It is not possible to discover all useless writes through a pure static analysis of the state machine. A run-time mechanism is needed to discover all such useless writes.

Since CoDeL implements designs as a Moore finite state machine, the clock gates for the registers are simply a function of the current state. Thus, simple combinational logic can be used to set up a clock gate. It should be noted that the register encoding the state is not clock gated. Thus, to ensure the state value stabilizes and setup and hold times are met for the register inputs, we use the falling edge of the clock to clock the gated registers. In effect, we have introduced a two-phase clocking mechanism. This allows us to clock a register only in the state where the value of the register needs to be updated. Otherwise, the register is not clocked. This is presented in figure 1.

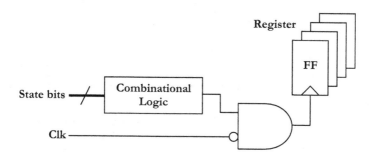

Fig. 1. Clock Gating Circuit

The minimum number of bits for a register which should be clock gated is left as a configurable parameter, ξ, which is an input to the CoDeL compiler. Thus, a register r is clock gated only if $\text{len}(r) \geq \xi$.

3   Power Savings Estimation Framework

The dynamic power savings obtained are divided into two parts. In the first part, we examine the saved power due to the removal of useless switching, while in the second part we examine the savings due to the reduction of clock fanning.

3.1   Useless Switching

For the entire state machine the total number of bits that are potentially written to, W, can be calculated as $W = \sum_{s=1}^{M} \sum_{w_i^s \in w^s} \text{len}(w_i^s)$, where w^s is the unoptimized set of written registers in state s. The optimized total number of written bits, $\tilde{W}$, needs to account for all those non-gated registers whose bit length is less than the threshold ξ.

$$\tilde{W} = \sum_{s=1}^{M} \left[\sum_{w_i^s \in \tilde{w}^s} \text{len}(w_i^s) + \sum_{w_i^s \in w^s, \text{len}(w_i^s) < \xi} \text{len}(w_i^s) \right].$$

To take into account that not all potential writes result in actual writes, the total number of written bits W needs to be reduced. Let η be a statistical quantity representing the fraction of total potential writes that are actual writes.

Not taking into account the clock gating overhead, the fraction of clock power saved due to the removal of useless switching, P_s, is proportional to the fraction of writes saved.

$$P_s = 1 - \frac{0.5\ \tilde{W}}{0.5\ \eta W} = 1 - \frac{\tilde{W}}{\eta W} \tag{1}$$

where the 0.5 factor is included to reduce the number of actual number of bits that change states. Here we assume that on average when a register value changes, only half of its bits change value.

3.2 Clock Switching

The total number of clocked register bit states is given by $C = M \times \sum_{i=1}^{N} \text{len}(r_i)$, where r_i is the ith register.

After clock gating, the number of clocked register bit states is given by

$$\tilde{C} = \sum_{s=1}^{M} \left[\sum_{w_i^s \in \tilde{w}^s, \text{len}(w_i^s) \geq \xi} \text{len}(w_i^s) + \sum_{\text{len}(r_i) < \xi} \text{len}(r_i) \right].$$

Not taking into account the clock gating overhead, the fraction of power saved due to the reduction in clock switching, P_c, is proportional to the fraction of clock cycles saved, given by

$$P_c = 1 - \frac{\tilde{C}}{C}. \tag{2}$$

3.3 Clock Gating Overhead

We call the additional power requirement for clock gating P_g, which is a monotonically increasing function of the number of clock gated bits and the frequency of changes in the state of these gates. We can approximate this overhead by summing the additional switching activity and the additional clocking requirement.

The proportion of additional switching activity, p_s, is

$$p_s = \frac{\sum_{s=1}^{M} \text{count}(w_i^s \in \tilde{w}^s, \text{len}(w_i^s) \geq \xi)}{0.5 \eta W} \tag{3}$$

where, as before, the 0.5 factor is used to reduce the number of bits that change states, based on the assumption that when a register value changes, half of its bits change value.

The proportion of additional clocking overhead, p_c, is given by

$$p_c = \frac{M \cdot \sum_{i=1}^{N} \{1 \text{ if len}(r_i) \geq \xi; 0 \text{ otherwise}\}}{C}. \tag{4}$$

The overall gating overhead can now be stated as

$$P_g = \alpha_s p_s + \alpha_c p_c, \tag{5}$$

where α_s is the fraction of dynamic power dissipation attributable to register switching activity and α_c is the fraction of dissipation attributable to clocking.

3.4   Total Power Saved

The total power saved P is the sum of savings due to the removal of useless switching, P_s, and the saving due to reduction in clock switching, P_c. We also need to take into account the clock gating overhead, P_g. The total power saving is then given by

$$P = \alpha_s P_s + \alpha_c P_c - P_g, \tag{6}$$

where, as before, α_s is the fraction of dynamic power dissipation attributable to register switching activity and α_c is the fraction of dissipation attributable to clocking.

In the power evaluation of our circuits, which use the TSMC 0.18-micron CMOS technology, we find that the dynamic power in non-clock-gated circuits is close to 99.5%. Further, experimentation shows that for our circuits $\alpha_s = 0.4$ and $\alpha_c = 0.6$ gives good approximations to dynamic power consumption. This means that approximately 60% of the dynamic power is attributable to clock switching, while 40% is due to the switching of other circuit elements.

It should be noted that the numbers for α_s and α_c presented above are simply guidelines and could vary considerably depending on the specific circuit and the underlying implementation technology. More accurate values will be obtained over time through simulation of a number of different circuits.

4   Evaluation

To evaluate CoDeL's power efficient compilation we use an implementation of four integer algorithms [1]:

- A simple 16-bit counter.
- A 5/3 Discrete Wavelet Transform using the lifting technique [11, 12]. The 5/3 DWT is used to perform lossless compression of images in the JPEG2000 standard [13].
- A multiplierless approximation to the eight-point Discrete Cosine Transform (DCT) [14]. The DCT forms the heart of the JPEG and MPEG standards [15, 16]. From [14] we use the C7 DCT based on Chen's factorization.
- An integer transform used in the H.264 (MPEG4 Part 10) standard [5]. H.264 is an important, new video compression standard suitable for very high data compression.

---

[1] This is because CoDeL does not currently support floating point or fixed point arithmetic. We are currently working on integrating a floating point unit into CoDeL to allow floating point calculations.

4.1 Implementation

All four modules are implemented using CoDeL. For synthesis we have used Synopsys tools with the TSMC 0.18-micron CMOS technology.

Table 1. CoDeL vs. VHDL code complexity

Module	CoDeL	Lines of Code	
		VHDL (No Clock Gating)	VHDL (Clock Gating)
Counter	13	98	144
DWT	116	719	1089
DCT	80	569	1124
H.264	33	181	358

Table 1 shows the code complexity, as measured by the number of lines of code, of the CoDeL description as compared to the VHDL description of the various designs. We see that the clock gated VHDL descriptions use nearly 10 times the number of lines of code as the CoDeL description. This shows that CoDeL is able to significantly reduce the complexity of describing power efficient hardware architectures.

5 Power Saving Results

The CoDeL compiler automatically implements clock gating as presented in section 2. Using the calculations presented in section 3, power savings estimates are obtained for the designs implemented. These are then verified through power analysis using the Power Compiler from Synopsys. All the results are presented for the gate level design, before placement and routing. We are currently working on getting more accurate results after placement and routing. For brevity, most numerical results are rounded to the nearest integer.

For synthesis, we initially used a 10 MHz clock resulting in a 100 ns maximum propagation delay constraint. To obtain the power dissipation in the circuits Synopsys was used to perform the calculations based on two methods. The first method uses no user specified switching activity annotation and relies on Synopsys' default, statistically based, annotations [17] to perform the power calculations. The second method uses switching activity annotation using simulation, where actual input data is provided.

Table 2 shows power, area and timing results for the non-clock-gated (NCG), Synopsys clock gated (SCG), and CoDeL clock gated (CCG) designs using a 10 MHz clock for synthesis. These results are obtained using method one where statistical switching activity annotation is used.

We see that in almost all cases CoDeL's clock gating produces more power efficient designs relative to no clock gating and Synopsys clock gating. Only the

Table 2. Clock gating results based on statistical analysis, 10 MHz clock (NCG = No Clock Gating, SCG = Synopsys Clock Gating, CCG = CoDeL Clock Gating)

	Power (μW)			Total Cell Area			Longest path (ns)		
	NCG	SCG	CCG	NCG	SCG	CCG	NCG	SCG	CCG
Counter	20	9	10	1919	1796	1971	2.21	1.48	1.42
DWT	376	184	134	55938	51645	57577	10.37	7.32	10.12
DCT	643	389	361	69538	63224	78441	6.36	4.84	6.04
H.264	231	153	140	20604	18364	23759	5.15	1.26	2.40

counter exhibits slightly higher dissipation when CoDeL clock gating is used compared to Synopsys clock gating.

We also see that the Synopsys clock gated designs exhibit reduced total cell area, while CoDeL clock gating increases cell area. The lower area with Synopsys clock gating is because clock gating allows Synopsys to use more area efficient TSMC cells to implement the sequential elements, namely the flip flops. Specifically, we discovered that the non clock gating designs (NCG) use the DFERPQ1 cells to implement the register flip flops, meanwhile the clock gated designs (SCG, CCG) use the simpler DFFRPQ1 cells. The increase in area using CoDeL clock gating can be attributed to the increase in combinational logic required to generate the clock enable signal.

The timing results show that the clock gated designs exhibit better timing than the non clock gated designs. This means that the clock gated designs can be clocked at a higher frequency. This is again due to the use of simpler flip flops in clock gated designs. The higher timing requirement for CoDeL clock gated designs is due to the addition of multi-stage combinational logic in generating the enable signal.

Table 3. Clock gating results based on simulation analysis (NCG = No Clock Gating, SCG = Synopsys Clock Gating, CCG = CoDeL Clock Gating)

	Power (μW)		
Module	NCG	SCG	CCG
Counter	21	10	10
DWT	273	41	31
DCT	337	19	13
H.264	113	7	5

Table 3 shows the power dissipation results using method two, where simulation is used to accurately annotate switching activity in the circuit. For all designs, other than the counter, the input data is provided from a 128×128 grayscale image of *Lena*[2]. Also, in all cases, a 10 MHz clock is used to clock the circuits in the simulations. We find, as before, that clock gating performed

---

[2] The standard grayscale *Lena* image is 512×512. We used IrfanView, which uses the Lanczos resampling algorithm, to reduce this to 128×128.

by CoDeL is more effective at reducing dynamic power dissipation than clock gating performed by the Synopsys Power Compiler.

Table 4. Power Savings (SCG = Synopsys Clock Gating, CCG = CoDeL Clock Gating)

| | | Measured using Synopsys | | | |
| | | Statistical (%) | | Simulation (%) | |
Module	Estimated (%)	SCG	CCG	SCG	CCG
Counter	28	55	50	52	52
DWT	51	51	64	85	89
DCT	43	40	44	94	96
H.264	36	34	39	94	96
Average	40	45	49	81	83

Table 4 provides the power savings obtained using clock gating. The first column presents the estimated power savings using the calculations presented in section 3. The other columns present statistical and simulation based measurements of dynamic power savings using automated clock gating using Synopsys and CoDeL. Since the estimation framework also implicitly uses statistical switching activity annotation, the statistical analysis performed using Synopsys provides a better comparison for our estimation framework than the simulation based analysis. The simulation based power analysis, however, is a more accurate estimate of the expected power savings in the final design.

We find that the power savings estimated using the analysis framework compares quite well to the power savings using statistical power analysis. We find that in all cases, other than the counter, CoDeL clock gating provides more power savings than Synopsys clock gating. The averages show that using a statistical analysis, CoDeL clock gating saves 49% power, while Synopsys clock gating saves 45%. Using simulation analysis, CoDeL clock gating saves 83% power, while Synopsys clock gating saves 81%. This is a reasonable result since the CoDeL compiler still lacks the ability to reuse states and provide automated pipelining. Therefore, some parts of the circuit may remain idle during processing. The addition of clock gating reclaims much of the power consumed in these idle sections.

To assess the scalability of our results, we also synthesized our circuits using stricter constraints and faster clocks. It was found that using Synopsys and the TSMC 0.18-micron CMOS technology the highest clock frequency for which all circuits could be successfully synthesized without any manual circuit optimization was 200 MHz.

Table 5 shows power, area and timing results for a 200 MHz clock using statistical switching activity annotation. Although the area and power requirements to support this frequency are higher, the relative power savings using Synopsys clock gating and CoDeL clock gating are within 2% of those obtained with a 10 MHz clock. Thus, we feel that our clock gating approach scales well as the circuit frequency is increased.

Table 5. Clock gating results based on statistical analysis, 200 MHz clock (NCG = No Clock Gating, SCG = Synopsys Clock Gating, CCG = CoDeL Clock Gating)

	Power (μW)			Total Cell Area			Longest path (ns)		
	NCG	SCG	CCG	NCG	SCG	CCG	NCG	SCG	CCG
Counter	402	189	191	1918	1797	1971	2.21	0.74	0.71
DWT	8436	4192	3178	72668	66972	76555	4.55	2.84	7.05
DCT	14200	8456	7732	93785	82938	97724	4.54	2.86	7.04
H.264	4830	3122	2876	24975	21609	27341	4.55	4.69	6.85

6   Conclusions and Future Work

We find that extending CoDeL to implement automated clock gating produces power efficient designs. The synthesized circuits that use CoDeL clock gating, at least in the examples we have used, are more power efficient than the circuits that use Synopsys clock gating.

We have studied the power efficiency using both switching activity annotated through simulation as well as through statistical methods. In virtually all cases, CoDeL outperforms Synopsys in clock gating. This is an indication of consistency of our clock gating techniques. Further, we find that the power savings obtained using CoDeL clock gating scale quite well to higher frequencies and still beat Synopsys' clock gating efforts.

We have also found that our power savings estimation framework provides estimates that are quite close to the power savings analyzed using statistical power analysis. Thus, the estimation framework is an effective tool for quickly approximating power savings at the behavioral level.

We are currently looking at ways to improve the efficiency of the designs generated by the CoDeL compiler by introducing state and register reuse and some form of automated pipelining. Also, we are currently in the process of incorporating automated power gating into CoDeL to reduce static dissipation in low voltage technology architectures.

References

1. Agarwal, N., Dimopoulos, N.J.: Using CoDeL to rapidly prototype network processor extensions. In: Proc. SAMOS IV. (2004) 333–342
2. Agarwal, N., Dimopoulos, N.: Power-efficient rapid system prototyping using CoDeL: The 2D DWT using lifting. In: Proc. IEEE PacRim 2005. (2005) 550–553
3. Agarwal, N., Dimopoulos, N.: Power efficient rapid hardware development using codel and automated clock gating. In: Proc. ISCAS 2006. (2006)
4. Sivakumar, R., Dimakopoulos, V., Dimopoulos, N.: CoDeL: A rapid prototyping environment for the specification and automatic synthesis of controllers for multiprocessor interconnection networks. In: Proc. SAMOS III. (2003) 58–63
5. Malvar, H.S., Hallapuro, A., Karczewicz, M., Kerofsky, L.: Low-complexity transform and quantization in h.264/avc. IEEE Trans. Circuits Syst. Video Techn. **13** (2003) 598–603

6. Palumbo, G., Pappalardo, F., Sannella, S.: Evaluation on power reduction applying gated clock approaches. In: ISCAS 2002. Volume 4. (2002)

7. Raghavan, N., Akella, V., Bakshi, S.: Automatic insertion of gated clocks at register transfer level. In: Twelfth International Conference On VLSI Design. (1999) 48–54

8. Cadenas, O., Megson, G.: Power performance with gated clocks of a pipelined cordic core. In: 5th International Conference on ASIC. Volume 2. (2003) 1226–1230

9. Benini, L., Siegel, P., Micheli, G.D.: Saving power by synthesizing gated clocks for sequential circuits. IEEE Design and Test of Computers **11** (1994) 32–40

10. Lang, T., Musoll, E., Cortadella, J.: Individual flip-flops with gated clocks for low power datapaths. IEEE Transactions on Circuits and SystemsII: Analog and Digital Signal Processing **44** (1997) 507–516

11. Gall, D.L., Tabatabai, A.: Subband coding of digital images using symmetric kernel filters and arithmetic coding techniques. In: Proc. of the Intl. Conf. on Acoustics, Speech Signal Processing. (1988) 761–764

12. Sweldens, W.: The lifting scheme: A new philosophy in biorthogonal wavelet constructions. In: Proc. SPIE 2569. (1995) 68–79

13. Rabbani, M., Joshi, R.: An overview of the JPEG2000 still image compression standard. Signal Processing: Image Communication Journal **17** (2001)

14. Liang, J., Tran, T.: Fast multiplierless approximation of the dct with the lifting scheme. In: Proc. SPIE Apps. of Dig. Img. Process. XXIII. (2000)

15. Pennebaker, W.B., Mitchell, J.L.: JPEG Still Image Data Compression Standard. Kluwer Academic Publishers, Norwell, MA, USA (1992)

16. Mitchell, J.L., Pennebaker, W.B., Fogg, C.E., Legall, D.J., eds.: MPEG Video Compression Standard. Chapman & Hall, Ltd., London, UK, UK (1996)

17. Synopsys: Power Compiler User Guide. Release w-2004.12 edn. Synopsys (2005)

An Optimization Methodology for Memory Allocation and Task Scheduling in SoCs Via Linear Programming

Bastian Ristau and Gerhard Fettweis

TU Dresden, Vodafone Chair Mobile Communications Systems
01062 Dresden, Germany
{ristau, fettweis}@ifn.et.tu-dresden.de

Abstract. Applications for system on chips become more and more complex. Also the number of available components (DSPs, ASICs, Memories, etc.) rises continuously. These facts necessitate a structured method for selecting components, mapping applications and evaluating the chosen configuration and mapping. In this work we present a methodology for the last named. We will consider optimization of memory allocation and task scheduling as a packing problem and minimize needed memory area. The results can be used as one element of an automated performance analysis for a given system on a high abstraction level. This analysis is essential for establishing a framework that iterates over a large quantity of possible systems. Considering a part of the H.264 codec as an example we will illustrate the results. Furthermore we will show that results can be retrieved fast compared to other NP-hard problems due to intelligent formulation of conditions within the linear program.

1 Introduction

In todays system on chip (SoC) design there is a big gap between register transfer level simulations and higher abstraction level models. Efforts have been made to close this gap in recent years. But commercial solutions still assume a given system and consider mainly the process of mapping tasks to the system components. The quality of the system still depends on the knowledge of the system engineer. From the research area frameworks are emerging that enable automatic iterations over various systems. Unfortunately, performance analysis of the chosen mapping often stays unrevealed, is forwarded to the next lower abstraction level or focuses on heuristics like list scheduling. In most cases also memory sizes are assumed as constraints and not as variables. Therefore, overall execution time or throughput is optimized.

But memory allocation and scheduling strongly influences die size, power consumption and moreover the whole communication architecture of the resulting SoC. Thus, an early proper evaluation for the chosen memory hierarchy is necessary. For evaluation exact algorithms are eligible, which are able to determine *how much memory is needed, when tasks have to start and how data can be stored without fragmentation*. We will present a methodology that solves this problem for application tailored SoCs via linear programming. In doing so we show that this problem can be regarded as modified packaging problem.

S. Vassiliadis et al. (Eds.): SAMOS 2006, LNCS 4017, pp. 89–98, 2006.

We will not focus on minimizing overall execution time but on minimizing used memory resources under a given timing constraint. This is done for mainly two reasons. First, in lots of applications in mobile networking a maximum overall execution time is given, e.g. time for decoding a picture within a video stream. Second, after a system is chosen and tasks are mapped to components and memories, the final die size is only influenced by used memory capacities. Hence, this minimization of used memory resources leads directly to minimization of necessary die size and silicon costs. Moreover, smaller memory capacities result in less energy consumption, which is crucial for embedded systems in mobile devices.

We think of the presented methodology as a starting point for evaluating systems configurations without time-consuming simulations and trial-and-error approaches. Together with automated analysis of other metrics, automatic iteration over and evaluation of various system configurations can be possible. The results can then be used for simulations on lower abstraction levels.

2   Related Work

A large contribution in closing the gap mentioned in section 1 has been done by the MESCAL [1] and Ptolemy [2] projects . These as many other tools (e.g. Artemis [3]) are based on the Y-chart approach [4]. It describes the need and a possible modus operandi for automatic iteration over various SoCs and different abstraction levels. Another approach based on integer linear programming and considering the entire mapping process is presented in [5].

As mentioned in section 1 the focus of this paper is restricted to scheduling. Pioneering work has been done by Liu and Layland back in 1973 [6] and Baruah et. al. [7]. Since then a lot of papers were presented treating scheduling in different ways. Many approaches focus on minimizing makespan, e.g. [8] and neglect optimization of memory requirements. An optimization methodology for energy consumption under a *given* memory size can be found in [9].

A possibility to minimize memory requirements is presented in [10]. Therein the authors focus on minimizing buffer requirements for all rate-optimal schedules. In contrast we consider all schedules meeting the (given) timing constraint. Furthermore multiple memories as well as restrictions on simultaneous memory accesses are included.

In some tools multi-objective optimization (MOO) is used, e.g. [11]. But we rejected optimizing both makespan and resources simultaneously. From the mathematical point of view MOO has some downsides. Firstly, it produces a set of pareto-optimal solutions, from which the preferred one has to be chosen manually. Secondly, the existence of more than one solution prevents solvers from efficiently making use of branch&bound techniques. Latter leads to significantly higher solving times and, therefore, the necessity to use suboptimal heuristics or genetic algorithms. However, if optimization of more than objective is wanted, our result is suitable for a first step optimization in an lexicographical objective environment.

A mathematical introduction with a collection of algorithms for classic scheduling problems mainly treating minimizing makespan can be found in [12]. An approach for a classification scheme regarding resource-constraint scheduling is presented in [13].

3   Methodology

The given problem "Minimizing total needed memory capacity via scheduling" can be formulated as a modified two-dimensional strip packaging problem (2D-SPP). The 2D-SPP describes the problem of packing boxes of fixed width and height into a strip of fixed width in such a manner, that total height is minimized and boxes are non-overlapping. It is described more detailed in [14].

We assume that the application is given as algorithm. Dependencies between the tasks (e.g. functions, operations) are data dependencies described by variables. In our model execution time of a task depends on the used component and memories. So execution time is fixed after mapping of tasks to components and memory. Components in this context are defined as elements processing tasks, such as Microprocessors, DSPs, ASICs, FPGAs, etc. A task itself consists of three phases:

1. *fetch,* in which needed data is transferred into the work memory,
2. *execute,* in which the task is performed by the assigned component,
3. *write back,* in which data is transferred into other memories for further processing.

Furthermore we presume a given maximal overall execution time by the standard specification. Therefore, the number of possible paths/branches caused by if/then conditions is finite and loops can be eliminated by series arranged tasks. In case of data dependent iteration counts each possible number of iterations is considered as one possible path.

Applying this scenario to the problem of scheduling tasks and packing variables into memory the x-axis is time (where maximum execution time is determining the width of the strip) and of the y-axis is memory capacity (Fig. 1). The given problem placing variables and scheduling tasks necessitates a slight modification of the classic 2D-SPP, because there are not only one but two kinds of boxes to be packed:

1. *Outer boxes* represent the life cycles of variables. A life cycle starts when the variable is initialized in or transferred into memory and ends when it is needed no longer or transferred into another memory. The life cycles (respectively memory requirements) of the variables are the lengths (heights) of the boxes.
2. *Inner boxes.* Life cycles consist of different phases: phases, where the variable is used by a task or for transfer, and phases, in which the variable is stored, but not accessed. The inner boxes are characterized by the times the variable is accessed by tasks or transferred to another memory. Consequently, these boxes are nested in the outer boxes. The widths of the inner boxes are determined by the execution times of the corresponding tasks, the heights again are given by the memory requirements.

Note that the width of the inner boxes is given by the execution time of the referring task and fixed after mapping. In difference to classical 2D-SPPs the width of the outer boxes is variable due to the mutable storage times of variables between tasks. The two kinds of boxes are resulting in two different kinds of condition blocks in the later given mixed integer linear program (MILP) as visualized in Fig. 1:

1. *Order conditions.* As a result of data dependencies between tasks the inner boxes cannot be packed arbitrary regarding the horizontal position, e.g. if task i has to be completed before task j starts. These dependencies are included by one-dim. order conditions.

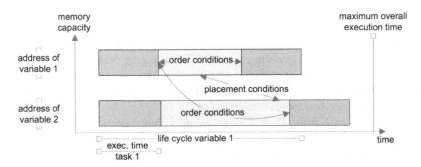

Fig. 1. Illustration of the scheduling problem interpreted as two-dimensional strip-packing problem. Outer boxes identify the life cycles and memory addresses of variables, inner boxes denote the execution times of tasks.

2. *Placement conditions.* This condition block is related to the two-dimensional placement conditions of the outer boxes (variables). In principle the positioning of these is free unless they do not overlap (respectively are not stored in the same memory address), but maybe restricted by order conditions referring to the inner boxes.

Fig. 1 illustrates only one possible path in the flowchart and one memory. Optimization however has to be simultaneous for all possible paths and existing memories. This is done by ensuring that all tasks that exist in two paths start at the same time and variables, whose life cycles overlap in two paths, are placed at the same memory address. To consider multiple memories multiple 2D-SPPs are merged in one superior 2D-SPP. Both are described more detailed in the following section.

4   Detailed Problem Formulation

We will now present the mathematical formulation of the verbal given modified 2D-SPP as mixed integer linear program. But before we start, we need some definitions.

4.1   Definitions

With $x_i \geq 0$ (respectively $w_i \geq 0$) we denote the start time (execution time) of task i. $y_i \geq 0$ ($h_i \geq 0$) specifies the start memory address (memory requirements) of variable i. W represents the maximum overall execution time. Furthermore we use the variables $u_{i,j}$, $b_{i,j}$ and $b'_{i,j}$ as follows:

$$u_{i,j} := \begin{cases} 1 \text{ if variable } i \text{ is placed below variable } j \\ 0 \text{ otherwise} \end{cases} \tag{1}$$

$$b_{i,j} := \begin{cases} 1 \text{ if variable } i \text{ is placed before variable } j \\ 0 \text{ otherwise} \end{cases} \tag{2}$$

$$b'_{i,j} := \begin{cases} 1 \text{ if task } i \text{ ends before task } j \text{ starts} \\ 0 \text{ otherwise} \end{cases} \tag{3}$$

c_n denotes the vector of available memory capacities for memory n, a_n the vector of areas for the respective memory capacities and $H \geq \max_n c_n$ a constant. Let

$$z_{n,k} := \begin{cases} 1 \text{ if capacity step } k \text{ is chosen for memory } n \\ 0 \text{ otherwise} \end{cases} \tag{4}$$

Supplementary we need some set definitions. Let

$$M^n_{g,v} := \left\{ (p,t) \,\middle|\, \begin{array}{l} \text{phase } p \text{ of task } t \text{ in path } g \text{ is accessing variable } v \text{ in mem-} \\ \text{ory number } n \end{array} \right\} \tag{5}$$

which is according to the set of all phase/task pairs accessing the variable v in path g and memory n. Within that set we denote the phase p and task t in which the life cycle of the variable v in memory n is beginning (ending) with $s_{M^n_{g,v}}$ $(e_{M^n_{g,v}}) \in M^n_{g,v}$.

$$M^n_g := \{M^n_{g,1}, M^n_{g,2}, \ldots\} \tag{6}$$

is the set of all variables allocated in memory n. Analogous we define $E^n_g := \{e_1, e_2, \ldots\}$ and $S^n_g := \{s_1, s_2, \ldots\}$. These are the sets of tasks being end and respectively start of the lifecycle of a variable in memory n and path g.

4.2   Placement Conditions

First all boxes have to be placed within the strip or in other words have to end before maximum overall execution time. This is done by

$$x_i + w_i \leq W \quad \forall i \in M^n_{g,v}, \ \forall g, n \tag{7}$$

To implement the corresponding vertical condition block we have to go into more detail. Since classic 2D-SPPs are NP-complete the range of solvable problems in finite time is limited. But the good news is that this special case of the problem (or to be more precise the minimization of needed memory resources) does not have to be solved exactly. Memory capacity is only available in discrete capacity steps, usually to the power of 2. So if memory is available for example in 32KBit and 64KBit it makes no difference if the capacity needed is 52KBit or 33KBit, as long as optimization cannot result in $\leq$32KBit and a solution $\leq$64KBit is capable. This characteristic is implemented by

$$y_i + h_i \leq \sum_k c_{n,k} z_{n,k} \quad \forall i \in M^n_g, \ \forall g, n \tag{8}$$

and

$$\sum_k z_{n,k} = 1 \quad \forall n \tag{9}$$

(8) guarantees that all outer boxes are placed below the chosen memory size, (9) makes sure that exactly one memory size is chosen for each existing memory. Considering as an example we will show in the following section that this minimization of memory capacity, not total needed memory, will result in considerable less time needed to find an optimal solution than minimizing total required memory resources.

Having ensured that all variables are placed within the memory and all tasks are completed before maximum execution time we have to ensure that two variables existing in the same path and memory are not allocated to the same memory address. That means all boxes (inner as well as outer ones) must not overlap. This is assured by

$$x_{e_i} + w_{e_i} - W + Wb_{i,j} \le x_{s_j} \tag{10}$$

$$y_i + h_i - H + Hu_{j,i} \le y_j \tag{11}$$

$$b_{j,i} + b_{i,j} \le 1 \tag{12}$$

$$u_{j,i} + u_{i,j} \le 1 \tag{13}$$

$$u_{j,i} + u_{i,j} + b_{j,i} + b_{i,j} \ge 1 \tag{14}$$

(10) – (14) hold $\forall i, j \in M_g^n, i \ne j, e_i \in E_g^n, s_j \in S_g^n, \forall g, n$. For each pair i, j of boxes (14) ensures at least one of the four conditions resulting from (10) and (11) is not redundant with $x_i \ge 0$ or $y_i \ge 0$ respectively. (12) and (13) prevent overlapping of the boxes. There is always one phase of a task constituting the start and end of the life cycle of a variable. So to prevent overlapping of the outer boxes, it is sufficient to postulate (10) only for the inner boxes delimiting an outer box.

To include if/then-conditions into the MILP (15) is added. It guarantees the placement of a variable existing in two possible paths g_1 and g_2 in the same vertical spot if at least one task is shared by the two paths.

$$y_{M_{g_1,v}^n} = y_{M_{g_2,v}^n} \quad \forall M_{g_1,v}^n \in M_{g_1}^n, M_{g_2,v}^n \in M_{g_2}^n : \exists (p,t) \in M_{g_1,v}^n \cap M_{g_2,v}^n, \forall n \tag{15}$$

Note, by definition a task existing in two possible paths is always started at the same time. However, if differentiated starting times are desired, a slight modification in terms of incorporating identifiers for the corresponding path by additional indices is necessary. It is also presumed that loops are eliminated. Remark that infinite loops do not exist due to the given maximum overall execution time resulting in a finite number of possible tasks.

The given set definitions also guarantee that two inner boxes with the same tag in different memories are located on the same spot horizontally. Hence, the starting time of the associated task is independent of the accessed memories. These facts and (15) are the only placement conditions between different paths and memories.

4.3 Order Conditions

The order conditions are defined by the application and can be derived from the flowchart. There are two different kinds of order conditions. Firstly, (16) denotes that task j is dependent on task i.

$$x_i + w_i \le x_j \tag{16}$$

Secondly, the number of simultaneously performed tasks by one component or the quantity of simultaneous memory accesses by different tasks can be limited. (17) and (18) are an example for such a limitation.

$$x_i + w_i - W + Wb'_{i,j} \le x_j \tag{17}$$

$$b'_{i,j} + b'_{j,i} = 1 \tag{18}$$

In the given case the number of simultaneous accesses to one memory by tasks is limited to one. Formulation for other cases can be adopted easily.

4.4   Objective Function

The objective function is given by

$$\sum_n \sum_k a_{n,k} z_{n,k} \rightarrow \min \qquad (19)$$

With (19) total area used by memory components on the system is minimized. Area in this model is given by the sum of areas of all used memory elements. Other components of the system are unaccounted because these elements are fixed after mapping. More sophisticated definitions for calculating die size can be integrated easily by modifying the objective and adding additional constraints.

5   Results

We have tested the methodology with a part of the H.264 video codec [15] from the Fraunhofer Hertz Institute Berlin, namely the function decodeMBInter. The problem characteristics are shown in table 1.

Table 1. Characteristics of the examined H.264-part

# of tasks	14
# of paths	14
# of variables	21

Fig. 2 illustrates the given data dependencies. Maximum overall execution time, times of tasks, memory requirements of the variables and memory capacity steps are a first estimate for a possible SoC configuration. Data dependencies were modified slightly to include possible parallel processing of tasks mapped to different components. Parallel processing of two tasks mapped to the same component was forbidden.

We assumed two components and two memories. One acting as system memory equipped with a single port and one representing a shared memory with double port. The mapping of tasks to components is shown in table 2. Note that tasks 1 and 14 denote dummy tasks identifying start and end. Consequently they do not have to be assigned to any components. Local memory for both components is the shared memory. To simulate memory transfers and the three phases fetch, execute and write back in our model a temporary variable is transferred from system to shared memory at the beginning of each task. After execution the variable is transferred back to system memory.

Optimization was done for the shared memory. The resulting MILP had 814 variables (thereof 748 binary) and 1491 constraints. Fig. 3 illustrates the result. As you

Table 2. Assumed mapping of tasks to components for the examined H.264-part

component	executed tasks
1	2 – 5
2	6 – 13

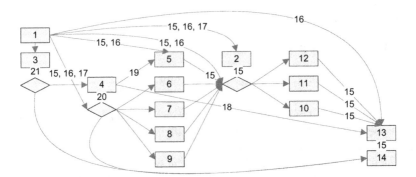

Fig. 2. Flowchart of the examined H.264-part. Numbers in the boxes identify the tasks, numbers beside the arcs label variables. Temporary variables needed only within the tasks are later referred by the number of the corresponding task. Task 1 and 14 denote additional inserted starting and ending tasks, which are not assigned to components.

can see the depicted solution is far away from minimum overall memory usage but optimal in respect to the chosen memory capacity step. The problem was solved in about 5 seconds on an AMD Dual Opteron System with 2.2 GHz processors each using CPLEX 9.1.

By contrast the solving time for minimizing needed memory capacity h (with modified condition (8): $y_i + h_i \leq h$ and without condition (9)) took more than 500 sec. or in this case $> 10,000\%$ compared to minimizing needed memory capacity step. It also illustrates the possible impact of a slightly different MILP formulation. The reason for this big difference is the utilization of the memory capacity steps as upper and lower bounds. If during the algorithm automatically generated lower bound and the capable

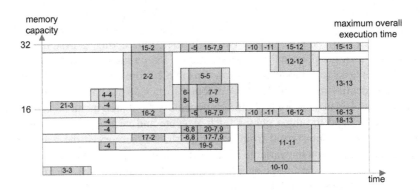

Fig. 3. Illustration of the optimized schedule of tasks and allocation of variables in respect to memory capacity step. Light blue boxes mark the outer boxes representing the life cycle of the variables, narrow boxes denote the phases in which a variable is transferred/initialized and blue boxes identify the inner boxes representing the tasks accessing the required variables. The labels of the boxes identify tasks – variables.

solution are in between the same two memory capacity steps the algorithm terminates. This behavior is illustrated in Fig. 3, where optimization is stopped after a solution of 32 Kbit is capable and a solution of 16 Kbit is ruled out.

We also performed a trade off analysis with a different system configuration. The shared memory was replaced by a single ported memory for each component. Optimization resulted in a required memory capacity of at least 32 Kbit for each component. Although single ported memory is smaller compared to double ported, the overall needed die size was almost the same for both configurations. For calculation we used custom designed memory elements by UMC/Virtual Silicon Technology.

6   Conclusions

In section 5 we have demonstrated a methodology for memory allocation and task scheduling applicable to real life problems of small size. The solution time shows that the full potential of the methodology is not tapped by the passed problem.

Furthermore our approach is highly flexible. The assumption that a task consists of the three phases, is not a must. Inclusion of additional phases or reduction to one phase is possible without large effort. Latter can be reasonable, if exact execution and transfer times are not known in an early design stage, but a first estimation model for scheduling is desired. For this case also data dependencies can be reduced to simple task dependencies. Moreover the methodology does not care what is stored in the memory. The MILP formulation holds for data as well as instruction code. Also, the type of memory to be optimized is arbitrary. Thus, scratchpad memory, register files, etc. can be simulated.

As mentioned in section 2 there exist methods for optimizing memory allocation under given memory capacities. Examination of possible combination of these methods with our methodology could lead to a refinement of existing high abstraction level models and consequently could be the next step for automated iteration over and performance evaluation of several systems.

References

1. Mihal, A., Kulkarni, C., Sauer, C., Vissers, K., Moskewicz, M., Tsai, M., Shah, N., Weber, S., Jin, Y., Keutzer, K., Malik, S. In: Developing Architectural Platforms: A Disciplined Approach. Volume 19. IEEE Design and Test of Computers (2002) 6–16
2. Lee, E.A.: Overview of the ptolemy project. Technical memorandum UCB/ERL M03/25, University of California, Berkeley, CA, 94720, USA. (2003)
3. Pimentel, A.D., Hertzberger, L.O., Lieverse, P., van der Wolf, P., Deprettere, E.F.: Exploring Embedded-Systems Architectures with Artemis. Computer **34** (2001) 57–63
4. Kienhuis, B., Deprettere, E., Vissers, K., van der Wolf, P.: An approach for quantitative analysis of application-specific dataflow architectures. In: ASAP '97: Proceedings of the IEEE International Conference on Application-Specific Systems, Architectures and Processors, Washington, DC, USA, IEEE Computer Society (1997) 338
5. Niemann, R., Marwedel, P.: Hardware/software partitioning using integer programming. In: EDTC '96: Proceedings of the 1996 European conference on Design and Test, Washington, DC, USA, IEEE Computer Society (1996) 473

6. Liu, C.L., Layland, J.W.: Scheduling Algorithms for Multiprogramming in a Hard-Real-Time Environment. J. ACM **20** (1973) 46–61

7. Baruah, S.K., Gehrke, J.E., Plaxton, C.G.: Fast scheduling of periodic tasks on multiple resources. Technical Report CS-TR-95-02, University of Texas, Austin, Austin, TX, USA (1995)

8. Jin, Y., Satish, N., Ravindran, K., Keutzer, K.: An automated exploration framework for fpga-based soft multiprocessor systems. In: CODES '05: Proceedings of the 2005 International Conference on Hardware/Software Codesign and System Synthesis. (2005) 273–278

9. Verma, M., Wehmeyer, L., Marwedel, P.: Dynamic overlay of scratchpad memory for energy minimization. In: CODES+ISSS '04: Proceedings of the 2nd IEEE/ACM/IFIP international conference on Hardware/software codesign and system synthesis, New York, NY, USA, ACM Press (2004) 104–109

10. Govindarajan, R., Gao, G., Desai, P.: Minimizing Memory Requirements in Rate-Optimal Schedules. In: ASAP '94: Proceedings ot the International Conference on Application Specific Array Processors. Volume Application Specific Array Processors, . Proceedings., International Conference on. (1994) 75–86

11. Dick, R.P., Jha, N.K.: MOGAC: a multiobjective genetic algorithm for the co-synthesis of hardware-software embedded systems. In: ICCAD '97: Proceedings of the 1997 IEEE/ACM international conference on Computer-aided design, Washington, DC, USA, IEEE Computer Society (1997) 522–529

12. Bruckner, P.: Scheduling Algorithms. 4th edn. Springer-Verlag (2003)

13. Brucker, P., Drexl, A., Möhring, R., Neumann, K., Pesch, E.: Resource-constrained project scheduling: Notation, classification, models, and methods. European Journal of Operational Research **112** (1999) 3–41

14. Belov, G., Chiglintsev, A., Filippova, A., Mukhacheva, E., Scheithauer, G., Shirgazin, R.: The two-dimensional strip packing problem: A numerical experiment with waste-free instances using algorithms with block structure. Preprint MATH-NM-01-2005 TU Dresden (2005)

15. Wiegand, T., Sullivan, G., Bjntegaard, G., Luthra, A.: Overview of the H.264/AVC video coding standard. In: Circuits and Systems for Video Technology, IEEE Transactions on. Volume vol.13, no.7., IEEE Circuits and Systems Society (2003) 560–576

Designing Wireless Sensor Nodes

Marcos A.M. Vieira[1], Adriano B. da Cunha[2], and Diógenes C. da Silva Jr.[2]

[1] Dept. of Computer Science, Federal University of Minas Gerais,
[2] Dept. of Electrical Engineering, Federal University of Minas Gerais,
Av. Antônio Carlos, 6627, Belo Horizonte, MG, Brazil
mmvieira@usc.edu, {adborges, diogenes}@cpdee.ufmg.br

Abstract. Wireless sensor networks are networks of large quantities of compact microsensors with wireless communication capability. Emerging applications of data gathering range from the environmental to the military. Architectural challenges are posed for designers such as computational power, energy consumption, energy sources, communication channels and sensing capabilities. This work presents the current state-of-the-art for wireless sensor nodes, investigating and analyzing these challenges. We discuss the characteristics and requirements for a sensor node. A comprehensive comparative study of sensor node platforms, energy management techniques, off-the-shelf microcontrollers, battery types and radio devices is presented.

1 Introduction

A wireless sensor network (WSN) is composed of many autonomous and compact devices called sensor nodes. The objective of this network is to collect data. The availability of integrated low-power sensing devices, embedded processors, wireless communication kits, and power equipment are enabling the design of sensor nodes.

Wireless Sensor Network has the potential for many applications and some already exists, for example in a large metropolis to monitor traffic density and road conditions; in engineering to monitor bridges and buildings structures; in a forest for fire detection, in other environments like oceans and air resources; in precision agriculture; in disaster recovery service; in condition based maintenance devices like powerplants; in biomedicine. Other applications include managing complex physical systems like airplane wings and complex ecosystems.

A sensor node is composed of a power unit, processing unit, sensing unit, and communication unit. The power unit has the purpose to supply the energy to the node. The processing unit collects and processes signals captured from sensors and transmit them to the network. Sensors devices are devices that produce a measurable response to a change in a physical condition like temperature and pressure. The wireless communication channel enables a medium to transfer signals from sensors to exterior world (provided by a gateway), and also an internal mechanism of communication to establish and maintain of WSN.

S. Vassiliadis et al. (Eds.): SAMOS 2006, LNCS 4017, pp. 99–108, 2006.

Power consumption is and will be the primary metric to design a sensor node. While there is the Moore's Law, that predicts doubling the number of transistors of microelectronic chips every 18-month, and Gilder's Law, which theorizes that the total communication bandwidth triples every year, there is no equivalent forecast for battery technology.

The objective of this work is to present the design considerations and discuss the component choices for a device for WSN. We present the state-of-the-art for sensor node architectures, investigating and analyzing some of the architectural challenges posed by these devices, including a survey of sensor node platforms and energy management techniques. A comparative study of component-off-the-shelf (COTS) such as microcontrollers, battery types, and radio devices, which are very important for system design, is presented. The design focus on individual components and not in subsystem level details. We also discuss some architecture issues and design trade-offs.

2 WSN Architecture

This section gives an overview of the WSN architecture. WSNs are networks composed of a large number of sensor nodes. The objective of these networks is to collect data. Sensor nodes are usually deployed over a desired area, then they wake-up, self-test and establish dynamic communications among them, composing a network [1].

Fig. 1 illustrates a WSN. Each dot represents a sensor node. Each device senses the environment, processes and usually transmits the data to gateway nodes. Gateway nodes transmit their data to an external observer called base station. Gateway nodes are ordinary sensor nodes or more complex devices, having more computational capabilities like greater radio range and more computational power. The discussion of gateway nodes is outside the scope of this work.

In a conventional network, such as cellular phone or local wireless networks, communication between computational elements is done through radio base stations, which represent a communication infrastructure. WSNs usually do not have such a communication infrastructure. That is why a wireless sensor

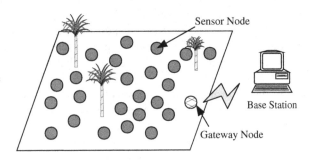

Fig. 1. Wireless sensor network architecture

network is considered as a special type of ad-hoc network, since its topology is dynamic, due to the fact that sensor nodes can wake-up joining the network, or go to sleep, leaving the WSN. An important characteristic is that the flow of data is typically unidirectional. The information flows from source nodes to gateway nodes.

A key resource of a WSN is the stored energy. Each sensor node is composed of a small battery, with limited capacity. It is almost unfeasible to recharge all battery since WSN can be composed of thousands of sensor nodes. Therefore, the WSN project focus, from hardware design to network protocols, is to save energy. Other sensor node restrictions include memory capacity and processing power.

A WSN tends to be application-dependent, in other words, the hardware and software requirements and the operation modes vary according to the application.

3   Characteristics, Requirements and Components

In this section we discuss some characteristics and requirements of a sensor node. The first question the designer should answer is if the sensor node will be a real-life sensor node or a prototype. While in a real product size and cost are essential requirements, a prototype focus the design in a system ease to expand with a number of sensors, robust and easy to reprogram. Following is the design considerations, characteristics and requirements when designing a prototype sensor node:

Energy-Efficiency. Sensor nodes must be energy efficient. Sensor nodes have a limited amount of energy that determines their lifetime. Hence, energy is the key resource, being the primary metric for analysis. Sensor node project should focus on energy-efficient COTS.

Low-Cost. It is desirable that sensor nodes be cheap since WSN may have hundreds or thousands of sensor nodes.

Wireless Communication. The sensor node needs to be wireless. In many applications, the environment being monitored does not have installed infrastructure for communications. Laying wires may be too difficult or expensive. The data rate is low, and a short range transceiver in a license free band is sufficient. The sensor node should receive and transmit, needing a bidirectional communication channel.

Processing. Each sensor node should be able to process local data, using filtering and data fusion algorithms to collect data from environment and aggregate this data.

Programmability. Since this node will be a test prototyping, it will be often reprogrammed for development of communication protocols and applications for WSN. Hence, the programming should be easy.

Expansibility. The hardware design must be expandable with a number of sensors to support a variety of applications. Some projects defined a generic sensor bus for future expansion.

Size. For demonstration purposes the devices should be reasonable small. But size is of less importance in our project since it does not need to be as small as a real-life wireless sensor nodes.

Power-Aware. The hardware should be able to estimate how much energy is available in order to allow algorithms to adapt themselves to the available power.

4   Sensor Node Functional Components

A sensor node, as shown in Fig. 2, is composed of four major blocks: power supply, communication, processing unit, and sensors. The power supply block has the purpose to power the node and usually consists of a battery and a dc-dc converter. The communication block consists of a bidirectional wireless communication channel. Most platforms use a short-range radio. Other solutions include laser and infrared media. The processing unit is composed of internal memory to store data and applications programs, a microcontroller to process data and an Analog-to-Digital Converter to receive signal from the sensing block. The sensing unit block links the sensor node to the physical world and has a group of sensors and actuators that depends on the application of the WSN.

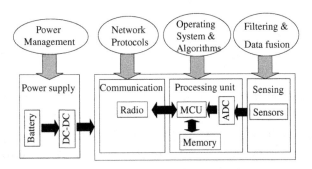

Fig. 2. Sensor node block diagram

Sensor nodes may also have a storage unit or a debugging unit. The storage unit is an external memory device that works as a secondary memory, keeping a data log. The debugging interface is used to program and test the sensor node, for example, programming interface, LEDs, serial interface, JTAG (IEEE 1149.1). This block can be omitted in a final sensor node product.

5 Processing Unit

Since the sensor node is expected to communicate, process and gather sensor data, sensor nodes must have processing units. The central processing unit of a sensor node determines to a large degree both the energy consumption as well as the computational capabilities of a sensor node. Many different types of CPUs can be integrated into a sensor node and they are discussed in this work. There are a large number of commercially available microcontrollers, microprocessors and programmable logic, which allows great flexibility for CPU implementations.

In general, microcontrollers are microprocessor with additional peripheral or support devices embedded in a single chip [2]. Microcontrollers include not only memory and the processor unit, but also non-volatile memory and interfaces such as UART, USB, SPI and I2C, and peripherals such as A/D Converters (ADCs), counters and timers. Therefore, a single chip microcontroller can interface to digital and analog sensors and to communication devices, such as a short-range radio module, to compose a sensor node.

The sensor node microcontroller needs to be energy-efficient, with different operating modes, and fast wake-up time. It does not need to have high computing power as a 32-bit microcontroller. The MCU should have an embedded system interface to facilitate the programming and debugging phases. An important feature is the start-up time, since the MCU of a sensor node will usually go to idle mode, but this feature is not very often divulged.

Static dissipation and dynamic dissipation are the two components that establish the amount of power dissipated in a CMOS (Complimentary Metal Oxide Semiconductor) circuit. The most important one is the dynamic dissipation because it is due to the switching transient current and the charging and discharging of load capacitances. In this case, the power dissipation is proportional to the clock frequency of the device and the capacitance of the load and the SQUARE of the voltage margin between low to high levels. Thus, dynamic power dissipation may be limited by reducing supply voltage, load capacitance and the frequency at which the logic is being clocked. That is why, applications should use low clock frequency for energy conservation and time keeping, but it also should use high clock frequency for fast reaction to events and fast burst processing. The faster it finishes processing, the longer it remains at low-power mode. Thus, changing the operating clock frequency is a much desired capability.

Table 1. Comparison of commercial microcontrollers

Characteristic	Bits	Flash	Power	Active
ATMEGA128L	8	128KB	5.5mA	@4MHz@3V
MSP430F169	16	60 KB	2mA	@4MHz@3V
StrongARM 1100	32	N/A	230mW	@133MHz
DragonBall MC9328MX1	32	N/A	120mA	@96MHz

Table 1 shows a comparison of actual microcontrollers. Microcontroller Control Units (MCUs) have many attributes like word size (number of bits), flash memory capacity, memory size, number of ADCs and timers, operating voltage, current consumption and power modes. In the rest of this section we will discuss some interesting MCUs for WSN.

The Texas Instruments MSP430F169 is a 16-bit, 8 MIPS, and a ultra-low power CPU. It has 60Kbytes of program memory and 2Kbytes of data memory. It is equipped with a full set of analog and digital processors. It has embedded debugging and in-system flash programming through a standard JTAG interface. Texas has developed a new member of this family, the MSP430F1611 with 10Kbytes of RAM.

The ARM family has floating-point computational capabilities, which makes it suitable for devices demanding more computational power, such as high performance gateways. The Intel SA1100 is a general-purpose, 32-bit RISC microprocessor based on the ARM architecture rated as the most efficient 32-bit low-power processor (in MIPS/Watt). The processor has three states: normal, idle and sleep that can be controlled to manage power consumption. Intel is upgrading the StrongARM SA-1110 processor-based designs to Intel PXA255 processor or Intel PXA26x processor family-based designs.

The Motorola DragonBall MC9328MX1 is a 32-bit CPU with a Bluetooth Accelerator radio interface, an Analog Signal Processing (ASP) Module, a Multimedia Accelerator (MMA), and a DPLL Clock and Power Control Module that provides power management capabilities.

The choice of MCU depends on application scenario. The ideal choice of microcontroller is the one that matches its performance level with application's need. Other factors that affect the selection of the proper microcontroller besides energy level include word size, peripherals, memory, speed, physical size, price, availability, personal experience, and vendor support.

The majority of current projects on wireless sensor node are using ATMEGA128L or MSP430. Projects that need simple microcontroller and the knowledge of personal experience are using the ATMEGA128L. Projects that need low-power capability and want to study and apply the Dynamic Voltage Scaling (DVS) technique and need more computing power are using MSP430 and ARM family CPUs.

It is desirable to know the time when an event happens, like keeping record when a sensor signal was read. Adding a real-time clock allows the sensor node to time and date stamp, and create a logbook. It is possible to create a real-time clock with the microcontroller (using the timer), but at the same time is also desired to put the microcontroller in the low-power mode to save energy, which implies in turning off the timer. This solution would make the software more complex. A simpler approach is to add a real-time clock device, usually external.

Many algorithms and applications require a large number of data to be stored. The amount of RAM in the microcontroller is limited. The solution to this problem is to add an external memory device that will work as secondary storage.

6 Power

The power supply block has the purpose to supply the energy to the node, and usually consists of a battery, but sometimes a DC-DC converter is used to boost the battery voltage. A voltage regulator can be added, whose purpose is to maintain the output voltage at a fixed value.

It might be possible to extend lifetime of a sensor node by extracting energy from the environment, such as light, vibration and RF. Continuum Control Corp. [3] has launched the iPower energy harvesters. These devices extract electric energy from mechanical vibrations, motion, or impact. Amirtharajah et al. [4] have demonstrated a MEMS system that extracts electric energy from vibrations.

There are two major power saving schemas, Dynamic Power Management (DPM) [5] and Dynamic Voltage Scaling (DVS) [6]. These techniques can be classified into static and dynamic. Static techniques are applied at design time, such as compilation and synthesis for low power. Dynamic techniques are applied at run time based on the variations in workloads. These techniques are called DPM.

The basic idea behind DPM is to shutdown the devices when not needed and get them back when needed. Turning off some components providing energy savings, but in many cases, it is not known beforehand when to turn on or off a particular device. A solution is a stochastic analysis to predict future events. An embedded operating system that is able to support DPM is also needed. For this approach, the devices should have, at least, the states: active, sleep and idle. Some CPUs offer several levels of active states with varying degrees of computational power and energy consumption, leading to richer power management possibilities. However, it is important to consider that moving between these operating modes involves power and latency overheads.

The main idea behind DVS is to change the power to match the workload, avoiding idle cycles. DVS reduces the power consumed by a processor by lowering its operating voltage and frequency. By varying the voltage along with the frequency, it is possible to obtain a quadratic reduction in power consumption. The problem is the fact that workloads are non-deterministic. For this approach, the microcontroller should permit to change its voltage supply and clock. Some approaches uses the StrongARM SA-1100 MCU since it can vary voltage and frequency from 59MHz/0.79V to 251MHz/1.65V.

7 Communication

Sensor nodes must communicate among themselves and also to a base station using a wireless communication channel. We explore optical and radio frequency (RF) channels. The sensor node communication channel needs to be bidirectional to support different operating modes, to be energy-efficient, allows setting the output power, and have relatively slow date rate. The range can vary from tens to about a hundred meters magnitude.

Optical Communication. Two technologies for optical communications are the laser and infrared. Laser communication has some advantages. It spends less energy than radio over larger range; it is secure, since there is no broadcast and if a channel is intercepted it would interrupt the signal; and there is no need for antennas. There are some disadvantages. It needs line of sight and the laser beam must be lined up with the receiver. Lasers are sensitive to atmospheric conditions and, finally, since the communication is directional and due to the fact that sensor nodes will be deployed randomly, this makes them not an attractive solution. Infrared communication is also directional. An interesting solution adopted by PushPin project [7] is to use an optical diffuser made of sandblasted polycarbonate tubing to create a more omnidirectional communication range within a plane. But, the node still needs to be aligned within that plane. PushPin project adopted the IrDA protocol. Its disadvantage is a short-range of about 1m. The advantage of infrared is no need for antennas.

Radio-Frequency. RF communication is based on electromagnetic waves. One of the most important challenges in RF communications devices is the antenna size. RF communication advantages are its ease of use, integrality, and well established in the commercial marketplace, which make it an ideal testing platform for sensor nodes. Several aspects affect the power consumption of a radio including the type of modulation, data rate, and transmission power. In general, radios can operate in three distinct modes of operation: transmit, receive, idle. Most radios operating on idle mode results in high power consumption, almost equal to receive mode, thus, it is important to shutdown the radio.

8   Sensing Devices

The sensing unit is composed of a group of sensors, which are devices that produce electrical signals to a change in a physical condition. Sensors can be classified as either analog or digital devices depending on the type of output they produce. This work does not intend to enumerate all sensor types, but to study their design trade-offs since many types of sensor exists, such as: magnetometer, accelerometer, light, temperature, pressure, and humidity. Given the diversity of sensors, there is no typical power consumption. The type of sensor to be used in a sensor node will depend on the application.

Besides energy consumption, another important feature of a sensor is its startup time, in other words, the minimum time after turned on to produce correct sample data. It is desirable that the startup time be as small as possible because it is required to turn off the sensors to reduce energy when they are not being used.

Analog sensors need an Analog-to-Digital Converter (ADC). In general, microcontrollers have embedded peripherals that include ADCs and sensor boards do not need dedicated ADCs. The MSP430 family is capable of 200,000 samples per seconds (ksps) of 12 bits divided in eight channels. For complex sensor boards that need higher sample rates or a larger channel number, the solution is to add ADCs to the sensor boards.

Depending on the sensor type, it can change the sensor node design. For example, an image sensor would need a very high communication bandwidth, which would require a communication block redesign. When designing a sensor node, it is desirable to build a sensor block that is easily expandable to support a variety of applications. Most of the sensor node prototypes define a sensor bus that works as an expansion connector.

9   The Bean Wireless Sensor Node

BEAN (Brazilian Energy-Efficient Architectural Node) [8] is a sensor node platform designed at the Federal University of Minas Gerais, Brazil. BEAN is the first sensor node that allows the measurement of power consumption of each architectural block. To our knowledge BEAN is the first sensor node designed in Brazil. Fig. 3 shows a picture of a BEAN prototype.

BEAN uses the MSP430F169 microcontroller. An external memory device was added to work as secondary storage. It is a 4 Mbit (512K x 8) serial flash memory and can be switched to a low power mode when it is not used. The communication channel uses the Chipcon CC1000 radio transceiver. It was desirable to design a sensor node that could be expandable to support a variety of applications. BEAN defines a sensor bus that provides a user interface for additional sensor boards. Each sensor node has a unique electronic identification. BEAN provides support for real-time application using an external real-time clock chip. Finally, for debugging objectives, BEAN has four LEDs, and a JTAG interface used to program and debug the microprocessor. Since BEAN is a prototype,

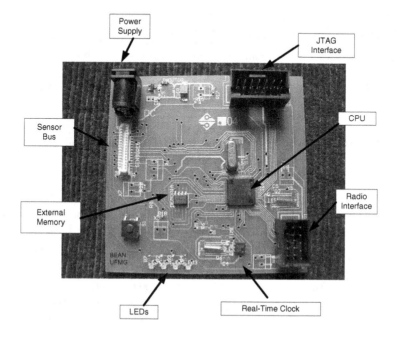

Fig. 3. BEAN prototype

it uses an external power supply, and an internal voltage regulator was added. The power budget for BEAN is about 10.3 μA at the power down state. During transmission power consumption is about 17 mA.

BEAN also includes software components and provides an Application Programming Interface (API). The API is a set of functionalities to control and configure and also provides services of the hardware components. The API communicates with an upper layer that is usually a WSN dedicated microkernel.

10   Conclusions

Wireless sensor networks present fascinating challenges for the application of distributed signal processing and distributed control. These systems challenge the applications of appropriate techniques to construct cheap processing units with sensing nodes considering energy constraints.

We presented the design considerations and components choices, investigating and analyzing some of the architectural challenges posed by these devices like computational power, energy consumption, energy sources, communication channels and sensing capabilities.

This work is a guideline for developers, who want to design a microcontroller based sensor node platform. We also discussed some architecture issues, design trade-offs, wireless communication channels, and impact on the WSN protocol stack.

References

1. L. B. Ruiz, J.M.N., Loureiro, A.A.F.: Manna: A management architecture for wireless sensor networks. IEEE Communication Magazine **41** (2003) 116–125
2. Berger, A.S.: Embedded Systems Design, An Introduction to Processes, Tools and Techniques. (2002)
3. Continuum Control Corporation: ipower. Available on: http://www.powerofmotion.com (2005)
4. R. Amirtharajah, S.M.: A micropower programmable dsp powered using a mems-based vibration-to-electric energy converter. In: IEEE Intl. Solid-State Circuits Conference. (2000) 362–369
5. Wang, A., Chandrakasan, A.: Energy efficient system partitioning for distributed wireless sensor networks. In: IEEE International Conference on Acoustics, Speech and Signal Processing. (2001) 905–908
6. Pillai, P., Shin, K.G.: Real-time dynamic voltage scaling for low-power embedded operating systems. In: ACM Symposium on Operating Systems Principles. (2001) 99–102
7. Lifton, J., Seetharam, D., Broxton, M., Paradiso, J.: Pushpin computing system overview: a platform for distributed, embedded, ubiquitous sensor networks. In: Pervasive Computing Conference - LNCS 2414. (2002) 139–151
8. Vieira, M.A.M.: BEAN: A computational platform for wireless sensor networks (in portuguese). Master's thesis, C. S. Dept. - Federal University of Minas Gerais, Belo Horizonte, Brazil (2004)

Design, Implementation, and Experiments on Outdoor Deployment of Wireless Sensor Network for Environmental Monitoring

Jukka Suhonen, Mikko Kohvakka, Marko Hännikäinen, and Timo D. Hämäläinen

Tampere University of Technology / Institute of Computer and Digital Systems
{jukka.suhonen, mikko.kohvakka, marko.hannikainen,
timo.d.hamalainen}@tut.fi

Abstract. This paper presents the design, implementation, and practical real world experiments of an energy optimized multi-hop wireless sensor network (WSN) targeted at environmental monitoring. The WSN is fully autonomous and consists of energy-efficient and scalable communication protocols and low-power hardware platform. Software tools are developed for configuring and analyzing large scale networks. The network has been deployed in outdoor environment consisting of 20 nodes covering over $2 \, km^2$ area. The results show that the multi-hop network works autonomously, reacts to environmental changes, and is able to operate temperatures down to -30 °C. The hardware nodes operating on 433 MHz frequency provide over 1 km communication distances, while still having sufficient throughput and low energy consumption. The deployed nodes had a lifetime of 6 months with a 1600 mAh battery, while generating 4 packets per minute.

1 Introduction

Wireless sensor network (WSN) is an emerging ad-hoc network technology that may consist of thousands of sensor nodes combining environment sensing, data processing, and wireless networking with extremely low energy and cost. Applications for WSN have been envisioned in home, outdoor, and industrial environments. An environmental sensor network can be deployed in hostile environments or over large geographical areas to provide accurate and localized data.

The vast number of sensor nodes introduces several challenges. The network must be scalable and autonomous, as the reconfiguration of individual nodes is not feasible. Also, since recharging or changing power sources is not practical or possible, the network must be extremely energy-efficient to allow a lifetime of even several years [1]. Still, the network must have adequate throughput and delay for the target application.

Few environmental monitoring applications utilizing WSN have been published. In NIMS [2], PC104 based devices use suspension cables to obtain low interference links to sensors deployed on the ground. Sensors perform complex data processing and aggregation, but the network itself is not suitable for large scale deployments. The implementation in [3] has wireless nodes that are inserted in glaciers. The network activity is low as sensors transmits readings to a base station once per day, which allows successful use of solar panels. [4] presents results with 25 multi-hop PicoNodes that utilize Bluetooth physical layer with a custom data link layer and energy aware routing scheme [5].

S. Vassiliadis et al. (Eds.): SAMOS 2006, LNCS 4017, pp. 109–121, 2006.

While the results in office environment show less than 4% packet loss, nodes have only few months lifetime with two 1400 mAh batteries. Implementations that are based on Mica II motes [6] have been published in [7], [8], and [9]. [7] introduces a multihop network that measures temperature in a vineyard consisting of 65 nodes. [8] presents a WSN for bird observation during four month deployment with 150 nodes. [9] describes a surveillance system for moving vehicles and consists of 70 nodes. Although the Mica platform provides adequate processing and sensor capabilities for most sensor applications, its energy consumption is too large to allow lifetime of years with low-capacity batteries. In general, the problem with the presented proposals is that the network has either too short lifetime, or the usage is limited to certain applications.

This paper presents a measurement network that uses our WSN, referred to as Tampere University of Technology WSN (TUTWSN). The network has been developed to address the challenges on WSNs, gather experiences on applying a WSN for practical purposes, and to create tools and methods for analyzing a large scale network. Furthermore, the network addresses how to cover large area with long-range multi-hop communications, while still having low energy consumption. The measurement network is presented in Fig. 1. Our ultra-low power hardware nodes utilize a long-range 433 MHz radio. A node has an energy-efficient and scalable TUTWSN protocol stack containing embedded sensor applications, TUTWSN routing protocol (TUTWSNR), and a TDMA-based Medium Access Control (MAC). The developed sensor applications provide control access to node configuration, gather temperature readings, and collect WSN self-diagnostics for network analyzation purposes. A sensor node referred to as *sink* collects data from other nodes by injecting *interests* into the network. An interest defines gathered data and collection intervals. A configuration software run on a PC is used to set the interests without tedious reprogramming. A *gateway* computer receives data from the sink and forwards it to a specifically designed remote database over TCP/IP through a IPSec/VPN tunnel. An easy-to-use web software has been implemented for viewing measurements and network status.

TUTWSN is the first WSN to provide extensive tool set for network analyzation and simulation. Cross-layer design has been used in network protocols to achieve energy-efficiency and scalability. Although TUTWSN is used to receive temperature and self-diagnostics packets in this paper, the network itself is bidirectional and symmetric, and can be used to transfer any data. Unlike other published environmental monitoring

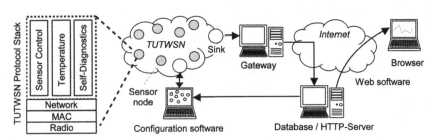

Fig. 1. Measurement network consisting of TUTWSN and network analyzation facilities. Protocol stack in sensor nodes contains communication protocols and sensor applications.

WSNs, TUTWSN has a long lifetime, while not being limited to a specific application. Also, the network can be implemented on nodes having very low memory and processing capabilities. The network is verified by an extensive deployment in outdoor environment. In our measurements, we use interests that instruct each node to send both its temperature and diagnostics information twice per minute. It should be noted that TUTWSN is autonomous, and does not need any user software or a connection to backbone networks to operate.

The rest of the paper is organized as follows. TUTWSN protocol stack is presented in Section 2. Section 3 presents data visualization and network analyzation software. The prototype hardware is presented in Section 4. Section 5 presents the deployment and discusses the obtained results. Section 6 concludes the paper.

2   TUTWSN Protocol Stack

The TUTWSN protocol stack contains MAC, routing, and application layers. TUT-WSN uses clustered mesh topology. A cluster consists of a *cluster head* and *subnodes* as shown in Fig. 2. A cluster head can receive and transmit data to any node within communication range, while subnodes save energy by communicating only with the cluster head. A sensor node can change its role between cluster head and subnode.

2.1   MAC Layer

TUTWSN MAC uses TDMA-based channel access, where each cluster operates on its own frequency (cluster channel). In addition, a common network channel is used to advertise and detect clusters. A cluster head maintains a periodic data exchange structure (access cycle) on its cluster channel as shown in Fig. 3. An access cycle consists of active and idle periods. Active period begins with a cluster beacon (CB) that is followed by a super frame. A super frame consists of two type of communication slots, reserved and ALOHA slots. Data is exchanged in reserved slots that provide collision free communication. Contention based ALOHA slots are used when joining a cluster and requesting a reservation. Cluster beacons signal cluster information, time schedules, and slot allocations within current the active period. The communication between cluster head and subnodes takes place in the active period. During the idle period cluster head sleeps, communicates with other clusters, and sends/receives periodically network beacons (NB) in the common network channel. A network beacon contains cluster timing and channel information that is required for other nodes to gain sync to the cluster.

The access cycle length and the number of ALOHA and reserved slots are adjustable parameters. The optimal access cycle length depends on the amount of the network traffic, because it causes a trade-off between delay, throughput, and energy consumption. Current implementation has 4 ALOHA slots, 8 reserved slots, and 2 s access cycle length. The parameters are selected by the expected traffic on the network.

2.2   Network Layer

In TUTWSNR, each node maintains a routing table to known sinks. A node selects the neighbor that minimizes cost to the sink as its next hop. The cost is calculated from

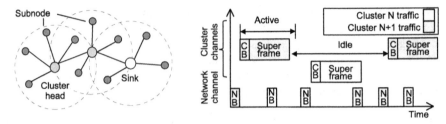

Fig. 2. TUTWSN clustered mesh network topology

Fig. 3. TDMA-based channel access in TUT-WSN MAC

the number of hops to the sink, remaining energy, link reliability, and thetransmission power required to reach the next hop cluster. Sender decided unicast transmissions is used to communicate with the next hop nodes. A node joins its next hop cluster in MAC layer, thus becoming a member of that cluster.

The routing begins with a setup phase. Initially, the sink sends route advertisement to its neighbors. When a cluster head receives new advertisement, it calculates a new cost to the sink based on the cost-field included in the packet and the cost that is required to reach the next hop cluster. If the cost decreases, the node changes its next hop and sends advertisement with updated cost to its neighbors. Eventually, all nodes have a route to the sink.

Sink asks data from nodes by declaring an interest that defines the type of data that the sink is interested in and reply generation interval (once, on change, or period). Furthermore, an interest can be limited to a certain group of sensor nodes by defining an area code or time-to-live field (hops from sink) into the interest. The interest is broadcast in the reverse direction of established gradients. When a node does not have a connection to the sink, it performs periodic network scans. After the node has detected its neighbors, the node request them for routes and interests. In this way, a node that is not part of the network establishes a route to the sink, when it is brought in the communication range of a connected cluster. After the routes have been established, extensive network scans are not needed.

2.3   Embedded Sensor Applications

Sensor nodes have three embedded sensor applications, sensor control, temperature, and WSN self-diagnostics. A light-weight operating system (OS) provides timer services and message passing between application layer and network stack. A sensor control application handles received control messages, thus allowing remote configuration of a node. Temperature and self-diagnostics applications generate packets, if the node has received an interest requesting for that data. Temperature application performs sensing on a digital sensor or reads value from analog-to-digital converter (ADC). The sensing interval is set in the related interest. Also, the interest includes measurement range that defines the values that cause generation of a reply packet to the sink that defined the interest. WSN self-diagnostics application maintains statistics of sensor voltage, buffer state, performed network scans, a list of known neighbor nodes, and transmitted/received traffic counters.

3   TUTWSN Prototype Hardware

The hardware architecture of the prototype is presented in Fig. 4. Arctic operating conditions set high requirements for components and batteries. Thus, all the components have extended temperature range ($-40\,°C$). The operation of the TUTWSN node is controlled by a Microchip PIC18LF4620 MCU. Available 64 kB program memory and 4 kB data memory are sufficient for TUTWSN protocol stack and application algorithms. 1 kB EEPROM is used for non-volatile configuration data, such as node address and node status log. The controller has high energy-efficiency and versatile power saving modes. Utilized clock frequency is 4 MHz resulting 1 MIPS performance. An internal 10-bit ADC is utilized for monitoring battery energy status.

Nordic Semiconductor nRF905 operating at 433 MHz license-free frequency band is used as radio transceiver. Totally 9 non-overlapping frequency channels are available between 433.050 MHz and 434.790 MHz. Radio data rate is 50 kbps, which is adequate for low data rate WSN applications. Internal transmission and reception buffers and Cyclic Redundancy Check (CRC) error detection reduce MCU loading. The radio has -100 dBm sensitivity and adjustable transmission power from -10 dBm to $+10$ dBm enabling long transmission range with efficient antennae. A folded dipole antenna is implemented directly on a printed circuit board. The antenna is selected due to a small size and low directivity. Antenna impedance is also near to the transceiver output impedance requiring only a minimum impedance matching. In addition, the antenna fits well in a slim tube enclosure selected for the nodes.

Temperature sensing is implemented by a Dallas Semiconductor DS620 sensor interfaced with a digital I2C bus. The sensor has $\pm0.5\,°C$ accuracy from 0 to $+70°C$ and an operating temperature range of $-55\,°C$ to $+125\,°C$. A CR123A primary lithium battery specified with 3 V / 1600 mAh capacity and from $-40\,°C$ to $+60\,°C$ operating temperature is selected as power source. Battery voltage is converted to 2.25 V supply voltage by a MAX1725 linear regulator. According to our measurements, linear regulators suit well for the WSN node current profile, which consists of very short and high current bursts, while around 99% of the time node is in low power sleep mode.

The implemented long-range TUTWSN prototype is presented in Fig. 5. The prototype is 255 mm x 21 mm sized, and encapsulated in a waterproof plastic enclosure.

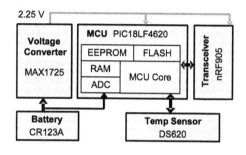

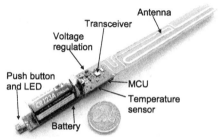

Fig. 4. TUTWSN prototype hardware architecture

Fig. 5. Long-range TUTWSN prototype

The prototype consists of two separate boards, one for MCU, radio, voltage regulation and temperature sensor, and other extension board for battery, push button, LED and I/O connector. Also, other types of sensors and energy scavenging circuits can be easily implemented in the extension board increasing flexibility for various applications.

3.1 Measured Static Power Consumption and Radio Range

The measured minimum power consumption of a prototype node at 3.0 V supply voltage is 31 μW, when all components are in sleep mode. The static power consumptions of individual components in active mode are presented in Table 1. According to the measurements, transceiver consumes significantly more power than the rest of prototype components. Transceiver in reception mode consumes 11.8 times the power of MCU. Data transmission at 10 dBm transmission power consumes 29.4 times the power of MCU. Thus, the transmission of 1 bit of data at 50 kbps data rate consumes energy equivalent to the execution of 647 instructions on MCU. For energy efficiency, both the transmission and reception time should be minimized.

Radio transmission ranges with four power levels are measured outdoors in an open space and line-of-sight conditions. One prototype is placed 1.5 m above a snowy ground and configured to periodically transmit beacons with the four possible power levels, while another node is moved away from the transmitter around 2 m above the ground, and is receiving beacons. The measured power levels with minimum and maximum

Table 1. The power consumption of the TUTWSN prototype components at 3.0 V supply voltage

Component	Power (mW)	Energy
MCU	3.14	3.14 nJ / instruction
ADC	0.51	29.6 nJ / sample
Temperature sensor	2.23	55.8 μJ / sample
Radio RX	37.4	844 nJ / bit [*]
Radio TX @ -10 dBm	27.0	609 nJ / bit [*]
Radio TX @ +10 dBm	90.0	2.03 μJ / bit [*]

[*] *256 bit packet, includes start-up trancient, MCU in sleep mode*

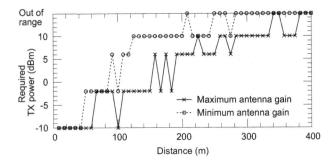

Fig. 6. Measured radio range versus transmission power

antenna gains are shown in Fig. 6. In an open space, a path loss increases quiteproportionally to the distance. At maximum gain, beacons transmitted at -10 dBm, -2 dBm, 6 dBm, and 10 dBm power levels are received until 58 m, 150 m, 250 m and 375 m distances, respectively. At minimum gain, the distances are 42 m, 83 m, 117 m and 240 m, respectively. A measured antenna directivity is around 2 dBi.

4   User Software for Network Analyzation

The configuration software communicates with a TUTWSN sink via a serial port interface. The software defines interests and writes them to the sink, which propagates

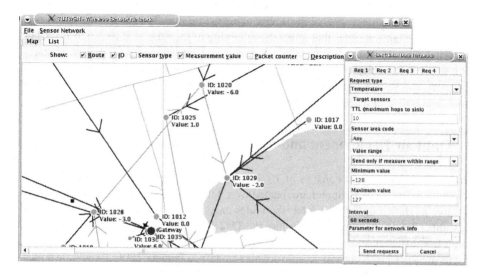

Fig. 7. Configuration software showing the real-time status and active routes in the network. A dialog for setting interests is presented on right.

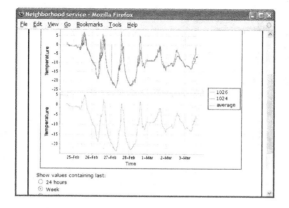

Fig. 8. Web software for local residents showing measurement history

interests to the network. Also, the software can configure a node by sending/receiving packets to the node through the sink. The adjustable node parameters contain description, area code used to select nodes in interests, sensor role (subnode/cluster head), and network wide configuration parameters that have a trade-off between performance and energy-usage (e.g. access cycle length). The configuration software connects to a database for storing received data, and analyzing earlier measurements and WSN self-diagnostics history. The self-diagnostics history allows to detect bottlenecks on network, find erroneous nodes, and predict the lifetime of a node based on a battery voltage usage history. Figure 7 shows the capture of the software on GNU/Linux desktop environment.

The web software is targeted at end-users and can be used with any device having a Web browser. The data is processed completely on server side with Java Servlets, which eases the requirements of the device using the service. The shown diagnostics information contain variables that affect the reliability of measured values, such as packet reception interval and the time of the last received measurement. The service starts with a selection of deployment area. Next, the map of the area containing sensors and last measured values is presented. A user can examine the measurement history of an individual sensor or a group of sensors, as shown in Fig. 8.

5   Outdoor Deployment and Measurement Results

The outdoor deployment consists of 19 nodes covering $2 \, km^2$ area. The nodes do not generally have line of sight and are located over 1 m above the ground, typically bound in a tree as shown in Fig. 9. So far, the nodes have been deployedover 4 months from November 2005 to March 2006. Because the TUTWSN protocol stack is under development, few different revisions of the protocols have been used. Therefore, the presented results measured with current version are obtained since January 2006. Two of the nodes are subnodes, while the rest of the nodes act as cluster heads.

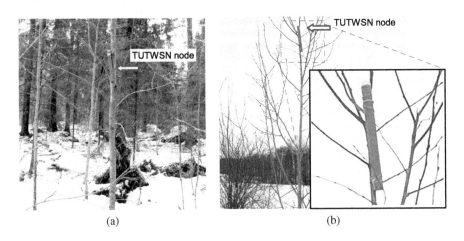

(a)   (b)

Fig. 9. The typical deployment of nodes in trees

5.1   Distribution of Traffic

Geographic locations of deployed sensor nodes (identified with numbers 1-18) and the distribution of transmitted traffic on selected nodes is shown in Fig. 10. Average successfully transmitted traffic per node is presented in Fig. 11. The bandwidth usage between temperature and self-diagnostics data was equal. Control traffic (route advertisements and interests) used less than 1% of bandwidth. Since nodes originate the same amount of traffic, the difference in traffic volumes is caused by forwarded data. The nodes located in the edge of the network transmit less data, since routing algorithm tries to minimize required energy and hops, thus preferring routes through centrally located nodes. The nodes 17 and 18 do not forward data, because they were configured as subnodes. Node 6 experienced high link error rates due to bad location, which resulted into low traffic. A significant portion of the traffic to the sink is forwarded via node 2. Node 2 sent 91% of its traffic (8.7 bit/s) to the sink, which corresponds to over 1/3 of the traffic received by the sink (17.8 bit/s). Although node 2 is located relatively close to the sink, other nodes have a to the sink through it because the sink is inside a building while the node 2 is outside. Thus, nodes have better connection to the node 2.

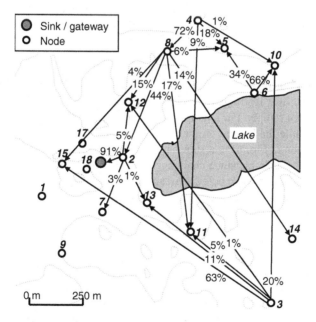

Fig. 10. Geographic locations of deployed sensor nodes and the distribution of transmitted traffic in selected nodes (node 16 is outside the picture, 250 m north of node 4)

A node had only one active next hop route at a time. Route changes are caused by a broken next hop link due to communication errors, or changes in network conditions that caused routing to change next hop node. An average time between route changes

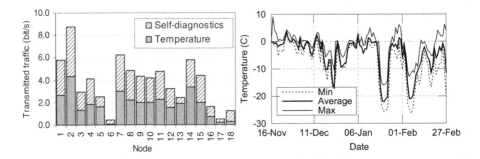

Fig. 11. Average transmitted traffic per node   **Fig. 12.** Measured minimum, maximum, and average day temperatures

was 30 minutes, caused typically by routing algorithm balancing the network load. Typical hop count from a node to the sink was 4, while the maximum count was 8.

The longest link is 1.1 km from node 3 to node 15. This is notably more than the measured communication ranges presented in Fig. 6. The difference is caused by reflections from the ground and buildings. The measured values were obtained in an opens space, while the deployment environment contains cliffs, icy surface of the lake, and other elements of terrain that can enhance the radio wave propagation.

5.2   Temperatures

Day temperatures during the measurement period are shown in Fig. 12. The temperatures are averaged over readings from all sensor nodes. The temperature changes significantly and often radiply. For example, on January 23, 2006 the lowest temperature was $-21.8\,°C$, while the highest temperature on the next day was $-5.2\,°C$. The rapid changes can be seen in Fig. 13 that shows temperature per hour on a selected sensor.

Temperature changes introduce challenges to the equipment and protocols. As the temperature alternates between below zero and above zero, the casing must be compact to prevent water damage. The MAC protocol must compensate clock drift, since the

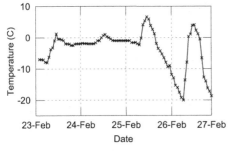

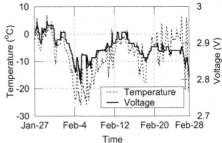

Fig. 13. Rapid environmental temperature changes on a selected sensor (node 8)   **Fig. 14.** The effect of temperature to voltage (node 8)

oscillating frequency of crystals depends slightly on temperature. On the deployment region, temperature does not change evenly and some nodes might be inside buildings.

5.3   Energy Consumption

A node measured its battery voltage with ADC. The voltage information was send to the sink in diagnostics packets. The energy consumption is calculated with drop in battery voltage. However, a short term development on voltage level cannot be used, as temperature affects the level. The effect is seen on Fig. 14 that shows temperatures and voltages measured on a selected node. Figure 15 presents voltages of two sensor nodes (2 and 8) and average voltage drop. The average voltage drop is calculated with linear regression, because the battery discharge rate is near linear between voltages 2.9 V and 2.6 V with presented temperatures and light load. The steeper voltage drop on node 2 is caused by heavy traffic. Figure 16 presents the voltages and incremental sum of transmitted and received packets on both nodes. The result indicates that it is beneficial to add a new node near a highly loaded node. In this way, the traffic between them averages and the network lifetime increases.

5.4   Discussion

The experiments are providing vast amount of information about the real operation of WSN nodes and radio links in forested, low temperature outdoor environment. According to the experiments, a forest attenuates radio wave propagation significantly. Achieved radio range in a forest has been below 100 meters, while the longest measured range has been near 1.5 km. An edge of the forest seems to operate as a reflector causing notable gain in antenna radiation pattern. Also, radio wave propagation has been notably affected by snowfall, rain, humidity, temperature, and the frost and snow in trees, ground, and around the nodes. Hence, the quality of radio links and the network topology changes dynamically although nodes are stationary.

Dynamic network topology affects significantly on the routing protocol operation. The experiments depict that the entire route to a sink must be considered in the route selection. As the difference between link qualities is very high, examining only next hop

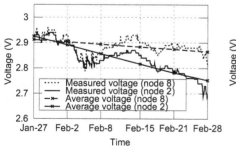

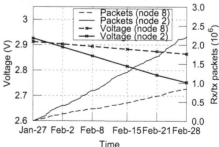

Fig. 15. Decrease in the battery voltage of two selected sensors

Fig. 16. Voltage decrease and transmitted/received packets in sensors

quality when determining a route leads to unsatisfactory performance. Since the environment affects radio wave propagation significantly, cost-effective routing paths do not typically follow geometrically reasonable routes. The utilized cost-gradient based routing seems to work well in outdoor multi-hop networks without line-of-sight.

The outdoor temperatures until March 2006 ranged from $-31.5\,°C$ to $12.0\,°C$. The high temperature variation reduced significantly the accuracy of crystals and thus, the accuracy of time synchronization. In the worst case scenario some nodes were inside buildings and other in outdoors resulting nearly 50 degrees difference in the operation temperature. The implemented hardware prototypes performed well during the whole test period. In some locations, nodes were not able to associate with the network for long periods of time. This was caused by poor radio link quality, not the hardware prototype itself. According to the reduction of battery voltages during the test period, an expected network lifetime is around 6 months. It should be noted that the network traffic consisted not only of temperature measurements but also diagnostics information, which increased load and decreased lifetime.

Although the expected lifetime is satisfactory, some improvements for the energy efficiency will be made. The high variation in temperature decreased significantly the accuracy of TDMA synchronization, therefore increasing idle listening time prior to beacon receptions. A significant energy save is achieved by an algorithm that dynamically compensates the crystal drift. A further energy save is achieved by an algorithm, which adjusts the access cycle lengths for each cluster head according to traffic conditions. According to our energy analysis, these improvements will decrease network energy consumption to a quarter, thus increasing expected network lifetime to around 2 years. For comparison, this equals to 3.5 years with 2xAA batteries.

6   Conclusions

This paper presents a complete measurement network based on a fully featured autonomous wireless sensor network. The network combines small energy consumption with adjustable network performance. The network protocols and hardware platform are energy-efficient, giving a node the lifetime of 6 months with a 1600 mAh battery during deployment in harsh outdoor environment. The future work will focus on implementing different services, such as positioning into sensor networks. The presented network allows fast implementation and testing of new ideas in practice.

References

1. Akyildiz, I.F., Weilian, S., Sankarasubramaniam, Y., Cayirci, E.: A survey on sensor networks. IEEE Communications Magazine **40** (2002) 102–114
2. M. A. Batalin et al: Call and response: Experiments in sampling the environment. In: Proceedings of the 2nd international conference on Embedded Networked Sensor Systems. (2004) 25–38
3. Martinez, K., Hart, J.K., Ong, R.: Environmental sensor networks. Computer **37** (2004) 50–56
4. Reason, J.M., Rabaey, J.M.: A study of energy consumption and reliability in a multi-hop sensor network. Mobile Computing and Communications Review **8** (2004) 84–97

5. Shah, R.C., Rabaey, J.M.: Energy aware routing for low energy ad hoc sensor networks. In: Wireless Communications and Networking Conference. (2002) 350–355
6. Hill, J.L., Culler, D.E.: Mica: a wireless platform for deeply embedded networks. IEEE Micro **22** (2002) 12–24
7. Beckwith, R., Teibel, D., Bowen, P.: Report from the field: Results from an agricultural wireless sensor network. In: Local Computer Networks. (2004) 471–478
8. Szewczyk, R., Mainwaring, A., Polastre, J., Anderson, J., Culler, D.: An analysis of a large scale habitat monitorin application. In: Proceedings of the 2nd international conference on Embedded Networked Sensor Systems. (2004) 214–226
9. T. He et al: Energy-efficient surveillance system using wireless sensor networks. In: Proceedings of the 2nd international conference on Mobile system. (2004) 270–283

LATONA: An Advanced Server Architecture for Ubiquitous Sensor Network

Chi-Hoon Shin[1], Soo-Cheol Oh[2], Dae-Won Kim[2], Sun-Wook Kim[2],
Kyoung Park[2], and Sung-Woon Kim[2]

[1] Department of Computer & Software Engineering, University of Science
and Technology, 52, Eoeun-dong, Yuseong-gu, Daejeon, 305-333, Korea
`cshin@etri.re.kr`
[2] Server Platform Research Team, Electronics and Telecommunications Research
Institute (ETRI), 161 Gajeong-dong, Yuseong-gu, Daejeon, 305-700, Korea
{`ponylife, won22, swkim99, kyoung, ksw`}`@etri.re.kr`

Abstract. The emerging Ubiquitous Sensor Network (USN) makes connection less datagrams and short event packets get popular. A large number of short term event packets of USN can cause serious problems, such as interrupt handling overhead and context switching overhead. Furthermore, heavy load of the packet security methods needs enough processing power. Then, the more USN develops, the more network overheads would be loaded into host CPU. To solve the problems, we propose a special server component including TOE (TCP/IP Offloading Engine) and H/W IPSec (IP Layer Security) for USN.

1 Introduction

In the last decade, there have been significant evolutions in the network environment [2,4,3,1,6]. Nowadays, the dominating packet type of network traffic is moving from the connection-oriented datagram to the connection-less datagram. This alteration is triggered by a popularization of the connection-less oriented applications such as Ubiquitous Sensor Network (USN) and multimedia streaming. In USN, integrated low power sensing devices will allow users to monitor remote objects Also, it can be used in many different contexts: in the field (vehicles, equipment, personnel), the office building (furniture, books, people), the hospital ward (syringes, bandages) and the factory floor (motors, small robotic devices) [23]. Then, enormous amount of the devices deployed in the various fields will produce a large number of short term event packets [16]. The large numbers event packets can cause serious problems, such as interrupt handling overhead and context switching overhead, on network servers.

To catch up with the performance demands of sensor network, servers need another device which is capable of offloading sensor packet processing from themselves. Nowadays, the wire communication speed has been getting fast three times a year. However, processor speed which has been getting fast only 1.8 times a year [5,2,3,6]. So, CPU has no margin to do other jobs [5,3,6]. The device should cover short term event packet and their security. Simultaneously, it is

S. Vassiliadis et al. (Eds.): SAMOS 2006, LNCS 4017, pp. 122–131, 2006.

good for the server that the device can offload high speed network burden from host CPU, since the CPU could get freedom for doing other works of server.

The Other bottleneck for servers is the security overhead. The packet communications without protection from a security method are vulnerable to various malfunction attacks. However, guarantee of the security of a large number of sensing devices will aggravate the server's performance degradation caused by the interrupt and context switching.Furthermore, the connection less datagram packets can not be protected by the widely used methods such as SSL (Secure Socket Layer) and TLS (Transport Layer Security) because those methods focus on over the transport layer. More lower lever security methods, like as IPSec and MAC layer security, can cover the problem [7,8].

As a solution, we propose a server component specialized for USN which includes a TOE (TCP/IP Offloading Engine) and an IPSec (IP Layer Security). We developed a network accelerator card - Leading Architecture for TCP Offloading & Network Acceleration (LATONA) - which can fully offload host network burden, accelerate processing of USN packets, and perfectly guarantee the security of the packets. In the remainder of this paper, we'll consider related works, show some basic knowledge for understanding of our approach, and describe our solution. Finally this paper shows the result data of some experiments comparing the performance differences between alternatives.

2   Related Works and Contribution

Most of the efforts towards improving the efficiency of the TOE have been targeted at addressing performance issues in area of the internet based storage such as ISCSI [2,4,3,1,6]. Also, most of the security researches have a bias towards VPN for the storage [17]. Various companies offer commercial security processor ICs to improve the performance of the storage VPN [20,19,18]. On the other hand, various organizations are actively involved in designing systems for USN. However, none of them have a method for connection between sensor node and server [23,21,22,24]. For example, Intel has a sensor network solution including sensors, gateways, and a server [21]. Nevertheless they do not consider server technology for handling the sensor traffic of real world.

Therefore, as far as we know, LATONA is first work to implement a server component specialized USN. If not, at least, it is certain that our work is first solution to adopt a full offloading hardware TOE and a hardware IPSec processor for processing USN packets.

3   Backgrounds

3.1   Transport Offload Engine (TOE)

The basic idea of a TOE is to offload the processing of TCP/IP protocols from the host processor to the hardware. The TOE can eliminate the delay caused by interrupt overhead, memory transfer, and etc. As depicted in figure 1, TOE

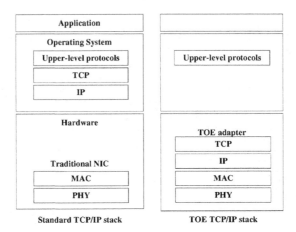

Fig. 1. Transport Offload Engine (TOE): comparison between Standard TCI/IP stack and TOE TCP/IP stack

processor can offload network burden from host using H/W network stack. This architecture makes host CPU free from network overhead, so that host CPU can concentrate with local processing without any of delay [4,3,6].

3.2 IP Layer Security (IPSec) Overview

IPSec is a fundamental security method for the network dominated by datagram. IPSec provides data confidentiality, data integrity, and replay protection for the whole IP datagram. It uses a symmetric key algorithm (like 3DES-CBC or AES-CBC) to encrypt the data. As described in figure 2, IPSec has ability to apply security with upper transport header directly. So it doesn't mind which transport protocol come onto network layer [7,8,17,9].

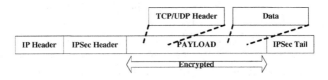

Fig. 2. IPSec Packet: IPSec encrypt or authenticate the payload including TCP/UDP header and data. There are IPSec header and IPSec tail (optional).

4   Implementation of LATONA Including H/W IPSec

Electronics & Telecommunications Research Institute (ETRI) developed an advanced TOE, the Leading Architecture for TCP Offloading & Network Acceleration (LATONA) with Hifn 8300 inline IPSec processor [12]. Though TOE has many advantages, previous TOEs are not suitable for optimal solution of USN. Most of the TOEs are focused on the Storage Market. They only consider large packet and use their own protocol stack, so that they could not guarantee the responsibility with event packet based applications [6].

4.1   Resource Management Architecture

The block diagram Figure 3 Shows the resource management architecture of LATONA. It is important how to manage connections (sockets) for processing of large number of event packets. As the figure shows, implementing connection manager using h/w pool and adopting tree mechanism for management of sockets can solve this problem. And LATONA reduce the overhead occurred by kernel data copies through zero copy technology where a data can directly pass between user buffer and TOE. These resource mechanisms are controlled by h/w doorbell. This doorbell includes an advanced interrupt mechanism for diminishing the interrupt overhead of event packets.

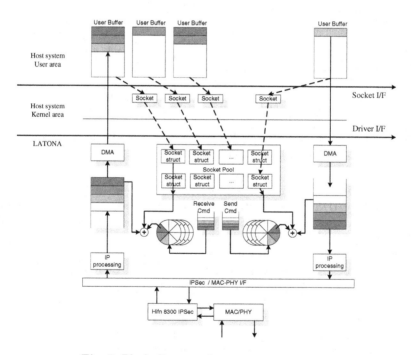

Fig. 3. Block diagram of resource management

4.2   Choice of H/W IPSec on LATONA

The S/W IPSec processing speed is very slow, because the IPSec is naturally computation oriented protocol. Then, the IPSec can cause serious bottleneck on network service because host normally has another burdens related with

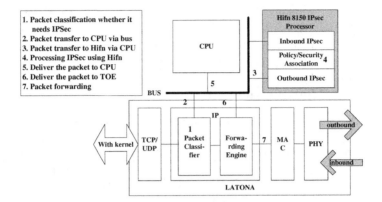

Fig. 4. Architecture of Look-aside IPSec LATONA: a view from high level block and operation sequence in the order of named in upper box of figure

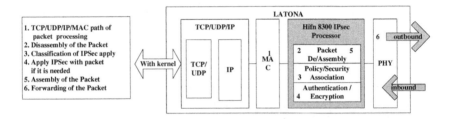

Fig. 5. Architecture of Inline IPSec LATONA: a view from high level block and operation sequence in the order of named in left box of figure

the security like firewall and virus protection. Therefore the IPSec has to be implemented by H/W design [11,9]. The combined system (H/W IPSec and TOE) can guarantee the security of datagram networks while preserving the bandwidth of gigabit networks. This system can be real as two types respectively, that are look-aside and inline architecture [9].

The look-aside IPSec processor implements partial functions (related with IPSec cryptography) of IPSec as H/W. The Figure 4 shows the architecture and outbound packet processing of look-aside system. The system consists of a LATONA and a Look-aside IPSec Processor (Hifn 8150) outside LATONA. And they communicate through the host bus. In this scheme, if there is a packet which needs IPSec service, the packet is sent out after IPSec processing and with bus transaction cost. More detail sequence is in a box upper Figure 4. It's evident that the system has better performance than the S/W IPSec system because it has an H/W cryptography engine. However it has some drawbacks such as difficult design and bus overhead.

The inline system completely offloads the host CPU from whole IPSec loads, providing significant additional cost saving compared to the look-aside system. The figure 5 shows the architecture and the outbound packet processing of the

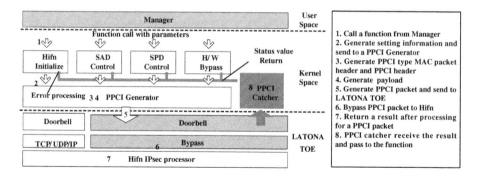

Fig. 6. S/w Architecture of LATONA for Inline IPSec: a view from high level block and operation sequence in the order of named in right box of figure

inline IPSec. The system consists of LATONA and a hifn 8300 inline IPSec Processor inside LATONA. And they are directly connected with wired interface. In this scheme, if there is a packet which needs IPSec service, the packet is sent out after IPSec processing and without bus transaction cost. More detail sequence is in a box upper Figure 5. This architecture can eliminate the bus overhead and bottleneck. Also it has the simple interface, so that designers are allowed to save the design cost.

There should be a Control Program to control Hifn processor. This program run initialization code and set tables for Hifn Processor operation such as Firmware download and GMAC interface initialization. More detail sequence is in a box upper Figure 6.

4.3   Specifications of LATONA

Here are simple specifications of LATONA.

- $TCP/IP protocol full offloading H/W (on Xilinx Virtex - II Pro FPGA)$
- $Standard PCI - Express bus interface (on Altera Stratix - GX FPGA)$
- $LSI GMAC \& Marvell GPHY$

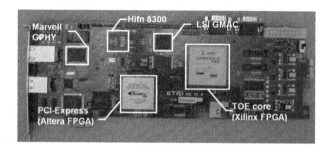

Fig. 7. LATONA TOE: FPGA version LATONA 2.0 with Hifn 8300

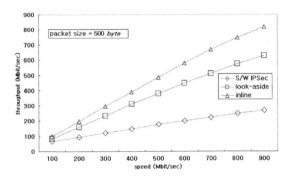

Fig. 8. Throughput of S/W, look-aside, and inline TOE IPSec system: measurement of throughput while sending speed of packet is increasing with a static packet size

As the security core of LATONA, Hifn8300 inline processor is adopted. As depicted in figure 7, Hifn8300 is located between PHY (Physical Layer) and MAC (Media Access Control Layer) of LATONA TOE. Hifn 8300 has 2 Gbps IPSec processing performance (full-duplex) and supports algorithms such as AES (CBC & CTR), DES/3DES, SHA-1, MD5, and AES-XCBC.

5   Some Experiments for IPSec

This paper shows the result data of some experiments comparing the performance among S/W only, H/W IPSec systems (look-aside and inline). The table 1 shows the condition of experiments. And the result is analyzed using the GTX protocol analyzer of Finisar[15].

Table 1. Condition of experiment: distinguished by the kinds of cores, traffics, and IPSec Modes

IPSec	CPU	Network	OS	Core	Traffic	IPSec setting
S/W only	Intel	3com	Linux-	IPSec-tools 0.6.2[14]	UDP using	ESP, tunnel
look-aside	Xeon	Gigabit	Fedora	Hifn8150[12]	packETH	HMAC-SHA1,
Inline	3.2G	Ethernet	3.0	Hifn8300[12]	1.2[13]	AES128

A. Measurement of the throughput of the IPSec TOE systems: We measure the throughput while interval time between each packet delay increases for the same packet size. As shown in the figure 8, for a fixed packet size, the inline system has outstanding performance. The throughput of the H/W system gradually increases as the sending speed increase whereas throughput increase rate of the S/W stack is getting weak. This overhead might seem to be caused by S/W computational overhead.

B. Measurement of the throughput while packet size increases: In the second experiment, we measure the changes of throughput during packet

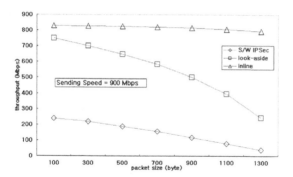

Fig. 9. Overhead of S/W, look-aside, and inline TOE IPSec system: measurement of throughput while packet size is increasing with a static sending speed

size is increasing for the same packet delay. As depicted in the figure 9, for a fixed sending speed, the throughput decrease rate of look-aside system gradually increase as the packet size increase. This overhead might seem to be caused by look-aside specific bus processing.

C. Approximation of the packet processing overhead: Through the above experiments, we can derive the main cause of the packet overhead. We estimate the overhead cost by some calculations. As figure 5 depicts, there are approximately 4 times of bus transfer between TOE and look-aside IPSec processor. Given that the packet size (1051 byte) and the bus (32bit, 133Mz), an approximation of packet processing overhead is possible.

Where B_{packet} is packet size, $C_{buspacket}$ is additional bus overhead, $S_{buspacket}$ is transmit time per packet, and $S_{1Gpacket}$ is processing time per packet on 1G network. As equation (3) of the above approximation, we can expect that look-aside TOE IPSec packet sending speed is two times slower than inline system speed. It's because the IPSec bus operation of look-aside spends same time as time which is necessary for packet processing with gigabit network stack. And we can know that the S/W IPSec packet cryptography cost is about 7 times more expensive than inline system. The overall result from the experiments is as follows in Table 2.

$$C_{buspacket} = (B_{packet} \times 8 \times 4) \div 32 = 1051 \qquad \text{(clock)} \qquad (1)$$

$$S_{buspacket} = \frac{C_{buspacket}}{133\,Mclock/\sec} \qquad S_{1Gpacket} = \frac{B_{packet} \times 8\,bit}{1\,Gbit/\sec} \qquad (2)$$

$$\therefore \quad S_{buspacket} : S_{1Gpacket} \approx 1 \qquad (3)$$

Table 2. Comparison among the systems: the S/W only, look-aside, and inline IPSec

metrics	S/W only	Look-aside	Inline	etc
Increase of Send speed	About 20% throughput compared with send speed	About 80% throughput compared with send speed	Almost 100% throughput compared with send speed	For sending speed
Increase Packet size	Bigger Packet size, less throughput	Bigger Packet size, less throughput	Almost 100% throughput compared with send speed	For sending speed
Cryptography overhead	760%[9]	0%	0%	For inline
Packet processing overhead	Maximum 100%	Maximum 100%	0%	For inline

6   Concluding Remarks

In this paper, we designed and implemented a server component (LATONA) for USN event packet service. It includes full TOE and hardware IPSec. Our approach can alleviate sensor network packet overheads as well as high speed network burden, so that host CPU can do other jobs. Also we classified which architecture is more suitable for the USN environment. Throughout some experiments and analysis of implementations, it was proven that the TOE system including the inline IPSec is an appropriated solution. The TOE system including the inline IPSec shows us the stable performance regardless of sending speed and packet size.

As a future work, we have a plan to expand the research area into the sensor security. The focus of the research is an implementation of key distribution protocol based on the IPSec TOE system. It is particularly challenging providing security in sensor networks due to the resource limitations of sensor nodes. The constrained energy budget of sensor nodes makes key distribute protocols such as IKE and Kerberos [17] developed for conventional wired networks impractical in large-scale sensor networks. We are interested in an implementation of a novel security key distribution protocol which is appropriate for the security between sensor node and the server based on the IPSec TOE.

References

1. G. Regnier et. al: TCP Onloading for Data Center Server. IEEE Computer, Vol. 37, Issue 11, Nov. 2004, pp 48-58
2. Renato John Recio: Server I/O Networks Past, Present, and Future", Proc.ACM SIGCOMM 2003 Workshop, Aug. 2003, pp. 164-178
3. Andy Currid: TCP Offloading to the Rescue", Queue, Vol. 2, No. 2, Issue 3, May 2004, pp. 58-65
4. "Intel I/O Acceleration Technology", http://www.intel.com
5. J. Mogul: TCP Offloading Is a Dumb Idea Whose Time Has Come. Proc. 9th Workshop on Hot Topics in Operating Systems, Usenix Assoc, 2003
6. Kyoung Park: Network I/O Acceleration Technologies. Summer Workshop, KISS, 2005

7. R.Oppliger: Internet and Intranet Security. Artech House, Norwood, Mass., 1998
8. R.Oppliger: Security at the internet layer. IEEE, 1998
9. Robert Friend: Making the gigabit IPSec VPN architecture secure. IEEE Computer, vol 37, pp. 54-60, 2004
10. A.P. Foong et al: TCP Performance Re-Visited. ISPASS, 2003
11. O.Elkeelany: Performance Analysis of IPSec protocol - encryption and authentication. ICC 2002
12. "Hifn IPSec Processors", http://www.hifn.com
13. "packETH", http://packeth.sourceforge.net
14. "IPSec-Tools", http://ipsec-tools.sourceforge.net
15. "Finisar GTX analyzer", http://www.finisar.com
16. Deepak Ganesan: Networking issues in wireless sensor networks. July 2004, Journal of Parallel and Distributed Computing
17. Srivaths Ravi et. al: System Design Methodologies for a Wireless Security Processing Platform. DAC2002, June 10-14, 2002
18. "Intel Corp., Enhancing Security Performance through IA-64 Architecture", http://developer.intel.com/design/security/rsa2000/itanium.pdf
19. K. Kant, R. Iyer, and P. Mohapatra: Architectural Impact of Secure Sockets Layer on Internet Servers. in Proc. Int. Conf. Computer Design, pp. 7-14, 2000
20. A. Goldberg, R. Buff, and A. Schmitt: Secure Server Performance Dramatically Improved by Caching SSL Session Keys. in ACM Wksp. Internet Server Performance, June 1998
21. "Intel Mote Reserch project website", www.intel.com
22. M. Hempstead, N. Tripathi, P. Mauro, G.-Y. Wei, and D. Brooks: An ultra low power system architecture for sensor network applications. In International Symposium on Com-puter Architecture, 2005
23. J. Hill, R. Szewczyk, A. Woo, S. Hollar, D. E. Culler, and K. S. J. Pister: System architec-ture directions for networked sensors. In Architectural Support for Programming Lan-guages and Operating Systems, pages 93-104, 2000
24. L. Nazhandali, B. Zhai, J. Olson, A. Reeves, M. Minuth, R. Helfand, S. Pant, T. Austin, and D. Blaauw: Energy optimization of subthreshold-voltage sensor network processors. International Symposium on Computer Architecture, 2005

An Approach for the Reduction of Power Consumption in Sensor Nodes of Wireless Sensor Networks: Case Analysis of Mica2

Adriano B. da Cunha and Diógenes C. da Silva Jr.

Dept. of Electrical Engineering, Federal University of Minas Gerais,
Av. Antônio Carlos, 6627, Belo Horizonte, MG, Brazil
{adborges, diogenes}@cpdee.ufmg.br

Abstract. This paper presents a novel solution for the effective reduction of power consumption in sensor nodes of wireless sensor networks. Possible alternatives to reduce the power consumption in generic sensor nodes are presented. After, these alternatives are evaluated for a specific sensor node, the Crossbow Mica2. The case analysis for this sensor node showed that, among the possible alternatives to reduce the power consumption, the radio communication channel presented the best opportunity. A novel solution that integrates the transmitted signal power control with the received information quality is presented in a dynamic mechanism called Maximal Survival Capacity.

1 Introduction

A Wireless Sensor Network (WSN) is composed of many autonomous and compact devices called sensor nodes. The objective of this network is to collect data. The availability of integrated low-power sensing devices, embedded processors, wireless communication kits, and power equipment are enabling the design of sensor nodes. WSN has the potential for many applications from monitoring large metropolis traffic density to road conditions; in a forest for fire detection; in precision agriculture; in condition based maintenance devices like powerplants; in biomedicine. Other applications include managing complex physical systems like airplane wings and complex ecosystems, and animal tracking.

A sensor node is composed of a power unit, processing unit, sensing unit, and communication unit. The power unit has the purpose to supply energy to the node. The processing unit collects and processes signals captured from sensors and transmit them to the network. Sensors devices are devices that produce a measurable response to a change in a physical condition like temperature and pressure. The wireless communication channel enables a medium to transfer signals from sensors to exterior world (provided by a gateway), and also an internal mechanism of communication to establish and maintain the WSN. Sensor nodes of WSN have limited resources, such as computational capacity, memory, communication and energy. In most applications, WSN will have large quantities of

S. Vassiliadis et al. (Eds.): SAMOS 2006, LNCS 4017, pp. 132–141, 2006.

distributed sensor nodes in remote or inhospitable places. That's why batteries are their main source of energy. Network lifetime depends on quantity of energy available and sensor nodes should balance their limited resources to increase the lifetime of the network.

The objective of this work is to present a novel approach to reduce the power consumption in sensor nodes. Several alternatives to reduce the power consumption are presented and analyzed. The case study focus at the Crossbow commercial sensor node called Mica2 Mote.

The Maximal Survival Capacity (MSC) is the ability of a WSN node to increase its operational lifetime. MSC is based on the amount of internal energy (supplied by its batteries) and the processing of the Maximal Survival Algorithm (MSA) which is based on the control of the node transmitted power and the quality of the received data at the base station.

2   Power Consumption in Sensor Nodes

To maximize the sensor node's lifetime after its deployment, aspects such as circuits, architecture, algorithms and protocols have to be energy efficient [1]. Once the system has been designed, it becomes necessary to identify how the power consumption is distributed among hardware components in the sensor node in order to obtain additional energy savings using Dynamic Power Management (DPM). The majority of the hardware components used, such as, microcontrollers, memories, and transceivers have at least two power management modes. Traditional Power Consumption reduction techniques use DPM and Static Power Management (SPM) which involves the control of power supply voltages and frequency of operation. In the case of WSN most used techniques are the Power Supply scaling, CPU Power states and peripheral Power Supply Control(on and off).

Microcontroller: Processing is effected by the microcontroller unit (MCU) of the sensor node. The MCU is composed by a central processing unit (CPU), a small internal program memory and, in general, a large data memory (usually non-volatile), and a set of peripherals such as timers, I/O modules and interfaces, and analog to digital converters. To increase the data memory capacity, an external is added and acts as a secondary memory not addressed in the CPU memory space. The MCU is responsible for the control of the sensors and execution of the communication protocols and algorithms of signal processing, applied to the data collected from the sensors. The StrongARM microprocessors from the Intel [2], microcontrollers AVR from the Atmel [3] and microcontrollers MSP430 of the Texas [4] are the MCUs often used in sensor nodes for WSN. DPM implemented in CPU makes possible the reduction of the power consumption in idle or sleep states. These modes permit that the application turn off modules not used. For example, the ATMEGA128L has six sleep modes, each one with a different set of internal modules turned on. There are also techniques that make possible the reduction of the power consumption in the active state of the MCU, such as DVS/DFS (Dynamic Voltage Scaling/Dynamic Frequency

Scaling) [5,6,7,8]. It should be noticed that the reduction of the voltage implies in a reduction of the operating frequency [5]. DVS is a technique used for power management in active states of the MCU, in which the power supply and the clock frequency are varied, depending on the processing demand [7]. The power supply is scaled for the application by means of the operational system and controlled at the physical layer with a DC-DC converter with variable voltage [5,7]. However, the hardware of the MCU must provide this type of functionality, as it is the case of the MCUs Intel StrongARM and the Crusoe, from Transmeta [9]. There are two types of power management supplied by CPUs in idle states. A mechanism of SPM, that is set in motion by the user and does not depend on the activities of the CPU. An example of a static mechanism is the power down mode. This mode is a way to reduce the unnecessary power dissipation and generally is implemented by the execution of a specific instruction. Exit of this mode occurs by means of an interruption or another event, not being possible to leave by means of the execution of another instruction. A mechanism of DPM [1,10,11] implements actions to control the power dissipation based in the dynamic activity of the CPU. For example, the CPU can disconnect some of its modules when the instructions that are being executed do not need them. To enter to, specially to exit from lower-power modes CPU consumes time and energy (without processing), and needs to adequately control its internal logic to avoid program and data corruption.

Transceiver: Wireless communication is carried by means of a radio frequency transceiver. This makes possible the communication of the sensor node with its neighbors and the external world. The characteristics that affect the consumption of energy of a transceiver include the type of modulation, transmission rate, transmission power and operational duty cycle [5,12]. The Chipcon CC1000 [13] and the CC2420 [14] are the transceivers often used in available commercial WSN platforms. An opportunity to reduce the consumption of the transceiver energy is to control the transmit power, since it can have an impact on the remaining battery capacity [15,16,17]. Several researchers have proposed simple modifications of IEEE 802.11 standard to incorporate power control. The main idea of these power control schemes is to use different power levels for RTS-CTS and data-ack. Specially, maximum transmit power is used for RTS-CTS, and the minimum required transmit power is used for data-ack transmissions in order to save energy [18]. Jung and Vaidya [19] have proposed a power control MAC protocol that periodically increases the transmit power to a maximum during the data packet transmission. With this change, nodes that can potentially interfere with the ack reception at the sender will periodically sense the channel as busy, and defer their own transmission. However, WSN differs from Ad Hoc Networks in two aspects: unidirectional data flow and a strong energy restriction. Thus, other questions and scenarios should be considered.

Power Supply: Usually, a battery is the energy source, but there are other energy sources that can be used, such as solar cells, ultra capacitors, vibrations cells, fuel micron-cells, etc [20].

Sensors: Sensors are responsible for the monitoring of interest phenomena, such as: temperature, pressure, luminosity, humidity, etc. They translate physical phenomena into electric signals and can be classified as analogical or digital devices, depending on the type of output they produce. The sources of energy consumption in sensors include sampling of the signal and the conversion of the physical signal for the electric signal, signal conditioning and analog to digital conversion.

3   Maximum Survival Capacity

Before implementing any technique of hardware for the reduction of the power consumption for the Mica Motes platform sensor node, a survey of the consumption for each hardware components is presented. The microcontroller used in this platform only makes possible the power management of sleep states, and no DVS mechanism is possible. Table 1 shows the consumption of the main hardware components.

It can be observed that the consumption is critical for the external memory and the transceiver. In the first case, the only alternative is to keep it in the standby mode. For the transceiver, besides the power down mode option, it has adjustable transmission power [13].

While focusing on the Mica2 platform, this technique can be applied to any WSN node. Mica2's CPU has a very simple low power facilities. MSC will not focus on CPU power savings since it varies from CPU to CPU. As shown below, the communication unit has the largest power budget in the node, and this value is much larger than the CPU (6mA versus 25.4 mA). MSC focus on the power consumption of the communication unit, controlling the Tx power, since Rx power is fixed.

In a real application, it will be necessary to configure the transmission power of the sensor node for a high value so that it can, effectively establish communication and to guarantee its survival. The direct consequence of a raised power

Table 1. Power consumption for the Mica2 node

Consumption Table	
MODE	CURRENT
ATMEGA128L	
Run	6mA
Sleep	10μA
External Memory (AT45DB041B)	
Write	15mA
Read	4mA
Stanby	2μA
CC1000 Transceiver	
Rx	8mA
Tx (5 dBm)	25.4mA
Power Down	0.2μA

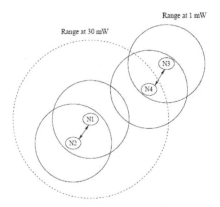

Fig. 1. Sensor node transmission power range and neighborhood interference [15]

transmission, for all sensor nodes or part of them, it is the interference that will occur between neighbors. Considering Fig. 1, if node N1 is configured with a transmission power of 30 mW, it will produce interference in node N4. This factor makes the dynamic adjustment of the transmission power essential, but, as it will be seen ahead, not satisfactory.

Once the power transmission has been adjusted for its minimum value necessary to establish communication with the base, an increase of the noise power in the transmission channel can occur and the base station starts to discard packets received from the sensor node. The problem is that such losses are not notified to the sender, i.e., all packets sent would be discarded until a reduction of the noise level occurs. Our proposal is to provide the sensor node with the Maximum Survival Capacity, whose characteristic is to integrate the control of the power of the transmitted signal and the quality of the information in a dynamic mechanism. Thus, beyond maximizing the probability of survival of the node, there will be reduction of the power consumption of the node quite effective while maintaining data communication. At least two reasonable justifications can be given for the necessity of maximizing the probability of survival of nodes: cost of commercial sensor nodes still high and the energy cost for network reorganization process, due to the deployment of new sensor nodes for the substitution of failed nodes. More clearly, the proposal is based on the following scenarios:

1. Launched node cannot communicate. The initial power is adjusted to the maximum value. Thus, the success in the establishment of the communication is maximized.
2. Launched node communicates and the packet received at base station does not contain error. The transmission power can be reduced.
3. Problems in the communication channel. After the transmission power is adjusted for the minimum value, the node stops communicating or occurs loss of packet in the base station. The transmission power must be increased.

Once these procedures are implemented, power consumption is effectively reduced, and the survival of the nodes after their launching is guaranteed even with the occurrence of problems in the communication channel. With the current RSSI level (Received Signal Strength Indicator) and the receiver sensitivity, these two values can be compared and the correct transmission power level determined by solving a control problem. The following variables must be determined: RSSI level, receiver sensitivity, proper action of control and number of lost packets of the base station.

Data formatting used is Manchester encoding and the signalling rate is 38.4 kbauds. The table supplied by the manufacturer [13] is used to obtain the receiver sensitivity. Based on this table, the sensitivity of the receiver was set to -97 dBm.

In the classic theory of control there are three basic control actions: proportional (P), integral (I) and derivative (D). Moreover, a combination of these basic actions of control can be made, such as PI, PD and PID. In the problem of control presented here, the action of control compares the value measured (RSSI + lost packets) with the desired value (reference) and acts in way to annulate the existing difference between them. In a WSN scenario, the action of ideal control to be implemented must be simple as possible, such that the power consumption for its processing is minimum and fast enough, so that the transceiver uses the minimum possible time at high transmission power levels. Another comment is that oscillations for the control action are highly undesirable, since it can represent an increase of the power consumption.

3.1 Maximum Survival Algorithm (MSA)

The Maximum survival algorithm (MSA), depicted in Fig. 2, behaves as follows: After launching of node, a process is initiated, called calibration phase: the base

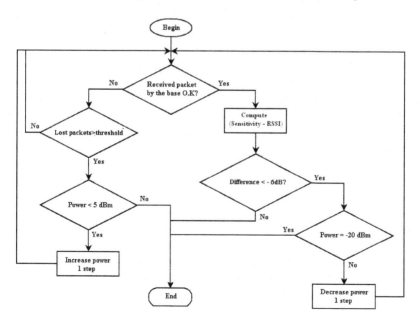

Fig. 2. The Maximum Survival Algorithm

station sends a message to the sensor node, that in turn, initiates the adjustment of its transmission power until it reaches the value of enough minimum power so that it can communicate with the base with quality: the amount of lost packets the base station is inferior to the established limit (through this experiment it was stipulated as three). Once that the ideal transmission power has been reached, it will only have new adjustment if there is loss of packet above the established limit. The monitoring of lost packets at the base verifies the occurrence of CRC errors, then a message is sent to the sensor node to obtain a new RSSI. MSA can be implemented in plain and hierarchical WSN, since it requires little computing power, thus incurring in a small amount of energy.

4   Experiments and Results

The base station was kept at a fixed position in the laboratory, while that the Mica2 node moved from the base station in multiples of the wavelength (λ). The frequency configured in the sensor node was of 914.077 MHz. The following sequence of distances based on the wavelength was used: $\lambda/10$, 1λ, 2λ, 3λ, 4λ, 5λ, 6λ and 7λ. The node started at the $\lambda/10$ position and was moved to next mark after ten minutes, totalizing 300 samples of voltage and current for each distance and for each one of the phases of experiments. In the first phase of the experiment, the node was configured with the maximum power transmission value (5 dBm). In second phase the node was configured using the MSA (maximum survival algorithm).

Fig. 3 shows the results of phase 1. In this phase Tx Power is fixed at 5 dBm. The maximum distance obtained was 7λ, since with a greater distance the

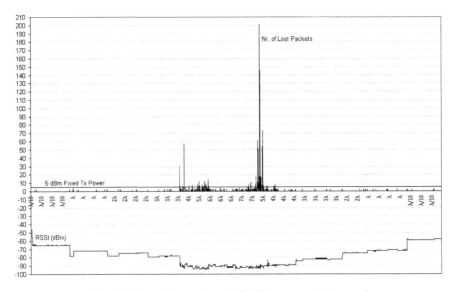

Fig. 3. Phase 1 experiment (5 dBm Fixed Tx Power)

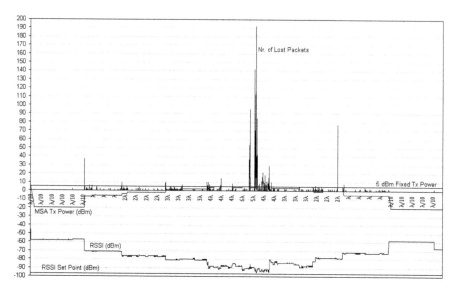

Fig. 4. Phase 2 with the Maximum Survival Algorithm

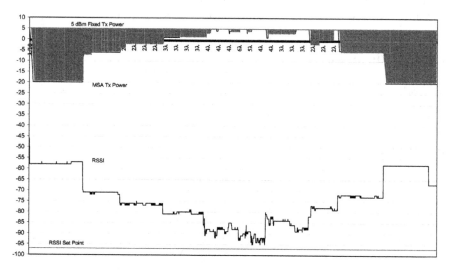

Fig. 5. MSA Power Consumption Reduction

communication was lost. The upper line in shows the number of lost packets and the bottom line the fixed value of the Tx power.

In the second phase the MSA was used with the same distance steps used in the first phase, see Fig. 4.

Reduction of the power consumption can be computed from the following data: voltage and current (at the output supply to the node) for each packet sent and the corresponding RSSI level for that packet at the receiver. This corresponds to the power used to transmit the packet. With data gathered from the two phases of the experiment, the difference between these values represents how much power consumption reduction was obtained using MSA. Fig. 5 shows the Phase 2 power savings. The gray area represents the energy saved under MSA. The upper line(5 dBm) is the maximum Tx power (Phase 1) and the second line is Tx power used in Phase 2. The third line is the RSSI level and the fourth line the set point for the minimum RSSI level (-97 dBm).

5   Conclusions

This work presented an effective solution that allows for the reduction of the power consumption in sensor node of a Wireless Sensor Network. Among the possible alternatives that had been studied, it was noticed that the performance in the transmission power of the transceiver presented the biggest gain in terms of consumption reduction. Thus, a solution was presented that integrates the adjustment of the power of the transmitted signal and the quality of the information in a dynamic mechanism, which was called Maximum Survival Algorithm. As a consequence, besides obtaining to maximal probability of node survival, a reduction of energy consumption was also obtained. The Maximum Survival Algorithm obtained an energy economy of 39.5% for the Mica2.

Acknowledgment

This work was supported by grants from Fapemig EDT 205/05 and CNPq Sensornet.

References

1. Sinhá, A., Chandrakasan, A.: Dynamic power management in wireless sensor networks. IEEE Design and Test of Computers **19** (2001) 62–74
2. Intel Corporation: Strongarm microprocessors. Available on: http://www.intel.com (2005)
3. Atmel Corporation: Avr 8-bit risc. Available on: http://www.atmel.com (2005)
4. Texas Instruments: Msp430 microcontrollers. Available on: http://www.ti.com (2005)
5. Srivastava, M.B.: Energy-aware wireless microsensor networks. IEEE Signal Processing Magazine **19** (2002) 40–50
6. P. Pillai, K.G.S.: Real-time dynamic voltage scaling for low-power embedded operating systems. In: Eighteenth ACM symposium on Operating systems principles. (2001) 89–102
7. Chandrakasan, A.: Power aware wireless microsensor systems. In: European Solid-State Circuits Conference (ESSCIRC). (2002) 47–54
8. Simunic, T., Benini, L., Acquaviva, A., Glynn, P., Micheli, G.D.: Dynamic voltage scaling and power management for portable systems. In: DAC '01: Proceedings of the 38th conference on Design automation, ACM Press (2001) 524–529

9. Transmeta Corporation: Crusoe microprocessor.   Available   on:
    http://www.transmeta.com (2005)
10. Simunic, T., Benini, L., Glynn, P., Micheli, G.D.: Event-driven power management.
    IEEE Transactions on Computer Aided Design of Integrated Circuits and Systems
    20 (2001) 840–857
11. L. Benini, A.B., Micheli, G.D.: A survey of design techniques for system-level
    dynamic power management. IEEE Transactions on VLSI Systems **8** (2000)
    299–316
12. Schurgers, C., Aberthorne, O., Srivastava, M.: Modulation scaling for energy aware
    communication systems. In: ISLPED '01: Proceedings of the 2001 international
    symposium on Low power electronics and design, ACM Press (2001) 96–99
13. Chipcon: Cc1000. Available on: http://www.chipcon.com (2005)
14. Chipcon: Cc2420. Available on: http://www.chipcon.com/ (2005)
15. Narayanaswamy, S., Kawadia, V., Sreenivas, R., Kumar, P.: Power control in ad-
    hoc networks: Theory, architecture, algorithm and implementation of the compow
    protocol. In: European Wireless, 2002. Next Generation Wireless Networks: Tech-
    nologies, Protocols, Services and Applications. (2002) 156–162
16. Su, N.M., Park, H., Bostrom, E., Burke, J., Srivastava, M.B., Estrin, D.: Aug-
    menting film and video footage with sensor data. In: PERCOM '04: Proceedings
    of the Second IEEE International Conference on Pervasive Computing and Com-
    munications (PerCom'04), IEEE Computer Society (2004) 3
17. Srivastava, A., Eustace, A.: Atom: A system for building customized program
    analysis tools. ACM SIGPLAN **39** (2004) 528–539
18. Agarwal, S., Krishnamurthy, S., Katz, R.H., Dao, S.K.: Distributed power control
    in ad-hoc wireless networks. In: Personal and Indoor Mobile Radio Communication
    (PIMRC01). (2001) F59–66
19. Jung, E.S., Vaidya, N.H.: A power control mac protocol for ad hoc networks. In:
    MobiCom '02: Proceedings of the 8th annual international conference on Mobile
    computing and networking. (2002) 36–47
20. Power Sources Review: Power sources for wireless sensor networks. Available on:
    http://www.eureka.gme.usherb.ca/memslab/docs/PowerReview-2.pdf (2005)

Energy-Driven Partitioning of Signal Processing Algorithms in Sensor Networks

Dong-Ik Ko, Chung-Ching Shen, Shuvra S. Bhattacharyya, and Neil Goldsman

Department of Electrical and Computer Engineering, and Institute for Advanced Computer Studies,University of Maryland, College Park MD 20742, USA
{dik, ccshen, ssb, neil}@eng.umd.edu

Abstract. In a sensor network, as we increase the number of nodes, the requirements on network lifetime, and the volume of data traffic across the network, it is often efficient to move towards hierarchical network architectures (e.g., see [5]). In such hierarchical networks, sensor nodes are clustered into groups, and their roles are divided into master and slave nodes for more efficient structuring of network traffic. The operational complexity of each sensor node and the amount of data to be transmitted across sensor nodes strongly influence the energy consumption of the nodes, which ultimately determines the network lifetime. This paper provides a new way of reducing data traffic across nodes by determining and exploiting the lowest data token delivery points within an application graph that is distributed across a network. The technique divides an application graph into two sub-graphs and then distributes each divided subgraph over a master node and its associated slave nodes. The buffer costs of the graph edges over the cutting line corresponds to the amount of data to be transmitted between nodes after allocating the two partial subgraphs such that one subgraph executes on a master node, and the other subgraph is distributed across the associated slave nodes. Since the energy consumption on each node is dominated by the transceiver, the reduced data traffic allows for reducing the turn-on time of the transceivers, and thereby leads to high energy savings. This technique also distributes the workload of sensor nodes in a systematic manner. The more balanced workload also contributes to efficient battery usage, and also improves the latency for processing the data frames captured by the sensor nodes.

1 Introduction and Related Work

The energy consumption of the nodes in a wireless sensor network must be carefully optimized to increase network lifetime. This paper develops an overall minimization of an energy consumption of a sensor network, and provides an efficient trade-off between latency and network lifetime by balancing the workload of the sensor nodes, and carefully determining the points in the application that must communicate across nodes so that the turn-on time of transceivers is minimized.

Many useful approaches have been suggested previously to reduce the energy consumption of sensor nodes. Shih et al. have distributed the FFT function over a master node and slave nodes to reduce energy consumption by moving the function

S. Vassiliadis et al. (Eds.): SAMOS 2006, LNCS 4017, pp. 142–154, 2006.

from a cluster head node to slave nodes [11]. Kumar, Tsiatsis, and Srivastava [8] explore energy and latency trade-offs by considering different computational capabilities for master and slave nodes. Other researchers have suggested a hierarchical, physical layer driven sensor network design to reduce data traffic and energy consumption of a sensor node in connection with the physical-layer network functions [10, 12]. In these latter approaches, the node optimization needs to be performed carefully in conjunction with the underlying protocol characteristics.

The technique that we develop in this paper is novel in that it analyzes the pattern of internal data exchange rates within an application to minimize the overall energy consumption of a sensor network, while also taking into account changes in latency due to distributed mapping, and application of a hierarchically clustered sensor network organization. The approach is especially suited for multirate signal processing applications, which exhibit complex and nonuniform patterns of data exchange across functional modules of the application.

Many sensor network applications or important application subsystems can be modeled efficiently with dataflow semantics. By analyzing a well-designed dataflow graph model of an application, operational efficiency can be effectively estimated and optimized at a coarse grain level for various kinds of target architectures (e.g., see [2, 3, 6]). Parameterized dataflow [1] is a form of dataflow that is especially well-suited to sensor network signal processing applications due to its integrated support for adaptation and reconfiguration at various layers of abstraction. Parameterized dataflow allows for dynamic change of variables and configuration settings that can be mapped to module- or subsystem-level parameters of an application.

This paper employs the DGT (dynamic graph topology) [7] method for modeling applications. DGT is a form of parameterized dataflow that emphasizes support for run-time flexibility by allowing for efficient, dynamic changes in application graph topologies based on run-time requests. In DGT semantics, the connections (dataflow edges) between actors (functional modules), as well as the amount of data produced and consumed by the actors can be changed, with the changes expressed in terms of dynamic parameters of the application. In the context of sensor network optimization, this feature can be used to integrate modeling of master/slave node relationships in a clustered network, and also modeling of dynamically changing application graph topologies that execute on sensor nodes.

2 DGT (Dynamic Graph Topology) Specifications

The DGT model allows for dynamic change of graph topologies through schedules that are pre-computed at a compile time. DGT is based on PSDF semantics [1], but is significantly more flexible than PSDF in that it allows graph actors and edges to be treated as dynamic parameters as well as the more standard types of parameters supported in the dynamic reconfiguration capabilities of PSDF. In DGT, as in PSDF, the data transfer rate of a port of an actor (i.e., the number of data values produced or consumed with respect to the incident edge) can be determined by a special subgraph, called the *init* graph. In this way, the consumption rate and production rate of selected ports can be determined dynamically, just before the invocation of the associated DGT graph. Additionally, in DGT, the *subinit* graph Φs can control the behavior of the associated body graph by dynamically changing the topology (interconnections between actors) of the associated body graph before each invocation (graph iteration) of the body graph. The set of possible graph topologies is predicted at compile time.

Figure 1 shows how a subinit graph can extract appropriate header information and set up parameters (X:param) with the required information for the associated body graph. An appropriate graph is selected from a set of possible graphs(G_1, G_2, G_3}by the subinit graph with (X:param). This mechanism is effective because many data streams for modern DSP applications are delivered in the form of frames, where each frame has a header part and a payload part, and the header part can be parsed to determine the appropriate graph topology.

Here, we classify actors and ports into two categories based on whether or not their behavior changes dynamically. Actors and ports that are not changed in the graph topology are called fixed actors (a_f) and fixed ports (p_f), respectively, while actors and ports having potential dynamic changes are named as varying actors (a_v) and varying ports (p_v). Here, one point that requires careful consideration is that a fixed actor(a_f) can have a varying port (p_v) since a fixed actor (a_f) can appear with different types of ports.

The *subinit* graph Φs dynamically sets up varying actors and varying ports based on data being delivered and produces an appropriate graph topology for the associated body graph. Deadlock-free operation and bounded memory requirements for each possible set of graph topologies are verified at compile time. At runtime, the *subinit* graph Φs sets up an appropriate graph topology for the associated body graph and selects an appropriate pre-computed schedule that also contains code and buffer size that is minimized for the configured graph. Code and buffer size minimization is obtained by a scheduling technique appropriately chosen depending on graph characteristics. In DGT, verification of validity of schedules can be performed at compile time and valid schedules can be guaranteed and can be ready to use at runtime without the overhead of fully dynamic scheduling. At runtime, *the subinit* graph Φs looks up pre-computed schedules in a table with the active set of parameter values.

3   Energy Consumption Optimization by Distribution of an Application

3.1   Application Cutting in a Sensor Network

In a clustered sensor network, each sensor node captures data from its set of one or more sensors. The captured data can be sent to the associated master node immediately, or the data can be processed to some degree within the slave node before it is sent to the master node. For the data processing functionality, each edge within the application dataflow graph may have different data transfer characteristics. It is useful to consider these characteristics carefully when dividing a dataflow graph for processing across a master- and slave-node pair.

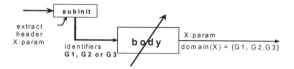

Fig. 1. Illustration of DGT semantics

Dividing an application graph in this manner generally allows us to reduce the amount of data that must be transmitted between the nodes, and it also allows us to balancing the workloads of sensor nodes. The amount of data that must be transmitted directly influences the turn-on time of the sensor node transceivers, which are major sources of energy consumption. Similarly, distributing the workload of an application for balanced processing increases network lifetime through balanced battery usage across the sensor nodes. Therefore, it is useful to partition dataflow graphs across sensor nodes with joint consideration of data transfer volume and workload balance.

Synchronous dataflow (SDF) is an especially useful model, due to its predictability and formal properties, for representing many signal processing applications [2, 9]. In SDF, the number of data values (tokens) produced and consumed by each actor is constant. As a result of this restriction, graphs can be scheduled statically based on the so-called repetition vector $_R$ »), which is a vector that is indexed by the actors in the graph, and gives the number of times that each actor needs to be invoked in a static schedule for the graph. Such a schedule can be repeated indefinitely with bounded memory requirements to process the indefinite-length data streams that are characteristic in the signal processing domain.

The number of tokens that are transferred across an edge in the dataflow graph in each schedule iteration can be obtained from the repetitions vector $_R$ » and the number of tokens produced by the source actor of the edge. Given a partition of the dataflow graph into two parts, the total number of tokens that must be transferred (buf_{tr}) across the partition can be obtained by summing up the token transfer volumes of the edges that cross the partition.

The repetitions vector can be obtained through (1) and (2) [9]:

$$T(e, v) = \begin{bmatrix} prd(e) & \text{if } v = src(e) \\ -cns(e) & \text{if } v = snk(e) \\ 0 & \text{otherwise} \end{bmatrix} \qquad (1)$$

$$T \bullet \vec{R} = 0 \qquad (2)$$

In (1), $prd(e)$ is the number of tokens produced onto edge e by each execution of $src(e)$, which denotes the source actor of e. Similarly, $cns(e)$ is the number of tokens consumed from e by each execution of $snk(e)$, which is the sink actor of e.

The total number of tokens buf_{tr} that cross a given partition in a schedule iteration can then be expressed as

$$buf_{tr} = \sum_{i=1}^{N_c} \sum_{j=1}^{Edge_{n_i}} \overrightarrow{R(n_i)} \cdot prd(e_j(n_i)) \tag{3}$$

where N_c is the number of actors whose outgoing edges cross the partition; $(n_1, n_2, \cdots, n_{N_c})$ is an ordering of the actors whose outgoing edges cross the partition; $Edge_{n_i}$ is the number of outgoing edges of actor n_i that cross the partition; and $e_j(n_i)$ is the j th outgoing edge of n_i that crosses the partition, based on some ordering of the outgoing edges.

Figure 2(a) illustrates how data transmission requirements can change depending the selection of a partition. Figure 2(a) provides four possible candidates for a "cutting line" to determine the partition. The edges that cross the cutting line determine the network data transfer volume that must be incurred on each graph iteration due to the associated application partition. The number shown inside each actor represents the processing complexity in terms of the actor execution time. The number on the left side of an edge represents the number of tokens produced by the source actor, and the number on the right side represents the number of tokens consumed by the sink actor.

In Figure 2, there are four edges, e0, e1, e2 and e3 . Figure 2(b) shows the repetition vector for Figure 2(a), and Figure 2(c) shows buf_{tr} for each cutting line candidate C0-C3 .

After a cutting line is determined for a graph, the graph is effectively divided into "left" and "right" subgraphs, where the left subgraph represents preprocessing of sensor

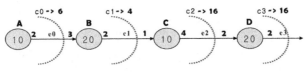

a) cutting line candidates

$$\begin{matrix} & A & B & C & D \\ \begin{matrix} e0 \\ e1 \\ e2 \end{matrix} & \begin{bmatrix} 2, & -3, & 0, & 0 \\ 0, & 2, & -1, & 0 \\ 0, & 0, & 4, & -2 \end{bmatrix} \end{matrix} \bullet \begin{bmatrix} R_1 \\ R_2 \\ R_3 \\ R_4 \end{bmatrix} = \begin{bmatrix} 0 \\ 0 \\ 0 \end{bmatrix} \implies \vec{R} = [3, \ 2, \ 4, \ 8]$$

b) Repetition vector

$$Buf_{tr, c0} = R_A \cdot buf_p(e_0(A)) = 3 \cdot 2 = 6$$
$$Buf_{tr, c1} = R_B \cdot buf_p(e_1(A)) = 2 \cdot 2 = 4$$
$$Buf_{tr, c2} = R_C \cdot buf_p(e_2(A)) = 4 \cdot 4 = 16$$
$$Buf_{tr, c3} = R_D \cdot buf_p(e_3(A)) = 8 \cdot 2 = 16$$

c) buf_{tr}s for each cutting line

Fig. 2. An illustration of partitioning (cutting line) trade-offs

signals and the right subgraph represents postprocessing. Accordingly, the left subgraph is allocated to the associated slave node, and the right subgraph is allocated to a master node.

Each cutting line in general leads to different workload distributions of an application graph, as well as different values of buf_{tr}. Intuitively,$C0$ leads to increased workload for the master node, since the master node is in charge of most of the data processing functionality. That value of buf_{tr} for $C0$ is 6 tokens. Similarly, $C3$ increases the workload of the slave node, while alleviating the workload of the master node; however, buf_{tr} for $C3$ increases to 16 tokens. As an alternative to $C0$ and $C3$, $C1$ allows for lower data transmission and more balanced workload distribution.

3.2 Cutting Algorithm

Cutting an application dataflow graph is an NP hard problem. However, in many sensor network applications, particularly those involving very simple, ultra-low cost/ power sensor node processing, the application graphs are of limited size, and are manageable by exact techniques. This paper uses an exhaustive search method for finding the best cutting line to target such applications and to demonstrate the potential of high-level, dataflow graph analysis for coordinating the processing across senor nodes.

More precisely, given an application dataflow graph Φ, our objective is to partition Φ into two subgraphs Φ_1 and Φ_2 . In this partitioning, we would like to minimize

$$buf_{tr, c_i(\Phi)} \tag{4}$$

subject to

$$\text{if } n \in \text{actors}(\Phi_2), \text{ then } \text{successors}(n) \subset \text{actors}(\Phi_2) \text{ and} \tag{5}$$

$$t(\Phi_1) - \delta t(\Phi_2) \leq \Omega \tag{6}$$

Here, $t(X)$ is the execution time of subgraph X , assuming that the subgraph is assigned to the same sensor node, and processing resources across the nodes are homogeneous. The formulation can easily be extended to handle heterogeneous processing resources, but for clarity and conciseness, we focus here on the homogeneous case. The subgraph execution time is obtained by adding the execution time estimates for the individual actors in the subgraph. Also, $\text{actors}(X)$ represents the set of actors in subgraph X, and given an actor n , $\text{successors}(n)$ represents the set of immediate graph successors of n . The constraint in (5) is necessary to avoid cyclic dependencies (potential deadlock) between the master and slave node.

The parameter δ is a coefficient that affects the load balancing aspect of the optimization. An appropriate choice for δ can be estimated by experimentation, or one can run the optimization multiple times for different values of δ and take the most attractive result. As the value of δ is increased, the workload of the master node is decreased, and the latency of the application is also generally decreased since the workload of the application is more distributed over slave nodes. The symbol Ω represents a tolerance for workload imbalance in conjunction with δ.

3.3 Effect on Energy Consumption

The total energy of a sensor node E can be divided into two parts: E_{radio} and E_{mc}, where E_{radio} represents the energy consumed by the transceiver, and E_{mc} represents the energy consumed by the microcontroller and the associated peripherals, such as the memory, UART, and ADC, apart from the transceiver. Thus,

$$E = E_{radio} + E_{mc} \tag{7}$$

The transceiver energy E_{radio} is usually dominant in the total energy consumption of a sensor node, and in the context of dataflow processing, this energy is proportional to the number of tokens that must be communicated. An optimal cutting of an application graph in terms of token transfer minimization across the cutting line therefore results in optimal streamlining of transceiver turn on time. In other words, by reducing buf_{t_r}, E_{radio} can be minimized under the workload balance constraints.

Each partitioned subgraph is mapped to a slave node or a master node. The operations of a subgraph apart from its transceiver-related operations are modeled by E_{mc}. Through a minor abuse of notation, we represent the energy consumption for data processing in an application $appl$ as $E_{mc}(appl)$. By distributing the application over a master node and a slave node, $E_{mc}(appl)$ can be divided into two sub energy consumption components: $E_{mc,s}(appl)$ and $E_{mc,m}(appl)$, corresponding respectively to the slave and master nodes. Thus, we have

$$E_{mc}(appl) = E_{mc,s}(appl) + E_{mc,m}(appl) \tag{8}$$

In a sensor network cluster that consists of a single master node and η slave nodes, the master node iterates η times to process data frames from all of its slave nodes. Then $E_{mc,m}$ is the total energy consumption for microcontroller-related functions by the master node during its η iterations of right-side-subgraph processing of data frames received from the slave nodes. The relationships among $E_{mc,m}$, $E_{mc,s}(appl)$, and $E_{mc,s}(appl)$ can be summarized as

$$\begin{aligned} E_{mc,m} &= \eta E_{mc,m}(appl) \qquad \text{and} \\ &= \eta(E_{mc}(appl) - E_{mc,s}(appl)) \end{aligned} \tag{9}$$

$$E_{mc,s} = E_{mc,s}(appl) \tag{10}$$

$E_{mc,s}$, which is the total energy consumption for microcontroller-related functions of a single slave node, is equal to $E_{mc,s}(appl)$ since data frames for an application graph are transmitted from a slave node to a master node, and for a single data frame, one iteration of a left-side (slave node) sub-graph is activated. Here, $E_{radio,m}$ is proportional to η since the transceiver of the master node should be turned on during the entire reception of η data frames from the η slave nodes.

The total energy consumed by the master node can be expressed as

$$E_m = E_{mc,m} + E_{radio,m} = E_{mc,m} + \lambda \eta E_{radio,s} \tag{11}$$

where λ is a coefficient that relates $\eta E_{radio,s}$ and $E_{radio,m}$. Since typically $\lambda \eta \gg 1$, the master node has significantly more energy consumption compared to the slave nodes. To reduce the overall energy consumption, the number of tokens that must be transmitted across the nodes should be minimized under the given workload distribution constraints.

3.4 Effect on Latency

The latency for processing a single data frame of a given application depends on the number of slaves in the network cluster, the network topology, and the volume of data contained in each data frame. For a cluster that consists of a single master node and η slave nodes, the latency $L(app)$ for processing a single application data frame can be expressed by (12), independent of the underlying transmission protocol.

$$L(app) = \eta L_{m,\,frame}(app) + L_{s,\,frame}(app) \qquad (12)$$
$$+ \eta L_{tr,frame}(app)$$

where $L_{m,\,frame}(app)$ is the latency of master node (right-side subgraph) processing for a single data frame, and $L_{s,\,frame}(app)$ is the corresponding latency of slave node processing. In total, a latency of $\eta L_{m,\,frame}(app)$ is induced on the master node to process the data from all of the slave nodes. The slave nodes, however, can operate in parallel, and thus, the latency required for slave node processing is independent of the number of slave nodes within the network cluster.

$L(app)$ also depends on the network delay for transmitting data frames across nodes. $L_{tr,frame}(app)$ thus denotes the latency for transmitting a single data frame from a slave node to the master node. The total transmission latency for delivering η data frames from the slave nodes becomes $\eta L_{tr,frame}(app)$.

Clearly, $L_{tr,frame}(app)$ depends on the data frame size. In particular, $L_{tr,frame}(app)$ is proportional to buf_{tr}.

Figure 3 shows three different cases of cutting line selection for an application example that involves maximum entropy spectrum computation. This application is based on an example in the Ptolemy II design environment [4]. The application can be divided into two subgraphs, which are allocated to master and slave nodes as illustrated in the figure. The dotted lines represent cutting line candidates. The application is characterized by a parameter n, called the *order* of the spectrum computation.

In Figure 3(a), the slave nodes capture raw data frames and send them directly to the master node, where the maximum entropy spectrum processing is performed. Here, buf_{tr} between a single slave node and the master node is 2^{n+1}. Therefore, the total data transmission for each data frame from the 5 slave nodes is $5 \times 2^{n+1}$.

In Figure 3(b), each slave node fully processes a data frame before sending to the master node. This is a fully distributed approach, which minimizes the workload of the master node. In this approach, each slave node sends 2^{n} tokens to the master node. Thus, the total data transmission from the 5 slave nodes is 5×2^{n}.

In Figure 3(c), on the other hand, the application graph is divided more evenly into two subgraphs A and B. A copy of subgraph A is assigned to each slave node, and B is allocated to the master node. The carefully-constructed cutting line between A and B reduces buf_{tr} to $(n + 1)$, which results in total slave-to-master data transmission of $5 \times (n + 1)$.

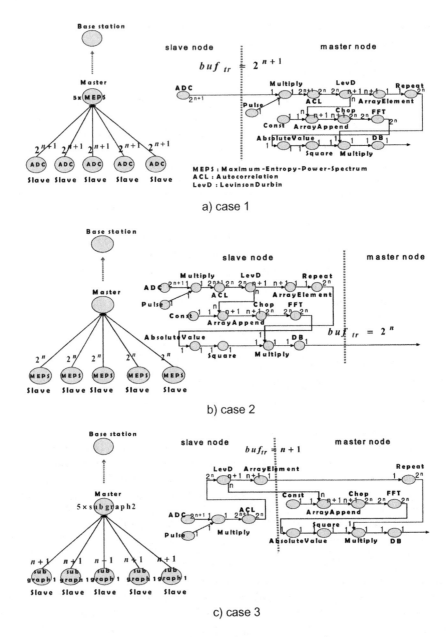

Fig. 3. Application mapping over sensor nodes

Without consideration of $L_{tr,\text{frame}}(app)$, the application latencies ($L(app)$) of the three cases in Figure 3 are related as ($L_{case1} > L_{case3} > L_{case2}$). Case 2 provides the maximal workload distribution by allowing raw data frames to be fully processed in the slave nodes. However, the greatly-reduced $L_{tr,\text{frame}}(app)$ of Case 3 offsets the increase in $L_{m, \, frame}(app)$ due to the increased workload of the master, while allowing reduced energy consumption because of reduced transceiver demands.

In summary, the example of Figure 3 illustrates the trade-offs that we can explore among processor workload balancing, latency cost, and transceiver requirements when considering different cutting lines for a multirate signal processing application.

3.5 Cutting Algorithm Under DGT Semantics

Each sensor node in a sensor network can be configured to execute different dataflow graphs depending on any changes in the network's functionality. This requirement leads naturally to a separate dataflow topology for each possible application configuration. As described in Section 2, DGT allows for modeling and software synthesis of a dataflow graph with alternative graph topologies under a single dataflow model. Under DGT semantics, the suggested cutting algorithm can be applied to each graph configuration to generate distributed subgraphs for each possible graph topology.

For example, suppose graph G can be configured into three different cases of graph topologies (G1,G2 or G3) depending on changes in sensor network functionality. Our cutting technique is then iteratively applied at compile time to generate a corresponding set of graph partitions $((G1_{sub1}, G1_{sub2}),(G2_{sub1}, G2_{sub2})$ and $(G3_{sub1}, G3_{sub2}))$ for (G1,G2 or G3), respectively. Under DGT semantics, GN_{sub1} is configured as a slave node at runtime, while its counterpart subgraph GN_{sub2} is set up for a master node. Thus, the suggested technique is applied to each possible graph topology at compile time to obtain an optimal dataflow graph distribution over the network. The compile time partitions derived by our integrated DGT/ graph-cutting techniqe are used at run time along with other relevant scheduling information to achieve a power efficient, adaptive operation of the network.

4 Experimental Results

We have developed experimental prototype platforms (Figure 4) for master and slave nodes using reconfigurable off-the-shelf components, including the Texas Instruments MSP430 microcontroller, the LINX Technologies 916MHz wireless transceiver, and a microphone sensor. The MSP430 provides a 16-bit processor core, along with a 12-bit ADC, 16-bit hardware timer, UART, 48kB program memory, and 10kB data memory.

Figure 5 and Figure 6 show experimental results where we measured the current consumption from our prototype platforms as they were running different partitionings of the maximum entropy spectrum application. In these experiments, we used TDMA operations for wireless communication. For the TDMA operations, we used 10 time slots per frame, and 250ms per time slot to guarantee that transmission and relevant computations can be completed within each slot.

Figure 5 shows experimental results for current consumption comparison in three different application mapping cases involving a single master node and three slave nodes when $n = 8$ is the application order. The amounts of data (in bytes) that must be transmitted and received between nodes in each slot under cases 1, 2, and 3 are, respectively, 512(2^{8+1}), 256(2^8 .) and 9(8+1).

Figure 5 shows that sensor node platforms consume much more current when the nodes are transmitting or receiving data compared to when the nodes are in their idle modes. Also, transceiver operation dominates the overall current consumption when data is being transmitted or received.

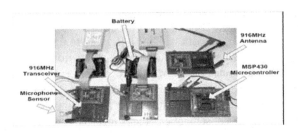

Fig. 4. MSP430-based sensor node platforms

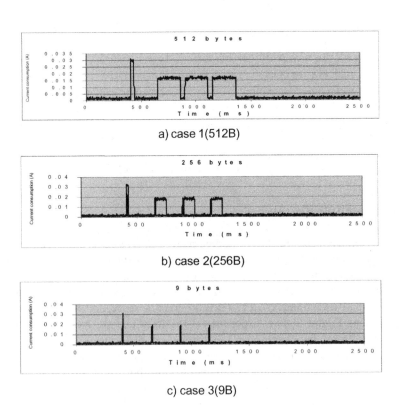

a) case 1(512B)

b) case 2(256B)

c) case 3(9B)

Fig. 5. Current consumption comparison of three application mapping

According to the results in Figure 5, we observe that case 3 of the suggested application cutting technique consumes 70.5% less energy than case 1 and 56.5% less than case 2. Here, the current and voltage for each sensor node are obtained by a digital storage oscilloscope. The power consumption for a time frame is obtained according to the sampling points for current and voltage values. The energy consumption within a TDMA time frame is calculated by integrating the power consumption over the time frame. Because the TDMA operations provide a periodic way to generate similar modes of operations for consecutive time frames, we calculate energy consumption results for several time frames and compute average values from these results.

Figure 6 shows how energy comparison varies as the application order parameter n is changed. For each order number, we measured current consumption and voltage on our prototype platforms, and calculated the average energy consumption based on the TDMA time frames. According to the results in Figure 6, we observe that as the order number is increased, the disparities between different application mapping cases become more prominent.

Table 1. Latency comparison for different values of order

order	3	4	5	6	7	8
case1	180ms	254ms	404ms	721ms	1364ms	2699ms
case2	64ms	92ms	150ms	270ms	515ms	1021ms
case3	146ms	191ms	280ms	474ms	864ms	1683ms

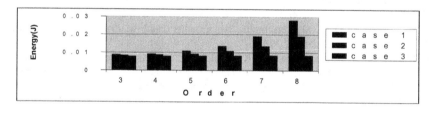

Fig. 6. Energy consumption comparison for different order values

Table 1 shows that as the application order increases, which results in increased data transmission, the relative latency gap between case 2 (best latency) and case 3 (best energy consumption) decreases. For any order, case 1, which is the conventional master-node-centric mapping, generates the worst latency and energy consumption pattern for our benchmark applications.

5 Summary

In this paper, we have developed a technique to partition an application graph into subgraphs to optimize the workload distribution and data transmission when mapping the application onto a hierarchical sensor network. The technique allows the overall energy consumption of a sensor network to be minimized without considerable loss of latency. In our future work, we will explore the integration of error correction into our partitioning framework to provide further savings in energy consumption.

References

[1] B. Bhattacharya and S. S. Bhattacharyya. Parameterized dataflow modeling for DSP systems. *IEEE Transactions on Signal Processing*, 49(10):2408-2421, 2001.

[2] S. S. Bhattacharyya, P. K. Murthy, E. A. Lee, *Software Synthesis from Dataflow Graphs*, Kluwer Academic Publishers, 1996.

[3] J. T. Buck, E. A. Lee, "Scheduling Dynamic Dataflow Graphs with Bounded Memory using the Token Flow Model", *Proc. ICASSP*, April, 1993.

[4] J. Eker et al., Taming heterogeneity — the Ptolemy approach. *Proceedings of the IEEE*, January 2003.

[5] W. Heinzelman, A. Chandrakasan, and H. Balakrishnan. Energy-efficient communication protocol for wireless microsensor networks. In *Proceedings of the Hawaii International Conference on System Sciences*, 2000

[6] A. Kalavade and P. A. Subrahmanyam, "Hardware / Software Partitioning for Multi-function Systems", *Proc. International Conference on Computer Aided Design*, pp. 516-521, Nov. 1997.

[7] D. Ko and S. S. Bhattacharyya. Dynamic configuration of dataflow graph topology for DSP system design. In Proceedings of the International Conference on Acoustics, Speech, and Signal Processing, pages V-69-V-72, Philadelphia, Pennsylvania, March 2005.

[8] R. Kumar, V. Tsiatsis, and M. B. Srivastava, Computation Hierarchy for In-network Processing, the 2nd ACM international conference on Wireless sensor networks and applications, pp. 68.77, 2003.

[9] E. A. Lee and D. G. Messerschmitt. Synchronous dataflow. *Proceedings of the IEEE*, 75(9):1235-1245, September 1987.

[10] S. Lindsey, C. Raghavendra, and K. Sivalingam, Data Gathering in Sensor Networks using the Energy Delay Metric. IEEE Transactions on Parallel and Distributive Systems, special issue on Mobile Computing, pp. 924-935, April 2002

[11] E. Shih, S. Cho, N. Ickes, R. Min, A. Sinha, A. Wang, and A. Chandrakasan, "Physical layer driven protocol and algorithm design for energy-efficient wireless sensor networks", in Proc. ACM MOBICOM'01, July 2001.

[12] M. Singh and V. K. Prasanna, System-Level Energy Tradeoffs for Collaborative Computation in Wireless Networks Norwell, MA: Kluwer, 2002.

Preamble Sense Multiple Access (PSMA) for Impulse Radio Ultra Wideband Sensor Networks

Jussi Haapola, Leonardo Goratti, Isameldin Suliman, and Alberto Rabbachin

Centre for Wireless Coomunications (CWC), University of Oulu, P.O. Box 4500 FIN-90014,
Oulu, Finland
{jhaapola, goratti, isam, rabalb}@ee.oulu.fi

Abstract. In this paper we propose preamble sense multiple access (PSMA), a random access MAC protocol capable of clear channel assessment in impulse radio-ultra wideband environment. Full compatibility with IEEE 802.15.4a contention access period is the key design criteria of PSMA, and the goal is to provide an alternative approach to the 802.15.4a envisioned slotted ALOHA and periodic preamble segment transmission schemes. The evaluation of PSMA consists of a traditional throughput analysis as well as energy consumption and delay analysis that takes into account the special features of impulse radio ultra wideband approach. From the analysis we can claim that PSMA has a very good energy and delay performance in addition to satisfactory throughput when the offered traffic to the channel is from low to moderate.

1 Introduction

Ultra Wideband (UWB) is a promising physical layer technology which potentially enables low power, low cost devices with applications for Wireless Personal Area Networks (WPAN) and for Wireless Body Area Networks (WBAN). UWB is a technology already exploited in radar systems for military applications since the 1960s. In the last few years UWB technology attracted renewed attention as a physical layer (PHY) for a wide range of applications like positioning and tracking, monitoring, and multimedia services. In 2002, the Federal Communications Commission (FCC) in the United States came out with the first regulatory on UWB allowing the use of the frequency spectrum between 3.1-10.6 GHz with emission limits of -41.25 dBm for outdoor hand-held systems [1].

Currently UWB is divided into two main physical layer technology branches: impulse radio-ultra wideband (IR-UWB) [2] using one very wide band for communications and multi-band, i.e., orthogonal frequency division multiplexing-ultra wideband (OFDM-UWB) [3] sponsored by the multi-band OFDM alliance (MBOA) and using several ultra wide OFDM channels for communcation. In this paper we limit ourselves to the IR-UWB that is the technology behind the current IEEE 802.15.4a draft [4].

IR-UWB utilizes extremely short pulses with correspondingly very wide bandwidths and very low emitted power. Because of these features, IR-UWB offers significant robustness against multipath fading [5] which makes UWB a suitable technology candidate for indoor applications, especially where power consumption and interference

S. Vassiliadis et al. (Eds.): SAMOS 2006, LNCS 4017, pp. 155–166, 2006.

levels are tightly constrained. With the IR-UWB approach, there are two main methods to generate the UWB signal: time-hopping (TH) and direct sequence (DS). These two systems offer the advantages of simple implementation due to their carrier-less nature and high processing gain. For the TH-UWB, which is used in this study, the most known modulation schemes are: pulse amplitude modulation (PAM) where the information modulates the amplitude of the signal and pulse position modulation (PPM), where the bit decision is made based on the pulses relative position in a slot [6].

For IR-UWB being a carrier-less signal, a medium access control (MAC) protocol based on carrier sensing (CS) is not well suited. The power of the clear channel assessment (CCA) done by the CS is clearly illustrated by superior throughput performance when comparing for example carrier sense multiple access (CSMA) [7] and ALOHA. For IR-UWB other, usually centrally coordinated or purely interference based, MAC approaches have been taken. Central coordination examples are the high data rate IEEE Std 802.15.3 [8] and the low data rate IEEE Std 802.15.4 [9] WPANs, and interference based approach example is $(UWB)^2$ [10], where the communication relies on the resilience of time hopping (TH) codes, the IR-UWB processing gain, and multi-channel access. The 802.15.4a draft proposal [4] has two options for IR-UWB contention access part: slotted ALOHA and an optional preamble segment detection (CCA) mode.

The Idea behind the optional CCA mode is the following. To enable CCA of IR-UWB signal at any time, a regular structure is introduced into the data portion of the frame by interleaving preamble segments in the PHY service data unit (PSDU) segments in time domain. The inserted preamble segments serve as a regular CCA structure of the frame. Effectively, the transmission of a frame starts with a full preamble sequence followed by the start-of-frame delimiter, followed by preamble segment and physical layer header. Then the transmission of the PSDU is a series of alternating preamble segment — PSDU segment portions starting and finishing in a preamble segment. When an another node is ready to send data it performs a CCA that is long enough to catch a preamble segment if there are any. If no segments are found transmission commences, otherwise a backoff is made and the process is repeated later.

In this paper, we propose a novel alternative method of utilizing CCA in IR-UWB environment, called the preamble sense multiple access (PSMA). The PSMA MAC protocol has been designed to provide a CSMA-like channel access for IR-UWB environment. Its salient features include the requirement of only one CCA before channel access, which saves time and energy because the IR-UWB preamble is long, unhindered communication on the channel for a duration of 2 time slots upon channel access, and low listening duty cycle even without any power saving mechanisms. To the authors' knowledge, the PSMA and the IEEE 802.15.4a optional preamble segment method are currently the only MAC protocols utilizing a CCA in IR-UWB sensor networks. The special properties of the IR-UWB channel are taken into account by using the IEEE 802.15.4a channel model [11] in MatLab simulator to derive two important parameters, probability of detection and probability of false alarm with respect to signal-to-noise ratio (SNR). These parameters are then taken into account in the energy and delay analysis of PSMA.

The PSMA and the IEEE 802.15.4a optional CCA method differ quite significantly from each other. The former has been designed to provide CCA functionality in slotted environment with a small preamble overhead and fixed (2 time slot) collision free communication time. The latter works in both slotted and un-slotted environment and provides CCA detection anywhere in the transmission, but the preamble overhead and CCA detection times easily become prohibitively expensive from the energy consumption point-of-view.

The rest of the paper is organised as follows. Section II describes how the IR-UWB characteristics are derived and taken into account. In section III the PSMA protocol is described, whereas its throughput, delay, and energy consumption are modelled in section IV. Section V presents the results and Section VI concludes the paper and describes future work.

2   Modelling IR-UWB to Probabilities

This investigation relies on IR-UWB employing pulse position modulation (PPM) where in each chip the signal is binary phase shift key (BPSK) modulated. Fig. 1 shows the signal structure. As one can observe the pulse can assume values of the phase $(1, -1)$ in each PPM slot. As described in the literature [2] these types of signals are carrier-less.

The original IEEE Std 802.15.4 standard was not designed for IR-UWB, therefore the carrier-less signals make conventional carrier sensing techniques practically impossible to use to detect the channel state. Recently, the task group TG4a took charge in order to provide an adaptation for IR-UWB and recently delivered PHY specifications [4]. A feasible alternative to regular carrier sensing consists of an approach based on the collection of the energy travelling through the channel that arrives at the receiving antenna.

The energy approach consists of integration, for a certain amount of time, of the signal present at the receiving antenna. The signal is integrated for a time window duration and based on the energy collected the decision, whether a useful signal is present on channel is made. Therefore, the integration time is a parameter affecting the performance of the energy collection and it will be taken into account in the MatLab simulations.

The access method proposed in this paper is based on preamble sensing. The IEEE Std 802.15.4 provides the feature to support slotted and un-slotted super frames (SF).

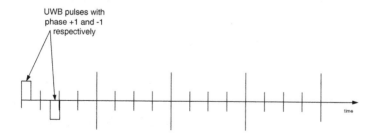

Fig. 1. The IEEE 802.15.4a UWB signal representation is a PPM-BPSK combination

When the SF is slotted, a node can start to sense the channel only at the commence of a boundary. In preamble sense access method, a node is able to detect only the presence of the preamble on the channel and cannot sense the channel busy in the middle of a communication in which the preamble is not present.

The capability of a device to detect the preamble is strictly related to the channel conditions. In fact, for the purpose of this investigation, several channel models are considered. The IEEE Std 802.15.4a PHY specifications indicate the following channels:

- *CM1*, home 7-23m LoS,
- *CM2*, home 7-23m NLoS,
- *CM3*, office 3-28m LoS, and
- *CM4*, office 3-28m NLoS,

where LoS indicates line-of-sight and NLoS non-line-of-sight. Depending on the channel conditions the efficiency of the energy collection approach method varies.

Based on the previous considerations, there exists a non-zero probability that the device may detect the presence of the preamble on the radio even when there is no preamble. This probability, called probability of false alarm P_{fa}, states for the probability that the channel may be sensed busy even when is not. On the other hand, it is possible to derive the probability of miss-detection, P_{md}, which represents the probability that a device misses the preamble even when it is present on the channel. The two probabilities have a different impact on the energy consumption and the system throughput. In fact the probability of false alarm indicates a waste of resources from the device because the channel is free and no transmissions occur. The probability of miss-detection instead, indicates a possible collision because the channel is sensed free when is already busy.

To define P_{fa} and probability of detection, P_d ($P_d = (1 - P_{md})$), it is necessary to define the following input parameters: the bandwidth W, the integration time T, the number of pulses per symbol N_p, the number of symbols in the preamble L_s, the noise variance σ_0^2, and the threshold ε. The W we have taken from [4] and use the mandatory channel with center frequency 3952 MHz. The T we have chosen to be 40 ns, a good compromise between the channel models and E_b/N_0. The N_p is chosen based on the [4] draft to be 15, and the values of 16 and 64 for L_s can be found from the same draft. With the parameters the probability of false alarm and the probability of miss-detection can be formulated to be

$$P_{fa} = Q\left(\frac{\varepsilon}{\sqrt{TWN_pL_s\sigma_0^4}}\right) \tag{1}$$

$$P_{md} = Q\left(\frac{\varepsilon}{\sqrt{TWN_pL_s\sigma_0^4 + 2L_sE_b}}\right), \tag{2}$$

where σ_0 is the variance of the additive white gaussian noise (AWGN) and ε is set based on the wanted probability of false alarm as defined below

$$\varepsilon = \left[\varepsilon : F\left(x|TWN_pL_s\sigma_0^2, \sqrt{TWN_pL_s\sigma^4}\right) = P_{fa}\right].$$

Here ε is the threshold to decide whether, on the receiving antenna, there is a useful signal or not. In the expression of ε, $F(x)$ is the cumulative density function of the random variable x and E_b is the energy carried by a bit. The energy is accumulated over $N_p L_s$ pulses.

The approach in this paper is to fix the probability of false alarm and assume a certain range of values for the preamble length L_s. Thus, by the mean of Eq. 1 it is possible to determine the threshold ε inverting the Q function. In order to have at least a probability of detection of 95 %, it is possible to derive, with MatLab, a set of curves varying the integration time T and the preamble length L_s. The curves are derived for the channel model $CM1$ and $CM2$. From the resulting graphs it is possible to derive the minimum preamble length that satisfies, for both channel models, the fixed constraint on P_d. The value of the preamble length must satisfy both channel models because from the MAC perspective there is no knowledge of the channel and therefore, a suitable preamble to minimize P_{fa} and P_{md} must be chosen. Table 1 presents the P_d for both $CM1$ and $CM2$ with varying SNR and fixed P_{fa}. It can be seen that $P_d > 0.95$ is difficult to get with $CM2$ when the typical SNR is between 15 dB and 30 dB. Therefore, in the later analysis we relax the criteria for $P_d > 0.95$ and see how lower values of P_d impact the energy consumption and the delay.

Table 1. Probability of detection P_d with varying SNR and preamble length, $P_{fa} = 0.05$

Preamble length (symbols), Channel model	SNR = 15dB	SNR = 20dB	SNR = 25dB	SNR = 30dB
16, *CM1*	0.9460	0.9992	1.0	1.0
32	0.9773	1.0	1.0	1.0
64	0.9926	1.0	1.0	1.0
16, *CM2*	0.6946	0.8472	0.9001	0.9360
32	0.7654	0.8690	0.9118	0.9443
64	0.8103	0.8852	0.9236	0.9530

3   Preamble Sense Multiple Access

Performing a CCA in IR-UWB environment is a difficult process; it requires a relatively good synchronisation and the knowledge of what is supposed to be detected. Therefore, a CCA done during another node's mid-transmission is not likely to detect the transmission. A predefined sequence of symbols can be detected even by using IR-UWB however, and it is exploited in the preamble sense multiple access (PSMA) MAC protocol as well as in the IEEE 802.15.4a draft.

In 802.15.4 type piconets, there is a piconet coordinator (PNC) which periodically transmits a beacon frame. This frame has an importance in providing information on the channel usage as well as providing for a rough periodic re-synchronisation of the piconet's nodes.

The principle of channel access method for PSMA can be found from Fig. 2. When a node has a higher layer arrival, it chooses an initial backoff from a set of allowed values. When the backoff timer fires, the node performs a preamble detection (CCA)

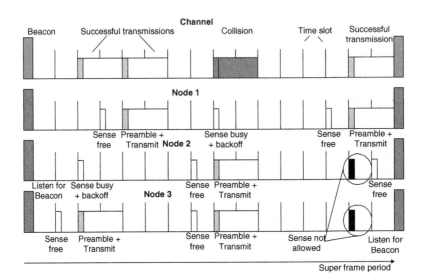

Fig. 2. Communication and channel access of the PSMA in 802.15.4a type piconet contention access period (CAP). Each super frame has 16 time slots and in the analysis all of them are used for CAP.

in the beginning of a backoff boundary. The PSMA and the 802.15.4a optional CCA method are almost identical up to here. Notice that a backoff boundary in the PSMA is the same as the time slot boundary whereas in 802.15.4a each time slot is divided into several (minimum 3) backoff boundaries. The PSMA and the 802.15.4a deviate from this point and we follow the PSMA approach. If no preamble is detected, the node begins transmission in the beginning of the next backoff slot boundary with a preamble immediately followed by the data. The data transmission and the acknowledgement have to be completed within two time slots. If the CCA indicated a detected preamble, the node makes a backoff according to the binary exponential backoff (BEB) rules and tries again later. The mechanism ensures that once a transmission has started, it can continue for a duration of two consecutive time slots without a collision. A collision can occur only if two or more nodes make a clear preamble detection CCA in exactly the same backoff boundary.

In PSMA the nodes have to refrain from performing a CCA in the second last backoff boundary of a super frame and refrain from starting transmission in the last time slot of a super frame. The limitations are valid only if we assume a data exchange of the whole PDSU size. Otherwise, communication that fits into one time slot still implicitly reserves two time slots and channel utilisation is wasted. Note that in the IEEE 802.15.4 optional mode the CCA is considerably longer because the assessment can begin at any backoff boundary and it has to be able to detect at least one valid preamble, i.e., the duration of 2 complete preamble segment lengths and the PSDU segment in between.

In IR-UWB, another collision is possible. in PSMA, if a node makes a preamble miss-detection it can begin transmission in the second time slot of an ongoing transmission. On the other hand, there is a possibility that a false alarm causes a node to backoff when the channel was free and prevent a collision of two nodes that schedule transmission in the same time slot. These misbehaviours also affect the IEEE 802.15.4 performance.

4   Throughput, Delay, and Energy Consumption

In the evaluation we assume the parameters presented in Table 2. Notice that in transmission, the actual transmitted power based on the FCC ruling on the Table 2 center frequency is approximately 37 μW. The powers in the table take into account the electronics of the transceiver and $M_{RX} = kM_{TX}$, where $k = 6$ [12].

In the analysis we consider a Poisson arrival rate g with infinite population and achieve the minimum worst-case performance. We use $2T_s$ to normalise the traffic, where $2T_s$ is the length of two time slots, i.e., the duration of a successful data transfer.

Table 2. Physical layer and MAC parameters used in evaluation of PSMA

Attribute	Value	Attribute	Value
Bandwidth (BW), 802.15.4a Channel 2	494 MHz	PSDU	127 bytes
Center Frequency	3952 MHz	Min Backoff exponent	2
Data Rate	0.842 Mbps	Max Backoff exponent	5
Transmitter Power Consumption, M_{TX}	20 mW	Beacon length	17 bytes
Receiver Power Consumption, M_{RX}	120 mW	Acknowledgement length	5 bytes
Sleep Power Consumption, M_{Slp}	0.2 mW	Preamble length	16,32,64 bytes

4.1   Throughput

In this section we derive the traditional, normalised throughput of PSMA without taking into account the effect of BEB, P_{fa}, or P_d. The throughput, S, follows the traditional formula of $S = U/(B + I)$, where U, B, and I are the average useful, busy, and idle periods, respectively. Average idle, busy, and useful periods are

$$I = \frac{T_s}{1 - e^{-gT_s}}, \qquad B = \frac{2T_s}{e^{-gT_s} - e^{-2gT_s} + e^{-3gT_s}}$$

$$U = \frac{CB}{2T_s}P_s, \text{ where } \quad P_s = \frac{gT_se^{-gT_s}}{1 - e^{-gT_s}}, \tag{3}$$

and P_s denotes the probability of no collision. In the above C is the communicated data within $2T_s$. With normalisation $a = C/(2T_s)$, $b = T_s/(2T_s) = 1/2$, and $G = 2gT_s$ the throughput S then becomes

$$S = \frac{aGe^{-bG}}{2(1 - e^{-bG}) + (e^{-bG} - e^{-2bG} + e^{-3bG})}. \tag{4}$$

4.2 Energy Consumption and Delay

The energy analysis follows largely the model proposed in [13] and the models are depicted in Fig. 3. Here we take into account the CCA misbehaviour probabilities P_{fa} and P_d. The probability of sensing the channel busy on CCA is $P_b = B/(B+I)$. The general solution for the transmit energy, E_{TX}, model is

$$E_{TX} = E_{Arrive} + P_{prob1}(E(A) + T_1) + (1 - P_{prob1})(E(BO) + T_2), \qquad (5)$$

$$E(A) = P_{prob2}E_{Success} + (1 - P_{prob2})(E(BO) + T_3), \qquad (6)$$

$$E(BO) = P_{prob3}(E(A) + T_4) + (1 - P_{prob3})(E(BO) + T_5), \qquad (7)$$

where P_{probX} are different probabilities (i.e., $P_{prob1} = (1 - P_{fa} - P_bP_d + P_bP_dP_{fa})$, $P_{prob2} = P_dP_s(1 - P_b)$, and $P_{prob1} = P_{prob3}$ in this case), E_{Arrive} is the expected energy consumption when coming to *Arrive* state, $E_{Success}$ is the expected energy consumption on reaching the *Success* state, and T_1, T_2, T_3, T_4, and T_5 are delays in the transition spent in a combination of transceiver nodes. For example, T_2 is equal to going to backoff, which consists of the transceiver spending the average first backoff delay in sleep mode and waking up to receive and performing a CCA in receive mode. $E(A)$ and $E(BO)$ represent the average energy consumed when arriving to *Attempt* and *Backoff* states, respectively. The general solution for reception energy, E_{RX}, model follows a similar approach.

The delay, D, is actually simple to derive from the above model by removing the effect of transceiver modes and only calculating the delay elements.

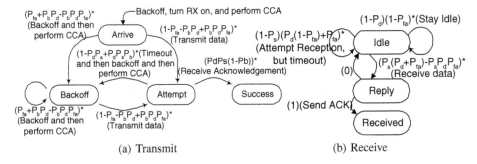

(a) Transmit   (b) Receive

Fig. 3. PSMA energy consumption models for transmission and reception. P_{fa}, P_d, P_s, and P_b are the probabilities of false alarm, detection, no collision, and busy when sensed, respectively.

5 Results

Fig. 4 illustrates the theoretical throughput of PSMA without the effect of P_{fa}, P_d, or BEB. As a comparison an ideal MAC is presented as the solid, non-symbol line indicating the theoretical maximum throughput any MAC protocol can have. Based on the figure the PSMA has a decent throughput when the offered traffic to the channel is small to moderate. When offered traffic reaches close to channel capacity ($G = 1$),

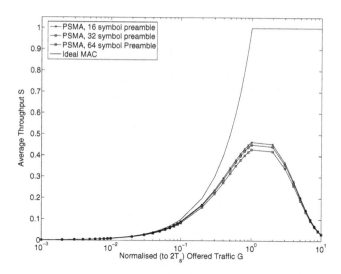

Fig. 4. PSMA throughput as a function of normalised offered traffic. Ideal MAC is a fictional one with maximum theoretical performance.

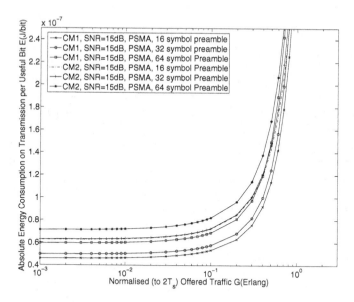

Fig. 5. PSMA Absolute energy consumption on transmission for channel models *CM1* (LoS) and *CM2* (NLoS) as a function of normalised offered traffic

there will be often several arrivals per time slot causing collisions, the effect of BEB would mitigate this effect as would choosing the initial backoff window exponent of 2 or 3. The traditional throughput (max. 37 % at $G = 1$) of slotted ALOHA also applies to the IEEE 802.15.4a case. If we compare the PSMA to that, a significant improvement is shown.

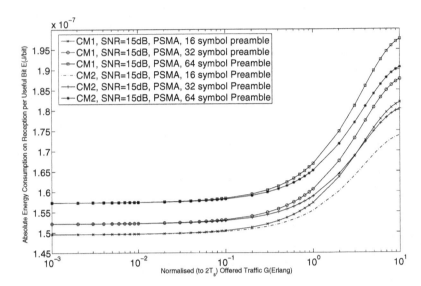

Fig. 6. PSMA Absolute energy consumption on reception for channel models *CM1* (LoS) and *CM2* (NLoS) as a function of normalised offered traffic

The absolute energy consumption per useful transmitted bit (J/bit) is depicted in Fig. 5. The term, useful, implies that only the protocol communication bits are beneficial, the rest is overhead. Overall, the energy per bit performance of the PSMA is very good, even until $G = 1$ where the energy consumption with any preamble length and any channel model is approximately 10 times more than with lower G. Also, the effect of channel model and the length of the preamble has a significant impact. For example, the energy consumption difference between the 16 symbol preamble and the 64 symbol preamble with *CM1* is approximately 30 %. As the channel becomes more difficult (*CM2*) causing the P_d to decrease, we can see that the difference between 16 symbol and 32 symbol preambles is nullified.

In addition to the initial preamble the IEEE 802.15.4a optional CCA mode transmits preamble segments between the PSDU segments. If we consider a 64 symbol preamble and 16 symbol preamble segments, and a PSDU segment of 127 symbols (1/8 of PSDU) in order not to make the CCA too long, the total preamble overhead of 802.15.4a is $(64 + 10 * 16 = 224$ symbols). This is 22 % of the PSDU length and 3.5 times the length of the PSMA total preamble.

In reception of Fig. 6 an interesting peculiarity can be observed. As the traffic on the channel increases, the amount of collisions increase. Having P_d lower is actually beneficial in this case since less colliding preambles will be detected and less time will be spent in unproductive receive.

Fig. 7 illustrates the delay behaviour as a function of G. As expected, the delay increases with longer preambles and more difficult channel models. The fractional difference between highest and lowest delays with low G is around 15 %. When G approaches 1, the delay rapidly grows to very high values.

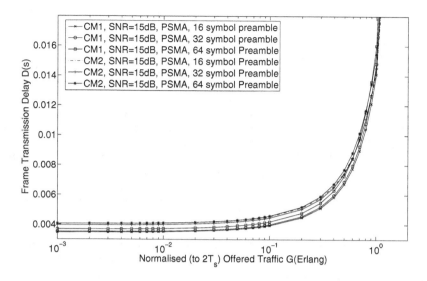

Fig. 7. PSMA delay (s) on transmission for channel models *CM1* (LoS) and *CM2* (NLoS) as a function of normalised offered traffic

6   Conclusions and Future Work

In this paper we have proposed preamble sense multiple access (PSMA), a random access MAC protocol capable of clear channel assessment in impulse radio-ultra wideband environment. The PSMA is compatible with the IEEE 802.15.4a contention access period, but only 1 CCA is required to ensure channel vacancy. The PSMA provides an alternative approach to the 805.15.4a slotted ALOHA and periodic preamble segment transmission schemes by offering higher throughput than slotted ALOHA, but lower preamble transmission requirements than the optional periodic preamble segment method. The PSMA was evaluated by a traditional throughput analysis and by an energy consumption and delay analysis that takes into account the special features of IR-UWB. The IR-UWB provides the probability of detection and the probability of false alarm, both of which have an impact on the MAC protocol performance. The analysis results show the PSMA to have a very good energy and delay performance as well as satisfactory throughput when the offered traffic to the channel is from low to moderate.

As future work, a Markov chain analysis is required to observe the impact of detection and false alarm probabilities on the throughput. In addition, the binary exponential backoff algorithm can be taken into account. A similar analysis will be made for the IEEE 802.15.4a optional preamble segment detection and ALOHA protocols. It is expected that based on these evaluations a number of significant conclusions on the usage of CCA methods in IR-UWB can be made.

References

1. FCC: Revision of Part 15: FIRST REPORT AND ORDER. Technical report, Federal Communications Commission (2002)
2. Win, M., Scholtz, R.: Ultra-wide Bandwidth Time-hopping Spread-spectrum Impulse Radio for Wireless Multiple-access Communications. IEEE Transactions on Communications **48, No. 4** (2000) 679–689
3. Batra, A., Balakrishnan, J., Aiello, G.R., Foerster, J.R., Dabak, A.: Design of a Multiband OFDM System for realistic UWB Channel Environments. IEEE TRANSCTION ON MICROWAVE THEORY AND TECNIQUE **52, No. 9** (2004)
4. P802.15.4a, I.: TG4a Drafting. Technical report, IEEE P802.15 Working Group for Wireless Personal Area Networks (WPANs) (2005) This document has been prepared to assist the IEEE P802.15.
5. Ramirez-Mireles, F.: On the Performance of Ultra-Wide-Band Signals in Gaussian Noise and dense Multipath. IEEE Transactions on Vehicular Technology **Volume 50, Issue 1** (2001) 244–249
6. Iacobucci, M., Di Benedetto, M.: Multiple access design for impulse radio communication systems. In: Proc. of IEEE International Symposium on Communications ICC. (2002)
7. Kleinrock, L., Tobagi, F.A.: Packet Radio in Radio Channels, Part 1: Carrier Sense Multiple Access modes and their throughput-delay characteristics. In: IEEE Transactions on Communications. IEEE (1975) 23(12): 1400–1416
8. IEEE-802.15.3: Part15.3: Wireless Medium Access Control (MAC) and Physical Layer (PHY) Specifications for High Data Rate Wireless Personal Area Networks. Technical report, The Institute of Electrical and Electronics Engineers, Inc. (2003) Draft P802.15.3/D17.
9. IEEE-802.15.4: Part 15.4: Wireless Medium Access Control (MAC) and Physical Layer (PHY) Specifications for Low-Rate Wireless Personal Area Networks (LR-WPANs). Technical report, The Institute of Electrical and Electronics Engineers, Inc. (2003) IEEE Std 802.15.4-2003.
10. Benedetto, M., Nardis, L., Junk, M., Giancola, G.: (UWB)2: Uncoordinated, Wireless, Baseborn Medium Access for UWB Communication Networks. Mobile Networks and Applications, Springer Science **10** (2005) 663–674
11. Molisch, A.F., Balakrishnan, K., Chong, C.C., Emami, S., Fort, A., Karedal, J., Kunisch, J., Schantz, H., Schuster, U., Siwiak, K.: Ieee 802.15.4a channel model — final report. Technical report, IEEE (2004) (Available online) http://www.ieee802.org/15/pub/TG4a.html.
12. Stoica, L., Tiuraniemi, S., Oppermann, I.: An Ultra Wideband Impulse Radio Low Complexity Transceiver Architecture for Sensor Networks. In: Proc. of IEEE International Conference on Ultra-Wideband (ICU) 2005. (2005)
13. Haapola, J., Shelby, Z., Pomalaza-Rez, C., Mähönen, P.: Multihop Medium Access Control for WSNs: An Energy Analysis Model. EURASIP Journal on Wireless Communications and Networking, Special Issue on Wireles Sensor Networks **2005** (2005) 523–540

Security in Wireless Sensor Networks: Considerations and Experiments

Panu Hämäläinen, Mauri Kuorilehto, Timo Alho,
Marko Hännikäinen, and Timo D. Hämäläinen

Tampere University of Technology, Institute of Digital and Computer Systems
P.O. Box 553 (Korkeakoulunkatu 1), FI-33101 Tampere, Finland
panu.hamalainen@tut.fi, mauri.kuorilehto@tut.fi, timo.a.alho@tut.fi,
marko.hannikainen@tut.fi, timo.d.hamalainen@tut.fi
http://www.tkt.cs.tut.fi/research/daci

Abstract. Wireless Sensor Networks (WSN) are seen as attractive solutions for various monitoring and controlling applications, a large part of which require protection. Due to the special characteristics of WSNs, e.g. low processing and energy resources and ad hoc networking, developing a reliable security solution becomes a challenging task. In this paper we survey various security aspects of WSNs, consisting of threats, attacks, and proposed solutions. We also present experiments with our own WSN technology (TUTWSN), concentrating on a centralized key distribution and authentication service. Our experiments suggest that a centralized scheme can be a feasible solution in certain WSN configurations.

1 Introduction

Wireless Sensor Networks (WSN), consisting of small, independent, collaborating wireless devices (*nodes*), have recently aroused considerable interest in industry and academic research communities [1]. WSNs are envisioned as cost-effective and intelligent solutions for various applications in automation, healthcare, environmental monitoring, safety, and security. For example, HVAC management, surveillance and alarm systems, and patient monitoring are among the expected WSN applications. The application tasks of the low-power and low-cost WSN nodes include sensing, processing, and exchanging data as well as acting according to the content of the collected data.

A large part of WSN applications require protection for the data transfer as well as for the nodes themselves [2]. For instance, unauthorized parties should not be able to access private patient information, suppress burglar alarms, or tamper with heating systems. Compared to other wireless technologies, such as Wireless Local Area Networks (WLAN), processing resources and power supplies are significantly more stringent in WSNs. This calls for very efficient security designs and implementations. Furthermore, ad hoc networking, multihop routing as well as node capturing and Denial-of-Service (DoS) threats place new challenges on the security of WSNs, specifically on key management, authentication, routing, and physical protection.

In this paper we survey various security aspects of WSNs—their security threats and proposed solutions. After the survey we present experiments with our own WSN

S. Vassiliadis et al. (Eds.): SAMOS 2006, LNCS 4017, pp. 167–177, 2006.

technology, called TUTWSN [3]. Our security experiments concentrate on an authentication service suited for centralized access control and key distribution in WSNs.

The paper is organized as follows. Section 2 introduces the various security threats inherent in WSNs. Section 3 reviews security architectures developed for WSNs. Key distribution is discussed in Section 4 and our experiments presented in Section 5. Finally, Section 6 concludes the paper.

2 Threats to WSN Security

WSNs share the security threats of other communication networks, consisting of message *interception*, *modification*, and *fabrication* as well as *interruption* of communications and operation (DoS) [4], illustrated in Fig. 1. However, the threats are specifically inherent in WSNs due their special characteristics which enable new forms and combinations of attacks.

Even though WSNs themselves have limited capabilities, an attacker can possess powerful tools, e.g. a laptop and a sensitive antenna, for making attacking more effective [5]. Attackers can be divided to *outsiders* and malicious *insiders* [5][6]. Whereas an outsider is not an authorized participant of a WSN, an insider may have the knowledge of all the secret parameters of a WSN, such as cryptographic keys, and thus is able to perform more severe attacks. An outsider can become an insider by compromising a WSN node. It is desired that a secure WSN blocks outsider attacks and that security only *gracefully degrades* (or, is *resilient*) in case of insider attacks [6].

2.1 Passive Attacks

Interception attacks, carried out by eavesdropping on transmissions, form the group of passive attacks on WSNs. A passive attack can either result in the disclosure of message contents or successful *traffic analysis* [4]. In traffic analysis an attacker finds out useful information through analyzing message headers, message sizes, and traffic patterns. In WSNs interception attacks can be performed by gathering information exchanged between nodes, particularly at data aggregation points [2]. Besides regular data transfer, routing information can be exploited for traffic analysis [2].

Discovering message contents, including exchanged routing tables, can be thwarted by encrypting transmissions, as long as encryption keys remain unknown to attackers. Analysis of traffic patterns can classically be deterred by maintaining a constant flow of encrypted traffic, even when there is nothing to transmit [2]. The solution is not suited

Fig. 1. Security threats in WSN communications: (a) interception, (b) modification, (c) fabrication, and (d) interruption

for WSNs as they should minimize the radio usage for power conservation. Another solution for hindering traffic analysis is to tunnel messages so that their final destinations addresses are encrypted.

2.2   Active Attacks

Active attacks on WSNs consists of modification and fabrication of information and DoS in its various forms [4]. Impersonation and message replay are two instances of fabrication. Modification includes changing, delaying, and reordering messages or stored data. Various modifications and fabrications can be prevented with cryptographic procedures. However, instead of directly tampering with data itself, in some WSN applications modifications can also be performed by affecting the sensed phenomenon, which cannot be restrained by using cryptography. For example, in a temperature monitoring application a sensor node can be relocated and heated, implying false readings. Of the methods for performing active attacks, WSNs are particularly vulnerable to node capturing, resource exhaustion, and tampered routing information.

Node Capturing. As WSN nodes are often deployed to publicly accessible locations, they are susceptible to capturing attacks [7]. After capturing a node, the attacker can attempt to discover its cryptographic keys or other sensitive information, to destroy it, or to reverse-engineer and modify its functionalities [8]. Compromising a single node can jeopardize even the whole WSN by allowing insider attacks. Regular node failures can also randomly cause similar effects as capturing attacks [2][6][8].

The countermeasures against node capturing consist of physical protection of nodes and applying compromise-tolerant and resilient security mechanisms, e.g. for key distribution. Proper physical protection is often considered too costly for WSNs. However, when the components of a node are integrated into a single chip, physical attacks are more difficult to perform. Also, the integration of smart card technologies with WSNs and mechanisms for wiping out sensitive information in case of physical tampering are potential solutions.

Resource Exhaustion. The capacity limitations of WSNs make them vulnerable to resource exhaustion attacks which can result in DoS. For example, battery draining can be realized by transmitting meaningless data to a node, keeping it active and possibly performing cryptographic message integrity verifications. As countermeasures, WSN security designs and implementations should be carefully tuned for high performance at low energy consumption and communication overhead. The transmission rates and number of connections for a node can also be limited for restricting attacks [8].

Routing Attacks. Despite that routing is an important aspect in WSNs, their routing protocols are often simple, and thus more susceptible to attacks than general-purpose ac hoc routing protocols [5]. A number of routing attacks for realizing DoS, performing selective forwarding of advantageous messages, and attracting traffic to a malicious destination for interception have been identified for WSNs [5]. The methods include routing information modifications, HELLO flooding, acknowledgement spoofing, as well as sinkhole, Sybil, and wormhole attacks. Routing information modifications can be used for creating routing loops, luring traffic, extending routes, and partitioning WSNs.

HELLO flooding and spoofed acknowledgements allow advertising non-existent or weak links. Sinkhole, Sybil, and wormhole attacks facilitate attracting traffic to a compromised node or to chosen parts of a WSN.

The countermeasures against routing attacks include link layer encryption and authentication for unicast, multicast, and broadcast transmissions, multipath routing, bidirectional link verification, and geographical routing [5]. Bidirectional link verification ensures that a link can equally be used for both directions. Geographical routing integrates location information to routing decisions.

3   Security Architectures for WSNs

As discussed, a large part of the attacks on WSNs can be prevented by means of cryptography. In this section we review selected cryptographic security architectures designed for WSNs, namely TinySec [9], SPINS [10], IEEE 802.15.4 [11], and ZigBee [12].

3.1   TinySec

TinySec [9] is a security architecture for protecting the link layer of WSNs. The design goal has been to provide adequate level of security with the limited resources of WSNs. TinySec provides services for data authentication by protecting transmissions with Message Authentication Codes (MAC) and confidentiality by encrypting transmissions. Encryption is performed with a block cipher in the Cipher Block Chaining (CBC) mode and MACs are computed with the cipher in the CBC-MAC mode. Applications can configure TinySec to apply only MACs or both MACs and encryption to transmissions. Freshness protection of messages is consciously excluded as it is consider too resource-demanding. Key distribution or entity authentication schemes have not been specified.

3.2   SPINS

SPINS [10] is a suite of WSN security protocols. It consists of two main components, Secure Network Encryption Protocol (SNEP) and μTESLA. Whereas SNEP provides services for data authentication and confidentiality of two-party communications, μTESLA is a protocol for the data authentication of broadcast messages. SPINS supports centralized key distribution, discussed in Section 4.

SNEP encrypts messages and protects them with MACs. Different keys, derived from a shared master key between the two communicating nodes, are used for each different purpose and communication direction. A counter value is included into messages for freshness. Encryption is performed with a block cipher in the counter (CTR) mode and data authentication in the CBC-MAC mode.

Instead of computationally expensive public-key algorithms, μTESLA uses symmetric-key cryptography. A broadcast message is protected with a MAC, for which the sender discloses the verification key at a pre-determined time instant. In order to work, it is required that the clocks of nodes are loosely synchronized and the sender has enough space for storing the chain of verification keys.

3.3   IEEE 802.15.4 and ZigBee

IEEE 802.15.4 [11] and ZigBee [12] are envisioned to be the first technologies enabling large-scale utilization of WSN-type solutions. The 802.15.4 standard defines optional cryptographic suites for providing either confidentiality, data authentication, or both. Confidentiality is achieved through encryption using Advanced Encryption Standard (AES) [13] in the CTR mode and data authentication through MACs in the CBC-MAC mode. The combination is offered with AES in the CTR with CBC-MAC mode (CCM). Freshness can also be provided. Each node can store keys for pairwise and group communications. The standard does not define key distribution or entity authentication mechanisms.

The ZigBee specification [12] builds on the security design of 802.15.4 by slightly modifying it and specifying services for key management and entity authentication. It uses separate keys for pairwise and network-wide communications. The keys can be either dynamically distributed or pre-installed into nodes. Protected distribution requires that nodes share a key with a Trust Center (TC), which is a device coordinating the network. Authentication is carried out with a challenge-response scheme. Instead of supporting the separate MAC and CTR suites of 802.15.4, ZigBee specifies a new mode of operation called CCM*. Also CCM* uses AES but in addition to the standard CCM operation, it offers encryption-only and MAC-only configurations.

4   Key Distribution in WSNs

Due to the multihop communications, large number of nodes, ac hoc networking, and resource constraints, distribution of secret keys becomes one of the most challenging security components of WSNs. In order to be applicable and secure, each of the security architectures described above requires a key distribution method. There exists various distribution solutions and keying mechanisms, suited for different WSN applications and deployment scenarios.

4.1   Public-Key Cryptography

Public-key cryptography is commonly used for key distribution in traditional computer systems, e.g. on the Internet. For WSNs the benefits of public-key mechanisms are the resiliency against node capturing, the possibility to revoke compromised keys, and scalability [14]. However, public-key algorithms are computationally intensive and public-key protocols require exchanging large messages, consisting of keys and their certificates. Therefore, the mechanisms are often considered poorly suited for WSNs. For example, the expensive computations and message exchanges can be exploited for DoS. Nevertheless, according to the recent research results [15][16][17], Elliptic Curve Cryptography (ECC) can be a feasible solution for some WSN applications. Still, as Section 5 will show, symmetric-key algorithms can be computed considerably more efficiently than ECC algorithms in typical WSN nodes.

4.2 Pre-distributed Keys

The simplest keying mechanism is to use a single, pre-installed symmetric key for the whole WSN. The solution results in the lowest resource and management requirements as well as enables nodes to create protected connections with all the other nodes in the network [9][14]. A drawback is that when a single node is compromised, the security of the whole WSN is lost. The solution also allows full-scale insider attacks. The effects of node compromises can be decreased e.g. by using the network-wide key only for setting up pairwise keys during the establishment of the WSN, erasing it afterwards [14]. However, this solution prevents adding nodes after the initial WSN deployment.

The other extreme is to pre-distribute unique keys for each pair of nodes [14]. The technique is resilient to node capturing as only the keys of compromised nodes are leaked. Also, key revocation can be supported [14]. The drawbacks are poor scalability and high storage requirements since in a WSN of n nodes each node has to store $n - 1$ keys, totalling $n(n - 1)/2$ keys for the network.

A solution between the network-wide and pairwise keys is to use group keying [9]. In this scheme a node shares a symmetric key with its neighbors. A group key compromise allows only accessing the communications within the group.

Depending on the WSN application and available resources, the described keying mechanisms can also be combined [18]. Each node maintains a certain number of pairwise and group keys and a network-wide key, which facilitate protected pairwise and group communications as well as local and global broadcasts.

Random Key Pre-distribution. WSN key distribution based on randomly chosen pools of symmetric keys has aroused interest in the research community. In the original scheme [19] a large set of keys is generated and distributed to nodes during the WSN setup. Each node is allocate a subset of the generated keys such that with a certain probability each pair of nodes end up sharing at least one key. After the allocation nodes perform key discovery in order to find out which of their neighbors they share keys with. The links protected with the discovered keys can be further used for agreeing on new keys, called *path-keys*, which enable direct communications with neighbors the nodes initially did not share a key with. The scheme has been further developed to be better resilient to node capturing e.g. by requiring larger number of overlapping keys [14] and exploiting WSN deployment information in advance [20].

The benefit of the random key pre-distribution over unique pairwise keys is the decreased amount of key storage and over network-wide keys the resiliency to node capturing. The mechanism also supports key revocation and re-keying [19]. However, in order to be applicable, the node density has to be high and uniform in the scheme. A drawback of the basic scheme [19] is that the randomly shared keys cannot unambiguously be used for entity authentication as the same keys can be shared by more than a single pair of nodes [14].

4.3 Centralized Key Distribution

Along with public-key cryptography, Key Distribution Centers (KDC) are utilized for providing authentication and key distribution services in communication systems, e.g. in WLANs. A KDC can be used in WSNs as well [10][14]. Nodes authenticate to a

KDC, which generates a symmetric key and securely communicates it to the nodes. For example, the TC of a ZigBee network operates as a KDC. It is required that nodes can establish secure channels to the KDC, e.g. through pre-shared symmetric keys, and that the KDC is trusted and has capacity for storing the channel establishment information of all nodes.

The storage requirements in WSN nodes are low as each node has to store permanently only a single key (node–KDC). Furthermore, since authentications and key establishments of a WSN are controlled in a centralized location, the scheme is resilient to node capturing, supports simple node revocation, and protects against node replication attacks [14]. The drawbacks of the scheme are that nodes establishing a connection must always first communicate with the KDC and that the KDC becomes an appealing target of attacks [14]. If the KDC is accessed through multiple hops, the authentication latencies increase, the energy consumption of the nodes close to the KDC grows, and they also become targets of DoS attacks. The situation can be alleviated by locating the KDC outside the hostile operation environment of the rest of the WSN [14] and distributing and/or replicating its functionalities.

5   Security Experiments with TUTWSN

A large part of WSN security research seems to have concentrated on the probabilistic key pre-distribution techniques as well as on the efficient implementation of cryptographic algorithms. In order to extend the evaluation of KDC-based solutions, we have developed a centralized WSN authentication service using our TUTWSN technology. The service can be used for both network access control and key distribution using only symmetric-key cryptography.

5.1   TUTWSN Overview

The main design goals for TUTWSN have been energy-efficiency and scalability [3]. TUTWSN uses a clustered topology, illustrated in Fig. 2(a). A cluster consists of a *headnode* and several *subnodes*. Special gateway nodes can be used for extending WSNs with other networking technologies (e.g. for locating a KDC in safe premises). The energy-efficiency derives from the medium access control protocol that uses Time Division Multiple Access (TDMA) for intra-cluster communications and Frequency Division Multiple Access (FDMA) for interleaving clusters. TUTWSN utilizes gradient-based multihop routing. The protocol stack is freely configurable for different application purposes. For more details, including the channel access mechanism, we refer to [3].

Several prototype platforms have been fabricated for TUTWSN. In the experiments of this paper we used the prototype presented in Fig. 2(b). It contains a PIC18F4620 nanowatt series Micro-Controller Unit (MCU) with 64 KB of code memory and 3986 B of data memory. The radio interface is a 2.4 GHz transceiver with 1 Mbit/s data rate. For our security experiments the payload size in a network packet is 22 B in the used TUTWSN configuration. The maximum payload data rate for a link is 1.4 kbit/s in both directions.

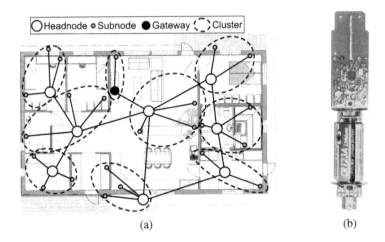

Fig. 2. (a) TUTWSN topology and (b) a prototype node

5.2   KDC-Based Key Distribution and Authentication Scheme

Our experimental key distribution and authentication scheme uses a similar authentication architecture and a same type of a protocol as Kerberos [21]. In contrast to Kerberos, the freshness of messages is ensured with *nonces* instead of timing information. Hence, nodes do not have to maintain clock synchronization but they require a random number generator.

The scheme is based on the KDC proposal of [10], which does not report an implementation. Instead of direct communications with the KDC, in our version all messages are communicated through a headnode, supporting the TUTWSN topology. Also, we have included authentication with the newly distributed key. The key agreement and authentication procedure can be performed between a headnode and a subnode or between two headnodes.

The scheme operates as follows. During the WSN deployment, each node is allocated a symmetric key K_X (consisting of an encryption key and a MAC key) which they share with the KDC (S). For authenticating and establishing a symmetric key K_{AB} between two nodes, A and a headnode B, the following protocol is applied:

1. $A \rightarrow B : N_A \mid A$
2. $B \rightarrow S : N_A \mid N_B \mid A \mid B \mid \mathsf{MAC}(K_B, N_A \mid N_B \mid A \mid B \mid S)$
3. $S \rightarrow B : A \mid \mathsf{E}(K_B, K_{AB}) \mid T \mid \mathsf{MAC}(K_B, A \mid \mathsf{E}(K_B, K_{AB}) \mid T \mid N_B \mid S \mid B)$
4. $B \rightarrow A : N_B' \mid S \mid T \mid \mathsf{MAC}(K_{AB}, N_A \mid N_B' \mid S \mid T \mid B \mid A)$
5. $A \rightarrow B : \mathsf{MAC}(K_{AB}, N_B' \mid A \mid B)$

where $T = \mathsf{E}(K_A, K_{AB}) \mid \mathsf{MAC}(K_A, \mathsf{E}(K_A, K_{AB}) \mid S \mid N_A \mid A \mid B)$ and I stands for concatenation. Above N_X is a nonce created by X, $\mathsf{MAC}(K, Y)$ is a MAC computed with the key K over the data Y, and $\mathsf{E}(K, Y)$ is the encryption of Y with the key K. K_{AB} is chosen by S, which is trusted by the nodes.

Message 1 of the protocol serves as a challenge from A to B and S. With Message 2, B requests K_{AB} from S, including N_B into the message for challenging S to prove its authenticity in Message 3. With Message 4, B proves A its knowledge of K_{AB} as it has been able to decrypt the key from Message 3 with K_B and compute the MAC over N_A. Finally, A proves B its knowledge of K_{AB}, which it has obtained from T, by transmitting the MAC computed over N_B'.

5.3   Implementation Experiments

In the experimental implementation of the key distribution scheme we used the AES cipher [13] with 128-bit keys for encryption as well as for MAC computations. For efficiency, we chose to carry out the encryption of K_{AB} in the Electronic CodeBook (ECB) mode. MACs are computed in the CMAC mode [22]. We chose the sizes of the protocol message fields so that each message fits at maximum into two packets of our TUTWSN configuration.

The implementation was carried out as software (C language) on the prototype nodes described in Section 5.1. For AES we utilized the assembly implementation of [23]. Our experimental implementation supports authentication of nodes that are at maximum two hops away from the KDC since multihop routing for the protocol messages is currently not included. For example, for covering the network of Fig. 2(a), increasing transmission power is required.

With the used TUTWSN configuration the protocol run takes about 2 s, in which the channel access and communication latencies dominate. For instance, the processing time for the largest message, Message 3, is below 100 ms in the TUTWSN prototype node. In networks of large number of hops and key requests, the increase of latencies can be reduced by allocating more processing power to the KDC and accessing it through uniformly deployed gateway nodes. Furthermore, the distance of nodes from the KDC (as the number of hops) can be shortened by increasing transmission power. Also, the KDC approach can be combined with certain amount of pre-distributed pairwise keys.

For evaluating symmetric-key and public-key cryptography on WSN nodes, Table 1 presents results for AES in our implementation as well as results from [16], which reports efficient ECC implementations on 8-bit microcontrollers, and from [17], which

Table 1. Evaluation of AES and ECC on WSN node platforms (the used data memory and code size are reported for MCUs, the gate area for ASICs)

Algorithm	Technology	Clock	Resources	Power	Exec. time	Energy
AES	PIC18F4620	4.0 MHz	45 B (data), 4400 B (code)	3.2 mW	6.5 ms	21 μJ
ECC [16]	ATmega128	8.0 MHz	282 B (data), 3682 B (code)	95 mW	810 ms	76 mJ
AES [25]	0.13 μm	150 MHz	3100 gates	5.6 mW	1.1 μs	5.9 nJ
ECC [17]	0.13 μm	0.5 MHz	19000 gates	0.39 mW	410 ms	160 μJ

reports results for ECC hardware implementations considering WSNs. We have computed the maximum power for ATmega128 according to the MCU data sheet [24]. We have also included initial results for our recent—yet unpublished—low-power, 8-bit AES encryption hardware implementation (standard-cell CMOS, 1.2 V) [25]. According to these results, symmetric-key algorithms have significantly higher performance both in software and in hardware. In software, the amount of consumed memory can be at the same level.

6   Conclusions

WSNs are seen as appealing solutions for numerous monitoring and controlling applications, a large part of which require protection. Due to their special characteristics, designing a reliable security solution for WSNs becomes a challenging task. Settling to trade-offs between the level of security and resource requirements is often needed. Similarly to the design of other aspects of WSNs, instead of attempting to develop a solution suited for all possible usage scenarios, for cost-efficiency the WSN security design should be developed considering the threat model of the target application. Our experiments with TUTWSN suggest that KDC-based key distribution mechanisms can be feasible solutions in certain WSN configurations, especially when a centralized, possibly physically protected location for network access control is desired. The KDC scheme and its implementation will be further developed and evaluated.

References

1. Stankovic, J.A., Abdelzaher, T.F., Lu, C., Sha, L., Hou, J.C.: Real-time communication and coordination in embedded sensor networks. Proceedings of the IEEE **91** (2003) 1002–1022
2. Avancha, S., Undercoffer, J., Joshi, A., Pinkston, J.: Security for Wireless Sensor Networks. [26] 253–275
3. Kohvakka, M., Hännikäinen, M., Hämäläinen, T.D.: Ultra low energy wireless temperature sensor network implementation. In: Proc. 16th IEEE Int. Symp. Personal Indoor and Mobile Radio Comm. (PIMRC 2005), Berlin, Germany (2005)
4. Stallings, W.: Network and Internetwork Security: Principles and Practice. Prentice-Hall, USA (1995)
5. Karloff, C., Wagner, D.: Secure routing in wireless sensor networks: Attacks and counter-measures. Elsevier Ad Hoc Networks **1** (2003) 293–315
6. Shi, E., Perrig, A.: Designing secure sensor networks. IEEE Wireless Comm. **11** (2004) 38–43
7. Perrig, A., Stankovic, J., Wagner, D.: Security in wireless sensor networks. Communications of the ACM **47** (2004) 53–57
8. Wood, A., Stankovic, J.A.: Denial of service in sensor networks. IEEE Computer **35** (2002) 54–62
9. Karlof, C., Sastry, N., Wagner, D.: TinySec: A link layer security architecture for wireless sensor networks. In: Proc. 2nd Int. Conf. Embedded Networked Sensor Systems (SenSys 2004), Baltimore, MD, USA (2004) 162–175
10. Perrig, A., Szewczyk, R., Tygar, J.D., Wen, V., Culler, D.E.: SPINS: Security protocols for sensor networks. Kluwer Wireless Networks (2002) 521–534
11. IEEE: IEEE Std. 802.15.4. (2003)

12. ZigBee Alliance: ZigBee Specification Version 1.0. (2004)
13. NIST: Advanced Encryption Standard (FIPS-197). (2001)
14. Chan, H., Perrig, A., Song, D.: Key Distribution Techniques for Sensor Networks. [26] 277–303
15. Gupta, V., Wurm, M., Zhu, Y., Millard, M., Fung, S., Gura, N., Eberle, H., Shantz, S.C.: Sizzle: A standards-based end-to-end security architecture for the embedded internet. Elsevier Pervasive and Mobile Computing (2005) 425–445
16. Gura, N., Patel, A., Wander, A., Eberle, H., Shantz, S.C.: Comparing elliptic curve cryptography and RSA on 8-bit CPUs. In Joye, M., Quisquater, J.J., eds.: Lecture Notes in Computer Science. Volume 3156. Springer (2004) 119–132
17. Gaubatz, G., Kaps, J.P., Öztürk, E., Sunar, B.: State of the art in ultra-low power public key cryptography for wireless sensor networks. In: Proc. Workshop on Pervasive Computing and Comm. Security (PerSec'05), Kauai Island, HI, USA (2005) 146–150
18. Zhu, S., Setia, S., Jajodia, S.: LEAP: Efficient security mechanism for large-scale distributed sensor networks. In: Proc. 10th ACM Conf. Computer and Comm. Security (CCS'03), Washington D.C., USA (2003) 62–72
19. Eschenauer, L., Gligor, V.D.: A key-management scheme for distributed sensor networks. In: Proc. 9th ACM Conf. Computer and Comm. Security (CCS'02), Washington D.C., USA (2002) 41–47
20. Du, W., Deng, J., Han, Y.S., Varshney, P.K.: A key predistribution scheme for sensor networks using deployment knowledge. IEEE Trans. Dependable and Secure Computing **3** (2006) 62–77
21. Kohl, J., Neuman, C.: The Kerberos network authentication service (V5). RFC 1510 (1993)
22. Dworkin, M.: Recommendations for Block Cipher Modes of Operation: The CMAC Mode for Authentication (Special Publication 800–38B). NIST. (2005)
23. Microchip Technology Inc.: Application note 953: Data Encryption Routines for the PIC18. (2005)
24. Atmel Corporation: 8-bit AVR Microcontroller with 128K Bytes In-System Programmable Flash – ATmega128 and ATmega128L, Rev. 2467M-AVR-11/04. (2004)
25. Hämäläinen, P., Alho, T., Hännikäinen, M., Hämäläinen, T.D.: Design and implementation of low-area and low-power AES encryption hardware core. Unpublished (2006)
26. Raghavendra, C.S., Sivalingam, K.M., Znati, T., eds.: Wireless Sensor Networks. 1 edn. Springer (2004)

On Security of PAN Wireless Systems

Ondrej Hyncica, Peter Kacz, Petr Fiedler, Zdenek Bradac,
Pavel Kucera, and Radimir Vrba

Brno University of Technology, Faculty of Electrical Engineering and Communication,
Kolejni 4, 612 00, Brno, Czech Republic
{xhynci00, xkaczp00}@stud.feec.vutbr.cz
{fiedlerp, bradac, kucera, vrbar}@feec.vutbr.cz
http://www.feec.vutbr.cz

Abstract. This paper describes security features of ZigBee and Bluetooth PAN
wireless networks. On examples of those two wireless systems are demonstrated challenges associated with utilization of present wireless systems for
applications requiring secure data exchange. Recent penetration of wireless
technologies into building and process automation applications even increases
the need to fully understand the limitations of the security concepts used.

1 ZigBee Security

ZigBee technology [1] is intended for low-cost low-power devices based on 8-bit
microcontrollers. The intended ZigBee application areas are home control, building
automation and plant control systems, including security related systems. For this
reason the security mechanisms are significant part of the ZigBee specification.

Security services defined within ZigBee standard comprise methods for frame protection, device management, encryption key establishment and key transport. The
ZigBee security depends on symmetric cryptographic mechanisms, which requires
that secret keys used for communication encryption are both distributed in a secure
manner and also kept securely within all devices. To reduce complexity of security
architecture within the ZigBee devices there is no cryptographic separation within
different stack layers inside a single device; the different stack layers and an application running on the device trust each other. Security is realized on device-to-device
basis and all layers within a device share common cryptographic keys.

Optimization of the security architecture to allow implementation on low power,
low memory CPUs resulted in following design choices:

The layer that originates a frame is responsible for its initial securing;
To prevent malevolent devices to use network services, NWK layer security shall
be used for all frames.
Only source and destination devices have to share a key, so secure data exchange
can be realized without the need to trust the route.

1.1 Security Keys

The security is based on a set of 128 bit encryption keys (network key, master key and
link keys) that are used at the Medium Access Control (MAC) Layer, Network Layer

S. Vassiliadis et al. (Eds.): SAMOS 2006, LNCS 4017, pp. 178 – 185, 2006.

(NWK) and the Application (APL) Layer. All layers share the same set of keys. The broadcasted communications are encrypted using the common Network key, while unicast communications are secured by Link keys. The Network key may be used by all stack layers, while the link keys and master key are used by the APL layer and its sub-layers only.

Link keys can be either pre-installed or acquired via network using (key-establishment and key-transportation mechanisms). To reduce re-use of link keys across various security services the services use keys derived from the link key by one-way function. Master key is used during key-establishment process for derivation of link keys.

Network key is acquired either via key-transport or pre-installation. Master key is acquired by key-transport or by pre-installation. As the security is based on shared-secret principles, the security of the network depends on secure initialization and secure storage of all the keys.

1.2 Layered Security Architecture

Physical and link layers of ZigBee technology is defined by IEEE 802.15.4 standard [2]. This standard defines CTR encryption, CBC-MAC authentication and a CCM mode, which combines CTR and CBC-MAC.

However, the ZigBee standard defines modified CCM mode denoted CCM* that defines also encrypted-only and integrity only modes. The CCM* eliminates the need to implement CTR algorithm while providing equivalent services. The CCM* uses AES-128 block cipher [3] and enables to use single key for all CCM* security levels.

To prevent unauthorized message replay the ZigBee standard defines nonce comprising 64 bit source address, 32 bit frame counter and 8 bit security control field. The nonce is included with all authenticated and/or encrypted frames.

Like the MAC layer the NWK and APL layers use AES-128 and CCM* for authentication and encryption. The NWK layer prefers link keys, however for broadcasted messages or when the appropriate link key is not available at the device a network key is used. The APL layer determines the appropriate keys to be used based on the purpose of the message.

1.3 ZigBee Network Security Modes

For secured networks the ZigBee defines a Trust Center, which is a device trusted by devices within a network. The Trust Center distributes the keys for purposes of end-to-end applications and network configuration management. The trust center may be used to assist during establishment of end-to-end secured connections either by distribution of link keys or by distribution of master keys.

In general two primary security modes for the Trust Center are defined – a Commercial mode (higher security) and Residential mode (lower security). In the residential mode static keys are used, which leads to reduced security. Network key updates are not supported in the residential mode. In the Commercial mode the keys are being updated during network runtime. In secured networks, the devices have to authenticate themselves before joining the network.

Table 1. ZigBee Security Levels

Security level	Security attributes	Data encryption	Frame integrity	Integrity code
0	None	No	No	0 bit
1	MIC-32	No	Yes	32 bits
2	MIC-64	No	Yes	64 bits
3	MIC-128	No	Yes	128 bits
4	ENC	Yes	No	0 bit
5	ENC+MIC-32	Yes	Yes	32 bits
6	ENC+MIC-64	Yes	Yes	64 bits
7	ENC+MIC-128	Yes	Yes	128 bits

The ZigBee standard defines four security levels for unencrypted communication and another four security levels for encrypted communication. The high security configuration uses 128 bit message integrity code and AES encryption with 128 bit key. The available ZigBee security levels are shown in table 1.

1.4 Is the AES-128 Based Security Sufficient?

The AES-128 cipher is considered to be sufficient for most commercial applications [5]. In June 2003, the US Government announced that AES-128 may be used for

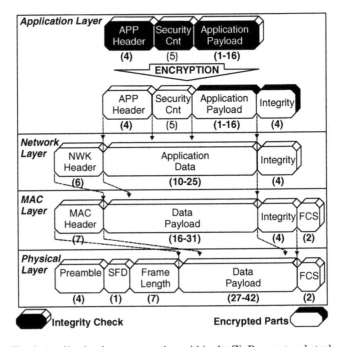

Fig. 1. Application layer encryption within the ZigBee protocol stack

classified information up to the level SECRET. Known AES attacks required either extremely high number of messages with artificial conditions that are unlikely on a real systems or execution of code directly on the on the same system that was performing AES encryptions. The NIST expects the AES-128 to be safe at least until the year 2036 [4].

However, the use of symmetric keys for key-distribution purposes in applications with hundreds of devices is not fortunate. Moreover it is impossible to predict what limitations in AES cipher will be found in the future. Utilization of single symmetric cipher algorithm for both data encryption and key exchange presents possible "single point of security failure" of the ZigBee security architecture. For this reason it is expected that ZigBee will be extended by asymmetric encryption methods for key distribution. Elliptic Curve Cryptography is proposed as a public-key asymmetric scheme for embedded systems [4] and for ZigBee [6].

2 Bluetooth Security

Bluetooth (BT) technology is intended for wireless connection between human-oriented devices (PC, keyboard, mouse, headset, mobile phone, PDA, GPS ...) [7]. IEEE approved Bluetooth-based wireless PAN standard in 2002 (IEEE 802.15.1 - Bluetooth v1.1 specification) [2].

The BT technology provides peer-to-peer communication over relatively close proximity. Typical application of BT is to create a temporary computer network; it is usually an ad hoc network. Computers communicate directly with each other; there is not a wireless access point, which can ensure security control over the network. Thus, security becomes a major concern because important data are exposed to the other member of the network not only in the meeting room but also anywhere in the above mentioned transmission range even not within your sight [10].

2.1 Security Items

In order to provide protection of the communication, the security at the link layer and application layer is ensured. Every Bluetooth device has four identification items used for the security features at the link layer [8]:

1. Bluetooth device address (BD_ADDR) - every BT transceiver has a unique 48 bits address that is derived from the IEEE802 standard. Structure of BD_ADDR is shown in Figure 2. BD_ADDR of the device is publicly known.
2. Private authentication key, which is always 128 bits random number used by the authentication algorithm.
3. Private encryption key is derived from the authentication key during the authentication process. The size of the key may vary between 8-128 bits due to different requirements imposed on cryptographic algorithms in different countries and due to the increasing computing power of the attackers.
4. A random number RAND, which can be derived from a random or pseudo-random process in the BT device. The RAND is always 128 bits and it is changed frequently.

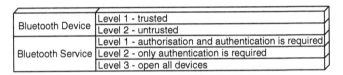

Fig. 2. Structure of the Bluetooth device address

Bluetooth can operate in one of three security models:
Mode 1 - non-security,
Mode 2 - security at the service level, after the communication channel is established,
Mode 3 - security at the link level, before the communication channel is established.
Different security levels for BT devices and services are shown in Figure 3.

Bluetooth Device	Level 1 - trusted
	Level 2 - untrusted
Bluetooth Service	Level 1 - authorisation and authentication is required
	Level 2 - only authentication is required
	Level 3 - open all devices

Fig. 3. Security Levels for devices and services

2.2 Key Management

The encryption key used during communication has a specific size and cannot be set by the user. The key's size is set by a factory and the Bluetooth baseband processing does not accept an encryption key given from higher software layers in order to prevent the user over-riding the permitted key size.

All security transactions between two or more parties are handled by the link key. The link key is a 128 bits random number which is used in the authentication routine and during the generation of the encryption key.

In order to accommodate for different types of applications, four types of link keys have been defined: the combination key KAB, the unit key KA (KB), the temporary key Kmaster, the initialization key Kinit.

The combination key KAB and the unit key KA (KB) are functionally indistinguishable. The unit key KA (KB) is generated in a single unit A (B). The unit key is generated once at installation of the Bluetooth unit. The combination key KAB is derived from information in both units A and B, and is therefore always dependent on two units. The master key Kmaster is a temporary key, which replaces the current link key. The initialization key Kinit is used as link key during the initialization process when there are not yet any unit or combination keys or when a link key has been lost. The key is derived from a random number, Personal Identification Number (PIN) code, and a BD_ADDR. This key is only to be used during initialization. The length of the PIN code used in Bluetooth devices can vary between 1 and 16 bytes.

2.3 Key Generation and Initialization

The link keys have to be generated and distributed among the Bluetooth units in order to be used in the authentication procedure. The exchange of the keys takes place during an initialization phase it consist of the following five parts: generation of an initialization key, generation of link key, link key exchange, authentication, generating of encryption key in each unit.

After the initialization procedure, the units can proceed to communicate, or the link can be disconnected. If encryption is implemented, the E0 algorithm is used with the proper encryption key derived from the current link key.

The initialization key is needed when two devices with no prior engagements need to communicate. During the initialization process, the PIN code is entered to both devices. The initialization key itself is generated by the E22 algorithm shown in Figure 4a, which uses the PIN code, the length of the PIN code L and a 128 bits random number IN_RAND generated by the verifier device as inputs.

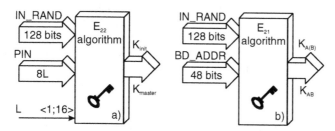

Fig. 4. a) Generation of an initialization key, b) Generation of a unit key and combination key

The unit key KA (KB) is generated with the key generating algorithm E21 - Figure 4b, when the BT device is in operation for the first time; i.e. not during each initialization. Once created, the unit key is stored in non-volatile memory and is rarely changed.

The combination key is generated during the initialization process if the devices have decided to use one. It is generated by both devices at the same time.

The master key is a temporary key of the link keys. It is generated by the master device by using the key generating algorithm E22 with two 128-bit random numbers and L=16.

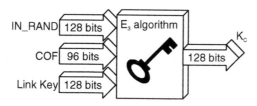

Fig. 5. a) Generation of an initialization key, b) Generation of a unit key and combination

The encryption key KC is derived by E3 algorithm, Figure 5, from the current link key, a 96 bits Ciphering OFfset number (COF), and a 128 bits random number. The COF is determined in one of two ways. If the current link key is a master key, then COF is derived from the master BD_ADDR. Otherwise the value of COF is set to the value of Authenticated Ciphering Offset (ACO), which is generated during the authentication procedure. The encryption key is automatically changed every time the BT device enters the encryption mode.

2.4 Encryption

The Bluetooth encryption system encrypts the payloads of the packets; the access code and the packet header are never encrypted. Encryption is done with a stream cipher E0, which is re-synchronized for every new payload, which disrupt so-called correlation attacks.

Depending on whether a device uses a semi-permanent link key (i.e. a combination key or a unit key), or a master key, there are several encryption modes available. If a unit key or a combination key is used, broadcast traffic is not encrypted. Individually addressed traffic can be either encrypted or not. If a master key is used, there are three possible modes: mode 1 - nothing is encrypted, mode 2 - broadcast traffic is not encrypted, but the individually addressed traffic is encrypted with the master key and mode 3 - all traffic is encrypted with the master key.

2.5 Authentication

The Bluetooth authentication scheme uses a challenge response scheme in which a claimant's knowledge of a secret key is checked through a 2-move protocol using symmetric secret keys; a successful authentication is based on the fact that both participants share the same key. First, the verifier sends the claimant a random number AU_RANDA to be authenticated. Then, both participants use the authentication function E1 with the random number, the claimants BT Device Address BD_ADDRB and the current link key to get a response. The claimant sends the response SRES to the verifier, who then makes sure the responses match.

When the authentication attempt fails, a certain waiting interval must pass before the verifier will initiate a new authentication attempt to the same claimant, or before it will respond to an authentication attempt initiated by a unit claiming the same identity as the suspicious unit.

2.6 Problems in the Bluetooth Security

The encryption scheme of BT has some serious weaknesses. The most important is a fact that E0 algorithm has flaw in the resynchronization mechanism and there were some investigation of conditional correlations in the Finite State Machine (FSM) governing the keystream output of E0. The best attack finds the original encryption key for two level E0 using the first 24 bits of 223.8 frames and with 238 comput-ations [9].

The generation of the initialization key is also a problem. The strength of the initialization key is based on the used PIN code. The E22 initialization key generation algorithm derives the key from the PIN code, the length of the PIN code and a random number, which is transmitted over the air. When using 4 digit PIN codes there are only 10.000 different possibilities; in fact most of the PINs are like "1111". Thus, the security of the initialization key is quite low.

The unique Bluetooth Device Address introduces another problem. When a connection is made that a certain Bluetooth device belongs to a certain person, it is easy to track and monitor the behavior of this person. For instance, with the appropriate equipment (easy accessible) it is possible to track BT devices from more than mile away [10]. The initial key exchange takes place over an unencrypted link, so it is especially vulnerable because there is no such thing as a secure location anymore.

Finally the well known Denial of Service (DoS) Attack. This nuisance is very simple; a constant request for response from a hacker's Bluetooth enabled computer to another Bluetooth enabled device such that it causes some temporary battery degradation in the receiving device. While occupying the Bluetooth link with invalid communication requests, the hacker can temporarily disable the product's Bluetooth services.

3 Conclusion

Security aspects are very important for wireless technologies due to easy access of the attackers to the communication medium. Anyone with the appropriate HW can scan radio communication, log it and use today's powerful computer performance to obtain sensitive information. BT technology has serious vulnerability due to E0 cryptographic algorithm.

ZigBee uses AES-128 algorithm that seems to be secure at present time. Side channels found in recent time shows vulnerability of this cipher - i.e. Bernstein in [11] showed attack based on time side channel. This is because of poor implementation of the algorithm in 32 bits processor. ZigBee technology is primary designed for devices based on 8 bits microcontrollers where the correct implementation without side channels will be even more challenging. Finally, the DoS attack is a common problem in wireless communication systems in general.

A security system is only as strong as its weakest link. With the ZigBee the possible weakness lies in secure key distribution and secure key storage at all the devices.

References

1. ZigBee Specification 1.0, ZigBee Alliance (2004)
2. IEEE 802.15.X, IEEE, http://www.ieee802.org/15/
3. Advanced Encryption Standard AES: http://advanced-encryption-standard.iqnaut.net/
4. Krasner J.: Using Elliptic Curve Cryptography (ECC) for Enhanced Embedded Security, Embedded Market Forecasters, American Technology International, Inc. (2004)
5. Ferguson N., Schneier B.: Practical cryptography, Wiley (2003)
6. Pereira R.: ZigBee And ECC Secure Wireless Networks, Electronic Design (2004) www.elecdesign.com
7. Bluetooth Special Interest Group SIG: http://www.bluetooth.com
8. Bluetooth specification Version 1.1, (February 22 2001)
9. Lu Y., Meier W., Vaudenay S.: The Conditional Correlation Attack: A Practical Attack on Bluetooth Encryption. Crypto'05, Santa Barbara (2005)
10. Ceung H.: How To: Building a BlueSniper Rifle, http://www.tomsnetworking.com/Sections-article106-page1.php (2005)
11. Bernstein D.: Cache-timing attacks on AES, http://cr.yp.to/antiforgery/cachetiming-20050414.pdf (2005)

Code Size Reduction by Compiler Tuning

Masayo Haneda[1], Peter M.W. Knijnenburg[1,2], and Harry A.G. Wijshoff[1]

[1] LIACS, Leiden University,
Niels Bohrweg 1, 2333CA Leiden, The Netherlands
{haneda, peterk, harryw}@liacs.nl
[2] University of Amsterdam,
Kruislaan 403, 1098 SJ Amsterdam, The Netherlands
peterk@science.uva.nl

Abstract. Code size is a main cost factor for many high volume electronic devices. It is therefore important to reduce the size of the applications in an embedded system. Several methods have been proposed to deal with this problem, mostly based on compressing the binaries. In this paper, we approach the problem from a different perspective. We try to exploit the back end code optimizations present in a production compiler to generate as few assembly instructions as possible. This approach is based on iterative compilation in which many different versions of the code are tested. We employ statistical analysis to identify the compiler options that have the largest effect on code size. We have applied this technique to *gcc* 3.3.4 using the MediaBench suite and four target architectures. We show that in almost all cases we produce shorter codes than the standard setting *-Os* does which is designed to optimize for size. In some cases, we generate code that is 30% shorter than *-Os*.

1 Introduction

Memory is a main cost factor for many high volume electronic devices and constitutes an increasing portion of the total product cost. Code size reduction therefore may reduce the direct cost of a product by reducing the size of required memory. On the other hand, a reduction in code size can also be used to fit more features into the same ROM which may enhance the value of a product. Many approaches have been proposed to reduce the code size of an application [1], ranging from code compression by means of, e.g., Huffman coding, to specific compiler based techniques like code factoring.

In this paper, we approach the problem from a different perspective. Instead of proposing yet another technique that may reduce code size, we want to explore the possibilities standard compiler optimizations can offer to decrease the number of generated assembly instructions. Although the number of assembly instructions is not directly proportional to the final size of the binary in general, it is a significant factor in the code compaction process. Moreover, our approach is orthogonal to the approaches mentioned above and can be used in conjunction with them, possibly leading to smaller compressed codes. Furthermore, our approach is easy to implement using a simple driver on top of the compiler. Modern compilers implement many optimizations that often can explicitly be turned on or off using compiler flags or switches. For example, *gcc* 3.3.4 has over 60

S. Vassiliadis et al. (Eds.): SAMOS 2006, LNCS 4017, pp. 186–195, 2006.

switches. Obviously, some optimizations, like loop unrolling or procedure inlining, can increase code size. Others, like dead code removal or strength reduction, can decrease code size. While these statements seem obvious, some care needs to be taken since it has been shown [2] that procedure inlining can actually decrease code size in some cases. This trivially holds when functions with only one call site are inlined or when the body of a function is smaller than the code needed to call and return from that function. However, it is clear that all options in a compiler may change the generated assembly code and thus may have an effect on code size. Whether they increase or decrease code size is largely unknown as is their effect on code size if we take into consideration the interaction of options. To the best of our knowledge, this paper is the first paper that systematically investigates how an existing production compiler can be tuned in order to reduce code size using over 50 options. We show that we can obtain a reduction in the number of assembly instructions in the generated code that can be as high as 30% over the standard -*Os* option of *gcc* that is designed to reduce code size.

Our method is based on statistical analysis of many versions of the code obtained by using different compiler settings. In previous work, we have used so-called the *main effect* of compiler options to tune the compiler for performance [3]. We have shown that the compiler settings obtained in this way produce faster programs than standard -*Ox* settings do. In the present paper, we use an improved statistical technique to optimize for size, namely, non-parametric inferential statistics.

In this paper, we only optimize for code size. We do not take into consideration the speed of the resulting code. Therefore, we may end up with a code that is short but may be too slow to be useful. In future work, we plan to integrate our approaches to code size and speed optimization. A possible solution is to optimize for size under speed constraints. In this case, possible candidate settings need to be profiled in order to check that they do not run too slow. Conversely, we can optimize for speed under code size constraints. Finally, a third possibility is to optimize for both at the same time by using a suitable function of both speed and size improvement.

This paper is structured as follows. In Section 2 we discuss related work. In Section 3, the statistical framework used in this paper is explained. In Section 4, we present our iterative algorithm to find a compiler setting. In Section 5, we discuss our experimental environment, and the results are shown in Section 6. In Section 7, we draw some conclusions.

2   Related Work

There exist some papers that study how the compiler can be used to reduce code size. One important transformation that is specifically geared toward code size reduction is code factoring [4]. This transformation can be seen as the inverse to function inlining. The assembly code is searched for repeating patterns that are encapsulated in a new function and the patterns are replaced by a call to this function. Cooper and McIntosh [5] improved the original idea. The *squeeze* binary-rewriting tool uses aggressive interprocedural optimization and code factoring [6]. Mathias et. al. [7] employ genetic algorithms to detect repeating patterns. The transformation reduces code size by

5 to 10%. As a drawback, code factoring can give rise to longer execution times by increasing the number of dynamic instructions and cache miss rates [8].

In a paper most related to the present paper, Cooper et. al. [9] propose to use genetic algorithms to search for short code sizes using a research compiler. However, they only employ 10 options, in contrast to the present approach which uses 53 options. It is not immediately clear that such large number of options will not lead to combinatorial explosion in their approach. Moreover, their compiler allows them to specify the order in which these optimizations are applied and the same optimization may occur several times in an optimization sequence. In contrast, we use an existing production compiler in which this order is fixed as is generally the case for production compilers. Hence, the technique from [9] is not immediately applicable to production compilers.

3   The Mann-Whitney Test

In this section, we discuss the statistical test we employ. First, we define a *null hypothesis* which negates the experimental hypothesis. When we want to know about the effectiveness of compiler option A for application B, the null hypothesis is

> **Null Hypothesis.** Compiler option A is *not* effective to reduce the size of application B.

Second, we conduct an experiment which contains two groups which are called the *control group* and the *experimental group*, respectively. The control group consists of the experimental runs that do not use compiler option A. The experimental group consists of the experimental runs which use compiler option A. The null hypothesis implies that the code sizes from these two groups are the same.

We employ Orthogonal Array [10] for the experimental design. Briefly, an Orthogonal Array (OA) is a matrix of zeroes and ones. The rows of an orthogonal array represent experiments to be performed and the columns of the orthogonal array correspond to the different factors whose effects are being analyzed. For the purposes of this paper, an OA has the property that for two arbitrary columns, the patterns, 00, 01, 10, and 11, occur equally often.

An OA has the property that any option is turned on and off equally often in the experiments defined by the rows of the OA. Moreover, for the rows that turn a certain option on, any other option is turned on and off equally often as well. The Orthogonal Arrays used in the present paper are taken from [11].

Since both experimental and control group consist of experiments where many different options are turned on, the code sizes of the members of each group can differ considerably. Therefore, taking the average code sizes for each group and comparing these averages is not accurate. Because of the large variation in each group, a difference between these averages could well be by pure chance. *Non-parametric statistics* are designed to deal with this situation [12]. It is capable of analyzing data without an underlying distribution by ranking the raw data first and analyzing the rankings.

The Mann-Whitney test is a well known test in inferential non-parametric statistics [12]. The Mann-Whitney test is based on the value of T which is the sum of ranks of the experimental group. In order to discuss how the test works, assume for simplicity that the two groups both contain N members and that the option to be analyzed is the only difference between the groups. It has been shown in [12] that if the null hypothesis is true, then T has a *normal distribution* although the underlying raw data does not have such a normal distribution. This distribution has mean

$$\mu = \frac{N(2N+1)}{2} \tag{1}$$

and standard deviation

$$\sigma = \sqrt{\frac{N^2(2N+1)}{12}} \tag{2}$$

Since T is normally distributed, we can apply 'ordinary' statistics on it. The Mann-Whitney test does not consider T directly but considers the test statistic z instead, which is given by

$$z = \frac{T - \mu}{\sigma} \tag{3}$$

That is, z measures how far T lies from the mean expressed in units of standard deviation. Then z is normally distributed also (with mean zero).

If the measured value of T is significantly different from μ, then we may conclude that the null hypothesis is false because it is highly unlikely that we measure such a value by chance. In order to decide whether T is significantly different from μ or, equivalently, whether its corresponding value z is significantly different from zero, we proceed as follows. Consider the function $P(t)$ given by

$$P(t) = \left(1 - 2 \cdot \int_0^t \frac{1}{\sigma\sqrt{2\pi}} e^{-\frac{1}{2}z^2} dz \right) \cdot 100\% \tag{4}$$

Then $P(t)$ expresses the chance to measure a value for z such that either $z \geq t$ or $z \leq -t$. A standard criterion [12] for "significant difference" is when the chance to measure a certain value of z is less than 5%. This threshold of 5% is called the *critical value* of the test. The corresponding value for t is 1.96. This means that the chance of measuring a value for z that is larger than 1.96 or smaller than -1.96 when the null hypothesis is true, is less than 5%[1]. This essentially means that the probability to reject the null hypothesis when it is in fact true, is less than 5%.

4   Methodology

This section describes our algorithm to determine a compiler setting for an application based on the statistical theory discussed in the previous section. The algorithm is given in Figure 1. It starts with a factor list which includes all compiler options. As explained in the Introduction, we use the number of assembly instructions in the generated code to obtain the test statistic for each compiler option. This statistic tells us which options have a significant effect, and whether they should be turned on or off. The compiler

---

[1] Equivalently, we can check whether $|z| > 1.96$ but the above formulation is more intuitive. There exists a simple algorithm to compute $P(|z|)$ from z given in [12].

– Choose an orthogonal array A from [11]. In our case, we start with 53 options and hence start with an OA with 56 rows.
– Repeat
  • Compile the application with each row from A as compiler setting and measure the number of assembly instructions generated.
  • Compute test statistic z for each compiler option with Equation (3).
  • If the test statistic meets $P(|z|) < 5\%$,
    ∗ If z is negative then the option has a positive effect, and the option is turned on.
    ∗ If z is positive then the option has a negative effect, and the option is turned off.
  • Remove the compiler options that have been selected from the factor list and remove the corresponding columns from A to obtain a smaller OA.
– Until
  • All options are set, or
  • No option with a significant effect is detected anymore.
– After the above loop, several options may not yet have received a value. We inspect the results for the last iteration and choose the row from the OA used there that gives rise to the shortest code to set these remaining options.

Fig. 1. Iterative Selection Algorithm

options whose settings are fixed are removed from the factor list, and the reduced factor list is used in the next iteration which uses a smaller Orthogonal Array. We obtain this smaller OA by dropping the columns that correspond to the options selected. It is easy to see that this procedure gives another Orthogonal Array. We then iteratively repeat the test to set more options until all options are set or the test fails to set another option because all P-values are too large. In the latter case, there will be very little variation in the OA and all different settings give rise to almost the same code size.

The algorithm starts to explore a large search space in which there is much variation, and it cuts down the search space every iteration, obtaining new small search spaces.

5   Experimental Environment

We have used *gcc* version 3.3.4 as our compiler. It contains over 60 options and we chose a subset of 53 options that are not described as experimental in the manual nor are options that may violate IEEE floating point standards, like *fast-math*. The resulting list of options is given is Fig 2. Note that in some cases, we have grouped a few options into one factor since the gcc manual explicitly states that these options should be turned on together [13]. For example, in factor 14, we have grouped all global common subexpression elimination options since they are enabled by default when *gcse* is enabled. Note also, that in factors 26 and 27, we turn on instruction scheduling together with a speculative scheduling option because the gcc manual states that this speculative scheduling option needs instruction scheduling, but we also have instruction scheduling as a separate option (22).

1	defer-pop
2	force-mem
3	force-addr
4	omit-frame-pointer
5	optimize-sibling-calls
6	inline-functions
7	merge-constants
8	strength-reduce
9	thread-jumps
10	cse-follow-jumps
11	cse-skip-blocks
12	rerun-cse-after-loop
13	rerun-loop-opt
14	gcse
	gcse-lm
	gcse-sm
	gcse-las
15	loop-optimize
16	crossjumping
17	if-conversion

18	if-conversion2
19	delete-null-pointer-checks
20	expensive-optimizations
21	optimize-register-move
22	schedule-insns
23	sched-interblock
24	sched-spec
25	schedule-insns2
26	sched-spec-load
	schedule-insns
27	sched-spec-load-dangerous
	schedule-insns
28	caller-saves
29	move-all-movables
30	reduce-all-givs
31	peephole
	peephole2
32	reorder-blocks
33	reorder-functions
34	strict-aliasing

35	align-functions
36	align-labels
37	align-loops
38	align-jumps
39	rename-registers
40	web
41	cprop-registers
42	tracer
43	unit-at-a-time
44	function-sections
45	data-sections
46	unroll-loops
	rerun-cse-after-loop
47	peel-loops
48	unswitch-loops
49	old-unroll-loops
50	branch-target-load-optimize
51	branch-target-load-optimize2
52	delayed-branch
53	prefetch-loop-arrays

Fig. 2. Options from gcc 3.3.4 used

We have configured *gcc* as a cross-compiler for the following platforms. We have used *mips* and *arm* which are two well known embedded RISC processors. We use the Motorola *m68k* which is a CISC processor that 25 years after its introduction still is a popular embedded processor. Current implementations are known as *68HC000*. We have also used a processor that is more specifically geared toward the embedded domain: the Renesas *M32R* processor.

We use the MediaBench benchmark suite for our test programs [14] except *pgp* and *ghostscript* that did not compile correctly on all platforms.

6   Results

6.1   Optimization Time Requirements

We let the algorithm run until completion when no more options are selected. The number of iterations required is between 5 and 12, with an average of 8. This means that on average we require 448 program compilations. Concerning the time it took to complete our iterative method, we performed our experiments on a P4 at 2.8 GHz platform. Depending on the size of the source code for the benchmark, it took between 30 minutes and 2 hours to complete the iterative procedure. Hence, when developing embedded applications, this time is certainly affordable. Please, note also that our approach is essentially 'for free': all that is required to implement it is a small driver on top of the compiler that generates different settings, compiles the source code using these settings, and counts the number of instructions in the assembly code. No complex new transformations or other adaptation of the compiler are needed.

6.2   Code Size Reduction

In this section, we show the results obtained from our iterative selection In Figures 3, we show the code size reduction for the *mips* with respect to the standard option *-Os*

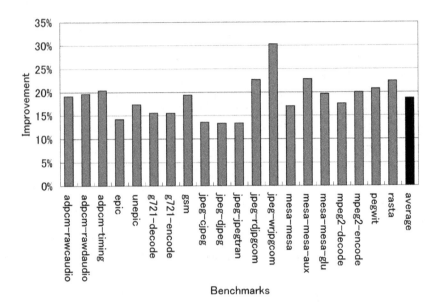

Fig. 3. Code size reduction with respect to –Os for mips

which is specifically geared toward code size reduction [13]. The figures for the other platforms are not included in this paper due to space restrictions and are available in [15]. The code size reduction is computed as follows. For an application A, let $S_s(A)$ be the size obtained by using -Os given by the number of instructions in the resulting assembly code, and let $S_n(A)$ be the size obtained from our new method. Then the code size reduction $R(A)$ is computed as $R(A) = \frac{S_s(A) - S_n(A)}{S_s(A)} \cdot 100\%$. This definition implies that when the code size obtained from our new method is larger than the size obtained from -Os, the reduction has a negative value. We immediately observe that in almost all cases, on all platforms, our method produced code sizes that are smaller than the code sizes produced by -Os. The amount of reduction is highly dependent on the platform used. For the *mips*, Figure 3 shows that high reductions are obtained for all benchmarks, with an average of 18%. For one benchmark, even a reduction of 30% is obtained. For the *m68k* and *M32R*, almost every benchmark is reduced in size w.r.t. -Os and in some cases reductions of 10 to 15% are achieved. On average, we reduce code size by 4 to 5% on these platforms which is the same reduction as is obtained from code factoring [1]. However, this last approach is much more complex to implement and moreover can be used in conjunction with our approach. We perform worst on the *arm*. The reason for this is that most options in *gcc* have little effect on code size for this architecture. We have observed that on the *arm* platform after a few iterations, the variance (standard deviation) in the 56 different settings tested becomes less than 0.5%. This means that there exist several hundreds of different settings that give rise to almost the same code size. In fact, there are more than one hounded settings that give rise toexactly the shortest code size found. We have also observed that on the *arm* platform -$O1$, -$O2$, -Os and our method give rise to almost the same code sizes. Only -$O3$ produces code sizes that are significantly larger, mainly due to inlining.

Nevertheless, also for the *arm* there exist two applications that are significantly reduced in size.

For each platform, there exist at least a few benchmarks that obtain a significant reduction in code size. On the other hand, there are no benchmarks that suffer a significant degradation in size, except one benchmark on the *arm*. As mentioned before, these code size reductions are obtained by carefully exploiting the existing code generator in *gcc* and are essentially 'for free'. This means that our method can be applied, the resulting code size can be compared to -*Os*, and the shortest code can be selected.

6.3   Compiler Settings

In Figure 4, we have shown the final selection of compiler options in the last iteration of our iterative method for the *mips*. The tables for the other platforms are left out from the present paper due to space restrictions and are available in [15]. In the table, '1' denotes that the option has been turned on, '0' that it has been turned off, and a blank space that it has not yet been decided. In the setting that is finally produced, these blanks are filled with values that give rise to the shortest code in the final iteration. However, the

	1	2	3	4	5	6	7	8	9	10	11	12	13	14	15	16	17	18	19	20	21	22	23	24	25	26	27
-Os	1	1	0	0	1	0	1	1	1	1	1	1	1	1	1	1	1	1	1	1	1	1	1	1	1	0	0
adpcm-rawcaudio			0	1					0					1	0		1	1									
adpcm-rawdaudio	0			1										1	0		1	1									
adpcm-timing			0	1			0				0			1	0			1									
epic-epic		1	0	1		0		0			1	1	1	0	0	1	1	1		1		0			0	0	0
epic-unepic	0	0	1		0				1	1				1	0	1	1	1		1		0			0	0	0
g721-decode	0	0	1		0				1	1				0	0	1	1	1		1		1	0		0		
g721-encode	0	0	1		0				1	1	1			0	0	1	1	1		1		1	1	1	0		
gsm	1	0	0	1	1	0		1			1	0		1	1	1	1	1		1		0	0	1	1	0	0
jpeg-cjpeg	0	0	1		0				1	1				0	0	1	0	1		1		0			0	0	0
jpeg-djpeg	0	0	1		0				1	1	1			0	0	1	0	1		1		0			0	0	0
jpeg-jpegtran	0	0	1		0				1	1	1			0	0	1	0	1		1		0			0	0	0
jpeg-rdjpgcom			1	1		0		1			1			0	0	1	1	1		0		0	1	1	0	1	1
jpeg-wrjpgcom			1		0		0	1	1	1				0	0	1	1	1		0		0			0	0	0
mesa-mesa	0	0	1		0				1	1	1	1		1	0	1	1	1		0	1	0			0	0	0
mesa-mesa-aux	1	1	1	1	1	0	1		1		1			0	0	1	1	1		0	1	1	1	1	0	1	
mesa-mesa-glu	1	0	1	1	0				0	1	1	1		0	0	1	0	1	1	0		0			0	0	0
mpeg2-mpeg2decode	1	0	1	1	0		1	1	1	1				0	0	1	0	1	1	0	1	0	1	1	0	0	0
mpeg2-mpeg2encode	1	0	1		0				1	1	1	0		1	0	1	0	1	1	1		0			0	0	
pegwit-pegwit	1	0	0	1		0		1	1	1	1			0	0	1	0	1		1		0			0	0	0
rasta-rasta	0	0	1		0				1	1	1	1		1	0	1	0	1		0		0			0	0	0

	28	29	30	31	32	33	34	35	36	37	38	39	40	41	42	43	44	45	46	47	48	49	50	51	52	53
-Os	1	0	0	1	0	1	1	0	0	0	0	0	0	1	0	1	0	0	0	0	0	0	0	0	1	0
adpcm-rawcaudio													0		0	0									0	
adpcm-rawdaudio				1	0								0		0	0									0	
adpcm-timing	1				0								0		0	0						0			0	
epic-epic					0		0					0	1		0	0						0			0	
epic-unepic	1				0		1							1	1	0	0			1					0	
g721-decode					1							0	0	1	0	0				1		0			0	
g721-encode					1							0	0	1	0	0									0	
gsm		1	0				1						1	1	1	0	0	0		1			1	0	0	
jpeg-cjpeg	1				0		1					0	1	1	0	0				1					0	
jpeg-djpeg	1				0		1					0	1	1	0	0				1	1				0	
jpeg-jpegtran	1				0		1					0	1	1	0	0				1	1				0	
jpeg-rdjpgcom			0									1	1	1	0	0									0	
jpeg-wrjpgcom						0						1	0	1	1	0						0			0	
mesa-mesa	1			1		1						0	1	1	0	0									0	
mesa-mesa-aux	1	1	1	1	0	1		1		1		1	1	0	1	0	0	1	1	1	1		1		0	
mesa-mesa-glu	1				0		1					1	1	1	0	0									0	
mpeg2-mpeg2decode			1		1	1	1	1		1		1	1	1	0	0		1	1	1	1			1	0	0
mpeg2-mpeg2encode	1				0		1					0	1	1	0	0				1	1		1		0	
pegwit-pegwit				1		1						1	1	1	0	0						0			0	
rasta-rasta					0	1	1		0		1	1		1	0	0	1	1			0	0		0	0	0

Fig. 4. Generated settings for mips

variance in this last iteration is very low, sometimes as low as 0.002%. This means that the effect of these options on code size is very low and it is not important which value they receive. For comparison purposes, we have also shown the setting *-Os*.

From the table, we observe that many options do not have much effect on code size for any benchmarks. Also, we observe that there are a few options (14, 15, and 43) that in our method are explicitly turned off mostly whereas they are turned on in *-Os*. This means that we measure a degradation in size. From this table, we see that *inline-functions* (6) is turned off in all cases, as is *loop-optimize* (15) and *tracer* (42). This last option performs tail duplication to enlarge superblock sizes. In many cases, instruction scheduling (22-27) and *reorder-blocks* (32) are turned off also. The option *omit-frame-pointer* (4) is turned on in almost all cases since it drops the instructions required to create this frame pointer. Remarkably, the loop unrolling option (46) is turned on in several cases. These observations are valid across benchmarks and platforms [15].

Many options are switched on or off depending on the application and platform, showing that compiler tuning for a particular application and platform can be worthwhile.

7   Conclusion

In this paper, we have proposed an iterative approach to setting compiler options in order to generate as few instructions in the assembly code as possible. We use a technique that is based on non-parametric inferential statistics, in particular, the Mann-Whitney test, to decide which options should be switched on or off. We have shown that our technique performs better in almost all cases considered than the standard *-Os* switch that is designed to optimize for size. However, this improvement is highly dependent on the target platform. For the *mips* platform, we obtain high reductions in code size of 18% on average over *-Os*. In some cases, we produce code that is 30% smaller than *-Os*. For the *m68k* and *M32R* we reduce code size by 4 to 5% on average, and 10 to 15% in some cases. Finally, for the *arm* gains are less and in one case we are even 5% larger than *-Os*. However, our technique is easy to implement and requires no adaptation of the compiler. Therefore, it can be worthwhile to try to optimize for size using our method and switching to *-Os* in the few cases it should fail.

References

1. Beszédes, A., Ferenc, R., Gyimóthy, T., Dolenc, A., Karsisto, K.: Survey of code-size reduction methods. ACM Comput. Surv. **35** (2003) 223–267
2. Cooper, K., Hall, M., Torczon, L.: Unexpected side effects of inline substitution: A case study. ACM Letters on Programming Languages and Systems **1** (1992) 22–32
3. Pinkers, R.P.J., Knijnenburg, P.M.W., Haneda, M., Wijshoff, H.A.G.: Statistical selection of compiler options. In: Proc. Workshop on Modeling, Analysis, and Simulation of Computer and Telecommunication Systems (MASCOTS). (2004) 494–501
4. Fraser, C., Myers, E., Wendt, A.: Analyzing and compressing assembly code. In: Proc. SIGPLAN symposium on Compiler Construction. (1984) 117–121
5. Cooper, K., McIntosh, N.: Enhanced code compression for embedded risc processors. In: Proc. Programming Language Design and Implementation (PLDI). (1999) 139–149

6. Debray, S., Evans, W., Muth, R., Sutter, B.D.: Compiler techniques for code compaction. ACM Trans. Programming Languages and Systems **22** (2000) 378–415
7. Mathias, K., Eshelman, L., Schaffer, J., Augusteijn, L., Hoogendijk, P., van de Wiel, R.: Code compaction using genetic algorithms. In: Proc. Genetic and Evolutionary Computation Conference (GECCO). (2000) 710–717
8. Sutter, B.D., Vandierendonck, H., Bus, B.D., Bosschere, K.D.: On the side-effects of code abstraction. In: Proc. Language, Compiler, and Tool for Emebedded Systems (LCTES). (2003) 244–253
9. Cooper, K., Schielke, P., Subramanian, D.: Optimizing for reduced code space using genetic algorithms. In: Proc. Languages, Compilers, and Tools for Embedded Systems (LCTES). (1999) 1–9
10. Hedayat, A., Sloane, N., Stufken, J.: Orthogonal Arrays: Theory and Applications. Series in Statistics. Springer Verlag (1999)
11. Sloane, N.: A library of orthogonal arrays. (http://www.research.att.com/~njas/)
12. Hollander, M., Wolfe, D.A.: Nonparametric Statistical Methods. Wiley Series in Probability and Statistics (1999)
13. GNU Consortium: GCC online documentation. (http://gcc.gnu.org/onlinedocs/)
14. : Mediabench. (http://cares.icsl.ucla.edu/MediaBench)
15. Haneda, M., Knijnenburg, P., Wijshoff, H.: Code size reduction by compiler tuning. Technical report, LIACS, Leiden Univeresity (2005)

Energy Optimization of a Multi-bank Main Memory

Hanene Ben Fradj, Sébastien Icart, Cécile Belleudy, and Michel Auguin

Laboratoire d'informatique, Signaux et Systèmes de Sophia-Antipolis,
Les Algorithmes, route des Lucioles-BP 121, 06903 Sophia-Antipolis cedex. France
{benfradj, sicart, belleudy, auguin}@i3s.unice.fr

Abstract. A growing part of the energy, battery-driven embedded system, is consumed by the off-chip main memory. In order to minimize this memory consumption, an architectural solution is recently adopted. It consists of multi-banking the addressing space instead of monolithic memory. The main advantage in this approach is the capability of setting banks in low power modes when they are not accessed, such that only the accessed bank is maintained in active mode. In this paper we investigate how this power management capability built into modern DRAM devices can be handled for multi-task applications. We aim to find, at system level design, both an efficient allocation of applications tasks to memory banks, and the memory configuration that lessen the energy consumption: number of banks and the size of each bank. Results show the effectiveness of this approach and the large energy savings.

1 Introduction and Related Work

Memories in SoCs become increasingly broad especially for multimedia application which handles a great quantity of data. According to ITRS prevision, embedded memory will continue to dominate SoC content in the next several years, approaching 94% of the die area by year 2014 [1]. As a consequence, the power consumption of memories increases tremendously. The main memory is consuming an increasing proportion of the power budget and thus motivates efforts to improve DRAM energy efficiency. On other hand, memories with multiple banks instead of a monolithic module appeared in several architectures. Recently, this kind of memory architecture was exploited to reduce energy dissipation by operating banks at different modes (Active, Standby, Nap, Power-Down) for example RAMBUS-DRAM technology (RDRAM) [2], Mobile-RAM of Infineon (SDRAM) [3]. To service a memory request (read or write), a bank must be in active mode which consumes most of the power. When a bank is inactive, it can be put in any low power mode (Standby, Nap, Power-Down). Each mode is characterized by its power consumption and the time that takes to transit back to the active mode (resynchronization time). The lower the energy consumption of the low power mode is, the higher the resynchronization time is (see table 1 [2]). Several techniques, which exploit the low power modes

S. Vassiliadis et al. (Eds.): SAMOS 2006, LNCS 4017, pp. 196–205, 2006.

of memories, were published recently. Those works can be classified in two categories. The first one tries to determine when to power down and into which low power mode its possible to transit the memory banks. These memory controllers policies are either hardware [4] or software [5] [6] oriented. The second category focuses on data allocation (dynamically or passively) to memory banks to minimize energy. The paper [7] studied the impact of loop transformations on banked memory architecture; [8] proposed an automatic data migration to reduce energy consumption in multiple memory banks by exploiting the temporal affinity among data. Authors in [9] proposed an integer linear programming (ILP) based approach that returns the optimal non uniform bank sizes and the mapping of data to banks. Our work is classified in the second category as we consider only one low power mode at once. We address the energy optimization in a multi-bank memory architecture but unlike the previous quoted works, we choose to operate at the system level of the co-design steps. In this level we can achieve larger energy savings. So the considered data granularity is the combined task's data and code. We noted that results in previous researches like [9] [8] [6] [7] can be added to our approach by optimizing the data and code allocation in each task. The focus of this paper is to find the optimal allocation of tasks to banks based on several parameters: task size, number of times the task was executed during the hyperperiod, memory access ratio, number of preemptions between tasks) and the corresponding memory configuration that lessens the memory energy consumption (optimal number of banks and optimal size of each bank). The paper is structured as follow: section 2 presents the memory architecture and the system model. In section 3 an estimation of a multi-banked main memory consumption is presented. In section 4 we focus on searching the low power tasks allocation to banks and the associated memory configuration (number of banks and banks size). Section 5 shows experiments and results obtained with our approach. We close the paper in section 6 with concluding remarks and future works.

2   Memory Architecture and System Model

For the architecture model, we consider a multi-bank main memory architecture. Each bank can be controlled independently and placed into one of the available low power modes. Each low power mode is characterized by the number of components being disabled to save energy. This multi-bank main memory communicates with an embedded processor through a L1 SRAM cache (figure 1). We consider real-time, multi-task embedded application. This application is described by a set of N periodic tasks; each task is characterized by temporal parameters namely (P_i: period, $wcet_i$: worst case execution time), ξ_i: memory access ratio and S_{T_i}: the task size (code and data). These tasks are scheduled according to the fixed priority and preemptive Rate Monotonic (RM) algorithm as shown in figure 2. ξ_i is the ratio of $wcet_i$ corresponding to cycles where the task T_i accesses to the memory, the number of memory accesses M_i of T_i is computed with the following equation:

$$M_i = \frac{\xi_i \times wcet_i}{100}$$

We define an allocation function noted ϕ that associates each task T_i belonging to a set of N tasks to a bank b_j belonging to a set of k banks.

$$\phi : \{T_1, T_2, ..., T_N\} \rightarrow \{b_1, b_2, ..., b_k\} \quad ; \quad \phi(T_i) = b_j$$

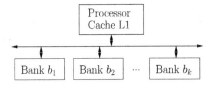

Fig. 1. Multi-bank main memory architecture

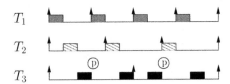

Fig. 2. RM schedule of the example task set during the hyperperiod

3   Energy Estimation and Models

3.1   Parameters Influencing Memory Consumption

Bank Size. The energy consumption monotonically increases with the memory size. The analytical model given in [10] illustrates that the memory energy consumption increases with the number of lines and columns in the memory. For the multi-bank main memory, several papers consider that the energy values given in table 1 (active, low power mode, resynchronization) increase by $\tau_1 = 30\%$ when bank size is doubled [9] [8]. In our approach, we consider that the size S_{b_j} of bank b_j is the sum of the size of all tasks T_i allocated to this bank:

$$S_{b_j} = \sum_{T_i / \phi(T_i) = b_j} S_{T_i}$$

So in the same architecture, the banks can have different sizes (non uniform bank sizes). We develop a mathematic formula that traduces the 30% of increase in memory energies consumption when the bank size is doubled for RDRAM technology. So with equation 1, we can determine the energy values per memory cycle of a bank b_j for a given size of S_{b_j}.

Table 1. Energy consumption (per cycle) and resynchronization times for different operating modes for 8 MB RDRAM bank size

Operating modes	Energy consumption (nJ)	Resynchronization cost (cycles)
Active	3.57	0
Standby	0.83	2
Nap	0.32	30
Power-Down	0.005	9,000

$$E_\alpha = E_{0\alpha}(1.3)^{Log2(\frac{S_{b_j}}{8})} \qquad (1)$$

$\alpha=\{$active, lp-mode, resynchronization$\}$, $E_{0\alpha}$: The energy values for the 8 MB bank size given in table 1.

Number of Banks and Communication. The multi-bank energy consumption depends also on the number of banks in the memory architecture. When we add a new bank, the sizes of banks decrease (less tasks per bank) as well as the energy values (active, low power mode and resynchronization). However, the energy consumption in the banks connecting increases. We assume that the energy consumption for communication increases by $\tau_2=20\%$ when we add a new bank to the architecture [11]. So for main memory architecture with k banks, the communication energy is described by equation 2.

$$E_{bus} = E_{0bus}(1.2)^{k-1} \qquad (2)$$

E_{0bus}: The bus consumption for one bank main memory architecture (monolithic memory). In our approach, τ_1 and τ_2 can be easily adjusted for different technologies.

Successivity and Preemption Between Tasks. We call successivity between task T_i and task T_j noted σ_{ij} when T_j begins its execution just after the end of T_i or when the higher priority task (T_i or T_j) preempts the other one. The successivity parameters are deduced from the application scheduling during the hyperperiod. They are exploited to minimize the number of resynchronizations of the memory banks and making the idle period of banks longer. The resynchronizations number of a bank b_j is computed as follows.

$$N_{resynchronization\_b_j} = \sum_{T_i/\phi(T_i)=b_j} N_{exeT_i} - \sum_{T_i,T_j/(\phi(T_i),\phi(T_j))=(b_j,b_j)} \sigma_{ij}$$

Where N_{exeT_i} is the number of executions of task T_i during the hyperperiod. From the RM schedule of figure 2, the successivities between the three tasks are: $\sigma_{12}= 3$, $\sigma_{13}= 4$, $\sigma_{23}= 3$. Considering the tasks allocation given in figure 3, the resynchronizations numbers of each bank are:

$N_{resynchronization\_b_1} = N_{exeT_1} + N_{exeT_3} - \sigma_{13} = 4$
$N_{resynchronization\_b_2} = N_{exeT_2} = 3$.

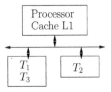

Fig. 3. Tasks allocation to 2 memory banks

By exploiting the successivity between tasks we can minimize the resynchronization numbers of banks and the energy associated. However, reducing the energy of resynchronisation by grouping in the same bank the tasks having the maximum number of successivities, can increase other energy contributions due for example to the increase in the size of the banks. In conclusion, minimizing separately each memory energy contribution cannot usually minimize the total memory consumption because of the strong interdependence between the memory parameters relevant to energy consumption. The problem can be modeled as a problem of allocation of tasks to banks with an objective of energy optimization.

3.2   Energy Models for a Multi-bank Memory

The energy consumption of a memory composed of k banks and a given allocation of N tasks to these banks is evaluated with equation 3.

$$E_{memory} = E_{access} + E_{nonaccess} + E_{lpmode} + E_{resynchronization} + E_{preemption} + E_{bus} \tag{3}$$

Unlike [9] we separate the active mode given in table 1 into two different operating modes: the read/write mode (access) and active but idle mode (nonaccess). E_{access}: the energy due to read or write accesses to the memory banks.

$$E_{access} = \sum_{b_j/j=1}^{k} \left(\sum_{T_i/\phi(T_i)=b_j} N_{cycles\_access\_T_i} E_{0access}(1.3)^{Log_2(\frac{S_{b_j}}{8})} \right)$$

$E_{nonaccess}$: the energy consumption when the memory banks are active but not servicing any read or write operation. This energy is essentially due to the co-activation of the memory bank with the task execution by the processor.

$$E_{nonaccess} = \sum_{b_j/j=1}^{k} \left(\sum_{T_i/\phi(T_i)=b_j} N_{cycles\_nonaccess\_T_i} E_{0nonaccess}(1.3)^{Log_2(\frac{S_{b_j}}{8})} \right)$$

E_{lpmode}: the energy consumed by banks when they are in low power mode

$$E_{lpmode} = \sum_{b_j/j=1}^{k} N_{cycles\_lpmode\_b_j} E_{0lpmode}(1.3)^{Log_2(\frac{S_{b_j}}{8})}$$

$E_{resynchronization}$: the energy consumption due to the transition of memory banks from a low power mode to the active mode to service a memory request.

$$E_{resynchronization} = \sum_{b_j/j=1}^{k} N_{resynchronization\_b_j} E_{0resynchronization} (1.3)^{Log_2(\frac{S_{b_j}}{8})}$$

$E_{preemption}$: the energy induced by context switches due to the preemption between tasks on the processor.

E_{bus}: the energy consumption in the bank interconnection.

$$E_{bus} = E_{0bus} (1.2)^{k-1}$$

$N_{cycles\_access\_T_i}$: the number of memory access cycles of task T_i to the memory bank.

$$N_{cycles\_access\_T_i} = M_i \times t_{accessM} \times f_{memory}$$

$N_{cycles\_nonaccess\_T_i}$: the number of memory cycles of task T_i when the memory bank is active but idle.

$$N_{cycles\_nonaccess\_T_i} = (wcet_i \times \frac{1}{f_{processor}} - M_i \times t_{accessM}) \times f_{memory}$$

$t_{accessM}$: the memory access time.

$f_{memory}, f_{processor}$ are respectively memory and processor frequency.

$N_{cycles\_lpmode\_b_j}$: the number of memory cycles, the bank b_j spends in low power mode.

$N_{resynchronization\_b_j}$: the resynchronizations number of bank b_j from low power mode to the active mode.

$N_{preemptions}$: the number of preemptions of tasks during the hyperperiod.

We note that $N_{cycles\_acessT_i}$, $N_{cycles\_nonacessT_i}$, $N_{preemptions}$ are application related constants, whereas N_{cycles_lpmode}, $N_{resynchronization\_b_j}$ are variables depending on the number of banks and the tasks allocation.

$E_{0access}$, $E_{0nonaccess}$, $E_{0lpmode}$, $E_{0resynchronization}$ are the energy values per memory cycle for a 8 MB bank size given in table 1.

$E_{context\_switch}$: the energy of preemption due to context switching.

4   Exploration Algorithm

Our aim is to find both; an allocation ϕ of tasks to a multi-bank memory and the number of banks and their respective sizes; so as to minimize the overall energy consumption due to the main memory structure. In this study, only a single low power mode is considered. The strong interdependence of the different parameters influencing memory consumption, as explained in the previous section, makes the problem NP-hard to solve. An exhaustive approach exploring all the configurations space was adopted. This technique allows to find the optimal solution, to compare the energy of all the configurations and to observe the behavior of the memory consumption according to the variations of tasks and system characteristics. First, the algorithm starts by finding all the banks configurations to arrange N tasks in a k memory banks with k = 1 to N. Each configuration is represented by a set of integers; the cardinal of the set (k) represents the number of banks in the memory architecture and the sets elements called tasks b_i represents the number of tasks in a bank b_i. Considering for example 4 tasks application, five bank configurations are possible : {4} ; {3,1} ; {2,2} ; {2,1,1} ; {1,1,1,1}. For a number of banks equals to 2, there are two different configurations for arranging tasks in banks. In the first one {3,1}: 3 tasks are allocated to the first bank and one task is in the second while in the second configuration {2,2} two tasks are allocated to each bank. Second for each configuration, there are several permutations of tasks in banks. For the configuration {3,1}, allocating tasks T_1, T_2 and T_3 in the first bank b_1 and task T_4 in b_2 does not consume the same energy as if we allocate tasks T_2, T_3 and T_4 in the bank b_1 and task T_1 in bank b_2. This is due for example, to the different number of banks resynchronizations or to the different banks sizes. The number of tasks permutations for a given bank configuration is evaluated by equation 4.

$$
N_{permutations} = \frac{\prod_{i=1}^{k} C_{N-\sum_{j=1}^{i} tasks\_b_j}^{tasks\_b_i}}{s!}
\tag{4}
$$

Where s is the number of banks in the memory architecture in which there are an equal number of tasks, N is the number of tasks in the task set and k is the number of banks. For the 4 tasks application example, there are 15 possibilities for arranging 4 tasks in a number of banks varying from 1 to 4. Once all tasks permutations are exhibited for all bank configurations, the energy of each solution is estimated based on energy models described in section 3.2. Then we select the tasks permutation that gives the minimum main memory energy.

5   Experiments and Results

We considered an Intel PXA270 processor with a first level cache and a main memory in RAMBUS RDRAM technology (table 2) with the Nap as low power mode (table 1). The application example is described in table 3. The L1 cache energy is deduced from an extended version of the original CACTI cache modeling tool called eCACTI (enhanced CACTI) [12]. It considers in addition to the dynamic consumption, the static dissipation of the SRAM cache.

Table 2. System parameters

Component	Parameters
Processor	Intel PXA 270, 624Mhz [13]
cacheL1	32 KB, 2 way set associative, 2 cycles latency
Main Memory	Rambus DRAM, $t_{Maccess} = 50$ns

Table 3. Task set example

Tasks	P_i (cycles)	wcet$_i$ (cycles)	S_{T_i} (MB)	ξ_i (%)
1	100,000	550	16	50
2	150,000	500	14	60
3	200,000	450	12	70
4	300,000	350	8	55
5	300,000	490	10	85
6	400,000	1,500	8	60
7	600,000	2,050	16	56
8	1,200,000	9,000	12	78

As first experiments, we plot the variation of the total main memory consumption versus the number of banks. Figure 4 illustrates the energy efficiency of a multi-bank memory architecture compared to monolithic module (single bank memory). The minimum consumption is obtained for the architecture with 4 banks (the optimal number of banks). Compared to the monolithic architecture, the energy savings is about 42%. Figure 5 depicts the optimal memory architecture and the corresponding optimal tasks allocation.

In figure 4, we remark also that the memory consumption decreases as long as were adding a new bank to the architecture until we reach the optimal number of banks (4 in our case). Exceeding this number, the memory consumption increases again. To understand this memory consumption behavior, we plot figure 6. It represents for each number of banks, the sum of all the memory energy contributions mentioned in equation 3.

Adding a new bank to the architecture means: first, smaller bank sizes thus a decrease in E_{access} and $E_{nonaccess}$. Second, more low power periods, resynchronizations of banks and consumption in the interconnection thus an increase in E_{lpmode}, $E_{resynchronization}$ and E_{bus}. We define two differential energy values:

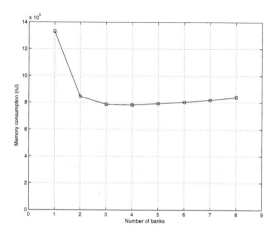

Fig. 4. Variation of multi-bank memory consumption versus the number of banks

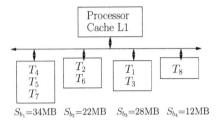

S_{b_1}=34MB S_{b_2}=22MB S_{b_3}=28MB S_{b_4}=12MB

Fig. 5. Optimal allocation

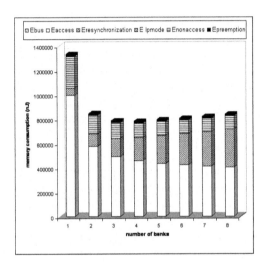

Fig. 6. Memory energy contributions

$$\Delta_1 = (E_{access} + E_{nonaccess})_{b=k+1} - (E_{access} + E_{nonaccess})_{b=k}$$
$$\Delta_2 = (E_{bus} + E_{lpmode} + E_{resynchronization})_{b=k+1} - (E_{bus} + E_{lpmode} + E_{resynchronization})_{b=k}$$

b: represents the number of banks in the memory architecture. We notice, while $\Delta_1 > \Delta_2$, that the total memory consumption decreases as the number of banks increases. However, when adding an extra bank does not significantly reduce $E_{access} + E_{nonaccess}$ but in other hand significantly increase $E_{lpmode} + E_{resynchronization} + E_{bus}$, the total energy consumption increases again. In figure 4 and figure 6, the fifth bank is responsible of re-increasing the memory consumption. So its not beneficial to add a supplementary bank to an architecture with four banks. These 2 values Δ_1 and Δ_2 can be used in future work to build an heuristic approach for tasks allocation to memory banks.

6   Conclusion and Future Work

For the multi-bank memory consumption problem, we proposed an exhaustive algorithm; at system level and for real-time applications; that returns the optimal allocation of tasks to banks (the optimal number of banks, the optimal sizes of banks). This approach can reduce the memory consumption by up to 40%. The exhaustive approach returns the optimal solution. Unfortunately, the exploration space is exponential in size and the computation time become quickly important. The exhaustive approach becomes impractical exceeding a set of 30 tasks, so employing such approach to take into account additional tasks that appears on-line (sporadic tasks) is impossible. As future work, we seek to propose an heuristic approach that is able to prune the configuration space, and to efficiently solve, in polynomial time, the power aware multi-bank main memory configuration and the corresponding tasks allocation. It will be interested also to extend this memory consumption optimization to multi-processor architecture with more accurate L1 and L2 cache models in the memory hierarchy.

References

1. SIA: International roadmap for semiconductors. (2001)
2. Rambus, Inc.: 128/144 MBit Direct RDRAM data sheet. (1999)
3. Infineon, Inc.: Mobile-RAM data sheet. (2004)
4. Delaluz, V., Kandemir, M., N.Vijaykrishnan, Sivasubramaniam, A., Irwin, M.: Dram energy management using software and hardware directed power mode control. HPCA (2001) 159–170
5. Delaluz, V., Kandemir, M., Sezer, U.: Improving off-chip memory energy behavior in a multi-processor, multi-bank environment. LCPC (2001) 100–114
6. Lebeck, A.R., X. Fan, H.Z., Ellis, C.: Power aware page allocation. ASPLOS (2000)
7. Kandemir, M., Kolcu, I., Kadayif, I.: Influence of loop optimizations on energy consumption of multi-bank memory systems. In Proc. Compiler Construction (2002)
8. Delaluz, V., Kandemir, M., Kolcu, I.: Automatic data migration for reducing energy consumption in multi-bank memory systems. DAC (2002)
9. Ozturk, O., Kandemir, M.: Nonuniform banking for reducing memory energy consumption. DATE (2005)
10. Itoh, K., Sasaki, K., Nakagome, Y.: Trends in low-power RAM circuit technologies. Proc. IEEE **83** (1995) 524–543
11. Benini, L., Macci, A., M, P.: A recursive algorithm for low-power memory partitioning. ISLPED (2000)
12. Mamidipaka, M., Dutt, N.: ecacti: An enhanced power estimation model for on-chip caches. Technical Report TR-04-28, Center for Embedded Computer Systems (2004)
13. Intel, Inc.: PXA 270 data sheet. (2005)

Probabilistic Modelling and Evaluation of Soft Real-Time Embedded Systems[*]

Oana Florescu[1], Menno de Hoon[2], Jeroen Voeten[1,3], and Henk Corporaal[1]

[1] Eindhoven University of Technology
[2] Chess Information Technology BV
[3] Embedded Systems Institute

Abstract. Soft real-time systems are often analysed using hard real-time techniques, which are not suitable to take into account the deadline misses rate allowed in such systems. Therefore, the resulting system is over-dimensioned, thus expensive. To appropriately dimension soft real-time systems, adequate models, capturing their varying runtime behaviour, are needed. By using the concepts of a mathematically defined language, we provide a modelling approach based on patterns that are able to express the variations appearing in the system timing behaviour. Based on these modelling patterns, models can be easily created and are amenable to average case performance evaluation. By the means of a case study, we show the type of results that can be obtained from such an evaluation and how these results are used to dimension the system.

1 Introduction

Due to the high time-to-market constraint in the embedded systems industry, accompanied by increasing demand for more functionality and tighter requirements on cost, speed (throughput) and energy consumption of the final product, the industry has shifted its focus from improving the system *implementation* phase to improving the system *design* phase. To this end, early evaluation of system properties is needed to make correct decisions that guarantee the satisfaction of the *functional* and *non-functional* requirements. This is where design space exploration and system-level performance modelling techniques come into scene. In the past, such techniques were applied mainly in the design of hard real-time systems. However, the higher demands on the quality of products require such techniques also for soft real-time systems, like DVD players for the synchronisation of the audio and video stream decoding, or printers for the accuracy of printing an image on a sheet. As no suitable techniques are available, the timing requirements of such systems are treated as hard, and consequently, the resulting system is over-dimensioned. However, as these requirements are not critical factors, instead of having all the deadlines met, one should be able to reason about the rate of deadlines misses which is allowed in soft real-time systems.

---

[*] This work has been carried out as part of the Boderc project under the responsibility of the Embedded Systems Institute. This project is partially supported by the Netherlands Ministry of Economic Affairs under the Senter TS program.

S. Vassiliadis et al. (Eds.): SAMOS 2006, LNCS 4017, pp. 206–215, 2006.

Contributions of the paper. In this paper, we present an approach for *probabilistic modelling and evaluation* of soft real-time embedded systems. The approach is based on the concepts of a formally defined general-purpose modelling language, POOSL, which enables creation of models that describe systems behaviour using probabilistic distributions. Based on this, we developed a library of *probabilistic modelling patterns* to be used when composing models for design space exploration of soft real-time systems. These patterns act like templates that can be used in any situation, reducing the necessary modelling effort. Based on them, we can analyse the *varying* timing behaviour (average case analysis) of the system, instead of considering only its worst case. The analysis results expose the degree to what extent the requirements can be met by a certain system architecture and decisions can be made with respect to reducing the performance of the necessary architecture for lowering the cost and the energy consumption.

Related research. An extensive overview of performance modelling and analysis methodologies is given in [1] and [2]. They range from analytical computation (Modular Performance Analysis [3], UPPAAL [4]) to simulation-based estimation (Spade [5], Artemis [6]). The analytical computation techniques are exhaustive in the sense that *all* possible behaviours of the system are taken into account, whereas simulation of models allows the investigation of a *limited* number of behaviours. Thus, the obtained analysis results are *estimates* of the real performance of the system. For credibility of results, models created in both types of techniques need to be amenable to mathematical analysis (see [7]), using mathematical structures like Real-Time Calculus [8], timed automata [9] or Kahn process networks [10]. As in general analytical approaches do not scale with the complexity of the industrial systems, simulation-based estimation of performance properties is used more often.

With respect to timing behaviour, an impressive amount of work has been carried out in the area of schedulability analysis (e.g. [11], [12], [13]) focussing on worst case. However, less work addresses the analysis of systems with probabilistic behaviour. For soft real-time systems, it is important to analyse the variations in the runtime behaviour to determine the likelihood of occurrence of certain undesired situations and, based on that, to dimension the system. In [14] and [7] it is showed that the techniques proposed in this area are quite restrictive. Some of them target certain application classes, being limited to uni-processor architectures or supporting only exponential distributions for expressing the probabilistic behaviour; other approaches address specific scheduling policies or assume highly-loaded systems. Overcoming these issues, the modelling approach presented in this paper can capture any kind of probabilistic distribution of system behaviour and any scheduling policy is allowed for the analysis of timing behaviour. Although the evaluation of the system properties is based on simulations, due to the formal semantics of the modelling language, the accuracy of the results can be determined.

The paper is organised as follows. The case study used throughout the paper to illustrate various ideas is presented in section 2. In section 3, the modelling approach is described together with the modelling language used, whereas the performance analysis method is presented in section 4 next to the results obtained for the case study. Conclusions are drawn in section 5.

2 Case Study

The case study discussed in this paper is an in-car navigation system. The system has three clusters of functionality: the man-machine interface (MMI) handles the interaction with the user; the navigation functionality (NAV) deals with route-planning and navigation guidance; the radio (RAD) is responsible for basic tuner and volume control, as well as receiving traffic information from the network. For this system, three application scenarios are possible: the ChangeVolume scenario allows users to change the volume; the ChangeAddr scenario enables route planning by looking up addresses in the maps stored in the database; in the HandleTMC scenario the system needs to handle the navigation messages received from the network. Each of these scenarios is described by a UML message sequence diagram, like the one shown in fig. 1. A detailed description of the system and of its scenarios can be found in [3].

The *problem* related to this system was *to find suitable platform candidates* that meet the timing requirements of the application. To explore the design space, a few platforms, presented in fig. 2, were proposed and analysed using Modular Performance Analysis (MPA) in [3]. MPA is an analytical technique in which the functionality of a system is characterised by the incoming and outgoing event rates, message sizes and execution times. Based on Real-Time Calculus, hard upper and lower bounds of the system performance are computed. However, these bounds are in general not exact, meaning that they are larger/smaller than the *actual* worst/best case. Thus, the analysis performed is conservative.

As the in-car navigation is a soft real-time system that allows a certain percentage of deadline misses, it is doubtfully interesting to explore if there is an

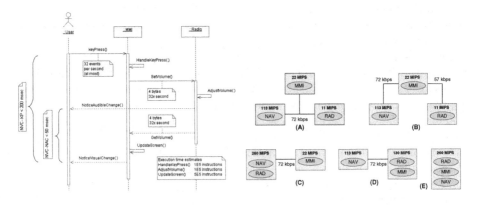

Fig. 1. ChangeVolume scenario   **Fig. 2.** Platforms proposed for analysis

architecture of lower cost and performance than what have been obtained with MPA that can still meet the timing requirements.

3 Modelling of the System

One of the approaches for performing systematic design space exploration is the Y-chart scheme introduced in [15]. This scheme makes a distinction between applications (the required functional behaviour) and platforms (the infrastructure used to perform this functional behaviour). The design space can be explored by evaluating different mappings of applications onto platforms. In the following subsections, first the modelling language POOSL is briefly presented and then the models of the application and of the platform are explained, whereas the environment model and the mapping are detailed in [16].

3.1 POOSL Modelling Language

The Parallel Object-Oriented Specification Language (POOSL) [17] lies at the core of the system-level design method called Software/Hardware Engineering (SHE). POOSL contains a set of powerful primitives to formally describe concurrency, probabilistic behaviour, (synchronous) communication, timing and functional features of a system into a single executable model. Its formal semantics is based on timed probabilistic labelled transition systems. This mathematical structure guarantees a unique and unambiguous interpretation of POOSL models. Hence, POOSL is suitable for specification and, subsequently, verification of correctness and analytical computation of performance for real-time systems. However, due to the state space explosion problem, simulation-based estimations are used for the evaluation of system properties.

The SHE method is accompanied by two simulation tools. SHESim is a graphical environment intended for incremental specification, modification and validation of POOSL models. Rotalumis is a high-speed simulator, enabling fast evaluation of system properties. Both tools have been proved to correctly simulate a model with respect to the formal semantics of the language ([18]).

3.2 Application Model

The functional behaviour of a real-time embedded system is implemented through a number of tasks that communicate with each other. In our approach, they are modelled as POOSL process objects. Using the primitives of the language, any kind of real-time behaviour can be expressed (e.g. concurrency, communication, data computations).

As an example, the HANDLEKEYPRESS (visualised in the UML diagram in fig. 1) task model is presented in fig. 3. The activation of the task is triggered by an event (i.e. turning the knob by the user). The computations performed by the task, modelled by the method COMPUTATION, impose a certain *load* on a CPU and have a deadline D, modelled by the **delay** statement. When the deadline expires, or when the computation finishes (if it takes longer than D) the result

HANDLEKEYPRESS()()
  | E : Event, R : Results |
  /* a new event E is received */
  in?event(E);
  par
    par
      COMPUTATION(E)(R)
    and
      delay D
    rap;
    /* the result R is sent */
    out!result(R)
  and
    /* handle another event */
    HANDLEKEYPRESS()()
  rap.

Fig. 3. HandleKeyPress task model

SCHEDULE()() | req, oldreq : Request |
  sel
    task?schedule(req);
    req *setCurrentLoad*();
    SchPolicy *scheduleRequest*(req);
    if (SchPolicy *hasHighestPriority*(req) == *true*)
    then
      sel
        toResource!execute(req)
      or
        toResource!preemption;
        fromResource?stopped(oldreq);
        toResource!execute(req);
        SchPolicy *update*(oldreq)
      les
    fi;
    SCHEDULE()()
  or
    fromResource?stopped(oldreq);
    task!executed;
    req := SchPolicy *removeRequest*(oldreq);
    if (req != *nil*)
    then toResource!execute(req) **fi**;
    SCHEDULE()()
  les.

Fig. 4. Scheduler model

is sent as a message to another task. By recursively calling HANDLEKEYPRESS method in the **and** branch of the outer **par** statement, it is ensured that another available message can be immediately received.

The *deadline* and the *load* (expressed as the number of instructions to be executed by a CPU) represent the parameters of a real-time task. As the COMPUTATION performed by a task usually depends on the incoming event, the *load* is not a fixed value, but varies between a minimum and a maximum (best case and worst case). These parameters affect the scheduling of tasks on a platform.

3.3 Platform Model

The platform on which the software runs is described as a collection of computation and communication resources. As there is no large conceptual difference between them (they receive requests, execute them and send back notification on completion), we have conceived a single model for both types of resources.

As a resource is usually shared by a number of concurrent tasks, a scheduler is needed to arbitrate the access. The modelling pattern for a scheduler is given in fig. 4. The scheduler can either receive scheduling requests from newly activated tasks (the outer **sel** branch), or notifications from the platform about completed requests (the **or** branch). In case of a newly activated task, the *setCurrentLoad* method sets its current load according to a probabilistic distribution which appropriately captures the fluctuations in the task load. The data object *SchPolicy* is an instance of a data class implementing the actual scheduling algorithm. For specifying different policies, different subclasses can be defined. *Any* type of policy can be modelled (e.g. EDF, RMA, round-robin). An EDF scheduling

RESOURCE()() | req: Request,
              loadLeft, tstart, tstop : Integer |
sch?execute(req);
delay initialLatency *sample*();
tstart := **currentTime**;
abort
  delay req *getLoad*() / throughput
with sch?preemption;
tstop := **currentTime**;
loadLeft := req *getLoad*() -
            (tstop - tstart) * throughput;
req *setLoad*(loadLeft);
sch!stopped(req);
RESOURCE()().

scheduleRequest(req : Request): SchPolicy
  | i, j : Integer |
  i := 1;
  while(req *getDeadline*() >
        list *get*(i) *getDeadline*()) **do**
    i:=i+1
  od;
  list *insert*(i, req);
  return self.

Fig. 5. EDF scheduling policy   **Fig. 6.** Resource model

policy is given as an example in fig. 5. A list is kept with all the ready requests, and the new request *req* is inserted in this list based on its deadline value. For the requests completed by the resource, the scheduler checks if the deadline was missed and monitors the percentage of misses during simulation.

Fig. 6 presents the resource model as a POOSL process. The parameters of this modelling pattern are the *initialLatency*, which is due to task context switch time, in case of a CPU, and to the time to transfer the first bit of a message, in case of a bus, and the *throughput*. While *throughput* of a resource has a constant value, the *initialLatency* may vary due to diverse factors (e.g. cache). Therefore, we have modelled it is as a data object of some distribution type. Furthermore, we have enabled preemption of the execution of a request on a resource using the **abort** statement. Once finished or preempted, the remaining execution time of a request is computed and the request is sent back to the scheduler.

4 Average Case Performance Analysis

The modelling patterns presented in the previous section can be used to automatically generate a Y-chart-compliant model of a system. Different application-platform configurations can be specified and evaluated. During the simulation of such a model, the scheduler reports if there are deadline misses. Furthermore, based on the POOSL semantics, it can be detected if there is a deadlock in the system. If all the deadlines are met and there is no deadlock during the simulation, then the corresponding platform is a *good* candidate that meets all the system requirements, although simulation completeness cannot be claimed. However, for soft real-time systems, it is allowed that a certain percentage of deadlines are missed. Thus, in this case, it is useful to keep track of the rate of deadlines missed and check if the underlying platform meets the requirements. With the modelling approach presented above, the average case behaviour can be monitored and an appropriate dimensioning of the system can be made.

Task name	Min [instr.]	Max [instr.]
HandleKeyPress	7.5E4	1E5
AdjustVolume	7.5E4	1E5
UpdateScreen	3.75E5	5E5
DatabaseLookup	3.75E6	5E6
ReceiveTMC	7.5E5	1E6
DecodeTMC	3.75E6	5E6

Scenario name	Deadline [ms]	Task name	f [1/s]
ChangeVolume	200	HandleKeyPress	32
		AdjustVolume	32
		UpdateScreen	32
ChangeAddr	200	HandleKeyPress	1
		DatabaseLookup	1
		UpdateScreen	1
HandleTMC	1000	ReceiveTMC	1/3
		DecodeTMC	1/3
		UpdateScreen	1/30

Fig. 7. Tasks loads in the case study   **Fig. 8.** Timeliness requirements

4.1   Analysis Results for the Case Study

For the case study considered in this paper (the in-car navigation system) we have assumed that the loads of all tasks variate according to a uniform distribution, based on the inspiration got from measurements of similar systems. As the UML diagrams provide only the worst case value of the load of each task, we have considered that the actual load varies between 75% and 100% of the value provided. The limits of the load variation for each task are given in fig. 7. Based on the MIPS rate of the CPUs on the proposed architectures, given in fig. 2, we can compute the execution times of tasks. Depending on the scenario in which it is used, a task may be called at different rates. The frequencies of tasks activations per scenario are given in fig. 8. Based on these activation rates, priorities were assigned to tasks according to the rate monotonic approach. The timing requirements of the system are specified in the UML diagrams as end-to-end deadlines for each scenario, provided also in fig. 8.

During simulations[4] of the system behaviour for each of the architectures proposed in fig. 2, the end-to-end delays were monitored. The results obtained were graphically plotted as distribution histograms, showing on the horizontal axis the values of the end-to-end delay and on the vertical axis the rate of occurrence of each value. As the parallel execution of two scenarios is likely to lead to more variation in the end-to-end delay, fig. 9 shows the distribution histogram for the HandleTMC scenario when it runs in parallel with ChangeVolume on architecture A. From such distribution histograms, the minimum (best case) and the maximum (worst case) values for the end-to-end delays can be deduced. Columns 3 and 4 in fig 11 show these values for all the combinations of scenarios running on architecture A. Moreover, the relative frequency of occurrence of the maximum value can also be deduced. During simulations, we have observed that the requirements are met for all the scenarios on all the proposed architectures and that the maximum delays are much smaller than the deadlines.

---

[4] By using the fast execution engine Rotalumis, a few minutes of system simulation represent several hours of runtime behaviour. The simulation was run until an accuracy of 99% of the results was reached.

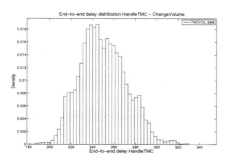

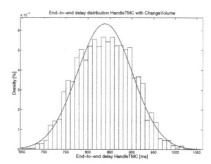

Fig. 9. HandleTMC distribution histogram on architecture A

Fig. 10. Distribution fitted over the HandleTMC distribution histogram on the improved A

Measured scenario	Active scenario	Min. delay [ms]	Max. delay [ms]	Mean delay [ms]	Max. delay [ms]
ChangeVolume	HandleTMC	28.17	47.82	49.66	58.48
HandleTMC	ChangeVolume	180.9	353.51	838.32	1056.06
ChangeAddr	HandleTMC	61.08	127.51	134.12	270.8
HandleTMC	ChangeAddr	132.59	204.06	349.712	496.03

Fig. 11. End-to-end delays of all scenarios

4.2   Dimensioning of the System

The in-car navigation system is a soft real-time system that allows a rate of 5% of deadline misses. Based on this, together with the utilisation rates of the resources, which were also monitored during simulation, and the observed maximum values of the delays, one can reason about possible platform performance reduction in order to reduce cost and energy consumption of the system.

In [3], where this case study was analysed using MPA, the authors investigated the robustness of architecture A. Therefore, in this paper we have also focussed on this architecture to reason about its resources. The utilisation of **MMI** is 88%. As the periods and loads of the tasks mapped on this processor are quite heavy, there is not much room for the decrease of its capacity. The **NAV** processor is used 6%. The histograms of scenarios ChangeAddr and HandleTMC showed a difference of 80ms and 200ms respectively between the worst case delays obtained and the requirements. Hence, we reduced **NAV** capacity to 40MIPS. The utilisation of **RAD** is 33%. The analysis showed a difference of 100ms for ChangeAddr and 200ms for HandleTMC respectively between the maximum delays and the deadlines. As there is potential for capacity reduction, we reduce the capacity of this processor to 5MIPS.

With this new configuration for architecture A, we resumed our simulations using the same variances in the task loads and the same task priorities. The distribution histograms of the end-to-end delays were plotted and, as an example, fig. 10 shows the histogram for the HandleTMC scenario. The mean and maximum values of the end-to-end delays for all the scenarios are presented in columns

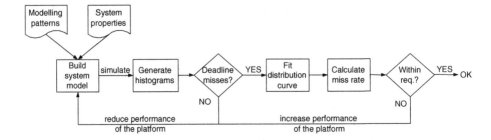

Fig. 12. Flow of the steps in the analysis approach

5 and 6 in fig. 11. From the confidence intervals calculated during simulation, we observed that the rate of deadline misses is within 5%, thereby fulfilling the requirements. In this way, we have found a better dimensioning of the system than what was found using MPA, reducing two of the processors with 65% (NAV) and respectively 55% (RAD).

Furthermore, in order to use such analysis results in an multi-disciplinary model of complex systems aiming at design trade-offs across disciplines, an abstraction of the timing behaviour of the software part is needed. To this end, we propose to fit the resulting distribution curves into known types of distribution. According to the *central limit theorem* in probability theory, due to the uniformly distributed loads of the tasks and to the fact that tasks in different scenarios are independent, the end-to-end delay of a scenario has approximately a normal distribution. Therefore, over the distribution histogram obtained from a simulation, a normal distribution curve is fitted. Fig. 10 shows such a curve fitted over the HandleTMC histogram. The parameters of the normal distribution are the mean value (μ) of 838.32 (ms) (the mean value of the delay) and the standard deviation (σ^2) of 3953.36 (ms). From such curves, the rate of deadline misses can be deduced, based on their characteristics. For example, the deadline for HandleTMC, which is 1000ms, can be found between two and three standard deviations from the mean. Thus, the probability of missing the deadline is less than 5%, which means the requirements are met. Furthermore, from these curves the probability of rare events occurrence can also be computed.

The analysis approach presented in this section is summarised in fig. 12 in which the steps to be performed for the analysis of a soft real-time system are provided.

5   Conclusions

As soft real-time systems are often analysed using hard real-time techniques, which are not suitable to account for the deadline misses rate allowed in such systems, the resulting system is over-dimensioned. To overcome this issue, in this paper, we have presented a modelling approach, based on the concepts of the POOSL language, that enables probabilistic modelling of soft real-time embedded systems. This approach relies on patterns that allow composition of system models consisting of tasks, resources and their associated schedulers, capturing the varying runtime system behaviour using distributions. By using them, models for design space exploration can be built easily.

Moreover, we presented an approach to perform average case performance analysis to appropriately dimension soft real-time systems. We show for a case study that, using this approach, we could reduce the dimension of the system with more than 50% than what was found using analytical techniques. Furthermore, we presented a way to make an abstraction of the analysis results of the timing behaviour to use it as input for multi-disciplinary models.

As future work, we aim at extending the probabilistic modelling patterns to cover for complex platforms like networks-on-chip, by taking into account memory components, routing algorithms and even batteries for the analysis of energy consumption.

References

1. Balsamo, S., et al.: Model-based performance prediction in software development: A survey. IEEE Trans. on Software Engineering **30**(5) (2004) 295–310
2. Gries, M.: Methods for evaluating and covering the design space during early design development. Integration, the VLSI Journal **38**(2) (2004) 131–183
3. Wandeler, E., et al.: System architecture evaluation using Modular Performance Analysis - A case study. (Accepted in the STTT Journal)
4. Behrmann, G., et al.: A tutorial on UPPAAL. In: Proc. of SFM. (2004) 200–236
5. Lieverse, P., et al.: A methodology for architecture exploration of heterogeneous signal processing systems. VLSI Signal Processing Systems **29**(3) (2001) 197–207
6. Pimentel, A.D., et al.: Exploring embedded-systems architectures with Artemis. Computer **34**(11) (2001) 57–63
7. Theelen, B.D.: Performance modelling for system-level design. PhD thesis, Eindhoven University of Technology (2004)
8. Chakraborty, S., et al.: A general framework for analysing system properties in platform-based embedded system designs. In: Proc. of DATE, IEEE (2003)
9. Alur, R., Dill, D.L.: A theory of timed automata. Theoretical Computer Science **126**(2) (1994)
10. Kahn, G.: The semantics of simple language for parallel programming. In: Proc. of IFIP Congress. (1974)
11. Liu, C., Layland, J.W.: Scheduling algorithms for multiprogramming in a hard real time environment. J. of ACM **20**(1) (1973) 46–61
12. Buttazzo, G.C.: Hard real-time computing systems: predictable scheduling algorithms and applications. Kluwer Academic Publishers (1997)
13. Bini, E., et al.: A hyperbolic bound for the rate monotonic algorithm. In: Proc. of ECRTS, IEEE (2001) 59–66
14. Manolache, S.: Analysis and optimisation of real-time systems with stochastic behaviour. PhD thesis, Linkpings University (2005)
15. Kienhuis, B., et al.: An approach for quantitative analysis of application-specific dataflow architectures. In: Proc. of ASAP. (1997)
16. Florescu, O., et al.: Performance modelling and analysis using poosl for an in-car navigation system. In: Appear in Proc. of ASCI. (2006)
17. (POOSL) http://www.es.ele.tue.nl/poosl.
18. Geilen, M.G.: Formal techniques for verification of complex real-time systems. PhD thesis, Eindhoven University of Technology (2002)

Hybrid Functional and Instruction Level Power Modeling for Embedded Processors

Holger Blume[1], Daniel Becker[1], Martin Botteck[2], Jörg Brakensiek[2], and Tobias G. Noll[1]

[1] Chair for Electrical Engineering and Computer Systems
RWTH Aachen University, Schinkelstr. 2, 52062 Aachen, Germany
[2] Nokia Research Center
Meesmannstr. 103, 44807 Bochum, Germany
{blume, becker, tgn}@eecs.rwth-aachen.de,
{martin.botteck, jorg.brakensiek}@nokia.com

Abstract. In this contribution the concept of Functional-Level Power Analysis (FLPA) for power estimation of programmable processors is extended in order to model even embedded general purpose processors. The basic FLPA approach is based on the separation of the processor architecture into functional blocks like e.g. processing unit, clock network, internal memory etc. The power consumption of these blocks is described by parameterized arithmetic models. By application of a parser based automated analysis of assembler codes the input parameters of the arithmetic functions like e.g. the achieved degree of parallelism or the kind and number of memory accesses can be computed. For modeling an embedded general purpose processor (here, an ARM940T) the basic FLPA modeling concept had to be extended to a so-called hybrid functional level and instruction level model in order to achieve a good modeling accuracy. The approach is exemplarily demonstrated and evaluated applying a variety of basic digital signal processing tasks ranging from basic filters to complete audio decoders. Estimated power figures for the inspected tasks are compared to physically measured values. A resulting maximum estimation error of less than 8 % is achieved.

1 Introduction

In the course of increasing complexity of digital signal processing applications, especially in the field of mobile applications, low power techniques are of crucial importance. Therefore, it is desirable to estimate the power consumption of a system at a very early stage in the design flow. By this means, it is possible to predict whether a system will meet a certain power budget before it is physically implemented. Necessary changes in the system or the underlying architecture will then be much less time and money consuming, because no physical implementation is required to determine its power dissipation.

Like any other architecture block the power consumption of a processor depends on several factors like the switching activity of the input data, the clock frequency and of course the executed task itself. Besides these dependencies

S. Vassiliadis et al. (Eds.): SAMOS 2006, LNCS 4017, pp. 216–226, 2006.
© Springer-Verlag Berlin Heidelberg 2006

there are many more processor-specific factors like the type and rate of memory accesses, the usage of specific architecture elements, different compiler settings, pipeline stalls and cache misses but also different programming styles or algorithmic alternatives which all strongly influence the power consumption of a task that is executed on a processor.

For this reason it is desirable to consider methodologies for power estimation that cover all significant influencing factors and provide a sufficient accuracy at moderate complexity. Such a methodology is presented in this paper and verified using exemplary vehicles. The paper is organized as follows: Chapter 2 shortly discusses several existing power estimation techniques in terms of their applicability to modern processor kernels. The following chapter describes the so-called Functional-Level Power Analysis (FLPA) approach in detail. Chapter 4 describes the required basics of the ARM940T general purpose processor architecture which is exemplarily modeled here. Chapter 5 explains the exemplary modeling of this processor architecture and works out the need for a hybrid FLPA/ILPA approach. A benchmarking of the hybrid FLPA/ILPA model is performed in chapter 6. Finally, a conclusion of the paper is given in chapter 7.

2   Classical Approaches for Power Estimation

One possible straight forward power estimation approach on processors is the so-called Physical-Level Power Analysis methodology. This approach is based on the analysis of the switching activity of all circuit nodes of the processor architecture. The requirement of this methodology is the availability of a detailed description of the processor architecture on transistor level, which is rarely given for modern processors and even more severe results in an extremely high computational effort. Architectural-Level approaches like [1] reduce this computational effort by abstracted modeling typical architecture elements like registers, functional units or load/store queues. Therefore, these methodologies can be mainly found in the development of high volume products like e.g. microprocessors. Due to their extremely high computational effort they are not suited to evaluate the power consumption of complete digital signal processing tasks performed on a processor in practical use with acceptable computation times.

Another possibility for power estimation for processors is the so-called Instruction-Level Power Analysis [2]. By means of low level simulations or physical measurements the energy consumption of each instruction out of the instruction set of a processor is determined. By analysis of the assembler code of a task it is possible to estimate the specific power consumption of this program performed on a certain processor. The advantage of this approach is to cope with so-called inter-instruction effects. In general, the energy consumption of a processor instruction depends on the previously executed instructions, what can be explained by means of Fig. 1 and Fig. 2.

At a certain stage of a processors pipeline, instruction words are transferred from the program cache into a register in the processor core for further processing. Fig. 1 shows the situation that an ADD instruction word replaces a MUL

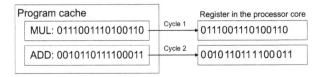

Fig. 1. Sequential execution of two *different* processor instructions

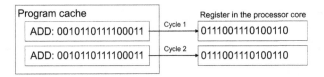

Fig. 2. Sequential execution of two *identical* processor instructions

instruction word in cycle 2. The numbers shaded by gray boxes show the bits in the register that switch their state in this case. In this example a Hamming distance (number of different bits of these two instruction words) of eight ($H_d=8$) is resulting. Of course the sequence of two identical instructions causes no switching activity ($H_d=0$), (Fig. 2). Effects like this occur in many stages of a processors pipeline and as a result of these effects the energy consumption of an instruction obviously depends on the previously executed instruction. The Instruction-Level Power Analysis methodology allows to cover such inter-instruction effects by measuring the energy consumption of groups of processor instructions, but the huge number of possible combinations makes this approach very complex. The effort will even grow, if Very-Long-Instruction-Word (VLIW) architectures shall be modeled due to their increasing word length and their ability to issue several operations in parallel.

A more attractive approach for power estimation is the Functional-Level Power Analysis (FLPA) methodology. This methodology has been introduced in [3] and was first applied in [4] to a digital signal processor. Furthermore, in [5] or [6] it could be shown that a good estimation accuracy can be achieved. Here, an extension of this methodology is presented in order to model even processor cores which feature a strong dependency of the corresponding power consumption on the performed instruction. According to this, a so-called hybrid FLPA/ILPA model is elaborated which advantageously combines the low modeling and computational effort of an FLPA model and the higher accuracy of an ILPA model.

3   Functional Level Power Analysis (FLPA)

The basic principle of the FLPA methodology is depicted in Fig. 3. In a first step the processor architecture is divided into functional blocks like fetch unit, processing unit, internal memory etc. By means of simulations or measurements it is possible to find an arithmetic model for each block that determines its power consumption in dependency of certain parameters. These parameters are for example the degree of parallelism, the access rate of the internal memory or the clock frequency. Most of these parameters can be automatically determined by a parser which analyzes the assembler file of a program code. The total power consumption is then given as the sum of the power consumption of each functional block.

The left side of Fig. 3 depicts the process of extracting parameters from a program implementing a task. In this second step it is possible after compilation to extract the task parameters from the assembler code. Further parameters can be derived from a single execution of the program (e.g. the number of required clock cycles). These parameters are the input values for the previously determined arithmetic models. Thus, an estimation of the power consumption of a given task can be computed. This approach is applicable to all kind of processor architectures without detailed knowledge of the processor architecture. Furthermore, FLPA modeling only requires moderate time effort.

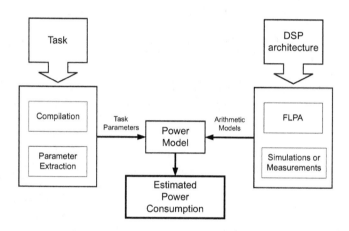

Fig. 3. The basic FLPA principle

4 Architecture of the ARM940T Processor

The 32 bit general purpose processor ARM940T is targeted for mobile applications, e.g. smart phones. Both hardware and instruction set architecture are based on the ARM v4T reference architecture (see e.g. [7]).

Like the ARM v4T, the ARM940T processor is based on a Harvard-architecture. The ARM940T consists of an ARM9TDMI Reduced Instruction Set Computer (RISC) -processor core and separate instruction and data caches (4KByte each). Additionally, the ARM940T provides interfaces for coprocessors and the special Advanced Microcontroller Bus Architecture (AMBA) interface, as well as the system configuration coprocessor (CP15), which is used to control e.g. the memory protection unit [8]. A block diagram of the ARM940T architecture is depicted in Fig. 4.

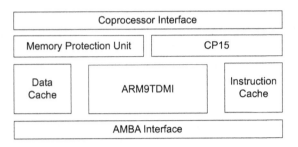

Fig. 4. Block diagram of the ARM940T architecture

The ARM9TDMI RISC-processor core consists of a five stage pipeline, which is controlled by a 32 bit instruction word. Each instruction word is derived from the standard ARM instruction set. The standard ARM instruction set itself is based on a load/store architecture. As a consequence, the source data of different instructions must be loaded separately into one or two source registers. The result is written back to a target register. Therefore, the instruction set can be divided into load/store and arithmetic instructions. However, branch and control instructions are supplied by the standard ARM instruction set. To improve the code density the ARM9TDMI processor core also features a dynamic instruction set exchange to the Thumb instruction set. These 16 bit instructions are compressed versions of a subset of the standard ARM instructions. The exchange is performed by dynamic decompression in the ARM9TDMI pipeline.

The CP15 coprocessor is accessed via the coprocessor interface using specific assembler directives. It enables and initializes the memory protection unit, which itself enables instruction and data regions in the main memory as well as in the instruction and data cache. Moreover, the memory protection unit sets and monitors access rules for the different instruction and data regions.

For the course of this modeling work, a so-called ARM Integrator Core Module featuring an ARM940T has been applied as reference platform. Internal processor states could be analyzed using a MultiICE in circuit emulation interface and an instruction set simulator (ARMulator).

5   Hybrid FLPA/ILPA Modeling of the ARM940T

In contrast to the FLPA modeling of some complex VLIW-DSP-architectures where the processor architecture had to be separated into up to seven functional blocks [5] for the modeling of the ARM940T only a separation into three different functional blocks is required. These are the ARM9TDMI processor core, the instruction cache and the data cache. According to the FLPA modeling concept each functional block is described by an arithmetic model, which itself describes the power consumption of the functional block. It can be found via simulations or measurements [5]. Hence, it is necessary to excite each block separately. This can be achieved by executing different parts of assembler code, which will be called scenarios in the following. Both, scenarios with and without cache misses have to be considered to model the ARM9TDMI processor core (execution unit) and the instruction and data caches.

In Fig. 5 the power consumption is depicted as a function of the frequency of the core clock while the ARM940T is executing exemplary SUB and MUL scenarios without cache misses (test loops featuring 1000 SUBs (single cycle op.) or 1000 MULs (three cycle op.)). The results show that there are significant differences between individual instructions and that for each instruction a nearly perfect linear frequency dependency results (avg. coefficient of determination, a measure that is used to determine how well a regression fits [9], for all operation types is $R^2_{avg} = 0.9993$, theoretical maximum for R^2 is 1). In the following, the according power consumption of a test loop with an instruction i at the frequency f without cache misses is denoted as instruction-specific offset $P_{inst\_spec}(i, f)$.

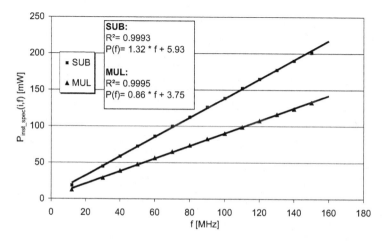

Fig. 5. Power consumption as a function of the frequency of the ARM940T core clock while executing SUB and MUL scenarios without cache misses

It has to be regarded, that the distribution of basic instructions significantly varies from application to application. Two exemplary distributions for a 4 tap 1D FIR filter and an MP3 (MPEG1/2 Layer3) decoder are depicted in Fig. 6.

Regarding the strong dependency of the power consumption on the operation which is performed and the significant difference of the distribution of instructions this shows, why it is required to extend the classical FLPA approach by an instruction dependent part. This new approach is denoted as hybrid FLPA/ILPA modeling. One key element of this approach is that for each application, respectively task, whose power consumption has to be determined, a dynamic determination of the distribution of instructions on the basis of the assembler code has to be performed.

Increasing the number of instructions in a test scenario (here more than 1024 instructions, due to the cache size and the instruction word length) leads to cache misses. As shown in Fig. 7, the power consumption is no longer a linear

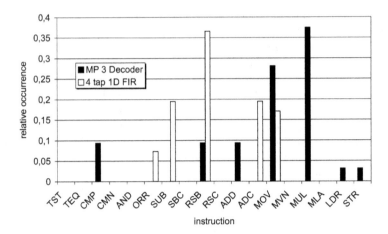

Fig. 6. The distribution of instructions within the most frequently used sections of the assembler code for a 4 tap 1D FIR filter and an MP3 decoder

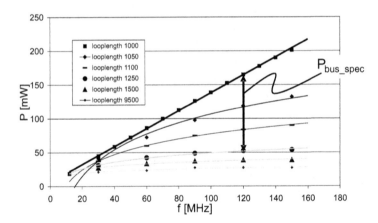

Fig. 7. Power consumption as a function of the frequency of the core clock while executing SUB test scenarios featuring cache misses

function of the core clock frequency while the processor is executing those test scenarios.

The difference at a given frequency between the instruction-specific offset and the actual power consumption of the ARM940T by executing such test scenarios with cache misses is called the bus-specific offset P_{bus_spec}. Hence, the number of cache misses would be an appropriate parameter influencing the model for P_{bus_spec}. Using the ARM instruction set simulator and cycle counter (ARMulator [10]) it is possible to derive various cycle counts (core clocks, memory bus clocks, etc.). These values are much more accurate than the number of cache misses which are also provided by the simulation environment [11]. Therefore,

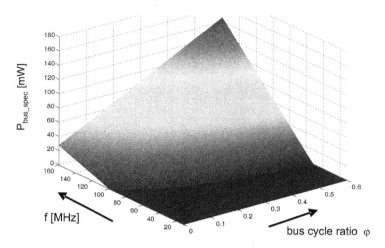

Fig. 8. Bus-specific offset of the ADD instruction

the bus-specific offset (see Fig. 8) can be modeled as a linear function of the ratio S/T. Here, the variable S denotes the number of bus cycles that are followed by data movement and the variable T denotes the total number of bus cycles. In the following, the ratio S/T is denoted as the bus cycle ratio φ. Using the relative share of instruction cache misses r_{icm} and the relative share of data cache misses r_{dcm} the bus cycle ratio is split into a bus cycle ratio caused by instruction cache misses φ_{inst} and caused by data cache misses φ_{data}, whereby the influence of the instruction and data caches apart from each other is considered. So with

$$\varphi_{inst} = r_{icm} \cdot \varphi \quad \text{and} \quad \varphi_{data} = r_{dcm} \cdot \varphi \tag{1}$$

the bus-specific offset is calculated by the equation

$$P_{bus\_spec} = P_{bus\_spec}(i, f, \varphi_{inst}) + P_{bus\_spec}(i, f, \varphi_{data}) \quad . \tag{2}$$

Besides the dependency on the bus cycle ratio φ the bus-specific offset is also a function of the frequency. It could be modeled as

$$P_{bus\_spec}(f, \varphi) = a \cdot \varphi + b \cdot f + c \cdot \varphi \cdot f + d \quad . \tag{3}$$

Negative values for $P_{bus\_spec}(f, \varphi)$ are not possible and clipped to zero. Finally, the actual power consumption of a given task can be calculated by

$$P_{act} = P_{inst\_spec} - P_{bus\_spec} \quad . \tag{4}$$

To estimate the complete power consumption of the ARM940T processor while executing a task, a profiler from the ADS1.2 framework [10] determines the share h_{label} of the execution time of the different parts of the assembler code which are produced by the compiler and which are denoted here as labels. The instruction distribution is determined for every label by a special parser

Table 1. Subset of parameters of the ARM940T hybrid FLPA/ILPA model

Instruction Class i	a	b	c	d
arithmetic (ADD, SUB, ...)	43.07	0.451	1.49	-44.6
logic (AND, CMP, ...)	48.68	0.462	1.42	-47.3
multiplication (MUL, MLA, ...)	194.82	1.436	-1.01	-133.6
load (LDR, LDRB, ...)	82.54	0.61	1.61	-60.7
...	...	...	...	...

which has been implemented as a C program, whereby the complete share h_i of every instruction class i in the label is extracted. The parser categorizes the instruction set into 6 different instruction classes. It has been analyzed by comprehensive inspections that 6 different instruction classes is an attractive compromise between estimation accuracy and modeling effort. Using less instruction classes significantly decreases the estimation accuracy while increasing the number of instruction classes only very marginally improves the estimation accuracy. Some exemplary parameters which are required to calculate $P_{bus\_spec}(f, \varphi)$ for some exemplary instruction classes are depicted in Table 1. The resulting hybrid FLPA/ILPA power model of the ARM940T can be summarized as follows

$$P_{act}(i, f, \varphi) = \sum_{label} h_{label} \cdot \left(\sum_i h_i \cdot (P_{inst\_spec}(i, f) - P_{bus\_spec}(i, f, \varphi)) \right) \quad (5)$$

6   Benchmarking of the Hybrid FLPA/ILPA Model

The estimated power consumption was compared to the measured values for a variety of tasks in order to benchmark the hybrid model (see Fig. 9). The

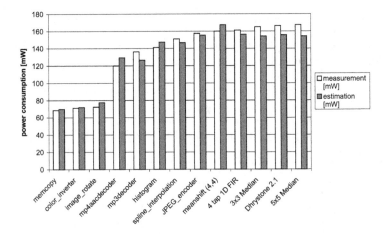

Fig. 9. FLPA estimation results and measurements for the AR940T architecture

comparison of estimated and measured values shows a maximum error of 7.8 % and an average error of 4.8 % for the power consumption.

As can be seen in Fig. 9, the variety of tasks which has been inspected on this platform features a dynamics concerning the according power consumption of more than 55 % (e.g. memcopy: 68.7 mW, 5x5 median: 165.0 mW). Thus, the estimation error is much smaller than the power consumption dynamics of the ARM940T. It is one of the key features of this modeling technique that it provides a very robust estimation accuracy while covering even a very wide range of applications with their according high power consumption dynamics. Some other available power models [12] can provide such an attractive estimation accuracy only for a limited range of applications with a corresponding small power dynamics. However, a power modeling approach can be applied only successfully if it is applicable also for a wide range of signal processing tasks.

7   Conclusion

Different approaches for power estimation for programmable processors have been analyzed. It has been shown that the concept of so-called Functional-Level Power Analysis (FLPA) has to be extended by an instruction dependent part in order to achieve high estimation accuracy even for embedded general purpose processor cores. According to this hybrid functional and instruction level modeling approach the processor architecture has been separated into several functional blocks. The power consumption of these blocks has been described in terms of parameterized arithmetic models. A parser which allows to analyze automatically the assembler codes has been implemented. This parser yields the input parameters of the arithmetic models like e.g. distribution of instructions or the type and number of memory accesses. An evaluation of this approach has been performed applying an ARM940T processor core and a variety of basic signal processing tasks. Resulting estimated power figures were compared to physically measured values. A maximum estimation error of 8 % for the absolute power consumption is achieved. This estimation error is much smaller than the dynamics of the power consumption for the inspected variety of tasks (55 %). The application of this methodology allows to evaluate efficiently different parameter settings of a programmable processor, different coding styles, compiler settings, algorithmic alternatives etc. concerning the resulting power consumption.

References

1. Brooks, D., Tiwari, V., Martonosi, M.: Wattch: A framework for architectural-level power analysis and optimizations. In: Proc. of the ISCA. (2000) 83–94
2. Tiwari, V., Malik, S., Wolfe, A.: Instruction level power analysis and optimization of software. Journal of VLSI Signal Processing **13** (1996) 1–18
3. Qu, G., Kawabe, N., Usami, K., Potkonjak, M.: Function level power estimation methodology for microprocessors. In: Proc. of the Design Automation Conference. (2000) 810–813

4. Senn, E., Julien, N., Laurent, J., Martin, E.: Power consumption estimation of a C program for data-intensive applications. In: Proc. of the PATMOS Conference. (2002) 332–341
5. Blume, H., Schneider, M., Noll, T.G.: Power estimation on a functional level for programmable processors. In: Proc. of the TI Devel. Conf., Houston. (2004)
6. von Livonius, J., Blume, H., Noll, T.G.: FLPA-based power modeling and power aware code optimization for a Trimedia DSP. In: Proc. of the ProRISC-Workshop, Veldhoven, Netherlands. (2005)
7. Furber, S.: ARM System-on-Chip Architecture. Addison-Wesley (2000)
8. ARM: ARM940T Tech. Ref. Manual, Rev2, ARM DDI 0144B. (2000)
9. Sachs, L.: Angewandte Statistik (in German). Springer Verlag (1996)
10. ARM: RealView ARMulator ISS User Guide, V. 1.4, ARM DUI 0207C. (2004)
11. ARM: App. Note 93 Benchmarking with ARMulator, ARM DAI 0093A. (2002)
12. Senn, E., Julien, N., Laurent, J., Martin, E.: Functional level power analysis: An efficient approach for modeling the power consumption of complex processors. In: Proc. of the IEEE DATE. (2004) 666–667

Low-Power, High-Performance TTA Processor for 1024-Point Fast Fourier Transform

Teemu Pitkänen, Risto Mäkinen, Jari Heikkinen, Tero Partanen, and Jarmo Takala

Tampere University of Technology, P.O. Box 553, FIN-33101 Tampere, Finland
{teemu.pitkanen, jari.heikkinen, risto.makinen, jarmo.takala}@tut.fi

Abstract. Transport Triggered Architecture (TTA) offers a cost-effective trade-off between the size and performance of ASICs and the programmability of general-purpose processors. This paper presents a study where a high performance, low power TTA processor was customized for a 1024-point complex-valued fast Fourier transform (FFT). The proposed processor consumes only 1.55 μJ of energy for a 1024-point FFT. Compared to other reported FFT implementations with reasonable performance, the proposed design shows a significant improvement in energy-efficiency.

1 Introduction

Fast Fourier transform (FFT) has an important role in many digital signal processing (DSP) systems. E.g., in orthogonal frequency division multiplexing (OFMD) communication systems, FFT and inverse FFT are needed. The OFMD technique has become a widely adopted in several wireless communication standards. When operating in wireless environment the devices are usually battery powered and, therefore, an energy-efficient FFT implementation is needed. In CMOS circuits, power dissipation is proportional to the square of the supply voltage [1]. Therefore, a good energy-efficiency can be achieved by aggressively reducing the supply voltage [2] but unfortunately this results in lower circuit performance. In this paper, a high performance, low power processor is customized for a 1024-point FFT application. Several optimization steps, such as special function units, code compression, manual code generation, are utilized to obtain the high performance with low power dissipation. The performance and power dissipation are compared against commercial and academic processors and ASIC implementations of the 1024-point FFT.

2 Related Work

Digital signal processors offer flexibility and, therefore, low development costs but at the expense of limited performance and typically high power dissipation. Field programmable gate arrays (FPGA) combine the flexibility and the speed of application-specific integrated circuit (ASIC) [3]. However, FPGAs cannot compete with the energy-efficiency of ASIC implementations. For a specific application, the energy-efficiency between these alternatives can differ by multiple orders of magnitude [4]. In general, FFT processor architectures can be divided into five categories: processors are based

S. Vassiliadis et al. (Eds.): SAMOS 2006, LNCS 4017, pp. 227–236, 2006.

on single-port memory, dual-port memory, cached memory, pipeline, or array architecture [5]. In [6], a reconfigurable FFT-processor with single memory based scalable IP core is presented, with radix-2 algorithm. In [7], variable-length FFT processor is designed using pipeline based architecture. It employs radix-2/4/8 single path delay feedback architecture. The proposed processor supports three different transform lengths by bypassing the input to the correct pipeline stage. In [5], cached memory architecture is presented, which uses small cache memories between the processor and the main memory. It offers good energy-efficiency in low voltage mode but with rather low performance. In [8], an energy-efficient architecture is presented, which exploits subtreshold circuits techniques. Again the drawback is the poor performance.

The proposed FFT implementation uses a dual-port memory and the instruction schedule is constructed such that during the execution two memory accesses are performed at each instruction cycle, i.e., the memory bandwidth is fully exploited. The energy-efficiency of the processor matches fixed-function ASICs although the proposed processor is programmable.

3   Radix-4 FFT Algorithm

There are several FFT algorithms and, in this work, a radix-4 approach has been used since it offers lower arithmetic complexity than radix-2 algorithms. The specific algorithm used here is a variation of the in-place radix-4 decimation-in-time (DIT) algorithm and the 4^n-point FFT in matrix form is defined as

$$F_{4^n} = \left[\prod_{s=n-1}^{0} [P_{4^n}^s]^T (I_{4^{n-1}} \otimes F_4) D_{4^n}^s P_{4^n}^s \right] P_{4^n}^{in} ;$$

$$P_{4^n}^s = I_{4^{(n-s-1)}} \otimes P_{4^{(s+1)},4^s} ; \quad P_{4^n}^{in} = \prod_{k=1}^{n} I_{4^{(n-k)}} \otimes P_{4^k,4} ;$$

$$P_{K,R}(m,n) = \begin{cases} 1, \text{iff } n = (mR \bmod K) + \lfloor mR/K \rfloor \\ 0, \text{otherwise} \end{cases} \tag{1}$$

where $\otimes$ denotes tensor product, P_N^{in} is an input permutation matrix of order N, F_4 is the 4-point discrete Fourier transform matrix, D_N^s is a diagonal coefficient matrix of order N, P_N^s is a permutation matrix of order N, and I_N is the identity matrix of order N. Matrix $P_{K,R}$ is a stride-by-R permutation marix [9] of order K such that the elements of the matrix. In addition, mod denotes the modulus operation and $\lfloor \cdot \rfloor$ is the floor function. The matrix D_N^s contains N complex-valued twiddle factors, W_N^k, as follows

$$D_N^s = \bigoplus_{k=0}^{N/4-1} \text{diag} \left\{ W_{4^{s+1}}^{i(k \bmod 4^s)} \right\} , \ i = 0,1,\ldots,3 ; \ W_N^k = e^{-j2\pi k/N} \tag{2}$$

where j denotes the imaginary unit and $\oplus$ denotes matrix direct sum. Finally, the matrix F_4 is given as

$$F_4 = \begin{pmatrix} 1 & 1 & 1 & 1 \\ 1 & -j & -1 & j \\ 1 & -1 & 1 & -1 \\ 1 & j & -1 & -j \end{pmatrix} . \tag{3}$$

4 Transport Triggered Architecture

Transport triggered architecture (TTA) is a class of statically programmed instruction-level parallelism (ILP) architectures that reminds very long instruction word (VLIW) architecture. In the TTA programming model, the program specifies only the data transports (moves) to be performed by the interconnection network [10] and operations occur as "side-effect" of data transports. Operands to a function unit are input through ports and one of the ports is dedicated as a trigger. Whenever data is moved to the trigger port, the operation execution is initiated.

When the input ports are registered, the operands for the operation can be stored into the registers in earlier instruction cycles and a transport to the trigger port starts the operation with the operands stored into the registers. Thus the operands can be shared between different operations of a function unit, which reduces the data traffic in the interconnection and the need for temporary storage in register file or data memory.

A TTA processor consists of a set of function units and register files containing general-purpose registers. These structures are connected to an interconnection network, which connects the input and output ports of the resources. The architecture can be tailored by adding or removing resources. Moreover, special function units with user-defined functionality can be easily included.

5 TTA Processor for Radix-4 FFT

An effective means to reduce power consumption without reducing the performance is to exploit special function units for the operations of the algorithm. These units reduce the instruction overhead, thus they reduce the power consumption due to instruction fetch. Here four custom-designed units tailored for FFT application were used.

The interconnection network consumes a considerable amount of power and, therefore, all the connections from ports of function units and register files to the buses, which are not really needed, should be removed. By removing a connection, the capacitive load is reduced, which reduces also the power consumption. Clock gating technique can be used to reduce the power consumption of non active function units. Significant savings can be expected on units with low utilization.

TTA processors remind VLIW architectures in a sense that they use long instruction words, which implies high power consumption on instruction fetch. This overhead can be significantly reduced by exploiting program code compression.

5.1 Arithmetic Units

Since the FFT is inherently an complex-valued algorithm, the architecture should have means to represent complex data. The developed processor uses 32-bit words and the complex data type is represented such that the 16 most significant bits are reserved for the real part and the 16 least significant bits for the imaginary part. Real and imaginary parts use fractional representation, i.e., one bit for sign and 15 bits for fraction. The arithmetic operations in the algorithm in (1) can be isolated into 4-input, 4-output blocks described as radix-4 DIT butterfly operation defined by the following:

$$(y_0, y_1, y_2, y_3)^T = F_4 (1, W_1, W_2, W_3)^T (x_0, x_1, x_2, x_3)^T \qquad (4)$$

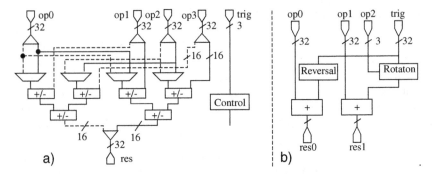

Fig. 1. a) Block diagram of complex adder. Solid lines represent real parts and dotted lines imaginary parts. ports op1-3 are operand ports and trigger port defines the operation. b) Block diagram of data address generator. op0: Base address of input buffer. op1: Base address of output buffer. op2: Butterfly column index. trig: Element index, trigger port. res0: Resulting address after field reversal. res1: Resulting address after index rotation.

where x_i denotes an input operand, W_i is a twiddle factor, and y_i is an output operand. One of the special function units in our design is complex multiplier, CMUL, which is a standard unit containing four 16-bit real multipliers and two 16-bit real adders. When the operand to the CMUL unit is a real one, i.e., multiplication by one, the other operand is directly bypassed to the result register. The CMUL unit is pipelined and the latency is three cycles. The butterfly operation contains complex additions defined by (3). In this work, we have defined a four-input, one-output special function unit, CADD, which supports four different summations according to each row in F_4. The motivation is that, in a TTA, the instruction defines data transports, thus by minimizing the transports, the number of instructions can be minimized. Each of the four results defined by F_4 are dependent on the same four operands, thus once the four operands have been moved into the input registers of the function unit, four results can be computed simply by performing a transport to trigger register, which defines the actual function out of the four possible complex summations. The block diagram of the CADD unit is illustrated in Fig. 1 a).

5.2   Address Generation

The N-point FFT algorithm in (1) contains two type of data permutations: input permutation of length N and variable length permutations between the butterfly columns. In-place computations require manipulation of indices into data buffer. Such manipulations are low-power if performed in bit-level. If the 4^n input operands are stored into a buffer in-order, the read index to the buffer, i.e., operand for the butterfly operation, can be obtained by bit field reversal. This reminds the bit reversal addressing in radix-2 algorithms but, instead of reversing single bits, here 2-bit fields are reversed [11], i.e., a $2n$-bit read index $r = (r_{2n-1}r_{(2n-2)}\ldots r_0)$ is formed from an element index (a linear counter) $a = (a_{2n-1}a_{2n-2}\ldots a_0)$ as

$$r_{2k} = a_{2n-2k-2} \; ; \; r_{2k+1} = a_{2n-2k-1} \; , \; 0 \leq k < n \tag{5}$$

This operation is implemented simply with wiring. In a similar fashion, the permutations between the butterfly columns can be realized in bit-level simply by rotation of two bits to the right. However, the length of the bit field to be rotated is dependent on the butterfly column index, s, in (1). The $2n$-bit read index $p = (p_{2n-1}p_{(2n-2)}\cdots p_0)$ is formed from the element index a as [11]

$$
\begin{cases}
p_{2k} = a_{(2k+2s)\ \mathrm{mod}\ 2(s+1)}, 0 \leq k \leq s \\
p_{2k+1} = a_{(2k+1+2s)\ \mathrm{mod}\ 2(s+1)}, 0 \leq k \leq s \\
p_{2k} = a_{2k}, s < k < n \\
p_{2k+1} = a_{2k+1}, s < k < n
\end{cases}
\tag{6}
$$

Such an operation can be easily implemented with the aid of multiplexers. When the generated index is added to the base address of the memory buffer, the final address to the memory is obtained. The block diagram of the developed AG unit is shown in Fig 1 b). The input ports of the AG units are registered, thus the base addresses of input and output buffers need to be store only once into operand ports op0 and op1, respectively. The butterfly column index is stored into operand port op2 and the address computation is initiated by moving an index to trigger port. Two results are produced: output port res0 contains the address according to input permutation and port res1 according to bit field rotation.

5.3 Coefficient Generation

A coefficient generator (COGEN) unit was developed for generating the twiddle factors, which reduces power consumption compared to the standard method of storing the coefficients as tables into data memory. In an radix-4 FFT, there are $Nlog_4(N)$ twiddle factors as defined by (2) but there is redundancy. It has been be shown that all the twiddle factors can be generated from $N/8 + 1$ coefficients [12] with the aid of simple manipulation of the real and the imaginary parts of the coefficients. The COGEN unit is based on a table where the $N/8 + 1$ are stored. This table is implemented as hard wired logic for reducing the power consumption. The unit contains an internal address generator, which creates the index to the coefficient table based on two input operands: butterfly column index ($s = 0, 1, \ldots, n-1$) and element index ($a = 0, 1, \ldots, 4^n - 1$). The obtained index is used to access the table and the real and imaginary parts of the fetched complex number are modified by six different combinations of exchange, add, or subtract operations depending on the state of input operands. The resulting complex number is placed in the output register as the final twiddle factor.

5.4 General Organization

The general organization of the proposed TTA processor tailored for FFT (FFTTA) processor is presented in Fig. 2. The processor is composed of eight separate function units and a total of 11 register files containing 23 general-purpose registers. The function units and register files are connected by an interconnection network (IC) consisting of 18 buses and 61 sockets. In addition, the FFTTA processor contains a control unit, instruction memory, and dual-ported data memory. The size of the data memory is 2048 words of 32 bits implying that 32-bit data buses are used. There is one 1-bit bus, which is used for transporting the Boolean values.

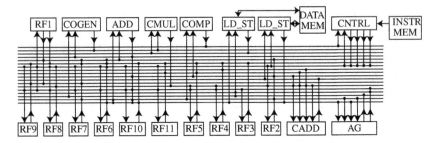

Fig. 2. Architecture of the proposed FFTTA processor. CADD: Complex adder. CMUL: Complex multiplier. AG: Data address generator. COGEN: Coefficient generator. ADD: Real adder. LD_ST: Load-store unit. COMP: Comparator unit. CNTRL: Control unit. RFx: Register files, containing total of 23 general purpose registers.

5.5   Instruction Schedule

In principle, an 4^n-point radix-4 FFT algorithm in (1) contains two nested loops: an inner loop where the butterfly operation is computed $4^{(n-1)}$ times and an outer loop where the inner loop is iterated n times. Each butterfly operation requires four operands and produces four results. Therefore, in a 1024-point FFT, a total of 10240 memory accesses are needed. If a single-port data memory is used, the lower bound for the number of instruction cycles for a 1024-FFT is 10240. If a dual-port memory is used, the lower bound is 5120 cycles.

In order to maximize the performance, the inner loop kernel needs to be carefully optimized. Since the butterfly operations are independent, software pipelining can be applied. In our implementation, the butterfly operations are implemented in a pipelined fashion and several butterflies at different phases of computation are performed in parallel. The developed 1024-point FFT code follows the principal code in Fig. 3.

In initialization, pointers and loop counters, i.e., butterfly and element indices, are set up. The input data is stored in order into data memory buffer. Another 1024-word buffer is reserved for intermediate storage and the final result. There is no separate code performing the input permutation but the address generation unit is used to access the input buffer in correct order with an address obtained from port res0 of AG in Fig.1b). The results of the first butterfly column are stored into the intermediate buffer with an address obtained from port res1 of AG. All the accesses to the intermediate buffer are done by using addresses from port res1 of AG.

In the prologue, the butterfly iterations are started one after each other and, in the actual inner loop kernel, four iterations of butterfly kernels are performed in parallel in pipelined fashion. The loop kernel evaluates also the loop counter. In the epilogue, the last butterfly iterations are completed and the loop counter of the outer loop is evaluated. The kernel contains the functionality of butterfly operations, which requires four triggers for memory reads and memory writes and corresponding address computations, four triggers for complex multiplier and four triggers for CADD unit. Since the branch latency is three cycles, the kernel can actually be implemented with four instructions. However, this approach results in a need for moving variables from an register to another. The reason is that parallel butterfly iterations need more than four intermediate

```
main() {
  initialization(); /* 9 instr. */
  for(stage=0; stage<5; stage++) {
    prologue(); /* 16 instr. */
    for(k=0; k<84; k++)
      kernel(); /* 12 instr. */
    epilogue; /* 21 instr. */
  }
}
```

Fig. 3. Pseudocode illustrating structure and control flow of program code

results, which need to be stored into register files. Since there is no mechanism to dynamically index the register accesses, the only way is to use the register files as first-in-first-out buffers. Such register copies introduce additional power consumption, in particular, since the moves require additional buses and increase the register activity.

The final implementation of the kernel was 12 instructions and by that way, it was possible to keep the intermediate results in a dedicated register without need to copy the values. This resulted significant savings in power consumption at the expense of lengthening the program code by eight instructions. The parallel code for 1024-point FFT contains a total of 58 instructions and the instruction length was 162 bits. The program spends 96% of the execution time in the kernel. The execution of 1024-point FFT takes 5234 instruction cycles, thus the overhead to the theoretical lower bound with dual-port data memory (5120 cycles) is only 2% (114 cycles). This overhead is negligible compared to overheads seen in typical software implementations.

5.6   Code Compression

TTA suffers from poor code density, which is mostly due to minimal instruction encoding that is used to simplify decoding. Minimal instruction encoding leads to long instruction words. The long instruction word consists of dedicated fields, denoted as move slots. Each move slot specifies a data transport on a bus. Each move slot consists of three fields: guard, destination ID, and source ID. The guard provides means for conditional execution. The destination ID specifies the address of a socket that is reading data from a bus. The source ID specifies the address of a socket that is writing data on a bus. In addition to move slots, instruction words may contain dedicated long immediate fields to define large constant values, e.g., for jump addresses.

The poor code density can be improved by compression. Compression also results in reduced power consumption as fewer bits need to be fetched from the program memory. Dictionary-based compression is one of the simplest compression approaches to improve the code density [13]. Dictionary-based program compression stores all unique bit patterns into a dictionary and replaces them in the program code with code words to the dictionary. Given a program with N unique instructions, the length of the code word is $\lceil log_2 |N| \rceil$ bits. During execution, the code word, fetched from the program memory is used to obtain the original instruction from the dictionary for decoding.

In order to reduce the power consumption of the FFTTA processor and improve the code density, dictionary-based program compression was applied. All the unique instructions of the program code were stored into a dictionary and replaced with indices pointing to the dictionary. This resulted in decrease in the width of the program memory from 162 bits to 6 bits. The decompression, i.e., the dictionary access was supplemented to the control unit without additional pipeline stage. The actual dictionary(8586 bits) was implemented using standard cells.

6   Performance Analysis

In order to analyse the characteristics of the FFTTA processor, the structures of the previous special function units were described manually in VHDL. The structural description of the FFTTA core was obtained with the aid of the hardware subsystem of the MOVE Framework [14], which generated the VHDL description.

Then the FFTTA was synthesized to a 130nm CMOS standard cell ASIC technology with Synopsys Design Compiler. This was followed by a gate level simulation at 250 MHz. Synopsys Power Compiler was used for the power analysis. The obtained results are listed in Table 1. It should be noted that the instruction and data memories take 40% of the total power consumption of 74mW with 1.5V supply voltage. If the supply voltage is reduced to 1.1V, the total power consumption will drop down to about 40 mW. However, this will reduce the maximum clock frequency.

Table 1. Characteristics of 1024-point FFT on FFTTA processor on 130 nm ASIC technology with 1.5V supply voltage

Clock Cycles	**5234**	Execution Time	**20.94 μs**	Power	**74 mW**
Clock Frequency	**250 MHz**	Area	**140 kgates**	Energy	**1.55 μJ**

Table 2 presents how many 1024-point FFT transforms can be performed with energy of 1 mJ. The results are presented for ten different implementations of the 1024-point FFT. For some implementations there are different operating voltage or clock frequency points listed. Spiffee processor [5] employs a high performance architecture and low supply voltages and it's dedicated for the FFT. The StrongArm SA-1100 processor [15] employs custom circuits, clock gating, and reduced supply voltage. The Stratix [16] is an FPGA solution with dedicated embedded FFT logic usign Altera Megacore function. The TI C6416 [17] is a digital signal processor and the Imagine [18] is a media processor. They were both created using pseudo-custom data path tiling. In addition, the TI C6416 employs pass-gate multiplexer circuits. The 1024-point FFT with radix-4 algorithm can be computed in 6002 cycles in TI C6416 when using 32-bit complex words (16 bits for real and imaginary parts) [19]. However, in-place computations cannot be used and the processor has eight memory ports while the FFTTA uses only two. The Intel Pentium-4 [20] is a standard general-purpose microprocessor. Rest of the processors are dedicated for the FFT. The custom scalable IP core Zhao [6], employs single memory architecture with clock gating. The custom variable-length Lin [7] FFT-processor employs radix-2/4/8 single-path delay algorithm. MIT FFT uses subreshold circuit techniques [8].

Table 2. The number of 1024-point FFTs performed with a unit of energy

Design	Tech. [nm]	Oper. voltage [V]	Clock freq. [MHz]	Exec. time [μs]	FFT/mJ	Design	Tech. [nm]	Oper. voltage [V]	Clock Freq. [MHz]	Exec. time [μs]	FFT/mJ
FFTTA	130	1.5	250	20.9	645		130	1.2	720	8.34	100
	600	1.1	16	330	319	TI C6416	130	1.2	600	10.0	167
Spiffee	600	2.5	128	41	67		130	1.2	300	21.7	250
	600	3.3	173	40	39	MIT FFT	180	0.35	0.01	250000	6452
SA-110	350	2	74	425.7	60		180	0.9	6	430.6	1428
	130	1.3	275	4.7	241	Lin	350	3.3	45.45	22.5	93
Stratix	130	1.3	133	9.7	173		350	2.3	17.86	57	133
	130	1.3	100	12.9	149	Zhao	180	-	20	281.6	43
Imagine	150	1.5	232	16.0	16	Intel P4	130	1.2	3000	23.9	0.8

Compared to other FFT designs the proposed FFTTA processor shows significant energy-efficiency. Only the MIT FFT outperforms the FFTTA. However, due to its long execution time, the MIT FFT is not usable in high performance designs. The performance of the FFTTA processor is still quite feasible although it does not provide the best performance. However, the performance can be scaled, i.e., the execution time can be halved by doubling the resources and memory ports. The memory size remains constant and it can be estimated that the energy-efficiency remains the same in terms of FFTs per energy unit.

7   Conclusions

In this paper, a low-power application-specific processor for FFT computation has been described. The resources of the processor have been tailored according to the needs of the application consisting of eight function units and 11 register files. Several methods for reducing the power consumption of the processor were utilized: clock gating, special function units, and code compression. The processor was synthesized on a 130 nm ASIC technology and power analysis showed that the proposed processor has both high energy-efficiency and high performance.

The described processor has limited programmability but the purpose of this experiment was to prove the feasibility and potential of the proposed approach. However, the programmability can be improved by introducing additional function units and loosening the code compression. In addition, different transform sizes can be supported by modifying the address generators and twiddle factor unit. This modifications are mainly addition of multiplexers, thuse significant increase in power consumption is not expected. In addition, the performance of the processor can be improved by adding computational resources implying need for higher data memory bandwidth

Acknowledgement

This work has been supported by the Academy of Finland under project 205743 and the National Technology Agency of Finland under research funding decision 40153/05.

References

1. Weste, N., Eshraghian, K.: Principles of CMOS VLSI Design: A Systems Perspective. Addison-Wesley, Reading, MA (1985)
2. Chandrakasan, A., Sheng, S., Brodersen, R.: Low-power CMOS digital design. IEEE Journal of Solid State Circuits **27** (1992) 473–483
3. Reeves, K., Sienski, K., Field, C.: Reconfigurable hardware accelerator for embedded DSP. In Schewel, J., Athanas, P.M., Bove, V.M., Watson, J., eds.: Proc. SPIE High-Speed Comp. Dig. Sig. Proc. Filtering Using Reconf. Logic. Volume 2914., Boston, MA (1996) 332–340
4. Chang, A., Dally, W.: Explaining the gap between ASIC and custom power: A custom perspective. In: Proc. IEEE DAC, Anaheim, CA (2005) 281–284
5. Baas, B.M.: A low-power, high-performance, 1024-point FFT processor. IEEE Solid State Circuits **43** (1999) 380–387
6. Zhao, Y., Erdogan, A., Arslan, T.: A low-power and domain-specific reconfigurable fft fabric for system-on-chip applications. In: Proc. 19th IEEE Parallel and Distrubuted Prosessing Symp. Reconf. Logic, Denver, CO (2005)
7. Lin, Y.T., Tsai, P.Y., Chiueh, T.D.: Low-power variable-length fast fourier transform processor. Proc. IEE Computers and Digital Techniques **152** (2005) 499–506
8. Wang, A., Chandrakasan, A.: A 180-mV subthreshold FFT processor using a minimum energy design methodology. IEEE J. Solid State Circuits **40** (2005) 310–319
9. Granata, J., Conner, M., Tolimieri, R.: Recursive fast algorithms and the role of the tensor product. IEEE Trans. Signal Processing **40** (1992) 2921–2930
10. Corporaal, H.: Microprocessor Architectures: From VLIW to TTA. John Wiley & Sons, Chichester, UK (1997)
11. Mäkinen, R.: Fast Fourier transform on transport triggered architectures. Master's thesis, Tampere Univ. Tech., Tampere, Finland (2005)
12. Wanhammar, L.: DSP Integrated Circuits. Academic Press, San Diego, CA (1999)
13. Lefurgy, C., Mudge, T.: Code compression for DSP. Technical Report CSE-TR-380-98, EECS Department, University of Michigan (1998)
14. Corporaal, H., Arnold, M.: Using transport triggered architectures for embedded processor design. Integrated Computer-Aided Eng. **5** (1998) 19–38
15. Intel: StrongARM SA-110 Microprocessor for Portable Applications Brief Datasheet. (1999)
16. Lim, S., Crosland, A.: Implementing FFT in an FPGA co-processor. In: The International Embedded Solutions Event (GPSx), Santa Clara, CA (2004) 230–233
17. Agarwala, S., Anderson, T., Hill, A., Ales, M., Damodaran, R., Wiley, P., Mullinnix, S., Leach, J., Lell, A., Gill, M., Rajagopal, A., Chachad, A., Agarwala, M., Apostol, J., Krishnan, M., Duc-Bui, Quang-An, Nagaraj, N., Wolf, T., Elappuparackal, T.: A 600 MHz VLIW DSP. IEEE J. Solid State Circuits **37** (2002) 1532–1544
18. Rixner, S., Dally, W., Kapasi, U., Khailany, B., Lopez-Lagunas, A., Mattson, P., Owens, J.: A bandwidth-efficient architecture for media processing. In: Proc. Annual ACM/IEEE Int. Symp. Microarchitecture, Dallas, TX (1998) 3–13
19. Texas Instruments, Inc. Dallas, TX: TMS320C64x DSP Library Programmer's Reference. (2003)
20. Deleganes, M., Douglas, J., Kommandur, B., Patyra, M.: Designing a 3 GHz, 130 nm, Intel® Pentium ®4 processor. In: Digest of Technical Papers Symp. VLSI Circuits, Honolulu, HI (2002) 230–233

Software Pipelining Support for Transport Triggered Architecture Processors

Perttu Salmela[1], Pekka Jääskeläinen[1], Tuomas Järvinen[2], and Jarmo Takala[1]

[1] Tampere University of Technology, P.O.Box 553, FIN-33101, Tampere, Finland
{perttu.salmela, pekka.jaaskelainen, jarmo.takala}@tut.fi
[2] Nokia Technology Platforms, P.O.Box 88, FIN-33721 Tampere, Finland
tuomas.jarvinen@nokia.com

Abstract. Many telecommunication applications, especially baseband processing, and digital signal processing (DSP) applications call for high-performance
implementations due to the complexity of algorithms and high throughput requirements. In general, the required performance is obtained with the aid of parallel
computational resources. In these application domains, software implementations
are often preferred over fixed-function ASICs due to the flexibility and ease of
development. Application-specific instruction-set processor (ASIP) architectures
can be used to exploit efficiently the inherent parallelism of the algorithms but still
maintaining the flexibility. Use of high-level languages to program processor architectures with parallel resources can lead to inefficient resource utilization and,
on the other hand, parallel assembly programming is error prone and tedious.

In this paper, the inherent problems of parallel programming and software
pipelining are mitigated with parallel language syntax and automatic generation
of software pipelined code for the iteration kernels. With the aid of the developed
tool support, the underlying performance of a processor architecture with parallel
resources can be exploited and full utilization of the main processing resources is
obtained for pipelined loop kernels. The given examples show that efficiency can
be obtained without reducing the performance.

1 Introduction

Rapid development and continually updated standards in all areas of telecommunications call for implementations with high-throughput, flexibility, configurability, and
even programmability. In [1] it was shown that the digital baseband functions of 3G
receiver will require approximately a total computational performance of 10 GIPS. For
such performance, processors relying on sequential execution of program code would
require unpractical clock frequencies. On the other hand, pure hardware implementation
does not possess the flexibility in form of programmability.

For the sake of increased design and manufacturing costs, using highly parallel
application-specific instruction-set processors (ASIP) is suggested in [2]. With the aid
of sufficient parallelism the clock frequencies and power consumption can remain at
practical level, while maintaining acceptable throughput. In addition, the programmability of the processor allows rapid development and alleviates updates. However,
mapping algorithms onto a parallel processor architecture is a challenging task. For
example, if a C compiler does not have the information that the memory accesses are

S. Vassiliadis et al. (Eds.): SAMOS 2006, LNCS 4017, pp. 237–247, 2006.

independent, they must be executed in the order defined in the source file and no parallelism can be exploited. Furthermore, if the target architecture contains special function units with operations, which are not part of the native operations of the used high-level language, the compiler has a challenging task on mapping operations onto such units. Manual assembly programming can be used to explicitly specify such parallel operations but this would be a tedious and error prone process due to the included details of the processor architecture and literally long instruction words of parallel processors.

One example of an ASIP with parallel resources is transport triggered architecture (TTA) [3]. In TTA, parallel computing resources can be tailored according to the requirements of the given application. TTA processors can be programmed with C language [4] but the scheduling of user defined special operations onto parallel function units especially in loops with short kernels is challenging. Quite often the user has already information of the efficient schedule for the special operations. For example, in [5] and [6], scalable FIR filtering and Viterbi decoding, respectively, were programmed in detailed assembly and they obtained full utilization of main computing resources in the pipelined loop kernel.

This paper represents a software development tool targeted in the area between detailed low-level assembly language and high-level C language. The applications are described with a parallel language, which excludes the lowest level details on how the parallel resources are used. The developed compiler tool will partially solve the allocation of resources. The language does not prohibit use of full parallelism available on the processor. In addition, the language includes high-level structures, which make the programming more intuitive. Especially, the tool supports automatic generation of software pipelined code for the loops. This is essential since the fully pipelined loops result in large sections of long instruction words, which calls for automatic code generation to avoid extensive manual programming work. The proposed method is demonstrated on parallel processors based on transport triggered architectures and the given experiments show that the high performance and full parallelism of the TTA can be exploited with minor efforts and typical loop based signal processing kernels can be developed rapidly.

2   Transport Triggered Architecture

A transport triggered architecture is an ASIP template [3] where parallel computing resources can be tailored according to the requirements of the given application. Basically, a TTA processor consists of functional resources, which are connected with an interconnection network and the network is controlled by a control unit. In Fig. 1, an example of TTA processor is shown. This processor contains basic units for simple arithmetic, units for accessing the memory, register files, and four special function units for multiply and accumulate (MAC). The processor is modular since unnecessary function units can be excluded and necessary special function units can be easily included. The interconnection network consists of buses, which are connected to the function units via sockets. Since the processor can be tailored, the interconnection network does not have to contain all the connections. Therefore, only the required connections are used and the unnecessary connections can be removed. This reduces the bus load and, therefore, reduces the power consumption and allows higher clock frequency.

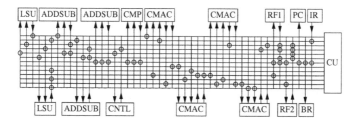

Fig. 1. Example of TTA processor tailored for FIR filtering. A circle denotes a connection between one of buses of the interconnection network and port of a function unit. LSU: Load and store unit. ADDSUB: Addition and subtraction unit. CMP: Comparison unit. CNTL: Processor status word. CMAC: MAC unit. RFx: Register file. PC: Program counter. IR: Immediate register. BR: Boolean register. CU: Control unit.

The syntax of the TTA processor assembly language consists of only one operation. The move operation, →, moves data from a source in left-hand side to a destination in the right-hand side. With non-terminals written in italics, the syntax of the move is

> *src* → *dst*
> *src* ⇐ number | register | *function_unit*
> *dst* ⇐ jump | register | *function_unit*
> *function_unit* ⇐ identifier . operation_port

In addition, the moves are followed by more detailed information in the form of four fields separated by slashes, i.e., [bus / immediate_unit / source_port / destination_port]. Furthermore, each move can be preceded with an optional Boolean guard, which allows conditional execution. The syntax allows also inversion of the guard. A list of parallel moves, separated by commas, constitute one instruction. Consecutive, sequentially issued instructions are separated with semicolons.

An example of a move, which transports value of register r2 to the operand port of an adder in function unit fu2 on bus zero and whose execution depends on value of Boolean b0, would be

> b0:r2 → fu2.add_o [m0 / – / ri_o1 / fu2_o].

Each move corresponds to a bus. If a bus is not used for any move, the no-operation (NOP) is denoted by three dots.

3   Software Pipelining

Software pipelining is a technique for executing the loops in such a way that several loop iterations are issued in parallel. An extensive study and comparison of software pipelining techniques is presented in [7]. Software pipelining is vital also for very long instruction word processors for the efficient utilization of available parallelism [8]. Since the software pipelining strives to issue several iterations of loop in parallel, in one extreme all the iterations of the loop are issued at the same time. In the other extreme, the software pipelining can not be used and the iterations are executed sequentially. An example of software pipelining principle is presented in Fig. 2, which shows how

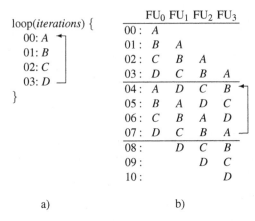

a)   b)

Fig. 2. Loop Example consisting of operations A, B, C, and D: (a) code excerpt and (b) pipelined iterations mapped to function units $FU_{0...3}$. Block of instructions at 04...07 is repeated according to the required number of iterations.

a total of four instances of loop iterations are executed in parallel. Depending on the total number of required iterations, four parallel instances are iterated by conditionally branching from instructions at 07 back to instructions at 04.

In general case, results of the computations of the loop body are used as operands in the next iteration. In this case, the delay between demand of operands in the next iteration and their completion in the previous iteration determines how soon the next iteration can be issued. For example, if the first operation of the loop accesses the memory and the memory pointer is updated, the update must take place also during the same single clock cycle to allow issuing next iteration in the next clock cycle. This practice, where new iterations are issued on consecutive clock cycles, is shown in Fig. 2(b). The example also shows that during any of the instructions 03...07, all the four operations A, B, C, and D are executed in parallel and, therefore, they must be mapped to four separate function units. On the contrary, in sequential loop in Fig. 2(a) the operations A, B, C, and D can share the same function unit. If a new iteration is issued on each instruction cycle, the maximum parallelism equals to the length of the sequential loop kernel.

4   Parallel Language with Software Pipelining

The developed parallel language is improved in two frontiers. First, the assembly language syntax is both simplified and extended to a intuitive form of the proposed language. Second, the language is enhanced with a loop construct, which pipelines the loop iterations.

4.1   Language Extensions

The program is divided into declarations and labeled program blocks consisting of statements. With non-terminals written in italics and excluding minor details the core syntax of the improved assembly language is given in Fig. 3. The syntax replaces the functionality of moves ($\rightarrow$) with assignment and operand passing, which are compiled to original low-level moves. Instead of list of moves, the program resembles a list of conventional function calls. Since the function units can produce several results, the syntax allows the left-hand side with several variables to be written in a similar syntax as in Matlab, e.g., radix-2 add-compare-select function returns two metrics and two bits as follows

$$[a, b, sela, selb] = \text{fu}1.\text{acs}(c, d, e, f); .$$

The parallel assignments or functions are separated with commas and consecutive operations with semicolons. If the right-hand side of the assignment is a function and the left-hand side is a register variable, operands will be passed to the function unit during the current clock cycle and the assignment to the left-hand side will be issued after the latency of the function unit. On the contrary, immediately available right-hand side is assigned on the current clock cycle.

The variables are divided into three classes: registers, Booleans, and bypass variables. Register and Boolean variables are automatically mapped to registers, register files, and Boolean registers of the processor. It is assumed, that the processor contains enough registers. The introduction of bypass variables is a novel contribution in the proposed syntax. The bypass variables behave like dynamically defined macros. When a bypass variable is used in the left-hand side of a function, its value will be set to a string, which defines the outcome port of the function unit. Later, when the bypass

program ⟸ *declaration-list block-list*
declaration ⟸ register variables | bypass variables | bool variables
block ⟸ *stmnts-block* | *loop-block*
stmnts-block ⟸ label: { *statement-list* }
loop-block ⟸ label: loop(*immediate*) { *statement-list* }
statement ⟸ *assignment* | *function* | *no-operation*
assignment ⟸ *lhs = rhs*
lhs ⟸ *single-lhs* | [*list-of-single-lhs*]
single-lhs ⟸ jump | variable
rhs ⟸ *number* | variable | *function* | *conditional*
function ⟸ identifier . operation(*operand-list*)
conditional ⟸ if(variable) *number* | variable | *function*
operand ⟸ number | variable
number ⟸ *immediate* | *long-immediate* | label
immediate ⟸ decimal | hexadecimal | octal | binary
long-immediate ⟸ '*immediate*'
no-operation ⟸ ...

Fig. 3. Syntax of the proposed parallel language

variable is used on the right-hand side or as an operand, it will be replaced with the saved presentation of result port. In the next example, value of $10 + a$ is stored in address 0xFF with the aid of bypass variable b:

$$b = \text{fu}1.\text{add}(10, a);$$
$$\text{fu}2.\text{st}(0\text{xFF}, b);$$

will be compiled to

$$10 \rightarrow \text{fu}1.\text{add\_o}, \text{r}1 \rightarrow \text{fu}1.\text{add\_t};$$
$$255 \rightarrow \text{fu}2.\text{st\_o}, \text{fu}1.\text{add\_r} \rightarrow \text{fu}2.\text{st\_t}; .$$

In the resulting assembly code, variable a resides in register r1 and details about accessed ports and buses are excluded. The example shows that, in reality, the variable b did not use any resources. Its value was obtained directly from the unit, which generated the value. The purpose of the bypass variables is to easily pass short life-time results of function units for later use. Their usage avoids extensive use of registers and reduces the size of the register files. Since usage of bypass variables does not increase the complexity of the processor, there is no practical limit on the number of bypass variables. For these reasons, the bypass variables encourage imperative programming style without reserving real registers.

The guarded moves are generated with conditional structures like, e.g.,

$$a = if(b) \; ful.add(a, 10);$$

where b is a Boolean variable. In a similar way as in the assembly language, the branching occurs when program counter is accessed via assignment to the *jump* keyword. Longer conditional branches can be created with conditional jumps to different code blocks, which is a typical compilation strategy for processors lacking conditional execution of single operation. However, jumping can be disadvantageous due to the jump latency.

4.2   Resource Allocation

The user does not have to provide detailed information about ports, units, and buses since the missing information is resolved automatically. The port names of the function units are defined systematically and, therefore, they can be derived easily. The function name consisting of the name of the function unit, dot, and operation is split and the port names are formed by concatenation of unit name, underscore, and a port letter, which indicate whether the port is a trigger, operand, or result port. For example, ful.add() will result in ports ful_r, ful_o, and ful_t.

When register variables are mapped to registers, two register files are assumed. The variables are mapped in the same order as they are defined. Thus, every other variable will get even register number and is mapped to the first register file and every second variable is mapped to odd registers in the second register file. The register files are also accessed via read or write ports. If there are several accesses to the same register file the next free read or write port is used. In other words, the processor must have as many ports for register file as the maximum number of parallel accesses in the program. However, in practice, extensive use of registers can be avoided by applying bypass variables when possible.

The mapping of compiled moves to the buses consists of several steps. First, the maximum parallelism M, i.e., the maximum number of parallel moves is obtained from the program. The M will be also the number of buses. Second, source-destination pairs are formed from every move of the program and their frequencies are counted, i.e., a distribution of source-destination pairs is generated. Third, M most frequent source-destination pairs, i.e., moves, are mapped to the M buses in consecutive order. Next, when deciding the bus for moves at current cycle, all the moves which are in the set of the most frequent M moves, are assigned to the previously determined buses. Thereafter, unassigned moves are mapped to the remaining free buses in consecutive order. The main purpose of this practice is to let the most frequent moves use always the same path along the interconnection network. Thus, they will never increase the complexity of the interconnection network by requiring extra connections.

4.3 Pipelining

All the program blocks preceded with the *loop* keyword and iteration count are pipelined. If there is a need for non-pipelined loops, they can be implemented by regular conditional jumps back to the beginning of loop body. In principle, the loops are pipelined in a similar manner as in Fig. 2. The pipelining algorithm basically copies the code of the loop body to be issued on consecutive clock cycles. An example loop is illustrated in Fig. 4(a). First, bypass variables for write address, data, and array index are created. The loop iterates 32 times and sets ith elements to i^2. Since the memory is byte wise addressable, the memory pointer is always incremented by four. Since the latency of the multiplication is two clock cycles, a new iteration can be issued on every clock cycle without conflict of multiplier resource if the result of multiplier is read in the same clock cycle when it becomes available. The pipelined loop is given in Fig. 4(b). For simplicity, the lowest level details about bus and interconnection network socket identification are

```
bypass addr, index, data;
init: {
    addr = 0x1F, index = 0;
}
main: loop(32) {
    index = fu4.add(index, 1);
    data = fu6.mul(index, index);
    addr = fu3.add(addr, 4);
    fu1.st(data, addr);
}
```
a)
```
00: 0→fu4.add_t, 1→fu4.add_o;
01: fu4.add_r→fu6.mul_o, fu4.add_r→fu6.mul_t, 1→fu4.add_o,
    fu4.add_r→fu4.add_t;
02: fu4.add_r→fu6.mul_o, 4→fu3.add_o, fu4.add_r→fu6.mul_t,
    31→fu3.add_t, 1→fu4.add_o, fu4.add_r→fu4.add_t;
03: fu4.add_r→fu6.mul_o, 4→fu3.add_o, fu4.add_r→fu6.mul_t,
    fu6.mul_r→fu1.st_t, 1→fu4.add_o, fu3.add_r→fu1.st_o,
    fu4.add_r→fu4.add_t, fu3.add_r→fu3.add_t;
04: fu4.add_r→fu6.mul_o, 4→fu3.add_o,fu4.add_r→fu6.mul_t,
    fu6.mul_r→fu1.st_t, 1→fu4.add_o, fu3.add_r→fu1.st_o,
    fu4.add_r→fu4.add_t, fu3.add_r→fu3.add_t;
05: fu4.add_r→fu6.mul_o, 4→fu3.add_o, fu4.add_r→fu6.mul_t,
    fu6.mul_r→fu1.st_t, 1→fu4.add_o, fu3.add_r→fu1.st_o,
    fu4.add_r→fu4.add_t, fu3.add_r→fu3.add_t;
06: fu4.add_r→fu6.mul_o, 4→fu3.add_o, fu4.add_r→fu6.mul_t,
    fu6.mul_r→fu1.st_t, 1→fu4.add_o, fu3.add_r→fu1.st_o,
    fu4.add_r→fu4.add_t, fu3.add_r→fu3.add_t;
07: fu4.add_r→fu6.mul_o, 4→fu3.add_o, fu4.add_r→fu6.mul_t,
    fu6.mul_r→fu1.st_t, 1→fu4.add_o, fu3.add_r→fu1.st_o,
    fu4.add_r→fu4.add_t, fu3.add_r→fu3.add_t;
08: fu4.add_r→fu6.mul_o, 4→fu3.add_o, fu4.add_r→fu6.mul_t,
    fu6.mul_r→fu1.st_t, fu3.add_r→fu1.st_o, fu3.add_r→fu3.add_t;
09: 4→fu3.add_o, fu6.mul_r→fu1.st_t, fu3.add_r→fu1.st_o,
    fu3.add_r→fu3.add_t;
10: fu6.mul_r→fu1.st_t, fu3.add_r→fu1.st_o;
```
b)
```
02: 0→b0; 03: 0→fu51.add_t, 0→fu51.add_o;
04: !b0:4→jump;
05: 1→fu51.add_t, fu51.add_r→fu51.add_o;
06: fu51.add_r→fu50.eq_t, 6→fu50.eq_o;
07: fu50.eq_r→b0;
```
c)

Fig. 4. Example loop, which sets ith array elements to i^2: (a) original loop, (b) pipelined loop, and (c) loop control code

excluded. The instructions 00, ..., 03 start iterations and the instruction 03 contains the last move of the first iteration. On the contrary to the example in Fig. 2 the first iteration must be issued as a special case. The first iteration uses values of bypass variables, which are set in the *init* block in Fig. 4(a). The values are copied to the code of the first iteration. Thereafter, during the rest of the iterations, the bypass variables have new values, which are the results of function units. For this reason, each loop block is read twice. The first pass sets initial values of bypass variables for the first iteration. The second pass sets the values for rest of the iterations.

The instructions 04, ..., 07 maintain full parallelism of four instances of loop iterations. All the instructions 04, ..., 07 are identical. The reason for repeating four instructions is the jump latency of the processor, i.e., the minimum size of the repeated block must be four instructions. Instructions 08, ..., 10 finish the iterations one by one and the last result is stored in instruction 10. Loop control code is given in Fig. 4(c). The control code is executed in parallel with the loop code in Fig. 4(b). Due to the jump latency, the jump instruction is issued on instruction 04. The instruction 03 sets the initial state of the loop counter.

For i loop iterations, the number of repetitions, R, for the loop kernel, whose length is L instructions, is

$$R = \max(0, \lfloor (i - 2L)/L \rfloor) \tag{1}$$

and the number of extra loop iteration instances, e, is

$$e = i - (2L + RL) . \tag{2}$$

The extra iteration instances are required when the remainder of the division in (1) is not zero. In practice, issuing extra iteration instances means that the loop is partially unrolled. The total number of generated loop iteration instances, N, is

$$N = 2L + e . \tag{3}$$

Since each iteration instance spans over four instructions in Fig. 4(b), the instruction number 10 contains the last moves.

The pipelining algorithm assumes that the next iteration can be started on the next clock cycle. This is a justified assumption for tight signal processing kernels, where the main computation resources are fully utilized, i.e., new operands are fed to the main function units on every clock cycle. The second assumption is avoidance of resource conflicts. Since all the moves of loop are issued in parallel, the function units in the original loop must be separate. Furthermore, to avoid conflicts of intermediate values, the generated outcomes, which are stored either in bypass or register variables, should be used on the next clock cycle. If longer life-time is required a new copy instance of the variable must be used on each clock cycle.

The jump latency and length of the loop control code in Fig. 4(c) set a minimum loop length of four instructions. For example, in Fig. 4(a), the *index* variable could be incremented in parallel with increment of *addr* variable, which results in loop kernel of three instructions. However, even if they are issued sequentially in the original code, both the operations are executed in parallel in the software pipelined code. In practice, such short loop kernels are rare if there is a three clock cycles long latency of memory load operations.

5   Case Studies

The performance of the software pipelining is exemplified by applying the loop construct to an iterative computation of two functions. In Table 1, the performance is given as clock cycles per iteration. The first function $\sum_{i=0}^{255} a_i b_i$ is an inner product and the second function $\sum_{i=0}^{255} (a_i - b_i)^2$ computes a sum of squares, which is needed when computing distances of multidimensional vectors. The samples a_i and b_i are loaded from the memory and a dual access to the memory is enabled. The results are stored to the memory after the computation. The source code of the pipelined loop is shown in Fig. 5(a). Due to the latencies of the function units NOP instructions must be used as shown in the source code.

As a second case in Table 1, the loop is created with a conditional jump to the beginning of code block, i.e., no software pipelining is applied. The program code for this function is shown in Fig. 5(b). As a third method in Table 1 the program is generated with C compiler. The compiler uses a modified version of gcc, which generates analogous sequential move instructions for typical assembly instructions found in general purpose processors. Next, a dedicated program, *scheduler*, is used to schedule parallel moves and allocate resources. Relatively modest performance is obtained since not even partial pipelining is applied. Therefore, the sequential execution is slowed down by

```
bypass addr1, addr2, data1, data2, prod, sum;
init: {
    addr1 = 0, addr2 = '1024', sum = 0;
}
main: loop(256) {
    data1 = fu1.ld(addr1), data2 = fu2.ld(addr2),
    addr1 = fu3.add(addr1, 4), addr2 = fu4.add(addr2, 4);
    ...;
    ...;
    prod = fu6.mul(data1, data2);
    ...;
    sum = fu5.add(prod, sum);
}
end: {
    fu1.st(sum, 0);
}
```
a)
```
bypass addr1, addr2, data1, data2, prod, sum;
bool b1;
init: {
    sum = fu5.add(0,0);
    addr1 = fu3.add(0, 0), addr2 = fu4.add('1024',0);
}
main: {
    data1 = fu1.ld(addr1), data2 = fu2.ld(addr2);
    addr1 = fu3.add(addr1, 4), addr2 = fu4.add(addr2, 4);
    jump = if(!b1) main:;
    prod = fu6.mul(data1, data2);
    b1 = fu50.eq(addr1, '1020');
    sum = fu5.add(prod, sum);
}
end: {
    fu1.st(sum, 0);
}
```
b)

Fig. 5. (a) Source code of the $\sum_{i=0}^{255} a_i b_i$ applying automatically generated software pipelined loop. Three dots, ..., is the mnemonic of the no-operation. Long immediates are denoted with quotes, short immediates without quotes. (b) Source code of the $\sum_{i=0}^{255} a_i b_i$. No software pipelining is applied.

Table 1. Clock cycles per iteration of inner product and sum of squared differences functions

	$\sum_{i=0}^{255} a_i b_i$	$\sum_{i=0}^{255}(a_i - b_i)^2$
Pipelined loop	1.04	1.05
Non-pipelined assembly loop	6.03	7.03
TTA compiled C code	7.04	8.04
C55x compiled C code	1.01	5.00

Table 2. Program source code size in the proposed language and parallel TTA assembly in bytes

		Proposed	Assembly	Ratio
$\sum_{i=0}^{255} a_i b_i$	pipelined	370	7954	0.05
	non-pipelined	451	1752	0.25
$\sum_{i=0}^{255}(a_i - b_i)^2$	pipelined	405	10270	0.04
	non-pipelined	504	2067	0.24

the latencies of the function units, e.g., the latency of load operation is three clock cycles and multiplication takes two clock cycles. Since not even partial pipelining is used the operations cannot overlap and they are issued sequentially. In all the TTA processor cases in Table 1, the processor contains sufficient resources, i.e., there is no performance bottleneck of lacking some computing resource. Thus, the effect of processor configuration is excluded.

For comparison, the same functions are executed on TI TMS320C55x digital signal processor [9] and the required clock cycles per iterations are shown in Table 1. The inner product is such a function that it lends itself to the MAC instruction available on C55x [10]. On the contrary, TTA processors in Table 1 use separate multiplier and adder units for MAC operation. Since C55x is dedicated to signal processing tasks it has an excellent performance on inner product and the C compiler is able to generate a hardware loop, where a single MAC instruction is repeated on every clock cycle. On the contrary, the second function requires sequential execution, which results in a performance penalty.

Finally, the size of the generated code is observed to exemplify reduction in manual programming work and the increase in abstraction level. The sizes of source code in introduced language and generated low-level assembly code are given in Table 2, which shows that when applying software pipelining the size of the original source is only 5% of the generated code. The tremendous decrease in code size justifies use of the developed language and tool support, when software pipelining is required. The Table 2 shows also that, even if the software pipelining is not applied, the size of the source code is only one fourth of the generated assembly code.

6   Conclusions

Parallel assembly programming is a demanding task calling for a support for automatic code generation. Especially, the software pipelining results in extensive parallelism and long instruction words. However, to achieve adequate performance for signal processing and telecommunication applications, the software pipelining is essential. Otherwise, the resources are only partially utilized and the performance is degraded. In this paper, the parallel language syntax for TTA processor was developed with intuitive presentation without loosing the expressiveness of the language. The capability to generate software pipelined code for the loops was the main achievement. The introduction of the by-pass variables allowed imperative programming style without reserving extra registers, thus, it results in lower complexity of the processor. The results showed that the effect in performance was outstanding. Finally, the sizes of the source and generated code showed the amount of saved manual programming work.

Acknowledgement

This work has been supported by the National Technology Agency of Finland under research funding decision 40441/05.

References

1. Kokozinski., R., Greifendorf, D., Stammen, J., Jung, P.: The evolution of hardware platforms for mobile 'software defined radio' terminals. In: IEEE Int. Symp. Personal Indoor Mobile Radio Commun. Volume 5., Freiburg, Germany (2002) 2389–2393
2. Keutzer, K., Malik, S., Newton, A.R.: From ASIC to ASIP: the next design discontinuity. In: IEEE Int. Conf. Computer Design: VLSI in Computers and Processors, Freiburg, Germany (2002) 84–90
3. Corporaal, H.: Microprocessor Architectures from VLIW to TTA. John Wiley & Sons Ltd (1998)
4. Corporaal, H., Arnold, M.: Using transport triggered architecture for embedded processor design. Integrated Computer-Aided Eng. **5** (1998) 19–38
5. Salmela, P., Järvinen, T., Sipilä, T., Takala, J.: Scalable FIR filtering on transport triggered architecture processor. In: Int. Symp. Signals Circuit Syst., Iasi, Romania (2005) 493–496
6. Salmela, P., Järvinen, T., Sipilä, T., Takala, J.: 256-state rate 1/2 Viterbi decoder on TTA processor. In: IEEE Int. Conf. Application-Specific Syst. Architectures Processors. Volume 2., Samos, Greece (2005) 370–375
7. Allan, V.H., Jones, R.B., Lee, R.M., Allan, S.J.: Software pipelining. ACM Computing Surveys **27** (1995) 367–432
8. Fisher, J.A., Faraboschi, P., Young, C.: Embedded Computing: A VLIW Approach to Architecture, Compilers and Tools. Morgan Kaufman Publishers Inc. (2004)
9. Texas Instruments: TMS320C55x Technical Overview. (2000) SPRU393.
10. Texas Instruments: TMS320C55x DSP Mnemonic Instruction Set Reference Guide. (2002) SPRU374G.

SAD Prefetching for MPEG4 Using Flux Caches

Georgi N. Gaydadjiev and Stamatis Vassiliadis

Computer Engineering Laboratory,
Electrical Engineering, Mathematics and Computer Science Dept.,
EEMCS, TU Delft, The Netherlands
G.N.Gaydadjiev, S.Vassiliadis@ewi.tudelft.nl
http://ce.et.tudelft.nl

Abstract. In this paper, we consider flux caches prefetching and a media application. We analyze the MPEG4 encoder workload with realistic data set in a scenario representative for the embedded systems domain. Our study shows that different well known data prefetch mechanisms can gain little reduction in the cache miss ratios when applied on the complete MPEG4 application. Furthermore, we investigate the potential improvement when dedicated prefetching strategies are applied to the sum of absolute differences (SAD) kernels in MPEG4. We propose a flux cache mechanism that dynamically invokes cache designs with dedicated prefetching engines that can fully utilize the available memory bandwidth. We show that our proposal improves the cache miss ratios by a factor close to 3x.

Keywords: Flux caches, Prefetching mechanisms, Reconfigurable architectures, Multimedia.

1 Introduction

Flux caches [1] have been proposed as a microarchitectural alternative hardware mechanism for improving the performance of memories when compared to the hardwired caches. They are based on two main assumptions. The first assumption regards the availability of technologies that can be reconfigured before and/or during program execution. The second assumption regards the changing memory access behavior from program to program and during program execution. Flux caches are cache hierarchy designs that change dynamically their hardware organization to capture the memory access requirements of a given program/program execution. Flux caches assume implicit and explicit dynamic cache calls to "redesign and place" new hardwired caches instead of having permanent and unchangeable caches. In order to establish the validity of the approach, this paper assumes a real application and considers prefetching- one of the cache design aspects. Our experiments with some well know prefetching mechanisms and dynamic execution suggest that the above conjunctures hold true. For the mechanisms considered we also provide guidelines of how to design a Flux cache for sum of absolute differences (SAD) prefetching in MPEG4. It is noted that our investigation is not intended to propose a novel cache prefetching mechanisms but it is rather focusing on cache adaptation to "fit" the application behavior.

S. Vassiliadis et al. (Eds.): SAMOS 2006, LNCS 4017, pp. 248–258, 2006.

The contributions of this paper can be summarized by the following:

- A careful investigation of the memory behavior of a real-life MPEG4 encoding application working on a representative workload;
- Identification of potential kernels that can benefit from a dedicated prefetch method;
- Special Flux cache organization to fully utilize the available main memory bandwidth;
- Improvement of the cache miss ratios by a factor close to 3x.

The rest of this paper is organized as follows: Section 2 briefly reviews the most relevant related work on prefetching. Section 3 describes our experimental methodology and introduces the MPEG4 flux cache design for optimal prefetching of SAD8 and SAD16 data. In Section 4 the performance results that support our idea are described. Finally, the discussion is concluded in Section 5.

2   Background

In this section we will provide only the background information needed directly in the reminder of this paper. It introduces the two major parts used in our work: the flux cache concept and a very brief classification of cache data prefetch mechanisms. This is mainly due to space limitations and the fact that cache prefetching techniques have been a topic of research for numerous years. The interested reader can refer to overview papers such as [2, 3] where an elaborated discussion is presented. In addition, due to the subject we investigate, our background information on cache prefetching will be limited to the data cache prefetching only.

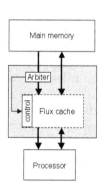

Fig. 1. Flux cache

Flux caches: Flux caches are fully customizable memory levels, envisioned for reconfigurable hardware implementation, that can be instantiated on demand. The flux cache reconfiguration can be performed before or during program execution. Implementations of arbitrary hardware cache design can be "programmed" under software or hardware control at runtime. The specific flux cache implementations are pre-determined at hardware/software co-design stage, i.e. by using application partitioning, monitoring, profiling or else. In its general form flux caches would require additional ISA support, however it has being shown that this is not always necessary, e.g. as in the MOLEN [4] polymorphic processor case (see [1]). The reconfiguration of the intended cache design is expected to introduce some reconfiguration overhead, although the benefits of using the flux cache during program execution are likely to compensate for it. The general flux cache organization is depicted in Figure 1.

The three main components of a flux cache are: the arbiter, the control unit and the reconfigurable HW area available for different cache instantiations. The flux cache parameters are usually implicit, however explicit calls (as it will be shown later in this text) can also be used. There is essentially a single *put* phase initiated by the arbiter after detection of a **put** instruction that interrupts the processor program flow until the hardware configuration is completed. The **put** instruction will be redirected to the control unit and interpreted accordingly. More precisely, the configuration microcode located at the targeted address will be loaded into the configuration memory to ensure the flux cache hardware structure. After the cache reconfiguration is completed (and all *valid* tags of the "new" cache are invalidated) the execution of the processor will continue with the execution of the next instruction keeping the processor execution consistency intact.

Prefetching for Data Caches classification: Prefetching has been extensively considered to improve cache performance. Data cache prefetching mechanisms the subject of our investigation can be divided into three major classes: *Software*, *Hardware* and *Hybrid HW/SW* data prefetching schemes. The software data prefetching has the potential of issuing requests for only the data that is expected to be used. This is due to the ability to have an application wide (compiler) view. The major drawbacks of the software data prefetching are the additional prefetch instructions overhead, the inability of the compiler to estimate run-time cache miss latencies and difficulty with prefetching of addresses unknown at compile time, e.g. pointer references. The hardware approaches have a zero processor overhead and direct access to run-time (latency) information. In addition, it has been shown that problems inherent to hardware prefetching such as memory bandwidth contention and cache pollution can be addressed effectively [5]. On the other hand, the hardware has no direct knowledge of future references and usually operates within a very limited scope. Furthermore, the hardware based mechanisms always trade between accuracy and coverage and can only exploit structured data access patterns. As expected, the hybrid hardware/software data prefetching approaches gain in popularity lately. A variety of schemes have been proposed ranging from prefetching of very specific access patterns to more generally applicable approaches [6, 7, 8, 9]. It should be noted that work in this area is often focused on multiprocessor machines.

The application of the flux caches for prefetching can benefit from the advantages of both the software and the hardware approaches. More precisely they can combine the compiler knowledge on references far ahead of the SW techniques with the zero processor overhead and run-time latencies awareness of the hardware approaches. Because flux caches will be called on demand (dynamically) multiple HW/SW schemes can coexist for single program execution. In addition, in respect to the proposed hybrid approaches, our proposal do not involve any additional ISA extension (see [1] for more information) and can instantiate any of the previously proposed schemes. In the next section we will show how specific memory intensive MPEG4 kernels can benefit form our approach. It should be noted that although here we focus on regular array accesses only, similar schemes can be applied for speeding up memory access to complex pointer structures (i.e. recursive pointers), sparse matrices or for support of novel vectorization mechanisms [10, 11].

3   MPEG4 Encoder Prefetching Investigation

In this section, before focusing on the envisioned solution we provide discussion of the methodology we used to perform our evaluation.

Methodology: We base our study on memory traces and the dinero IV [12] trace driven cache simulator for L1 and L2. Although the traces used in this study became rather huge (hundreds of gigabytes), we did not have the means to perform direct hardware measurements - widely accepted as the second preferred method for cache performance evaluation [13]. The dinero style application traces for this study where obtained using a modified in-order SimpleScalar 4.0 simulator [14].

As our benchmark we selected a complete MPEG4 encoder application and a set of representative workloads. This in contrast with the widely used Mediabench and EEMBC benchmark suites that concentrate on small kernels and limited datasets. In order to avoid library calls overhead we created a single statically linked executable based on xvidcore v.1.1.0 library and xvid_encraw.c raw format MPEG4 encoder. As dataloads we used five of the widely used video conferencing test sequences: *foreman, carphone, claire, miss america* and *grandma*. We obtained those from the Stanford Center for Image Systems Engineering web site [15]. All video sequences used are in raw format, YUV concatenated with sub-sampled UV components. The image dimensions are 144 lines x 176 pixels per line (or *Quarter Common Intermediate Format* (QCIF)) with 30 frames per second as specified by ITU H.261 video conferencing standard [16]. The sequence lengths are: 400 (for foreman), 382 (carphone), 494 (claire), 150 (miss america) and 870 (grandma) frames respectively. The produced MPEG4 output is in "raw" format m4v that was found sufficient for our study. We validated the correctness of the compressed output by using $ffmpeg$ [17]. We limited our study to only five out of nine available sequences after we found that the data loads play a minor role for the data miss ratios. As an example, the miss ratios found vary from 0.26 (foreman) to 0.32 (claire) for exactly the same 2k direct mapped data cache configuration. This is why only the best performing *foreman.qcif* encoding scenario will be considered in this study. This to investigate our proposal under worst case conditions.

For our experimental cache we use 2k split instruction and data direct mapped cache with 16 byte lines with no sub-blocks. This in attempt to evaluate the effects of the proposed mechanisms instead of working at the noise levels. In addition, we aim at a solution for simple embedded processors (without any SIMD extensions) and MPEG4 encoding. The findings in the text hereafter are general and will show similar relative improvements on arbitrary chosen realistic data cache sizes, applications and workloads.

Performance Evaluation: To identify the potential targets that may benefit from prefetching "on demand" we used both code execution profiling as well as memory trace analysis. Profiling results show that SAD8 and SAD16 are responsible for 35.58% and 9.07% of the application cumulative execution time. In addition, the memory trace analysis indicated that 39.7% of the total data

Table 1. MPEG4 encoder cache miss ratios and memory fetches

	miss ratios			fetches	
	demand	prefetch	total	prefetch	total
always	0.265	0.2501	0.2582	1,754,619,345	*3,822,878,836*
load	0.2682	0	0.2682	0	2,068,259,491
miss	0.2649	0.8399	0.3717	471,670,789	2,539,930,280
OBL[a]	0.2682	0	*0.1451*	1,754,619,345	*3,822,878,836*
tagged	0.2645	0.84	0.3756	494,668,112	2,562,927,603
on demand	0.2682	-	0.2682	-	2,068,259,491

[a] *in dinero VI prefetch distance 1 with sub-block placement disabled*

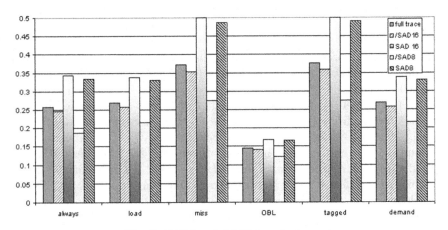

Fig. 2. SAD8 and SAD16 cache impact

memory reads are due to SAD8 (and 11.06% for SAD16) that makes both kernels primary candidates for prefetch optimizations.

We first started with evaluation of the existing prefetch techniques implemented in dinero IV. Table 1 depicts the miss ratios of a 2k/16bytes direct mapped data cache for our executable and video sequence (MPEG4 encoder and foreman.qcif). This table shows that the traditional prefetch strategies do not have significant impact on the miss ratios for the considered workload. The only strategy that shows some improvement (reduction from 26.8 down to 14.5 %) is the *one block look ahead* (OBL). This scheme initiates a prefetch of block $a + 1$ when block a is accessed. Such behavior fits well with the memory access patterns of the investigated MPEG4 kernels as will be shown later in this paper. A major drawback of OBL (as in the case with always prefetch) is the doubled number of main memory accesses compared to the "no-prefetch" scheme presented in the last row of Table 1. The always prefetch (25.8%) performs very similar to a cache design without any prefetch (26.8%), while the prefetch on miss (37.2%) and the tagged prefetch (37.5%) show degradation in the miss ratios for this particular application. The prefetch on load (26.8%) is applying essentially the demand fetch policy (no prefetch) since we have not defined any sub-blocks in our experimental data cache. The latter fact will cause disabling of the sub-block placement and respectively the load-forward-prefetch as explained in the dinero IV documentation.

```
uint32_t sad8_c(const uint8_t * const cur,
        const uint8_t * const ref,
        const uint32_t stride)
{
    uint32_t sad = 0;
    uint32_t j;
    uint8_t const *ptr_cur = cur;
    uint8_t const *ptr_ref = ref;
    for (j = 0; j < 8; j++) {
        sad += abs(ptr_cur[0] - ptr_ref[0]);
        sad += abs(ptr_cur[1] - ptr_ref[1]);
        sad += abs(ptr_cur[2] - ptr_ref[2]);
        sad += abs(ptr_cur[3] - ptr_ref[3]);
        sad += abs(ptr_cur[4] - ptr_ref[4]);
        sad += abs(ptr_cur[5] - ptr_ref[5]);
        sad += abs(ptr_cur[6] - ptr_ref[6]);
        sad += abs(ptr_cur[7] - ptr_ref[7]);
        ptr_cur += stride;
        ptr_ref += stride;
    }
    return sad;
}
```

Fig. 3. SAD8 C code

Next, we produced partial memory traces to investigate the relative behavior of the SAD8 and SAD16 kernels compared to the "reminder" of the application code. Again, we based out experiments on the same cache organization and size for the sake of a common reference for comparison. The main question was how the different parts of the investigated workload will influence the cache performance. The results are summarized in Figure 2. As it can be seen on this figure, the identified kernels perform worse than the full application when using the same cache size. In general, the "overall" code (/SAD16, read as *not* SAD16, and /SAD8 on Figure 2) shows a very minimal improvement of a couple of per-cents compared to the complete application figures. Considering the significant contribution of both kernels to the total number of MPEG4 encoder memory reads, we took a closer look at their internal structure.

The C-code of the SAD8 kernel is shown on Figure 3. SAD16 loop has a similar structure with twice as long body and doubled number of iterations. As it can be seen the memory accesses of the SAD operation are predominately reads of array elements. In addition, the memory access pattern of the

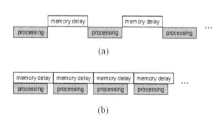

Fig. 4. SAD8 execution diagrams

complete loop is 100% deterministic and is basically predefined by the three input parameters. This is an advantage that should be exploited.

Please note that all software prefetching techniques will fail to fully schedule the complete loop access pattern, since the stride is continuously adjusted from call to call and not known at compile time. Although this loop can be optimized by applying specific SIMD instructions (for ISA extensions like MMX, AltiVec and 3DNow!), the memory bandwidth requirements will remain unchanged.

The solution: SAD Flux Cache. Taking into account that the stride is usually much bigger than the cache line size, the SAD8 and SAD16 execution is envisioned to involve many stall cycles due to the main memory latency as indicated on Figure 4(a).

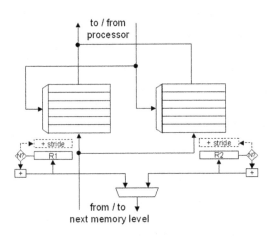

Fig. 5. SAD8 prefetch flux cache

In such case the processor is supposed to wait for the main memory to provide the requested data that is often not resident in the cache. Please note that by processing we mean the execution of all instructions involved in a single loop iteration. The reference to the $ptr\_cur[0]$ and $ptr\_ref[0]$ will bring all of the elements needed (and maybe more data) into the cache line (indicated as "memory delay" in our figure).

The optimal case will be to have a prefetch strategy in hardware (prefetch engine) that mimics the memory access patterns of both SAD8 and SAD16 kernels. Considering the fact that the start addresses and the stride are changed dynamically, it should be possible to pass this information to the prefetch engine on run-time (every time the procedure call is initiated). This ideally should be done without any additional burden for the processor ISA.

It should be noted that all of the above can be done fairly easy by applying a specialized flux cache (a very small cache installed/deinstalled on demand). The proposed organization is shown in Figure 5. It consists of two stream buffers that are filled from the main memory locations indicated by the values stored in $R1$ and $R2$. The flux cache control is not only responsible for incrementing the two pointers but will also check for the loop boundaries and apply the stride offset when necessary. We apply the two stream buffers to fully utilize the available main memory bandwidth by exploiting properties like interleaving. Since the prefetching is completely decoupled from the program execution and there are two "channels" applied, the memory accesses can be performed in a back to back fashion as shown in Figure 4(b).

```
uint32_t sad8_c(const uint8_t * const cur,
      const uint8_t * const ref,
      const uint32_t stride)
{
    uint32_t sad = 0;
    uint32_t j;
    uint8_t const *ptr_cur = cur;
    uint8_t const *ptr_ref = ref;
    __asm("movtx xr1,cur");
    __asm("movtx xr2,ref");
    __asm("movtx xr3,stride");
    __asm("movtx xr4,#8");
    __asm("set $SAD_prefetch_flux");
    for (j = 0; j < 8; j++) {
        sad += abs(ptr_cur[0] - ptr_ref[0]);
        ... ... ... ... ... ... ... ... ...
        sad += abs(ptr_cur[7] - ptr_ref[7]);
        ptr_cur += stride;
        ptr_ref += stride;
    }
    __asm("set $2k_16_DM_LRU");
    return sad;
}
```

Fig. 6. Modified SAD8 C code

This is possible since both data addresses are known at advance (and are usually far away from each other), so the location of each memory read can be perfectly predicted and pre-scheduled. This all results in a highly effective prefetch strategy that in addition has a limited hardware cost.

The proposed flux cache will be installed before the execution of the SAD loop and its interface works as follows. The $R1$ and $R2$ are the two address pointers to the current (cur) and the reference (ref) arrays. These pointers are passed to the hardware prefetch engine together with the stride ($stride$) and the loop length ($N = 8$ or 16) parameters on subroutine call boundary. We envision an implementation of the proposed engine in the MOLEN polymorphic processor scenario: flux cache plus exchange registers bank for parameters passing. Please note that this is a slightly more complicated MOLEN utilization than the one described in [1]. The stream buffers size is limited and envisioned to be no more than two loop iterations, e.g. 32 entries in case of SAD16. The required buffer length can be estimated from the ratio of the average memory latency and the expected loop execution time (both measured in processor cycles). In addition, very limited control logic for scheduling of the fetches from the main memory is required. The hardware complexity of such control logic is in the order of four binary counters and one multiplexor. Please note that any specific memory burst mode can be implemented into the prefetch controller to exploit the particular memory bandwidth and resources (e.g. DMA controllers) available in the specific targeted system. The latter does not necessarily increase the complexity of the proposed control hardware.

The modified SAD8 loop for the MOLEN programming paradigm [18] is shown in Figure 6. The four additional *movtx* MOLEN instructions at the beginning are to "instruct" the SAD prefetch engine about the array access pattern and the loop boundaries as described earlier. We added the inline assembly code by hand, however the generation and the scheduling process can be integrated in the MOLEN compiler [19]. Please note the mapping of the flux cache *put* onto the MOLEN *set* instructions as previously proposed in [1].

As indicated earlier the same flux cache can be used for both SAD8 and 16 without any future modifications. The selection between the two kernels is done by the constant stored in $xr4$ (8 or 16). After loop completion the cache configuration used for the "overall" MPEG4 application code is to be restored by the second *set* instruction. Please note that the reconfiguration latency is not a major point of concern. Assuming sufficient hardware resources are available, and considering the limited size of the proposed SAD flux cache, both flux caches (SAD_prefetch_flux and 2k_16_DM_LRU) can be resident in the configuration memory (the reconfigurable hardware) at the same time. This will reduce the configuration overhead of the two *set* operations down to a trivial multiplexer switch of the address and the data busses. In addition, such scenario will prevent the cold start effects for the flux cache used for the "overall" code. For the SAD flux cache the cold start is a minor concern, since such a behavior is inherent to its functionality, e.g. the pointers and the stride are reused in very rare situations among two subsequent calls. The only overhead of the proposed flux cache will remain the four additional register to register transfer *movtx* instructions that have no impact on the main memory bus utilization.

4   Results

The improvements of the cache miss ratios of the proposed design are shown in Figure 7. The four bars (from left to right) represent the following cases: no flux cache (the base for the comparison), flux cache for SAD16 only, SAD8 flux cache and general SAD (8 and 16) flux cache as proposed in Section 3. The "remainder" of the code is using a similar 2k/16 direct mapped data cache as in the reference case (complete application without flux cache). It is interesting to note that 2k

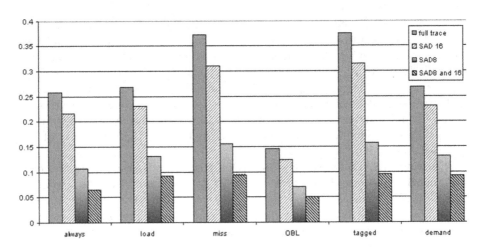

Fig. 7. MPEG4 encoder 2K DM cache and flux cache for the kernels

direct mapped cache without prefetch in combination with a SAD flux cache for the SAD8 kernel only performs better (cache miss ratio of 13%) than a 2k DM cache with OBL prefetch strategy (14.5%) that is the best performing standard prefetch mechanism for the complete application. In addition, when our flux cache is applied to both kernels the miss ratios are reduced down to the range 4.5% (for OBL) - 9.5% (for tagged prefetch). That is an improvement by near 3x. When our flux cache is applied the number of prefetches (and their impact on the main memory bus) will be reduced by a number close to the cumulative SAD8 and SAD16 memory read accesses. This forms one additional advantage of our proposal especially in the envisioned constrained embedded system context.

5 Conclusions

In this paper, we investigated the data memory access behavior of xvid MPEG4 encoder, identified kernels that can benefit form a dedicated prefetch mechanism and proposed a flux cache design to cope with it. More precisely, we studied the memory patterns of SAD8 and SAD16 during the MPEG4 encoding process. We proposed a flux cache design that optimally utilizes the main memory bandwidth with a trivial hardware complexity. We showed that our approach can reduce the data cache miss ratios by a factor close to 3x and expect to significantly reduce the number of main memory accesses when the proposed prefetching is applied. Our study focused on rather small data cache sizes (the case for very small, power constrained embedded systems) however similar relative improvements are envisioned for any realistically chosen configuration.

References

1. Gaydadjiev, G.N., Vassiliadis, S.: Flux caches: What are they and are they useful? In: Proceedings of the 5th International Workshop on Computer Systems: Architectures, Modelling, and Simulation (SAMOS 2005). (2005) 93–102
2. VanderWiel, S.P., Lilja, D.J.: Data prefetch mechanisms. ACM Computing Surveys **32** (2000) 174–199
3. Smith, A.J.: Sequential program prefetching in memory hierarchies. IEEE Computer 11 **12** (1978) 7–21
4. Vassiliadis, S., Wong, S., Gaydadjiev, G.N., Bertels, K., Kuzmanov, G., Panainte, E.M.: The molen polymorphic processor. IEEE Transactions on Computers (2004) 1363– 1375
5. Lin, W.F., Reinhardt, S.K., Burger, D.: Reducing DRAM latencies with an integrated memory hierarchy design. In: HPCA. (2001) 301–312
6. Gornish, E.H., Veidenbaum, A.: An integrated hardware/software data prefetching scheme for shared-memory multiprocessors. Int. J. Parallel Program. **27** (1999) 35–70
7. Chen, T.F.: An effective programmable prefetch engine for on-chip caches. In: MICRO 28: Proceedings of the 28th annual international symposium on Microarchitecture, Los Alamitos, CA, USA, IEEE Computer Society Press (1995) 237–242

8. Zhang, Z., Torrellas, J.: Speeding up irregular applications in shared-memory multiprocessors: memory binding and group prefetching. In: ISCA '95: Proceedings of the 22nd annual international symposium on Computer architecture, New York, NY, USA, ACM Press (1995) 188–199

9. Wang, Z., Burger, D., McKinley, K.S., Reinhardt, S.K., Weems, C.C.: Guided region prefetching: a cooperative hardware/software approach. In: ISCA '03: Proceedings of the 30th annual international symposium on Computer architecture, New York, NY, USA, ACM Press (2003) 388–398

10. Corbal, J., Espasa, R., Valero, M.: Three-dimensional memory vectorization for high bandwidth media memory systems. In: MICRO 35: Proceedings of the 35th annual ACM/IEEE international symposium on Microarchitecture, Los Alamitos, CA, USA, IEEE Computer Society Press (2002) 149–160

11. Kuzmanov, G., Gaydadjiev, G.N., Vassiliadis, S.: Visual data rectangular memory. In: Proceedings of the 10th International Euro-Par Conference (Euro-Par 2004). (2004) 760–767

12. Edler, J., Hill, M.D.: Dinero IV trace-driven uniprocessor cache simulator. (1998) http://www.cs.wisc.edu/~markhill/DineroIV.

13. Smith, A.J.: Cache Memories. Computing Surveys **14** (1982) 473–530

14. Burger, D., Austin, T.M., Bennett, S.: Evaluating future microprocessors: The simplescalar tool set. Technical Report CS-TR-1996-1308 (1996)

15. (http://ise.stanford.edu/labsite/ise_test_images_videos.html)

16. (http://www.itu.int/rec/recommendation.asp?lang=en\&parent=T-REC-H.261)

17. (http://ffmpeg.sourceforge.net)

18. Vassiliadis, S., Gaydadjiev, G.N., Bertels, K., Panainte, E.M.: The molen programming paradigm. In: Proceedings of the Third International Workshop on Systems, Architectures, Modeling, and Simulation. (2003) 1–10

19. Panainte, E.M., Bertels, K., Vassiliadis, S.: Compiling for the molen programming paradigm. In: Proceedings of the 13th International Conference on Field Programmable Logic and Applications (FPL'03). (2003) 900–910

Effects of Program Compression

Jari Heikkinen and Jarmo Takala

Tampere University of Technology, P.O. Box 553, FIN-33101 Tampere, Finland
{jari.heikkinen, jarmo.takala}@tut.fi

Abstract. The size of the program code has become a critical design constraint in embedded systems, especially in handheld devices. Large program codes require large memories, which increase the size and cost of the chip. In addition, the power consumption is increased due to higher memory I/O bandwidth. Program compression is one of the most often used methods to reduce the size of the program code. In this paper, two compression approaches, dictionary-based compression and instruction template-based compression, were evaluated on a customizable processor architecture with parallel resources. The effects on area and power consumption were measured. Dictionary-based compression reduced the area at best by 77% and power consumption by 73%. Instruction template-based compression resulted in increase in both area and power consumption and hence turned out to be impractical.

1 Introduction

Embedded systems are nowadays widely used in many consumer products, such as automobiles, home automation, and portable electronics. Portable embedded systems, like cellular phones, personal digital assistants (PDA), game consoles, and media players, are often limited by constraints on size, weight, battery life, and cost. Therefore, reducing the chip area and its power consumption has become crucial in designing this kind of embedded systems. As the embedded applications are becoming more complex, the sizes of the programs are also increasing. This results in need for larger memories and, consequently, to systems, where the memory might already consume more area than the processor core [1]. Large memories also increase the power consumption, and hence reduce the battery life. Therefore, minimizing the program size is important in reducing the area and power consumption of embedded systems.

The increased complexity of embedded systems requires also more processing power from the underlying processing hardware. Recently, very long instruction word (VLIW) architectures have gained considerable popularity in embedded systems, especially in digital signal processing (DSP), due to their modularity and scalability. VLIW architectures provide more processing power by exploiting the instruction level parallelism (ILP). Operations are executed in parallel in concurrently operating functional units (FU). The FUs are controlled by a long instruction word that contains dedicated fields for each FU. This kind of an instruction encoding leads to poor code density as the full processing power of the architecture cannot always be fully utilized [2]. Poor code density increases the size of the program code even further. In addition, more power is consumed as the long instructions increase the program memory I/O bandwidth.

S. Vassiliadis et al. (Eds.): SAMOS 2006, LNCS 4017, pp. 259–268, 2006.

The size of the program code can be reduced through program compression. The program is compressed during compile-time and stored in compressed form in the program memory. During execution, the compressed instructions are fetched from the program memory and decompressed back to original form before they are decoded inside the processor core. The decompressor can be located in or outside the processor core.

Several compression methods have been proposed for VLIW architectures. In one of the earliest approaches, no-operations (NOP) were eliminated from the instructions [2]. A "mask" identifier, preceding each instruction, specified which fields were present in the instruction word. A similar approach was presented in [3], where NOPs were eliminated by using multiple instruction formats, or instruction templates, that provided operation slots for only a subset of all the functional units. In [4], a dictionary-based compression method was applied to VLIWs. Frequently used instruction words were stored into a dictionary and occurrences of these instructions in the program code were replaced by codewords. Dictionary-based compression was also applied in [5], where the non-time-critical part of the program was compressed using *superinstructions* that correspond to frequently used instruction patterns. In [6], an approach to minimize the number of dictionary entries was presented. The dictionary entries were chosen so that all the instructions of the program code were at most a specified maximum Hamming distance from a dictionary entry. Bit toggling information was used to restore the original instruction. Entropy encoding is another fairly commonly used approach to improve the code density. It exploits the fact that some symbols are used more frequently than others. Therefore, the shortest codes are allocated to the most frequent symbols and vice versa. Entropy encoding has been applied on VLIWs by means of arithmetic coding, e.g., in [7], and Huffman encoding, e.g., in [8].

In this paper, dictionary-based compression and instruction template-based compression approaches are implemented in hardware and evaluated in terms of area and power consumption. These kind of statistics are rarely reported for the program compression approaches. The two compression alternatives are evaluated on a customizable processor architecture, transport triggered architecture, that reminds VLIW architectures. Two customized processors are designed for a set of applications from the DSP application domain. The program codes of the applications, compiled on the two processors, are then compressed using the two compression alternatives. The processor designs are implemented in hardware and synthesized onto a 130nm technology to obtain the area and power consumption statistics.

2   Dictionary Compression

Dictionary-based compression methods use the principle of replacing substrings, e.g., words in a text, with a codeword that identifies that substring in a dictionary [9]. The dictionary contains a list of substrings and a codeword for each substring. As the codeword is smaller than the original substring, compression is achieved. During decompression the codeword is used to fetch the original substring from the dictionary.

Dictionary-based program compression is based on the fact that instructions in a program code are typically highly repetitive [10]. Furthermore, often only a small part of the instruction set provided by the processor is used. This indicates that the program can be executed with a set of much shorter instructions. This can be achieved by storing all the unique instructions of a program into a dictionary and by replacing the instructions in the program code with indices to the dictionary. Given a program with N unique instructions, the length of the codeword is $\lceil log_2|N| \rceil$ bits. Thus, the size of the program memory is reduced. During program execution the compressed instructions need to be decompressed. Decompression is fairly straightforward. The codeword (dictionary index), fetched from the program memory is used to obtain the original uncompressed instruction from the dictionary for decoding and execution. The dictionary, typically implemented using ROM or standard cells, introduces an additional cost in the control hardware of the processor core.

3   Instruction Templates

Most programs contain parallelism for the VLIW compiler to exploit. However, programs contain also parts where data dependencies limit the parallelism resulting in sequences of instructions that contain only few operations. As most VLIW architectures are tailored for the highly parallel parts, the less parallel parts result in large number of NOPs and waste of instruction bits.

A method using multiple instruction formats, or instruction templates, to avoid explicit specification of NOPs for VLIW and EPIC architectures has been proposed in [3]. An instruction template provides operation slots only for a subset of the functional units. The rest of the functional units receive NOPs implicitly. For each instruction, a fixed-width template selection field is added at the beginning of the instruction to specify the used template. From its value the instruction decoder obtains the number of fields in the template, their widths, and their bit positions.

This compression scheme results in variable-width instructions, and, consequently, more complex instruction fetch and decompression. During decompression, the template selection field is inspected and according to its value the bits of the instruction template are forwarded to the decoder, supplemented with NOPs for the operation slots that did not have a field in the template. The remaining bits are shifted at the beginning of the instruction register and the bits of the next fetched program memory packet are concatenated with the bits in the instruction register. A buffer is needed before the decompressor to avoid overflow in the instruction register.

4   Evaluation Methodology

The compression methods were evaluated in terms of area and power consumption on a customizable processor architecture, transport triggered architecture (TTA), which is a class of statically programmed ILP architectures that reminds VLIW architectures [11]. In the TTA programming model, the program specifies only the data transports (moves) to be performed by an interconnection network. Operations occur as a "side-effect". A TTA processor consists of a set of functional units and register files, which are connected to an interconnection network consisting of buses through input and output sockets, as illustrated in Fig. 1. The architecture is extremely flexible and modular and it allows easy inclusion of special functional units with user-defined functionality.

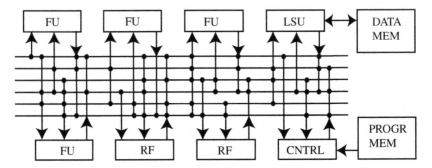

Fig. 1. TTA processor structure. FU: functional unit. RF: register file. LSU: load-store unit. CN-TRL: control unit. Dots express connections between buses and sockets.

As TTA resembles VLIW, it also suffers from poor code density. The poor code density is mostly due to minimal encoding, which leads to long instruction words. Instead of containing fields for the concurrently operating functional units like in VLIW, TTA instruction word contains dedicated fields, called move slots, for each bus to define the data transports. Each move slot contains three fields, as illustrated in Fig. 2. The guard field provides means for conditional execution. The destination ID field contains the address of the socket that reads data from the bus. The source ID field specifies the address of a socket that is writing data on the bus. During decoding these addresses are compared against the hardwired socket IDs. When the IDs match, a proper action is taken. In addition, the instruction word usually contains at least one dedicated long immediate field to define long immediate values, e.g., large constants and jump addresses. Another reason for poor code density is that the hardware resources are typically tailored for the highly parallel sections of the program. The less parallel parts result in large number of null data transports that waste instruction bits.

The two compression methods, dictionary-based and instruction template-based compression approaches have been evaluated theoretically on TTA in [12, 13]. According to the theoretical evaluations, based on the program memory bit sizes, the instruction template-based compression approach is more effective. However, practical hardware implementations give more accurate statistics as the theoretical evaluation does not take into account the actual implementations of the decompressor. Preliminary results of implementing the dictionary-based compression on TTA have been reported in [14], but with unoptimized decompression structures that have been optimized in this work.

For the hardware implementations of the two compression approaches, two TTA processors were designed for four benchmarks from the digital signal processing domain. The benchmarks realized two versions of the discrete cosine transform (DCT); two-dimensional (2-D) 8×8 DCT and 1-D 32-point DCT, and 1024-point Radix-4 fast Fourier transform and Viterbi decoding. The two TTA processors were designed using the design space explorer of MOVE framework [15], which is a semi-automatic design environment for designing application-specific instruction set processors. Two configurations, a cost-efficient configuration (A) and a configuration being a compromize between cost and performance (B) were chosen. The resources, i.e., buses, functional units, and registers of these configurations are described in Table 1. The statistics of

move slot 0			move slot 1			move slot 2			
G(3)	S(9)	D(6)	G(3)	S(9)	D(5)	G(3)	S(9)	D(7)	LI(32)

Fig. 2. Structure of instruction word. G: Guard field. S: Source ID field. D: Destination ID field. LI: Long immediate field. (x): x-bit field.

the benchmarks compiled on the two processor configurations using the compiler of the MOVE framework are illustrated in Table 2.

The program codes were compressed using the two compression methods. Dictionary compression was applied at three different symbol granularity levels; at instruction level, at move slot level, and at ID field level. At instruction level, unique bit patterns to be stored into a dictionary were searched inside full instructions. At move slot level, instructions were divided into parallel streams according to move slot boundaries and unique bit patterns were searched inside these streams. At ID field level, instructions were divided to even smaller streams, according to source and destination ID field boundaries. For the instruction template-based compression, the cases of having 4 and 16 instruction templates were applied.

The structural hardware descriptions (VHDL) of the two TTA processor cores were created using the hardware subsystem of the MOVE framework. The control paths of the processors were then modified to decompress the compressed instructions back to the original form. The decompressors for the both compression approaches were added to the decode stage of the three-stage TTA pipeline [11] to avoid an additional pipeline stage that would have increased the cycle count. In addition, for the instruction template-based compression, a buffer had to be added to the instruction fetch stage to avoid overflow in the instruction register. Data and program memories were configured so that the same memories could be used for all the four benchmark applications. A single-ported, 1kB data memory was chosen for the configuration A and a 1kB dual-ported data memory for the configuration B. For the uncompressed program memories, a 512 word, 128-bit memory (8kB) was used for the configuration A, and 512 word, 192-bit memory (12kB) for the configuration B. The compressed program memories were configured to match the widths and lengths of the compressed program codes.

The processors were synthesized using a 130nm CMOS standard cell technology using the Synopsys Design Compiler version 2003.06. The processors were synthesized with a timing constraint of 200MHz. Data and program memories (SRAM) were

Table 1. Hardware resources of the two TTA processor configurations

Conf.	Buses	Functional units	Registers	Instr. width [bits]
A	5	1 multiplier, 1 load-store, 1 ALU, 1 compare, 1 shifter, 1 logic, 1 sign extend	19	128
B	8	1 multiplier, 2 load-stores, 2 ALUs, 1 compare, 3 shifters, 1 logic, 2 sign extend	52	192

Table 2. Statistics of the benchmark applications compiled on the two TTA processors

Application	Conf.	Instruction count	Code size	Clock cycles
32-point	A	484	7744	466
DCT	B	441	10584	423
2-D 8x8	A	163	2608	22959
DCT	B	137	3288	19455
1024-point	A	315	5040	282547
FFT	B	149	3576	123667
Viterbi	A	367	5872	2710738
decoding	B	253	6072	1568227

included as presynthesized macro cells. The switching activities for the power analysis were obtained from the gate-level simulations run on ModelSim.

Table 3 shows the areas of the uncompressed processor designs. The area of the instruction memory is comparable to the area of the processor core. In the configuration A they are equal, in the configuration B the area of the instruction memory is approximately 60% of the area of the processor core. Data memory turned out to consume most of the area. This was due to the lack of I/O support in the current architecture, which meant that all the input and output data had to be stored into the data memory. The average power consumptions, when running the four benchmarks, were on average 41 mW for the configuration A and 71 mW for the configuration B. Instruction memory consumed on average 16.1 mW on configuration A and 25.7 mW on configuration B, i.e., close to 40% of the total power consumption.

5   Experimental Results

The results of the evaluations are presented in Fig. 3 for the configuration A, and in Fig. 4 for the configuration B. Figures 3(a) and 4(a) illustrate the results in terms of area. Figures 3(b) and 4(b) illustrate the results in terms of power consumption. The areas and power consumptions are shown for the program memory and the control logic of the processor core as these were the only parts affected by the compression. The results are presented for the four benchmark applications. In addition, an average over the four benchmarks is included. For the dictionary compression, results are given for three symbol granularity levels; instruction level, move slot level, and ID field level. For the instruction template-based compression, results are shown for the cases

Table 3. Areas of the reference designs

Configuration.	data memory [kgates]	instr. memory [kgates]	Processor core [kgates]	Total [kgates]
A	104	32	31	167
B	410	48	80	538

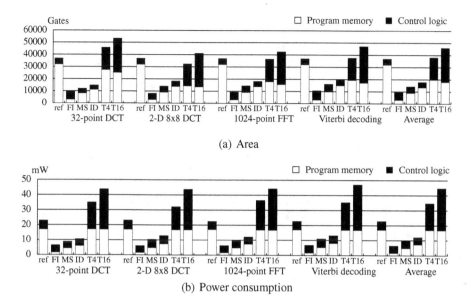

(a) Area

(b) Power consumption

Fig. 3. The obtained results on configuration A. The graph illustrates the areas and power consumptions of the program memory and the control logic for the uncompressed case (ref), for the dictionary-based compression at full instruction level (FI), at move slot level (MS), and at ID field level (ID), and for the instruction template-based compression using 4 templates (T4) and 16 templates (T16).

of having 4 and 16 templates. The obtained results indicate that from the two experimented compression alternatives the dictionary-based compression is effective in reducing both area and power consumption. On the other hand, the instruction template-based compression turned out to be unusable as it resulted in increase in both area and power consumption.

With dictionary-based compression, area and power consumption decrease remarkably on all symbol granularities. The best reduction in both area and power consumption is achieved at full instruction level. The area is reduced on average 74% on configuration A and 77% on configuration B. The power consumption is reduced on average 72% and 73%, respectively. Even though most of the instructions are stored into the dictionary as the probability of finding exactly identical instructions is small, the synthesis tool can efficiently minimize the logic of the dictionary, resulting only small additional area and power consumption due to the dictionary. The drawback of this approach is highly limited programmability. The program can be modified only if all the instructions of the modified program can be found from the original dictionary. As TTA instructions are long and are composed of several smaller fields, the number of possible combinations is huge and the probability that all the instructions of the modified code can be found from the original dictionary is small. An alternative would be to use RAM to implement the dictionary, but the results would be worse, as is shown in [14].

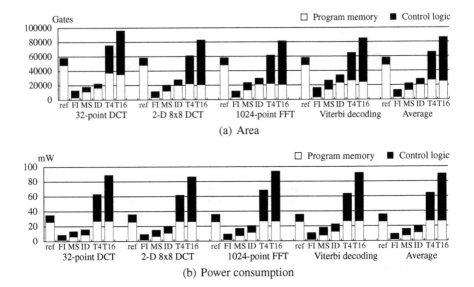

Fig. 4. The obtained results on configuration B. The graph illustrates the areas and power consumptions of the program memory and the control logic for the uncompressed case (ref), for the dictionary-based compression at full instruction level (FI), at move slot level (MS), and at ID field level (ID), and for the instruction template-based compression using 4 templates (T4) and 16 templates (T16).

The programmability can be maintained better when the dictionary-based compression is made at move slot level. As the bit patterns are smaller, the probability of finding the correct bit pattern from the dictionary for the modified code is higher. Therefore, to maintain the programmability at move slot level, it is sufficient that all the move slots of the modified code can be found from the corresponding move slot dictionaries. The area and power consumption reductions at move slot level are slightly worse compared to compression at full instruction level. The area is reduced on average 62%, and power consumption 56%, on both configurations. Even though the area and power consumption of the control logic is smaller compared to compression at full instruction level, the program memory is bigger and dissipates more power. This is due to the increased width of the compressed instruction as it is composed of several dictionary index fields.

Even better possibilities to modify the program can be achieved when the compression is applied at ID field level as the bit patterns stored into the dictionary are even smaller than at move slot level. At ID field level, the area is reduced on average 52% on configuration A and 51% on configuration B. The power consumption is reduced on average 46% on configuration A and 45% on configuration B. The area and power consumption of the control logic is smaller compared to other levels of dictionary-based compression, but the area and power consumption of the program memory are higher because the compressed instruction word becomes wider as it is composed of several indices to the source and destination ID dictionaries.

Despite the good theoretical compression ratios, instruction template-based compression approach turned out to be unusable on TTA when it was implemented in hardware as it resulted in increase in both area and power consumption. The increase is mostly due to the complex decompression procedure. As the compressed instructions are variable-width, the decompression logic turns out to be fairly complex because it requires shifting and alignment logic to construct the original instruction. In addition, a buffer is needed in the instruction fetch logic to avoid overflow in the instruction register. This additional logic results in larger area increase in the control unit than is reduced in the program memory. The decompression logic consumes also a significant amount of power. In addition, the power consumption of the program memory remains mostly unchanged even though its size decreases. This is due to the increased width of the program memory and the fact that the power consumption of a memory is more dependent on the width of the memory than its length. Due to these two reasons, the instruction template-based compression turns out to increase power consumption.

6 Conclusions

In this paper, dictionary-based and instruction template-based compression approaches were evaluated in terms of area and power consumption. These two compression methods were evaluated on two customized processors that were designed for four benchmarks from the DSP application domain. Dictionary-based compression was evaluated with three distinct symbol granularities and instruction template-based compression with two distinct numbers of templates.

Best reductions in area and power consumption were achieved when the dictionary-based compression was applied at full instruction level. On average, the area was reduced 74% on configuration A and 77% on configuration B. Power consumption was reduced on average 72% and 73%, respectively. The drawback of this approach is highly limited programmability. The programmability can be maintained better when the compression is applied at lower symbol granularity levels, but with worse area and power consumption reductions.

The instruction template-based compression approach turned out to be unusable compression approach, as it resulted in increase in both area and power consumption. This was mostly due to variable-width instructions that resulted in complex decompressor that required large area and consumed significant amount of power.

The practical hardware implementations of the compression approaches showed that theoretical evaluations are not enough to fully evaluate the goodness of a compression approach as they do not take into account the implementation details of the decompression logic. According to theoretical compression ratios the instruction template-based compression method was more effective than the dictionary-based compression, but when the compression approaches were implemented in hardware, dictionary-based compression significantly outperformed instruction template-based compression.

As TTA reminds VLIW architectures and the instruction formats are comparable, similar results could be achieved also on customizable VLIW architectures where the decompressor can be implemented inside the processor core. Because the compression approaches consider only the occurrence of a group of bits, it does not matter whether the bits actually represent an operation or a data transfer. VLIW instructions, just like

TTA instructions, can be divided into smaller fields to experiment dictionary-based compression on different symbol granularity levels. The division can be made, e.g., according to operation slot boundaries, or divide the operation slots to even smaller fields according to opcode and operand fields. The instruction template-based compression may perform better on VLIW as it has been especially designed for it.

References

1. Araújo, G., Centoducatte, P., Azevedo, R., Pannain, R.: Expression tree based algorithms for code compression on embedded RISC architectures. **8** (2000) 530–533
2. Colwell, R.P., Nix, R.P., O'Connel, J.J., Papworth, D.B., Rodman, P.K.: A VLIW architecture for a trace scheduling compiler. IEEE Trans. Comput. **37** (1988) 967–679
3. Aditya, S., Rau, B.R., Johnson, R.C.: Automatic design of VLIW and EPIC instruction formats. Technical Report HPL-1999-94, Hewlett-Packard Laboratories (2000)
4. Nam, S.J., Park, I.C., Kyung, C.M.: Improving dictionary-based code compression in VLIW architectures. IEICE Trans. Fundamentals of Electronics, Commun. and Comput. Sciences **E82-A** (1999) 2318–2124
5. Hoogerbrugge, J., Augusteijn, L., Trum, J., van de Wiel, R.: A code compression system based on pipelined interpreters. Software - Practice and Experience **29** (1999) 1005–1023
6. Ros, M., Sutton, P.: A Hamming distance based VLIW/EPIC code compression technique. In: Proc. Int. Conf. on Compilers, Architectures and Synthesis for Embedded Systems, Washington, DC, U.S.A. (2004) 132–139
7. Xie, Y., Wolf, W., Lekatsas, H.: A code decompression architecture for VLIW processors. In: Proc. 34th Annual Symp. Microarchitecture, Austin, TX, U.S.A. (2001) 66–75
8. Larin, S.Y., Conte, T.M.: Compiler-driven cached code compression schemes for embedded ILP processors. In: Proc. 32nd Annual Symp. Microarchitecture, Haifa, Israel (1999) 82–92
9. Witten, I.H., Moffat, A., Bell, T.C.: Managing Gigabytes: Compressing and Indexing Documents and Images. Morgan Kaufmann Publishers, San Francisco, CA, U.S.A. (1999)
10. Lefurgy, C., Mudge, T.: Code compression for DSP. Technical Report CSE-TR-380-98, EECS Department, University of Michigan (1998)
11. Corporaal, H.: Microprocessor Architectures: From VLIW to TTA. John Wiley & Sons, Chichester, UK (1997)
12. Heikkinen, J., Cilio, A., Takala, J., Corporaal, H.: Dictionary-based program compression on transport triggered architectures. In: Proc. IEEE Int. Symp. on Circuits and Systems, Kobe, Japan (2005) 1122–1125
13. Heikkinen, J., Rantanen, T., Cilio, A., Takala, J., Corporaal, H.: Evaluating template-based instruction compression on transport triggered architectures. In: Proc. 3rd IEEE Int. Workshop System-on-Chip for Real-Time Applications, Calgary, AB, Canada (2003) 192–195
14. Heikkinen, J., Takala, J., Corporaal, H.: Dictionary-based program compression on TTAs: Effects on area and power consumption. In: Proc. IEEE Workshop on Sig. Proc. Systems, Athens, Greece (2005) 479–484
15. Corporaal, H., Arnold, M.: Using transport triggered architectures for embedded processor design. Integrated Computer-Aided Eng. **5** (1998) 19–38

Integrated Instruction Scheduling and Fine-Grain Register Allocation for Embedded Processors*

Dae-Hwan Kim and Hyuk-Jae Lee

School of Electrical Engineering and Computer Science, P.O.Box #054,
Seoul National University, San 56-1, Shilim-Dong, Kwanak-Gu, Seoul, Korea
dhkim@capp.snu.ac.kr, hjlee@ee.snu.ac.kr

Abstract. This paper proposes a new integration technique, called IRIS (Integrated Register allocation and Instruction Scheduling), to combine instruction scheduling and register allocation. Both register allocation and instruction scheduling are performed simultaneously at each variable reference where the selection between serialization by scheduling and spilling by register allocation is determined. To make a right selection, the costs of serialization and spilling are estimated with a cost model proposed to reduce the complexity of the estimation. Experiments show that IRIS achieves significant improvements when compared to widely-used existing techniques.

1 Introduction

For embedded systems, both speed improvement and code size reduction are important goals of an optimizing compiler. An efficient instruction scheduling is necessary for fast execution while an intelligent register allocator is required for code size reduction. Instruction scheduling and register allocation make a significant impact on each other. Therefore, even an efficient instruction scheduling or a register allocation can reduce the overall performance of a program if they give a negative effect on each other. In order to achieve the best optimization results, techniques of integrating instruction scheduling and register allocation have been extensively studied [1], [5], [8], [9].

Any register allocation is required to reduce register requirement to the number of machine registers. To meet this requirement, a traditional register allocator spills an instruction, i.e., does not allocate a register to an instruction. For a register allocator integrated with an instruction scheduler, it has another option, called serialization which prohibits overlapped live ranges of variables by adding precedence constraints among instructions. For an integrated register allocator and instruction scheduler, the decision to select spilling or serialization is important for its performance.

In previous approaches [5], [8], serialization is preferred to spilling. However, serialization is not as efficient as spilling for certain architectures and/or program contexts. For example, pipeline stalls caused by serialization in a heavily nested loop are more expensive than the cost of spill in less frequently executed regions. To make

---

* This work was supported by Korea Research Foundation Grant (KRF-2003-003-D00341).

S. Vassiliadis et al. (Eds.): SAMOS 2006, LNCS 4017, pp. 269–278, 2006.

a right choice, a precise estimation of the costs of serialization and spilling is essential. Berson et al. [1] compute the costs for both spilling and serialization, and then selects the one with the minimum cost. However, the spill cost is computed for the spill-everywhere technique which inserts a store after every definition and a load before every use. Thus, the spill cost is somewhat overestimated since it assumes more spill instructions than are necessary.

In addition to the imprecise comparison of spill and serialization, the limitation of graph-coloring approach for global register allocation gives another source of severe performance degradation. The main advantage of the graph-coloring approach is its simplicity by abstracting each variable as a single node of an interference graph. However, the simple abstraction results in the loss of information about program context. Contrary to the global decision of the register allocation where variables are allocated only once throughout a function, instruction scheduling is basically a local transformation that is sensitive to the local order of instructions. The mismatch between the global decision of register allocation and the local decision of instruction scheduling often reduces the efficiency of the integration of register allocation and instruction scheduling.

This paper proposes a new integration of global register allocation and local instruction scheduling addressing the two issues described above. To overcome the limitation of the graph-coloring register allocation, this paper employs the fine-grain approach for register allocation recently proposed by Kim and Lee [6]. The fine-grain approach performs register allocation at every reference of a variable in the order of a variable reference flow. The register allocation becomes a local decision so that it can be effectively combined with instruction scheduling. Thus, both register allocation and instruction scheduling are performed simultaneously at each reference in the variable reference flow. To address another issue of making a right decision between spilling and serialization, the costs of various possible schedules and register spills are estimated and the schedule and register allocation with the minimum cost are selected. Henceforth, the proposed integration technique is referred as IRIS (Integrated Register allocation and Instruction Scheduling).

The rest of this paper is organized as follows. Section 2 introduces the register allocation proposed in [6]. Section 3 presents the proposed algorithm for the integration of register allocation and instruction scheduling. Section 4 presents the cost model of the integrated algorithm. Section 5 shows experimental results and Section 6 presents conclusions.

2 Fine-Grain Register Allocation

Kim and Lee in [6] propose a fine-grain approach for register allocation such that register allocation is performed at every reference of a variable in the order of a variable reference flow. It improves the efficiency by using information about the flow of variable references of a program. For each reference, the costs of various possible register allocations are estimated by tracing a possible instruction sequence resulting from the register allocations. A cost model is formulated to reduce the scope of the trace. This section briefly introduces the register allocation.

For a given program, the fine-grain approach constructs a varef-graph (variable reference flow graph) that represents a partial order of variable references in the program. Each node of this graph represents a variable reference and an edge represents a control flow of the program, i.e., the execution order of the variable references of the program. Fig. 1 shows an example program with the corresponding varef-graph. For illustration, the number of each statement is given in the leftmost column in the program. Each node in the graph represents the reference of a variable whose name is given inside the circle. The number in the upper right of the circle is the node number. Note that this number is different from the statement number because one statement can have multiple variable references, and consequently, correspond to multiple nodes in the varef-graph. In Fig. 1, the reference of variable 'a' at statement (1) is represented by node '1'. The program has two additional references of variable 'a' that are represented by nodes '2' and '5', respectively. Variable 'b' is referenced three times at statements (3), (4), and (5) and the corresponding nodes are '3', '4', and '6', respectively. Note that statement (5) has references of two variables 'a' and 'b' which are represented by nodes '5' and '6', respectively. An edge represents a partial execution order. Statement (1) is supposed to be executed first, and the corresponding node '1' is the root node. Statement (2) is supposed to be executed next, and the corresponding node '2' is the successor of node '1'. Statements (3) and (4) are executed next to the statement (2), and therefore the corresponding nodes '3' and '4' are successors of node '2'. Statements (3) and (4) must be executed exclusively, and therefore, there is no edge between nodes '3' and '4'. Statements (5) and (6) are executed next in sequence.

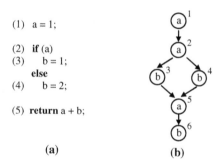

(1) a = 1;

(2) **if** (a)
(3)   b = 1;
     else
(4)   b = 2;

(5) **return** a + b;

(a)   (b)

Fig. 1. Fine-grain register allocation (a) example program (b) variable reference flow graph (varef-graph)

With the order given by the varef-graph, register allocation is performed at every reference of a variable (i.e. every visit of a node in the varef-graph). The visit order is a modified breadth-first order that is the same as the breadth-first order with the modification that guarantees a successor node to be always visited later than its predecessor. The register allocation continues until all nodes in the varef-graph are visited. When no register is available, the fine-grain allocator preempts a register from a previously assigned variable if the preemption reduces the execution cost of a program. To select the register with maximum cost reduction, the preemption cost and benefit are analyzed for all possible registers for preemption. The cost estimation often requires large computation with exponential complexity. Thus, a mathematical model for the simple estimation of an approximated cost is derived and a heuristic with a reasonable amount of computation is developed based on the cost model [6].

3 Integrated Register Allocation and Instruction Scheduling

Consider the program with the flow graph shown in Fig. 2. It consists of four basic blocks, B1, B2, B3, and B4. The four boxes in the figure represent the basic blocks. The contents of each basic block are given inside the box for B1, B3, and B4. For B2, the program code and its dependence dag are shown separately in the right. In the left of each box, the number in the parenthesis represents the number of iterations of a basic block. Basic block B2 is iterated 100 times and needs to be carefully optimized. In the dag of B2, each statement corresponding to the node is given below the circle and the statement number is given inside the circle. The cost of an edge is also given to represent the required latency between instructions. It is assumed that a multiply instruction takes 3 cycles, a load/store instruction takes 4 cycles, and all the other instructions are executed in a single cycle. If the number of registers is sufficient, one possible optimal schedule is '1'→'2'→'4'→'3'→'5'→'6', and it requires 6 cycles. If the number of registers is five, this schedule runs out of registers at statement '4' because the number of live-in variables is three, 'x', 'y', and 'z', and each of nodes '1', '2', and '4' requires a new register. In this case, previous approaches attempt to reduce register demands by serialization. One approach, called integrated prepass scheduler (IPS) [5] schedules node '3' instead of node '4'. Similarly, another approach called a scheduler-sensitive global register allocator (SSG) [8] adds a dag edge from node '3' to node '4'. The final schedule is '1'→'2'→'3'→'4'→'5'→'6'. This rescheduling requires 7 cycles with one pipeline stall between '2' and '3'. Considering 100 iterations of B2, the total execution cycles of B2 is 700.

Serialization is not the only choice that the integrated scheduler can make. Register spilling is the alternative. Consider the case when 'y' in node '2' is spilled partially,

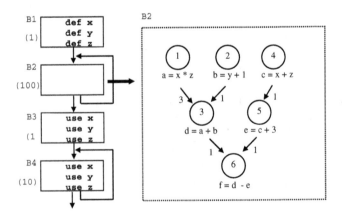

Fig. 2. Example program and a dependence dag

i.e., it is spilled not in the entire program but only in a certain part of the program. For example, 'y' is spilled after the execution of '2'. In this spilling, a load of 'y' in B3 and a store of its reaching definition of 'y' in B1 are required. Note that no load is required for 'y' at node '2' because it is guaranteed to be in a register until the execution of node '2'. Because this selection frees one register after the execution of node '2', the fastest schedule, '1'$\rightarrow$'2'$\rightarrow$'4'$\rightarrow$'3'$\rightarrow$'5'$\rightarrow$'6', is allowed. Although the partial spilling requires spill code of 'y' in less frequently executed blocks, B1 and B3, it achieves the optimal schedule for the most frequently executed block of B2 and does not require spill code in B2 and B4. Thus, the partial spill results in the better performance than serialization.

IRIS, a new integrated instruction scheduling and register allocation, extends the register allocation presented in the previous section and performs instruction scheduling and register allocation at the same time at an every visit of a node in the varef graph. When there are enough registers, IRIS focuses on instruction scheduling and selects an instruction to reduce pipeline stalls. This scheduling scheme is the same as CSP (Code Scheduling for Pipelined processors) presented in [5]. The instruction scheduling based on the CSP scheme continues until the scheduler runs out of registers. When no register is available, IRIS selects one between serialization and spilling. The choice of spilling avoids the possibility of instruction rescheduling and searches a register to be assigned to the current instruction. In this case, the register should be preempted from another instruction. The preemption requires the insertion of spill instructions resulting in the increase of execution cycles. Among many registers, the one with the minimum increase of execution cycles is selected. The other choice of serialization avoids a register preemption and reschedules another instruction that does not increase register pressure. This selection may introduce extra pipeline stalls. To make the best selection between the two possible choices, it is essential to have a cost model to allow a fair comparison between serialization and spilling. The cost model for register allocation defined in [6] is modified and extended to have a new cost model. More details of the cost model are discussed in Section 4.

4   Cost Estimation

The success of IRIS heavily depends on the precise cost analysis of serialization and spilling. However, the problem of analyzing this cost is equivalent to the problem of finding both the optimal schedule and the register allocation. Since this problem is NP-complete [7], an approximated cost with reasonable complexity is derived in this section.

Suppose that no register is available when a node 'm' is considered for scheduling. IRIS needs to select between serialization and spilling. With the choice of spilling, IRIS schedules the node 'm' first and preempts a register from another node. The additional execution time due to the preemption is represented by a preemption penalty and denoted as PenalyPreempt(m) where 'm' is the node which is supposed to acquire a register preempted from another node. Here, the term, preemption instead of spill is used in order to use the same terminology as [6]. With the other choice of serialization, IRIS searches a new node 'n' that does not increase register pressure, and therefore, does not require a preemption. However, scheduling of this node may cause an additional pipeline stall. The increase of the execution time caused by the additional pipeline stall is represented by a stall penalty and denoted as

PenalytStall(n). Then, ScheduleCost(n) represents the additional execution time caused by both a preemption and a pipeline stall and is defined as the summation of the preemption penalty and the stall penalty.

$$\text{ScheduleCost (n)} = \text{PenaltyStall(n)} + \text{PenaltyPreempt(n)}. \tag{1}$$

For the derivation of Eq. (1), consider, first, the stall penalty. A node is called *ready* when all its predecessors are scheduled, and called the *first-ready node* when it is the first node in the CSP order among ready nodes. The scheduling of the first-ready node demands no additional scheduling cost. Thus, the stall penalty of the first-ready node is defined as zero. For a node, 'n', that is not the first-ready node, its stall penalty is defined as follows. If the node 'n' is not ready or increases register pressure, PenaltyStall(n) is defined as infinity. This definition prevents the schedule of the node that is neither ready nor good for register allocation. For ready nodes that do not increase register pressure, the stall penalty is defined as the increased execution cycles, i.e., the execution cycles of the new schedule subtracted by that of the CSP schedule. Let G be unscheduled nodes in the dependence graph. Let CSP(G) be the schedule in the CSP order and $CSP_n(G)$ be the schedule where 'n' is scheduled first and the remaining unscheduled nodes in G are scheduled in the CSP order. Let Cycles(S) be the execution time of schedule S. Then, PenaltyStall of a node 'n' is defined as:

$$\text{PenaltyStall(n)} = 10^d * [\text{Cycles}(CSP_n(G)) - \text{Cycles}(CSP(G))]$$
$$\qquad \text{if n is ready and does not increase register pressure,} \tag{2}$$
$$\infty \qquad \text{otherwise.}$$

Here, d is the loop depth for the node 'n' and is zero if the node 'n' is not inside a loop. The term, 10^d is multiplied in order to give a weight to a nested loop. Any local instruction scheduling can be used for the proposed integrated approach with Eq. (2) by replacing CSP( ) with the appropriate cost model of the local schedule. List scheduling [4] based on the CSP scheme is one of the most widely-used techniques for local instruction scheduling. In this technique, a priority is assigned to each node to determine which ready node to be scheduled next. A common strategy for priority assignment uses the *latency weighted depth* of a node [4] which is the longest weighted path from 'n' to a leaf node. The weight of a node is the latency of the operation associated with the node. Then, the priority of a node 'n' is defined as:

$$\text{priority(n)} = \max \left(\forall l \in \text{leaves(G)}, \ \forall p \in \text{paths(n,...,l)} \ \sum_{p_i=n, \, p_i \in p}^{l} \text{latency}(p_i) \right) \tag{3}$$

where latency(p_i) is the latency of node 'p_i', leaves(G) represent all leaf nodes, and paths(n,...,l) does all paths from node 'n' to node 'l'. With Eq. (3), Cycles (CSP(G)) is replaced by priority(k) where k is the first-ready node in the CSP order. In addition, Cycles ($CSP_n(G)$) is replaced by priority(n) . Thus, the stall penalty becomes

$$\text{PenaltyStall(n)} = 10^d * [\text{priority(n)} - \text{priority(k)}]$$
$$\qquad \text{if n is ready and does not increase register pressure,} \tag{4}$$
$$\infty \qquad \text{otherwise,}$$

where node 'k' is the first-ready node in the CSP order.

Now, consider the derivation of PenaltyPreempt(n). For this derivation, the cost model proposed for the fine-grain register allocation in [6] is modified for the comparison with serialization. First, PenaltyPreempt(n) is set to zero if node 'n' does not increase register pressure. If node 'n' increases register pressure, the node 'n' must preempt a register 'r' assigned to another node. Let VarHold(n,r) denote the variable that holds register 'r' when the register allocation is performed for node 'n', and NodeHold(n,r) denote the set of nodes that reference VarHold(n,r) and precede 'n' while no other nodes referencing VarHold(n,r) exist between NodeHold(n,r) and 'n'. The nodes that are most likely to be spilled by the register preemption are the ones that reference VarHold(n,r) next to NodeHold(n,r). Therefore, this set of nodes is defined as *the preemption impact set* denoted by ImpactSetPreempt(n,r) and spill costs are estimated for the nodes in this set. If there is no path from NodeHold(n,r) to a next reference of VarHold(n,r) including node 'n', the next reference is not included in the preemption impact set. This is because the insertion of a reload instruction is not necessary at the next reference. Reference [6] explains more details about the preemption impact set.

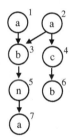

Fig. 3. Example varef-graph for preemption impact set

Consider the varef-graph in Fig. 3. Assume that both nodes '1' and '2' hold register 'r1', and the register allocator visits node '5'. Then, VarHold(5,'r1') = 'a', and NodeHold(5,'r1')= {1,2}. The next reference of VarHold(5, 'r1') is {7}. For both nodes '1' and '2', there exists a path to '7' that includes node '5'. Thus, ImpactSetPreempt(5, 'r1') = {7}. This indicates that the preemption of 'r1' at node '5' causes node '7' to be spilled.

Let PenaltyPreempt(n,r) denote the preemption penalty for the case when node 'n' preempts register 'r'. All the nodes in the preemption impact set are likely to be spilled. Thus, PenaltyPreempt(n,r) is defined as the summation of the execution times of the nodes in the preemption impact set

$$PenaltyPreempt(n,r) = \sum_{m \in ImpactSetPreempt\,(n,r)} cost(m). \qquad (5)$$

Here, cost(m) represents the estimated execution cycles of the additional load/store instructions when node 'm' is spilled. In the estimation of cost(m), a load/store instruction is necessary not only for the execution of the node 'm' itself but also for reaching definitions of the node's referencing variable. Therefore, the execution times caused by the insertion of the store instructions for the reaching definitions should also be included in cost(m). Let ReachingDef(m) denote the set of reaching definitions of node 'm'. Let NodeCost(m) denote the estimated execution time of each node 'm'. Then, cost(m) is defined as follows:

$$cost(m) = NodeCost(m) +$$
$$\sum_{k \in ReachingDef(m),\ k \notin ImpactSetPreempt\,(n,r)} NodeCost(k). \qquad (6)$$

Note that reaching definitions in ImpactSetPreempt(n,r) are not included in Eq. (6) because they should be added just once in the evaluation of PenaltyPreempt(n,r).

Consider the evaluation of NodeCost(k). If node 'k' is already spilled, no additional cost is necessary. Thus, NodeCost(k)=0 in this case. In the other cases when the node is not visited yet or allocated to the same register, the cost is simply the estimated execution time of the node. Thus, the NodeCost(k) is defined as follows:

$$\text{NodeCost(k)} = 0 \quad \text{if 'k' is already visited and spilled,}$$
$$\text{time(k)} \quad \text{otherwise,} \tag{7}$$

where time(k) is the estimated execution time of node 'k'. For a fair comparison with Eq. (4), the execution time should be estimated in the same manner as Eq. (4). Thus, time(k) is defined as

$$\text{time(k)} = \text{latency(k)}* 10^d \tag{8}$$

where d is the loop depth. Eq. (5) gives the preemption cost for a register r. Assume that a target processor has R registers, $r_0, r_1, \ldots, r_{R-1}$. Among the R registers, the one with the minimum preemption penalty is chosen. Thus, the preemption penalty of a node 'n' is defined as:

$$\text{PenaltyPreempt(n)} = \min_{i \in \{0, 1, \ldots, R-1\}} \text{PenaltyPreempt(n, } r_i). \tag{9}$$

5 Evaluation

To evaluate the efficiency, IRIS is implemented in the intermediate code of `lcc` [3] targeted for a hypothetical machine. This target assumes a load/store, register-oriented, three-address instruction format, and pipelined with interlock architecture that is similar to the one used by previous research, IPS in [5] and SSG in [8]. Two different simulations are performed for low latency and high latency architectures, respectively. For the low latency, delays are similar to IPS; an add instruction takes 2 cycles, a multiply/divide instruction takes 3 cycles, a load/store instruction takes 4 cycles, and all the other instructions are executed in a single cycle. The high latency architecture assumes 3, 6, and 8 cycles for add, multiply/divide, and load/store instructions, respectively. The benchmark programs are the livermore program, linpack program, DCT computation, inverse DCT computation, huffman computation, stanford bench-mark, and jccoefct program that controls the JPEG coefficient buffer.

The simulation is for the comparison with other integrated scheduling and allocation techniques, IPS and SSG. For SSG, a BMW approach is used. Postpass scheduling (POSTPASS) is also implemented because it is widely used for comparison. POSTPASS performs list scheduling [4] first and then processes Briggs' graph-coloring register allocation next [2]. Fig. 4 shows the speed-ups over POSTPASS for the low latency architecture. The number of registers is changed from 12, 16, to 20. As the number of registers increases, the average improvement of IRIS over POSTPASS changes from 29%, and 36%, to 34%, respectively. When compared to SSG and IPS, the average improvements of IRIS are 14.5% and 25.9%, respectively.

The improvement over IPS is achieved because IRIS selects the better choice between serialization and spilling while IPS always chooses serialization. Another reason for the improvement is the support of the partial spilling by IRIS while spilling is not allowed in IPS. Thus, in IPS, when no ready instruction can reduce register pressure, register pressure can be increased continuously, which degrades the overall performance. After IPS is completed, spilling is handled by a postpass register allocator with a spill-everywhere technique. SSG also employs the spill-everywhere

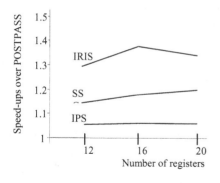

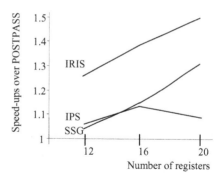

Fig. 4. Speed-up of IRIS, SSG and IPS over POSTPASS for the low latency architecture

Fig. 5. Speed-up of IRIS, SSG and IPS over POSTPASS for the high latency architecture

approach and prefers serialization. In addition, the serialization of SSG often adds unnecessary constrains on scheduling. It also prefers the original sequential ordering of instructions in serialization while other ordering may be more beneficial.

Fig. 5 shows the speed-ups over POSTPASS when latencies are high. As the number of registers increases from 12, and 16, to 20, the average improvement of IRIS changes from 25%, and 38%, to 50%, respectively. When compared to SSG and IPS, the average improvements of IRIS are 20.5% and 27%, respectively. This result shows that greater improvements are achieved when the latencies are high.

Consider the complexity of IRIS. The variable flow graph can be constructed by classical reaching definition analysis [7]. The complexity of a dependence dag build is $O(n^2)$ where n is the number of instructions in a program. The worst-case complexity of scheduling is $O(n^2)$ because it requires each unscheduled instruction to be inspected at each scheduling of a node. Note that the complexity of scheduling is $O(n)$ in most real applications. The complexity of the register allocation is $O(N^2)$ [6] where N is the number of nodes in the varef-graph. For the derivation of a preemption impact set, the search space is localized because the next reference of a variable is generally close to the node. Thus, the complexity may not increase as N increases in many programs and the time complexity of the proposed approach is close to $O(N)$ in these programs. As n is generally larger than N, the total complexity of IRIS is $O(n^2)$, and $O(n)$ in practice.

6 Conclusions and Future Work

The proposed integration of register allocation and instruction scheduling improves the posspass scheduling, IPS proposed in [5], and SSG proposed in [8] by an average of 35.3%, 26.5%, and 17.5%, respectively. Although the widely-used list scheduling is employed in this paper, other instruction schedulers can also be used for the proposed integration approach. Evaluation for the integration with various other instruction schedulers remains as future work. The instruction scheduling in IRIS is limited to the local level, and the integration with a global scheduler is another topic for future work.

References

1. Berson, D. A., Gupta, R., and Soffa, M. L.: Integrated instruction scheduling and register allocation techniques. In Proceedings of LCPC 1998 (1998), 247-262.
2. Briggs, P., Cooper, K.D., Kennedy, K., and Torczon, L.: Coloring heuristics for register allocation. In Proceedings of ACM PLDI'89 (1989), 275-284.
3. Fraser, C.W., and Hanson, D.R.: A Retargetable C Compiler: Design and Implementation. Benjamin/Cummings (1995).
4. Gibbons, P.B, and Muchnick, S.S.: Efficient instruction scheduling for a pipelined architecture. In Proceedings of CC'86 (1986), 11-16.
5. Goodman, J. R., and Hsu, W. C.: Code scheduling and register allocation in large basic blocks. In Proceedings of Supercomputing'88 (1988), 442-452.
6. Kim, D. H. and Lee, H. -J.: Fine-Grain Register Allocation based on a Global Spill Costs Analysis. In Proceedings of SCOPES'2003 (2003), 255-269.
7. Muchnick, S. S.: Advanced compiler design and implementation. Morgan Kaufmann, SanFrancisco CA (1997).
8. Norris. C., and Pollock. L. L.: An experimental study of several cooperative register allocation and instruction scheduling strategies. In Proceedings of MICRO'95 (1995), 169-179.
9. Pinter, S.: Register allocation with instruction scheduling: A new approach. In Proceedings of ACM PLDI'93 (1993), 248-257.

Compilation and Simulation Tool Chain for Memory Aware Energy Optimizations *

Manish Verma[1], Lars Wehmeyer[1], Robert Pyka[1], Peter Marwedel[1], and Luca Benini[2]

[1] Department of Computer Science XII, University of Dortmund, 44221 Dortmund, Germany
[2] DEIS, University of Bologna, 40136 Bologna, Italy

Abstract. Memories are known to be the energy bottleneck of portable embedded devices. Numerous memory aware energy optimizations have been proposed. However, both the optimization and the validation are performed in an ad-hoc manner as a coherent optimizing compilation and simulation framework does not exist as yet. In this paper, we present such a framework for performing memory hierarchy aware energy optimization. Both the compiler and the simulator are configured from a single memory hierarchy description. Significant savings of up to 50% in the total energy dissipation are reported.

1 Introduction

Contemporary portable devices are experiencing an ever-increasing spiral of feature enhancement and device convergence. Today's mobile devices, besides acting as phones, also serve as PDA, MP3 player, digital camera and also as a video game console. Fast processors, large memories and aggressive energy optimization techniques are required to support all the aforementioned features in a portable device. It is expected that future devices will have even faster processors and larger memories, both of which are extremely power hungry. As a consequence, a lot of research effort is being directed towards energy optimizations.

The memory subsystem has been identified as the energy and performance bottleneck of the entire system. This problem is expected to aggravate in the future as the performance gap between the processor and the memory is growing. This phenomenon is also known as the "Memory Wall Problem" [1]. Memory hierarchies are constructed to improve the energy dissipation and the performance of the memory subsystem. In addition, the application is optimized to efficiently utilize the memory subsystem.

In order to perform a fast and efficient design space exploration, a coherent framework for code-optimization and system simulation is required: A framework which can optimize the application code for a given memory hierarchy and also evaluate the optimization by simulating the optimized executable on the same memory hierarchy. Unfortunately, most contemporary memory optimizations are performed at the source-level with a complete disregard to the compiler generating the executable. Often, the simulation framework is also a stopgap solution such that every new memory hierarchy requires manual intervention and recompilation of the entire simulation framework. In this paper, we present a coherent framework called Memory Aware C Compilation (MACC) framework.

---

* This work has been partially supported by the European ARTIST Network of Excellence and the German Research Foundation (DFG).

S. Vassiliadis et al. (Eds.): SAMOS 2006, LNCS 4017, pp. 279–288, 2006.

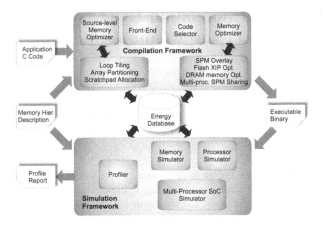

Fig. 1. Workflow of MACC Framework

Figure 1 presents the workflow of the MACC framework. The MACC framework is partitioned into the compilation and the simulation framework, both of which share the memory hierarchy description and the energy database. The compilation framework, depending upon the memory hierarchy, optimizes the application code and generates the executable binary. This binary is then simulated and profiled by the simulation framework and the system statistics are reported. These statistics are used to evaluate the system and the optimizations. The main advantages of the MACC framework are that it includes the only energy optimizing compilation framework known to the research community and a highly configurable processor independent memory hierarchy simulator. We start by explaining the compilation framework of the MACC framework.

2   Compilation Framework

The compilation framework shown in the upper half of Figure 1 provides the user with a rich set of memory optimizations. It optimizes the energy consumption of the system by efficiently utilizing the memory hierarchy. Besides the application source file, it requires the memory hierarchy description file, an XML representation of the memory hierarchy, as input. The memory hierarchy can also be designed by the user with the help of a GUI (*cf.* Section 4.1 for additional details). In addition, the compilation framework has access to the energy database which contains the instruction-level energy model of the processor as well as the energy and timing models of various memories. The compilation framework supports the ARM7 processor and includes numerous optimizations supporting memories *viz.* SRAM/Scratchpad, Cache, Loop Cache, DRAM and Flash. The framework is being extended to support an ARM based Multi-processor SoC [2]. The compilation framework is divided into the following tools:

1. *Source-Level Memory Optimizers:* perform memory related optimization at the source code level.
2. *Front-End:* converts the application source code into an intermediate representation (IR) and performs several traditional optimizations (*e.g.* dead code elimination)

3. *Code Selector:* converts the IR into the assembly code of the application and performs several low-level optimizations (*e.g.* peephole optimization).
4. *Backend Memory Optimizer:* performs memory optimizations at assembly level in cooperation with the linker to generate the executable binary of the application.

The memory aware compilation framework started as a research endeavor and has matured into a fairly stable framework. It is based upon ICD-C [3] and Lance [4] compilation frameworks. It supports all ANSI-C data types and can compile and optimize applications from Mediabench, MiBench, DSPStone and UTDSP benchmark suites.

All optimizations are performed on the set of memory objects (*MO*). A memory object is a part of the application program (*e.g.* variable, array tile, function, basic block etc.) whose mapping onto the memory hierarchy enables various memory optimizations. Subsections 2.1 and 2.2 describe the source-level and the backend memory optimizations, respectively.

2.1 Source-Level Memory Optimizer

The source-level memory optimizer is the highest level optimization phase of the compilation framework. It includes several optimizations also present in the backend memory optimizer, albeit at a coarser granularity level. The main benefit of the source-level optimizer is its inherent retargetability. The optimized application can be compiled for any other processor resulting in similar gains.

The source-level memory optimizer is based primarily on the ICD-C framework. It features a lossless object oriented intermediate representation for C programs. Most important for our optimizer is the capability to write out the IR to a file conforming to the C standard. The set of memory objects considered by the optimizations consists of global variables and functions. The memory optimizer includes the following optimizations:

1. Non-Overlayed Scratchpad Allocation [5]
2. Scratchpad Overlay (with support for DMA) [6]
3. Array Partitioning [7]
4. Array Tiling

The first two approaches are also present in the backend memory optimizer and will be presented in detail in the following section. The focus of *array partitioning* approach are applications containing large arrays which are accessed through irregular index functions. These arrays cannot be allocated onto small and energy efficient scratchpad memories. Consequently, the *array partitioning* approach divides the large array into two smaller partitions such that the allocation of one of the two partitions to the scratchpad memory is guaranteed. Additionally, the application source code is modified such that the irregular index functions correctly access the two array partitions. If the application under consideration contains only arrays with affine index functions, the *array tiling* optimization can be used. It generates several equal sized partitions or tiles of the arrays. These tiles are then swapped in and out of the scratchpad memory at runtime, based upon their live-ranges.

2.2 Backend Memory Optimizer

The backend memory optimizer includes numerous optimizations for various memories. Unlike most of the current approaches, the optimizations consider both the data and instructions for optimization. The memory optimizer includes optimizations for scratchpad, instruction cache, loop-cache, DRAM and Flash memory. Scratchpad allocation approaches reduce the energy dissipation of the system through the improved utilization of the scratchpad memory. Trace generation based instruction cache optimization is used to improve the spatial locality of the application.

The backend memory optimizer is the last optimization step of the compilation framework. It works in conjunction with the assembler and the linker and produces the optimized executable by mapping all the memory objects to the assigned memories. The optimizations are performed at a finer level than in the source level memory optimizer as the set of memory objects is composed of global variables, basic blocks and the stack. Some of the important memory optimizations are enumerated below:

1. Non-Overlayed Scratchpad Allocation [5]
2. Partitioned Scratchpad Allocation [8]
3. Scratchpad Overlay (with DMA support) [6]
4. Instruction Cache Optimization [9]
5. Pre-loaded loop cache Optimization [9]
6. DRAM memory optimization [10]
7. XIP Flash Memory Optimization [10]

Non-overlayed scratchpad allocation [5] maps the best set of memory objects onto the scratchpad memory which remain allocated onto the scratchpad for the entire execution time of the application. Each memory object *mo* has two parameters: (a) $E_{profit}(mo)$ quantifies the energy reduction that can be achieved by assigning the memory object on the scratchpad memory and (b) $size(mo)$ returns the size of the memory object. The best set of memory objects is chosen such that the total energy benefit is maximized and the aggregate size of the memory objects in the best set is less than the scratchpad size. The allocation problem can be formulated as the following:

$$\text{Maximize:} \qquad E_{profit}^{Total} = \sum_{mo} E_{profit}(mo) * x_{mo}$$
$$x_{mo} * size(mo) \leq ScratchpadSize \;\; \forall mo \in MO \;\; x_{mo} \in \{0,1\}$$

It can be easily seen that the non-overlayed scratchpad allocation is the well-known knapsack problem. If a number of partitioned scratchpad memories are being used instead of one single scratchpad, additional savings are possible since smaller memories are faster and consume less energy per access. The above equations have to be reformulated to take into account the increased freedom of allocating the memory objects to a number of scratchpad memory partitions. Additionally, the leakage energy dissipation of a large number of scratchpad memories was also studied in our experiments to let the compiler choose those memory partitions that are most profitable in order to minimize the overall system energy dissipation.

The *scratchpad overlay* optimization uses the fact that a memory object is not required by the application for its entire execution time. In other words, memory objects also have *live-ranges*. Therefore, memory objects with non-conflicting live-ranges can be assigned to the same location onto the scratchpad. The approach also takes into account the spilling of memory objects to the main memory in order to maximize the total energy reduction. The overlay approach [6] was found be similar to the *global register allocation* approach and both optimal and near-optimal solutions were presented.

The memory optimizations [9] for a cache based architecture are also present in the backend memory optimizer. The included approaches improve the spatial locality of the application code by generating *traces*. Additionally, scratchpad and loop cache allocation approaches are also included. These approaches utilize a scratchpad or a loop-cache as an instruction buffer and map the instruction sequences to minimize the number of cache misses and the total energy dissipation of the system.

If a DRAM main memory is used in the system, considering per-access costs for memory accesses is insufficient due to the state-dependent behavior of a dynamic RAM. A corresponding energy model is integrated into our evaluation framework. It also supports the power management features commonly found in DRAM chips today. This can be exploited in an optimization that allocates memory objects to a scratchpad memory in order to maximize the time that the main DRAM memory can be kept in the power down state.

Most embedded systems today carry Flash memories to permanently store configuration information or the application's binary code. In contrast to the prevailing "Store-and-Download" approach, where code and data is first copied and then accessed from the faster main memory, the "eXecute-In-Place" (XIP) feature allows the memory objects to be accessed directly from the Flash memory. The corresponding optimization determines a trade-off between the copy costs and the slower Flash memory access times. The main benefit of this optimization is that it significantly reduces the main memory requirements of the system.

3   Energy Database

A fine-grained, accurate and exhaustive energy database is an essential component of the entire MACC framework. An evaluation board (AT91EB01) [11] featuring an ARM7 processor was chosen to generate an accurate energy database. Current measurements were performed on the board to determine an instruction level energy model for the ARM7 processor. A measurement based energy model was also determined for the SRAM main memory of the board. The energy model for the processor and the memory was found to be 98% accurate [12]. Behavioral energy models for memories have also been found to be very accurate. Consequently, we used behavioral models for the memories whose current consumption could not be measured. The accurate energy model for the MPSoC, accounting for the processors, memories and the interconnect, was obtained from ST Microelectronics.

4   Simulation Framework

The presented simulation framework allows simulation of a system consisting of an ARM7 processor attached to a customizable memory hierarchy. The processor simulator provided by ARM Ltd. is used to generate the instruction trace. The instruction trace is fed into the memory simulator which simulates the specified memory hierarchy. The profiler accesses the instruction trace, the memory simulator and the energy database to compute the system statistics (*e.g.* execution time in CPU cycles and energy dissipated by the processor and the memory hierarchy). In addition, it computes the application statistics (*e.g.* number and type of accesses to each global variable). Currently, we are integrating the ARM-based MPSoC [2] into the simulation framework.

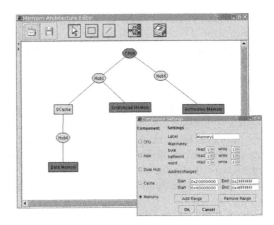

Fig. 2. Example MEMSIM memory hierarchy configuration

4.1 Memory Simulator

In order to efficiently simulate different memory hierarchy configurations, a flexible memory hierarchy simulator (MEMSIM) was developed. Memory regions with different access characteristics, a number of different cache parameters, loop caches and scratchpad memories are currently supported. MEMSIM reads the XML description of the memory hierarchy and a memory access trace of a program. The development of MEMSIM enabled us to overcome limitations of pure instruction set simulation and also of the currently available cache and memory simulation frameworks. The technical requirements for MEMSIM, e.g. cycle true simulation, flexibility and configurability were achieved by using object oriented design principles in the design and implementation phase. All components of the memory hierarchy are derived from one uniform base class, which enables the easy and seamless integration of memory models into the simulation framework. Since the overall structure of MEMSIM is comparable to a subset to the simulation framework offered in SystemC and this modeling language has evolved to a fairly stable tool, it would be also possible to develop such a simulator in SystemC.

While a variety of cache simulators are available, none of them seemed suitable for an in-depth exploration of the design space of a memory hierarchy. In addition, scratchpad memories, loop caches and DRAM memories should also be considered. This flexibility is missing in previously published memory simulation frameworks which tend to focus on one particular component of the memory hierarchy. Therefore, the development of this new memory simulator was necessary. To avoid the high complexity of implementing a cycle-true instruction set simulator for a particular processor, MEMSIM runs as a post-pass to processor simulation. The sequence of executed instructions and memory accesses is fed into MEMSIM and the accesses to each memory are computed accordingly. By encapsulating the trace reader functions in classes of their own with a defined interface, it is possible to use a variety of available processor simulators by only adjusting the internal implementation of the trace reader functions. The trace based approach introduces a constrain to the way the simulator has to generate the memory access log. Since in a suitable tracefile each entry represents a completed memory access, no interleaving of accesses is allowed.

All components of the simulated memory hierarchy are implemented as abstract components. All instantiated components inherit from virtual C++ base classes and implement the functionality required to perform as a part of the memory hierarchy. To connect the different components to each other, the concept of so-called hubs is used. Compared to real hardware hubs serve as a kind of addresspace selector and multiplexer. Using hubs, it is only necessary to consider the connection of each memory component to its neighboring hub, which in turn connects to other memory components. An example memory hierarchy is shown in Figure 2. Memory accesses in MEMSIM are first considered at the level of the processor and are subsequently passed to the corresponding memory hierarchy elements. The decision about which component an access is routed to is taken by the hubs, considering e.g. the address of the access. When it is availble, the requested memory element is then passed back to the processor.

A graphical user interface is provided so that the user can comfortably select the components that should be simulated in the memory hierarchy. The GUI generates a description of the memory hierarchy in the form of an XML file which is then processed by MEMSIM in order to instantiate the memory components, connect and simulate them.

4.2 MPSoC Simulator

The MPSoC simulation framework, presented in Figure 3, is a SystemC based cycle true simulator. It is capable of simulating a runtime configurable number of processing units, which are connected through a single bus to memories and I/O devices. The most common setup is to use a simulation of an ARM7 core for the processing unit, and an AMBA bus simulation for the interconnection. There are also other combinations of buses (i.e. STbus) and processing units available.

As shown in the figure, each ARM-based processing unit has its own private memory, which can be a unified cache or separate caches for data and instructions. A wide range of parameters may be configured, including the size, associativity and the number of wait states. Besides the cache, a scratchpad memory of configurable size can be attached to each processing unit. The recent development of the simulator targets the hardware requirements in streaming media applications, therefore offering "smart memories" which are basically scratchpad memories accompanied by DMA units.

The MPSoC simulator does not support a configurable multilevel memory hierarchy. The memory hierarchy consists of caches, scratchpads and the shared main memory. Currently, an effort is being made to integrate MEMSIM into the simulator. Finally, it provides a number of semaphores which may be used to synchronize inter-processor communications.

The simulator offers various reporting and tracing facilities. At the lowest level it may report waveform diagrams of the performed bus actions. It is further able to report memory access traces. This feature is most important for the integration into the MACC simulation framework. Besides the simple access based trace files, sophisticated statistics may be generated, including precise information about the amount of cycles spent in bus actions, processing and waitstates.

4.3 Profiler

The profiler uses the trace file, the memory hierarchy simulator and computes the access to each memory in the memory hierarchy. These accesses are then mapped to timing and

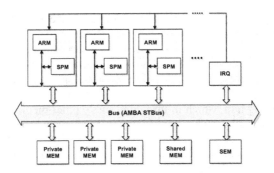

Fig. 3. Multi-process SoC (MPSoC) Simulator

energy models of the processor and the memories to compute the execution time and the energy dissipation of the entire system during the execution of a given application. The profiler also receives as input a mapping of the memory objects present in the application source code and their addresses in the application executable. Therefore, the profiler is able to back-annotate each fetched or executed address within the system to the corresponding memory object. This enables the profiler to gain in-depth knowledge about the application and the system under simulation. This extensive information as a tabulated report file is then presented back to the users. Some of the contents of the report file are enumerated below:

1. Energy consumption, number of accesses and size of every function and basic block
2. Energy consumption, number of accesses and size of every variable
3. Execution order of the basic blocks
4. Energy Consumption and number of accesses to each memory
5. Energy Consumption of the processor
6. Number of executed instruction and execution time (CPU Cycles)

5   Experimental Results

In this section, we first compare the scratchpad overlay and the non-overlayed scratchpad allocation approaches. The values shown in Figure 4 are average values over varying scratchpad size in the range of 128 to 1024 bytes. According to the figure, applying a more sophisticated allocation strategy, which takes into account the temporal distribution of memory object usages, results in a significant reduction in energy consumption and execution time. Average reductions of more than 40% and 20% in the energy dissipation and the execution time, respectively, related to the 100% baseline of the non-overlay approach, for the *edge detection* benchmark are reported.

Furthermore a comparison of the scratchpad overlay memory optimization technique included in the MACC against a cache based system is presented in Figure 5. Similar to the previous figure, these are average values for each benchmark obtained by varying scratchpad and cache sizes in the range of 128 to 1024 bytes. In this case as well, the scratchpad overlay approach demonstrates energy savings of over 30% for the *adpcm* benchmark. Average performance improvement of about 20% is also reported for the same benchmark.

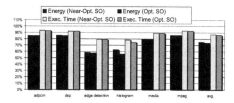

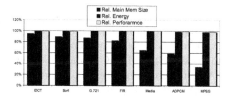

Fig. 4. SPM overlay vs. Non-Overlayed allocation

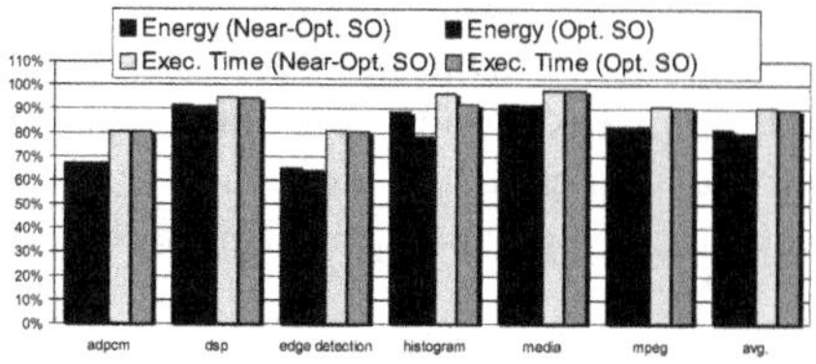

Fig. 5. SPM overlay vs. Cache based system

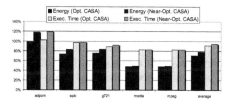

Fig. 6. Instruction Cache optimization vs. Preloaded loop cache optimization

Fig. 7. Results for XIP Optimization

The memory optimization using the scratchpad as an instruction buffer achieves significant energy and runtime savings compared to the preload loop cache optimization. The memory optimizations reduce the number of conflict cache misses while the loop cache optimization buffers frequently executed instructions. In this particular case, we achieve energy savings of about 50% and execution time reductions of close to 20% for the *mpeg* benchmark. The results are illustrated in Figure 6, which shows the average values for each benchmark. The scratchpad size has been varied in the range from 128 to 1024 bytes. The size of the direct mapped instruction cache has been fixed to 2048 bytes. Exploiting the reduced energy dissipation of a DRAM memory in the power down state leads to significant energy savings. By allocating memory objects to a scratchpad memory in such a way as to maximize the power down periods of the DRAM main memory, substantial energy savings of up to 80% compared to a system without scratchpad memory and no power down times for the used DRAM were achieved. Since both allocation results and obtainable savings are similar to the static scratchpad allocation scheme that uses energy per access as the cost function (in contrast to maximizing the power down time of the main memory), no specific results are given for the sake of brevity.

Figure 7 shows the obtained results when the Flash memory used in an embedded system is capable of executing code using the XIP technique. An intrapage access time of 20*ns* is assumed for the used Flash memory. The leftmost bar shows the percentual amount of DRAM main memory that is still required despite also using Flash memory to execute instructions: for the *mpeg* benchmark, 65% of the previously used DRAM main memory is not required when XIP is being used. The gains concerning energy and performance of XIP compared to an execution from the faster DRAM are marginal, as shown by the second and third bars in the figure. For the *mpeg* benchmark, both the energy dissipation and the number of executed cycles are reduced by a maximum of about 2%. This shows that the large savings with respect to the required main memory capacity do not incur any overhead concerning energy or performance for the considered setup. Taking into account that the amount of main memory is an important cost factor for embedded systems, the exploitation of XIP functionality should be considered during the design and optimization of embedded systems.

6   Conclusions and Future Work

In this paper, we presented the MACC framework, a coherent compilation and simulation framework for performing and evaluating memory aware energy optimizations. The framework features an energy optimizing compilation framework for the Uni- or Multi-process ARM SoCs and a highly configurable simulation framework. In addition to optimization of the application for a given memory hierarchy, the framework enables fast and efficient memory hierarchy design space exploration. In the future, we would like to extend the MACC framework for homogeneous and heterogeneous MPSoCs.

Additional information and a complete list of publications concerning MACC can be found at [13].

References

1. Wulf, W.A., McKee, S.A.: Hitting the Memory Wall: Implications of the Obvious. IEEE Computer Architecture News **23** (1995)
2. Francesco, P., Marchal, P., Atienza, D., Benini, L., Catthoor, F., Mendias, M.: An Integrated Hardware/Software Approach for Run-Time Scratchpad Management. In: Proc. of DAC, San Deigo, CA, USA, DAC (2004)
3. ICD: Informatik Centrum Dortmund e.V.: ICD-C Compiler Development Framework, (http://www.icd.de/es/icd-c/icd-c.html)
4. ICD: Informatik Centrum Dortmund e.V.:   LANCE Retargetable C Compiler, (http://www.icd.de/es)
5. Steinke, S., Wehmeyer, L., Lee, B.S., Marwedel, P.: Assigning program and data objects to scratchpad for energy reduction. In: Proc. of DATE, Paris, France (2002)
6. Verma, M., Wehmeyer, L., Marwedel, P.: Dynamic Overlay of Scratchpad Memory for Energy Minimization. In: Proc. of CODES+ISSS, Stockholm, Sweden (2004)
7. Verma, M., Steinke, S., Marwedel, P.: Data Partitioning for Maximal Scratchpad Usage. In: Proc. of ASPDAC. (2003)
8. Wehmeyer, L., Helmig, U., Marwedel, P.: Compiler-optimized Usage of Partitioned Memories. In: Proceedings of the 3rd Workshop on Memory Performance Issues (WMPI2004), ACM International Conference Prodeedings Series, ISBN: 1-59593-040 (2004) 114–120
9. Verma, M., Wehmeyer, L., Marwedel, P.: Cache-aware Scratchpad Allocation Algorihm. In: Proc. of DATE, Paris, France (2004)
10. Wehmeyer, L.: Fast, Efficient and Predictable Memory Accesses – Optimization algorithms for memory architecture aware compilation. Ph.D.-thesis, unpublished (2005)
11. ATMEL: Atmel Corporation, (http://www.atmel.com)
12. Steinke, S., Knauer, M., Wehmeyer, L., Marwedel, P.:   An Accurate and Fine Grain Instruction-Level Energy Model Supporting Software Optimizations. In: Proc. of PATMOS, Yverdon-Les-Bains, Switzerland (2001)
13. Department of Computer Science XII, University of Dortmund: MACC: Memory Aware C Compilation Framework, (http://ls12.cs.uni-dortmund.de/research/macc/)

A Scalable, Multi-thread, Multi-issue Array Processor Architecture for DSP Applications Based on Extended Tomasulo Scheme

Mladen Bereković[1] and Tim Niggemeier[2]

[1] IMEC, Belgium, and TU Delft, Netherlands
mladen.berekovic@imec.be
[2] IBM Deutschland Entwicklung GmbH, Germany
niggemei@de.ibm.com

Abstract. A scalable, distributed micro-architecture is presented that emphasizes on high performance computing for digital signal processing applications by combining high frequency design techniques with a very high degree of parallel processing on a chip. The architecture is based on a superscalar processor model with out-of-order execution, that supports specialized, complex DSP function units, and simultaneous instruction issue from multiple independent threads (SMT). Consequent application of fine clustering reduces the cycle-time for wire-sensitive building blocks of the processor like the register file and leads to a distributed architecture model, where independent thread processing units, ALUs, registers files and memories are distributed across the chip and communicate with each other by special networks, forming a "network-on-a-chip" (NOC) [1]. The communication protocol is a modified version of Tomasulo's scheme [2], that was extended to eliminate all central control structures for the data flow and to support multithreading. The performance of the architecture is scalable with both the number of function units and the number of thread units without having any impact on the processors cycle-time.

1 Introduction

Today's typical embedded DSP systems are built around system-on-chip architectures [3], [4], consisting of one or more DSP and RISC cores, that are interconnected by a standardized on-chip peripheral bus like the ARM-AMBA [5], Multi-AMBA, or a similar proprietary busses.. These system architectures favor a model of lower-performance, lower-power, embedded processor cores that are assisted by one or more hardwired accelerators for specialized tasks like filter or bitstream processing. Making the hardwired coprocessors more programmable leads to a "softening of hardware" [6], with many small, configurable processors and DSPs on a single-chip that share several custom function specific coprocessors or even reprogrammable and reconfigurable hardware blocks [7]. An on-chip communication network is needed to keep as many of these cores busy as possible, leading to networks-on-chip architectures [1].

We propose a different architecture framework for network-on-chip architectures that offers a very high parallelization potential for DSP applications. It is based on a simultaneously multithreaded processor model where multiple independent thread units si-

S. Vassiliadis et al. (Eds.): SAMOS 2006, LNCS 4017, pp. 289–298, 2006.

multaneously issue multiple instructions to a large array of function units, where they are processed in a dataflow-manner.

Although this work fits nicely into Meerbergen's definition of an NOC, it differs in three terms. First, it is based on a different processor model, a superscalar, out-of-order processor with SMT extensions instead of a static VLIW architecture. Second, the dynamically scheduled processors use switched router networks for both resource sharing and explicit communication between the processors or thread units. Third, function specific accelerator units that are embedded as application specific instructions are shared between all threads, leading to a higher utilization of these modules. The following section discusses the details of the overall microarchitecture and explains the developed modifications to the scheduling mechanism in contrast to the classical Tomasulo scheme. The third section discusses related work. Finally, Section 4 summarizes the main conclusions of this work.

2   Extending Tomasulo's Scheme for Clustered Architectures with Explicit Operand Transport

The proposed architecture takes on Tomasulo's original design and extends it with superscalar and SMT features. Fig. 1 shows the resulting architecture that is distributed along the FUs that serve as basic building blocks. The heterogeneous array of small processing units is connected by a network for operand and instruction communication. In contrast to classic centralized schedulers, forwarding of result tags is replaced with dedicated operand transport instructions. Each FU forms a separate cluster with a private register file. The register files of the thread units are distributed to the local register files of the FU-clusters. This offers two advantages: First, every local register file needs only 2 write and one read port, independent of the number of threads and issue slots. This makes the architecture more scalable in terms of issues per cycle and cycle

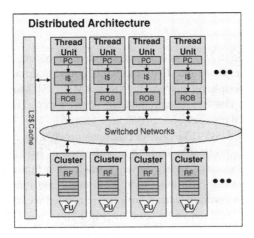

Fig. 1. Distributed SMT processor overview. RF= register file, ROB= reorder buffer, FU= function unit.

time. The second is that the total number of registers can be significantly increased, paving the way for large instruction windows that typically support a large number of "in-flight" instructions, without having effecting the cycle time.

This work makes some essential modifications to Tomasulo's original scheme to eliminate the costly tag matching process: After the register renaming table is read during instruction decode stage, all dependence information is available to build the dynamic signal-flow graph. In analogy to the "Transport Triggered Architectures" [28], or TTAs, the instruction is then split into three subinstructions: a (mathematical) function and two helper instructions that move the two source operands from the place of their generation, i.e. the physical reservation station (=register, cluster) read from the renaming table, to the place where the operation is performed, i.e. the destination reservation station (register/cluster) in the function unit to which the instruction has been dynamically assigned. These helper transport instructions inherently have knowledge of the physical location of both, their source and their destination operands, since these are directly reflected by their reservation station numbers and function units. The helper transport instructions, consisting of a simple pair of reservation station or rename register numbers (src, dest), are sent to the physical address of the source. As soon as the source data gets available the helper transfer instruction is executed, i.e. the data is send to the destination register via the switched operand network. This way, a precise point-to-point communication link is established between producer instruction and producing function unit on one side and consumer instruction and consuming function unit on the other side. The dependence graph is early resolved into a signal-flow graph during the rename stage. This reduces the complexity of the transform process significantly when compared with a central instruction scheduler implementation. The central instruction scheduler checks *all completing* versus *all waiting* instructions for *all threads* using a content addressable memory (CAM), whereas the renaming logic only needs to perform a (renaming) table access for all decoded instructions *within a single thread*.

To explain the mechanism of the helper copy instructions, consider the following example sequence of 4 instructions:

$$a : R4 \;\; <- \;\; R0 + R8; \qquad b : R2 \;\; <- \;\; R0 * R4$$

The physical registers are addressed with two index sets: one for the FU and one for the register number within the FU. So (5,10) denotes the 10th register in FU (cluster) 5. Suppose that FU1 is an adder and FU2 is a multiplier unit.

After the first clock cycle, logical register R4 is assigned to FU1, register 1 (=R(1,1)), and instruction a is moved to FU1 (adder). A set of copy instructions for the two source operands is generated. After the second cycle, instruction b is moved to FU4 (multiplier) and R2 is assigned to FU4, R1 (=R(4,1)). A second set of copy instructions are generated. So the first two instructions become after renaming:

$$
\begin{aligned}
&a : R(1,1) \;\; <- \;\; R0 + R8; &\quad &b : R(2,1) \;\; <- \;\; R0 * R(1,1); \\
&a1 : cp \;\; R0 \;\; -> \;\; R(1,1); &\quad &b1 : cp \;\; R0 \;\; -> \;\; R(4,1); \\
&a2 : cp \;\; R8 \;\; -> \;\; R(1,1); &\quad &b2 : cp \;\; R(1,1) \;\; -> \;\; R(4,1);
\end{aligned}
$$

The cp instructions are sent to their appropriate source operand destinations, e.g. b2 is sent to FU1, register 1 and stored in the appropriate field of the cp operand buffer for

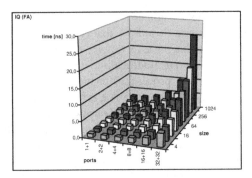

Fig. 2. Timing Estimates for different scheduler configurations using CACTI 3.0

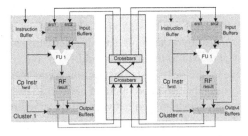

Fig. 3. Modified Tomasulo architecture with distributed registerfile and instruction scheduling

R(1,1). Once the data is available, the cp instruction is executed and the data send to R(4,1) and stored in its input operand buffer.

Fig. 2 shows the simulated timing estimates for different configurations for the fully associative (CAM-based) instruction-scheduler (window) obtained from CACTI 3. What can be seen is the superlinear increase in delay with the number of ports. Also, large register file sizes lead to significantly higher delay. From these numbers it can be concluded that an optimized clustered architecture is built using memory blocks with only few ports and issue slots. Fig. 3 shows the resulting cluster data path architecture. The local register file stores the function unit's result data that is addressed by the destination register. Each register file entry has two associated entries in the operand buffer memories, that replace the original reservation stations. A third memory, the cp instruction buffer, contains entries to store a cp instruction for the register's result. This way, a precise point-to-point communication link is established between producer instruction and producing function unit on one side and consumer instruction and consuming function unit on the other side. The dependence graph is early resolved into a signal-flow graph during the rename stage. This reduces the complexity of the transform process significantly when compared with a central instruction scheduler implementation. The instruction scheduler checks *all completing* versus *all waiting* instructions for *all threads* in a content addressable memory (CAM), whereas the renaming logic only needs to perform a (renaming) table access for all decoded instructions *within a single thread*.

The cluster memories are of small size and have a limited port number, e.g. 2 ports for the reservation stations that serve as input buffers. An architecture with 16 function

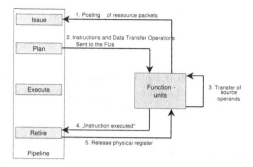

Fig. 4. Pipelining scheme

units (=clusters) with a moderate 32 registers each would already have 512 physical registers, which is more than any available processor offers.

The encapsulation of the whole processing logic in small clusters with local interconnects and fully pipelined in- and outbound communication makes very high frequency realisations possible. A recent implementation of a comparable execution core cluster (2x 32bit ALU, 32-entry x 32-bit register file, 8 entry x 2 scheduler loop) on a 130nm, six-metal, Dual VT CMOS technology consumed 2.3 mm2 and yielded 5 GHz [29].

Fig. 4 shows the basic steps pipelining scheme, although not in full cycle-true details, the delays between the operand transfers are left out for example. The basic pipeline steps are:

1. The Function Units post their free resources via a global resource broadcasting network (FU2Rename network) to the Thread Units (TUs). The TUs pick up these resources autonomously according to their individual needs. A free resource consists of a package containing
   - a free (destination) register
   - An associated entry in the two operand buffers (typically the same register address)
   - An entry in the local instruction window
2. The instruction renaming stage consumes the free resources and the corresponding sub-instructions are created on-the-fly in the decode Issue and Plan stages, where tzey are also sent to the FUs via the Rename2FU Network
3. In the FUs the instructions are stored in the local instruction windows and the necessary data transfer operations are performed (on availability of their source operands) and the data is axchanged directly between the FUs on the FU2FU data network.
4. The FUs notify back the TUs via the FU2Retire network that the instructions have executed and are ready for retirement.
5. The Retire stage in the Tus retires the instructions and notifies back the FUs about the release of the _overwritten_ destination register (from prvious valus, that has to be stored in the rename tables as well).

3   Simulation Results with MPEG-4 Kernels

Cycle-true simulations of two typical and computation-intensive DSP kernels from MPEG-4 [3] were performed on an RT-level simulator of the architecture: global motion compensation (GMC), which is equivalent to an affine warping of a 16x16 pixel block and deblocking. The benchmarks were hand-optimized in Assembler for the architecture.

Fig. 5 and Fig. 6 show the results for the MPEG-4 GMC subtask, which is equivalent to an affine warping of a 16x16 pixel block. The GMC is one of the most performance critical kernel loops of the MPEG-4 standard. The benchmarks were hand-optimized in Assembler for the architecture without compiler-support and exploit multi-threading. This approach is different from General-Purpose processors, but is typically employed on DSPs.

For all simulation runs the same configuration with 64 FUs was used except that the number of thread units was increased to the number of parallel running threads. The register-files size is 256 registers each, as is the reorder buffer size (and hence the instruction window). Each thread has a local L1 I-cache of 32kB, and a maximal fetch and issue bandwidth of 16 instructions. There is a shared L1-D-cache, that is connected to the Load/Store units. All L1-caches are backed up by a larger 4MB L2-cache. However, for the current simulations, the L1-D cache hit-rate was set to 100% to explore the full performance potential. The branch prediction uses a simple shared array of 2-bit counters.

The simulation results show that if enough data bandwidth is available, the performance scales with the number of threads. The lower single-thread performance is caused by inter-cluster latencies and branch miss-predictions. This benchmark had a 40% miss-prediction rate, which results in significant IPC losses (30%) between issue and retire stages (see the two difference between the red and the blue rows), even in a multi-threaded environment. It is interesting to note that this loss gets smaller as the

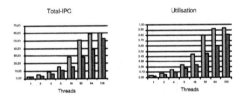

Fig. 5. GMC simulation results for 1 to 128 threads. The left bar shows the Issue-IPC, the right bar retire-IPC.

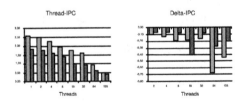

Fig. 6. Simulated Thread IPC results for 1..128 threads

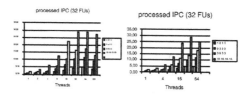

Fig. 7. Simulation results: 32 FUs, 1 to 128 threads. Left: GMC. Right: MPEG-4 Deblocking filter. The different bars represent different network bandwidth.

number of threads increases, which is caused by the fact that resource contention between the thread units leads also to lower issue rates per thread and therefore to fewer unsued or wasted execution cycles. The high utilization rates of the FUs in the above simulations show however that multi-threading effectively compensates the high latencies for data-forwarding between dependent instructions. Another conclusion is that, in the presence of multiple available threads to run, speculation does not yield better results.

The simulations results shown in Fig. 7 were obtained from simulations with different bandwidth configurations of the internal networks. With 1 denoting a single word bandwidth and 16 denoting 16 word bandwidth, for example for the data communication network.

The simulation results show that if enough network bandwidth is available, the performance scales with the number of threads. The lower single-thread performance is caused by inter-cluster latencies and branch miss-predictions. The high utilization rate of the FUs for higher thread numbers (IPC>15) shows however, that multi-threading effectively compensates the high latencies for data-forwarding between dependent instructions.

4   Related Work

Previous work on DSP processor architectures has mainly been focused instruction-level parallelism, particularly on statically scheduled, VLIW processing. These architectures offer good compiler support for a moderate parallelism of 2-8 (peak) instructions per cycle, but run out of steam for larger parallelisms. Furthermore, their main advantage, the simpler hardware compared to dynamically scheduled ooo-execution models diminishes with the huge demand for registers and for more register file ports. A main disadvantage of VLIW architectures is their inability to dynamically react to cache misses and resource contention leading to frequent performance-limiting stalls [30], and making it inadequate for simultaneous multithreading.

Only few studies have been performed so far that investigate multithreading, out-of-order execution, or SMT for digital signal processing applications [31]. With the rapid increase of the transistor budget that is available on chips, DSP chip multi-processors are beginning to surface and it is to be expected that this trend is going to continue.

Previous studies [32] have identified the instruction window design to be a major limiter for more (future) processor speed. Several studies have advocated improvements for larger window sizes and higher frequency designs [33], while other designs eliminate associative compares altogether from the instruction scheduling [34].

Clustering has been proposed by many researches to address the complexity problems of large instruction windows and register files and it is employed in several recent processor designs. Studies of clustered architectures include the Multi-Scalar project, Trace Processors, EDF [35], Hierarchical Scheduling Windows, and Transport Triggered Architectures (TTAs) [36]. In contrast to this work TTAs are based on static VLIW techniques and compiler-generated scheduling. Other approaches include array processors like the UT/Austin Grid architecture [37], MIT's RAW project [38], and Stanford's IMAGINE stream processor project.

5 Conclusion

We propose a distributed SMT processor architecture as a scalable network-on-chip platform for dynamically reconfigurable digital signal processing. Although well suited for multiprocessing, it combines all characteristics needed by DSP applications in a single processor framework. Like the very popular VLIW processors it supports multiple instruction issue and offers a very large number of registers, but it avoids the performance degrading stalls in instruction issue due to cache misses. Just as VLIW processors it supports the embedding of special function units that can perform parallel vector instructions, or complex functions like filtering. Also, fine-clustering offers a path to high frequency implementations, but unlike VLIW processors, multithreading effectively compensates the related IPC losses. The architecture shares the system-on-chip processing model with multiple heterogeneous ASIP cores on a chip, each specialised for a specific task, communicating with each other over specialised on-chip networks. However, it offers more flexibility for resource sharing especially for the costly, high-performance, specialised function units. Furthermore, it offers fast context switches and a fine-grained and fast communication scheme between threads that is based on hardware CSPs channels. Large scale clustered SMT processors with many shared specialised or configurable function units come very close to the ideal of a softening of hardware and offer an attractive alternative to both, pure FPGA implementations and to costly ASIC designs.

References

1. L. Benini, G. de Micheli, "Networks on chip: A New SOC Paradigm," IEEE Computer, Vol. 35, no. 1, Jan. 2002, pp. 70-78.
2. R. M. Tomasulo, "An efficient algorithm for exploiting multiple arithmetic units", IBM Journal on Research and Development, Vol.11, no.1, January 1967, pp. 25-33.
3. M. Bereković, H.-J. Stolberg, P. Pirsch, "Multi-Core System-On-Chip Architecture for MPEG-4 Streaming Video," Transactions on Circuits and Systems for Video Technology (CSVT), Vol. 12, No. 8, August 2002, pp. 688-699.
4. P. Pirsch, M. Bereković, H.-J. Stolberg, J. Jachalsky, "VLSI Architectures for MPEG-4 Video," VLSI Conference, Taipei, April 2003.
5. ARM AMBA Specification, www.ARM.com.

6. F. Vahid, "The Softening of Hardware," IEEE Computer, Vol. 36, no. 4, April 2003, pp. 27-34.

7. H. Zhang, J.M. Rabaey et al., " A 1V Heterogeneous Reconfigurable Processor IC for Baseband Wireless Applications," Proc. Int'l. Solid-State Circuits Conference (ISSCC), San Francisco, February 2000.

8. J. L. van Meerbergen, "Lecture slides: Complex Multiprocessor architectures," www.ics.ele.tue.nl/ jef/education/5p520/index.html.

9. ISO/IEC JTC/SC29/WG11 N4668, "Overview of the MPEG-4 standard," Jeju, March 2002.

10. M. Berekovic, P. Pirsch, J. Kneip, "An Algorithm-Hardware-System Approach to VLIW Multimedia Processors," Journal of VLSI Signal Processing Systems, Vol. 20, No. 1-2, October 1998, pp. 163-180.

11. A. Allan, D. Edenfeld, W. H. Joyner, A. B. Kahng, M. Rodgers, and Y. Zorian, "2001 Technology Roadmap for Semiconductors," IEEE Computer, Vol. 35, no. 1, January 2002, pp. 42-53.

12. M. H. Lipasti and J. P. Shen "Modern Processor Design", McGrawHill, 2002.

13. M. Berekovic, H. J. Stolberg, M. B. Kulaczewski, P. Pirsch, H. Moeller, H. Runge, J. Kneip, B. Stabernack, "Instruction Set Extensions for MPEG-4 Video," Journal of VLSI Signal Processing Systems, Vol. 23, No. 1, October 1999, pp. 7-50.

14. J. P. Wittenburg, W. Hinrichs, J. Kneip, M. Ohmacht, M. Berekovic, H. Lieske, H. Kloos, P. Pirsch, "Realization of a Programmable Parallel DSP for High Performance Image Processing Applications," Design Automation Conference (DAC) 1998, June 1998, pp. 56-61.

15. R. Lee, "Accelerating Multimedia with Enhanced Microprocessors," IEEE Micro, Vol.15, no. 2, March/April 1995, pp. 22-32.

16. N. Slingerland, and A. J. Smith, "Measuring the Performance of Multimedia Instruction Sets," IEEE Transactions on Computers, Vol. 51, no. 11, November 2002, pp. 1317-1332.

17. Texas Instruments, "TMS320DM642 Technical Overview," Application Report SPRU615, Sep. 2002.

18. M. S. Lam, and R. P. Wilson, "Limits of Control Flow on Parallelism", Proc. 19th Ann. Int'l Symp. on Computer Architecture, June 1992, pp. 46-57.

19. D. M. Tullsen, S. J. Eggers, and H. M. Levy, "Simultaneous Multithreading: Maximizing On-Chip Parallelism", Proc. 22th Ann. Int'l Symp. on Computer Architecture, June 1995, pp. 392-403.

20. R. P. Preston, et.al "Design of an 8-wide Superscalar RISC with Simultaneous Multithreading", Solid-State Circuits Conference (ISSCC2002), San-Francisco, Ca, Febr. 2002, pp.469-471.

21. S. Palacharla, N.P. Jouppi, J. Smith, "Complexity Effective Superscalar Processors", Proc. 24th. Int'l. Symp. on Computer Architecture, June 1997, pp. 206-218.

22. B. Ackland et al., "A Single Chip, 1.6-Billion, 16-b MAC/s Multiprocessor DSP," IEEE J. Solid-State Circuits, Mar. 2000, pp. 412-424.

23. H.-J. Stolberg, M. Berekovic, L. Friebe, S. Moch, S. Fluegel, X. Mao, M. B. Kulaczewski, H. Klussmann, P. Pirsch, "HiBRID-SoC: A Multi-Core System-on-Chip Architecture for Multimedia Signal Processing Applications," Proceedings Design, Automation and Test in Europe (DATE2003) - Designer's Forum, March 2003, pp. 8-13.

24. K.I. Farkas, P. Chow, N. P. Jouppi, and Z. Vranesic, "The Multicluster Architecture: Reducing Cycle Time through Partitioning", Proc. 30th. Int'l. Symp. On Microarchitecure, Dec. 1997, pp.149-159.

25. R. E. Kessler, "The Alpha 21264 Microprocessor", IEEE Micro 19(2), March 1999, pp. 24-36.

26. R. Ho, K. W. Mai, M. A. Horowitz, "The Future of wires", Proceedings of the IEEE, 89(4): 490-504, Apr. 2001.

27. V. Agarwal, M.S. Hrishikesh, S. W. Keckler, and D. Burger, "Clock Rate versus IPC: The End of the Road for conventional Microarchitectures", Proc. 27th Ann. Int'l. Symp on Computer architecture, June 2000, pp. 248-259.
28. H. Corporaal, "Microprocessor Architectures from VLIW to TTA," John Wiley & Sons, 1998.
29. S. Vangal et. al., "5-Ghz 32-bit Integer Execution Core in 130-nm Dual-VT CMOS," IEEE Journal of Solid-State Circuits, vol. 37, no. 11, November 2002.
30. M. Berekovic, P. Pirsch, J. Kneip, "An Algorithm-Hardware-System Approach to VLIW Multimedia Processors," Journal of VLSI Signal Processing Systems, Vol. 20, No. 1-2, October 1998, pp. 163-180.
31. Y.-K. Chen, R. Lienhart, E. Debes, M. Holliman, and M. Yeung, "The impact of SMT/SMP Designs on Multimedia Software Engineering: A Workload Analysis Study," Fourth International Symposium on Multimedia Software Engineering, December 2002.
32. David W. Wall, "Limits of Instruction-Level Parallelism", Fourth International Conference on Architectural Support for Programming Languages and Operating Systems, April 1991, pp. 176-188.
33. M. Brown, J. Stark, and Y. Patt, "Select-Free Instruction Scheduling Logic, " Micro-34, 2001, pp. 204-213.
34. S. Weiss, and J.E: Smith, "Instruction Issue Logic in Pipelined Supercomputers," IEEE Trans. on Comp., vol. C 33, No. 11, Nov. 1984, pp. 1013-1022
35. T. Sato, Y. Nakamura, and I. Arita, "Revisiting Direct Tag Search Algorithm on Superscalar Processors," in Workshop on Complexity-Effective Design, June 2001
36. H. Corporaal, "Microprocessor Architectures from VLIW to TTA," John Wiley & Sons, 1998.
37. R. Nagarajan, K. Sankaralingam, D. Burger, and S. Keckler, "Design Space Evaluation of Grid Processor Architectures, " Micro-34, 2001, pp.40-53.
38. M. B. Taylor et al., "The RAW Microprocessor: A Computational Fabric For Software Circuits and General-Purpose Programs," IEEE Micro, Vol. 22, no. 2, March/April 2002, pp. 25-35.

Reducing Execution Unit Leakage Power in Embedded Processors

Houman Homayoun* and Amirali Baniasadi

Electrical and Computer Engineering Department
University of Victoria, Victoria, Canada
houman@houman-homayoun.com, amirali@ece.uvic.ca

Abstract. We introduce low-overhead power optimization techniques to reduce leakage power in embedded processors. Our techniques improve previous work by a) taking into account idle time distribution for different execution units, and b) using instruction decode and control dependencies to wakeup the gated (but needed) units as soon as possible. We take into account idle time distribution per execution unit to detect an idle time period as soon as possible. This in turn results in increasing our leakage power savings. In addition, we use information already available in the processor to predict when a gated execution unit will be needed again. This results in early and less costly reactivation of gated execution units. We evaluate our techniques for a representative subset of MiBench benchmarks and for a processor using a configuration similar to Intels Xscale processor. We show that our techniques reduce leakage power considerably while maintaining performance.

1 Introduction

The goal of this work is to reduce leakage power in embedded processors. In recent years, we have witnessed a rapid complexity increase in the embedded space. As a result, embedded processors power dissipation has become one of the major barriers in their deployment in mobile devices. Meantime, as the semiconductor technology scales down, leakage (standby) power will account for an increasing share of processor power dissipation [1, 2].

In most processors, including embedded processors, computational units power dissipation accounts for a considerable share of total power dissipation. However, and as we show in this work, computational units may be idle for long periods of time depending on the applications required resources. During such idle periods, execution units consume energy without contributing to performance.

We investigate embedded processors and show that there is an opportunity to reduce leakage power dissipated by idle execution units. In particular, we show that execution units may be idle for long periods of time. Identifying such idle periods accurately provides an opportunity to reduce power while maintaining performance.

---

* The author was with the University of Victoria, Electrical and Computer Engineering Department when this work was done.

S. Vassiliadis et al. (Eds.): SAMOS 2006, LNCS 4017, pp. 299–308, 2006.
© Springer-Verlag Berlin Heidelberg 2006

To reduce power dissipation, we turn off the voltage supply for execution units that are detected to be in their idle time.

One way to detect idle execution units is to monitor the units and to gate them if they are idle for a consecutive number of cycles [3]. This is referred to as time-based power gating. This approach has two inefficiencies. First, the time overhead associated with this method could be costly. Particularly the energy savings are very sensitive to the time needed to wakeup gated units. Second, as we show in this work, different functional units have different idle time distributions. While some execution units may be idle for long periods there are others that stay idle for short periods. Therefore, a one-size-fits-all approach fails to provide optimal results across all units.

In this work we introduce new heuristics to address both inefficiencies. We improve previously suggested techniques by using different idle time detection thresholds and by using control dependency and decode information to wakeup gated execution units early in embedded processors.

In particular we make the following contributions:

1. We show that there is an opportunity in the embedded space to reduce leakage power by identifying idle execution units.
2. We improve previously suggested leakage reduction techniques as we detect idle periods more effectively. Consequently we increase energy savings.
3. We reactivate gated (but needed) units earlier than the time they are re-activated using previously suggested methods. Consequently, we reduce the performance cost.

Note that there is a timing overhead associated with power gating. We take into account this overhead in this study.

The rest of the paper is organized as follows. In section 2 we discuss related work. In section 3 we discuss power gating in more detail. In section 4 we discuss our motivation and present our techniques. In section 5 we review methodology, present our analysis framework and present performance and power savings results. Finally, in section 6 we offer concluding remarks.

2   Related Work

Leakage power may become a more serious issue in embedded processors where applications may require long periods of inactivity [4, 5]. Accordingly, previous study has introduced many techniques to reduce leakage in different processor units (e.g., [6, 7, 8, 9, 10]). Powell et al., explored an integrated architectural and circuit level approach to reducing leakage energy dissipation in instruction caches [6]. Kaxiras et al. proposed an approach to reduce the L1 cache leakage energy by turning off the cache line not likely to be reused [11]. Bai et al optimized several components of on-chip caches to reduce gate leakage power [12]. Kao and Chandrakasan suggested dual-threshold voltage techniques for reducing standby power dissipation while still maintaining high performance in static and dynamic combinational logic blocks [7]. Johnson et al., modified circuits considering state dependence. They identified a low leakage state and inserted leakage control transistors only where needed [8]. Durate et al., studied and compared three leakage power reduction techniques: Input Vector Control, Body Bias Control and Power Supply Gating. They investigated their limits and benefits, in terms of the potential leakage reduction, performance penalty and area and power overhead [9]. Rele et al.,introduced an approach to combine compiler, instruction set, and microarchitecture support to turn off functional units that are idle for long periods of time for reducing static power dissipation by idle functional units using power gating [10]. Our work is different from previous work as it targets embedded processors. We show that there is a motivating opportunity in the embedded space to apply power gating. Moreover, we take advantage of embedded processor characteristics such as in-order execution to improve previously suggested gating techniques.

3   Power Gating

Power dissipation in a CMOS circuit can be classified to dynamic and static. Dynamic power dissipation is the result of switching activity while static power dissipation is due to leakage current. Among all factors influencing the static power the subthreshold leakage is considered to be an important contributor. Subthreshold leakage current ($I_{leakage}$) flows from drain to source even when the transistor is off (see figure 1(a)). Static power dissipation can be computed using the following:

$$P_{static} = V_{cc}.I_{leakage} = V_{cc}.N.K_{design}.K_{tech}.10^{\frac{-V_T}{S_t}} \qquad (1)$$

The parameters in equation 1 are divided to two categories: technology dependent and design dependent. V_{cc}, N and K_{design} are technology independent and may be varied independently targeting a specific design model. V_T is a technology dependent parameter. As the technology scales down, V_T decreases which results in an increase in static power.

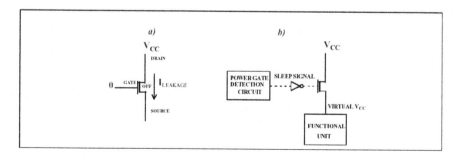

Fig. 1. a) Turned off transistor dissipating leakage power b) Schematic showing major blocks exploited in power gating

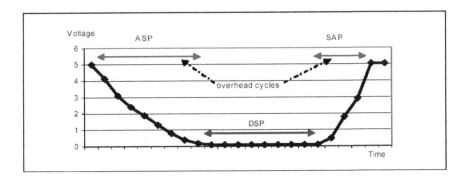

Fig. 2. Transition states in power gating

We use power gating to block V_{cc} and reduce leakage power to zero. In figure 1(b) we present how power gating is achieved using a header transistor to block voltage supply from reaching a circuit unit. The power gate detection circuit decides when is the appropriate time to turn off the voltage supply. Once the sleep signal is generated, and after a transition period, the V_{cc} signal will be blocked from reaching the functional unit.

Applying power gating comes with timing overhead. To explain this in more detail in figure 2 we present transition states associated with power gating.

As presented, the power gating process includes three separate intervals. We refer to the first interval as the active to sleep transit period (ASP). ASP starts the moment we decide to power gate a unit and ends when the voltage supply is completely blocked. We refer to the second interval as the deep sleep period or DSP. This is the period where the functional unit is gated and therefore does not dissipate power. Power dissipation reduction depends on how often and for how long units stay in DSP. We have to wakeup a unit as soon as its idle period ends. For example, in the case of integer ALU, this is when an instruction requires the unit to execute. Turning on the voltage supply to wakeup a unit takes time. The third interval presented in figure 2 represents this timing overhead and is the time needed to reactivate a unit. We refer to this period as the sleep to active transition period (SAP).

While saving leakage power during ASP and SAP is possible, in this study we assume that power reduction benefits are only achievable when a unit is in DSP. As such we refer to ASP and SAP as timing overheads associated with power gating. Hu et. al, provide a detailed explanation of the three intervals [3].

4   Motivation and Heuristics

Through this study we report for a representative subset of MiBench benchmarks [13] and for a processor similar to that of Intels XScale processor (more on this later in section 5).

In figure 3 we present energy savings achievable by ideal (but not practical) power gating. We assume that the percentage of execution units idle cycles

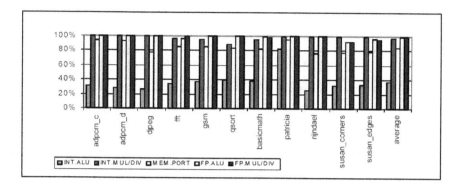

Fig. 3. Leakage power reduction achieved by ideal power gating

indicates maximum leakage power reduction possible by using power gating. We also assume that the timing overhead with power gating is zero. As a result the data presented in figure 3 serves as an upper bound for our leakage power savings. Bars from left to right report average savings for integer ALU, integer multiplier/divider, memory ports, floating point ALU and floating point multiplier/divider.

In figure 3, and as an indication of potential leakage power savings, we report how often each of the five units used in the Intels XScale are idle. On average, three of the units, i.e., integer multiplier/ divider, floating point ALU and floating point multiplier/divider are idle more than 95% of cycles. Average idle period is least for integer ALU (40%). We conclude from figure 3 that there is motivating opportunity in embedded processors to exploit idle times and to power gate execution units to reduce leakage power dissipation. However, identifying idle times early enough is a challenging problem. Moreover, reactivating the gated execution units soon enough is critical since stalling instruction execution could come with a performance penalty.

As explained earlier time-based power gating monitors the state of each execution unit and turns it off after the number of consecutive idle cycles exceeds a pre-decided threshold. We refer to this threshold as the idle detect threshold (IDT). In the following sections we extend time-based power gating to reduce leakage power further.

4.1 Multiple IDTs (MIDT)

In figure 4 we report how changing the idle detect threshold or IDT impacts power gating. We assume that the active to sleep period is 3 cycles. We also assume that returning an execution unit from sleep to active takes 5 cycles [3].

In 4(a) bars from left to right report average percentage of cycles each execution unit is gated for the benchmarks studied here for IDT values 5, 10, 20, 50, 100 and 150.

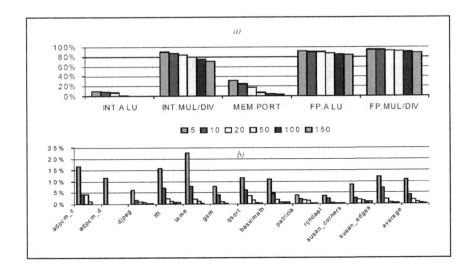

Fig. 4. a) Average leakage power savings achieved by power gating for different IDT values for ASP=5 and SAP=3. Higher is better. b) Performance cost associated with power gating for different IDT values for ASP=5 and SAP=3. Lower is better.

In 4(b) we report performance cost for the benchmarks studied here for different IDT values. Average performance slowdown is 10.9%, 4.1%, 1.9%, 0.9%, 0.3%, 0.3%, for IDT values 5, 10, 20, 50, 100 and 150 respectively.

A closer look at figure 4 reveals that none of the IDT values provide acceptable results across all execution units and for all applications. Lower IDT values (i.e., 5, 10 and 20) provide high power savings but come with high performance cost. Higher IDT values (i.e., 50 and 100), on the other hand, maintain performance but can reduce power savings dramatically. This is particularly true for integer ALU and memory port.

To provide better insight in figure 5 we report idle time distribution for each execution unit. As presented, idle time distribution is quite different from one execution unit to another. As such using a single IDT for all execution units is inefficient. To address this issue we use a different IDT for each execution unit. We refer to this method as multiple IDT or MIDT. To pick the right IDT for every execution unit we took into account many factors including how often the execution unit becomes idle and how long it stays idle. After testing many alternatives we picked IDT values 20, 80, 40, 100 and 140 for integer ALU, integer multiplier/divide, memory ports, floating point ALU and floating point multiplier/ divider respectively. Note that multiple IDT could be implemented easily by using programable registers.

4.2 Early Wakeup

In figure 6 we report how changes in SAP impact performance. Note that SAP is the time required to reactivate an execution unit by turning on the power supply. SAP depends on the circuit parameters and may change from one design

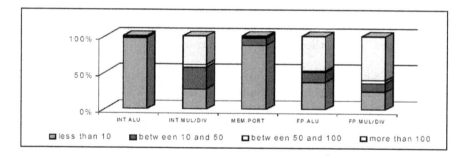

Fig. 5. Idle time distribution for different execution units

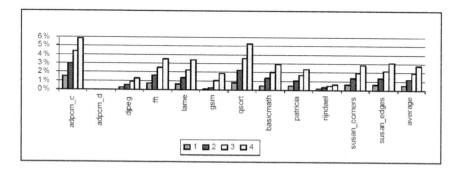

Fig. 6. Performance cost associated with power gating for different SAP values for IDT=20 and ASP=5. Lower is better.

to another. We assume that IDT and ASP are 20 and 5 respectively. Bars from left to right report for SAP values of 1, 2, 3 and 4 respectively. As expected the longer it takes to reactivate a gated execution unit the higher the performance penalty would be. Average performance cost is 0.5%, 1.2%, 1.9% and 2.7% for different SAP values.

We conclude from figure 6 that long wakeup periods can harm performance seriously. One way to reduce performance cost is to reactivate gated units as early as possible. To reactivate gated execution units sooner we suggest two methods:

First, we use control dependencies to wakeup execution units in advance. We refer to this method as the branch-aided wakeup or BAW technique.

Second, we use information available at the decode stage to wakeup the needed execution units at least one cycle earlier than when they become active in conventional power gating. We refer to this technique as the decode-aided wakeup or DAW.

Branch-Aided Wakeup (BAW). Note that embedded processors such as Intels XScale use inorder issue. As such once a branch instruction is issued, the following basic block should issue sequentially. To take advantage of inorder instruction issue we store information regarding whether integer ALU and memory ports are used inside a basic block. We limit the stored information to the these two execution units since our study shows that long wakeup periods for the two units impact performance more seriously compared to other execution units. Moreover,limiting the technique to the two units will reduce the overhead associated.

We use an 8-entry table to record the required information. The table is indexed using the branch instruction address associated with the basic block. Each entry stores two bits. The first bit records if any instruction within the basic block uses the integer ALU and the second bit records if any instruction uses the memory port.

At fetch, and in parallel with accessing the branch predictor, we probe the 8-entry table. We reactivate the execution units if the table indicates that they will be needed by the following basic block. We take no action if the execution units are already active. Note that possible misspeculations are not costly from the performance point of view since all they do is to reactivate an execution unit which will not be used.

We use a 3-bit register to store the index associated with the latest fetched branch. For example, when an issued instruction is dispatched to the integer ALU, we update the entry associated with the last branch fetched, i.e., we set the first bit in the entry to 1 indicating that the integer ALU will be used by the basic block. We use the 3-bit register to find and update the table entry associated with the last fetched branch.

The area overhead associated with this techniques is very small. We use a 3-bit register and an 8- entry table which contains eight 2-bit fields. The total area requirement is equivalent to 19 bits which is negligible.

Decode-Aided Wakeup (DAW). In this method we start the activation process of the gated execution units at decode and immediately after recognizing the opcode. Note that in conventional power gating execution units are activated when a ready to execute instruction is detected. DAW, on the other hand, uses the already available information at decode and starts reactivation at least one cycle before the instruction becomes ready. This in turn reduces the timing overhead associated with power gating.

5   Methodology and Results

In this section we report our analysis framework and simulation results. To evaluate our optimization techniques we report performance and leakage power reduction. We use a subset of MiBench benchmark suite [13] compiled for MIPS instruction set. In this work, similar to earlier studies [3], we assume that the percentage of cycles a functional unit stays in DSP indicates net leakage savings achieved by using power-gating.

For simulation purpose we used a modified version of simplescalar v3.0 toolset [14]. We modeled a single issue in-order embedded processor with an architecture similar to Intels XScale core. Table 1 shows the configuration we used.

In figure 7 we report how our optimizations impact performance and leakage power savings. We also report results for a combined technique where multiple

Table 1. Configuration of the processor model

Issue Width	In-Order:2	Inst/Data TLB	32-entry,full-associative
Functional Units	1 I-ALU, 1 F-ALU,1 I-MUL/DIV 1 F-MUL/DIV	L1 - Instruction/ Data Caches	32K, 32-way SA, 32-byte blocks, 1 cycle
BTB	128 entries	L2 Cache	None
Branch Predictor	Bimodal, 128 entries	Register Update Unit	8 entries
Main Memory	Infinite, 32 cycles	Load/Store queue	8 entries

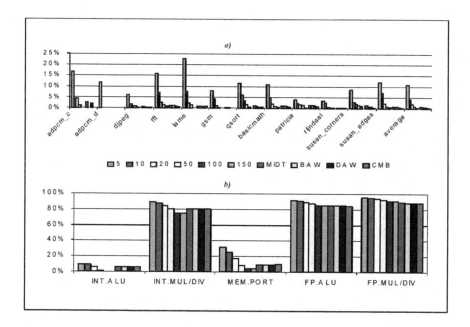

Fig. 7. a) Performance cost. b) Leakage power reduction for the methods discussed.

IDT, BAW and DAW are applied simultaneously. We refer to the combined technique as CMB. For the sake of comparison we also include results achieved when all execution units use the same IDT. Bars from left to right report for IDT values 5, 10, 20, 50, 100, 150, multiple IDT (MIDT), BAW, DAW and CMB.

We limit our discussion to comparing the CMB method to methods where a single IDT is used across all execution units. Nonetheless, it is important to note that similar comparisons could be made for each of the three optimizations. Note that as explained earlier single IDT results in either high performance cost (for low IDTs) or low energy savings (for high IDTs). CMB, however, maintains performance for all benchmarks (see figure 7(a)). While average performance costs are 10.9% and 4.2% for IDT values 5 and 10, average performance cost is reduced to 0.3% for CMB.

Average leakage energy savings are 0.1% and 3% for integer ALU and memory ports for IDT values 100 and 150 respectively. For CMB, average savings for integer

ALU and memory port are increased to 6.5% and 11% respectively (see figure 7(b)). Note that CMB maintains high energy savings for other execution units.

6   Conclusion

In this paper we analyzed how power gating could be exploited in embedded processors to reduce leakage power. We extended previous work by introducing three optimization techniques to reduce leakage power while maintaining performance. Our techniques used control dependency, instruction decode information and idle time distribution. We showed that it is possible to reduce leakage power while maintaining performance for an embedded processor similar to Intels Xscale and for a representative subset of MiBench benchmarks.

References

1. Borkar, S.: Design challenges of technology scaling. IEEE Micro **19** (1999) 23–29
2. Butts, J.A., Sohi, G.S.: A static power model for architects., In Proceedings of the 33rd Annual IEEE/ACM International Symposium on Microarchitecture (December 2000)
3. Hu, Z., Buyuktosunoglu, A., Srinivasan, V., Zuyuban, V., Jacobson, H., Bose, P.: Microarchitectural techniques for power gating of execution units., In proceedings of ISLPED (2004)
4. Unsal, O.S., Koren, I.: System-level power-aware design techniques in real-time systems. Volume 91, NO. 7., In proceedings of the IEEE (July 2003)
5. Jejurikar, R., R., G.: Dynamic voltage scaling for systemwide energy minimization in real-time embedded systems., In proceedings of ISLPED (2004)
6. Powell, M., Yang, S., Falsafi, B., Roy, K., Vijaykumar, T.: Gated-vdd: A circuit technique to reduce leakage in deepsubmicron cache memories., In proceedings of ISLPED (2000)
7. Kao, J., Chandrakasan, A.: Dual-threshold voltage techniques for low-power digital circuits. IEEE Journal of Solid State Circuits **35** (2000)
8. Johnson, M., Somasekhar, D., Cheiou, L., Roy, K.: Leakage control with efficient use of transistor stacks in single threshold cmos. IEEE Transactions on VLSI Systems **10** (2002)
9. Durate, D., Tsai, Y.F., Vijaykrishnan, N., Irwin, M.J.: Evaluating run-time techniques for leakage power reduction., ASPDAC (2002)
10. Rele, S., Pande, S., Önder, S., Gupta, R.: Optimizing static power dissipation by functional units in superscalar processors., In International Conference on Compiler Construction (2002)
11. Kaxiras, S., Hu, Z., Martonosi, M.: Cache decay: exploiting generational behavior to reduce cache leakage power., In proceedings of ISCA (2001)
12. Bai, R., Kim, N., Sylvester, D., Mudge, T.: Total leakage optimization strategies for multi-level caches., ACM Great Lakes Symposium on VLSI (2005)
13. Guthaus, M., Ringenberg, J., Ernst, D., Austin, T., Mudge, T., Brown, R.: Mibench: A free, commercially representative embedded benchmark suite, IEEE 4th Annual Workshop on Workload Characterization (WWC-4) (December 2001)
14. Burger, D., Austin, T.M., Bennett, S.: Evaluating Future Microprocessors: The SimpleScalar Tool Set.Technical Report CS-TR-96-1308, University of Wisconsin-Madison. (July 1996)

Memory Architecture Evaluation for Video Encoding on Enhanced Embedded Processors

Ali Iranpour and Krzysztof Kuchcinski

Lund University, Department of Computer Science,
SE-22100 Lund, Sweden
{ali.iranpour, krzystof.kuchinski}@cs.lth.se

Abstract. In this paper we investigate the impact of different memory configurations on performance and energy consumption of the video encoding applications, MPEG-4 and H.264. The memory architecture is integrated with SIMD extended embedded processor, proposed in our previous work. We explore both dedicated memories and multilevel cache architectures and perform exhaustive simulations. The simulations have been conducted using highly optimized proprietary video encoding code for mobile handheld devices. Our simulation results show that the performance improvement of dedicated memories on video encoding applications is not very significant. The multilevel cache-based architecture processes approximately 17 frames/s compared to 19-22 frames/s for 512 KB dedicated on-chip zero-wait state memory. Thus it is difficult to justify using dedicated memory for this kind of embedded systems, when energy consumption and cost of implementation are also considered.

1 Introduction

The video encoding applications implementing standards such as MPEG-4 and H.264 are computationally and memory intensive. These applications are becoming a dominant portion of today's computing workloads for handheld embedded devices. Since, embedded devices have limited energy supply and size they need to be designed carefully to fulfill these confined demands. With this in mind, these devices have other design challenges than high-performance designs. The key is to increase the performance just enough to meet the requirements with as little cost overhead as possible.

An important characteristic of video processing applications is the presence of data localities. This provides the possibility to use a special memory architecture that reuses data efficiently. Choosing the right memory solution is important in order to provide sufficient performance and manageable energy consumption. The memory solutions range from dedicated memories [1-4] to standard memory hierarchies [5-7].

The research on data reuse in media applications provides contradicting conclusions. Some authors argue that data reuse is ineffective for these applications [8]. They however concentrate on computational kernels only. Other authors draw different conclusions when the whole video processing application is considered [7]. Their paper confirms the existence of data locality for video encoding applications such as MEPG-4 for non-SIMD architecture, and the authors state that specific memory system optimizations fails to improve MPEG-4 performance. In this paper we examine Single

S. Vassiliadis et al. (Eds.): SAMOS 2006, LNCS 4017, pp. 309 – 320, 2006.

Instruction Multiple Data (SIMD) enhanced embedded processor and video encoding applications specifically developed for mobile applications.

We use two proprietary video encoding applications provided by Ericsson AB specifically developed with focus on very low complexity algorithms, which influences both computations and memory traffic. This is important when evaluating memory architecture.

In our previous work [12] we have proposed SIMD extension for embedded processor to address the problem of high computation requirements for video encoding. In this paper we examine the impact of different memory architectures on performance and energy consumption of our architecture. We evaluate standard *multilevel cache hierarchy* against *dedicated memory* because the standard code can be run without rewriting that provides system flexibility.

The structure of the paper is as follows. Section 2 describes our video encoding applications. In Section 3 basic information of our extended processor architecture is given and in section 4 the memory architecture is discussed. Section 5 presents the method used in our approach. In section 6 we present and discuss our experimental results. In Section 7, we discuss related work and in Section 8 we give some concluding remarks.

2   Video Application

The two video standards used in our research are MPEG-4 [9] and H.264 [13]. Both are block based and one could view H.264 as the next step after MPEG-4. Looking at the optimized implementations of H.264/AVC encoders, time complexity is about 3.4 times higher for H.264 than MPEG-4 [14]. There are different phases involved in video encoding, such as Motion Estimation (ME), Motion Compensation (MC), Discrete Cosine Transform (DCT), quantization (Q) and variable length coding (VLC) [9]. The MPEG-4 and H.264 implementations selected for our research are full proprietary video encoding applications provided to us by Ericsson AB [11].

By profiling both MPEG-4 and H.264 video encoding applications we have identified the main computationally intensive operations. Our MPEG-4 application allows for full search (FS) and optimized search (OS) modes, with the last being more realistic for mobile devices. In MPEG-4 the most time consuming operations are in motion estimations Sum-of-Absolute-Differences (SAD), DCT as well as SAD_Intra. These operations account for 25-80% of the entire encoding time in case of MPEG-4 [15].

Two different H.264 implementations were evaluated. H.264 Ultra light (UL) comparable in quality to MPEG-4 and H.264 FAST comparable to the reference implementation [10]. The profiling of H.264 FAST and UL while performing encoding of the foreman test sequence shows the suitable operations for data parallelism account for approximately 40% of encoding time. These operations are Sum-of-Absolute-Transformed-Differences (SATD) and interpolation where they are significant part of the overall encoding time.

The main difference between our two implementations of H.264 encoder is the time complexity of the encoders and the quality of the encoded video sequence. The H.264 UL implementation is the simpler of the two and on average performs more efficiently than MPEG-4. The H.264 FAST encoder is more computationally demanding. This encoder performs well against the H.264 reference code [10] even though the time complexity of our encoder is significantly lower, approximately a speedup with a factor of 100 with an average bit-rate increase of less than 20%, than the reference encoder. This corresponds to approximately 700 times fewer SAD calls and 35 times fewer SATD calls [11].

The most often executed operation of video encoding, as identified by our profiling, use pixel arrays that represent frames. Macroblock (MB) is the main block of data where in MPEG-4 it consists of 8x8 pixels or 16x16 pixels. H.264 uses variable block sizes where macroblocks are partitioned into smaller MB 16x8, 8x8, 8x4 and 4x4. The frames are allocated in consecutive memory locations represented as pixel arrays. The allocated size for each frame is the frame size plus a border of 16 pixels surrounding the frame to deal with edge macroblocks when these are moved. The allocated memory for each section with screen size, QCIF (176x144) is 35 KB, CIF (352x288) is 122 KB and VGA (640x480) is 343 KB.

3 Processor Architecture

For the purpose of this study we have extended an embedded processor (MIPS based) with a specialized SIMD unit. This unit is designed in such a way that it supports specific operations found in video encoding algorithms such as MPEG-4 and H.264. Media applications and in particular video encoding is well tailored for SIMD based solutions, as there is abundance of data-level-parallelism [8,16,17]. In addition, SIMD design is highly efficient in exploiting the structure and resources of the processor.

Our SIMD unit proposed in our previous work [12] is a pipelined unit with specific instructions that increase the overall performance. The baseline architecture contains a MIPS CPU with SIMD unit as well as the cache hierarchy and the main memory. The second architecture extends the baseline architecture with dedicated memory SIMDMeM. A more detailed schematic of the MIPS core and the SIMD unit microarchitecture is depicted in fig. 1. SIMD unit is integrated in the flow of the

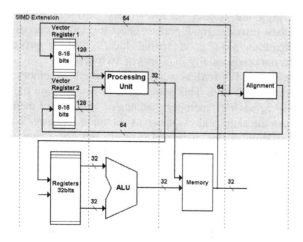

Fig. 1. The proposed SIMD architecture

instruction pipeline of the processor. At the instruction decode stage, SIMD instructions are identified and redirected to SIMD unit. The SIMD unit executes load and arithmetic instructions. It has two vector registers VR1 and VR2 that can be configured either as 16X8-bits or 8X16-bits registers. The bandwidth of the memory interface is 64-bits, thus resulting in two or three load accesses for loading each vector register. Three accesses are needed for alignment of data.

Five arithmetic and five memory instructions have been added to the MIPS ISA to support the SIMD extension. The new instructions follow the same ISA as the other processor instructions. The load instructions perform the loading of vector registers (VR1 and VR2). The arithmetic instructions work on the two vector registers.

Instruction SIMDSAD16 performs first 16 absolute value operations in parallel and then a tree of adders (together 15) sums all these values. SIMDSAD8 performs two 8x8 MB SAD operations. SIMDSATD first performs a Hadamard transform and then calculates SAD on the difference array. SIMDFIR performs a FIR filtering in half pixel interpolation. SIMDAVG performs average value for two pixel values for quarter-pixel calculation. The vector-processing unit is pipelined and has several stages, depending on used adders and technology. The speed-up for our SIMD using different SIMD instructions is approximately 6-7 times for SIMDSAD/SIMDSATD, three times for SIMDFIR and two times for SIMDAVG.

4 Memory Architecture

The memory system and cache utilization stands out as one of the main issues, when introducing our SIMD support. As this affects many parts of the system, we need to investigate the architectural design tradeoffs. We investigated three different solutions, one using the standard memory hierarchy, the other introducing a zero-wait state separate memory for the SIMD unit, SIMDMeM, and a third using a dedicated zero-wait state frame memory. As the impact of this memory on the overall encoding performance was the focus, we evaluated a memory sufficiently large to hold all data we need.

We evaluated both the impact of level-1 and level-2 caches on the overall performance. Caches provide good performance for video encoding applications, since these applications have good spatial locality. Many procedures in these applications access data sequentially in blocks of 16 bytes.

Our SIMD memory SIMDMeM, acts as a tightly coupled memory (TCM), holding all data used by the SIMD unit. This provides a zero-wait state memory for SIMD calculations, thus removing memory latencies from the memory hierarchy. SIMDMeM also use the same address space as the main memory. We do not discuss any specific organization of this dedicated memory but our assumptions provide an ideal model. A real dedicated memory cannot provide better performance than the model used in our studies. As we will show even with this assumption, the overall performance of the encoder is not improved very much comparing to the standard cache hierarchy.

An alternative solution would be an on-chip zero-wait state frame memory. The minimum size for this on-chip memory is dependent mainly on frame size and number of reference frames used. The memory footprint for our H.264 encoder with screen size of QCIF (176x144) and four reference frames is at least 512 KB. This solution reduces the energy costs of off-chip communication, at the same time, a 512 KB for on-chip fast memory might be difficult to justify in an embedded system.

5 Methodology

For verification of our architecture we used the two proprietary video encoding applications presented in section 2. Instruction Set Simulator (ISS), which is based on SimpleScalar toolset was used for the evaluation. This toolset provides an infrastructure for architectural modeling [18]. To estimate power we integrated the power estimation tool Wattch [19] into our system. The switching information for registers, functional units and buses was collected and used by Wattch for power calculation. The SimpleScalar cycle accurate model sim-outorder, modeling an in-order processor, with MIPS ISA has been chosen. We compile our video applications with the MIPS gcc compiler included in SimpleScalar toolset at optimization level – O3. Three memory configurations were used in our experiments: a separate level-1 instruction and data cache together with a unified level-2 cache, dedicated memory SIMDMeM, and on-chip frame memory. Table 1 illustrates configuration of the system with the underlined values representing the memory architecture configuration proposed after our investigation presented in section 6.

We evaluated two different architectures, baseline SIMD extended with standard memory hierarchy and SIMD extended with dedicated memory. The processor clock speed was set at 650 MHz in all the simulations with 90 nm process power model. The energy model for the off-chip memory includes the memory and communication energy consumption. The memory hierarchy latency for the system is 6 cycles for level-1 cache miss for the first chunk of data and 1 cycle for the consecutive chunks. A cache level-2 miss gives 45 cycles latency for the first chunk of data and 5 cycles for the consecutive data chunks when fetching data from the main off-chip memory.

Table 1. Cache architecture, dedicated memory SIMDMeM and on-chip frame memory with the chosen size and configurations (underlined in the table)

	Size (KB)	Line size (Bytes)	Associativity	Replacement policy
Inst. Cache	8/**16**/32/64	16/**32**	**2**	**LRU**
Data Cache	8/16/**32**/64/128/256/512/1024	8/16/**32**	1/2/**4**/8/16	**LRU**
Unified Cache	64/**128**/265/512/1024/2048	32/**64**/128	**4**	**LRU**
SIMDMeM	**128**	-	-	-
On-chip Frame memory	**512-768**	-	-	-

Table 2. MPEG-4 and H.264 configuration

	Screen size	Quantization	Search algorithm	Comments
MPEG-4	QCIF/CIF	15	Full Search/ IGRADD	Half-pixel enabled
H.264 Ultra Light (UL)	QCIF	30	IGRADD	Ref. frames 4
H.264 FAST	QCIF	30	IGRADD	Ref. frames 4

Table 2 illustrates the configuration chosen for the MPEG-4 and H.264 encoders. The screen resolutions chosen was QCIF (176x144) and CIF (352x288). H.264 is restricted with the screen resolution of QCIF as our encoder for the moment supports this size. Test sequences chosen in our experiments were foreman, mobile and news [20]. The main difference between these sequences is the amount of processing they need to encode the sequences. The mobile sequence is the most demanding sequence in terms of processing. In order to measure the overall performance of the system we used frames per second, which in our case is more relevant as we are performing video encoding. As we are dealing with handheld, battery driven embedded devises we use total energy consumption rather than power consumption. For evaluating cache performance we use miss rate, which is a common practice. But as we will point out later, blindly using miss rate alone can be misleading, as cache accesses influence the total energy consumption.

6 Experimental Results and Discussion

In sub-section 6.1, we evaluate the level-1 instruction and data cache size and their configurations for video encoding. In sub-section 6.2 we present our evaluation of the level-2 cache and its impact on performance and cache miss rate. Sub-section 6.3 deals with the energy consumption of the architecture. The results obtained in section 6.1-6.3 are then used to select an appropriate cache configuration when comparing with dedicated memory. In sub-section 6.4, we present the performance results for encoding applications on the evaluated architectures for both standards cache hierarchy and dedicated memory. Finally, we discuss experimental results and their implications in sub-section 6.5.

6.1 L1 Cache Configuration

To find the optimal cache configuration for our two encoding applications we performed extensive simulations for different cache configurations. We have chosen separate instruction and data cache architecture. The evaluated data cache sizes for

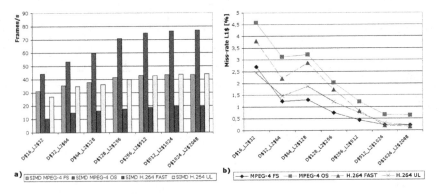

Fig. 2. a) Frame rate for MEPG-4 and H.264 with different level-1 cache sizes. b) Miss rate for MEPG-4 and H.264 with different level-1 data cache sizes.

level-1 cache were 8, 16, 32 and 64 KB, which are the most common sizes used. The increased data cache size has positive effect on encoded frames per second (frames/s) as shown in fig. 2a, but this comes at the expense of increased energy (fig. 5a) as discussed later. Based on the analyses of miss rate for level-1 data cache, fig. 2b, we can conclude that the level-1 data cache already at 32 KB has a miss rate between 1.2-3.1% for all applications. This provides a performance of 30 frames/s for most applications except H.264 FAST.

Fig. 3a shows performance for 4, 8 and 16 KB instruction cache sizes. Caches larger than 16 KB are not shown in figures, but we have observed that there is no significant miss rate improvement and are not realistic for embedded systems. Looking at the frame rate depicted in fig. 3a, going from 8 to 16 KB instruction cache gives a significant improvement for our application. An important factor is the level-1 instructions cache miss rate, which is as high as 29% for 4 KB and 20% for 8 KB going down to 4.3% for 16 KB instruction cache.

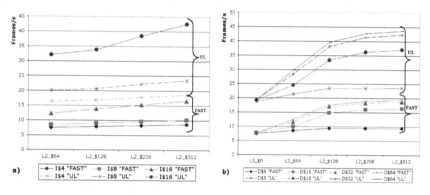

Fig. 3. Frame rate for H.264 FAST and UL with different level-2 and level-1. a) Instruction cache sizes and b) data cache sizes.

Cache associativity is another key issue for cache performance. The number of cache accesses decrease when we go from direct mapped to 2-way, 4-way associativity. Our experiment shows that going beyond this to 8-way and above provides no significant improvement. As our results show, the low miss rates in level-1 cache indicates the high reuse of data in level-1 cache. The main bandwidth bottleneck is between level-1 cache and processing unit. In our architecture a 64-bits bus handles this. Our simulations indicate 16 KB being right size for level-1 instruction and 32 KB for level-1 data cache.

6.2 L2 Cache and Its Impact

Fig. 3b illustrates the impact of level-2 cache for encoding foreman test sequence. This test sequence can be considered as good average since similar results were observed for both mobile and news test sequence. As in previous sub-section the presented results are for H.264 encoding. The results of MPEG-4 indicate a similar pattern. We observe the potential benefits of reducing the size of level-1 cache with small performance degradation on the overall encoding. If the size of level-1 is below 8 KB the size of level-2 cache has no impact on overall performance. Cache level-1 of 16 KB and above provides significant improvement with added level-2 cache. The optimal size, when taking into account miss rate as well as energy consumption and performance, of level-2 cache is 128 KB. This is true for all test sequences.

The impact of introducing a level-2 cache, which is significantly slower but larger than level-1 cache, is apparent on overall performance. We observe a miss rate improvement when going from 20-16% for 64 KB level-2 cache to 8-4% for 128 KB and below 1.5% for 512 KB. An important issue is the impact of level-1 cache on level-2 cache. The observation made for instruction cache, that a larger level-1 cache gives a higher miss rate in level-2 cache, is also true for level-1 data cache.

In fig. 3b there is a break at 128 KB where the curve flattens and we observe less noticeable improvement with increased level-2 cache size. The same results were also obtained and verified for encoding MPEG-4, but due to space limitations we only present H.264 encoding results.

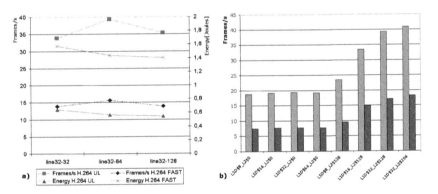

Fig. 4. a) Frame rate and energy consumption for different level-2 cache line sizes. b) The impact of level-2 cache on performance while encoding foreman with H.264 UL and FAST.

As shown in fig. 4a the optimal line size for level-2 cache, which in our study was 64-bytes. The positive impact of increased level-2 line size both saves energy as well as lowers the miss rate. At the same time the number of accesses are almost identical. This has more impact on the overall system performance than level-1 line size. Going beyond 64-bytes does not give any significant improvement on the overall perfor-mance and has negative impact on the overall energy consumption.

Fig. 4b shows the overall improvement in video encoding performance that can be obtained by introducing a level-2 cache. The significant performance jump can be observed when we use level-2 cache together with a large enough level-1 cache. In our case this is at 32KB for level-1 data cache and 128 KB level-2 unified cache. Going beyond this has no significant overall improvement.

6.3 Energy Consumption

Fig. 5a depicts the total energy consumption of the system with caches and off-chip memory. The total energy consumption includes also our SIMD unit but it is usually lower for SIMD enhanced architecture even though we have introduced a new component in the processor architecture [11]. The energy consumption of different cache configurations while performing video encoding on the foreman test sequence shows that the optimal point is at 128 KB level-2 cache, 32 KB level-1 data cache and 16 KB level-1 instruction cache sizes. As can be seen this is true both for H.264 FAST and H.264 UL, similar results were obtained for MPEG-4 as well. Fig. 5b shows the energy consumption when encoding MPEG-4 as well as H.264 with the final memory architecture. The overall energy consumption is almost identical for both SIMD and SIMDMeM.

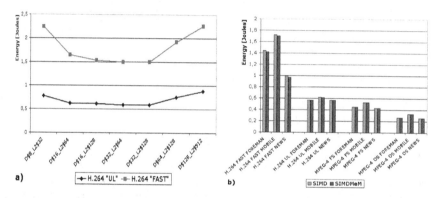

Fig. 5. a) Energy consumption for H.264 (FAST) and (UL) for encoding foreman test sequence with different level-2 data cache sizes. b) Energy consumption for MPEG-4 (FS) (OS) and H.264 (FAST) (UL) for test sequences foreman, mobile and news.

6.4 Dedicated Memory vs. Cache

The three memory configurations were standard cache hierarchy as discussed earlier and dedicated memory SIMDMeM for SIMD unit, as well as dedicated frame memory. The optimal cache configuration we found in previous sub-sections was used for our evaluation (see table 1). Fig. 6 shows the performance of our two memory architectures for H.264 FAST and UL as well as MPEG-4 when encoding the three different test sequences foreman, mobile and news.

The performance of SIMD and SIMDMeM are almost identical which shows the impact of adding a dedicated memory to SIMD unit has no significant impact over standard cache memory organization. With regards to energy consumption in fig. 5b we do not see any significant difference between the two memory architectures.

We have also evaluated the most optimistic data memory hierarchy, where all frame data used for encoding is in dedicated zero-wait state frame memory. The encoding of foreman results in 22 frames/s compared to 17.5 frames/s for SIMD and 18.6 frames/s for the SIMDMeM solution. The increased energy consumption from using a standard memory hierarchy with off-chip frame memory compared to using an on-chip zero-wait state frame memory is 0.35 J. This includes off-chip memory and communications for our chosen standard memory hierarchy configuration (see table 1). As stated before, the main arguments against an on-chip solution is the added costs in terms of size and practicality of having at least 512KB for on-chip zero-wait state memory. The justification for this solution in an embedded system is extremely hard especially when the gains are still relatively small.

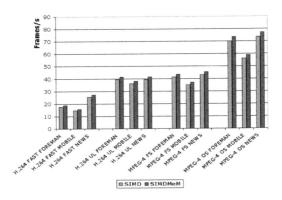

Fig. 6. Frame rates for MPEG-4 (FS) (OS) and H.264 (FAST) (UL) while encoding the test sequences foreman, mobile and news

6.5 Summary

The addition of dedicated memory for the SIMD unit has no significant benefit when performing video encoding, both for H.264 as well as MPEG-4, and regardless of the test sequence used. The benefit of increasing the size of level-1 data cache beyond 32 KB has no substantial improvements on the overall performance, as well as it may even reverse affect for the energy consumption. The introduction of level-2 cache, to hide the latencies between the level-1 cache and main memory, has more significant impact on the overall performance as well as energy consumption. This has also the positive side effect of being able to reduce level-1 cache size. In terms of using a dedicated SIMDMeM or dedicated on-chip frame memory the increase in performance is relatively small only by 4.5 frames for the dedicated frame memory.

7 Related Work

Most work on video encoding has been done using kernels [8,21], or using non-optimized code [3,4,7,22,23]. This approach makes it difficult to draw right conclusions for how an entire video encoding application behaves. In our study we use proprietary video encoding applications, ensuring that we have correct workloads for evaluation of our memory architectures.

The high bandwidth requirements of video encoding applications are important architectural design issues [22]. Multilevel caches, together with special instructions for computationally intensive application kernels, are discussed in [21] as important performance boosters. The authors of [6,7] propose to use bandwidth hierarchy to address the memory bandwidth problem. By removing the latency through usage of memory hierarchy the performance degradation was negligible and thus illustrated the potential of balanced memory architecture. We also use cache hierarchy but we test it with the SIMD unit that has higher bandwidth requirements. Our approach of using the standard memory hierarchy has the added benefit of not needing to optimize the data placement and having the added cost of dedicated memory.

Utilizing a level-2 cache has been a performance improvement factor in high performance processors. As more computationally demanding applications are executed on embedded systems, level-2 cache has been proposed for embedded domain as well. There are though not many studies done in this regard. In [6] the authors briefly discuss CPU utilization and transaction traffic when introducing level-2 cache for video decoding. Their finding is that both CPU utilization and transaction traffic decrease with increased level-2 cache size. In [7], the authors study performance of non-SIMD high performance processors for MPEG-4. Their architectures utilize large 1-8 MB level-2 cache, which improves the overall performance through reduction of traffic to main memory. In none of these works the emphasis has been on evaluating the actual impact of level-2 cache. The work has been on high performance general purpose processors using MPEG-4 reference code. In [6] there is a study on performance improvement for embedded processors when introducing level-2 cache. This work looks at MPEG-4 decoding which has some similarities to encoding but is much less performance demanding. We use video encoding and an embedded processor with an SIMD unit. This puts different requirements on memory bandwidth.

Dedicated memories have been proposed to improve performance of application specific systems, for example in [3,4]. The authors in [24] propose a HiBRID multi-core system on chip architecture with 4KB dedicated memory to compute macroblocks. In our work we have evaluated dedicated memory architectures against multilevel cache hierarchies.

8 Conclusions

In this paper we have performed extensive simulations on our SIMD extended processor and show that using standard multilevel cache hierarchy achieve almost the same performance as a dedicated memory for the SIMD processing unit for video encoding. As video encoding is highly data centric the importance of a well-balanced memory is crucial. An important issue for this exploration is the use of realistic application workloads specifically implemented for handheld embedded devices when exploring different design trade-offs. We examine two solutions, one that utilizes the standard cache hierarchy (two levels) and the other one that uses a dedicated zero-wait-state memory. Our results show, against common belief, that the use of the standard cache based architecture achieves almost the same performance as SIMD dedicated memory architecture for full video encoding applications. We have made conservative assumptions in our energy models for dedicated memory but the overall difference in energy consumptions was negligible.

References

1. V.A. Chouliaras et al., "A Multi-Standard Video Accelerator based on a Vector Architecture," IEEE Trans. Consum. Elec., Vol.51, No.1, Feb. 2005.
2. J.L.Nunez. and V.A. Chouliaras, "High-performance Arithmetic Coding VLSI Macro for the H264 Video Compression Standard," IEEE Trans. Consum. Elec., Vol.51, No.1, Feb. 2005.
3. Y.-W.Huang, B.-Y.Hsieh, T.-C.Chen and L.-G.Chen, "Hardware Design for H.264/AVC Intra Frame Coder," in Proc. of IEEE ISCAS'04, Vol. 2, II-269-272, 2004.
4. R.G.Wang, J.T.Li and C.Huang, "Motion Compensation Memory Access Optimization Strategies for H.264/AVC Decoder," in Proc. of IEEE ICASSP'05, Vol. 5, pp.97-100, 2005.
5. A.Stevens, "Level 2 Cache for High-performance ARM Core-based SoC System," White-paper ARM, Jan. 2004, http://www.arm.com/.
6. A.Asaduzzaman et al., "Cache Optimization for Mobile Devices Running Multimedia Applications," in Proc. IEEE ISMSE'04, pp. 499-506, 2004.
7. S.A.McKee, Z.Fang and M.Valero, "An MPEG-4 Performance Study for non-SIMD, General Purpose Architectures," in Proc. of IEEE ISPASS 2003, pp. 49-57, 2003.
8. J.D.Owens et al., "Media Processing Applications on the Imagine Stream Processor", in Proc. of IEEE ICCD'02, pp. 295-302, 2002.
9. MPEG-4: ISO/IEC JTCI/SC29/WG11, "ISO/IEC 14469:2000-2: Information on technology-coding of audio-video objects–Part 2:Visual," ISO/IEC, Genf, Switzerland, Dec. 2000.
10. H.264/AVCSoftwareCoordination,JM,http://iphome.hhi.de/suehring/tml/
11. C.Priddle, "H.264 video encoder optimization with focus on very low complexity algorithms," M.S. thesis, Uppsala University, April 2005.
12. A.R..Iranpour and K.Kuchcinski, "Evaluation of SIMD Architecture Enhancement in Embedded Processors for MPEG-4," in Proc. IEEE DSD'04, Sep. 2004.
13. Joint Video Team (JVT) of ISO/IEC MPEG, ITU-T VCEG "Text of ISO/IEC 14496 10:2004 Advance Video Coding Standard (second edition)", ISO/IEC JTC1/SC29/WGII/N6359, Munich, Germany, March 2004.
14. V.Lappalainen, et al., "Performance of H.26L Video Encoder on General-Purpose Processor," Kluwer Journal of VLSI Sig. Proc., Vol. 34, No. 3, pp. 239-249, 2003.
15. A.R.Iranpour and K.Kuchcinski, "Analyses of Embedded Processors for Streaming Media Applications," in CAECW-8, Feb. 2005.
16. V.Lappalainen, T.D.Hämäläinen and P.Liuha, "Overview of Research Efforts on Media ISA Extentions and Their Usage in Video Coding" IEEE Trans. Circuit and System for Video tech., Vol. 12, No. 8, Aug. 2002.
17. S.Vassiliadis, B.Juurlink and E.Hakkennes, "Complex Streamed Instructions: Introduction and Initial Evaluation" in Proc. 26th Euromicro Conference, Vol.1, pp. 400-408, 2000.
18. T.Austin et al., "SimpleScalar: An infrastructure for computer system modeling," IEEE Computer, Vol. 35, Issue 2, pp. 59-67, Feb. 2002.
19. D.Brooks, V.Tiwari and M.Martonosi, "Wattch: A Framework for Architectural-Level Power Analysis and Optimizations," in Proc. ISCA'00, pp. 83-94, June 2000.
20. Test sequences, http://www.chiariglione.org/mpeg/
21. F.Franchetti, S.Kral, J.Lorenz and C.W.Uberhuber, "Efficient Utilization of SIMD Extensions," in IEEE Proceedings, Vol. 93, No. 2, Feb. 2005.
22. J.-C.Tuau, T.-S.Chang and C.-W.Jen, "On the Data Reuse and Memory Bandwidth Analysis for Full-Search Block-Matching VLSI Architecture," in IEEE Trans. Circuit and Syst. For Video tech., Vol. 12, No.1, Jan. 2002.
23. C.-Y.Cho, S.-Y.Huang and J.-S.Wang, "An Embedded Merging Scheme for H.264/AVC Motion Estimation," in Proc. of ICIP 2003, Vol. 1, I-909, 2003.
24. H.J.Stolberg et al., "HiBRID-SoC:A Multi-Core SoC Architecture for Multimedia Signal Processing" Journal VLSI Signal Processing System, Vol. 41, pp. 9-20, 2005.

Advantages of Java Processors in Cache Performance and Power for Embedded Applications

Antonio Carlos S. Beck, Mateus B. Rutzig, and Luigi Carro

Instituto de Informática – Universidade Federal do Rio Grande do Sul
Caixa Postal 15064 – 90501-970 – Porto Alegre, RS, Brazil
{caco, mbrutzig, carro}@inf.ufrgs.br

Abstract. Java, with its advantages as being an overspread multiplatform object oriented language, has been gaining popularity in the embedded system market over the years. Furthermore, because of its extra layer of interpretation, it is also believed that it is a slow language while being executed. However, when this execution is done directly in hardware, advantages because of its stack nature start to appear. One of these advantages concerns the memory utilization, impacting in less accesses and cache misses. In this work we analyze this impact in performance and energy consumption, comparing a Java processor with a RISC one based on a MIPS with similar characteristics.

1 Introduction

While the number of embedded systems does not stop growing, new and different ones, like cellular phones, mp3 players and digital cameras, keep arriving at the market. At the same time, they are getting more complex, smaller, more portable and with more stringent power requirements, posing great challenges to the design of embedded systems. Additionally, another issue is becoming more important nowadays: the necessity of reducing the design cycle.

This last affirmative is the reason of why Java is getting more popular in embedded environments and replacing day by day traditional languages. Java has an object oriented nature, which facilitates the programming, modeling and validation of the system. Furthermore, being multiplatform, a system that was built and tested in a desktop can migrate to different embedded systems with a small number of modifications. Moreover, Java is considered a safe language and has a small size of code, since it was built to be transmitted through internet.

Not surprisingly, recent surveys reveal that Java is present in devices such as consumer electronics (digital TV, mobile phones, home networking) as well as industrial automation (manufacturing controls, dedicated hand held devices). It is estimated that more then 600 million devices will be shipped with Java by 2007 [1][3]. Furthermore, it is predicted that more then 74% of all wireless phones will support Java next year [2][4]. This trend can be observed nowadays, where most of the commercialized devices as cellular phones already provide support to the language. This means that current design goals might include a careful look

S. Vassiliadis et al. (Eds.): SAMOS 2006, LNCS 4017, pp. 321–330, 2006.

on embedded Java architectures, and their performance versus power tradeoffs must be taken into account.

However, Java is not targeted to performance or energy consumption, since it requires an additional layer in order to execute its bytecodes, called Java Virtual Machine (JVM), responsible for the multiplatform feature of Java. And that is why executing Java through the JVM could not be a good choice for embedded systems.

A solution for this issue would be the execution of Java programs directly in hardware, taking off this additional layer, but at the same time maintaining all the advantages of this high level language. Using this solution highlights again another execution paradigm that was explored in the past [5]: stack machines. Since the JVM is a stack machine, obviously a hardware for native Java execution should follow the same approach, in order to maintain full compatibility.

Furthermore, embedded applications today are not as small to fit in the cache and, at the same time, they are not as large to use configurations of traditional desktop environments either. Nevertheless, in nowadays embedded systems they can consume until 50% of the total energy of the system [6] and occupy a significant part of the total area of the chip. Adding these facts to all the constraints cited before explains why cache memories have gained more importance in the embedded domain.

Hence, in this paper we show the advantages of Java machines regarding energy consumption and performance of the cache memory when comparing to traditional RISC ones, considering the particularities of embedded systems. We demonstrate that, thanks to the particular execution method based on a stack, these machines have less memory accesses and less cache misses concerning the instruction memory. This way, the designer can take advantage of all benefits of a high level language such Java, shrinking the design cycle and at the same time increasing the overall performance - proving that Java can also be a high performance and low power alternative when executed directly in hardware.

This work is organized as follows: Section 2 shows a brief review of the existing Java processors and some recent works concerning cache memory for embedded systems. In Section 3 we discuss the processors used in the evaluation and its particularities. Section 4 presents the simulation environment and shows the results regarding performance of the cache memory on the systems with various configurations. The last section draws conclusions and introduces future work.

2   Related Work

In the literature, one can rapidly find a great number of Java processors aimed at the embedded systems market. Sun's Picojava I [7], a four stage pipelined processor, and Picojava II [8], with a six stage pipeline, are probably the most studied ones. Even though the specifications of such processors allow a variable size for the data and instruction caches, there is no study about the impact of stack execution on these cache memories.

Furthermore, we can cite some works regarding cache memory specifically for embedded systems. In [9], compiler techniques, memory access transformations and loop optimizations are used in order to decrease the number of cache accesses, hence increasing performance and saving power. In [10] a technique aimed at reconfiguring the cache by software in order to change its associativity configuration with the objective of saving power is presented. In [11], taking advantage of the frequent values that widely exist in a data cache memory, a technique is proposed to reduce the static energy dissipation of an on-chip data cache. Other approaches, such as the use of scratchpads in the embedded domain [12], have been applied as well.

In this specific work, we study the effect of cache memories in Java based embedded systems, and why it differs from traditional ones because of its stack machine architecture.

3   Architectures Evaluated

It is very hard to compare two different architectures, even when they are of the same family. Comparing two different hardware components that execute instructions in a different way is even more difficult. As a consequence, in this work we try to make general characteristics, such as number of pipelines stages, equivalent.

3.1   Architeture Details

The RISC processor used is based on the traditional MIPS-I instruction set [13]. It has a five stages pipeline: instruction fetch, decode and operand fetch, execution, memory access and write back. This MIPS implementation has 32 registers in its bank.

The Java processor used is the Femtojava [14], which implements a subset of Java instructions. It does not support dynamic allocation of objects neither garbage collection. Consequently, all objects are statically allocated in Java programs. This processor has the same number of pipeline stages that the RISC one has. However, the structure of the pipeline is a little different, as showed in Figure 1.

The first stage is instruction fetch, as in the MIPS processor. The second stage is responsible for decoding instructions. The next one is the operand fetch. It is important to note that, in opposite to the MIPS processor, operand fetch cannot be made at same time as decoding, because it is not known previously which operands to fetch (this data is not intrinsically available in the opcode), as in MIPS architecture. On the other hand, there is no instruction that accesses the register bank and the memory at the same time. As a consequence, the memory access, which is a separated pipeline stage in the MIPS, is made in the forth stage together with the execution. The write back to the register bank is the last stage, as in the MIPS processor. The stack in the Java processor is implemented in an internal register bank. In our benchmark set, the stack does not increase more than 32 values. Hence, there are 32 registers in the bank implementing the

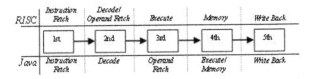

Fig. 1. Differences in the pipeline stages between the two processors

stack, the same number of registers used in the MIPS processor. However, it is important to mention that local variables in the Java processor are also saved in the stack (hence, in the internal register bank). It facilitates passing parameters between methods, since Java uses the concept of frames. On the other hand, local variables in the MIPS processor are saved in the main memory, not in the register bank. In order to keep the comparison as fair as possible, in all our benchmark set we implemented these local variables as global. This way, there will be accesses to the main memory in both processors. Moreover, data in the memory will also be accessed in static variables (such as vectors) and information about methods.

3.2   Computacional Methods

To better illustrate the difference between these two paradigms, let's start with an example. In RISC machines, to make a sum of two operands, just one instruction is needed:

$$add\ r1,\ r2,\ r3$$

where r2 and r3 are the source operands and r1 is the target. In stack machines, however, this operation needs three different instructions:

$$push\ OP1,\ push\ OP2,\ add$$

At first sight, this characteristic could be considered as a disadvantage. However, stack machines keep the operands always in the stack. This means that the next instructions will use operands that are already present in the stack, generated by the instructions executed before. Hence, the push instructions are not needed anymore. As more operations are executed, more data is reused from the stack. Since it is well known that each basic block usually has more than just on single operation, stack machines can be very economic concerning number of instructions. This characteristic will reflect in the instruction cache hits and misses, as it will be shown in next section.

Another important issue is the size of the instructions. In Java, they have a variable length: 1, 2 or 3 bytes; in opposite to the MIPS instructions, with a fixed size of 4 bytes. This way, the Femtojava is implemented to fetch 4 bytes at each cycle, in order to avoid bubbles in the pipeline. This makes also the comparison easier: the size of each word in the cache memory has exactly the same size. Adding the smaller size of the instructions with the stack paradigm leads to an incredible difference in the number of instruction cache misses, as we show in the next section.

4   Results

Three steps were necessary to gather the results. Firstly, using a SystemC description of both processors, traces of memory accesses for each application were generated. Then, another simulator, which in turn uses the traces generated before, was used. It has as additional inputs: cache size, associativity and spatial locality, in order to better explore the design space. After that, the cache simulator gives as output the number of cache misses and hits depending on the input's configuration.

Finally, using this information, the ECACTI tool [15] was used for the power consumption evaluation. It is very important to mention that this simulation also takes into account the static power. Statistics for the off-chip memory consumption as the bus were taken from [17], considering this memory working at 50Mhz, 2V, implemented in a 0.25 technology. Five different types of algorithms were chosen and simulated over the architectures described in Section 3: Sort (bubble, heap, select and quick); IMDCT - an important part of the MP3 (plus three unrolled versions); algorithm to solve the Crane problem; the Cordic, a shift-add algorithm for computing trigonometric; and three algorithms that belong to the Java Grande Benchmark set [16]: Lufact, that solves a N x N linear system using LU factorization followed by a triangular solve; SOR, performs 100 iterations of successive over-relaxation on a N x N grid; and Sparse, which is a sparse matrix multiplication. Each algorithm has two versions, in Java and C, compiled by Sun´s Java Compiler [18] and GCC [19], respectively.

First of all, we analyze the number of memory accesses of both processors. Remember that, as explained earlier, the stack in the Femtojava is implemented in a register bank instead of using the main memory. Table 1 demonstrates the number of accesses in the data and instruction memories. Dividing the table, the first and second columns show the number of accesses of each architecture, and the last column demonstrates the relative difference of accesses that the RISC architecture has, when compared to the Femtojava. As it can be seen, in the average, the Femtojava has fewer accesses in instruction memory and almost the same in data one. There is an enormous difference concerning the instruction memory, and the reason for that was explained in the last section. In the next sub-sections we analyze the impact of this fact in the performance and power consumption. For the experiments with the cache, we analyzed instructions and data caches separately, varying its size (64, 128 and 2048 lines); spatial locality (one and two words per line); and associativity (direct mapped, 2-way and 4-way associative).

4.1   Performance

Firstly, we demonstrate in table 2 the number of instruction and data cache misses in both processors, using different cache configurations (because of space limitations, we are considering direct mapped and 4-way associative cache with 64 and 2048 lines without exploring spatial locality). As can be observed in this table, concerning instruction cache accesses, the configuration that benefits the most the Femtojava (configuration that results in the bigger difference of cache

Table 1. Number of Accesses in the Data Memory

	Instruction Memory			Data Memory		
	Femtojava	MIPS	Difference	Femtojava	MIPS	Difference
Bubble 10	898	2697	3,003341	875	921	1,052571
Bubble100	96508	314240	3,256103	112933	113412	1,004241
Heap 10	849	3274	3,856302	743	1028	1,38358
Select 10	686	1915	2,791545	638	633	0,992163
Quick 10	793	2538	3,200504	860	987	1,147674
IMDCT N	13475	39241	2,912134	10741	8664	0,806629
IMDCTu1	8316	22173	2,666306	6305	4231	0,671055
IMDCTu2	7848	19740	2,515291	6003	3912	0,651674
IMDCTu3	3824	5998	1,568515	4234	2143	0,506141
Sparse	162620	602572	3,705399	115609	131753	1,139643
SOR	198613	777951	3,916919	197112	231980	1,176894
Lufact	14233	60658	4,261786	12617	22927	1,817151
Cordic	353	780	2,209632	358	352	0,98324
Crane	7700	23703	3,078312	8097	9877	1,219835
		Average =	3,067292		Average =	1,039464

misses between the Java and MIPS processors when dividing the total number of memory accesses by the number of cache misses) is the follow: 64 lines; 2 words per line and associativity of 4. For the MIPS processor: 2048 lines, 2 words per line and direct mapped. Even in this last configuration, though, there is a huge advantage in instruction cache misses for the Femtojava.

It proves that, no matter the cache configuration, always stack machines will present advantages in instruction memory accesses when comparing to conventional RISC ones. We repeat the same analysis used before, but now for the data cache. The best configuration for the Femtojava is: 2048 lines; 2 words per line and associativity 2; and for MIPS: 64 lines, 1 word per line and direct mapped. In this case, depending on the algorithm, there is a small advantage for the Femtojava. Another important thing to note is that there is almost no difference

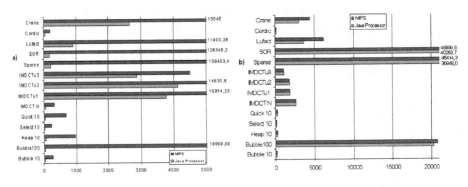

Fig. 2. Average number of cache misses: a) Instruction Cache b) Data cache

Table 2. Cache Misses: Instruction and Data Caches

	Femtojava				MIPS			
	Direct Mapped		4-Way Associative		Direct Mapped		4-Way Associative	
	Size 64	Size 2048	Size 64	Size 2048	Size 64	Size 2048	Size 64	Size 2048
	Instruction Misses							
Bubble 10	44	44	44	44	701	162	855	162
Bubble100	46	46	46	46	42210	161	93577	161
Heap 10	83	81	82	81	2275	342	2784	342
Select 10	34	34	34	34	495	122	783	122
Quick 10	47	47	47	47	1945	175	2092	175
IMDCT N	86	85	86	85	551	246	1001	246
IMDCTu1	7410	534	7544	534	22173	19033	22173	19033
IMDCTu2	7847	1065	7847	1065	19740	19740	19740	19740
IMDCTu3	3824	3824	3824	3824	5998	5998	5998	5998
Sparse	686	187	268	187	474916	1098	547256	1156
SOR	213	209	213	209	407200	1793	568243	1510
Lufact	2025	753	1355	398	26497	6727	32331	4353
Cordic	60	59	60	59	541	168	419	168
Crane	5221	1986	5492	1233	20287	13157	19780	12703
	Data Misses							
Bubble 10	150	150	152	150	171	171	187	171
Bubble100	21746	18767	23167	18902	22363	18909	23367	19154
Heap 10	221	221	244	221	258	256	276	258
Select 10	131	131	131	131	124	124	125	124
Quick 10	201	201	204	201	282	233	247	243
IMDCT N	3017	2925	2933	2906	2961	2904	2925	2902
IMDCTu1	2185	2114	2126	2101	2127	2096	2122	2098
IMDCTu2	2096	2028	2038	2012	2042	2012	2034	2009
IMDCTu3	1489	1360	1137	980	1192	1111	1026	977
Sparse	48559	28509	40046	28960	48392	43165	45285	43265
SOR	56741	41886	38963	27757	58144	38855	51532	40120
Lufact	4328	3123	4403	3364	6877	5627	6635	5673
Cordic	141	141	141	141	144	143	146	143
Crane	3137	2865	3176	2972	4434	4350	4840	4215

between different cache configurations: the proportion of misses in data caches
is almost the same, no matter its configuration.

Finally, figures 2(a) and 2(b) shows the average number of data and instruction
cache misses for each algorithm of the whole benchmark set considering all possible configurations (18 in the total). This graph summarizes what was affirmed
before: an expressive difference in instruction cache misses and equivalence in
the data ones, with a small advantage for the Femtojava in some algorithms.

4.2 Power and Energy Consumption

In this sub-section we analyze the power spent by cycle and the total energy consumption caused by cache misses. As could be expected, the energy consumption

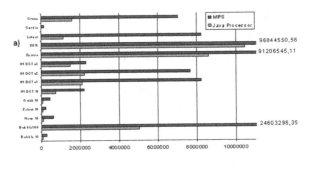

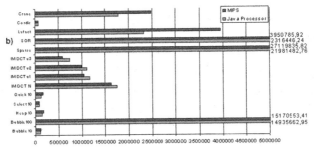

Fig. 3. Average total energy consumption: a) Instruction Cache b) Data Cache

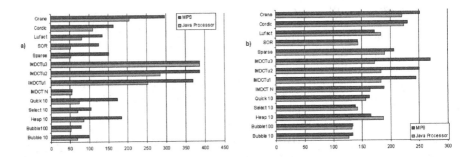

Fig. 4. Average power consumption: a) Instruction Cache b) Data Cache

is directly proportional to the number of misses, showed before. This way, huge energy savings concerning the instruction memory is achieved, and a very similar consumption in data memory is obtained. Finally, we demonstrate the average power and energy consumption for each algorithm considering the whole set of cache configurations.

As it is demonstrated in Figure 4(a) for instruction cache, there is less power consumption in the Femtojava: since there is less cache misses, less accesses to the off-chip memory is necessary. Moreover, as there are less overall memory accesses, the difference in energy consumption between the two processors is even higher (figure 3(a)).

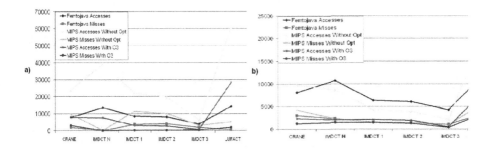

Fig. 5. Comparison:number of instruction accesses when using GCC optimization: a)Instruction Cache b)Data Cache

Concerning the data cache, power is saved because there are less off-chip memory accesses per cycle (figure 4(b)) in the Femtojava. However, as depending on the algorithm there are more accesses in the Java architecture, the total energy consumption can be higher than in the MIPS hardware (figure 3(b)).

In all results showed above, no optimization flags were used to make the comparison as far as possible, since optimizations as forcing values to be in the registers, loop unrolling and method inlining are not available for Java Compilers yet - although they are possible to be made in java bytecodes. However, in order to analyze the impact of such optimization in the results, in the figure 5(a) and 5(b) we make a first analysis, comparing the number of memory accesses and cache misses (instruction and data memory, respectively) of the Femtojava Processor with the MIPS processor when the benchmarks are compiled with the higher possible level of optimization (-O3). As can be observed, in certain cases there is a huge impact in the number of accesses.

It is very likely that these common optimizations will be included in future versions of Java compilers and, as a consequence, the advantages of stack machines concerning memory accesses will remain, as we demonstrated when we compared both architectures with the same level of compiler resources.

5   Conclusions and Future Work

Java became popular mainly because it is an object oriented language and for its ease of use. It is also common sense that it is a slow language while being executed. In this paper we showed that when executing Java directly in hardware, advantages start to appear. In the case of the memory system, specifically instruction caches, stack machines can at the same time have a higher cache hit ratio that besides increasing the overall performance, reflects in less dynamic and static power consumption, while the data memory presents very similar results - when comparing equivalent configurations. This way, besides decreasing the design cycle, Java can also bring advantages concerning performance, area and power consumption. Our next step is to compare complete architectures of both processors.

References

1. The Embedded Software Strategic Market Intelligence. Java in Embedded Systems. http://www.vdc-corp.com/
2. S. McAteer. Java will be the dominant handset platform. www.microjava.com/articles/perspective/zelos/.
3. D. Mulchandani. Java for Embedded Systems. Internet Computing, 31(10):30-39, May 1998.
4. Lawton, "Moving Java into Mobile Phones", Computer, vol. 35, n. 6, 2002, pp. 17-20.
5. P. Koopman, Stack Computers: The New Wave, Halsted Press, 1st edition, 1989
6. S. Segars, "Low power design techniques for microprocessors," Int. Solid-State Circuits Conf. Tutorial, 2001.
7. J. M. O'Connor, M. Tremblat, "Picojava-I: the Java Virtual Machine in Hardware", IEEE Micro, vol. 17, n. 2, Mar-Apr. 1997, pp.45-53
8. Sun Microsystems, PicoJava-II Microarchitecture Guide, Mar. 1999.
9. W. Shiue, C. Chakrabarti, "Memory Design and Exploration for Low Power, Embedded Systems", The Journal of VLSI Signal Processing - Systems for Signal, Image, and Video Technology, Vol. 29, No. 3, Nov. 2001, pp. 167-178
10. C. Zhang, F. Vahid, W. Najjar, "A highly configurable cache architecture for embedded systems", Proceedings of the 30th annual international symposium on Computer architecture (ISCA), 2003
11. C. Zhang, J. Yang, F. Vahid," Low Static-Power Frequent-Value Data Caches", Proceedings of the. Design, Automation and Test in Europe Conference (DATE), 2004
12. R. Banakar, S. Steinke, B. Lee, M. Balakrishnan, P. Marwedel, "Scratchpad Memory: A Design Alternative for Cache On-chip memory in Embedded Systems", Proc. of the 10th International Workshop on Hardware/Software Codesign, CODES, 2002
13. J. L. Hennessy, D. A. Patterson, Computer Organization and Design: The Hardware/Software Interface, Morgan Kaufmann Publishers, 3th edition, 2005
14. A.C.S.Beck, L. Carro, , "Low Power Java Processor for Embedded Applications". In: IFIP 12th International Conference on Very Large Scale Integration, Germany, 2003
15. G. Reinman and N. Jouppi. Extensions to cacti, 1999. Unpublished document.
16. D. Gregg, J. Power, "Platform Independent Dynamic Java Virtual Machine Analysis: the Java Grande Forum Benchmark Suite", Joint ACM Java Grande - ISCOPE Conf. Proc., 2001
17. K. Puttaswamy, K. Choi, J. C. Park, V. J. Mooney, A. Chatterjee, P. Ellervee. "System Level Power-Performance Trade-Offs in Embedded Systems Using Voltage and Frequency Scaling of Off-Chip Buses and Memory", ISSS'02., October, 2002
18. Java Tecnology Homepage, http://java.sun.com/
19. GCC Homepage, http://gcc.gnu.org/

CARROT – A Tool for Fast and Accurate Soft Error Rate Estimation

Dimitrios Bountas and Georgios I. Stamoulis

Department of Computer and Communications Engineering
University of Thessaly
37 Glavani St.
Volos 38221, Greece
{dibountas, georges}@uth.gr

Abstract. We present a soft error rate (SER) analysis methodology within a simulation and design environment that covers a broad spectrum of design problems and parameters. Our approach includes modeling of the particle hit at the transistor level, fast Monte-Carlo type simulation to obtain the latching probability of a particle hit on all nodes of the circuit, embedded timing analysis to obtain the latching window, and fine-grained accounting of the electrical masking effects to account for both the effects of scaling and of pulse duration versus the period of the system clock to get an estimate of the maximum SER of the circuit. This approach has been implemented in CARROT and placed under a broad design environment to assess design tradeoffs with SER as a parameter.

Keywords: SER, combinational circuits, simulation.

1 Introduction

Particle hits first became an issue for memories but with the continuously shrinking feature sizes and shrinking supply voltages, these issues have become significant in the design of any modern integrated circuit. Soft errors induced in memory structures and latches have been extensively studied and there are empirical models covering their contribution to the overall SER of the circuit [1]. These models work well as the laws of physics along with the electrical behavior of the device suffice for the adequate description of the phenomenon.

The contribution of combinational logic blocks is intrinsically more complicated and not as straight-forward, since the current pulse induced by the particle hit and the localized electrical behavior of the device describe only the generation of a single event upset and not its latching into one of the sequential elements, which would transform it to a soft error. The resulting voltage pulse on the gate output can be eliminated by i) the electrical behavior of the gates it has to cross to reach a latch; the pulse may not be wide enough and it will be filtered out by the inertial delay of the gate, ii) the logic behavior of the circuit; the pulse may be blocked at a gate if the output of the gate does not change logic state due to the pulse, which is a function of

S. Vassiliadis et al. (Eds.): SAMOS 2006, LNCS 4017, pp. 331–338, 2006.

the circuit inputs and the gate structure and iii) the timing of the signals, as the pulse may not overlap with the sampling range of the flip-flop it drives.

Several approaches with varying levels of detail have been proposed for the estimation of the SER due to combinational logic that can be categorized as follows:

a. direct simulation of the SEU within a circuit-level framework. Tools such as SEMM [2] use Monte-Carlo simulation for achieving high levels of accuracy but at a high price for simulation time.

b. mixed-mode simulation. The approach suggested by Dynamo [3] attempts to reduce the simulations required by a static approach initially, and processes the remaining ones through a mixed-mode simulator, where the current injection part is simulated at the circuit level, while the rest of the circuit at the timing level.

c. hybrid methods such as SERA[4] and SEUPER_FAST [5]. SERA uses a combination of mathematical and simulation methods to arrive at a SER estimate without the overhead of detailed circuit simulation. It simplifies gates between the charge injection point and the latch input nodes to equivalent inverters and performs and electrical simulation over the simplified circuit. SEUPER_FAST is a simulator at a very high level of abstraction that does not consider either circuit or logic simulation but models SER through a mathematical model.

d. logic-level simulation coupled with glitch and delay analysis. This category includes FAST [6], ASERTA [7], and ASSA [8], and tries to decouple the three factors (electrical, logic, and timing masking) that limit SEU latching. FAST compares the use of a standard event-driven simulator to assess SEU propagation and latching with a zero-delay fault simulator, while using a timing simulator to model the charge injection. ASERTA is using lookup tables for charge insertion, zero-delay simulation for logical masking, a ramp model for electrical masking, and pulse duration for timing masking. ASSA uses and extended timing window for timing masking, probability propagation for logic masking, and a noise rejection curve for electrical masking.

All of the aforementioned approaches have their drawbacks either in terms of accuracy or in terms of runtime. Furthermore, they tend to restrict the control that a designer has over the level of abstraction that is suitable for the design at hand, as well as the side effects of changes to enhance SER. The major source of the error introduced by approaches such as FAST, ASERTA, and ASSA stemmed from the decoupling of the three SEU latching prevention factors. Indeed, this permitted the use of zero-delay simulators for logic masking as well as lookup tables and simplified models for capturing electrical and timing effects.

We are proposing a new SER estimation approach that alleviates the restrictions that limit the accuracy while preserving the significant speedup of a zero-delay fault simulation approach. Our approach uses a zero-delay Monte-Carlo fault simulator that has been augmented by capabilities for handling timing and electrical masking at a fine grain level, within the main flow of fault simulation. This allows the appropriate weighting of the random effects, which is not possible in the flow suggested by ASERTA and ASSA. Our SER simulator, CARROT, also permits the use of charge injection, pulse propagation, and timing analysis methods of varying detail, so that the user can choose between simulation speed or accuracy.

The aim of this paper is to include SER estimation within a larger design framework and permit trading off SER for timing, power, area, and/or leakage.

The rest of the paper is organized as follows. Section 2 describes the soft-error analysis methodology that we are proposing, Section 3 presents results for all ISCAS85 and ISCAS89 benchmark circuits, and Section 4 contains the concluding remarks.

2 Soft Error Analysis

We assume a standard sequential digital circuit that can be described by an array of flip-flops controlled by one clock and combinational logic driven by flip-flop outputs and driving flip-flop inputs.

We also assume that the Soft Error Rate (SER) of a circuit is defined as the fraction of Single Event Upsets (SEUs) that are captured by the memory elements of the circuit, and that an SEU can occur with uniform probability over the clock period.

2.1 Electrical Modeling

A high-energy particle hit can interact with silicon atoms and generate a number of electron-hole pairs [9], which can flip the state of a logic node. This phenomenon is modeled by a current source with exponential decay as in [10].

$$I(t) = I_0(e^{-t/a} - e^{-t/b})$$

Different particle energy levels will produce a different number of electron-hole pairs which will be reflected into I_0. The circuit node that is affected can be either a gate output or an internal node of a gate. In both cases the particle hit appears as voltage pulse at the gate output. Since the particle energy level can be described as a random variable, the width of the output voltage pulse can also be described as a random variable with a probability density function (pdf) that can be approximated by Monte-Carlo electrical simulations of the charge injection circuits.

Simplifying assumptions can be made on the pdf (uniform or normal) and on the random nature of the pulse width (one can assume that the voltage pulse width is fixed for a specific gate to just one value).

Our approach can work equally well with a fixed value as well as with any pdf for the pulse width. In the latter case, the pdf is propagated through the circuit to the flip-flop inputs. During the propagation, the pdf is altered to account for electrical masking and is then used to calculate the latching probabilities of the SEUs it describes. Our approach requires that the pdf be discretized into a user-defined number of levels to enable its propagation through the circuit. The largest quantization value can be equal to the period of the clock, since for pulse widths larger than that, timing masking has no effect.

The propagation process is intertwined with the logic and timing masking process and will be described in detail in the next subsection.

The probability of a particle hit on a specific node is proportional to the area of the node as the flux of particles through the circuit is considered uniform. Any deviations from this assumption should be quantified by a flux distribution over the area of the circuit, and by the location of the node within the chip. Thus, for non-uniform flux distributions, placement data are required.

2.2 SER Propagation and Electrical/Logic/Timing Masking

This is the main part of this work, which addresses the issues raised by the interaction of a logic level simulator, like the fault simulator that we are using, and the masking phenomena. This is precisely the point where loss of accuracy can occur due to either modeling or systematic difficulties. Instead of decoupling the analysis for the three masking effects, and recombining their effects at the end of the process, we opted to analyze them in every step in order to maintain the required granularity for accurate estimates without resorting to simplifying assumptions.

As in FAST and ASERTA, CARROT also uses a zero-delay fault simulator to estimate the effect of logic masking on the probability of latching the incorrect value due to an SEU. However, unlike the aforementioned approaches, the effects of logic and timing masking are engrained into the zero-delay logic simulation in order to eliminate the error resulting from:

i) an SEU latched in more than one flip-flop
ii) different arrival times and latching probabilities in different flip-flops
iii) differential pulse propagation behavior along different paths from the upset gate to the latch inputs.

After the pdf for the voltage pulse width at the output of the gate being affected by a SEU is calculated and discretized a circuit would be like the one Figure 1, where the pulse widths fall into N levels. The probability of an SEU on the node has been calculated as proportional to the upset node area.

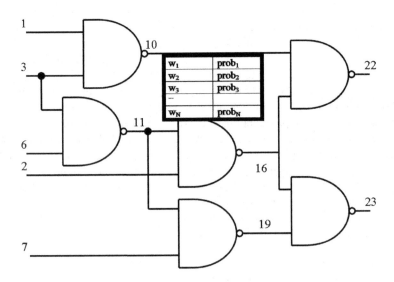

Fig. 1. Modeling of the pdf

We model the SEU as a stuck-at-fault and proceed through a Monte-Carlo fault simulation of the circuit. The number of input vectors is user defined, and the input probability for every input to the combinational block is determined by an RTL simulation in order to capture the effects of the input vectors on SER.

At the end of the Monte-Carlo fault simulation we preserve to flip-flop input vectors for further analysis. It must be noted here that we can now calculate the effect of logic masking on the flip-flop inputs. However, this is result requires further processing as the electric and timing masking effects are not accounted for yet.

In order to model electrical masking we chose the modeling of ASERTA, although the modeling in ASSA or any other could be used without impeding the subsequent analysis. Thus, we estimate the output pulse duration according to the following:

$$
\begin{array}{lll}
0 & \text{if} & w_i < d \\
2(w_i - d) & \text{if} & d < w_i < 2d \\
w_i & \text{if} & w_i > 2d
\end{array}
$$

where w_i is the input pulse duration and d is the inertial delay of the gate. It must be noted here that we apply this function to all the entries in the table containing the discretized pdf of the pulse width.

For the timing masking we add a basic timing analysis capability by capturing the minimum and maximum pulse arrival times at each node, as shown in Figure 3. At the charge injection node both are 0. The timing at the output of each gate is propagated as follows:

$$
\begin{aligned}
\min_o &= \min(\min(\text{all inputs to the gate})) + d \\
\max_o &= \max(\max(\text{all inputs to the gate})) + d
\end{aligned}
$$

where $\min_o$ and $\max_o$ are the min and max for the output node of the gate. For this purpose only the inputs of each gate activated by the upset node are considered.

A significant point is that we do not propagate pulse width information nor min/max timing information to outputs of gates that are not activated by the fault, i.e. their faulty and fault free outputs are identical. This helps eliminate false paths in both electrical and timing analysis.

A second point that needs attention is the handling of the pdf in reconvergent fanout nodes. In such a case we update the pdf as follows:

$$
w_i = \max(w_{i,1}, w_{i,2})
$$

where w_i is the updated pulse width, and $w_{i,1}$, $w_{i,2}$ the pulse widths being merged.

The above analysis is repeatedly applied to the fanouts of gates being activated until we reach the flip-flop inputs.

The last step is the calculation of the latching probabilities that includes the timing masking effects. In order to achieve that we require the pulse width pdf, the minimum and maximum arrival times and the logic vectors at the end of the fault simulation at every flip-flop input.

For each pulse width entry in the pdf we calculate the probability that it will be latched in a flip-flop. For each experiment in the Monte-Carlo simulation we check which flip-flop inputs are at an erroneous state from logic masking. From these we select the ones whose equivalent pulse width entries are not zero, i.e. the pulse has not been eliminated due to electrical masking, and we merge their minimum/maximum windows as follows:

$$bit\_min = min(of\ all\ selected\ nodes)$$
$$bit\_max = max(of\ all\ selected\ nodes)$$

Then the timing masking probability p_j would be:

1	if	*bit_max-bit_min+wi+setup+hold>T*
(bit_max-bit_min+wi+setup+hold)/T	if	*bit_max-bit_min+wi+setup+hold<T*

where T is the clock period, setup the setup time of the flip-flop, and hold the hold time of the flip-flop.

The total latching probability is the sum of the above probabilities for all Monte-Carlo experiments over the number of experiments. The overall SER due to an upset at a specific node is the sum of the product of the pulse width probabilities by their respective total latching probabilities. Consequently, the overall SER of the circuit is the sum of the products of the SER for each node by the SEU probability calculated by the particle flux.

3   Results

The methodology described in Section 2 has been implemented in C++ tool (CARROT) and run on most of the ISCAS85 and ISCAS89 benchmark circuits. The combinational examples were assumed to have flip-flops at both primary inputs and outputs. The pdf was discretized into 10 levels, while 10000 vectors were used for the Monte-Carlo simulations, which is more than adequate to ensure high-confidence estimation of the probabilistic quantities required for the SER analysis (confidence level of more than 95%). The results are shown in Table 1. The reported execution times are on a Pentium4™ with 512MB of RAM. It should be noted that memory usage did not exceed 200MB.

4   Conclusion

This paper presents a new approach to SER estimation in combinational circuits. The proposed approach allows the accurate assessment of the effects of electrical, logic, and timing masking while still permitting a fast logic-level simulation for their evaluation. Both the pulse width modeling and the glitch absorption algorithm can be user defined for further flexibility and accuracy.

The method described above has been implemented in CARROT, which has become part of a broader simulation environment to assess the tradeoffs between SER and other design considerations such as timing, power, and leakage. Further research will be towards assessing circuit design solutions for SER enhancement.

Table 1. CARROT execution time for ISCAS85/89 benchmark circuits

Circuit Name	Nodes	Inputs	Gates	DFFs	Exec. time
S27	17	4	13	3	<1sec
S208_1	125	10	115	8	<1sec
S208	149	10	139	8	<1sec
S298	169	3	166	14	1sec
S386	284	7	277	6	2sec
S382	196	3	193	21	2sec
S344	240	9	231	15	2sec
S349	224	9	215	15	2sec
S400	203	3	200	21	2sec
S444	211	3	208	21	2sec
S526	280	3	277	21	4sec
S526N	280	3	277	21	4sec
S420	252	19	233	16	1sec
S510	293	19	274	6	3sec
S420_1	313	18	295	16	2sec
S832	457	28	429	5	7sec
S820	443	18	425	5	7sec
S641	517	35	482	19	8sec
S713	539	35	504	19	9sec
S953	496	16	480	29	11sec
S838_1	641	34	607	32	8sec
S838	641	34	607	32	8sec
S1238	768	14	754	18	17sec
S1196	762	14	748	18	16sec
S1494	1213	8	1205	6	39sec
S1488	1211	8	1203	6	33sec
S1423	1008	17	991	74	51sec
S5378	3053	35	3018	179	5.9min
S9234	7002	19	6983	228	35.3min
S9234_1	7019	36	6983	211	34.5min
S13207	9608	31	9577	669	1.1h
S13207_1	9609	32	9577	638	1.1h
S15850	12115	14	12101	597	1.7h
S15850_1	12178	77	12101	534	1.6h
S35932	21278	35	21243	1728	7.8h

Acknowledgements. The authors would like to acknowledge the help of Nestor Evmorfopoulos, Dimitrios Karampatzakis, Maria Kozyri, and Antonios Dadaliaris in support of this work.

References

1. International technology roadmap for semiconductors, http://public.itrs.net/, 2002.
2. Murley, P.C., and Srinivasan, G.R.: Soft-error Monte Carlo modeling program, SEMM, IBM Journal of Research and Development, vol. 40, no. 1 (1996) 109–118.
3. Yang F.L., and Saleh R.A.: Simulation and analysis of transient faults in digital circuits, IEEE Journal of Solid-State Circuits, vol. 27, no. 3 (1992) 258–264.
4. Zhang, M., and Shanbhag, N.R.: A soft error rate analysis (SERA) methodology," in Proceedings of International Conference on Computer Aided Design (2004) 111–118.
5. Baze, M.P., Buchner, S.P., Bartholet, W.G., and Dao, T.A.: An SEU analysis approach for error propagation in digital VLSI CMOS ASICs, IEEE Transactions on Nuclear Science, vol. 42, no. 6 (1995) 1863–1869.
6. Cha, H., Rudnick, E.M., Patel, J.H., Iyer, R.K., and Choi, G.S.: A gate-level simulation environment for alpha-particle-induced transient faults, IEEE Transactions on Computers, vol. 45, no. 11 (1996) 1248–1256.
7. Dhillon , Y.S., Diril, A.U., Chatterjee, A.: Soft-error tolerance analysis and optimization of nanometer circuits, in Proceedings of Design, Automation, and Test in Europe (2005) 288–293.
8. Zhao, C., Bai, X., Dey, S.:A scalable soft spot analysis methodology for compound noise effects in nano-meter circuits, in Proceedings of Design Automation Conference (2004) 894-899.
9. Lantz, L.: Soft errors induced by alpha particles, in IEEE Transaction on Reliability, vol. 45, no. 2 (1996) 174-179.
10. Messenger, G.C: Collection of charge on junction nodes from ion tracks, IEEE Trans. Nucl. Sci., vol. NS-29, no. 6 (1982) 2024-2031.

A Scheduling Strategy for a Real-Time Dependable Organic Middleware

Uwe Brinkschulte, Alexander von Renteln, and Mathias Pacher

Institute for Process Control and Robotics
University of Karlsruhe (TH)
{brinks, renteln, pacher}@ira.uka.de

Abstract. This paper presents the architecture and conception of a dependable organic middleware based on the yet existing, *not organic* middleware OSA+. We show a scheduling strategy which assigns missions in real-time to a distributed set of platforms in the scope of a fabric automation scenario. The missions are distributed to different robots by the organic middleware whose scheduling includes organic aspects like self-organization, self-optimization and self-healing.

Keywords: Self-organization, organic real-time scheduling, OSA+ middleware, self-healing.

1 Introduction

Nowadays, it is a challenge to manage complex missions in fabric automation in respect to performance, robustness and flexibility because there is only a limited number of robots which have to be used in an optimal way. Another aspect is that robots might have to overtake missions from defect robots.

The SIMON project at the University of Karlsruhe deals with these challenges [9] in the scope of a fabric automation scenario by trying to add organic features to a middleware. This means that the middleware is intended to have some life-like properties as *self-configuration*, *self-healing* and *self-optimization* to e.g. distribute the missions to robots or to autonomously re-schedule a mission in case of a robot failure. By having this self-x features, the dependability of the system is considerably increased. In this paper, we present the architecture of the organic middleware and its scheduling strategy which holds the mentioned organic features.

The paper is structured as follows: In section 2, we present related work and similar approaches to our work. In the following section 3, we present a short introduction of the OSA+ middlware. Section 4 presents the concept of execution paths, which is important for the scheduling strategy. In the sections 5, 6 and 7, we explain pre-conditions and assumptions made for the scheduling of the organic middleware, and in section 8, the scheduling is explained in detail. Section 9 concludes the paper.

2 Related Work

A lot of different middleware systems have been developed to provide a homogeneous view over a heterogeneous network like CORBA [10], Java RMI [11], DCOM [12] and

S. Vassiliadis et al. (Eds.): SAMOS 2006, LNCS 4017, pp. 339–348, 2006.

Microsoft's .NET framework [13]. In contrast to our middleware, the softwares above cover no organic aspects.

Self-organization has been a research focus for several years. Publications like [15] deal with basic principles of self-organizing systems, like e.g. emergent behavior, reproduction etc. Regarding self-organization in computer science, several projects and initiatives can be listed. IBM's Autonomic Computing project [4,5] deals with self-organization of IT servers in networks.

The German Organic Computing Initiative has been founded in 2003. Its basic intention is to improve the controllability of complex embedded systems by using principles found in organic entities [14].

Regarding self-organization in middleware, current middleware approaches provide features for load-balancing. Middleware architectures fulfilling organic computing principles are rare. In [3], the use of middleware for self-healing is investigated, but none of the presented approaches deals with fabric automation.

Another approach towards an organic middleware is AMUN developed at the university of Augsburg [8]. It consists of four main parts: The *Transport Interface* which decouples the communication from the transport platform and the *Event Dispatcher* which is responsible for the delivery of incoming and outgoing messages. The *Service Interface and Service Proxy* is the connector between the AMUN middleware and services which build an application and the *Autonomic Manager* which configures the services on a platform. Our approach is more fine grained than the AMUN approach because our Autonomic Manager will even configure the jobs to be executed by services. In this way, our organic middleware is able to react to changes in its environment in a faster and more fine grained way. Another difference is that our algorithms support real-time properties which is not concerned by AMUN.

3   The OSA+ Middleware

OSA+ is a service oriented middleware for distributed real-time systems [7]. It provides an uniform view over a heterogeneous network, protocols and OS features and simplifies distributed application development. In OSA+, the active communication parts are *services*. A service realizes certain functionalities which are made public to the execution environment through an interface. This interface can be accessed in a platform and a language independent manner. In our case, the service interface is accessed through *jobs*. A job consists of an order and a result. The order is sent from one service to another to state what functionality the service should do, for which data, and when the action should be performed. After the service executes the order, a result is sent back. The communication of jobs is accomplished by a platform. The platform facilitates the plugging of services which can communicate with each other.

An important aspect regarding the OSA+ middleware consists of the flexible way it adapts to different environments. In this respect, OSA+ is using the *micro-kernel* concept. The core of the middleware, the micro-kernel, has a minimum foundation of functionalities and is independent from the execution environment (no hardware nor operating system dependent parts).

The adaptation of the middleware is done by a set of special services provided by the developer, which extend the functionality of the core. These services are plugged into the platform according to the user needs, and realize tasks like the *MemoryService* which allocates memory for jobs and services at run-time by accessing the memory management and the *ProcessService* which introduces the multi-tasking and multi-threading facilities of the hardware and operating system to the middlware. Besides, the *Communication services* make use of the available communication systems, e.g. TCP/IP, serial, etc. These services provide a transparent use of communication between different hardware platforms. The *EventService* handles timer events or events caused by other hardware components. It is used as a monitoring tool and signals if jobs cannot hold their time constraints.

Another aspect of the OSA+ mddleware is that is designed to offer support for real-time and introduces only small overhead at run-time which is acceptable for most applications [7].

4 Execution Paths

In [6], we described the idea of *execution paths* in detail. The idea is that missions are splitted in sequences of atomic jobs which can directly be executed by services of the middleware.[1] Splitting the mission introduces some dependencies to be considered: If we look at the mission "Bring a sparepart from place A to place B", then the resulting sequence of atomic jobs is as follows:

"Drive(A)"
"PickUp(grab, sparepart)"
"Drive(B)"
"PickUp(unload, sparepart)"

Considering the set of atomic jobs, we notice that the jobs have to be executed sequentially because it is useless to drive to B and unload the sparepart before having picked it up at position A. We also notice that the jobs have to be executed by the same robot since it is also useless if e.g. one robot drives to A and picks up the sparepart while another robot drives to B and tries to unload the sparepart now located on the first robot.

Generalizing this example, we identify three kinds of dependencies between atomic jobs: Let A and B be atomic jobs and X and Z be a service and a resource respectively, which are able to execute A and B. There is a

1. **temporal dependency** between A and B if and only if B has to be executed after the finishing of A.
2. **service dependency** between A and B if and only if A and B have to be executed by the same service. This means if A is executed by X then B has to be executed by X, too.
3. **resource dependency** between A and B if and only if A and B have to be executed on the same resource. This means if A is executed by any service running on resource Z then B has to be executed by any service running on Z, too.

---

[1] In fact, the concept is more general. It can be used to split real-world tasks/missions in sequences of jobs to be executed by humans or computers and not only by a middleware, see [6].

The temporal and the resource dependencies are motivated and explained in the example. The service dependency is used for e.g. database accesses. If there is a job storing a value in a database of a certain service, the value can only be read out from another job by accessing the same database service.

Knowing the dependencies, we define an execution path as follows:

*An **execution path** is a finite set of atomic jobs which have to be executed in a certain order by one resource.*

The execution of an execution path is not interruptible and after finishing the execution path, the resource has to be in an initial state.

This definition is very intuitive as it follows the idea to form the missions by atomic jobs. It includes the temporal dependencies given by the "certain order", and it also includes the resource dependencies since the atomic jobs of the execution paths are claimed to be executed by one resource.

By initial state (in the definition), we mean a pre-defined state of the resource. This specification was claimed in order to ease the scheduling of the Autonomic Manager. If the robot has e.g. a mechanical arm, the initial state of the robot is that the arm is in a zero-position. The claim eases the scheduling of the execution paths because the Autonomic Manager does not have to include this information in the scheduling decision.

The additional specification that the execution of the execution path is not interruptible means that once an execution path has started it can not be interrupted by another execution path (it forms a logical unit like a transaction). The reason is that a resource or a service might be in a state different from the initial state while executing the execution path. Therefore, it is neither guaranteed that the other execution path can be started nor that the first execution path can be resumed after finishing the interrupt.

A mission given by the user consists of one or several execution paths, see fig. 1. We assume as a precondition that missions are organized in a way that there are no dependencies between different missions.

But it is also possible, that there are dependencies between different execution paths of a mission, see also fig. 1. In [6], we described the problems arising from dependencies between different execution paths and presented several ways to handle them.

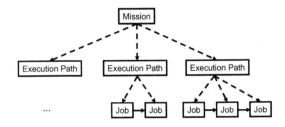

Fig. 1. A mission is partitioned into execution paths

In the following sections, we will describe a scheduling scheme for the execution paths to resources respectively to services. The scheduling is able to hold real-time constraints and covers the above mentioned organic properties.

5   Assumptions for the Organic Middleware

In our scenario, we assume that the user decomposits the missions to execution paths. The basic idea of the organic middleware is now that the assignment of execution paths to resources and services is done by the middleware autonomously. It introduces self-configuration, self-optimization due to reassignment of execution paths under changing conditions and self-healing due to reassignment of execution paths in case of resource failure. This is done by the Autonomic Manager (AM) (see fig. 2). As there is an AM running on each resource, one master is elected by a de-centralised master election [1].

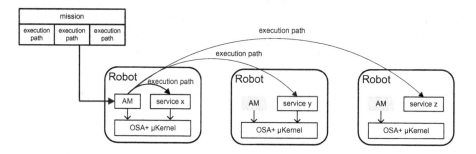

Fig. 2. Mission scheduling by the Autonomic Manager

Additionally, several parameters are assigned to the resources which describe impor-tant properties of them. Since the parameters are application dependant, the user has to define them.

Nevertheless, we can identify two kinds of categories of these parameters:

- **static parameters** and
- **dynamic parameters**

Static parameters are all parameters which do not vary during time. These parameters describe features of a resource e.g. if a resource is able to move or to grab an object.

In contrary to static parameters, dynamic parameters are able to vary. Parameters like the amount of power left in the battery of a robot or the number of items on the cargo area are examples for dynamic parameters. During the execution of jobs/execution paths on the resources, these dynamic parameters may vary due to the power consumption or the charging of the resources.

6   A Scheme for the Parameter Prediction

To be able to choose between all possible assignments of the execution paths to the resources, it is necessary to know the development of all the dynamic parameters.

Therefore, we need to predict the variation of the dynamic parameters if a resource will execute a job respective an execution path. If we know the parameter prediction of the different assignments of execution paths, we can choose the best one.

Since the middleware does not know about the semantics of a job, some information has to be given by the application. For parameter prediction three types can be distinguished:

Relative value given by the application. For some jobs, the variation of a parameter is directly given by the job. We explain this by an example: Let's consider the dynamic parameter "number of spareparts on the robot". If there is a job "Load(sparepart, 3)" which means that three spareparts have to be charged on the robot, the predicted parameter value of the job is increased by 3.

Therefore, the applicant has to give the information about *the modification of the parameter* in this case.

Absolute value given by the application. For some other jobs, the absolute value of a parameter of the job executed is given by the application job. Let's consider the dynamic parameter "Distance to target" and the job "Drive(target)". If a robot executes this job, the distance to the target will be predicted to be "0" after. Therefore, the application has to give the information about *the new value of the parameter*.

Value calculated by the middleware. For the most of the jobs, the AM can *predict* the parameter variation by the following equation:

$$r_{new} = r_{old} - (M * c_{job} + d_{job})$$

Hereby, r_{new} and r_{old} are n-dimensional vectors containing the values of the n dynamic parameters to be considered in this scenario. r_{old} are the parameter values before and r_{new} are the parameter values after executing the job. The modification of the parameter values is predicted by the term $M * c_{job} + d_{job}$ where M is a $n \times n$ matrix containing the connections between the parameters. This matrix is universal for the whole scenario but can be modified by the user for each job if necessary (see next section). The vector c_{job} depends on the job and announces the parameters necessary to predict the dynamic parameter variation. d_{job} is a constant vector also defined for this job. Notice that we assume the parameter variation to be calculated linearly.

7   The Calling Scheme

The mission and thus its set of execution paths is send to the AM by an XML file which is structured as shown in fig. 3. Its structure is almost self-explaining and therefore, we only mention some of the parameters in the XML file in detail.

The root element of the container is the *mission* element and contains at least one *execution path*. Each execution path contains at least one *job* which has four subelements: *restrictions*, *weightings*, *dependencies* and *instruction*. In restrictions, the user is able to claim minimal or maximal values of parameters, e.g. the minimal power level needed to execute a job. The weightings include job or execution path specific modifications of the matrix M. The dependencies mentioned in section 4 are included in the dependencies

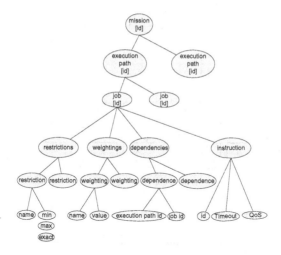

Fig. 3. Tree illustrating the XML format

elements. Finally, the *instuction* element contains an instruction along with a timeout and an optional quality of service value. Figure 3 illustrates the format of the XML file.

8   The Scheduling of the Autonomic Manager

In this section, we will explain the scheduling algorithm of the AM. The AM will firstly do a parameter prediction as mentioned in section 6 for all possible assignments of execution paths to resources and services. After finishing, it will compare the results by some relations and choose the best one according to the relation.

The first step of scheduling - the parameter prediction. In the first step, the AM builds up a prediction tree for a mission. The root of this prediction tree is the current status of each resource. Hereby, the current status of a resource are the current values of all of its dynamic parameters. These values are included in a resource vector.

From this starting point, the AM begins to predictively schedule the first execution path - the one with the highest priority - to the different robots. For this purpose, the AM checks if the jobs of the execution path can be executed by the services of these resources (this is done by checking the static parameters). If this is possible, the AM predicts the parameter modifications according to section 6 and creates a new leaf in the prediction tree for each possible assignment of the execution path. Each leaf contains the modified values of the dynamic parameters according to the predicted assignment. These modified values are also represented by a modified resource vector. In this step, the AM also checks if the restrictions (mentioned in section 7) can be met. If they can be met, the branch is continued and otherwise, the branch will not be explored for the next execution paths.

After finishing the predictive assignment of the first execution path, the AM starts to assign the second execution path in the same way as the first execution path was

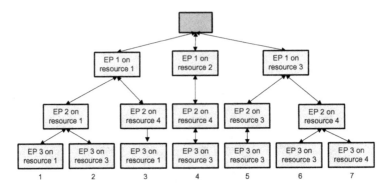

Fig. 4. A prediction tree assigning 3 execution paths to 4 resources

scheduled. The main difference is, that this prediction now starts from the leafs of the first prediction, see fig. 4.

This procedure is repeated for all of the mission's execution paths and as a result of the first step, we get a complete prediction tree.

The second step of scheduling - choice of the best leaf. In a second step, the AM has to choose the best leaf and thus the best assignment of execution paths according to the dynamic parameters. Since the AM has to compare the leafs, it combines the parameter vectors of all of the leafs' resources in the following *combination vector* m_{leaf}:

$$m_{leaf} := \begin{pmatrix} m_1 \\ m_2 \\ ... \\ m_n \end{pmatrix} = \begin{pmatrix} min\{r1_{res_1}, r1_{res_2}, ..., r1_{res_k}\} \\ min\{r2_{res_1}, r2_{res_2}, ..., r2_{res_k}\} \\ ... \\ min\{rn_{res_1}, rn_{res_2}, ..., rn_{res_k}\} \end{pmatrix}$$

Each of its parameter values contains the minimum of the parameter values of one type of a leaf's robots, e.g. power. This scheme guarantees for each robot of a leaf a minimum parameter value calculated in the combination vector thus presenting a lower bound for the parameters.

Using the combination vector for each leaf, the AM has to compare them to find the best suited assignemnt of execution paths.

We implemented two different strategies to compare the combination vectors:

Comparison by vector length. When using this strategy, the AM compares the length of the different leafs' combination vectors. It calculates the length of a combination vector m_{leaf} by the following formula:

$$\|m_{leaf}\|_1 = \sum_{i=1}^{n} |m_i|$$

After computing the length of the different combination vectors, the AM compares them using the "$\leq$" relation in $\mathbb{R}$. Then the AM selects the vector with maximum length. If there are several vectors with the same maximal length, then the according leaf which is the first in the tree will be chosen.

This comparison strategy can be used if all of the the parameters have the same priority or if the applicant has no certain information about the priorities of the parameters.

Comparison by priority. Another strategy is to order the combination vectors by priority. Let's consider the two combination vectors m_{leaf} and v_{leaf} of two different leaves:

$$m_{leaf} = \begin{pmatrix} m_1 \\ m_2 \\ ... \\ m_n \end{pmatrix} \text{ and } v_{leaf} = \begin{pmatrix} v_1 \\ v_2 \\ ... \\ v_n \end{pmatrix}$$

Then, $m_{leaf} \leq_P v_{leaf}$ if and only if

$m_1 < v1$ **or**
$m_1 = v_1$ and $m_2 < v_2$ **or**
...
$m_1 = v_1$ and $m_2 = v_2$ and ... and $m_{n-1} = v_{n-1}$ and $m_n < v_n$ **or**
$m_1 = v_1$ and $m_2 = v_2$ and ... and $m_{n-1} = v_{n-1}$ and $m_n = v_n$

This means, the vector with the highest value in the first row is greater than the other vector. If the first value is the same in both vectors, the values in the second rows are decisive and so on.

This comparison is useful if the applicant knows exactly which parameters are the most important ones. It is more restrictive than the first strategy and might allow better scheduling if the parameters are suited.

Organic and real-time properties of the scheduling strategy. The presented scheduling assigns the execution paths to the services and resources autonomously thus it is self-configuring. As the current parameter values of the resources are continuously refreshed by a monitoring unit, the scheduling is also self-optimizing since it includes these values. We also include self-healing since the dependent execution paths of a mission are rescheduled if a resource fails.

The scheduling is also able to meet real-time constraints because the creation of the tree is interruptible which means that the AM is able to interrupt the tree computing at each point of time (if this is necessary). Then, it uses the existing tree to choose the best assignment of execution path and can use the execution time of the robots to complete the scheduling.

9   Conclusion and Further Work

In this paper, we presented a new idea to realize a real-time dependable organic middleware. We introduced the idea of execution paths and a real-time scheduling scheme by which the execution paths are assigned to services and resources, respectively. The scheduling scheme includes organic features like self-configuration, self-optimization and self-healing. We implement the presented middleware in the SIMON project at the University of Karlsruhe.

As future work, we plan to evaluate the scheduling scheme in detail. Especially, we have to categorize the different kinds of parameters to get rules how to set the values in the parameter matrix to model the fabric automation scenario as well as possible.

Acknowledgment

The SIMON project is funded by the **Landesstiftung Baden-Wuerttemberg**.

References

1. RICHARD JOHN ANTHONY, "Emergence: a Paradigm for Robust and Scalable Distributed Applications", *Proceedings of the International Conference on Autonomic Computing (ICAC'04)*, 2004
2. A. BECHINA, U. BRINKSCHULTE, F. PICIOROAGA AND E. SCHNEIDER, "OSA+ Real-Time Middleware. Results and Perspectives", *International Symposium on Object-Oriented Real-Time Distributed Computing (ISORC)*, Vienna, Austria, 2004
3. C. BUSCHMANN, S. FISCHER AND N. LUTTENBERGER, "Middleware for Swarm-like Collections for Devices", *IEEE Pervasive Computing Magazine, Vol. 2, No. 4*, 2003
4. IBM, Autonomic Computing, http://www.research.ibm.com/autonomic/
5. J. O. KEPHART AND D. M. CHESS, "The Vision of Autonomic Computing", *IEEE Computer*, pp. 41-50, 2003
6. MATHIAS PACHER, ALEXANDER VON RENTELN AND UWE BRINKSCHULTE, "Towards an Organic Middleware for Real-Time Applications", *ISORC 2006, Ninth IEEE International Symposium on Object and component-oriented Real-time distributed Computing*, Korea, 2006
7. FLORENTIN PICIOROAGA, "Scalable and Efficient Middleware for Real-time Embedded Systems. A Uniform Open Service Oriented Microkernel Based Architecture", PhD thesis, Strasbourg, 2004
8. WOLFGANG TRUMLER, JAN PETZOLD, FARUK BAGCI AND THEO UNGERER, "AMUN - An Autonomic Middleware for the Smart Doorplate Project", *UbiSys '04 - System Support for Ubiquitous Computing Workshop at the Sixth Annual Conference on Ubiquitous Computing*, 2004
9. THE SIMON PROJECT, University of Karlsruhe (TH), http://simon.ira.uka.de
10. Object Management Group: The common object request broker: Architecture and specification. Revision 3.0, July 2002
11. Sun Microsystems: Java Remote Method Invocation Specification. Revision 1.8, 2002 http://java.sun.com/j2se/1.4/docs/guide/rmi/
12. G. EDDON AND H. EDDON, "Inside Distributed COM", *Microsoft Press*, 1998
13. MICROSOFT CORPORATION, The .Net framework, http://www.microsoft.com/net/default.mspx
14. VDE/ITG (EDITOR), "VDE/ITG/GI-Positionspapier Organic Computing: Computer und Systemarchitektur im Jahr 2010", *GI, ITG, VDE*, 2003
15. RANDALL WHITAKER, "Self-Organization, Autopoisesis, and Enterprises" http://www.acm.org/sigs/sigois/auto/Main.html

Autonomous Construction Technology of Community for Achieving High Assurance Service

Kotaro Hama[1], Yuji Horikoshi[2], Yosuke Sugiyama[1], and Kinji Mori[1]

[1] Department of Computer Science, Tokyo Institute of Technology
2-12-1 Ookayama, Meguro, Tokyo 152-8552, Japan
{hama@mori., sugiyama@mori., mori@}cs.titech.ac.jp
http://www.mori.cs.titech.ac.jp/
[2] horikoshi@smg.co.jp

Abstract. In the retail business under the evolving market, the users solicit continuously to utilize the appropriate services based on their preferences and situations. Such requirements can not be satisfied with the conventional centralized system, due to the dynamic changes of user requirements. Autonomous Decentralized Community System (ADCS) has been proposed to realize a system that satisfies such requirements. The system realizes flexibility to cope with dynamic changes in the environment, but since ADCS is a pure decentralized system, the system has no existence that monitors the whole system to maintain timeliness, which is an essential factor for assurance. In this paper, Autonomous Construction Technology is proposed to improve the response time, which integrates and divides a community in order to achieve the optimal size depending on the changes in environment. The effectiveness is verified through simulation.

1   Introduction

The recent advancement in information and communication technology enabled various information services that are available anytime, anywhere and for anyone. However, the increase in the variety of information service often perplexes the users by providing too many options. Also, for the provider of information services, or Service Providers (SP), the selection of appropriate services is becoming increasingly difficult. According to these backgrounds, information services considering users' preference and situation are becoming more important. To provide such services, Community Service is proposed to offer adequate services through mutual cooperation among Local Majority, which consists of users who have similar preferences or are in similar situations [1]. In such a system, adaptability is regarded as an important property to assure the quality of services depending on a requirement level.

This paper reports the proposition of Autonomous Construction Technology. The objective is to realize high assured services which achieves high dependability and timeliness depending on the number of community members. This paper is structured as follows. Next section presents the application and system requirements. Section 3 describes ADCS in detail, and section 4 exposes Autonomous Construction Technology. Section 5 shows the effectiveness of the technology by showing the improvement in response time and the last section is the conclusion.

S. Vassiliadis et al. (Eds.): SAMOS 2006, LNCS 4017, pp. 349–358, 2006.

2   Application and Requirements

2.1   Community Service

User requirements towards information services are becoming more advanced, like the services that consider users' situations and preferences. For wide area information services, it is difficult for SP to provide adequate services for all users, since the target users not always have the same similarities. However, places like department stores where people often have the same preferences, it is possible to collect user requests in certain area to provide suitable services. Thus, by grasping user groups that are in the same situation as community, it is possible for SP to provide adequate services efficiently. Some location-aware systems using mobile terminals for providing services based on user locations have been reported [2][3]. These technologies have described a basic concept of service mediation platform, but they assume that each service is provided to static area and considers no dynamic situations.

In Community Service, the members of a community cooperate to aggregate requests, and then SP provide services based on the requests [4]. Community members are obliged to cooperate between other members for request aggregation and service distribution, whereas SPs are obliged to provide adequate services to the community. However, both members of a community and SP have the merits by adopting Community Service. Users are able to enjoy exclusive services only for the members of a certain community. The benefit of Community Service increase as the number of community members increase. On the other hand, SPs are able to collect requests from users with less effort, since the community members cooperate to aggregate requests themselves. To meet the community requests, SP simply provide adequate services according to the aggregated requests, instead of answering all users one by one. Thus, Community Service simplifies SP's operation and increases efficiency.

2.2   Application Requirements

For Community Service, users and SPs have the following application requirements.

– Assurance for merits of cooperation: Since users are obliged to cooperate with other community members, the merits for cooperation must be assured for each member of community.
– Adequate service utilization/provision: SP's services should provide services that considers the user requirement level as accurate as possible.

2.3   System Requirements

To realize the application requirements described, the system is required to satisfy flexibility and timeliness. Since users' situation changes dynamically, Local Majority and its requirement level also changes. Therefore, it is necessary for SP to correspond to accommodate to such changes. Also, users wish to receive services that reflect their requirements as much as possible. However, such requirements often change as users' situation and preference change. Therefore, SPs must compose and distribute the services as quick as they can. Thus, a system must satisfy flexibility and timeliness.

3   Autonomous Decentralized Community System

3.1   System Architecture

Autonomous Decentralized Community System (ADCS) is a system that realizes flexibility by enabling the members of the system to autonomously cooperate to achieve particular objectives. The system is structured based on Autonomous Decentralized System (ADS) [5]. In order to provide services, the nodes in ADCS autonomously form a group or community, in accordance with service property. The nodes in ADCS autonomously decide to join or leave a certain community and to cooperate with other members. Such autonomous decisions of each node is realized with Autonomous Control Processor (ACP) that judges and processes based only on local information, such as storage storing user requests and Neighboring Nodes Table (NNT), which indicates the directions of neighboring nodes for a certain node [6]. When a node receives a message, each node autonomously judges whether the message should be taken into the node or not, by checking the node's NNT and the service property of the message. As a result, nodes that received the message will form a community. The overview of the system architecture is shown in fig. 1.

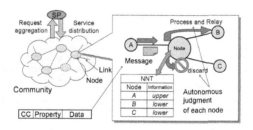

Fig. 1. System Architecture

The nodes are supposed to be base stations for wireless communications and connect SPs and users through mobile terminals. The nodes transmit data between physically neighboring nodes and broadcast messages to the users within the cover-area of each cell. SPs and users communicate with the physically nearest node. The area covered by community of nodes is called service area. In order to form a community according to the contents of services, autonomous distribution technology based on time-distance is proposed [6]. Time-distance indicates the time to physically travel from one place to another, and community can be formed depending on the time-distance for each service. Time-distance is measured by autonomous collaboration between each base station. By each base stations having the values of time-distance between each node, SP can provide services like "advertisement of exclusive service only for users that are with in 30 minutes far from the SP". Such services can be regarded flexible, since the time distance between each node is updated real-timely by autonomous collaboration between each node. In this case, the trigger for community formation is the distribution of advertisement, and community vanishes when the service of SPs terminates.

3.2   Process and Communication

When a community member receives a message from the SP, the member relays the message only to the lower members depending on the service property of the message. Each node possesses time-distance table for its neighboring nodes, which is used as judgment data when relaying messages. Thus, it is able to provide services only to the users that actually require them, which realizes flexible information system. When a community receives service from a certain SP, the first node that receives the message from the SP is regarded as the leader of the community. All requests from the community will be aggregated by the leader, and will be transmitted to the SP through the leader.

3.3   Response Time Model

To clarify the discussions on response time, the above figure describes on the model for response time in ADCS. Service provision is composed from 3 steps of request aggregation to the leader, access to the SP and service distribution. Therefore, total response time T can be divided into 3 steps, time of aggregation T_a, time for SP-access T_s and time for community distribution T_c. T can be expressed as the following simple equation. Hereinafter, we will discuss on modeling of T_a, T_s and T_c.

$$T = T_a + T_s + T_c \tag{1}$$

Time of aggregation T_a. @The transmission delay between each node for a single request is assumed to be constant and is expressed as t_t (time for transmission). Also, the number of hops (transmission of message between nodes) between the leader and the farthest node within the community is expressed as D_L. When considering about response time of community as a whole, it is necessary to regard the worst value. Therefore, time of aggregation T_a can be expressed as follows. It is necessary to note that T_a does not concern about the delay of request processing at each node.

$$T_a = D_L t_t \tag{2}$$

Time for SP-access T_s. @Assume that message processing at SP takes t_p (time for processing) for a single request. The transmission delay between the leader and the SP is t_t as explained above. Also, let total number of request from leaders be m. All SPs have message queue, and processes requests as LIFO (Last In First Out). The model assumes that all requests arrive at the same time, and does not concern about rejection of requests due to queue overflows. The validity of such an assumption comes from the fact that requests arose from dynamic changes in situation is more likely to be simultaneous rather than random-arrive. Since the model considers community as a whole, it is necessary to regard the worst processing time for T_s as following.

$$T_s = m t_p + 2 t_t \tag{3}$$

Time for community distribution T_c. @Assume that the definition for t_t and D_L be the same asfor request aggregation. Since it is necessary to assure response time for all members of community, again we regard the worst time for service distribution as follows.

$$T_c = D_L t_t \tag{4}$$

Since ADCS is based on the concept of ADS, response time will not deteriorate by the concentration of SP access like it does in centralized systems. This is because there will be only one user accessing the SP from request aggregation. However, when changes in the contents of services cause enlargement in the size of community, or when there is a great increase in the number of users in a certain community, response time for service provision deteriorates. The deterioration is caused by the increase in the number of hops between the furthest node to the leader of community. Also, for SP access time T_s, the increase in the number of requests is causing the deterioration in response time.

4   Autonomous Construction Technology

4.1   Community Division

As discussed before, deterioration in response time is caused by the increase in the number of hops D_L between the farthest node and the leader of the community. Also, while aggregating requests within a community, SP will be wasting the processing power since it takes time for community requests to reach the SP. Considering such a fact, we introduce the concept of community division. In community division, a community is divided into multiple smaller communities and enables each sub-community to aggregate requests and distribute services concurrently. The concept of community division is first proposed in [6]. However, the main purpose of community division in [6] is to improve the dependability. For an assure system that satisfy both dependability and timeliness, improvement in response time is still considered as an important problem to be solved. In this research, our objective is to improve the timeliness in Community Service with the concept of community division. Response time model after community division can be expressed as follows.

$$T = T_a + T_s + T_c \tag{5}$$
$$= D_L t_t + nmt_p + 2t_t + D_L t_t \tag{6}$$
$$= 2D_L t_t + nmt_p + 2t_t \tag{7}$$

In the equation, n is the number of sub-community, and it is noteworthy that D_L decreases as the number of sub-community increases. Therefore, when each sub-community's size decrease, T_a and T_c will be improved due to the decrease in D_L, but T_s will deteriorate due to the increase in n. On the other hand, when each sub-community size enlarges, T_s will improve but T_a and T_c will worsen. Thus, there exist a tradeoff between sub-community size and the response time. Thus, there exists an optimum size for sub-community size, so it is possible to realize the best response time by adjusting the size of sub-community.

4.2   Problems

From the discussions so far, the optimal size for sub-community alters depending on the size of community as a whole. Therefore, to improve response time, it is necessary to adjust the size of sub-community depending on the community size.There are several solutions considered to achieve such a task. The simplest solution is to place a centralized observer to monitor changes in the number of community, which lacks in flexibility and deterioration in response time. Another possible solution is to enable each node in community to monitor its response time from the SP all the time, and adjust the community size by trial-and-error. However, such a solution requires complicated operations for keeping the consistency between each node. Such problems are caused by the fact that each node in community not possessing global information to make decisions on which community to belong. In this research, we propose a solution for this problem by Autonomous Construction Technology, which adopts the concept of threshold.

4.3   Threshold and Community Construction

The size for each sub-community is determined by threshold D_{thH}. The threshold D_{thH} is calculated by the leaders of community by monitoring the response time from the SP and their sub-community size. When distributing messages from the SP, a leader attach the threshold value to the message and send it to the lower nodes. Thus, each member of the sub-community is able to update their values of D_{thH} when receiving messages from the SP. As a result, the value of D_{thH} will adapt to the size of community, and the structure of community will be optimized. The figure below shows the overview of how to calculate the threshold D_{thH} from monitoring. Total response time T can be regarded as a function of $f_T(d_L)$, where d_L is the size of sub-community. The graph of $f_T(d_L)$ is V-shaped as shown in the figure. By observing the derivative of such a function $f_T'(d_L)$, it is possible to determine the tendency of function $f_T(d_L)$ at the size of monitoring sub-community $\hat{d}_L$. If the function is in trend of decreasing, the leader should judge to increase the sub-community size by enlarging the threshold. On the other hand, if the function has trend of increasing, the leader can adjust the sub-community into smaller size to increase the response time of the community as a whole. Thus, it is possible to adjust sub-community size into optimal size without any existence of centralized monitors.

4.4   Autonomous Construction Technology

Each node in ADCS posses information D_{thH} and D_{thL}, which are thresholds to judge that sub-community is too large or too small respectively. Also, each node posses D_L and D_B that are distance from its leader and boundary nodes respectively. Each node posses SubComID, Sub-community ID for each node.

Between each node in community, two types of message are interchanged. From a SP to the community, service messages are transmitted. The fields in service messages are shown in table 2 on the left. On the other hand, from a community to the leader, request messages are transmitted. The fields in request messages are shown on.

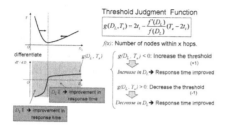

Fig. 2. Calculating Threshold

Table 1. Service Message and Request Message Parameters

Sign	Content		Sign	Content
CC	Content code for service message		CC	Content code for request message
SubComID	Sub-community ID		SubComID	Sub-community ID
SPAddr	SP Address		Generator	The node ID for the generator of this message
Sender	Address for the message sender	@		
nHops	Number of hops for the message			
D_{thH}	Field for updating each node's D_{thH}		flagBoundary	Flag to indicate boundary
D_{thL}	Field for updating each node's D_{thL}		D_L	Distance between leader to the boundary
$D_{Arbitrator}$	Priority for sub-community			
Data	Service Data		Data	Request Data

Autonomous Construction Technology is composed from autonomous division technology and autonomous integration technology. In autonomous division technology, sub-community size is decreased by increasing the number of leaders in the community. On the other hand, autonomous integration technology decreases the number of leaders to make each sub-community larger. In the discussion on technology, we call non-leader nodes as normal nodes, to distinct from leader nodes. The overview of Autonomous Construction Technology is shown below.

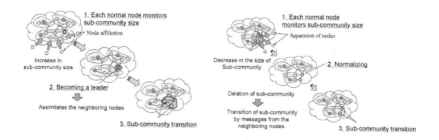

Fig. 3. Autonomous Construction Technology

Autonomous Division Technology. @When sub-community size increase by affiliation of new nodes, each normal node detects whether the distance from the leader D_L is exceeding the threshold D_{thH} or not. If so, the normal node judges that the sub-community it belongs is too big and becomes a leader itself. Therefore, a new sub-community will be created, and the neighboring nodes that are near the new leader will transit to the new sub-community. When a node receives a message, the node regards the distance from the leader D_L as $nHops + 1$ of the received message. Thus, each node increment the $nHops$ field of the received message as the message transmits. When a node receives a message from its leader with $nHops$ field that is bigger than the node's D_{thH}, the node detects that the sub-community has become too large and the node becomes a leader. When a node becomes a leader, it executes the following procedures.

1. Set the own D_B field to 0
2. Set the own D_L field to 0
3. Set the own SubComID field to the own node ID
4. Set all neighboring nodes are lower nodes

When a node receives messages from other sub-communities, the node decides to transit sub-community or not, depending on the following.

1. If, the own D_L > the received message's $nHops + 1$ A then transit to the sub-community with lower D_L value
2. When the own SubComID is set to NULL, transit to the received message's sub-community

Also, for a node that is about to transit sub-community executes the following procedures.

1. Becomes a normal node
2. Set the own SubComID field to the received message's SubComID
3. Set the own D_L field to the received message's $nHop + 1$
4. Set the own D_B field to the received message's $nHops + 1$
5. Set the sender of the message as "upper" in the node's NNT, and set all the other nodes are "lower" nodes.

Autonomous Integration Technology. @When nodes separate from the community, some sub-communities may be too small to exist. The leader of each sub-community detect whether the own sub-community is too small or not by checking the D_B on the message from the boundary nodes. If the leader judges that the sub-community is too small, it becomes normalized and the sub-community vanishes. Boundary nodes are nodes that are placed on the boundary of each sub-community. When such nodes send request messages to the leader, they attach additional information as a flag to indicate that the node is a boundary node. A node is regarded as a boundary node when it satisfies the following.

1. Receiving messages with other sub-community's ID on SubComID field
2. Receiving annul messages from all neighbors that are set as "lower" nodes

The message from boundary nodes are transmitted to the leader just like the normal message, but when it reaches the leader, it is used as information for the leader to find out the own sub-community size by checking the largest D_B field out of all messages from its boundaries. When a leader receives a boundary message with D_{thL} that is smaller than its own D_B, the leader judges that the sub-community is too small. D_{thL} is also a threshold for a node to judge whether the sub-community is too small or not. When a leader normalizes, it executes the following procedures. As a result from the following procedures, the node will be independent and can be regarded as the same state as the initial state where nodes first affiliate communities.

1. Set the own SubComID field to NULL
2. Set the own D_{thL} field to the maximum value available
3. Set all nodes in NNT to "lower" nodes

5 Simulation and Evaluation

The objective for simulation is to verify the effectiveness of Autonomous Construction Technology by evaluating the improvement in response time. The simulation is done under the condition where community members increase periodically. The network topology used in the simulation is a hexagonal mesh network, which is widely adopted in actual networks for base stations of wireless communication.

Table 2. Parameters Used in Simulation

Sign	Logical time	Assumption time	Outline
t_t	15	150[ms]	Link transmission delay
t_p	10	100[ms]	Request processing time
$T_{JoinInterval}$	500	5000[ms]	Node entry interval
$T_{ServiceTimer}$	300	3000[ms]	Service message interval
$T_{Boundary}$	900	9000[ms]	Boundary message interval
$T_{Promotion}$	500	5000[ms]	Leader timer interval
$T_{AdaptCheck}$	400	4000[ms]	Threshold updating interval

In evaluation of response time, we have compared the response time for Autonomous Construction Technology with various values of D_{thH} with the case without such a technology, under the situation where number of members in community increase gradually. At the initial state of simulation, the number of node is 1, then increase the number of node periodically depending on $T_{JoinInterval}$ until the total number of node reach up to 721. As shown in the result displayed on fig 4, for D_{thH} value of 1, 2 and 3, it is better not to adopt community division. However, for D_{thH} as 7, the result shows some improvement in response time under the situation where the total number of node is 721. For the case not adopting community division, the average response time is 5200 [ms] under the situation where number of node is 721. On the other hand, the case adopting the technology with D_{thH} value of 7, the average response time improved

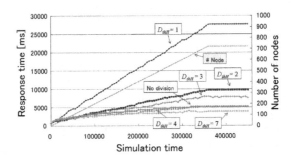

Fig. 4. Number of Nodes and Response Time

to 3900 [ms]. Thus, there exists appropriate value for D_{thH} depending on the number of nodes in a community. Therefore, adjustment of the size for D_{thH} by calculating the threshold improves the response time of a community for different number of nodes.

6   Conclusion

Community Service, which is provided through cooperation among Local Majority, has been proposed to provide services in accordance with users' situations and preferences. In this paper, we proposed Autonomous Construction Technology to improve response time for ADCS under the situation where the number of members shifts dynamically. Also, we have evaluated the effectiveness of such a technology through simulation. The result verified the effectiveness of Autonomous Construction Technology.

References

1. T.Ono, K.Ragab, N.Kaji and K.Mori, "Service Oriented Communication Technology for Achieving Assuarance," International Workshop on Assuarance in Distributed Systems and Networks (ADSN02), IEEE, pp69-74, July 2002.
2. J.Hightower, G. Borriello, "Location Systems for Ubiquitous Computing", IEEE *Computer*, vol.34, no.8, pp.57-66, 2001.
3. N.Marmasse, C.Schmandt, "Location-Aware Information Delivery with ComMotion", HUC2000, LNCS1927, pp.157-171, 2000.
4. N.Kaji, K.Ragab, T.Ono and K.Mori, "Service Oriented Community System for Mobile Commerce", Proc. of SSGRR2002, July
5. K.Mori, "Autonomous Decentralized Systems: Concept, Data Field Architecture and Future Trends," Proc. of ISADS93, pp28-34, March 1993.
6. T.Ono, N.Kaji, Y.Horikoshi, H.Kuriyama, K.Ragab, and K.Mori, "Autonomous Decentralized Community Construction Technology to Assure Quality of Services", in Proc. of the 10th IEEE International Workshop on Future Trends of Distributed Computing Systems (HASE), pp299-305, May 2002, pp84-89.
7. Matei Ripeanu, "Peer-to-Peer Architecture Case Study: Gnutella Network", In Int'l. Conf. on Peer-to-Peer Computing (P2P2001), August 2001.

Preventing Denial-of-Service Attacks
in Shared CMP Caches

Georgios Keramidas, Pavlos Petoumenos, Stefanos Kaxiras,
Alexandros Antonopoulos, and Dimitrios Serpanos

Department of Electrical and Computer Engineering,
University of Patras, Patras, Greece

Abstract. Denial-of-Service (DoS) attacks try to exhaust some shared resources
(e.g. process tables, functional units) of a service-centric provider. As Chip
Multi-Processors (CMPs) are becoming mainstream architecture for server class
processors, the need to manage on-chip resources in a way that can provide
QoS guarantees becomes a necessity. Shared resources in CMPs typically
include L2 cache memory. In this paper, we explore the problem of managing
the on-chip shared caches in a CMP workstation where malicious threads or just
cache "hungry" threads try to hog the cache giving rise to DoS opportunities.
An important characteristic of our method is that there is no need to distinguish
between malicious and "healthy" threads. The proposed methodology is based
on a statistical model of a shared cache that can be fed with run-time
information and accurately describe the behavior of the shared threads. Using
this information, we are able to understand which thread (malicious or not) can
be "compressed" into less space with negligible damage and to drive
accordingly the underlying replacement policy of the cache. Our results show
that the proposed attack-resistant replacement algorithm can be used to enforce
high-level policies such as policies that try to maximize the "usefulness" of the
cache real estate or assign custom space-allocation policies based on external
QoS needs.

1 Introduction

In application domains that range from information access to electronic commerce,
many services are susceptible to attacks by malicious clients that can significantly
degrade their performance. One kind of attack, called Denial-of-Service (DoS) attack,
is a malicious attempt by a single person or a group of people to cripple an online
service. This can have serious consequences for companies such as Amazon and eBay
which rely on their online availability to do business. In the past, many companies fell
victim to DoS attacks resulting in a damage of million of dollars [14][15]. Moreover,
service providers may be forced by the customer requirements to provide specific
QoS guarantees. In this case, the providers must assure the service quality of their
services by assigning a specific amount of resources (i.e. CPU cycles). On the
architecture front, processor designers are fast moving towards multiple cores on a
chip to achieve new levels of performance. The target is to hide as much as possible

S. Vassiliadis et al. (Eds.): SAMOS 2006, LNCS 4017, pp. 359–372, 2006.

the long memory latencies. CMPs are becoming the dominant architecture for many server class machines [8][9][10]. For reasons of efficiency and economy of processor area, the sharing of some chip resources is a necessity. The shared resources in CMPs typically include the lower level caches. Those shared resources in CMPs create a need for fair and efficient management policies. A trivial solution would be to statically partition the shared resources among the running threads. However, this design point is inefficient in resource utilization when the demand is not uniform.

From another point of view, having caches shared between threads provides a vastly more dangerous avenue of attack —a DoS attack [16]. A malicious application can abuse the shared cache rendering the whole system practically inoperative, since the L2s are a critical element in the performance of all modern computers. Furthermore, according to [18], even through a DoS attack is usually intentional and malicious, such types of attacks can sometime happen accidentally. For example, one person running a memory or CPU intensive program in a multiuser machine can cause all the other users of the system to experience an extreme slowdown even if the running program is not by nature malicious. Furthermore, poor programming, either in choice of algorithm or in implementation, can also cause programs to consume resources disproportionately. This is in accordance to the problem of attack detection: sometimes it is impossible to distinguish between memory or CPU intensive applications from DoS attacks, since they operate indentically. Hence, a desirable characteristic of all the methods against DoS is to manipulate the system threads in a fair and/or efficient manner without the need to distinguish between malicious and normal threads.

To model and understand cache sharing we have built a new theoretical framework that accurately describes applications interplay in shared caches. Our cache model, named StatShare, is derived from the StatCache statistical cache model [6], which yields the miss ratio of an application for any cache size. While the StatCache model uses the number of memory references as its unit of time, StatShare uses the number of cache replacements at the studied cache level [4] as the unit of time. This allows for a natural mapping of the cache statistics to the shared cache level. This further leads to a very efficient implementation of the StatShare which enables on-line analysis feeding a dynamic resource scheduler. StatShare can predict miss rate with great success as a function of the active cache ratio used by an application.

We also demonstrate how online StatShare results can be used as inputs to a resource sched-uler. We model and evaluate a cache resource sharing strategy based on Cache Decay, originally proposed for leakage reduction [7]. Our proposal introduces important differences. A decayed cacheline is simply available for replacement rather than turned-off for leakage. Thus, hits on decayed lines are allowed. Secondly, the decay interval is measured not in cy-cles but in CAT time.

Our modified attack resistant cache replacement algorithm has the added advantage that it does not need to classify a thread (client) as malicious or not malicious permanently, but instead computes this based on recent behavior. Hence, our algorithm performs a kind of dynamic check on thread's behavior. This is an important feature, since it is possible that a normal thread may be misclassified as malicious, through this classification will change with time. As an example, a thread that has poor locality may have a low hit rate (and try to hog the cache), resulting in its being identified as malicious, by our approach, and its eventual compression into less space. However, this does not significantly impact the performance, because the thread is already experiencing a low hit rate and hence higher latencies.

Structure of this paper. Section 2 surveys related work and reviews the StatCache model. Section 3 presents our StatShare model. Section 4 describes how cache decay can be intergrated into the StatShare model and provide attack resistant high-level cache management policies. Section 5 presents implementations and Section 6 our results. Section 7 summarizes the paper.

2 Related Work

Cache Partitioning Schemes. The issue of cache fairness has been initially investigated by Kim et al. [2]. They introduce a set of metrics for fair cache sharing and they implemented a static partitioning algorithm for the OS scheduler, and a dynamic three-part algorithm (ini-tialization, rollback and re-partitioning) for shared-cache partitioning. Their algorithms are based on stack-distance counters but do not restrict the cache replacement algorithm to LRU. Their partitioning algorithm is based on counters and partitioning registers. When a process is under-represented in the cache it starts to pick its victims from other processes, while when it is over-represented, it picks its victims among its own lines.

In [3], Kim et al. extend their previous work with three performance models that predict the impact of cache sharing on co-scheduled threads. The input to the models is the isolated second-level cache stack distance of the applications and the output is the number of extra second-level cache misses for each thread due to cache sharing. Suh et al. [1] studied partitioning the cache among sharers by modifying the LRU replacement policy. The proposed mechanism used in their scheme is the same as the one used by Kim et al. [2], but their focus is in performance and not fairness.

Denial-of-Service at the Architectural Level. One of the initial attempts to prevent DoS attacks at the architectural level was the one introduced by Soderquist and Leeser [19]. The authors proposed the idea of cache locking where the locked cachelines were not allowed to be removed from the cache, quaranteeing freedom from DoS attacks. In their approach, a dynamic cache locking technique, aided by custom processor instructions, treat locked cache lines as additional registers.

Recently, many researchers studied the issue of DoS attacks in the context of SMT processors. Because multiple threads share many resources (pipeline, execution units etc.) in a SMT, there are many opportunities for a malicious thread to launch a DoS attack by abusing shared resources. Grunwald and Ghiasi describe a form of attack in which a malicious process repeatedly flushes the trace cache of a SMT by executing self modifying code. Because the trace cache is shared among all the processes, the flushing degrades the performance of all threads [16]. Hasan et al. study DoS attacks based on power density [17].

The above techniques try to address the DoS attacks by stalling the application that is suspected of malicious behavior. This may be a working solution for SMTs but it is less attractive for CMPs, because CMPs have most of their resources unshared. A stalled core in a CMP environment will lead in underutilization of the whole system. Furthermore, a service-targeted system may become unable to provide services even if no malicious threads are running on it [3][18]. In this scenario, the previous techniques will not detect a DoS attack, rendering the whole system practically inoperative. The problem becomes more serious when specific services require QoS guarantees.

The Statcache Model. StatCache is a technique for estimating an application's miss rate as a function of cache size based on a very sparse and easily captured fingerprint of certain performance properties [6]. The application property measured is the reuse distance of the application's memory accesses, i.e., the number of memory references between two consecutive accesses to the same cachline. Unlike stack distance, which measures the number of unique memory references between two consecutive accesses to the same cacheline, the reuse distance can easily be captured using functionality supported in today's hardware and operating systems.

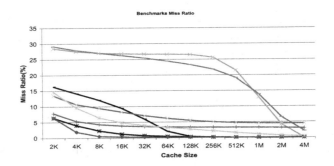

Fig. 1. StatCache results for selected SPEC2000

The reuse distances of an application's all memory accesses is most easily represented as a histogram $h(i)$, where $h(0)$ is the number of references to the same cache line with no other intervening memory references, $h(1)$ is the number of accesses with one intervening access, and so forth. The shape of this histogram is the performance fingerprint of an application. The shape can cheaply be approximated by randomly picking every the Nth access and measuring its reuse distance. Experiments have shown that sampling every $10^{7}th$ access is sufficient for long-running applications [6]. StatCache uses an application's histogram together with a simple statistical model of a cache and a simple numerical solver to derive the miss rate of the application as a function of cache size.

Figure 1 shows StatCache results for a number of SPEC2000 benchmarks for various cache sizes. This figure provides our motivation for managing the cache and prevent the hog of the cache by cache greedy applications (either they are by nature malicious or not).

As it is evident from Figure 1 many programs have flat areas in their miss-rate curves, where a change in their cache size results in virtually no change in their miss rate. Such areas can be exploited to release cache space for other programs than can benefit from more cache space (as suggested by their miss-rate curves).

3 StatShare: A Statistical Cache Model in Cat Time

In this section, we describe the basic principles of our statistical model. A necessary compromise to construct our model is to assume a fully-associative cache with random replacement.

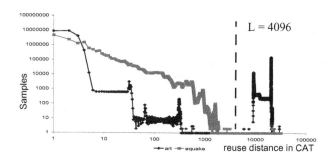

Fig. 2. CAT reuse distance histograms for art and equake (both axes log scale)

CAT Time. The reuse distance of a cacheline is measured as the number of intervening events -a notion of time- between two consecutive accesses to this cacheline. In [6], reuse distances are measured as the number of other intervening accesses. In contrast, we measure reuse distances with a different notion of "time." Our time is measured in Cache Allocation Ticks (CAT) [4], or in other words, cache replacements. The CAT clock can be advanced with two different ways: by snooping the cache replacements irrespective of the thread that causes the replacement in the shared cache (we call this a global CAT clock) or by using the replacements of the particular thread that is replaced (we call this local or per-thread counters). Our theory is independent of which clock, global or local, we use for a thread's histogram, as long as we always relate the global clock to the size of the cache and the local clock to the thread's footprint in the cache. Both ways have each own positives and negatives, but we omitted such analysis due to lack of space. For the didactic purpose of this section, we will assume global CAT as our notion of time. The importance of CAT time stems from the fact that it allows for a natural mapping of the cache statistics to the studied cache level.

CAT Reuse-Distance Histograms. The reuse distance histogram of a program measured in CAT time is denoted as: $h(i)$, $i = 0,\infty$. Figure 2 shows the histograms for two SPEC2000 programs, art and equake, sharing a 256KB cache. The histograms are collected in a time window of 200M instructions and in this case we see reuse distances of up to a few tens-of-thousands CAT.

As we can see from the histograms art shows a "binary" distribution of reuse distances, with the bulk of samples at short reuse distances, but also with a significant bulge beyond L ($L=4096$, the size of the cache in cachelines). This bulge signifies than many of the items that art accesses, do not "fit" in the cache and produces a significant number of misses. It is responsible for the behavior of art which hogs the cache and squeezes its companion thread to a very small footprint. In contrast, equake shows a distribution of reuse distances that decreases slowly to the right. The meaning of this distribution, as we will show, is that equake is already in a compressed state (we cannot squeeze it further without serious damage to its miss ratio) but it can benefit from expansion to a larger footprint. In general many programs behave either like art or like equake. artlike programs are prime candidates for management-com-pression.

Basic Probability Functions. The centerpiece of the StatShare model are the f and f-*bar* functions. These functions give the probability of a miss (f) or a hit (f-*bar*) for an item in the cache with a given reuse distance. The f-functions coupled with the reuse-distance histograms of threads produce the rest of the information of our statistical model. The f-functions concern a specific replacement policy. As we have mentioned, for the didactic purposes of this section we will assume a fully-associative (FA), random replacement cache where the notion of time is given by a global CAT counter.

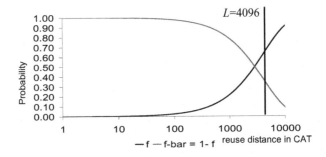

Fig. 3. f and f-*bar* for Random replacement in a FA cache

Under this scenario, any item in a such cache of size L (in cachelines) has $1/L$ probability of being replaced at any miss or $(1–1/L)$ probability of remaining in the cache. If an item has a CAT reuse distance of i, then after i misses (or replacements), it has a probability of remaining in the cache of $(1–1/L)^i$ and a probability of having been replaced of $1–(1–1/L)^i$. We call this miss probability function f, in contrast to the hit probability denoted as f-*bar*:

$$f(i) = 1-\left(1-\frac{1}{L}\right)^i \qquad \overline{f(i)} = 1-f(i) = \left(1-\frac{1}{L}\right)^i$$

Once we have a CAT reuse distance histogram for a thread it is easy to calculate its hits and misses by multiplying it with the f-*bar* and f functions respectively:

$$hits = \sum_{i=0} \tilde{h}(i) \times \overline{f(i)} \qquad misses = \sum_{i=0} \tilde{h}(i) \times f(i)$$

The results of these formulas agree with our simulation results with very high accuracy. However, in order to get an accurate count of misses we must take into account cold misses. Cold misses are estimated when we collect samples for the reuse distance histograms of a thread. In short, dangling samples with no observed reuse distance correspond to cold misses [5].

4 Integrating Decay and LRU Replacement in the Model

The StatShare model gives us all the necessary theoretical information on which application we can "compress" to release space for the benefit of system as a whole. It is a good approximation for relatively large caches (greater than 64KB) of moderate to high associativity (greater than 2) with LRU replacement, such as the likely L2 or L3 caches in CMPs [8][9][10]. In this section we describe in abstract terms the StatShare model for LRU replacement and decay. We will not expand in details but give the basic information needed to support our decay-based management policies. In addition, as we will show in rest of this section, using *local* CAT counters in combination with a decay-driven replacement algorithm, we can precisely control the thread's cache footprint. This characteristic allows us not only to prevent malicious or cache-greedy applications to abuse the shared cache, but it can be used as a methodology to enforce high-level policies such as policies that try to assign custom cache-space-allocation based on external QoS.

4.1 Per-Thread Histograms

Since in this paper we are interested in indentifying unique cache-greedy applications in a shared cache, we use *per-thread* CAT clocks that are advanced by cache replacements of cachelines belonging to a specific thread, regardless of the thread that causes the replacement. In this way, the CAT clock is insensitive to the status of the whole shared cache, but dedicated to the status (cache requirements) of each individual thread. Collecting histograms of each thread using their own CAT counters creates "pure" histograms which accurately describe the cache behavior of the thread *confined to its space in the cache*. This means that the term L, which is the cache size in cachelines with the global CAT counter, is now replaced by the active ratio (in cachelines) of each thread.

LRU Replacement. With LRU replacement in a FA cache, the probabilities of a miss or a hit change with respect to those of random replacement. In short, the LRU f-functions are much more steep than the random f-functions and reach their bounds right at L. This is evident, for example, for the f function which reaches 0 just at L since nothing can remain in an LRU FA cache after seeing L replacements.

However, the shape of the f-functions before L is complex to derive. Because LRU, unlike random, is not memoryless, the miss and hit probabilities depend on the state of the cache which in turn implies that the f and f-*bar* functions depend on the reuse-distance histograms of the threads. In other words the behavior of LRU depends on the applications.

Assume that we have an application which has a miss rate of 1 —it has no hits. The f-*bar* (hit probability) function in this case is a step function: everything with a reuse distance larger than L is guaranteed to be a miss since an item that lives through L replacements is guaranteed to be thrown out of the cache. (However, the only compatible histograms with this *f-bar* function have no samples inside L otherwise they would have hits.)

Now assume that we introduce hits into the cache by having some histogram samples inside

L. Hits affect how quickly an item with a given reuse distance moves down the LRU chain. Assume, for example, an item at a position x in the LRU chain (items enter in position 1 and fall out of the cache at position $L+1$). This item is pushed down in the LRU chain either from new items that enter at the top via replacements, or by hits on *older* items, located below the item in question, which bring them at the top of the LRU chain. The number of possible hits on items located after x is a function of the application's reuse distance histogram. The end result is that the more hits we have the faster an item with a reuse distance less than L can be evicted increasing the probability of misses in small reuse distances.

The end result is that f-function are very steep around L (or the equivalent active ratio), and their form at reuse distances less than L depends on the hit ratio and the thread's actual reuse-distance histogram.

Decayed *f* and *f-bar* Functions. Decay modifies the *f*-functions of the decayed applications. Once we apply decay to one of the threads that share the cache, the underlying replacement policy of the cache (LRU or Random) is changed, since decayed cachelines take precedence for eviction.

The effect of decay on LRU *f*-functions is to effectively make them step functions: the f-bar function is one almost up to the decay interval D and then rapidly falls to 0. The explanation is the following: if we decay a thread at a reuse distance D, all its items with smaller reuse distances can be hits as long as there are decayed lines available for replacements. Our modified replacement algorithm chooses a decayed line to replace if there is one available. In addition, decayed items are certain misses since they decay and are replaced. However, for performance reasons we allow hits on decayed items. This results in a discrepancy between our model and our implementation since the decayed f-functions are step function only if decayed items are misses. Thus our models are pessimistic in their assessment of performance.

Cache Management. StatShare gives us all the elements required to make informed decisions and construct high-level cache management policies. Using the StatShare outputs, we are able to understand which thread (malicious or not) can be "compressed" into less space with negligible damage and to drive accordingly the underlying replacement policy of the cache by selecting the appropriate decay intervals. This characteristic allows us not only to prevent malicious or cache-greedy applications to abuse the shared cache, but it can be used as a methodology to enforce high-level policies.

The management policy we examine in this paper is as follows:

- We collect reuse-distance histograms using local (per-thread) CAT counters.
- We assess the "threat" that each thread poses based on its reuse-distance histogram. Threads are sorted according to their DoS threat level.

- We assess the performance impact of decaying the most threatening threads using decayed LRU *f*-functions and we choose an appropriate decay interval for each. Decay intervals are restricted to a small set of *L*-fractions (e.g., *L*, *L*/2, *L*/4, etc.).

Finally, we propose as the appropriate place for using StatShare, the operating system and in particular the thread scheduler. This is because a sampling period is required at the end of which a management decision can be made. Managing the cache must be performed periodically, since threads change behavior in different program phases. In addition, threads are created, suspended, or killed dynamically and each change requires a new management decision. The sampling period must be long enough to have the time to collect useful histograms for the threads. For example, in our evaluation the sampling window is 45M instructions. Finally, Quality-of-Service guarantees that must be taken into account can be easily handled at the OS level. For example, if it is desired externally to give specific space to specific threads, this can be taken into account in the scheduler for adjusting decay intervals to satisfy such requirements.

5 Practical Implementations

In this section we show that the abstract theory can be translated into realistic run-time implementations.

Reuse-Distance Histogram Collection. At first sight, the nature of the reuse-distance histograms, which potentially span values from 0 to infinity, seems impractical for run-time collection. There are two techniques that make histogram collection not only practical but even efficient: *sampling* and *quantization*.

Sampling is a technique that was also used in StatCache [6][5]. Instead of collecting reuse distances for all accesses, we select few accesses at random, and only trace those for their reuse distance. The resulting histogram is a scaled version of the original but with the exact same statistical properties. Sampling allows for efficient run-time tracing. In our evaluation our sampling ratio is 1:1024, i.e., we select randomly one out of 1024 accesses.

The second fundamental technique that allows a practical implementation of StatShare is the *quantization* of the reuse distance histogram. Normally, it would be impractical to collect and store a histogram with potentially many thousands of buckets. However, samples with small reuse distances are statistically more significant than the ones with very large reuse distances. We use 20 buckets for quantization. In this way, the histograms can be collected in a set of 20 32-bit registers per thread, that are updated by hardware and are visible to the OS similarly to other "model-specific" registers such as performance counters. We have verified that the outputs of StatShare are practically indistinguishable using either quantized or full histograms.

Decay Implementations and Replacement Policies. Our modified replacement algorithm is very simple: we replace *any* decayed cacheline (randomly) if there is one in the set, or —if there is not— we use the underlying LRU replacement policy.

In order to hold the decay information, we use a set of registers (visible to the OS) to store the decay intervals of each thread. Non-decayed threads have an "infinite" decay interval corresponding to the largest value of these registers. Cachelines are tagged with the CAT clock which is updated every time a hit or a replacement occurs in the corresponding cacheline. CAT tags can be made just a few bits long [4]. At the time of replacement, the CAT tag of each cacheline is subtracted from the thread CAT clock. If the result is greater than the decay interval of the corresponding thread, the cacheline is decayed and can be chosen for replacement. This check starts at a random place in a set and proceeds until either a decayed line is found or the entire set has been checked. In our methodology, the only decision we make is which decay intervals to use for the various threads.

6 Evaluation

For our simulations we have modified an SMT simulator [12] to model a CMP architecture with 2 to 4 cores. Each core is a modest 2-way out-of-order superscalar. The memory hierarchy consists of private L1s —instruction and data— and a shared, 8-way set-associative, 64B-line L2 cache. The memory latency is 250 cycles. Our intention is to isolate the data accesses behavior of applications, hence we use a relatively large instruction L1 (1MB) to preclude instruction misses from polluting the L2.

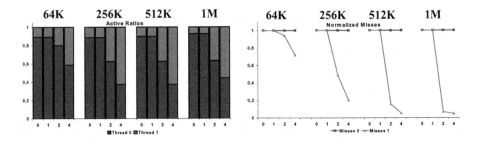

Fig. 4. Tramp vs. Gzip: active ratios and miss ratios for various decay intervals

We use a subset of the most memory intensive SPEC2000 benchmarks for our evaluation: art, gzip, equake, mcf and parser. To emulate the impact of a malicious thread, we write our own malicious program —named tramp— which is designed to be a greedy consumer of the L2. The tramp program scans continuously a very large memory array (bigger than the L2) accessing one byte out of 64 bytes (the size of the L2 block size). In every iteration, a read and a write operation are performed. With this way, the best case miss ratio of the tramp program can be equal to 50%.

To understand the behavior of decay in relation with StatShare's outputs, we have simulated a set of co-scheduled applications where one or two of them are decayed. The workload consists of 2 and 4 threads. In some sets, the tramp program has the role of the greedy application, while in some others the same role is taken by the two most memory intensive benchmarks of the SPEC2000 suite —art and mcf. Although our methodology allows any decay interval to be chosen in order to manage a thread, we have constrained the choice of decay intervals to be binary fractions of the corresponding cache size.

All our simulations are for 200M instructions per thread. We simulate after skipping 1B instructions for art and gzip, 2B for mcf, parser, and vpr, and 3B for equake. After skip we warm up the caches for 50M instructions. Management decisions are taken every 45M instructions. In the rest of this Section we discuss results for five representative cases.

tramp—gzip. In this example art shares the cache with gzip. Figure 4 shows the active ratios and the miss ratios of the two threads for the four caches we consider, and for four decay intervals (decay is applied to tramp). Every set of bars corresponds to a specific cache size (noted on top of the set). The x-axis shows the decay intervals. The first bar (tagged with a 0 label), for each set, stands for infinite decay interval, while the values 1, 2, and 4 correspond to L, $L/2$, and $L/4$ respectively (L is the cache size measured in cachelines).

As we can see from Figure 4, our methodology successfully manages to equally divide the cache between the two threads. With an $L/4$ decay interval both applications have almost the 50% of the cache in all cache sizes. The value of our cache management technique can be seen not only for the active ratios, but for the miss ratios too (miss ratios are normalized to the non-decayed case). tramp is already experiencing a high miss ratio, so compressing it will not significantly impact its performance (as it can be seen from the graph). On the other hand, gzip is the kind of application (as it is shown by the statcache curves —Figure 1), that can benefit from its space expansion and reduce its miss ratio. The more space it gets the more hits it generates. In the 64K cache, gzip starts (at non decayed state) with 87% miss ratio and ends up ($L/4$ decay interval) with 62% miss ratio resulting in a normalized reduction of almost 30%. In the 1MB case, the benefit is more pronounced. gzip starts with 21% miss rate and ends up with a miss ratio less than 1%. This corresponds to a normalized reduction of 96%. In all cases, the miss ratio of tramp is always constant at 50%.

tramp—equake. In this case we examine tramp with another SPEC2000 program — equake. Figure 5 shows the active ratios and the miss ratios for the four cache sizes and for the 4 decay intervals (infinite, L, $L/2$, $L/4$).

As Figure 5 indicates tramp begins (before decay) by clearly "hogging" the cache having more than 90% of the cache in the non-decayed state (same results as in the previous example). Once it is decayed, it releases space for the benefit of equake. However, in contrast to gzip, equake cannot exploit its increased space except in the case of the 64K cache. This is evident also from the StatCache curves. Giving more space to equake produces very few additional hits.

mcf—parser. Our third example is mcf co-scheduled with parser. mcf is one of the two most memory intensive programs of the SPEC2000 suite (the other is art).

mcf is chosen for decay since it decays better than parser and occupies the most space in the cache (Figure 6). mcf's decay benefits parser with up to a maximum reduction of miss ratio of 23.5% for the 64K, 47% for the 256K, 34% for the 512K, and 25% for the 1M cache. mcf experiences a slightly increase of 3% in the miss ratio only in the case of 1M cache.

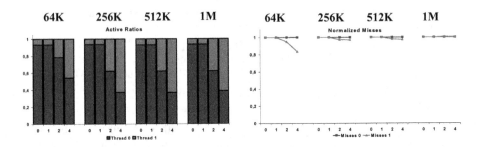

Fig. 5. Tramp vs. equake: active ratios and miss ratios for various decay intervals

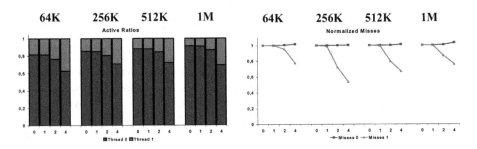

Fig. 6. Mcf vs. parser: active ratios and miss ratios for various decay intervals

tramp—gzip—parser—vpr. In this example, we evaluate our methodology when the L2 cache is shared among 4 threads —tramp, gzip, parser, and vpr. Figure 7 shows the active ratios and the miss ratios in this case.

The interesting observation that can be made from Figure 7 is that tramp must be decayed "harder" in order to see significant changes in its active ratio. Thus, we expand the decay intervals up to $L/16$ (our management algorithm always picks tramp as the decayed application). In the 2M case and for decay interval equal to $L/16$, tramp's miss ratio is increased by 2%, while its cache footprint has been decreased by a factor of 2.9 compared to the non decayed case. The released space by tramp benefits the other 3 applications. gzip increases its space by 1.3x, parser by 1.7x, and vpr by 1.4x. These expansions lead to a decrease in miss ratio of 10% for gzip, 2% for parser and 18% for vpr.

tramp—art—equake—gzip. Finally, we give a 4-thread example where decay is applied to two applications —tramp and art— since they both pose significant threat for DoS and can be significantly compressed. This two-thread decay management decision works very well since, when only tramp is decayed, its released space is occupied directly by art. art's aggressive behavior does not let the other two threads benefit from tramp's compression. On the other hand, even though art increases its cache footprint, its miss ratio does not show considerable improvements. Figure 8 presents the active ratios and miss ratios for this example. The first bar of every set corresponds to the non-decayed case (none of the applications are decayed). In the rest of the bars, tramp has a constant decay interval equal to $L/16$, while art's decay intervals are shown in the x-axis (L, $L/2$, $L/4$, $L/8$, $L/16$).

As we can see from Figure 8, equake and gzip benefit from art's and tramp's compression. In the 1M cache, equake increases its space by 4x and gzip by 2.5x. However, equake, in contrast to gzip, cannot exploit its increased space leading to a meagre 2% decrease (improve-ment) in its miss ratio while gzip experiences an impressive 43% decrease. The results are analogous for the other cache sizes with a big difference in art's behavior in the 2M cache. As we can see from Figure 1, art is no longer in its flat area, so if we try to compress it, we will destroy its performance, as it is evident from Figure 8 (2M case). art is not a good candidate for decay in this case.

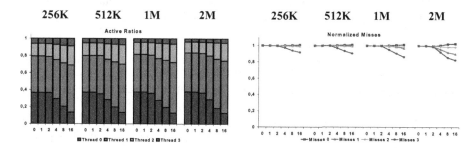

Fig. 7. Tramp-gzip-parser-vpr: active ratios and miss ratios for various decay intervals

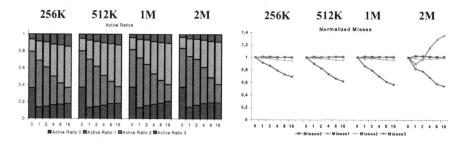

Fig. 8. Tramp-art-equake-gzip: active ratios and miss ratios for various decay intervals

7 Conclusions

In this paper, we demonstrate a new management methodology for shared caches in CMP systems, that utilizes statistical run-time information of the application behavior in order to deal with Denial-of-Service attacks. Our methodology does not need to distinguish between malicious programs and "greedy" but not-by-nature malicious programs, since these two categories behave similarly in terms of reuse distance histograms. This leads us to a more generalized approach, where dealing with DoS attacks is similar to enforcing QoS constraints or sharing the cache in a fair way.

The proposed methodology is evaluated using a detailed CMP simulator running the most memory intensive SPEC2000 applications and a "tramp" program which is designed to be an excellent consumer of the shared cache. Our results indicate that our attack-resistant cache management methodology makes it possible to identify which application (malicious or not) can be "compressed" into less cache space with negligible damage and modify accordingly —in run-time— the underlying replacement algorithm of the cache using decay. Our results show significant benefits across the board with minimal damage for the managed threads.

References

[1] G. E. Suh, S. Devadas, and L. Rudolph. "A new memory monitoring scheme for memory-aware scheduling and partitioning" High-Performance Computer Architecture HPCA'02, 2002.

[2] S. Kim, D. Chandra and Y. Solihin. "Fair cache sharing and partitioning in a chip multiprocessor architecture" Parallel Architectures and Compilation Techniques, PACT'04, 2004.

[3] D. Chandra, F. Guo, S. Kim and Y. Solihin. "Predicting inter-thread cache contention on a chip multi-processor architecture" High-Performance Computer Architecture HPCA'05, 2005.

[4] M. Karlsson and E. Hagersten. "Timestamp-Based Selective Cache Allocation" In High Performance Memory Systems, edited by H. Hadimiouglu, et al., Springer-Verlag, 2003.

[5] E. Berg, H. Zeffer, and E. Hagersten. "A Statistical Multiprocessor Cache Model" International Symposium on Performance Analysis of Systems and Software (ISPASS-2006), USA, 2006.

[6] E. Berg and E. Hagersten. "Fast Data-Locality Profiling of Native Execution" ACM SIGMETRICS 2005, Canada, 2005.

[7] S. Kaxiras, Z. Hu, M. Martonosi. "Cache Decay: Exploiting Generational Behavior to Reduce Cache Leakage Power" International Symposium on Computer Architecture ISCA'28, 2001.

[8] P. Kongetira, K. Aingaran, and K. Olukutun. "Niagara: A 32-Way Multithreaded SPARC Processor" In IEEE Micro, 2005.

[9] K. Krewell. "Power5 Tops on Bandwidth." In Microprocessor Report, 2003.

[10] K. Krewell. "Double Your Opterons; Double Your Fun." In Microprocessor Report, 2004.

[11] J. Hennessy and D. Patterson. "Computer Architecture: a Quantitative Approach." Morgan-Kaufmann Publishers, Inc., 2nd edition, 1996.

[12] R Goncalves, E Ayguade, M Valero and P Navaux "A Simulator for SMT Architectures: Evaluating Instruction Cache Topologies" 12th Symposium on Computer Architecture and High Performance, (SBAC-PAD 2000), 2000.

[13] R. L. Mattson, J. Gecsei, D. R. Slutz, and I. L.Traiger. "Evaluation techniques for storage hierarchies" IBM Systems Journal, 1970.

[14] CNN. 'Immense' network assault takes down Yahoo, 2000. Available at http://www.cnn.com/2000/TECH/computing/02/08/yahoo.assault.idg/index.html.

[15] Netscape. Leading Web sites under attack, 2000. Available at http://technews.netscape.com/news/0-1007-200-1545348.html.

[16] D. Grunwald and S. Ghiasi. "Microarchitectural denial of service: insuring microarchitectural fairness" International Symposium on Microarchitecture MICRO-35, 2002.

[17] J. Hasan, A. Jalote, T. N. Vijaykumar, and C. E. Brodley. "Heat Stroke: Power-Density-Based Denial of Service in SMT" High Performance Computer Architecture HPCA'05, 2005.

[18] Techtarget.com. Technology terms: Denial of service. Available at http://http://whatis.techtarget.com /definition/0,289893,sid9 gci213591,00.html.

[19] P. Soderquist and M. Leeser. "Optimizing the Data Cache Performance of a Software MPEG-2 Video Decoder" In ACM Multimedia 97 - Electronic Proceedings, 1997.

A Method for Router Table Compression
for Application Specific Routing in Mesh Topology NoC
Architectures

Maurizio Palesi[1], Shashi Kumar[2], and Rickard Holsmark[2]

[1] DIIT, University of Catania, Italy
mpalesi@diit.unict.it
[2] Jönköping University, Sweden
{Shashi.Kumar, Rickard.Holsmark}@ing.hj.se

Abstract. One way to specialize a general purpose multi-core chip built using NoC principles is to provide a mechanism to configure an application specific deadlock free routing algorithm in the underlying communication network.
A table in every router, implemented using a writable memory, can provide a
possibility of specializing the routing algorithm according to the application requirements. In such an implementation the cost (area) of the router will be proportional to the size of the routing table. In this paper, we propose a method to
compress the routing table to reduce its size such that the resulting routing algorithm remains deadlock free as well as has high adaptivity. We demonstrate
through simulation based evaluation that our application specific routing algorithm gives much higher performance, in terms of latency and throughput, as
compared to general purpose algorithms for deadlock free routing. We also show
that a table size of two entries for each output port gives performance within 3%
of the uncompressed table.

1 Introduction

Routing topology and routing algorithm are the two most important aspects which distinguish various proposed NoC architectures [1,2,3]. Fixed tile size based two dimensional
mesh topology is favored by many research groups because of its layout efficiency and
resulting good electrical properties of the signals. It is possible to envision that application area specific NoC chips will soon become off the shelf products like FPGA chips.
One can easily imagine that one such chip could be useful for multi-media applications.
Such a heterogeneous multi-core chip will be next in line to the current superscalar DSP
chips and will provide an order higher computational power than the current DSPs.

The one mechanism to specialize such a chip for a specific application, or a set of
concurrent applications, will be through configuring the routing algorithms in the underlying communication infrastructure. The routing algorithm in such an application
area specific NoC chip must provide deadlock free communication with a high degree
of adaptivity and low latency. Many deadlock free routing algorithms, like e.g. Odd-
Even [4] and the Turn Model [5], have been proposed in literature for mesh topology networks. In these algorithms, deadlock freedom is achieved at a high loss of
adaptivity. Boltin *et al.* [1] have proposed hard coded paths for deadlock safe routing for an application for an irregular mesh topology NoC. A non-minimal deadlock

S. Vassiliadis et al. (Eds.): SAMOS 2006, LNCS 4017, pp. 373–384, 2006.
© Springer-Verlag Berlin Heidelberg 2006

free routing algorithm is described for an irregular mesh topology NoC with regions in [6]. Duato has proposed a general theory to develop adaptive deadlock free routing algorithms for any communication network which uses worm-hole switching technique [7].

Most of the deadlock routing algorithms proposed in literature are general purpose and have been designed to handle worst case communication patterns in the network. A NoC system specialized for a set of applications can be regarded as a semi-static system. Here we can have the information about the set of pairs of cores which communicate and other pairs which never communicate after task mapping step. But it may not be possible to know the dynamic variations in the communication traffic among the cores. This information about the communication topology can be incorporated in Duato's theory to design highly adaptive routing algorithms. We call such algorithms as Application Specific Routing Algorithms (APSRAs) [8].

The most natural way to implement an APSRA will be to provide a table in every router which will guide an incoming flit to an appropriate output port of the router. A table implemented using a writable memory can provide a possibility of specializing the routing algorithm according to the application requirements (in the same way as different functions can be configured in a SRAM based FPGA). Like in FPGAs, we even have a possibility of dynamically updating a routing algorithm. However, the implementation of this routing table will constitute a major part of the router cost (area). In this paper, we propose a method to compress the routing table to reduce its size such that the resulting routing algorithm remains deadlock free.

We have analyzed the cost saving possible with our lossless compression method for various sizes of mesh topology NoC. We have also compared the performance of APSRA which uses limited size router tables generated by our methodology with a general purpose deadlock free routing algorithm. The results justify the use of APSRA methodology and our router table compression method.

2   Application Specific Routing Algorithm

In [7] Duato has proposed a general theory to develop adaptive deadlock free routing algorithms for communication networks which use wormhole switching technique. Duato's method is based on generating a *Channel Dependency Graph* (*CDG*), in which every channel is a node and there is a directed edge from a node i to j if channel j can be used after channel i for some communication among resources in the network. A cycle in the *CDG* indicates a possibility of a deadlock. Duato's method takes only the network topology as input and generates many routing algorithms which will work for all possible situations in the network. In [8] we extended Duato's theory and presented a method to generate routing algorithms for communication networks when the communication graph of the application is known. We applied the extended method to generate a routing algorithm for a mesh topology network.

Figure 1 shows the block diagram of the APSRA methodology. There are two main blocks. The first one implements the APSRA methodology whose inputs are:

- A *Communication Graph* where each vertex t_i represents a task, and each directed arc (t_i, t_j) represents the communication from t_i to t_j.

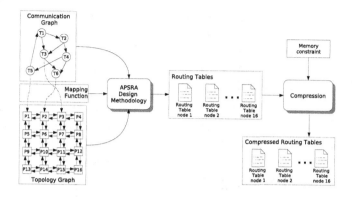

Fig. 1. Block diagram of the APSRA methodology

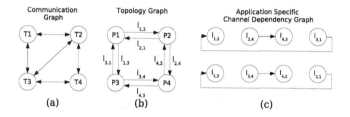

Fig. 2. An example of application specific channel dependency graph (c) for a given topology graph (a), communication graph (b) and a fully adaptive minimal routing

- A *Topology Graph* where each vertex p_i represents a node of the network, and each directed arc (p_i, p_j) represents a physical unidirectional channel (link) connecting node p_i to node p_j. (In this paper we focus on mesh topologies).
- A *Mapping Function* $M : T \rightarrow P$ which maps a task $t \in T$ on a node $p \in P$.

For the sake of example, let us consider the 2×2 mesh depicted in Figure 2(a). Let us suppose a communication graph, CG, in which each task communicates with each other task except for task t_1 and t_4 as shown in Figure 2(b). As mapping function let us consider $M(t_i) = p_i$. The APSRA methodology starts by considering a fully adaptive minimal routing and builds the CDG. Then, by exploiting the CG it extracts from the CDG a sub-graph named *Application Specific Channel Dependency Graph* ($ASCDG$). The difference between CDG and $ASCDG$ is that the latter does not contain any channel dependencies between channel pairs that do not belong to any admissible source/destination path for the current routing. Figure 2(c) shows the $ASCDG$ for our example. In [8] we demonstrated that if the $ASCDG$ is acyclic then routing is deadlock free. In our example, $ASCDG$ is acyclic therefore we can assure that minimum fully adaptive routing is deadlock free for this specific communication graph. More in general, if the $ASCDG$ contains some cycles, in [8] we presented an heuristic to break these cycles in order to minimise adaptiveness degradation.

The outputs of APSRA methodology is a set of routing tables one for each node of the network. Unfortunately, as we will see in the next sections, the size of each routing table grows linearly with network size. For this reason we introduce a second block, named *Compression*, which performs routing table compression. It gets as inputs: a) the set of routing tables generated by APSRA, and b) a constraint about the maximum routing table size. The compression algorithm (which will be discussed in Section 4) tries to reduce the size of routing tables in such a way as compressed routing tables size do not exceed a user defined threshold. However, sometimes, this operation is not lossless and the cost to pay is a reduction of adaptiveness. At any rate, in all our experiments the reduction in adaptiveness is very low: in the worst case less than 6 percent against a reduction in routing table size of 66 percent.

3   NoC Router Functionality and Design Options

A NoC router will have to perform the same functionality as a traditional computer network router, which is basically to help packets sent into the network reach their destination. Due to the on-chip physical constraints, size and power consumption needs to be given higher consideration while designing NoC routers. This will make complicated routing schemes infeasible. An overview of a generic router for mesh topology NoC is shown in Figure 3(a). The router has five input and five output ports, one for each direction plus one for the local resource. There could be packet buffers to manage variations in traffic. The functionality of finding the route for a packet can be split into a routing function and a selection function. A crossbar switch connects the input and output ports. When a packet enters an input port the routing function has to decide to which output a packet should be forwarded. This is in the simplest case done by examining the destination address in the header of a packet. For more advanced routing schemes additional information in the header could also be used.

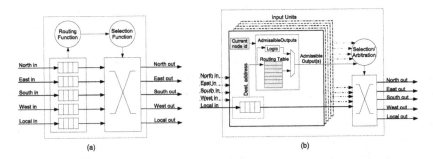

Fig. 3. Generic mesh topology router (a). Table-based NoC router (b).

If the used routing algorithm is adaptive, it is possible that the routing function returns multiple output choices. In the case that these outputs are not occupied by other packets, a selection has to be made among these. This corresponds to the selection function. There are several schemes that can be used, for example (pseudo) random selection or selection according to a favoured dimension. It is also possible to use look-ahead techniques that sense distant congestion and try to avoid this. If a crossbar is used packets headed for non-conflicting outputs can be simultaneously routed. There could be a situation where several packets simultaneously want to use the same output. In this case, arbitration between these has to be performed, for example by using round-robin, random or priority policies.

One way to implement the routing function is to design it in hardware logic. For simple routing functions, this results in small and fast routers which can be repeatedly implemented throughout the network. This method has been used by several NoC proposals [1,9].

Another way, mainly used in non on-chip networks, to implement the routing function is to use a routing table [10], depicted in Figure 3(b). Index to the table, where the admissible outputs are stored, is the destination address or a function of the destination address. The values of the table are dependent on which router, or even in which input of a router it is implemented. Using a table gives the possibility to implement more complex routing functions and also the possibility to change it. A disadvantage is that a table can take large space if many destination addresses should be stored. We believe therefore that compressing the table will be of high importance in the NoC context. In this case there would be some encoding logic to find the right table position. As we show later in the paper, routers with small routing table sizes are sufficient for APSRA methodology based routing.

4 Router Table Compression

Looking at Figure 3(b), the *AdmissibleOutputs* block determines the set of admissible output ports through which a header flit can be forwarded to reach a given destination. There is an *AdmissibleOutputs* block for each input. It contains a routing table RT_{ipn}^{curr} where the subscript *ipn* represents the input port name (North, East, South, West and Local) and the superscript *curr* indicates the current node id. A RT_{ipn}^{curr} consists of a memory addressed by a destination node id *dst* which returns the set of admissible output port(s) which can be used to reach the destination *dst*.

The total number of bits to store in a generic router is:

$$S_{u1} = Size(RT_{North}^{curr}) + Size(RT_{East}^{curr}) + Size(RT_{South}^{curr}) + Size(RT_{West}^{curr}) + Size(RT_{Local}^{curr}) \quad (1)$$

If we consider a $H \times W$ mesh based NoC it is simple to show that:

$$S_{u1} = 12 \times (1 + H \times W - H - W) \quad (2)$$

Since we are dealing with shortest path routing, for a given *ipn* the destination will be in the opposite quadrants with respect to *ipn*. For instance, if *ipn* is *West* then destination will be either in the first or in the fourth quadrant. For this reason it is possible to reduce the number of bits to store the admissible outputs from 4 to 3 (i.e., it is enough to store the *North, East,* and *South* output directions). If we do that, we have to specialise the *AdmissibleOutputs* block for a given input port. In this case the total number of bits to store in a generic router is:

$$S_{u2} = 9 \times (1 + H \times W - H - W) \quad (3)$$

The main problem of this approach is that a great deal of memory locations are wasted. Since in real cases a node communicates with only a small subset of network nodes, many table entries are never used. An alternative approach is to store the admissible output ports for a set of destinations rather than for a given destination. Let us consider a generic input port, for the sake of clarity let us consider the west input port. If a router receives a flit from its west input port the destination will be in the first and forth quadrant. The problem is to choose the admissible output ports in accordance with the complete routing table generated by APSRA. There are five alternatives: North, South, East, North & East, South & East. The basic idea is to associate a color to each of these 5 alternatives (e.g., North=Red, South=Green, East=Blue, North & East=Purple, South & East=Yellow). Then label each destination with a color. (For instance, if for destination d it is admissible to use outputs North and East, destination d is labeled with color purple). Finally destinations are clustered based on their color.

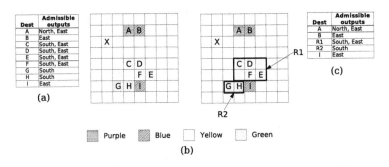

Fig. 4. (a) Routing table before compression. (b) Color based clustering. (c) Compressed routing table.

For example let us consider the routing table associated to the west input port of node X shown in Figure 4(a). After coloring each destination, a color based clustering is performed [Figure 4(b)]. The constraint is that clustering is performed by means of rectangular regions. In this way it is no more necessary to store the set of all the destinations but only the set of the regions [Figure 4(c)].

Figure 5 shows the block diagram of the *AdmissibleOutputs* block which uses the compressed routing table. The block *InRegion* checks if a destination *dst* belongs to a region identified by its top left corner (TL register) and its bottom right corner (BR register). If this condition is satisfied the output *directions* assumes the value of the *Color* register and output *hit* is set. The same figure shows also the pseudo-code of the *InRegion* block for a west input port.

For a $H \times W$ mesh based NoC and M *InRegion* blocks per input port the total amount of bits to store is:

$$
\begin{aligned}
S_c &= number\ of\ inputs \times M \times [Size(Color) + Size(TL) + Size(BR)] \\
&= 5 \times M \times [3 + (\lg_2 W + \lg_2 H) + (\lg_2 W + \lg_2 H)] \\
&= 5 \times M \times [3 + \lg_2 (W \times H)^2]
\end{aligned}
\tag{4}
$$

From Equations (2), (3), and (4) with $M = 4$ the compression technique starts to be effective from 7×7 mesh size. The saving in terms of the number of bits to store grows

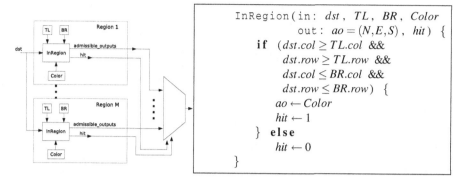

```
InRegion(in: dst, TL, BR, Color
         out: ao = (N,E,S), hit) {
  if (dst.col ≥ TL.col &&
      dst.row ≥ TL.row &&
      dst.col ≤ BR.col &&
      dst.row ≤ BR.row) {
    ao ← Color
    hit ← 1
  } else
    hit ← 0
}
```

Fig. 5. Block diagram of the *AdmissibleOutputs* block using the compressed routing table and Pseudo-code of the *InRegion* block of a west input port

very fast with the mesh size (e.g., 14% for 7×7, 47% for 8×8, 84% for 9×9, and so on).

The factor M is the number of *InRegion* blocks operating in parallel on different regions. In other words it represents the available size of router table in a NoC router. APSRA methodology produces a routing table for every router for any given application mapped on the NoC. Each of these routing tables will be compressed using color based clustering method. Let M' represent the size of the compressed table in a given router. If $M' \leq M$ then it is possible to map each region into a *InRegion* block. Otherwise, if $M' > M$, there are not enough *InRegion* blocks to host all the regions. It is possible to manage the latter situation by performing a further level of compression at the cost of a loss of adaptiveness. Let us consider again Figure 4(b) where the number of detected regions was $M' = 5$ (A, B, R1, R2, I). If $M = 4$ we have to remove at least one region. To do this we can restrict the set of admissible output ports for destination A from {North, East} to {East}. Doing that the color of destination A changes from purple to blue and the application of the color-based clustering now returns $M' = 4$ regions (R3, R1, R2, I) as shown in Figure 6.

Of course, it is possible to reiterate this method to increase the compression ratio at the cost of a degradation of adaptiveness. For instance, it is possible to merge region

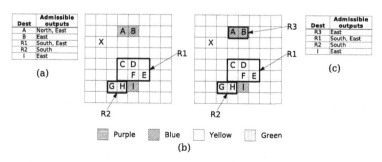

Fig. 6. Example of routing table compression with loss of adaptivity (a) Initial table (b) Color based clustering (c) Compressed routing table

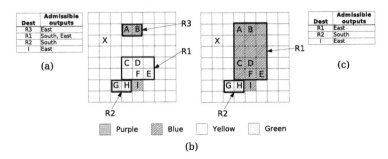

Fig. 7. Size constrained compression of routing table (a) Initial table (b) Color based clustering (c) Compressed routing table

R3 and region R1 restricting the set of admissible outputs for the destinations belongs to R1 from {South, East} to {East} as shown in Figure 7.

Finally, Figure 8 shows the pseudo-code for routing table compression. The function RoutingTableCompression requires as inputs the set of routing tables obtained by APSRA (*RT*) and the maximum number of regions a router can manage (*M*). The output is the set of compressed routing tables. The BuildColorMatrix function returns the color matrix *cm* for a given routing table. The ColorClustering function perform the color-based clustering of a color matrix and returns the set of the located regions $\mathscr{R}$. The RestrictRouting try to merge some regions by restricting the set of admissible output ports for some destinations.

```
RoutingTableCompression      (inout :  RT ,
                              in :  M)  {
    for  (p ∈ P)
        for  (l ∈ Lin(p))  {
            cm ← BuildColorMatrix    (RT(p,l))
            ℛ ← ColorClustering    (cm)
            while  (|ℛ| > M)  {
                RestrictRouting    (cm,ℛ,RT(p,l))
                cm ← BuildColorMatrix    (RT(p,l))
                ℛ ← ColorClustering    (cm)
            }
        }
}
```

Fig. 8. Pseudo-code for the routing table compression

4.1   ColorClustering Function

Clustering of the color matrix is carried out by expanding each color as much as possible in a rectangular fashion with the constraint that the expanded region of a color c' cannot contain any other color $c'' \neq c'$. The pseudo code of the function ColorClustering is shown in Figure 9. The input of the function is the color matrix *cm*. The output is aset of

```
ℛ ColorClustering  (in : cm) {        RestrictRouting  (in : cm , ℛ
  while (cm is not fully covered) {                       inout : RT(p,l))
    c ← GetAColoredElement  (cm)     {
    R ← GetRawRegion (c,cm)            R ← GetCandidateRegion  (cm,ℛ)
    while (R contains impurities) {    if (R = ∅)
      p ← GetImpurity (R,c)              abort ();
      R ← CutOffImpurity  (p,R)        else
    }                                  {
    ℛ = ℛ∪{R}                            nc ← GetNewColor  (cm,R)
    Freeze (cm,R)                        ChangeColor  (cm,RT(p,l),nc,R)
  }                                    }
}                                    }
```

Fig. 9. Pseudo-code of the ColorClustering function and RestrictRouting procedure

regions $\mathscr{R}$. As said before, a region is identified by three attributes: the top left corner, the bottom right corner, and a color. The external loop iterates until the set of regions covers all the colored elements of the color matrix. That is, for each colored element c of the color matrix cm there exists one and only one region $R \in \mathscr{R}$ that contains c. First, a colored element c is extracted using function GetAColoredElement. Then, by using function GetRawRegion, a region R containing all the colored elements of the same color of c is extracted. Of course, R could contain some impurities (i.e., colored elements with a different color than c). In this case, for each impurity p, extracted by function GetImpurity, R is reshaped in such a way as to cut-off the impurity p from R. This is performed by function CutOffImpurity which objective is to maximise the *density* of the reshaped region. The density of a region R is the number of colored elements in R reduced by the number of impurities in R. Finally, when the region R is impurities free, it is inserted in the regions set $\mathscr{R}$ and the area of cm in correspondence of R is marked with a particular color code that avoid other colored elements to expand and overlap R (function Freeze).

4.2 RestrictRouting Procedure

The procedure RestrictRouting tries to reduce the number of regions by means of adaptivity reduction for some source destination pairs. The pseudo code of the procedure is shown in Figure 9. The input of the procedure are the color matrix cm and the set of regions $\mathscr{R}$. The current routing table $RT(p,l)$ is an input/output parameter. First of all, the candidate region R is extracted from $\mathscr{R}$ by using function GetCandidateRegion. The candidate region is the minimum density region whose color has a cardinality of 2. The cardinality of a color is defined as the number of output directions the color represents. If no region respects this constraint routing table cannot be compressed anymore. Otherwise, function GetNewColor returns the color nc used to fill region R. To explain how this color is calculated, let us suppose the original color of R is yellow. We remind that yellow represents South & East output directions, green represents South output direction and blue represents East output direction. Let the average of the Euclidian distances between each point of R and each green (blue) point of cm be d_{green} (d_{blue}).

If $d_{green} < d_{blue}$ then nc is *green* else nc is *blue*. Finally, function ChangeColor fills region R of cm with color nc. This function also update routing table $RT(p,l)$ consequently (i.e., destinations that belongs to R are now reachable by using output ports defined by nc).

5   Evaluation Experiments and Results

In this section we analyse the degradation in both adaptiveness and overall performance due to routing table compression. We consider three communication traffic scenarios: *random*, *locality*, and *hot spot*. For random and locality traffic we define the *communication density*, ρ, as the ratio between the number of communications and the number of tasks. The communication graphs are generated randomly based on two different assumptions. In the random scenario, each task can communicate with every other task with equal probability. In the locality scenario, tasks communicate with a probability depending on the distance of the nodes where they are mapped on (probability decrease with distance). Finally, in the hot spot traffic scenario some nodes are designated as the *hot spot nodes*, which receive hot spot traffic in addition to regular uniform traffic. Given a hot spot percentage h, a newly generated packet is directed to each hot spot node with an additional h percent probability. We consider hot spot nodes located at the center of the mesh [nodes $(3,3)$, $(4,3)$, $(3,4)$, $(4,4)$] with 20% hot spot traffic.

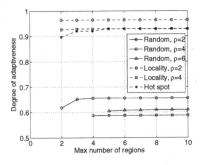

Fig. 10. Max number of regions versus degree of adaptiveness for random, locality, and hot spot communication traffic

Figure 10 shows the degree of adaptiveness after compression of the routing tables for different values of the factor M for a 8×8 mesh. For random communication traffic the compression is lossless downto $M = 4$ and $M = 5$ for $\rho = 2$ and $\rho = 4$ respectively. For locality communication traffic compression is lossless downto $M = 3$ and $M = 2$ for $\rho = 2$ and $\rho = 4$ respectively. For hot spot traffic compression is lossless downto $M = 5$. If the lossless hypotesis is relaxed the degradation of adaptiveness is less than 2% for random and locality traffic with $\rho = 4$, 6% for random traffic with $\rho = 2$, and 3% for hot spot traffic.

Finally, we evaluate dynamic performances of APSRA before and after routing table compression using a flit-accurate simulator developed in SystemC (Figure 11). As

performance metrics we choose *throughput* and *delay*. The evaluations are made on a
8 × 8 network using wormhole switching with a packet size randomly distribuited between 2 and 10 flits. In our model, each router has an input-buffer size of 2 flits. The
maximum bandwidth of each link is set to 1 flit per cycle. We use the source packet
generation rate as load parameter with Poisson packet injection distribution. For each
load value, latency values are averaged over 60,000 packet arrivals after a warm-up session of 30,000 arrived packets. The 95 percent confidence intervals are mostly within
2 percent of the means. If multiple output ports are available for a header flit, the output whose connected input port has the minimum buffer occupied is choosen. As traffic

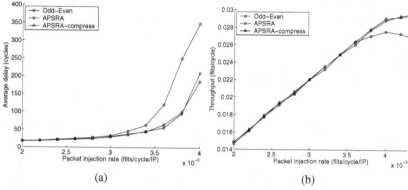

(a)   (b)

Fig. 11. Delay variation (a) and throughput variation (b) under *hot spot* traffic

scenario we use *hot spot* traffic which is considered to be more realistic than typical synthetic traffic such as uniform, transposte, etc. For this traffic scenario the average degree
of adaptiveness of APSRA is 0.93. Applying our compression technique, adaptiveness
reduces to 0.90 with a minimum number of regions equal to two. This extremely low
degradation in adaptiveness is also confirmed from the dynamic behaviour point of
view: there is no appreciable difference between APSRA and APSRA-compressed in
both delay and throughput. Moreover, we see that APSRA, in both its natural and compressed form, outperform Odd-Even adaptive routing [4].

6   Conclusions

In this paper, we have highlighted the importance and one possibility of developing application area specific NoC chips for mass production. Such a chip will have a capability of configuring a routing algorithm using the communication topology information of
already mapped applications. We have argued that a natural way to provide this configuration possibility is to implement the routing function as a table in a writable memory
in each router in the communication infrastructure. We have described a cluster based
scheme for lossless compression of these tables. An extension of this scheme for table
size constrained compression is also described. Through analysis and simulation based
evaluation we demonstrate that by using very small fixed sized tables we loose less than
3% performance as compared to uncompressed table.

We are aware that in any network with fixed size router tables there is always a finite probability that we may not be able to route all required communications. The routability problem may be solved by modifying task mapping on the NoC resources. In the worst case, there is a possibility that routing requirements of an application cannot be satisfied with any possible mapping. Then we must use a NoC chip with larger router tables. It will be interesting to study the routability property as a function of the table size using synthetic as well as real applications.

The proposed method can easily be extended for non-homogeneous mesh topologies as well as other topologies. The configurability of the table based router comes at an extra cost of hardware. It will be interesting to compare the hardware cost of the router implementing this scheme with cost of routers implementing general purpose deadlock free routing algorithms like Odd-Even routing. We believe the availability of writable tables in routers will open up many new possibilities for NoC usage as a dynamically configurable computing structure.

References

1. Bolotin, E., Morgenshtein, A., Cidon, I., Kolodny, A.: Automatic and hardware-efficient SoC integration by qos network on chip. In: IEEE International Conference on Electronics, Circuits and Systems, Tel Aviv (2004)
2. Dally, W.J., Towles, B.: Route packets, not wires: On-chip interconnection networks. In: Design Automation Conference, Las Vegas, Nevada, USA (2001) 684–689
3. Guerrier, P., Greiner, A.: A generic architecture for on-chip packet-switched interconnections. In: Design Automation and Test in Europe, Paris, France (2000) 250–256
4. Chiu, G.M.: The odd-even turn model for adaptive routing. IEEE Transactions on Parallel Distribuited Systems **11** (2000) 729–738
5. Glass, C.J., Ni, L.M.: The turn model for adaptive routing. Journal of the Association for Computing Machinery **41** (1994) 874–902
6. Holsmark, R., Kumar, S.: Design issues and performance evaluation of mesh NoC with regions. In: IEEE Norchip, Oulu, Finland (2005) 40–43
7. Duato, J.: A new theory of deadlock-free adaptive routing in wormhole networks. IEEE Transactions on Parallel and Distribuited Systems **4** (1993) 1320–1331
8. Palesi, M., Holsmark, R., Kumar, S., Catania, V.: APSRA: A methodology for design of application specific routing algorithms for NoC systems. Technical Report DIIT-TR-01-060406, Dip. di Ingegneria Informatica e delle Telecomunicazioni, Univ. di Catania (2006)
9. Wang, X., Siguenza-Tortosa, D., Ahonen, T., Nurmi, J.: Asynchronous network node design for network-on-chip. In: International Symposium on Signals, Circuits and Systems. Volume 1. (2005) 55–58
10. Vaidya, A.S., Sivasubramaniam, A., Das, C.R.: LAPSES: A recipe for high performance adaptive router design. In: Fifth International Symposium On High-Performance Computer Architecture, Orlando, Florida, USA (1999) 236–243

Real-Time Embedded System for Rear-View Mirror Overtaking Car Monitoring

Javier Díaz, Eduardo Ros, Sonia Mota, and Rodrigo Agis

[1] Dep. Arquitectura y Tecnología de Computadores, Universidad de Granada, Spain
[2] Dep.Informática y Análisis Numérico, Universidad de Córdoba, Spain
{jdiaz, eros, ragis}@atc.ugr.es, smota@uco.es

Abstract. The main goal of an overtaking monitor system is the segmentation and tracking of the overtaking vehicle. This application can be addressed through an optic flow driven scheme. We can focus on the rear mirror visual field by placing a camera on the top of it. If we drive a car, the ego-motion optic flow pattern is more or less unidirectional, i.e. all the static objects and landmarks move backwards while the overtaking cars move forward towards our vehicle. This well structured motion scenario facilitates the segmentation of regular motion patterns that correspond to the overtaking vehicle. Our approach is based on two main processing stages: first, the computation of optical flow using a novel superpipelined and fully parallelized architecture capable to extract the motion information with a frame-rate up to 148 frames per second at VGA resolution (640x480 pixels). Second, a tracking stage based on motion pattern analysis provides an estimated position of the overtaking car. We analyze the system performance, resources and show some promising results using a bank of overtaking car sequences.

1 Introduction

The blind spot in the rear-view mirror and the driver distractions are sources of multiple accidents. A camera can be placed in the car allowing us to detect the overtaking car, using optical flow algorithms. This can be used to generate alert signals to the driver. The optical flow driven scheme has several properties that can be very useful for car segmentation. Basically, focusing on the optical flow field, we should find static objects and landmarks moving backwards (due to our ego-motion) and the overtaking cars moving forward towards our vehicle. We should take into account the perspective deformation. The optical flow of a moving object is not homogeneous, the parts of the object that are far away from the camera seem to move slower than the ones that are closer, so you can find a set of different velocities, which changes continuously, along the same object.

On-board cameras have been used for lane tracking [1] and also in front/back vision for obstacle avoidance [2], but the application we address here focuses on a different field of view, the rear-view mirror and is important to emphasise that we have to deal with the perspective deformation. This scenario forces to use sophisticated clustering techniques, such as neural networks, when only sparse

S. Vassiliadis et al. (Eds.): SAMOS 2006, LNCS 4017, pp. 385–394, 2006.

features are used [3]. But in the presented approach we focus on an optical flow dense map to devise a more robust system based on a simple centroid computation for car tracking system. An accurate system will need to overcome this problem. We also require the proposed algorithm to be robust enough to detect movement using a non static camera. The movement of the host vehicle is a very important source of artefacts and for the application addressed here is critical that the algorithm used can *"clean"* these noisy patterns.

The work scheme that we have developed is composed of two different stages. In the first step, using a high performance motion estimation circuit, we compute the optical flow. Second, using very simple filtering operations and optical flow templates, we get a saliency map that can be used to estimate the car position in the image. In section 4, we show some results of the proposed system for several overtaking car sequences.

Some companies, such as Mobileye N.V. [4], Volvo [5], and Fico S.A. [6], have apparently developed some aids to lane-change decision making but no reports on their technical details, processor type or the performance of these approaches are available. This seems to suggest that the addressed application has in fact a high potential impact and the existing solutions are still under development. In our approach the whole system has been implemented on an embedded device to fit in the automobile market. In this environment, FPGAs seem to be a good option due to the intensive computation required, interfacing capabilities with automobile buses and packing possibilities inside the car. Furthermore, taking into account that complex vision processing systems are still being developed for automobile applications, the capability of the FPGA to be reconfigured to new processing schemes is a very valuable feature. This also encourages its utilization on these applications rather than other approaches based on ASIC/ASIP that fit better more market standard products.

2 Algorithmic Description

The proposed application needs the generation of alert signals to the driver to prevent traffic accidents. What we do is to estimate the car position and the confidence level. After that the alert signal generation is straightforward.

The problem has been solved using two main processing stages. First, motion is estimated using a gradient-based optical flow sensor described in [7]. In previous works, Lucas & Kanade (L&K) gradient based method [8], [9] is highlighted as a good candidate to be implemented on hardware with affordable hardware resources consumption [10], [11], [12] and good accuracy. The optical flow allows us to easily filter the overtaking car as shown on Fig. 1.

This scenario requires fulfilling to main aspects on the motion estimation stage. First, in order to detect the car as soon as possible, high image resolution is desirable. Second, since the relative inter-vehicles speed can be quite high, this motivates a specific purpose computing architecture for high frame-rate processing to achieve reliable tracking. This hard constraint requires a specific design strategy, making unviable the utilization of devices such as the one described in [10] which implemented a coarse grain pipeline processing scheme of only 6 stages being able to process just 3,5 Mpixels per second. We utilize a novel superpipelined and intensively parallelized architecture for optical flow processing with more than 70 pipelined stages that achieve a data throughput of one pixel per clock cycle. This customized DSP architecture is capable of processing up to 45 Mpixels/s arranged for example as 148 frames per second at VGA resolution (640x480 pixels). This is of extreme interest in order to use high frame-rate cameras which allows the estimation of high confidence motion information [13] to improving the tracking stage. This new system outperforms previous approach [10] thanks to the fine-grain pipeline, an improved image differentiation technique, and a novel memory management unit which enables the utilization of FIR temporal filters.

 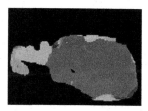

Fig. 1. Car segmentation using optical flow. Dark greys represent rightward movements (the car) and light greys leftward motion (the landscape). We can see that the proposed model gives us very uniform object segmentation therefore car tracking can be done easily.

In the second stage we calculate the overtaking car position and reliability on such measurement. Relaying on the advanced sensor used for motion computation, a simple tracking system based on motion filtering templates has been developed achieving very promising results. The method is described on the next section.

a. Car Tracking: Post-processing optical flow steps

The main operations to be implemented can be summarized as follows:

1. Pattern selection. We consider only rightward movements. While the overtaking manoeuvres, the overtaking car is moving to the right side of the image so we do not need to consider leftward velocities. If we note V_x the x component of the velocity, V_y the y component and k for the minimum reliable velocity component module, the velocities set that we use should verify:

$$v_x > k \quad and \quad |v_y| \leq v_x \qquad (1)$$

2. Saliency map generation. This step uses the previous information and isolates the main motion features which work as the input saliency map of the next stages; It is realized by using optical flow filtering templates. The proposed system computes the number of motion pixels grouping on spatial neighbourhoods of 15x15 pixels. Each template count the number of motion pixels presented at his neighbourhood. A feature will pass to the next stage if it has enough active points, where the limit threshold depends on the estimate car position. Due to the rear-view mirror perspective the threshold grows rightward according to the vehicle size. The final saliency maps clear spurious patterns and correct the image perspective to give reliable data to the next computation stage.

3. Centroid computation. A simple centroid computation of the saliency map provides us the car position estimation but, it is correct only for continuous car overtaking of only one vehicle. Some more complex and realistic situations need to be solved, as described bellow:

- Multiple car overtaking. For the addressed application a multi-target tracking system is not necessary. We only want to know if there is at least one car in a dangerous situation. What we have done is to use a car position iterative computation with several stages. In the first one we use all the saliency map points of the whole image to give the car position estimation. It will be the correct position if there is only one car. When there are several targets in the system, the main goal is to detect the position of the car that is closer to us. For this purpose, we focus on the right area of the image, using the computed centroid position as left image boundary. We try to calculate a centroid of the limited image if we have significant features. Otherwise we choose the previously calculated value. We can repeat this computation several times until the estimation converges or we can use a fixed number of iterations. For our system we have used only three iterations to get adequate results.

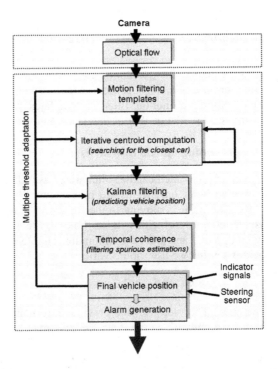

Fig. 2. Processing stages implemented for the rear-view mirror overtaking monitor

- Static overtaking: An overtaking car seems to stop (and it vanishes in the optical flow field) because it moves at our own velocity. In this situation we need to maintain the estimated car position during a certain time. We implement a simple memory system based on the Kalman filter which has been proved to be very useful in resolving many problems involved in predicting the position of moving targets [14], [15] and is even useful for complex motion prediction [16]. It predicts the car position based on the estimated centroid velocity and previous position. The process model used makes the assumption that velocity is constant and the noise can be seen as an acceleration of the object.

The processing stages are schematically described on Fig. 2. The final system could be improved based on the signal indicators steering information for the alarm generation and is planned as future work.

3   System Architecture and FPGA Resources Consumption

The global system architecture is represented on Fig. 3. We have implemented a very regular datapath (without requiring specific interrupt handling) with a very deep pipeline structure (more than 70 stages) in order to achieve high performance.

The synchronization between the different processing units (frame-grabber, motion processing core and tracking unit) is done using specific memory data buffers which solves the problem associated to the different clock frequencies. The computing platform used to ZBT SSRAM memories whose capabilities have been exploited using a specifically designed Memory Management Unit (MMU) described on [7] that minimizes data delays and latencies. It is especially useful for the temporal filtering stage of the motion processing unit because it enables the use of FIR temporal filters which provide more stable estimations.

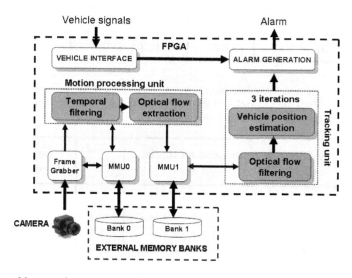

Fig. 3. Overtaking monitor system architecture. All the processing stages and interfaces have been implemented using the FPGA as element control and processing unit. The whole system requires two external memory banks, a camera and vehicle interfaces for the alarm generation and external inputs encoding vehicle information such as speed, steering or lateral indicators.

The memory interchange strategy makes use of delays between processing units as synchronization technique. This makes possible the design of a very deep pipeline processing structure without using branch predictions that would degrade the performance. The high system throughput is based on this deep pipeline and on the parallel scalar units of different stages designed according to the Lucas & Kanade algorithmic complexity. Well balanced units are used to achieve a final system throughput of one estimation per clock cycle.

The performance of the optical flow unit makes possible to take advantage of high frame-rate cameras reducing the speed range to be processed (more time resolution) and leading to accurate tracking. Each stage has been designed with customized bit-widths from 8 (in the first stage) to 19 bits (in the last stage) with fixed-point and floating point data representation depending on required precision. More details about this architecture are given in [7].

In the tracking unit the templates computation has been implemented using convolution kernels which collect the information of the neighbourhood of each pixel. The iterative process only requires some boundary image control to choose the area in which the centroid is computed. Finally, the Kalman filtering uses simple arithmetic operations which are computed once per frame.

Table 1. Basic stages gates resources consumption (results taken from the DK synthesizer [17])

Pipelined stages	NAND gates	FFs	Memory bits	Max clock frequency (MHz)
Interfaces + hardware controllers	65881	2363	18208	45
Motion Processing core	1145554	6529	516096	45,5
Tracking core	12087	751	0	71

Table 2. System resources required on a Virtex II XC2V6000-4 for the whole overtaking car system monitor (Mpps: mega-pixels per second and it's the maximum system processing clock frequency, EMB stands for *embedded memory blocks*)

Slices / (%)	EMBS / (%)	Embedded multipliers / (%)	Mpps	Image Resolution	Fps
8250 (24%)	29 (20%)	12 (8%)	45.49	640x480	148
10073 (29%)	29 (20%)	12 (8%)	45,5	640x480	148

The gates consumption estimation of the different subcircuits is given on Table 1. Note that the tracking unit, provided that is implemented using iterative computation, allows efficient resources sharing (thus representing a relatively inexpensive stage). On the other hand, the motion processing unit requires the intensive exploitation of the parallelism capabilities of the FPGA device (representing the most expensive module in terms of chip area). The interfaces and hardware controllers also require a considerable number of resources. Global system resources are shown in Table 2 after synthetization. It requires less than 2 million gates Virtex-II FPGA.. The tracking stage is processed sequentially only requiring 5% of the whole FPGA slices. This represents 17% of the global hardware resources consumed by the complete system.

4 Illustrative System Results

Evaluating the accuracy and efficiency of the system for real image sequences is not an easy task. Visual inspection of the results can give us some "quality estimations" to evaluate the performance but it is not a definitive "quality evaluation procedure". For our test we have considered that the tracking is done correctly if the estimated car position given by the algorithm belongs to the car's pixels. We have tested the algorithm in different overtaking car sequences provided by Hella [18] with different vehicles and whether conditions. At the beginning of the overtaking maneuvering, when the vehicle is very small our system confidence measure is not reached. This means that we have not enough information but we have already unreliable position estimations. This has been marked as black squares in the figures. When the car is larger, confidence measures begin to be reached but without temporal consistency and, finally, the system is able to track accurately the vehicle until the end of the overtaking sequence. Reliable position is drawn in the figures using a white cross. For all the evaluated sequences, this situation is reached for very far distances of the overtaking car so the system performance is good for safe distances.

An important problem occurs when the overtaking car velocity is equal to our car velocity, so the relative vehicle velocity will be around zero. In this situation the Kalman filtering allows us to keep the car position but the confidence value will not be reached, as it is seen in Fig. 4. The system memory allows us to keep the car position under the confidence threshold (see black square in the third frame). Alert signal system can use the estimation position and memory consistency to decide if we are in a dangerous situation or not.

Fig. 4. Overtaking with relative static situation with a black car in a shinny day. Sequence recorded using a conventional CCD camera.

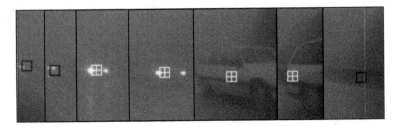

Fig. 5. Car in a foggy and rainy day. Sequence recorded using a high dynamic range camera.

Fig. 6. Car in a cloudy day. The car moves with the lights switched off. Sequence recorded using a high dynamic range camera.

In different whether and light conditions the kind of camera sensor is crucial and strongly motivates the use of high dynamic range cameras. The sequence of Fig. 5 and 6 tests our system capability for very low contrast sequences. The weather conditions in the sequence of Fig. 5 are really bad, in these situations lights become a very important source of information. Here the system needs closer cars to reach the confidence value to begin the car tracking reliably. In Fig. 6 we test the robustness of the system to low contrast scenarios. This sequence has more contrast but the car has switched off the lights. As it can be seen the results are correct.

The sequence of Fig. 7 shows a complex scene. Several cars are doing the overtaking in a highway. Each car is numbered using brackets. The figure shows different frames of the sequence and the dangerous car position estimations. As we explained in section 3.4 the system only marks the closest car (the most dangerous in the scene). One important problem occurs when we have multiple lanes. Motion information from monocular viewing can not give us information about car distance so it is difficult to know in which lane is detected the approaching car. We can use the road white lines to do that but the important issue is to be able to discriminate whether the situation is dangerous or not. Our system is useful if it prevents us of changing lane when another vehicle is present in a dangerous situation. This problem will be addressed in the future.

In this figure we can see the car estimation inertia. It should be noted that when the system looks for a new car, the estimation is over the confidence threshold but in a wrong position. This occurs because the saliency map obtained from the optical flow has reliable information about the car position but the Kalman filter needs two or

Fig. 7. Multiple cars overtaking in a highway in a cloudy day. Numbers above the cars are used to facilitate interpreting the scene. Sequence recorded using a high dynamic range camera.

three frames to update its parameters. We can use a more complex model for the car tracking but, thinking in hardware implementation of an embedded system, it can represent an unnecessary computation overload, since for a real time system that computes 25 frames/s this delay of the alert signal is not significant.

5   Conclusions

We present a monitor system to track the overtaking cars using the rear-view mirror perspective. Basically, we use two steps, first we compute the optical flow using a high parallel and superpipelined optical flow system that gives us a robust method for estimating the motion cues. The second step generates a saliency map that represents reliably car points that are used to compute the overtaking car position.

The results shown are very promising, because the system is very robust and stable, even for very difficult image sequences with bad visibility conditions. The utilization of FPGA technology fits quite well the necessities of automotive technology due to the reconfigurability and scalability of these devices.

Future work will address the integration of the vehicle signals into the alarm generation decision unit and also will address the topic of how alerting the driver. We also plan to address the scalability of the system in the future to enable its implementation on smaller devices.

Acknowledgements

This work was supported by the Spanish National Project DEPROVI (DPI2004-07032), by the EU grant DRIVSCO (IST-016276-2).

References

1. Apostoloff, N., Zelinsky, A.: Vision In and Out of Vehicles: Integrated Driver and Road Scene Monitoring. Int. J. of Robotics Research, 23: 4-5, (2004), pp. 513-538.
2. Dagan, E., Mano, O., Stein, G.P., Shashua, A.: Forward collision warning with a single camera. IEEE Intelligent Vehicles Symposium, 14-17 (2004), pp. 37-42.
3. Mota, S., Ros, E., Díaz, J., Tan, S., Dale, J., Johnston, A.: Detection and tracking of overtaking cars for driving assistance. Early Cog. Vision Workshop, Isle of Skye, Scotland, UK, 28 May- 1 June, (2004). (http://www.cn.stir.ac.uk/ecovision-ws/schedule.php).
4. Mobileye N.V. Blind Spot Detection and Lane Change Assist (BSD/LCA). Web link: http://www.mobileye.com/general.shtml.
5. Volvo BLIS system. Web link: http://www.mynrma.com.au/blis.asp.
6. Ficosa Digital blind spot detector. Web link: http://www.ficosa.com/eng/home_noticiaseventos.htm.
7. Díaz, J., Ros, E., Mota, S., Rodríguez-Gomez, R.: Highly parallelized architecture for image motion estimation. LNCS, Int. Workshop on Applied Reconfigurable Computing, ARC2006, Delft, Netherlands March 1-3, 2006. (accepted for publication).
8. Lucas B., Kanade T.: An Iterative Image Registration Technique with Applications to Stereo Vision. In Proc. DARPA Image Understanding Workshop, (1981), pp. 121-130.
9. Barron. J., Fleet, D.J., Beauchemin, S.S.: Performance of Optical Flow Techniques. IJCV 12:1, 1994, pp. 43-77.
10. Díaz, J., Ros, E., Ortigosa, E. M. and Mota, S.: FPGA based real-time optical-flow system. IEEE Trans. on Circuits and Systems for Video Technology, vol. 16: 2, (2006) pp. 274-279.
11. McCane, B., Novins, K., Crannitch D. and Galvin B.: On Benchmarking Optical Flow. Computer Vision and Image Understanding, vol. 84, (2001) pp. 126–143.
12. Liu, H.C., Hong, T.S., Herman, M., Camus, T., and Chellappa, R.: Accuracy vs. Efficiency Trade-offs in Optical Flow Algorithms. CVIU., vol.72, 3, (1998) pp. 271-286.
13. Lim, S., Apostolopoulos, J.G., Gamal, A.E.: Optical flow estimation using temporally oversampled video. IEEE Trans. on Image Processing, vol. 14:8, (2005), pp. 1074-1087.
14. Dellaert F., Thorpe C.: Robust car tracking using Kalman filtering and Bayesian templates. In Proceedings of SPIE: Intelligent Transportation Systems, vol. 3207, (1997).
15. Gao, J., Kosaka, A., Kak, A. C.: A multi-Kalman filtering approach for video tracking of human-delineated objects in cluttered environments. Computer Vision and Image Understanding, 99:1, (2005) pp. 1-57.
16. Jung, S.-K., Wohn, K.-Y.: 3-D tracking and motion estimation using hierarchical Kalman filter. IEE Proc.-Vis. Image Signal Process, 144 :5, (1997) pp. 293 – 298.
17. Celoxica company. Web site and products information available at: www.celoxica.com.
18. Dept. of predevelopment EE-11, Hella KG Hueck & Co., Germany, www.hella.de.

Design of Asynchronous Embedded Processor with New Ternary Data Encoding Scheme

Je-Hoon Lee, Eun-Ju Choi, and Kyoung-Rok Cho

Dept. of Computer and Communication Eng., Chungbuk Nat'l Univ.,
San 12, Gaeshin-Dong, Cheongju-City, Chungbuk-Do, Rep. of Korea
{leejh, ejchoi}@hbt.chungbuk.ac.kr, krcho@cbucc.chungbuk.ac.kr

Abstract. This paper presents a low-power implementation of the asynchronous 8051 processor, called A8051 and it employs a new data encoding method, RT/NRT encoding, to reduce switching activities. The paper focuses on power analysis of the proposed data encoding based on the experimental design of A8051. The proposed data encoding method is devised to meet the DI assumption using Ternary logic. This method reduces not only the number of wires but also the switching activities. In terms of switching activities, the proposed ternary encoding can reduce 26% comparing to conventional ternary encoding. A8051 using RT/NRT encoding shows 24% higher instruction per energy metric comparing to A8051 using dual-rail encoding.

1   Introduction

Previous research indicates that asynchronous processors are promising alternatives to synchronous processors to reduce power [1–9]. In the past, many implementations of asynchronous processors have been evaluated. The asynchronous counterpart to the ARM processor, AMULET3, and a 32-bit processor TITAC-2 demonstrated the advantages of asynchronous design methodology [2,3]. There are asynchronous CISC processor like a Lutonium and A8051 [8,9].

In asynchronous design, there are two types of delay models depending on whether or not both wire and gate delays are known: The DI (delay-insensitive) delay model and the bounded-delay model. The DI delay model assumes that an asynchronous circuit operates regardless of the gate and wire delays. Thus, the DI delay model does not require the precise latency of each circuit module and wiring delay. However, it requires a specified data encoding for generating a completion signal that indicate that execution has completed for each module. To generate the completion signal, various data encoding schemes have been introduced, such as a dual-rail, 1-of-4, and M-of-N encoding [10–13]. However, these encoding schemes need either dual data lines to generate completion signals or more switching activities than the bounded delay model.

Recently, a new data encoding method using MVL (multi-value logic) logic was introduced [14–16], which needs smaller number of data lines because it has an intermediate value to represent the invalid state. However, it does not reduce switching activities on the data communication comparing to 1-of-4 data

S. Vassiliadis et al. (Eds.): SAMOS 2006, LNCS 4017, pp. 395–405, 2006.
© Springer-Verlag Berlin Heidelberg 2006

encoding. For instance, the MiniMIPS microprocessor used 1-of-4 codes extensively, cutting the switching activity in half comparing to the classical dual-rail encoding [17]. The classical ternary encoding conveys 2 bits of information using 4 half-swings as opposed to the two full-swings that would be required if 1-of-4 encoding were chosen.

In this paper, we devise a new ternary encoding scheme, called RT(return to ternary)/NRT(non-return to ternary) to reduce the number of switching activities compared with the classical ternary encoding. We adapt this encoding scheme to the experimental design, A8051, to evaluate how much this encoding scheme can reduce the power dissipation. A8051 is a previously designed our implementation of an asynchronous 8051 processor [9]. It uses dual-rail data encoding and it was implemented using Hynix 0.35-μm CMOS technology and its performance analysis was discussed in [9]. The new version, A8051v2 uses RT/NRT data encoding scheme instead of dual-rail encoding one. Both versions of A8051 have a same architecture and implemented using the same fabrication technology, Hynix 0.35-μm CMOS technology. The only difference is the encoding scheme that is adapted in A8051. Since A8051v2 is ready for fabrication, the power analysis of A8051v2 was simulated using post layout extractions and the performance and power consumption of both processors were compared.

RT/NRT encoding using MVL is used to reduce switching activities. It has three logic levels; the logical high and the logical low represent the valid data '1' and '0,' respectively, while an intermediate value represents the invalid data, *spacer*. This reduces the number of data lines and diminishes the amount of switching activities. Our results show that this encoding scheme leads in 26% reduction in switching activities and achieves 24% power reduction compared to the conventional ternary encoding.

This paper is organized as follows. Section 2 describes the features of the proposed A8051. Section 3 discusses the features of RT/NRT data encoding. Section 4 presents the experimental results and analysis of the power reduction for each proposed method. Finally, Section 5 concludes the paper.

2   Features of the Proposed A8051

Intel 8051 is probably the most popular embedded processor used in controllers for industrial systems because of its small size and low cost. There are many synchronous and asynchronous counterparts to Intel 8051 [6–9,19–21]. Lutonium is a latest version of asynchronous 8051 [8], which shows performance 200MIPS at 1.8V. The A8051 shows average performance 75.1 MIPS at 3.3V. It has 255 instructions and is fully compatible with the ISA of Intel 8051. However, there are many differences in respect to the instruction execution scheme and the system architecture [9].

First, A8051 has a simpler instruction execution scheme compared to Intel 8051. Some instructions in Intel 8051 can access both register and memory for operands and destinations within an instruction cycle. These instructions need 2 or 4 machine cycles cause redundant activities during the instruction cycle

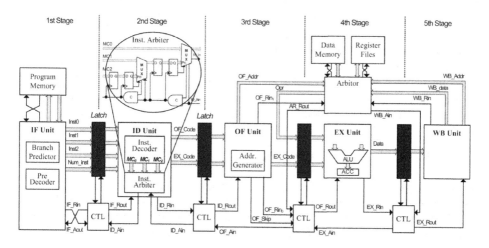

Fig. 1. The proposed architecture of A8051

to keep the pipeline regulation of instruction. These redundant activities lead to pipeline stalls when the second machine cycle of these instructions are executed in the pipeline [19]. The proposed instruction execution scheme of A8051 eliminates the unnecessary stage operation in the instruction cycle, and instead replaces the repetition of the entire machine cycle to the local repetition of OF (operand fetch) and EX (execution) stages. The ISA of A8051 is divided into seven groups according to the execution scheme.

Secondly, A8051 also employs a flexible pipeline architecture that reduces the unnecessary operations caused by the complicated pipelining. A8051 has five pipeline stages as shown in Fig. 1. Since all instructions do not require all pipeline stages, A8051 accompanies stage skipping to skip some of the stages that do not need any operations. There are two types of stage skipping. The first type is early termination of pipeline that occurs when the remaining stages are not necessary to complete the operation. The second type involves skipping only one stage, especially the OF stage. It can be skipped the redundant stages instead of operating these stages. The skipping stage makes the stage have no work to a transparent stage.

For example, some instructions do not need to fetch operands from either memory or register file. In this case, OF Unit asserts *OF_Skip* signal goes to high instead of generating an address for the operand as shown in Fig. 1. It indicates that there will be no operand from memory. Additionally, A8051 allows multi-cycle operations in the OF and EX stages to avoid pipeline hazards. Multi-cycle instructions are replaced two or three microinstructions to perform the subsequent pipeline stages repeatedly. These micro instructions are issued simultaneously to instruction arbiter. Instruction Arbiter can transfer these microinstructions to the subsequent pipeline stages, OF unit, in regular order reducing the number of stages to be executed.

Finally, each stage in A8051 communicates using the four-phase handshaking protocol with CTL and Latch as shown in Fig. 1. The architecture in Fig. 1 is based on the DI delay model using the proposed ternary data encoding. To adapt the proposed data encoding scheme to A8051, we modified the handshaking blocks and we add IVD(intermediate value detector), TVT(ternary value transmitter), and ZD(zero detector) logics. We also modified the combinational logics to adequate a MVL logics.

3   RT/NRT Data Encoding

In this paper, an asynchronous encoding method using a MVL is proposed to reduce not only the number of wires but also the switching activities. Furber and Mukaidono also introduce a ternary data encoding to design asynchronous circuit with DI model, which can reduce the number of data lines [5–7]. However, it increases the switching activities compared with 1-of-4 encoding. Thus, this paper proposes RT/NRT encoding to reduce switching activities without violating the DI assumption. This section presents the features of RT/NRT data encoding and how can it save the power.

3.1   Data Encoding Methods for DI Asynchronous Circuit

DI asynchronous circuits assume that the circuit designer do not know amount of the gate delay and wire delay. Figure 2 shows the handshaking model for DI asynchronous circuits. Each module uses a handshaking protocol to communicate with other modules that needs a completion signal of each module. This is major difference between the asynchronous circuit with the DI delay model and the bounded delay model. Fig. 3 shows data encoding schemes for DI circuits [10–16]. Data encoding scheme decides a number of data lines and signal transitions for handshaking. For example, both dual-rail and 1-of-4 encoding schemes require 2n wires for transferring n-bit data. 1-of-4 encoding scheme can reduce switching activities by 50% compared to the conventional dual-rail encoding. However, it also needs double wires compared to the bundled data asynchronous circuit [11]. To reduce the number of wires, the ternary data encoding scheme is used because it only requires n wires for transferring n-bit data [14–17].

Thus, we employ ternary encoding to save data lines. In addition, we modify it to reduce the switching activities. The proposed RT/NRT ternary encoding is

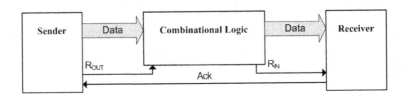

Fig. 2. Handshaking model for DI circuit

Information bit	D	D̄
Invalid	0	0
Valid '0'	0	1
Valid '1'	1	0
Not used	1	1

(a) Dual-rail

Information bits	Code
Invalid	0000
Valid '00'	0001
Valid '01'	0010
Valid '01'	0100
Valid '11'	1000

(b) 1-of-4

Information bit	D
Intermediate	V_I
Valid '0'	V_L
Valid '1'	V_H

(c) Ternary

Fig. 3. Various data encoding scheme

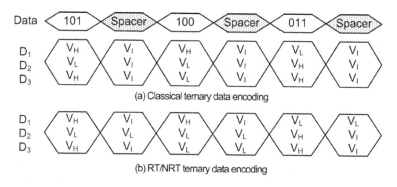

(a) Classical ternary data encoding

(b) RT/NRT ternary data encoding

Fig. 4. Comparison between classical ternary and RT/NRT ternary data encoding

similar with a conventional ternary in terms of using three logical levels such as 0, 1, and intermediate value, V_I. V_H represents valid data '1', V_L represents valid data '0', and V_I represents invalid data, i.e., *spacer*. The only difference between the classical ternary encoding and the proposed ternary encoding depends on whether all the data lines transit to intermediate value or not. In the conventional ternary encoding, after the valid data transfer is complete, the data lines must transit to intermediate value to represent invalid state, *spacer*. When all the data lines transit to intermediate value, the receiver identifies this as the invalid state as shown in Fig. 4(a). However, in the proposed RT/NRT data encoding, not all the data lines transit to intermediate value because the receiver can identified the validity of data transfers when more than one data transition to intermediate value occurs as shown in Fig. 4(b). In the RT/NRT encoding scheme, data lines that transfer zeros do not change to the intermediate value, which reduces switching activities. That is to say, when the sender transfers logical data '1' and then receives an acknowledgement signal from the receiver, the data transit to logic value, V_I that indicates a *spacer* state. In contrast, when the sender transfer logical '0' data and then receives an acknowledgement signal from the receiver, the data always remains as '0' as shown in Fig. 4. However, the receiver can identify exactly when data becomes the invalid. In the conventional

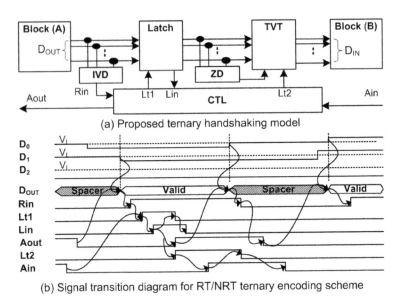

(a) Proposed ternary handshaking model

(b) Signal transition diagram for RT/NRT ternary encoding scheme

Fig. 5. The handshaking model and timing diagram of RT/NRT ternary encoding scheme

ternary encoding scheme, the receiver transfers data as an invalid data when all data received transits to the intermediate value. In the proposed encoding scheme, the receiver transfers data as an invalid data when more than one data lines changes to the intermediate value. Therefore, switching activity is reduced without violating the DI assumption. It is an exception condition that all of transferring data are zero because it is impossible to determine the validity of them. In this case, all data line transit logic level V_I the same as in the classical ternary encoding scheme.

Figure 5 illustrates the 2-phase handshaking model and timing diagram for the controller. The combinational blocks A and B communicate based on this protocol. The output of Block A is validated by asserting *Rin* high, which forces the latch to store the current output by activating *Lt1*. After the latch saves the valid output of Block A and the TVT (ternary value transmitter) logic outputs the data, the completion signal *Ain* returns to an initial state, *spacer*. The send data procedure is *data valid* → *Rin*↑ → *Lt1*↑ → *Lin*↑ → *Aout*↑ → *spacer*. Note that * ↑ and * ↓ means that signal * is rising and falling. Continuously the data path is refreshed with a procedure *spacer* → *Rin*↓ → *Aout*↓ → *data valid*. In addition, zero detectors needs to detect all zero inputs, which cause the only exception condition.

As shown in Fig. 6, the proposed ternary handshaking model requires additional blocks such as IVD (intermediate value detector) and TVT logic. The IVD logic is responsible for detecting the intermediate value, which identify whether or not the transferring data is valid. The TVT logic allows output to transition to logical high, logical low, and the intermediate value. If all the inputs are

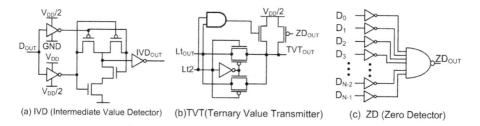

(a) IVD (Intermediate Value Detector)   (b)TVT(Ternary Value Transmitter)   (c) ZD (Zero Detector)

Fig. 6. Condition Detector Logic

valid, the receiver identifies that inputs are valid. In contrast, if there is one or more output are the intermediate value, the receiver considers the input data as invalid. The ZD logic is responsible to detect all zero inputs which cause the only exception. In this case, it is impossible to determine the validity of them. Thus, when all input data is all zeros, ZD logic makes the latch enable to output intermediate value, V_I after it receive an acknowledge signal 'high' from the next block.

Equation (1) shows the signal transition ratio for the asynchronous circuit using RT/NRT data encoding. As the data bandwidth increases, the ratio of signal transition decreases to 26%. These results indicate that the RT/NRT encoding scheme has the potential to reduce the switching activity by 26% compare with the classical ternary encoding scheme.

$$a_n = a_1 + \sum_{k=1}^{n-1}(b_1 \times r^{k-1}) = 12.5 + \sum_{k=1}^{n-1}(6.25 \times 0.5^{k-1})(n = 2, 3, 4, \cdots) \quad (1)$$

4   Power Analysis

A8051 was synthesized using Hynix 0.35-mum CMOS technology with a supply voltage of 3.3V. This processor has a complexity of about 105,000 transistors including 16KB memory and occupies 16 mm^2 silicon areas. The post-layout of A8051 was simulated using Nanosim from Synopsys. The simulation results of both performance and power consumption are obtained by executing the test-bench program, Dhrystone V2.1 [22].

Two different versions of A8051 were evaluated to show the efficiency of the RT/NRT encoding scheme. A8051v1 is designed based on the conventional dual-rail data encoding and A8051v2 is designed using the RT/NRT data encoding. A8051v1 resulted in an average performance of 75.5 MIPS and consumed an average power of 46.0mW with the test-bench program. A8051v2 resulted in an average performance of 75.1 MIPS and consumed an average power of 34.9mW. The performance of A8051vX is limited by the memory access speed. A8051v2 shows significant power saving even though it has the same performance with A8051v1.

The comparison results among A8051 and other counterparts are summarized in Table 1. Both performance and power consumption were evaluated with the

Table 1. Performance comparisons with other versions

Processor	Lutonium [18]	Asynch 80C51 [7]	CIP51 [21]	H8051 [20]	A8051v1 [9]	A8051v2
Pipeline	Asynchronous Pipeline	Asynchronous Non-pipeline	Synchronous Pipeline	Synchronous Pipeline	Asynchronous Pipeline	Asynchronous Pipeline
Tech.	0.18–μm	0.5–μm	0.35–μm	0.35–μm	0.35–μm	0.35–μm
Performance (MIPS)	200 MIPS at 1.8V	4 MIPS	23 MIPS	4 MIPS	75.5 MIPS	75.1 MIPS
MIPS/Watt	1,800 MIPS/W	444 MIPS/W	-	80 MIPS/W	1,641 MIPS/W	2,146 MIPS/W

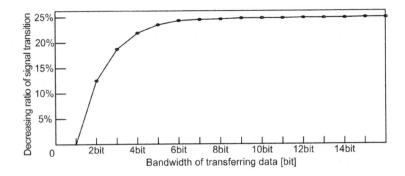

Fig. 7. Decreasing ratio of signal transition in RT/NRT scheme according to bandwidth of data

test-bench program. As shown in the Table. 1, A8051v2 runs about 18.8 times faster than H8051 with 48MHz clock and 3.3 times faster than CIP51 with 50MHz clock. For H8051, this result in energy per instruction metric of 80 MIPS/Watt, while A8051v2 gives 2,146 MIPS/Watt. Thus, A8051 shows 26.8 times higher energy per instruction metric than the synchronous non-pipelined counterpart of H8051. In addition, A8051v1 that uses conventional dual-rail data encoding scheme shows performance of 75.5 MIPS and 1,641 MIPS/Watt. On the other hand, A8051v2 using RT/NRT data encoding scheme achieves 24% power reduction. These results say that the proposed asynchronous pipeline architecture and data-encoding scheme save power and achieve higher performance compare to the synchronous and asynchronous counterparts. Also Lutonium [18] shows higher performance and MIPS/Watt than other synchronous designed counterparts.

Figure 7 shows the signal transition ratio for the circuit using RT/NRT data encoding. As the data bandwidth increases, the ratio of signal transition decreases to 26%. These results indicate that the RT/NRT encoding scheme has the potential to reduce the switching activity by 26% compare with the classical ternary encoding scheme. Comparison of the results of power consumption for data transmission scheme is shown in Fig. 8 that is on a ripple carry adder using variable data inputs. In terms of power consumption, the RCA with the proposed data encoding can reduce 45% comparing to conventional dual-rail reduction and it shows 25% power reduction comparing to the conventional ternary encoding.

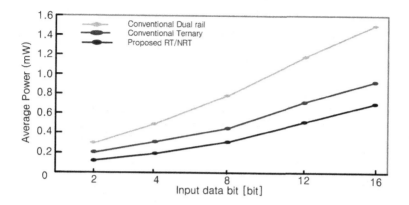

Fig. 8. Power consumption comparison among three schemes according to the number of input

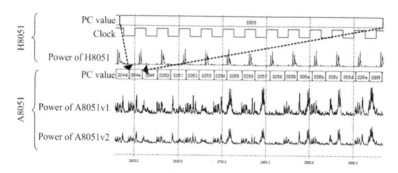

Fig. 9. Power consumption comparison between H8051 (synchronous) and A8051 (proposed)

From the power saving result of A8051v2 indicates that the RT/NRT data encoding scheme is better than the conventional dual-rail data encoding scheme as shown in Fig. 9. It can reduce not only switching activities but also the number of data lines. The performances of the two versions, A8051v1 and A8051v2, are almost the same. However, power consumptions of the two versions are 46.0mW for A8051v1 and 34.9mW for A8051v2, respectively. This means that the design with the RT/NRT encoding scheme consumes about 24% less power.

5   Conclusion

In this paper, a new design methodology for the asynchronous processor, A8051, was presented. The A8051 employ a new RT/NRT data encoding scheme, simplified control schemes, and well-tuned pipeline architecture, which enhances system performance. Power saving result of A8051v2 indicates that the RT/NRT data encoding scheme is better than the conventional dual-rail data encoding scheme. The performances of the two versions, A8051v1 and A8051v2, are almost the same. However, power consumptions of the two versions are 46.0mW for A8051v1 and 34.9mW for A8051v2, respectively. This means that the design with the RT/NRT encoding scheme consumes about 24% less power. Consequently, the proposed RT/NRT data encoding reduce the number of wires by half compared with the conventional dual-rail and 1-of-4 encoding. Our results show that the performance of A8051 is 18.8 times faster than a conventional synchronous design. In terms of power, the RT/NRT data-encoding scheme results in 24% power saving.

Acknowledgments

This work was supported by the Korea Research Foundation Grant funded by the Korea Government (MOEHRD, Basic Research Promotion Fund) (KRF-2005-214-D00101) and the Regional Research Centers Program of the Ministry of Education & Human Resources Development in Korea.

References

1. M. B. Josephs, S. M. Nowick and C. H. Van Berkel, "Modeling and design of asynchronous circuits," Proc. IEEE, vol. 87, pp.234–242, Feb. 1999.
2. S. B. Furber, J. D. Garside and D. A. Gilbert, "AMULET3 : a high-performance self-timed ARM microprocessor," Proc. ICCD'98, pp.247–252, 1998.
3. T. Nanya, et al., "ITAC-2 : an asynchronous 32-bit microprocessor based on scalable delay-insensitive model," Proc. ICCD97, pp.288–294, 1997.
4. M. Renaudin, P. Vivet, and F. Robin, "ASPRO-216 : a standard-cell QDI 16-bit RISC asynchronous microprocessor," Proc. 4th Int'l Symp. On Advanced Research in Asynchronous Circuits and Systems, pp.22–31, 1998.
5. C. Kelly, V. N. Ekanayake, and R. Manohar, "SNAP : A sensor-network synchronous processor," Proc. Int'l Symp. On Advanced Research in Asynchronous Circuits and Systems, pp. 24–35, 2003.
6. J. M. C. Tse and D. P. K. Lun, "ASYMPU : A fully asynchronous CISC microprocessor," Proc. ISCAS, pp. 1816–1819, 1997.
7. H. V. Gageldonk, K. V. Berkel, A. Peeters, D. Baumann, D. Gloor, and G. Stegmann, "An asynchronous low-power 80C51 microcontroller," Proc. Int'l Symp. On Advanced Research in Asynchronous Circuits and Systems, pp. 96–107, 1998.
8. A. J. Martin, M. Nystrom, K. Papadantonakis, P. I. Penzes, P. Prakash, C. G. Wong, J. Chang, K. S. Ko, B. Lee, E. Ou, J. Pugh, E. Talvala, J. T. Tong, and A. Tura, "The Lutonium : sub-nanojoule asynchronous 8051 microcontroller," Proc Int'l Symp. Advanced Research in Asynchronous Circuits and Systems, pp. 14–23, 2003.
9. J. -H. Lee, Y. H. Kim, and K. -R. Cho, "Design of a fast asynchronous embedded CISC microprocessor, A8051," IEICE trans. on Electron, vol. E87-C, no. 4, pp. 527–534, Apr. 2004.
10. S. Hauck, "Asynchronous design methodologies: an overview," Proc. IEEE, vol.83, no.1, pp.69–93, Jan. 1995.

11. J. Bainbridge, and S. B. Furber, "Delay insensitive system-on-chip interconnect using 1-of-4 data encoding," Proc. Int'l Symp. On Advanced Research in Asynchronous Circuits and Systems, pp. 118–126, Apr. 2001.
12. Renaudin, "Generalized 1-of-M QDI asynchronous adder," Proc 3rd Acid-WG Workshop, pp. 27–28, Jan. 2003.
13. W.J. Bainbridge, W.B. Toms, D.A. Edwards, S.B. Furber, "Delay-Insensitive, Point-to-Point Interconnect using m-of-n codes," Proc. Int'l Symp. On Advanced Research in Asynchronous Circuits and Systems, pp. 132–140, May 2003.
14. R. Mariani, R. Roncella, R. saletti, and P. Terreni, "On the realization of delay-insensitive asynchronous circuits with CMOS ternary logic," Proc. Int'l Symp. On Advanced Research in Asynchronous Circuits and Systems, pp. 54–62, 1997.
15. Y. Nagata and M. Mukaidono, "B-ternary asynchronous digital system under relative delay," IEICE Trans. Information and System, vol. E86-D, no.5, pp. 910–919, May 2003.
16. T. Felicijan and S. B. Furber, "An asynchronous ternary logic signaling system," IEEE trans. on VLSI, vol, 11, no. 6, pp. 1114–1119, Dec. 2003.
17. A. Efthymiou and J. D. Garside, "Adaptive pipeline structures for speculation control," Proc Int'l Symp. Advanced Research in Asynchronous Circuits and Systems, pp.46–55, 1999.
18. A. J. Martin et al, "The design of an asynchronous MIPS R3000," Proc. Advanced Research in VLSI, pp. 164–181, 1997.
19. Intel, Microprocessor and Peripheral Handbook, 1987.
20. Hynix, HMS99C52 Datasheet, 2003.
21. Cygnal, C8051F0xx Family Datasheet, 2002.
22. W. J. Price, "A benchmark tutorial," IEEE Micro, vol. 9, pp. 28–43, Oct. 1989.

Hardware-Based IP Lookup Using n-Way Set Associative Memory and LPM Comparator

SangKyun Yun

Department of Computer and Telecommunications Engineering, Yonsei University
234 Magiri, Heungeop, Wonju, Gangwon, 220-710, Korea
skyun@yonsei.ac.kr

Abstract. IP lookup process becomes the bottleneck of packet transmission as IP traffic increases. Hardware-based IP lookup is desirable for high-speed router. However, the IP lookup schemes using an index-based table are not efficient due to heavy prefix expansion. In this paper, efficient hardware-based IP lookup schemes using n-way set associative memory and a LPM comparator is proposed. It reduces memory requirements to about 50% or below compared with previous scheme and provides faster updating speed. It also completes an IP routing lookup with two memory accesses.

1 Introduction

The increased bandwidth in the Internet puts great demands on network routers. The IP lookup remains one of the major performance bottlenecks for faster packet processing in routers. Since the introduction of classless interdomain routing (CIDR) in 1993 [1], the IP lookup has been designed based on the longest prefix matching (LPM) algorithm that has more computational overhead than an exact match operation. For high speed routers, the LPM problem has been solved with hardware-based schemes.

While designing the hardware-based IP lookup scheme, reducing routing table space and ensuring fast routing table reconstruction are important design considerations. Reducing routing table space enables the IP lookup engine to be implemented using recent FPGAs including memory blocks. In this paper, we propose a hardware-based IP lookup scheme requiring smaller memory space and faster updating speed than previous hardware-based scemes.

2 Previous Schemes and Motivations

2.1 Previous Schemes

Hardware-based IP lookup schemes include indirect table lookup, direct ternary CAM (TCAM) match, a combination of two previous schemes, table lookup using hashing, and finite-state-machine (FSM) based lookup.

In indirect table lookup schemes [2,3], a routing table is divided into two parts: the segment table and the next hop arrays (NHA). The segment table consists of 2^{16} entries indexed with 16 leftmost bits of an prefix. An entry of the segment table stores either next hops of routes or pointers to the corresponding NHA. The NHA has next hops of

S. Vassiliadis et al. (Eds.): SAMOS 2006, LNCS 4017, pp. 406–414, 2006.

routes for destination IP addresses with prefix length > 16. The NHA is indexed with remaining rightmost bits of a prefix. The size of NHA depends on the length of the longest prefix within the segment and may be reduced by considering common bits of prefixes.

In TCAM schemes [4,5], a ternary content addressable memory(TCAM) is used as a forwarding table. TCAMs perform parallel search and can store "don't care" values in addition to 0's and 1's. The ternary capability of TCAMs makes them an attractive solution for the IP lookup based on the longest prefix matching. Although TCAM scheme achieves fast IP lookup without any prefix expansion, it has some shortcomings: small capacity, more power consumption, more cost, complicated updating. All these limit its usage.

A priority TCAM IP-routing lookup scheme proposed by Lin [6] is the combination scheme which consists of a compact IP routing lookup block and a priority TCAM block. The compact IP-routing lookup block processes the IP-routing entries with prefix length ≤ 24 and the priority TCAM block processes IP-routing entries with prefix length > 24. The compact IP-routing lookup block requires smaller index-based NHAs than other indirect table lookup schemes [2,3] by fully considering common bits of prefixes.

In table lookup scheme using hashing [7], hashing function reduces the memory requirement by taking the longer address and producing a shorter index field. However, this scheme requires parallel hashing in each prefix length and collision processing. In FSM-based lookup schemes [8,9], the IP lookup problem is translated into implementation of a finite state machine or binary decision diagram on reconfigurable hardware. However, it requires reconfigurable hardware that can be modified on the fly and the updating process is complex.

2.2 Motivations

Although the number of Internet hosts is growing exponentially, the routing prefixes with a router are still in sparse distribution. There are more than 100,000 routing prefixes over a total of 2^{16} segments in today's backbone router [10]. For most segments, there are fewer or even no routing prefixes. Only approximately 12% of all the segments have a NHA and approximately 55% of all NHAs have eight or less prefixes. This sparse distribution characteristic of prefixes makes index-based NHA schemes [2,3,6] inefficient in aspects of both memory requirement and updating speed.

For example, consider three prefixes 192.168.20/22, 192.168.72/23, and 192.168. 128/22 within a segment 192.168. The bit patterns from the 17th bit to the 24th bit of three prefixes are 000101**, 0100100* and 100000** where * denotes "don't care". Since the longest prefix length is 23 and the 19th bit is common, the NHA corresponding to segment 192.168 in Lin's scheme [6] has $64(= 2^6)$ entries in spite of only three prefixes. From the 17th bit to the 23th bit except the 19th bit of IP addresses is used as an index of the NHA. Index-based NHA schemes are also characterized by poor updating speed since each prefix corresponds to multiple NHA entries due to prefix expansion.

Therefore, a more efficient IP lookup scheme with regard to both the memory requirement and updating speed, is required.

3 Proposed IP Routing Scheme

In this section, we propose an efficient hardware-based IP lookup scheme using n-way set associative memory and a LPM comparator. The architecture for the proposed scheme consists of TCAM, a segment table, a NHA table, a LPM comparator, and glue logics as shown in Fig. 1. The proposed IP lookup scheme is based on the priority TCAM IP-routing lookup scheme proposed by Lin [6], but the NHA table is implemented using a n-way set-associative scheme like cache memory systems instead of index-based scheme.

In the proposed scheme, TCAM contains routing entries with a prefix length > 24 like in Lin's scheme . Routing entries with a prefix length $\leq$ 24 are stored in the segment table or the NHA table. The segment table contains 2^{16} entries, each of which represents a next-hop or a pointer to the corresponding NHA. If a segment has only a prefix with length 16, the segment table entry stores a next-hop; otherwise, it stores a pointer to the NHA.

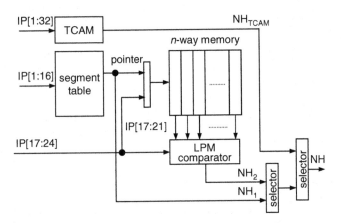

Fig. 1. Architecture for the proposed IP lookup scheme

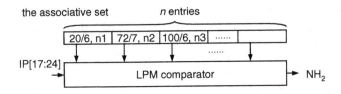

Fig. 2. The set-associative NHA scheme

The NHA table stores NHAs corresponding to segments. It is implemented in n-way memory, where n entries with the same address can be simultaneously accessed and the collection of them is called a set. Each IP address is associated with a set in the NHA table. Each NHA entry consists of two parts: a prefix/length and a next hop. Although the set-associative scheme requires longer entry width than the index-based scheme, it requires much smaller number of NHA entries because of few prefix expansions. During the IP lookup operation, the LPM comparator compares a destination IP address with n prefixes stored in the associative set in parallel and determines an entry with the longest matched prefix among them. Fig. 2 shows a corresponding NHA of segment 192.168 with three prefixes described in section 2.2

3.1   Construction of the NHA Table

Let $N(s)$ be the number of prefixes within a segment s. Let $p[x]$ and $p[x:y]$ be the xth bit and from the xth to the yth bits of the address p, respectively and let $p[x, y, \cdots, z]$ be the concatenation of $p[x]$, $p[y]$, $\cdots$, $p[z]$. The NHA size of a segment s is basically 2^k sets, where $k = \log_2(N(s)/n)$. In a NHA with 2^k sets, a prefix p is associated with a set selected by the k-bit set selection index which is part of $p[17:21]$. Each prefix entry is stored in an empty entry of the associative set. Some prefixes may be associated with multiple sets since some bits of the set selection index are don't care.

Let $|S_i|$ be the number of prefixes associated with a set i of a NHA. If $|S_i| > n$, a set i is called an overflow set. If there is an overflow set in a NHA, the NHA size must be increased until there is no overflow set. The set selection index for each NHA size has been determined by the simulation to reduce occurrences of overflow sets as follows: for 2, 4, 8, 16 and 32 sets, the set selection indexes are $p[19]$, $p[19:20]$, $p[18, 20:21]$, $p[17, 19:21]$, and $p[17:21]$, respectively.

Table 1. Routing prefixes of a segment $A.B$ and its NHA construction

prefix/length	$p[17:24]$	NHA with 2 sets	NHA with 4 sets
A.B.4/24	00000100	set selection index= $p[19]$	set selection index=$p[19:20]$
A.B.5/24	00000101		
A.B.12/22	000011**	set 0 = {4/24, 5/24, 12/22,	set 0 = {4/24, 5/24, 12/22,
A.B.13/24	00001101	13/24, 64/22, 128/19,	13/24, 64/22, 128/19}
A.B.64/22	010000**	24/21, 80/23, 216/23}	set 1 = {128/19, 24/21,
A.B.128/19	100*****	set 1 = {32/20}	80/23, 216/23}
A.B.24/21	00011***		set 2 = {32/20}
A.B.80/23	0101000*	set 0 is an overflow set	set 3 = { }
A.B.216/23	1101100*		
A.B.32/20	0010****		128/19 has two entries

For example, consider the construction of 8-way set associative NHA of segment $A.B$ with prefixes listed in Table 1. The NHA size is initially 2 sets because segment $A.B$ has 10 prefixes. However, set 0 is an overflow set since it has nine prefixes and The NHA size must be increased. In the NHA with 4 sets, there is no overflow set and the construction is completed. An entry 128/19 is stored into both set 0 and set 1 since $p[20]$ is don't care.

If an NHA has a few prefixes, many of n entires in a set are not used. For additional reduction in memory space, a segment with a few prefixes is allowed to use part of an associative set. The corresponding entries of a small NHA with $1/2^k$ set are selected by rightmost k bits of $p[12:16]$.

3.2 Lookup Operation

For an incoming packet with a destination IP address p, $p[1:16]$ selects an entry of the segment table. If the entry contains a next hop, the next hop is returned, and the lookup operation is completed. Otherwise, it contains a NHA pointer/size and the lookup operation in the NHA table is performed. The address of an associative set is the concatenation of the NHA pointer and the set selection index. Each IP address is associated with only one set in the NHA table since an IP address has no don't care bit. $p[17:24]$ is simultaneously compared with n prefixes in an associative set and the longest prefix matched prefix is determined. This operation is performed in n-way memory and a LPM comparator. If a matched entry is found, the LPM comparator outputs the next hop of the entry. Otherwise, the LPM comparator outputs the default next hop.

The destination IP address is also compared with TCAM entries. If a matched entry is found in the TCAM, the result of the TCAM is chosen as the next hop by the selector. Otherwise, the result of the LPM comparator or the segment table is chosen.

3.3 Update Operation

When a route is updated or inserted, it is compared with all entries in its associative set. If a matched entry is found, the route is an updated route and replaces the matched entry. Otherwise, the route is an inserted route. If there is an empty entry in the associative set, the route is inserted into the empty entry; otherwise, the new NHA with double size is allocated and reconstructed.

When a route is deleted, it is compared with all entries in its associative set. If a matched entry is found, it is simply deleted. Otherwise, no operation is performed since there is no deleted route in the NHA. If an updated, inserted or deleted route is associated with multiple sets, this procedure is repeatedly performed for multiple associative sets.

3.4 Entry Formats

The entry formats of the segment table and the NHA table in the proposed scheme are shown in Fig. 3. The pointer/size of the segment table entry and the prefix/length of the NHA table entry use compact formats, reducing the entry width.

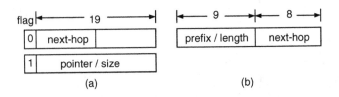

Fig. 3. The entry formats: (a) segment table entry (b) NHA table entry

A segment table entry consists of 1-bit flag and 19-bit NHA pointer/size. If the flag is 0, the pointer/size field is a next hop; otherwise, it represents a NHA pointer and the NHA size. Let (x, y) be the concatenation of x and y. The format of the pointer/size field is as follows.

1. If the NHA size is 2^k sets, the pointer/size field is $(ptr[16:k], 1 << k, 0)$, where $<<$ is shift left operator and thus, $1 << k$ is a $(k+1)$ bit value, $10\cdots0$
2. If the NHA size is part of a set, the pointer/size field is $(ptr[16:0], 1, 1)$. The NHA size is represented by rightmost bits of $ptr[16:0]$.

If the NHA size is 2^k sets $(k \geq 1)$, the pointer to the associative set is the concatenation of $ptr[16:k]$ and k bit set selection index. If the NHA size is equal to or less than a set, the NHA pointer is $ptr[16:0]$.

The NHA table entry consists of 9-bit prefix/length and 8-bit next hop. The 9-bit prefix/length represents the prefix and its prefix length in compact format as follows:

If the length of prefix p is m bits, the prefix/length field is $(p[17:m], 1 << (24-m))$.

For example, the prefix/length value of prefix $A.B.32/20$ $(0010****)$ is 001010000. A 9-bit prefix/length value of an NHA entry is converted into a 8-bit prefix and 8-bit prefix mask in the LPM comparator.

3.5 LPM Comparator

For a destination IP address, the LPM comparator compares IP[17:24] with n prefixes stored in the associative set in parallel and determines an entry with the longest matched prefix among them. Fig. 4 shows the architecture of the LPM comparator, which consists of n matched bit pattern generator, the longest prefix resolver, and a selector.

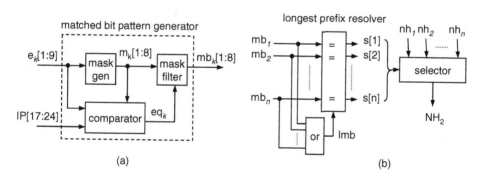

(a)   (b)

Fig. 4. The architecture of the LPM comparator

A matched bit pattern generator outputs a matched bit pattern by comparing an IP address with a prefix of each NHA entry. A mask generator outputs 8-bit bit mask, $m_k[1:8]$ from 9-bit prefix/length of the k-th NHA entry, $e_k[1:9]$ as follows:

$$m_k[j] = e_k[j+1] \vee e_k[j+2] \vee \cdots \vee e_k[9] \quad (j = 1, 2, \cdots, 8)$$

where $\vee$ is OR operator. For example, if a prefix/length e_k is 011010000, a bit mask m_k is 11110000. If $m_k[j]$ is 0, the j-th bit of the prefix is don't care. A comparator compares a prefix of the k-th NHA entry with the IP address in bitwise as follows:

$$cmp_k[j] = (e_k[j] \oplus IP[16+j]) \wedge m_k[j] \quad (j = 1, 2, \cdots, 8)$$

where $\oplus$ is exclusive-OR operator and $\wedge$ is AND operator. If the values in the j-th bit are not matched, $cmp_k[j]$ is 1. Since a don't care bit is a matched bit, if $m_k[j]$ is 0, then $cmp_k[j]$ is 0. If all bits of cmp_k are zero, eq_k is 1 and it means that the IP address is matched with the prefix of the k-th NHA entry.

A mask filter outputs the matched bit pattern mb_k of each NHA entry. A matched bit pattern represents the location of matched bits. For example, if mb_k is 11110000, matched bits are leftmost 4 bits, and if mb_k is 00000000, there is no matched bit. If eq_k is 1, mb_k is equal to m_k; otherwise mb_k is 0 since the IP address is not matched with the k-th entry.

The longest prefix resolver determines the location of the longest prefix entry by generating n bit selection signal $s[1:n]$, each bit of which corresponds to each NHA entry, from n matched bit patterns. Let 1^x0^y be the concatenation of x consecutive 1's and y consecutive 0's. A matched bit pattern is the form of $1^x0^{8-x}(x = 0, 1, \cdots, 8)$. The longest matched entry is an entry which generates a matched bit pattern with the largest x. The matched bit pattern of the longest matched prefix, lmb is the same as the result of bitwise OR operation of all matched bit patterns. The longest prefix resolver outputs n-bit selection signal $s[1:n]$ by comparing each matched bit pattern mb_k with the longest matched bit pattern lmb. If eq_k is 1 and mb_k is equal to lmb $s[k]$ is 1 and the k-th entry is the longest prefix matched entry; otherwise, $s[k]$ is 0.

A selector outputs the next hop of the longest prefix entry selected by the selection signal s from n next hops. If there is no matched entry, a selector outputs a default next hop.

4   Performance Evaluation

The performance of the proposed scheme and Lin's scheme is evaluated under realistic prefix data, obtained from the CIDR aggregated prefix routing table [10] in January 2005. Table 2 presents the characteristics of three prefix data sets and the NHA memory requirements for two schemes.

The memory requirements of the proposed scheme are obtained by simulation and are measured for four cases: 8-way, 16-way, 32-way, and 64-way set associative schemes. It can be seen that the memory requirements are reduced to approximately half or below

Table 2. Comparisons of NHA memory requirement

		AS1221	AS4637	AS6447
Prefixes		104,668	103,139	115,496
Nonempty segments		22,492	22,447	22,482
Segment with NHA		7,801	7,760	8,190
Prefixes with Length>24		217	1	1,485
Lin's scheme [5]		1149K	1144K	1205K
Proposed scheme	8-way set associative	571K	564K	638K
	16-way set associative	359K	351K	399K
	32-way set associative	304K	299K	336K
	64-way set associative	298K	295K	330K

of that of Lin's scheme, although the NHA entry size in the proposed scheme (17-bit) is larger than that in Lin's scheme (8-bit). Increasing the set associativity *n* decreases the memory requirement, but makes a LPM comparator more complex. A 16-way set associative scheme is a reasonable choice. In addition, the size of the segment table is also reduced since its entry size is the smaller (20-bit) than in Lin's method (32-bit).

Fig. 5 presents the distribution of NHA sizes in the proposed scheme using 16-way set associative memory. About 75% of NHAs is single set or less in size and this reduces the memory requirements.

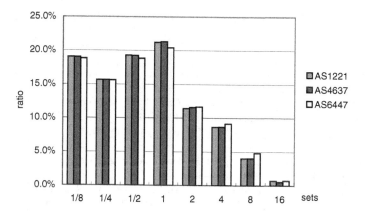

Fig. 5. The distribution of NHA sizes (16-way)

During lookup operation, the proposed scheme requires at most two memory accesses, where one is the segment table or TCAM and the other is the NHA table. Previous schemes are characterized by poor update speed since each prefix corresponds to multiple NHA entries due to heavy prefix expansion. In the proposed scheme, above 90% of all prefixes corresponds to a single set without prefix expansion and fast updating speed is achieved. However, the proposed scheme requires additional logic such as LPM comparator.

5   Conclusions

The routing prefixes with a router are still in sparse distribution, even as the rapid increase of Internet hosts is maintained. Previous IP routing schemes using an index-based NHA are inefficient in aspects of both memory requirement and updating speed, due to heavy prefix expansion. In this paper, a new hardware based IP lookup scheme using *n*-way set associative memory and LPM comparator is proposed. The LPM comparator compares an IP address with multiple prefixes in parallel and determines the longest matched entry. The proposed scheme can significantly reduce memory requirements to approximately 50% or below compared with Lin's scheme. In addition, it completes an IP lookup operation with at most two memory accesses and provides faster updating speed. Thus, the proposed scheme is an efficient hardware-based IP lookup scheme.

Acknowledgement

This work was supported by Yonsei University, Magi Research Fund, 2004.

References

1. Fuller, V., Li, T., Yu, J., Varadhan, K.: Classless inter-domain routing (CIDR): and address assignment and aggregation strategy, RFC1519 (1993)
2. Huang, N.F., Zhao, S.M.: A novel IP-routing lookup scheme and hardware architecture for multigigabit switching routers. IEEE J. Selected Areas in Communications 17 (1999) 1093–1104
3. Wang, P.C., Chan, C.T., Chen, Y.C.: High-performance IP routing table lookup. Computer Communications 25 (2002) 303–312
4. Ravikumar, V.C., Rabi, N.M.: TCAM architecture for IP lookup using prefix properties. IEEE Micro 24 (2004) 60–69
5. Akhbarizadeh, M.J., Nourani, M., Cantrell, C.D.: Prefix segregation scheme for a TCAM-based IP forwarding engine. IEEE Micro 25 (2005) 48–63
6. Lin, P.C., Chang, C.J.: A priority TCAM IP-routing lookup scheme. IEEE Communications Letters 7 (2003) 337–339
7. Lim, H., Seo, J., Jung, Y.: High speed IP address lookup architecture using hashing. IEEE Communications Letters 7 (2003) 502–504
8. Desai, M., Gupta, R., Karandikar, A., Saxena, K., Samant, V.: Reconfigurable finite-state machine based IP lookup engine for high-speed router. IEEE J. Selected Areas in Communications 21 (2003) 501–512
9. Sangireddy, R., Somani, A.K.: High-speed IP routing with binary decision diagrams based hardware address lookup engine. IEEE J. Selected Areas in Communications 21 (2003) 513–520
10. Huston, G.: CIDR report, http://www.cidr-report.org (2005)

A Flash File System to Support Fast Mounting for NAND Flash Memory Based Embedded Systems

Song-Hwa Park[1], Tae-Hoon Lee[1], and Ki-Dong Chung[2]

Dept. of Computer Science, Pusan National University,
Kumjeong-Ku, Busan 609-735, Korea
[1]{downy25, withsoul}@melon.cs.pusan.ac.kr,
[2]kdchung@pusan.ac.kr
http://apple.cs.pusan.ac.kr*

Abstract. In embedded systems, NAND flash memory is typically used as a storage medium because of its non-volatility, fast access time and solid-state shock resistance. However, it suffers from out-place-update, limited erase cycles and page based read/write operations. Flash file systems such as JFFS2 and YAFFS, allocate memory spaces using LFS (Log-structured File System) to solve these problems. Because of this, many pieces of a file are scattered through out flash memory. Therefore, these file systems should scan entire flash memory to construct the data structures during the mounting. This means that it takes a long time to mount such file systems on a large chip. In this paper, we design and propose a new flash memory file system which targets mobile devices that require fast mounting. We experimented on the file system performance and the results show that we improve the mounting time by 64%–76% as flash usage compared to YAFFS.

1 Introduction

Embedded computing systems such as mp3 player, digital camera and RFID reader should be able to provide an instant start-up time [1]. In these systems, flash memory is widely used as storage system because of its benefits. It is non-volatile, meaning that it retains data even after power is turned off and consumes relatively little power. In addition, flash memory offers fast access times and solid-state shock resistance. These characteristics explain the popularity of flash memory for embedded systems.

There are two major type of flash memory according to the gate type and structure of the memory cell: NOR flash and NAND flash. For NOR flash memory, the page size is typically 1 byte, meaning that each byte can be read and written individually. For NAND flash memory, on the other hand, the page size

---

* This work was supported by the Regional Research Centers Program (Research Center for Logistics Information Technology), granted by the Korean Ministry of Education & Human Resources Development.

S. Vassiliadis et al. (Eds.): SAMOS 2006, LNCS 4017, pp. 415–424, 2006.

is typically 512 bytes, so it offers higher read/write performance than NOR flash memory. As a result, it is widely used as the secondary storage systems [2].

Despite the advantages of NAND flash memory, it has several hardware characteristics that make straightforward replacement of existing storage media difficult. Firstly, it suffers from inability that does not provide the update-in-place. In ordinary writing, it can transit from one state (called initial state) to another, but it can't make the reverse transition. As a result, block erase operation is required for rewriting the contents of a block. Secondly, it can not be read or programmed smaller than a page (e.g. 512B, 2KB). Lastly, blocks have limited endurance due to wear out on the insulating oxide layer around the charge storage mechanism used to store data. Therefore the erase operation must be done evenly to all blocks to avoid wearing out specific blocks which would affect the usefulness of the entire flash memory. This is usually named as wear leveling or cycle leveling [3][4].

As the conventional file systems cannot be applied directly to flash memories due to above mentioned limitations, new flash file systems such as JFFS2 [5] and YAFFS [6] were developed. JFFS2 is a journaling file systems based on flash memory that keep metadata to avoid errors and corruption. Files are broken into several smaller nodes, which contain the actual data. When update operation occurs, a new node is created and the updated data is written to the node. Therefore, JFFS2 must scan the entire flash memory space at mounting time to collect the scattered data. Then the collected data are reorganized in RAM. It takes a long time and memory consumption is enormous. YAFFS is the first file system that is designed specifically for NAND flash memory and outperforms JFFS2 with respect to mount time and amount of memory consumption. However, it also has a long mounting time problem because it scans the spare areas of every block to check validation of data. In cases of JFFS2 and YAFFS, the flash mount time heav-ily depends on the flash capacity and stored data size.

Since flash chip capacity is increasing every year, the flash mounting time will soon become the most dominant reason of the delay of system start-up time [8]. Our goal is to design and implement a fast NAND flash file system. To support fast mounting, we keep the location of the required data such as block information, metadata during the mounting.

This paper is organized as follows. In Section 2, we describe JFFS and YAFFS, the flash file systems, respectively. In Section 3, we present our proposed file system to support fast mounting. The evaluation results are presented in Section 4, and the con-clusion is shown in Section 5.

2   NAND Flash File Systems

In this section, we introduce the flash file system, JFFS2 and YAFFS.

2.1   JFFS2

JFFS was originally developed for the 2.0 kernel by Axix Communications in Sweden. It is a journaling file system designed for small NOR ($\leq$ 32MB) flash memory. David Woodhouse and others improved JFFS and developed JFFS2 which addresses the issues of JFFS by providing compression, automatic leveling and NAND flash mem-ory support [9].

JFFS2 consists of simply a list of nodes and log entries. Each node contains actual data to be inserted into files or delete instructions and a log entry contains information about write operations on file. Nodes are written to flash sequentially starting at the first block. When update operation occurs, the updated data is written to other place since JFFS2 is based on LFS (Log-structured File System) to solve the out-of-place problem [8]. This makes the related nodes and log entries on the same file scattered throughout the flash memory. In order to collect the scattered data, JFFS2 scans all nodes and log entries to construct file system at mounting time. Also it checks the consistency and executes a garbage collection thread during the mounting. The gar-bage collection thread copies valid nodes in one block to another block, then erases blocks to get free space. Therefore, JFFS takes a long mounting time and consumes large amount of main memory.

Even though JFFS2 solved and improved the problems of JFFS, it has still some problems when applied to the NAND flash memory. Firstly, the arbitrary size of jour-naling nodes causes a fragmentation of pages on NAND flash memory. Secondly, JFFS2 has faced the serious problems such as slow mounting and wasteful memory consump-tion as NAND flash chips become larger. To overcome these problems, the JFFS3 [8] draft was issued and developed.

2.2   YAFFS [6][11]

YAFFS (Yet Another Flash Filing System) is the first file system designed specif-ically for NAND flash memory. It was designed and developed by Charles Man-ning of the company Aleph One. Instead of using a kind of translation layer such as FTL on flash devices to emulate a normal hard drive, it places the file system directly on the flash chips. Fig. 1 shows the organization of YAFFS. It works on a small NAND flash memory which consists of several blocks. Generally, a small NAND flash memory is composed of 32 pages and each page has spare area which contains the additional information on corresponding page.

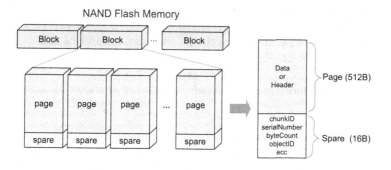

Fig. 1. Flash memory structure of YAFFS

In YAFFS, data is stored on NAND flash in chunks. Each chunk is the same size as a page and has a unique id (referred as chunkID). A chunk can hold either an object header or file data. If chunkID of a chunk is zero, the chunk holds an object header which describes a directory, file, symbolic link or hard link. Otherwise, the chunks holds file data and the value of chunkID indicates the position of the chunk in the file [12]. The spare area contains the information about the corresponding chunk such as chunkID, serialNumber, byteCount, objectID and ECC and others. When a chunk is no longer valid, YAFFS marks a particular byte in the spare area of the chunk as dirty. When entire pages of a block are marked as dirty, YAFFS erases the block and re-claim the space. If free space on the device is low, YAFFS chooses a block that has some number of dirty pages and valid pages. In this case, the valid pages are moved to a new block according to garbage collection and the old pages are marked as dirty. YAFFS marks every newly written chunk with a serial number that is monotonically increasing. Thereby when YAFFS scans the flash, it may detect multiple data chunks of one file that have identical ChunkID. It can choose the latest chunk by taking the greatest serial number. However, the data chunks are scattered throughout flash mem-ory, YAFFS should scan the entire flash memory at mounting time. This means that the mounting time of YAFFS heavily depends on the flash capacity and the stored data size the same as JFFS2.

3   A NAND Flash File System to Support Fast Mounting

In this section, we describe the NAND flash file system architecture which supports fast mounting.

3.1   On-Flash Data Structures

In this paper, we aim to provide fast mounting without regard to the flash memory capacity and amount of stored data. To satisfy this requirement, we propose a file system architecture in flash memory as is shown in Fig 2. In case of JFFS2 and YAFFS, the related data are spread all around flash memory. This scheme causes long mounting time. Therefore, keeping the location of the related data is the key to support fast mounting.

In the proposed architecture, the flash memory is managed as separated two areas, Location Information Area (referred as LIA) and General Area (referred as GA). Es-pecially, LIA maintains the latest location information. It occupies the several groups of blocks and firstly read during the mounting. GA is the remaining area except LIA in flash memory. In this area, all sub-areas such as metadata, data and block information are stored. Let us show the characteristics of each sub-area one by one.

Location Information Area. LIA keeps the latest location information where the metadata and block status are written. LIA is set to a fixed size and used in a round-robin manner. *Loc_Info*, the data structure for location information, is described in the left side of Fig. 2. It is a page-size data structure due to the

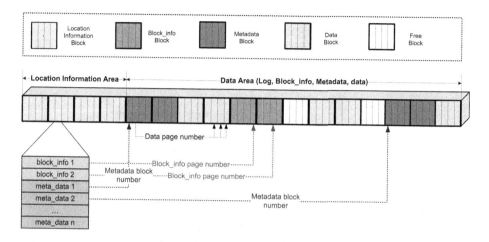

Fig. 2. The proposed flash file system architecture in flash memory

limitation of NAND flash memory I/O unit. *Loc_Info* consists of block_info and meta_data fields. Block_info fields point to the location where the latest block information are written. Array of meta_data field stores the latest addresses of the metadata sub-area where the metadata are stored. The number of index in the array limits the maximum number of files in the file system. In Fig. 2, the maximum number of files is 16,205.

General Area. GA includes all sub-areas such as metadata, file data and block_info. These sub-areas except data block are managed based on segment unit. Let us show the characteristics of each sub-area. First, metadata area consists of a number of independent segments which composed of several blocks. We store all metadata for objects such as files, directories, hard links and symbolic links in this area. Fig. 3 shows the *Meta_Data* structure of the proposed

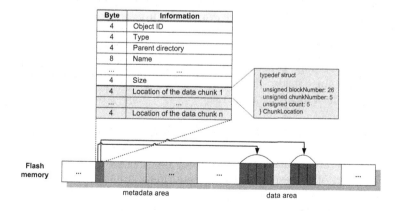

Fig. 3. An example of management of a file using Meta_Data

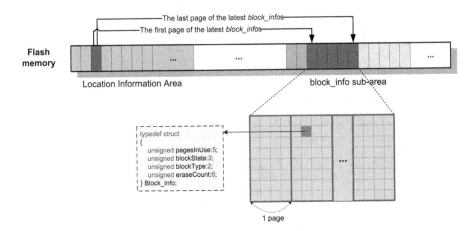

Fig. 4. Block_Info data structure containing status of all blocks in flash

file system. Unlike the conventional flash file system such as JFFS2 and YAFFS, the proposed file system contains file locations in metadata. Since all *Meta_Data* structures are belonged to metadata sub-area, we can construct the data structures in RAM by only scanning the metadata sub-area during the mounting.

Second, block_info area stores the *Block_Info* data structures that contain the newly updated status of all blocks in flash memory. For each block, *Block_Info* keeps the information of the number of pages in use, block status, block type and etc. as shown in Fig. 4. We make use of this information to determine policies such as new block allocation and garbage collection. When unmounting the file system, the latest *Block_Info* structures are written to flash memory.

3.2   In-Memory Data Structures

A procedure which mounts the file system includes constructing of block status and creating the data structure for object in RAM. A directory, file, hard link and symbolic link are abstracted to objects. Object structures are created for run-time support of operations on opened file and are managed by a list. For a file, Fnodes forms a tree structure that speeds up the search for data chunks in a file. The memory consumption of the proposed file system is similar to that of YAFFS since it also maintains the data structure for block information, metadata and data locations in RAM.

Block_Status data structure. The block_info area stores the *Block_Info* data structures that contain the status of all blocks in flash memory. The *Block_Status* data structures are created in RAM using the *Block_Info* data. These contain the information of corresponding block information and are managed by using an array. The index of an array denotes the corresponding block number. The *Block_Status* in RAM reflects the change on block status in flash memory. The Fig. 5 shows an example of *Block_Status* update. As an application performs

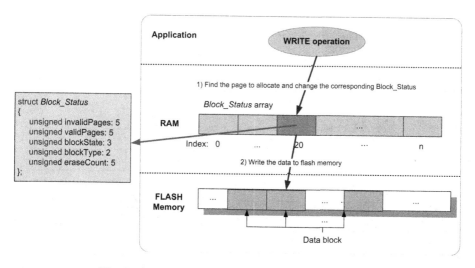

Fig. 5. An example of Block_Status update in RAM

write operation, we allocate the space using the *Block_Status* information in RAM. The 20th block status is changed as the pages in the block are allocated for write operation. When unmounting the file system, the updated *Block_Status* information is stored in block_info area.

Object data structure. An object can be a directory, file, hard link or symbolic link. During the mounting, the Object structures are created in RAM by loading *Meta_Data*s in metadata area. The relationship between these two structures is illustrated in Fig. 6. An Object knows about its corresponding metadata

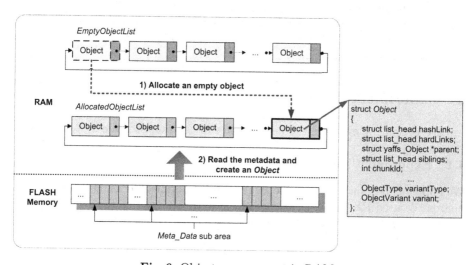

Fig. 6. Object management in RAM

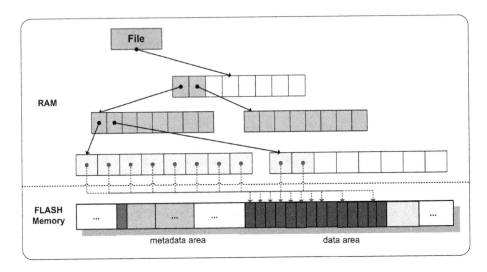

Fig. 7. Fnode data structure

location in flash memory. Modifications to the directory, file, hard link or symbolic link are reflected in the Object as they occur.

Fnode data structure. The file locations are maintained by a tree structure as described in Fig. 7. For a file, the *Fnode* data structures are created in RAM for managing its data location. The *Fnode* structures form a tree structure that speeds up the search for data chunks in a file. Depending on where it is in the tree, each *Fnode* holds the dif-ferent information. If it is at the lowest level, then it points to the data location. Otherwise, it points to lower-level *Fnodes*. When the file is created, it is assigned only one low-level *Fnode*. When the file expands past what a single *Fnode* can hold, then it is assigned a second *Fnode* and an internal node is added to point to the two *Fnodes*. As the file grows, more low-level *Fnodes* and high level *Fnodes* are added.

4   Experimental Results

In this section, we evaluate the performance of the proposed file system.

4.1   Experiment Environment

We implemented our proposed file system and experimented using an embedded board. We used PXA255-Pro III board made by Huins. Fig. 8 summarizes the PXA255-Pro III board specification. We used 64 MB Samsung NAND flash memory for our experiments. The block size of the memory is 64 KB and the page size is 512 B. Even though JFFS2 supports NAND flash memory, it doesn't manage bad blocks and has longer mounting time than YAFFS because of checking file

Hardware specification

Item		Specification
CPU		Intel PXA255 (Turbo Mode: 400 MHz, Normal Mode: 200 MHz)
SDRAM		128 MB SDRAM (32 BIT, 100 MHz)
Flash Memory	NOR	32 MB (Intel)
	NAND	64 MB (Samsung)

Fig. 8. PXA255-Pro III board specification

consistency and performing garbage collection. So we compare the performance of the proposed file system with that of YAFFS.

The performance metric was the mounting time. Since the mounting time of flash file system heavily depends on data size and flash memory usage, we evaluated performance by increasing the flash memory usage. For experiments, we created test data with reference to write access denoted as in [13]. The average file size is around 22KB and most files are smaller than 2KB.

4.2   Mounting Time Performance

Fig. 9 shows the average mounting times of YAFFS and the proposed file system. We measured the mounting time by increasing the flash memory usage from 10% to 80%. The result explains that the mounting time for YAFFS is uniformly high. This is because YAFFS should scan the entire flash memory regardless of flash memory usage to construct the data structures. In contrast

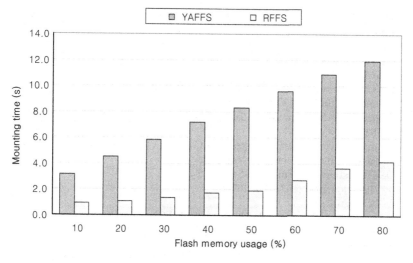

Fig. 9. Mounting time comparison according to flash memory usage

to YAFFS, mounting time of proposed file system is in proportion to amount of block_info and metadata areas. So we improve the mounting time of YAFFS by 64%–76%.

5 Conclusions

In this paper, we designed a new NAND flash file system, which provides fast mounting. To support fast mounting, we divide flash memory into Location Information Area and General Area. LIA is fixed in location and includes the block addresses for important file system data except file data. During the mounting, we can construct the data structures in RAM using the location information. GA includes the real data for file system such as metadata, file data and block information.

We evaluated our proposed file system by experiments. According to results, we improved the mount time by 64%–76% as flash usage compared to YAFFS.

Although we do not mention in this paper, we are developing the effective wear-leveling algorithm suitable for embedded system. Also we are planning to develop journaling mechanism in order to provide file system consistency against sudden system faults.

References

1. T.R. Bird: Methods to Improve Bootup Time in Linux. In Proc. of the Ottawa Linux Symposium (OLS). Sony Electronics (2004).
2. Two Technologies Compared: NOR vs. NAND. www.m-sys.com/NR/rdonlyres/24795A9E-16F9-404A-857C-C1DE21986D28/229/NOR_vs_NAND5.pdf
3. M. L. Chang, P. C. H. Lee, R. C. Chang: Managing Flash Memory in Personal Communication Devices. Proc. of IEEE Symp. on Consumer Electronics (1997) 177–182 erlin Heidelberg New York (1996)
4. Mei-Ling Chiang, Paul C. H. Lee Ruei-Chuan Chang: Cleaning Policies in Mobile Computers Using Flash Memory: Journal of System and Software ibr. 1 (1997) 108–121
5. David Woodhouse: JFFS: The Journaling Flash File System. Technical Paper of RedHat inc. (2001)
6. YAFFS Spec. http://www.aleph1.co.uk/yaffs/yaffs.html.
7. M.Resenblum and J.K.Ousterhout: The Design and Implementation of a Log-Structured File System: ACM Transaction on Computer Systems Vol.10. (1992) pp.26–52
8. Samsung Electronics: Advantages of SLC NAND Flash Memory. http://www.samsungelectronics.com/
9. Flash Filesystems for Embedded Linux Systems. http://linuxjournal.com/node/4678/.
10. JFFS3 Design Issue. http://www.linux-mtd.infradead.org/tech/JFFS3design/
11. YAFFS. http://en.wikipedia.org/wiki/YAFFS
12. Understanding the Flash Translation Layer(FTL) specification. Intel (1997)
13. G. Irlam: Unix File Size Survey. http://www.base.com/gordoni/gordoni.html

Rescheduling for Optimized SHA-1 Calculation

Ricardo Chaves[1,2], Georgi Kuzmanov[2],
Leonel Sousa[1], and Stamatis Vassiliadis[2]

[1] Instituto Superior Técnico/INESC-ID. Rua Alves Redol 9, 1000-029 Lisbon,
Portugal
http://sips.inesc-id.pt/
[2] Computer Engineering Lab, TUDelft. Postbus 5031, 2600 GA Delft,
The Netherlands
http://ce.et.tudelft.nl/

Abstract. This paper proposes the rescheduling of the SHA-1 hash function operations on hardware implementations. The proposal is mapped on the Xilinx Virtex II Pro technology. The proposed rescheduling allows for a manipulation of the critical path in the SHA-1 function computation, facilitating the implementation of a more parallelized structure without an increase on the required hardware resources. Two cores have been developed, one that uses a constant initialization vector and a second one that allows for different Initialization Vectors (IV), in order to be used in HMAC and in the processing of fragmented messages. A hybrid software/hardware implementation is also proposed. Experimental results indicate a throughput of 1.4 Gbits/s requiring only 533 slices for a constant IV and 596 for an imputable IV. Comparisons to SHA-1 related art suggest improvements of the throughput/slice metric of 29% against the most recent commercial cores and 59% to the current academia proposals.

1 Introduction

In current days, cryptography systems are the support for many innovations in both the industrial and the private sectors, being used from high security demanding applications, such as in banking transactions, to low security applications, like television. Three major classes of encryption algorithms exist: public key algorithms, symmetric key algorithms, and hash functions. While the first two are used to encrypt and decrypt data, the hash functions are unidirectional and do not allow the processed data to be retrieved. They are however extremely useful in data authentication and message integrity checks. Currently the most common hash functions are the MD5 and the SHA-1.Collision attacks have been found for both hash functions, however, while for MD5 they are computationally feasible on a standard desktop computer [1], the current SHA-1 attacks still require a massive computational power [2] (around 2^{69} hash operations), making it unfeasible in practical attacks for the time being.

Hash functions have the particularity of generating a small fixed length output value, the digest message or hash value, that is highly correlated with the input

S. Vassiliadis et al. (Eds.): SAMOS 2006, LNCS 4017, pp. 425–434, 2006.

data, which can be significantly larger (up to 2^{64} bits). The most important characteristics of these functions is the fact that virtually no information about the input data can be obtained from the outputted hash value. An adequate hash function has a very low probability of two different input data streams generating the same hash value. The Secure Hash Algorithm 1 (SHA-1) was approved by the NIST in 1995 as an improvement to the SHA-0, and is currently used in the main security applications, such as SSH, PGP, and IPSec.

As shown in the next section, the SHA-1 computational structure is quite straightforward and with a big data dependency, not allowing for efficient pipelining. Some works improve the SHA-1 computational throughput by unrolling the calculation structure, causing a significant increase on the required hardware [3, 4]. The fully rolled architecture proposed in this paper achieves a high throughput for the SHA-1 calculation, via the rescheduling of some operations, with a minimal area increase. The proposed SHA-1 core has been implemented within the reconfigurable co-processor of a Xilinx Virtex II Pro MOLEN prototype [5]. Implementation results of the proposed SHA-1 core indicate:

- A throughput of 1.4 Gbits/s with 533 Slices (2.7 Mbps per slice);
- An efficiency improvement to related art by 29% to 59%.

The hybrid implementation results indicate:

- 150x speedup with respect to the software implementation;
- 670% improvement to related art;

The paper is organized as follows. Section 2 presents an overview on the SHA-1 hash function and its computational characteristics. Section 3 describes the proposed architecture and the computational rescheduling of the SHA-1 core and the block expansion. Section 4 presents the obtained experimental results and compares them to other state-of-the-art SHA-1 implementations, both from academia and commercial companies. Section 5 concludes this paper with some final remarks.

2   SHA-1 Hash Function

In 1993 the Secure Hash Standard (SHA) was first publishes by the NIST, however some weakness were found and in 1995 a revised algorithm was published [6].This revised algorithm is usually referenced as SHA-1. The SHA-1 produces a single output message digest (the output hash value) of 160-bit from an input message. The input message is composed by multiple blocks of 512 bits each. Afterwards, the input block is expanded into 80 32-bit words (denoted as W_t), one 32-bit word for each round of the SHA-1 processing. Each round computation comprises additions and logical operations, such as bitwise logical operations (in f_t) and bitwise rotations to the left (denoted by $RotL^i$), as depicted in Figure 1.

The function (f_t) calculation depends on the round being executed, as well as the value of the constant K_t; the SHA-1 80 rounds are divided into four groups of

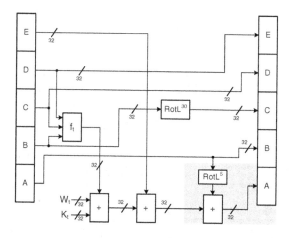

Fig. 1. SHA-1 Round calculation

20 rounds each. Table 1 presents the values of K_t and the logical function executed, according to the round. In this Table, $\wedge$ represents the bitwise AND operation and $\oplus$ represents the bitwise XOR operation.

The initial values of the A to E variables in the beginning of each data block calculation correspond to the value of the current 160-bit hash value, H_0 to H_4. After the 80 rounds have been computed, the A to E 32-bit values are added to the current Hash values. The Initialization Vector (IV) of the hash value for the first block is a predefined constant value. The output digest message is the final hash value, after all the data blocks have been computed. To better illustrate the algorithm a pseudo code representation is depicted in Figure 2. In some higher level applications such as the keyed-Hash Message

Table 1. SHA-1 functions and constants

Rounds	Function	K_t
0 to 19	$(B \wedge C) \oplus (\overline{B} \wedge D)$	0x5A827999
20 to 39	$B \oplus C \oplus D$	0x6ED9EBA1
40 to 59	$(B \wedge C) \oplus (B \wedge D) \oplus (C \wedge D)$	0x8F1BBCDC
60 to 79	$B \oplus C \oplus D$	0xCA62C1D6

Authentication Code (HMAC) [7] or when a message is fragmented, the initial hash value (IV) may differ from the constant specified in [6].

Data block expansion: In the SHA-1 algorithm the computation described in Figure 1 is performed 80 times (rounds), in each round an 32-bit word obtained from the current data block is used. However, each data block only has 16 32-bits words, resulting in the need to expand the initial data block to obtain the remaining 64 32-bit words. This expansion is performed by computing (1), where $M_t^{(i)}$ denotes the first 16 32-bit words of the i-th data block.

$$W_t = \begin{cases} M_t^{(i)} & 0 \leq t \leq 15 \\ RotL^1(W_{t-3} \oplus W_{t-8} \oplus W_{t-14} \oplus W_{t-16}) & 16 \leq t \leq 79 \end{cases} \qquad (1)$$

```
for for each data_block do

    W_t = expand(data_block)
    a = H_0 ; b = H_1 ; c = H_2 ; d = H_3 ; e = H_4

    for t= 0, t≤79, t=t+1 do
        Temp = RotL^5(a) + f_t(b,c,d) + e + K_t + W_t
        e = d
        d = c
        c = RotL^30(b)
        b = a
        a = Temp
    end for

    H_0 = a + H_0 ; H_1 = b + H_1 ; H_2 = c + H_2
    H_3 = d + H_3 ; H_4 = e + H_4
end for
```

Fig. 2. Pseudo Code for SHA-1 function

In order to assure that the input message is a multiple of 512 bits, as required by the SHA-1 algorithm, it is necessary to pad the original message. This message padding also comprises the inclusion of the original message dimension to the padded message, which can be used to validate the size of the original message.

3   SHA-1 Implementation

As depicted in Figure 1, the computational structure of the SHA-1 algorithm is rather straightforward. However, in order to compute the values of one round the values from the previous round are required. This data dependency imposes a sequentiality in the processing, preventing parallel computation between rounds. The only parallelism that can be efficiently explored is in the operations of each round. Some approaches [3] attempt to speedup the processing by unrolling the computation. With this technique, a speedup can be achieved, since the computation is performed as soon as the data becomes available. However, this approach carries with it a mandatory increase in the required circuit area. Other approaches, e.g. [4], even try to increase the throughput via the usage of a pipelined structure. However, this makes the core unusable in real applications, since one data block can only be processed when the previous one has been concluded, due to the data dependency of the algorithm.

In this paper, we propose a functional rescheduling of the SHA-1 hardware units, in order to obtain the throughput increase of the unrolled architectures, while maintaining the hardware requirements identical to the fully folded ones.

Operations rescheduling: From Figures 1 and 2 it can be seen that the bulk of the SHA-1 round computation is oriented for the A value calculation. The remaining values do not require any computation, apart from the rotation of B, their values are given by the previous value of the variables A to D.

Given that the value of A is calculated with the addition of the previous value of A along with other values, no parallelism can be exploited due to the data dependency, as depicted in (2).

$$A_{t+1} = RotL^5(A_t) + [f(B_t, C_t, D_t) + E_t + K_t + W_t] \qquad (2)$$

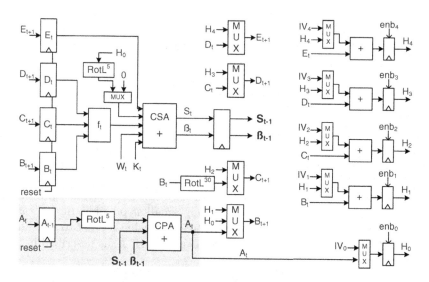

Fig. 3. SHA-1 rescheduling and internal structure

Nevertheless, since only the parcel $RotL^5(A_t)$ of (2) depends on the variable A_t, and all remaining parcels depend on variables that require no computation and do not depend on the value of A_t, some pre-computation can be performed. In (3) the parcel of (2) that does not depend of the value A is pre-computed, producing the carry (β_t) and save (S_t) vectors of the partial addition. The following holds:

$$S_t + \beta_t = f(B_t, C_t, D_t) + E_t + K_t + W_t \tag{3}$$

The calculation of the value of A_t, when part of its value is pre-computed on the previous computational cycle, is described in the following:

$$A_t = RotL^5(A_{t-1}) + (S_{t-1} + \beta_{t-1}) \tag{4}$$
$$S_t + \beta_t = f(B_t, C_t, D_t) + E_t + K_t + W_t$$

By splitting the value A computation and rescheduling it to different computational cycles, the critical path of the SHA-1 algorithm is significantly reduced. Since the calculation of the function $f(B, C, D)$ and the partial addition are no longer in the critical path, the critical path of the algorithm is reduced to a 3 input adder and some additional selection logic, as depicted in Figure 3. With this rescheduling an additional clock cycles is required since in the first clock cycle the value A is not calculated, (A_{-1} is not used) and in the last additional cycle the values $B_{81}, C_{81}, D_{81}, E_{81}$ are also not used. This extra additional cycle however, will be masked in the calculation of the value of the hash of each data block, as explained below.

After the 80 rounds of the SHA-1 algorithm for each data block, the final value of the internal variables (A to E) is added to the current hash value H, which remains unchanged until the end of each data block calculation, as depicted in

Figure 2. This final addition is performed by one adder for each 32 bits of the 160-bit hash value. However, the addition of the value H_0 is performed directly in the round calculation, in the CSA adder. With this option, an extra full adder is saved and the H_0 value calculation, that depends on the value A, is performed with less one clock cycle. Thus the calculation of all the hash value is concluded in the same cycle and the additional clock cycle caused by the value A calculation rescheduling is masked.

Hash value initialization: For the first data block, the internal hash value has to be initialized. This is performed by adding the Initialization Vector (IV) with zero, with this zero value being generated by resetting the internal values registers. This value is afterwards loaded to the internal values (B to E), through a multiplexer. Once more the value A initialization is performed in a distinct form in order to maintain the critical path as small as possible. In this case the value of H_0 is not set to the register A, instead the value A is set to zero and the value of H_0 directly introduced into the calculation of A, as described in (5).

$$S_0 + \beta_0 = f(B_{H_1}, C_{H_2}, D_{H_3}) + E_{H_4} + K_0 + W_0 + RotL^5(H_0)$$
$$A_1 = RotL^5(A_0) + (S_0 + \beta_0) = RotL^5(\,0\,) + (S_0 + \beta_0) \qquad (5)$$

The IV can be the constant value defined in [6] or application dependent, e.g. the HMAC or in hashing fragmented messages. In the first case the multiplexer that performs the selection between the IV and the current hash value can be removed and the constant value set with the set/reset signals of the hash value registers.

In order to minimize the power consumption of the this SHA-1 core the internal registers are disabled when the core is not being used, thus reducing the amount of internal switching.

Data block expansion: As previously mentioned, the 512 bits of each data block has to be expanded in order for the 80 32-bit words (W_t) to exist. Since this expansion has to be performed for each data block,(1), it becomes more efficient to perform this operation in hardware. The implementation of the data block expansion described in (1), is composed by: delays, implemented by registers, and XOR operators. Finally the output value W_t is selected between the original data block, for the first 16 words, and the computed values, for the remaining values. Figure 4 depicts the implemented structure. It should be noticed that part of the delay registers have been placed after the calculation, in order to eliminate this computation from the critical

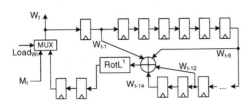

Fig. 4. Register based SHA-1 block expansion

path, since the value W_t is connected directly to the the SHA-1 core. The 4-bit XOR computation is a well suited operation for the 4-bit LUT, present in most CLBs of the Xilinx FPGAs. The one bit left rotate operation can be implemented directly in the routing process, not requiring additional hardware.

SHA-1 polymorphic processor: To create a practical platform to use and test the developed SHA-1 core, a wrapping interface has been added in order to integrate this units in the MOLEN polymorphic processor. The MOLEN paradigm [5] is based on the co-processor architectural paradigm, allowing the usage of reconfigurable custom designed hardware units. In this computational approach, the non critical part of the software code is executed on a General Purpose Processor (GPP) while the critical part, in this case the SHA-1 computation, is executed on the Custom Computing Unit (CCU). Since the hardware implemented function is called as a standard software function, the software development costs are minimal. Like in a software function, the code for the parameters passing though the XREG is included by the compiler [5].

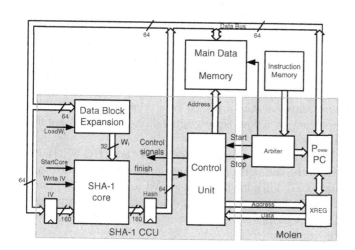

Fig. 5. SHA-1 polymorphic implementation

4 Performance Analysis and Related Work

In order to compare the architectural gain of this operation rescheduling with the current related art, the resulting core has been implemented in a Xilinx VIRTEX II Pro (XC2VP30-7) using the ISE (6.3) Xilinx tools. A CCU using this SHA-1 core has also been designed for the MOLEN polymorphic processor [5]. This polymorphic architecture uses the FPGAs embedded PowerPC running at 300 MHz, with a main data memory running at 100 MHz.

SHA-1 core: The SHA-1 core has also been implemented on a VIRTEX-E (XCV400e-8) device (Our-Exp.), in order evaluate the proposed core and compare it with the folded and the unfolded design proposed in [3]. The presented results in Table 2 for the VIRTEX-E device are for the SHA-1 core with a constant initialization vector and without the data block expansion module. When

Table 2. SHA-1 core performance comparisons

Design	Lien [3]	Lien [3]	Our-Exp.	CAST [8]	Helion [9]	Our-Cst.	Our +IV
Device	Virtex-E	Virtex-E	Virtex-E	XCV2P2-7	XCV2P-7	XCV2P30-7	XCV2P30-7
Expansion	no	no	no	yes	yes	yes	yes
IV	cst.	cst.	cst.	cst.	cst.	cst.	yes
Slices	484	1484	388	568	564	533	596
Freq. (MHz)	103	73	135	127	194	230	227
TrPut.(Mbps)	659	1160	840	802	1211	1435	1420
TrPut/Slice	**1.4**	**0.8**	**2.2**	**1.4**	**2.1**	**2.7**	**2.4**

compared with the folded SHA-1 core proposed in [3], a clear advantage can be observed both in terms of area and throughput. Experimentations suggest 20% less reconfigurable hardware occupation and 27% higher throughput, resulting in a 57% improvement on the throughput/slice metric, by adopting the proposed SHA-1 core. When compared with the unfolded architecture, the proposed core has a 28% lower throughput, however the unrolled core proposed in [3] requires 280% more hardware, resulting in a low throughput/slice, 2.75 times smaller than the core proposed in this paper.

Table 2 also presents the SHA-1 core characteristics for the VIRTEX II Pro FPGA implementation. Both the core with a constant initialization vector (Our–Cst.) and the one a variable IV initialization (Our+IV) are presented. These results also include the data block expansion block. The results are compared in Table 2 with the related art, including the most recent and efficient commercial SHA-1 cores known by the authors.

When compared with the leading market SHA-1 core from Helion [9], the proposed architecture requires 6% less slices while achieving throughput 18% higher. These two results originate a gain on the throughput/slice metric of about 29%.

For the SHA-1 core capable of receiving a IV other than the constant specified in [6], a slight increase in the required hardware occurs. This is due to the fact that the IV can no longer be set by the set/reset signals of the registers. This however has a minimal effect in the cores performance, since this loading mechanism is not located in the critical path. The decrease of the throughput/slice metric to 2.4 caused by the additional hardware for the IV loading is counterbalanced by the capability of this SHA-1 core (Our+IV) to be used in Message Authentication applications, like the HMAC, and in the processing of fragmented messages.

Polymorphic SHA-1 implementation: For this Polymorphic implementation of the SHA-1 hash function, the core (Our +IV) with Initial Vector loading has been used. Implementations results of the SHA-1 CCU indicate a device occupation of 813 slices (see Table 4). After receiving the start signal, the SHA-1 CCU starts by reading from the exchange register the location in the main data memory of the IV and after this, the value of IV itself is read from the memory. While reading the IV from the memory, the control units also reads from the exchange register the begin and end addresses of the data to be hashed. Once the SHA-1 CCU has been initialized, it goes into

Table 3. SHA-1 polymorphic performances

Bits	Hardware		Software		
	Cycles	(Mbps) ThrPut	Cycles	(Mbps) ThrPut	Kernel SpeedUp
512	396	389	38280	4.01	97
1024	642	479	76308	4.03	119
128k	63126	623	9766128	4.03	155

a loop where it reads a 512 bit block from the main memory and computes the hash function. This loop is repeated until the current data address becomes equal to the data end address read from the exchange register. Upon conclusion, the 160 bits of the digest message are written to memory. The SHA-1 CCU is working at the main data memory maximum frequency, which is approximately half of the SHA-1 maximum frequency. Table 3 presents the comparison between the purely software implementation of the SHA-1 hash function and the MOLEN polymorphic approach.

Table 4. Hybrid SHA-1

Design	Lu [10]	Our +IV
Device	XCV2P100	XCV2P30-7
Slices	3441[1]	813
Freq. (MHz)	145	100
TrPut.(Mbps)	304	624
TrPut/Slice	0.1	0.77

Even though the SHA-1 algorithm can be efficiently implemented in software, achieving a throughput above 4 Mbit/s, the usage of this hybrid approach allows for a speedup up to 150 times. Note that for data streams with only a few data blocks, a lower speedup is obtained, due to the initial overhead required for the SHA-1 CCU initialization. Even so, a speedup of approximately 100 times is still achieved in the worst case. For data streams with several data blocks, the achieved speedup tends to 150 times. If throughputs above 623 Mbit/s are required, the SHA-1 core can operate at a different frequency than the main data memory. Since the SHA-1 only reads from the memory 20% of the time, a buffer can be used in order to compensate the lower bandwidth of the memory. This technique requires a more complex hardware structure and additional hardware resources.

This hybrid computational approach is compared with the related art in [10]. As depicted in Table 4, the proposed implementation is able to achieve a 100% higher throughput with significantly less hardware resources, thus a 670% better throughput/slice metric is obtained.

5   Conclusion

The proposed rescheduling in the SHA-1 function operations allows the computation of each round of the algorithm in two distinct clock cycles. This rescheduling permits the exploration of parallelization technics, without increasing the required hardware. With the merging of the calculation of the final value of the lower bits of the digest message (H_0) with the round computation of the value

---

[1] Synthesis results for the SHA-1 core only. An estimated value for the slice utilization has been used, for a ratio of 0.58 Slices per LUT, obtained in our SHA-1 core.

A, the extra cycle created by the reschedule is concealed, thus not affecting the average throughput. Two SHA-1 cores have been developed, one that uses a constant *IV* and a second one that allows for different initialization vectors, in order to be used in HMAC and in the processing of fragmented messages. Even though, core with the *IV* loading requires some additional hardware for the registers initializations, this however does not influence the throughput, since it is not located in the critical path. A polymorphic SHA-1 processor has also been proposed, capable of speeding up the hash function computation by 150%, when compared to a fully software implementation running on a PowerPC at 300MHz, at a cost of 5% occupation of a VIRTEX II Pro 30 (833 slices). When compared to the four loop unfolded architectures, the proposed core is only 28% slower, however, it requires 280% more logic, thus our core has a throughput/slice metric 172% higher. To our best knowledge the proposed core is 18% faster that any commercial SHA-1 core and academia folded art, while achieving a reduction on the required hardware. These two factors result in an improvement of the throughput/slice metric of 29% when compared with commercial products and 59% to the current academia art. The proposed core achieves a throughput of 1.4Gbits/s with 4% occupation of the used device (533 slices).

Evaluation prototype: An evaluation prototype of the hybrid SHA-1 processor is available for download at: http://ce.et.tudelft.nl/MOLEN/applications/SHA/

References

1. Klima, V.: Finding MD5 collisions a toy for a notebook. Cryptology ePrint Archive, Report 2005/075 (2005)
2. Wang, X., Yin, Y.L., Yu, H.: Finding collisions in the full sha-1. In Shoup, V., ed.: CRYPTO. Volume 3621 of Lecture Notes in Computer Science., Springer (2005) 17–36
3. Lien, R., Grembowski, T., Gaj, K.: A 1 Gbit/s partially unrolled architecture of hash functions SHA-1 and SHA-512. In: CT-RSA. (2004) 324–338
4. Sklavos, N., Alexopoulos, E., Koufopavlou, O.G.: Networking data integrity: High speed architectures and hardware implementations. Int. Arab J. Inf. Technol. **1** (2003)
5. Vassiliadis, S., Wong, S., Gaydadjiev, G.N., Bertels, K., Kuzmanov, G., Panainte, E.M.: The Molen Polymorphic Processor. IEEE Transactions on Computers **53** (2004) 1363–1375
6. NIST: Announcing the standard for secure hash standard, FIPS 180-1. Technical report, National Institute of Standards and Technology (1995)
7. NIST: The keyed-hash message authentication code (HMAC), FIPS 198. Technical report, National Institute of Standards and Technology (2002)
8. CAST: SHA-1 Secure Hash Algorithm Cryptoprocessor Core. http://http://www.cast-inc.com/ (2005)
9. HELION: Fast SHA-1 Hash Core for Xilinx FPGA. http://www.heliontech.com/ (2005)
10. Lu, J., Lockwood, J.: IPSec Implementation on Xilinx Virtex-II Pro FPGA and Its Application. In: Proceedings. 19th IEEE International Parallel and Distributed Processing Symposium. (2005) 158b – 158b

Software Implementation of WiMAX on the Sandbridge SandBlaster Platform

Daniel Iancu[1], Hua Ye[1], Emanoil Surducan[1], Murugappan Senthilvelan[1],
John Glossner[1,2], Vasile Surducan[1], Vladimir Kotlyar[1], Andrei Iancu[1],
Gary Nacer[1], and Jarmo Takala[3]

[1] Sandbridge Technologies, One North Lexington Ave., White Plains, NY 10601, USA
{diancu, huaye, esurducan, msenthilvelan, jglossner, vsurducan, vkoltyar,
aiancu, gnacer}@sandbridgetech.com
[2] Delft University of Technology, Computer Engineering, EE, Delft, The Netherlands
[3] Tampere University of Technology, Tampere, Finland
jarmo.takala@tut.fi

Abstract. This paper describes a Sandbridge Sandblaster system implementation including both hardware and software elements for a WiMAX 802.16e system. The system is implemented on the fully functional multithreaded Sandblaster multiprocessor SB3010 SoC chip. The entire communication protocol, physical layer and MAC, has been implemented in software using pure ANSI C programming language and it executes in real time. In this paper, we also present a radio propagation analysis specific to the Samos island at the workshop location, and the DSP execution performance.

1 Introduction

WiMAX [1] is a long range, fixed, portable, or mobile wireless technology specified in the IEEE 802.16 standard. It provides high-throughput broadband connections similar to 802.11 wireless LAN systems but with much larger range. Possible applications for WiMAX include: "last mile" broadband connections, hotspot and cellular backhaul, and high-speed enterprise connectivity for businesses. Since the IEEE 802.16 standard defines a Media Access Control (MAC) layer that supports different physical layers and also defines the same Logical Layer Control (LLC) level 1 for different Local and Wide Area Networks (LAN and WAN), it opens up the possibility of bridging different communication networks together. A common MAC allows multi-mode and multi-radios easier implementations and at the same time it also simplifies system management and roaming issues. A multi-mode multi-radio system has historically been implemented using either multiple separate chip sets or specific System on Chip (SoC) solutions with replicated internal hardware. Recently, a more cost effective approach has gained in popularity. A Software Defined Radio (SDR) implements the entire physical layer in software and is capable of dynamically switching waveform execution and thus reusing existing silicon resources. Our WiMAX implementation described in this paper, is an SDR solution.

2 WiMAX System Background

The WiMAX 802.16 standard specifies a high throughput non-line-of-site (NLOS) communications link along with connectivity between network endpoints. It specifies

S. Vassiliadis et al. (Eds.): SAMOS 2006, LNCS 4017, pp. 435–446, 2006.

Table 1. Frequency bands, maximum power at the antenna and *EIRP*, NA: Not available

Parameters / Country	CE	CE	US	US
Frequency band [MHz]	2400–2483.5	5470–5725	2400–2483.5	5725–5850
Maximal power to antenna [mW]	NA	NA	200	1000
EIRP [dBm]	20 [100 mW]	30 [1 W]	23 [200 mW]	53 [200 W]

an RF spectrum in the 2 to 66 GHz range, including both licensed and unlicensed bands. The maximum bit rate as currently defined is 70 Mbps. The spectrum allocation and the maximum power at the antenna input, for both licensed and unlicensed bands are also specified in [1]. Table 1 lists the maximum power allowed by the standard at the antenna input and the Effective Radiated Power (ERPC) compared to an isotropic radiator, for different geographic areas.

Receiver Sensitivity Calculation. The receiver sensitivity is the measure of the signal strength for a specified modulation mode and bit-error rate (*BER*) that must be present at the receiver input in order to be able to detect the radio frequency signal and to demodulate correctly the transmitted data. The receiver sensitivity (P_{rx}) is a function of the Receiver Noise Floor (*NF*) and the Signal to Noise Ratio (*SNR*). The theoretical receiver sensitivity can be expressed as

$$P_{rx} = SNR + NF \tag{1}$$

where $SNR = (E_b/N_0)(R/B)$, E_b is the energy required per bit of information, N_0 is the thermal noise in 1Hz of bandwidth, R is the system data rate, and B is the system bandwidth.

The *BER* for a BPSK modulation system, with Additive White Gaussian Noise (AWGN) is given by

$$BER = \frac{1}{2}\text{erfc}(E_b/N_0)^{1/2} \tag{2}$$

where erfc($\cdot$) is the *complimentary* error function. The theoretical values of the *BER* as a function of E_b/N_0 are presented in Table 2.

The receiver Noise Floor (N_F) is the sum of thermal noise (N_0) and the noise figure (*N*) of the receiver as follows

$$N_F = N + N_0 \tag{3}$$

where $N_0 = kTB$, is the thermal noise power measured in Watts, N is the noise figure of the receiver, k is the Boltzman constant, T is the system absolute temperature usually

Table 2. Theoretical values of *BER* as a function of E_b/N_0

BER	10^{-2}	10^{-3}	10^{-4}	10^{-5}	10^{-6}	10^{-7}
E_b/N_0 [dB]	4.3	6.8	8.4	9.6	10.6	11.3

Table 3. Receiver sensitivity for BPSK modulation at $BER = 10^{-6}$

Modulation	R/B	E_b/N_0	N_0 [dBm]	N [dB]	SNR	P_{rx} [dBm]
BPSK	1/2	10.6	-113	7.5	7.6	-85.4

assumed to be 290 K, and B the channel bandwidth measured in Hz. All these entries are summarized in Table 3 and they are in accordance with the standard recommendations.

Link Budget Calculation. The link analysis provides the estimation of the required transmitted power level in order to cover for a desired range [2]. The sum of *EIRP* (transmitted power plus antenna gain) and receiver absolute sensitivity $|P_{rx}|$ must be equal to the sum of link loss (*LL*) and Fade Margin (*FM*) [3,4]. The link loss includes the Path Loss (*PL*), at frequency F over the range D, and the external Microwave Circuit Loss (*MCL*) (switch, antenna cables, and connectors) and is shown in the following:

$$EIRP + |P_{rx}| = PL(D,F) + FM + MCL. \tag{4}$$

To estimate the maximum range with a given *EIRP* and receiver sensibility P_{rx} it is necessary to estimate the fading loss, the RF front-end external circuit loss and to calculate *PL*. Table 4 illustrates the path loss versus distance D for the most popular propagation models. In Table 4, the columns refer to the following:

- CCIR: [4] Empirical model for the combined effect of free-space path loss and terrain-induced path loss published by CCIR-Committee Consultative International des radio Communication, now ITU-R.
- Hata: [4] Based on Okamura *et al.* (Empirical curves).
- Hata-l.city: Large City model (building height greater than 15m).
- Hata-s.city: Medium to Small City model.
- Hata-suburb: Suburban model.
- Hata-open: Free space model.
- ITU: Line of sight (LOS), experimentally tested for D larger than 3 km as follows

Table 4. Link budget for different channel models, path loss (*PL*) given in dB at 2.45 GHz

D [km]	CCIR	Hata-l city	Hata-s city	Hata suburb	Hata open	ITU	WI-LOS	WI-NLOS	SPLM
2	120.4	142.4	125.4	112.4	91.7	105.3	118.3	129.7	141.6
2.5	123.9	146.0	128.9	116.0	95.2	106.2	120.8	133.4	146.6
3	126.8	148.8	131.8	118.9	98.1	107.0	122.8	136.4	150.6
3.5	129.2	151.3	134.2	121.3	100.5	107.9	124.6	139.0	154.0
4	131.3	153.4	136.3	123.4	102.6	108.6	126.1	141.2	157.0
5.5	136.4	158.4	141.4	128.4	107.6	110.4	129.7	146.4	164.0
6.5	139.0	161.1	144.0	131.1	110.3	111.4	131.6	149.2	167.7
11	147.3	169.4	152.3	139.4	118.6	115.0	137.5	157.9	179.3
12	148.7	170.7	153.7	140.8	120.0	115.6	138.5	159.3	181.2

Table 5. Maximum range for the unlicensed frequency bands: * calculated with Hata Open model, 0 dB antenna gain and 12 dB loss and ** calculated with Hata Suburban model, 0 dB antenna gain and 12 dB loss

Frequency band [MHz]	2400–2483.5	5470–5725	2400–2483.5	5725–5850	5725–5795 5815–5850
EIRP [dBm]	20 (100 mW)	30 (1 W)	23 (200 mW)	53 (200 W) 30 dBm in the antenna	36 (4W)
*Max LOS [km]	3	5.5	3.58	23.8	8
**Max NLOS range [km]	0.8	1.23	1	5.3	1.8

$$PL(\text{dB}) = 92.45 + 20\log(D + F) \qquad (5)$$

where D is measured in km and F in GHz.
- WI: "Walfish-Ikegami" is an empirical and semi deterministic model for mobile radio propagation (COST-231 project). WI has a good fit for the frequencies in the range of 800 to 2000 MHz and the range of 0.02 to 5 km.
- WI-LOS: [4] No obstruction in direct path (LOS) (base station antenna height 30 m)
- WI-NLOS: [4] No-line-of-sight (NLOS). For the path loss calculation the following values have been used:
  - Base station antenna height (hb) : 4–50 m,
  - Terminal antenna height (hm): 1–3 m,
  - Building separation (b): 20–50 m,
  - Width of street (if not specified, $b/2$ is recommended), and
  - Angle of the incident wave to streets (assumed 90 degrees).
- SPLM: [5] Suburban Path Loss Model it is a modified Hata-Okamura model.

For the Samos island case, we have chosen the values for Hata-open and Hata-suburban models. The maximal distance possible to be covered within the maximum range of the allowable EIRP values, specified in the standard, are presented in Table 5. For the theoretical analysis we have considered a 0 dB gain antenna, $FM = 10$ dB fading loss and $MCL = 2$ dB loss.

3   System Description

Figure 1 shows a satellite map of Samos Island. Our goal is to connect Agios Konstantinos to Kokkari through a WiMAX link. There is 5.5 km between Agios Konstantinos and Kokkari but there is no direct LOS path. In order to meet the link budget for the unlicensed band a repeater is required. Based on the receiver sensitivity calculations and availability, for our demonstrations we used a standard off-the-shelf 802.11 WiFi transceiver which supports 7 MHz bandwidth operation mode and meets our estimated

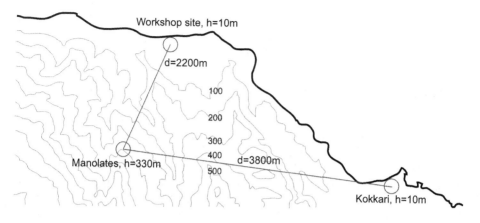

Fig. 1. Map of the demo place

sensitivity requirements. Using the 802.11 front-end also gives us the option of executing IEEE 802.11 a/b/g standard on the same platform.

A repeater must be able to support the Full Duplex Mode (FDD) mode on two different bands, for instance we can receive on the 2.4 GHz band and transmit on the 5.6 GHz band or vice-versa. Since the WiFi front-end supports only a TDD mode, there is need for two transceiver chips for each system. We note that we can also make use of the additional WiFi transceiver for Multi Input Multi Output (MIMO) communication modes. To summarize, the end to end system consists of: (a) TDD mode platforms at both ends on either 2.4 or 5.6 GHz and (b) a repeater in between, in FDD mode with LOS to both ends.

A hardware block diagram is illustrated in Fig. 2. The hardware components of both the end unit and repeater are identical. The RF front-end consists of two RF transceiver chips and one high rate sampling AD/DA (Analog-to-Digital/Digital-to-Analog converter) directly connected to the SB3010 Sandblaster evaluation board through a high speed parallel interface. Power amplifiers are connected to each transmitter and band-pass filters are placed between the antennas and the receivers. The system can operate

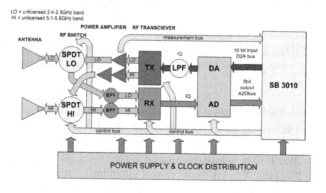

Fig. 2. Hardware block diagram of the WiMAX system

with a single antenna employing Rx/Tx switches or two separate Tx and Rx antennas. We describe results for the second case. All serial controls for the various chips are generated by software executing on the SB3010.

4   Sandblaster Platform

The SB3010 chip [6] consists of four Sandblaster DSP cores connected by a unidirectional deterministic and opportunistic ring network. The SB3010 chip is fabricated in 90 nm and each DSP core runs at 600 MHz. Each DSP core has a branch unit, a scalar Arithmetic Logic Unit (ALU), a Single Instruction Multiple Data (SIMD) vector unit and a load/store unit. These execution resources are time multiplexed equally among 8 threads per core. Each thread has its own set of scalar and SIMD vector registers.

Instruction Set Architecture. Each thread executes 64-bit compound instructions. A compound instruction can contain up to three concurrently executed compound operations. For example a load can be issued in parallel with an arithmetic operation and a branch. The following instruction computes the inner product of a vector with itself:

```
Label:
    vmulred %ac3, %vr7, %vr7, %ac3 ||
    lvu %vr7, %r8, 8 ||
    loop 0, %lc0, Label
```

The "vmulred" operation multiplies each of four 16-bit elements contained in the vector register %vr7 with itself and accumulates the products into an accumulator register %ac3. At the same time, the lvu operation increments the scalar register %r8 by eight and loads the next four values from the resulting address. The loop instruction decrements the loop count register %lc0 and repeats the instruction if the register is non-zero. Each Sandblaster core is capable of completing an instruction from a thread on every 600 MHz cycle provided there are no stalls due to memory access. In particular, each core is capable of completing a 4-way multiply-accumulate (MAC) instruction at every 600 MHz cycle. *Across four cores this adds up to 4×600×4=9600 million MACs per second.* Since core execution resources (ALU, branch, etc.) are shared equally among the eight threads - we can view a core as an 8-way multiprocessor with each processor running at 600 MHz / 8 = 75 MHz. We denote this performance as a "thread cycle". *In the rest of the paper, we report memory latencies and algorithm complexity using thread cycles.*

Memory Structure. Each core has a 32 kB *instruction cache*. Data memory is not cached and is divided between a 64 kB Level 1 (L1) and 256 kB Level 2 (L2) memory. A load from L2 memory incurs a pipeline stall. Stores into L2 are issued through a FIFO and do not block unless the FIFO is full. In practice up to four threads can simultaneously store into L2 without blocking. The L1 memory is divided into eight banks of 8 kB each. A particular implementation detail is that there is no penalty if the parity (odd/even) of the thread is the same as the parity of the bank. There is a single cycle penalty both for loads and for stores if the parities of the thread and the bank do not match. The instruction in the inner product example will complete within a single thread cycle, if it is executed on an even thread and %r8 points into an even bank. The compiler tries to ensure memory affinities and the processor tools can automatically generate linker scripts that optimize memory access.

Programming Environment. The Sandblaster programming tools include: a supercomputer-class vectorizing compiler, a fast simulator, and real-time operating system (RTOS) that implements POSIX threads standard [7]. *Our WiMAX implementation is written entirely in ANSI C using POSIX API for thread management.* We rely on the optimizing compiler to produce highly efficient machine code from straight-forward C source. The compiler automatically vectorizes most of the loops that occur in signal processing and media applications. It performs semantic analysis of input programs and automatically recognizes saturating arithmetic in ANSI C [8]. For example the single-instruction loop for an inner product is generated automatically from the following source:

```
int i, s;
for (I = 0, s = 0; I < N; i++)        {
    s += A[k]*A[k];
}
```

The Sandblaster simulator is capable of executing over 100 million instructions per second on a 3 GHz x86 computer [9]. The Sandblaster RTOS is capable of multiplexing an arbitrary number of software threads onto hardware threads. Software threads can be designated as pinned or non-pinned. Pinned threads are removed from the general thread scheduler and by convention, their stacks are allocated to L1 memory. Non-pinned threads can be rescheduled any time the operating system chooses and can be allocated based on the scheduling policy implemented in pthreads.

5   WiMAX Algorithms

The physical layer transmitter pipeline for the OFDM PHY as specified in IEEE 802.16 [1] is shown in Fig. 3(a). The OFDM signaling format was selected in preference to competing formats such as single-carrier (SC) CDMA due to its superior multipath performance, permitting significant equalizer design simplification to support operation in NLOS fading environments. Figure 3(b) shows the 802.16 OFDM PHY receiver block diagram. The back-end signal processing block is the reverse of the transmitter pipeline shown in Fig. 3(a). Note that a Reed-Solomon (RS) decoder is not required for the 2.9 Mbps BPSK mode.

Figure 4 shows the 802.16 OFDM PHY front-end signal processing block diagram. The inputs to the A/D converter are the I and Q baseband signals coming from the RF chip. The I/Q signals are first 2:1 decimated and filtered to the FFT sampling frequency F_s. The FFT sampling frequency is proportional to the channel bandwidth (B) as shown in the following:

$$F_s = \lfloor nB/8000 \rfloor 8000 \qquad (6)$$

where $\lfloor \cdot \rfloor$ is floor function. In our implementation, $B = 7$ MHz, $n = 8/7$, $F_s = 8$ MHz, and, therefore, the ADC sampling frequency will be at $2F_s = 16$ MHz.

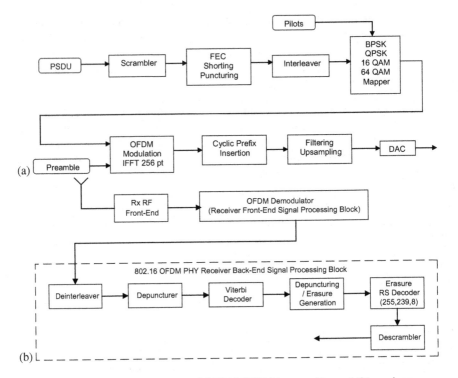

Fig. 3. Block diagrams of 802.16 OFDM PHY (a) transmitter and (b) receiver

The Automatic Gain Control (AGC) block calculates the new value required to establish the appropriate control bits used to set the gain level for the two gain stages in the RF chip based on the signal energy measurements as follows

$$E = \sum_{i=0}^{N-1} \left[r_I(i)^2 + r_Q(i)^2 \right] \tag{7}$$

where $r_I(i)$ and $r_Q(i)$ are the decimated I/Q signals and N is the number of samples in a symbol including the guard period.

The AGC algorithm runs under coarse setting and fine setting. In the coarse setting mode, the AGC monitors the input energy E and once the incoming signal is detected, an initial AGC setting is calculated by comparing the measured energy level E with a preset target energy level. The AGC coarse setting will allow the Voltage controlled Gain Amplifier VGA to pull the input signal within the ADC's dynamic range. Once the coarse setting is complete, the AGC gain will be kept constant while the receiver goes through a training process to achieve synchronization with the transmitter.

The AGC then enters a fine setting mode where the energy E measured during the preamble symbol duration will be compared with the preset energy target. Based on this measurement the LSB of the VGA control bits are adjusted accordingly.

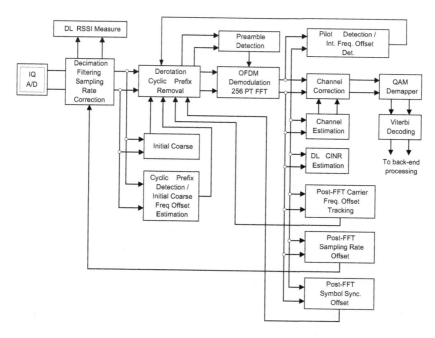

Fig. 4. 802.16 OFDM PHY front-end signal processing block diagram

The derotation operation is performed in time domain as follows

$$r'_I(i) + jr'_Q(i) = (r_I(i) + jr_Q(i)) e^{\frac{-j2\pi\Delta f}{F_s}}, \quad i = 0 \ldots N - 1 \tag{8}$$

where j is the imaginary unit. The purpose of the derotation is to correct for the frequency offset Δf that is detected by the initial coarse estimation and fine tracking. The cyclic prefix is then removed and the remaining I and Q samples are further used in the OFDM demodulation.

Both short and long preambles are defined to assist in channel estimation, timing, and carrier frequency estimation. The time domain periodicity properties of the preamble can be exploited to detect the preamble sequence and symbol boundary. The following equations are used to detect the preamble sequences:

$$c(j+n) = \sum_{i=0}^{127} r(i+n)r(i+j+n); \tag{9}$$

$$n_{max} = \arg\left(\max_{n} \sum_{j=0}^{L-1} \sqrt{(\Re[c(j+n)])^2 + (\Im[c(j+n)])^2}\right) \tag{10}$$

where $r(k)$ is a complex signal sample after decimation and L is the number of samples in the guard period. The autocorrelation peak at position n_{max} indicates the presence of preamble sequence and its starting sampling position.

The coarse fractional carrier frequency offset can be estimated as

$$\Delta f = \frac{F_s}{2\pi} \tan^{-1} \left(\frac{\Im[c(n_{max})]}{\Re[c(n_{max})]} \right). \tag{11}$$

After the initial coarse symbol timing and frequency offset estimation, fine estimation and adjusting algorithms are required in the frequency domain. There are eight pilot signals inserted in each data-bearing OFDM symbol. These are used to perform post FFT carrier frequency offset tracking, symbol synchronization tracking, and sampling rate offset tracking.

Channel estimation is performed when receiving the long preamble symbol that has 100 pilots spaced two subcarriers apart (excluding the DC subcarrier). The transmitted pilots can be represented as X_s, $s = 0, 1, \ldots, 99$. The corresponding received subcarriers at the pilot locations can be represented as Y_s. The channel frequency response at the pilot subcarrier locations can be represented as H_s. The least-square estimate of the channel frequency response at the pilot subcarrier location s, $\tilde{H}_s$, is given by the following equation:

$$\tilde{H}_s = \frac{Y_s}{X_s}, \quad s = 0, 1, \ldots, 99. \tag{12}$$

The channel frequency response at the remaining 100 non-pilot subcarriers can be readily estimated using linear interpolation.

It is mandatory that the Down Link (DL) receiver measures and reports the mean and standard deviation of the ratio of the Received Signal Strength Information and the Carrier to Interference and Noise Ratio (RSSI / CINR) to the Base-Station (BS) within a strict time requirement. Both RSSI and CINR measurements are performed using preamble sequences. The QAM demapping is Gray coded and the implementation supports up to four soft bit demapping.

6   Multithreaded Multiprocessor Implementation

The WiMAX transmit and receive algorithms are implemented as concurrent multi-threaded pipelines. The pipelines consist of all the processing steps such as FFT, filtering, scrambling, etc. To implement a pipeline on Sandblaster processor we have (a) aggregate steps into stages, and (b) decided how to assign threads to the computations within a stage.

The WiMAX transmitter is a simpler algorithm and we use it to illustrate our partitioning methodology. There are four steps: (a) OFDM data symbol/preamble generation, (b) FFT, (c) filtering, and (d) data copy to D/A converter. Based on profiling of the sequential ANSI C implementation, we allocate 2 processor threads for symbol generation, three threads for FFT, two threads for filtering and one thread for copying data to the D/A. The total number of threads is eight and thus the WiMAX transmitter may be implemented in a single Sandblaster processor core. The pipeline implementation is shown in Fig. 5(a). Symbol generation and filtering are *partitioned* naturally across two threads. Each thread works on either the I channel or the Q channel. To avoid the overhead of partitioning the FFT, we *replicate* FFT processing across three threads. Each thread works on a different symbol.

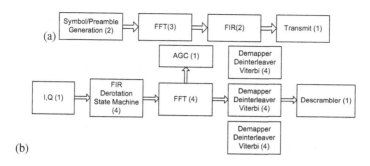

Fig. 5. (a) Transmitter and (b) receiver pipeline; each box is a team, the size of each team is in parenthesis

Our implementation illustrates two methods for partitioning work to threads: either we partition a unit of work (an OFDM symbol in this case) across multiple threads, or we process multiple units of work concurrently. In general, we might have multiple units processed concurrently, with each unit being partitioned across a *team* of threads. Therefore, for each stage we have to specify (a) the number of concurrent teams and (b) the number of threads in each team. The partitioning of work within each team is dependent on particular computation.

Using this strategy, the FFT stage is assigned to three teams. Each of the teams has a single thread. Symbol generation is assigned to one team of two threads, same as filtering. The D/A copy is assigned to a single team of one thread. We use double buffering to communicate between stages. When data is communicated between a stage with one team and a stage with multiple teams (e.g., symbol generation to FFT, FFT to filtering), round-robin scheduling is used to decide which team is communicated with.

The WiMAX receiver has two major modes of operation: startup and steady-state. During the startup process the receiver goes through several states of a state machine until reaches the steady state. The receiver runs through a startup process to achieve synchronization with the transmitter as follows: State 1: Initial energy detection and initial AGC setting, State 2: Coarse carrier frequency offset estimation and correction, State 3: OFDM symbol synchronization via preamble sequence, State 4: Integer frequency offset detection and correction, and State 5: Steady-state processing.

In the steady-state mode, the following functions are performed: (a) I/Q signal decimation and filtering, (b) energy monitoring and AGC fine tuning, (c) I/Q signal derotation, (d) OFDM demodulation via 256 point FFT per OFDM symbol, (e) post-FFT 4*64 preamble detection, (f) symbol timing offset tracking via 4*64 preambles, (g) carrier frequency offset tracking via data symbol pilots, (h) channel estimation via 2*128 preambles, and (i) data symbol processing: channel correction, demapping, deinterleaving, Viterbi decoding, and descrambling. In the implementation, we view steady-state processing as a pipeline. We combine the initial state machine onto one of the stages. The assignment of stages to threads is shown in Fig. 5(b). Overall, the receiver uses 24 threads (3 cores). The state machine is run within one of the threads along with the FIR/derotation team. Depending on the state transition, data is either passed to the FFT stage (in State 5) or to the thread responsible for the four initial states.

The receiver performance for 2.9 Mbps has been tested according to IEEE802.16 specifications. The targeted receiver SNR was 3.0 dB when using BPSK modulation with 1/2-rate convolutional coding. The measured receiver SNR was 1.59 dB when using 4-bit soft decoding. The simulation has been performed in the Sandblaster simulator. The Sandblaster SB3010 chip is sufficient for a complete ANSI C implementation of the entire physical layer processing. All results have been validated on the hardware development board including complete RF and baseband processing.

7   Conclusion

We have presented a real-time implementation of 2.9 Mbps WiMAX on the Sandblaster SDR platform. Our work demonstrates that a software implementation of WiMAX, suitable for mobile applications can be achieved on the same platform along with other communication protocols [10,11].

References

1. IEEE: IEEE standard for local and metropolitan area networks Part 16: Air interface for fixed broadband wireless access systems. Std. 802.16, IEEE (2004)
2. Zyren, J., Petrick, A.: Tutorial on basic link budget analysis. AN9804.1, Intersil (1998)
3. Miller, L.E.: LinkCalc: NIST Link Budget Calculator. NIST, Gaithersburg, MA. (2005) v. 1.23.
4. Miller, L.E.: General Purpose Propagation Loss Calculator Propagation Models: CCIR-Hata Walfisch-Ikegami (WIM). NIST, Gaithersburg, MA. (2005)
5. Erceg, V., Hari, K.V.S., Smith, M.S., Baum, D.S., Sheikh, K.P., Tappenden, C., Costa, J.M., Bushue, C., Sarajedini, A., Schwartz, R., Branlund, D., Kaitz, S., Trinkwon, D.: Channel models for fixed wireless applications. IEEE 802.16a WG document 802.16.3c-01/29r4, IEEE (2001)
6. Glossner, J., Mougdill, M., Iancu, D., Nacer, G., Jintukar, S., Stanley, S., Samori, M., Raja, T., Schulte, M.: The Sandbridge Sandblaster convergence platform. White paper, Sandbridge Technologies (2005) http://www.sandbridgetech.com/documents/sandbridge_white_paper_2005.pdf.
7. Nichols, B., Buttlar, D., Proulx-Farrell, J.: Pthreads Programming: A POSIX Standard for Better Multiprocessing. 1st edn. O'Reilly & Associates, Sebastopol, CA (1996)
8. Kotlyar, V., Moudgill, M.: Detecting overflow detection. In: Proc. IEEE/ACM/IFIP Int. Conf. Hardware/Software Codesign and System Synthesis, Stockholm, Sweden (2004) 36–41
9. Glossner, J., Dorward, S., Jinturkar, S., Moudgill, M., Hokenek, E., Schulte, M., Vassiliadis, S.: Sandbridge software tools. In: Proc. Int. Workshop Systems, Architectures, Modeling, and Simulation, Samos, Greece (2003) 142–148
10. Glossner, J., Iancu, D., Lu, J., Hokenek, E., Moudgill, M.: Software-defined communications baseband design. IEEE Communications Magazine **41** (2003) 120–128
11. Glossner, J., Iancu, D., Nacer, G., Stanley, S., Hokenek, E., Moudgill, M.: Multiple communication protocols for software defined radio. In: Proc. IEE Colloquium on DSP Enable Radio, Livingston, Scotland (2003) 227–236

High-Radix Addition and Multiplication in the Electron Counting Paradigm Using Single Electron Tunneling Technology

Cor Meenderinck and Sorin Cotofana

Delft University of Technology, Computer Engineering Lab
Postbus 5031, 2600 GA, Delft, The Netherlands
{cor, sorin}@ce.et.tudeft.nl

Abstract. The Electron Counting (EC) paradigm was proved to be an efficient methodology for computing arithmetic operations in Single Electron Tunneling (SET) technology. In previous research EC based addition and multiplication have been implemented. However, the effective performance of these schemes is diminished by fabrication technology imposed practical limitations. To alleviate this problem high radix computation was suggested. In this paper we present a high radix EC addition scheme and a high radix EC multiplication scheme. For both arithmetic operations, we first briefly present the normal (non high radix) EC schemes. Second, we present the high radix schemes and explain their functionality. Third, we explain the implementation of the high radix schemes in details. Finally, we present simulation results and evaluate the schemes in terms of delay and area cost.

1 Introduction

It is generally expected that current semiconductor technologies, i.e., CMOS, cannot be pushed beyond a certain limit because of problems arising in the area of power consumption and scalability. A promising alternative is Single Electron Tunneling (SET) technology [1], which has the potential of performing computation with lower power consumption than CMOS and is scalable to the nanometer region and beyond [2].

Several proposals have been made to implement computational operations using SET technology and these implementations are mainly categorized in two types (see for example [1,3]). The first type of implementation represents logic values by voltage (see [3] for an overview) while the second type of implementation represents bits by single electrons. Single Electron Encoded Logic (SEEL) [4] is an example of the latter.

Using the second type of implementation, arithmetic units can be designed in conventional logic design styles, e.g., using Boolean and/or threshold gates (see for example [4]). The Electron Counting (EC) paradigm [5], on the other hand, uses a novel design style and appears promising as an efficient computational paradigm for the implementation of SET based arithmetic operations, e.g., addition and multiplication. Previous EC based adder and multiplier implementations assumed that an unlimited amount of electrons could be transported within the EC building blocks, which does not hold true in practice. Therefore, a limit to the operand size of the previous proposed schemes

S. Vassiliadis et al. (Eds.): SAMOS 2006, LNCS 4017, pp. 447–456, 2006.

is implied by the available SET fabrication technology. One way to alleviate this problem is to do high-radix computation [6]. In this paper we propose a high-radix EC addition scheme and a high radix EC multiplication scheme.

The remainder of this paper is organized as follows. Section 2 briefly describes the single electron tunnel phenomenon and introduces the EC paradigm. Section 3 introduces the proposed high radix addition scheme, explains the implementation details and presents simulation results. In Section 4 the high radix multiplication scheme is proposed and explained in details. The scheme is verified by means of simulation. Section 5 concludes the paper.

2 Background

SET circuits are based on tunnel junctions which consist of an ultra-thin insulating layer in a conducting material (see Figure 1). In classical physics no charge transport is possible through an insulator. However, when the insulating layer is thin enough the transport or *tunneling* of charge can be controlled in a discrete and accurate manner, i.e., one electron at a time. Tunneling through a junction becomes possible when the junction's current voltage V_j exceeds the junction's critical voltage [7] $V_c = \frac{q_e}{2(C_e + C_j)}$, where $q_e = 1.602 \cdot 10^{-19}C$, C_j is the capacitance of the junction, and C_e is the capacitive value of the remainder of the circuit as seen from the junction. In other words, tunneling can occur if and only if $|V_j| \geq V_c$.

Electron tunneling is stochastic in nature and as such the delay cannot be analyzed in the traditional sense. Instead, for each transported electron one can describe the switching delay as $t_d = \frac{-ln(P_{error})q_e R_t}{|V_j| - V_c}$, where R_t is the junction's resistance and P_{error} is the chance that the desired charge transport has not occurred after t_d seconds. In this paper we assume $R_t = 10^5 \Omega$ and $P_{error} = 10^{-8}$.

Note that the implementations discussed in here are technology independent. SET tunnel junctions can for example be implemented by classical semiconductor lithography or by carbon nanotubes [8]. Therefore, circuit area is evaluated in terms the total number of circuit elements (capacitors and junctions).

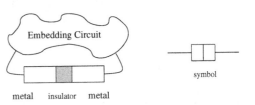

Fig. 1. Schematic representation of the tunnel junction

As mentioned in the introduction, there are many ways to do computation using SET technology of which the Electron Counting paradigm seems to exploit the potential of SET most of all. In the EC paradigm, the ability to control the transport of individual electrons is utilized to encode integer values X directly as a charge Xq_e. Once binary values have been encoded as a number of electrons, one can perform arithmetic operations directly in electron charges, which reveals a broad range of novel computational schemes.

3   High-Radix EC Adder

A basic (non high radix) EC based addition scheme was first proposed in [5]. Figure 2 depicts a 2-bit instance of this addition scheme, which functions as follows. Each bit of the inputs A and B is connected to the V input of an $MVke$ building block. This block, once enabled, adds Vkq_e charge to the charge reservoir, where V is the magnitude of the input, k is a build in constant, and q_e is the absolute charge of one electron $(1.602 * 10^{-19}$ C). In other words, the $MVke$ block removes Vk electron from the charge reservoir. The build in constant k is adjusted to the weight of the corresponding input bit of the $MVke$ block. Thus, the total amount of electrons removed from the charge reservoir is $\sum_{i=0}^{1}(a_i 2^i + b_i 2^i)$, which is equal to the sum of the inputs. The results of the addition is converted back to the digital domain using three PSF building blocks, which each implementing a Periodic Symmetric Function (PSF).

A possible implementation of the $MVke$ building block (Figure 3.1) was proposed in [6] and operates as follows. While R (reset) and V are zero and input E (enable) is set to '1', the voltage over junction 1 (C1) approaches it's critical voltage. If now V is set to '1' the critical voltage is exceeded and one electron tunnels from node M to node N. As a result of this event a positive charge is present on node M, which causes the voltage over junction 2 (C2) to exceed it's critical voltage and so one electron tunnels from node P to node M. This process of two tunnel events continues until the voltage over junc-

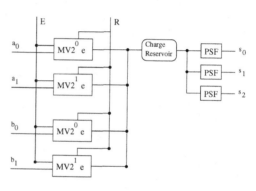

Fig. 2. 2-bit EC addition scheme

tion 1 has dropped below the critical voltage again. The number of electrons k that is removed from the charge reservoir is proportional to the magnitude of both V and C_v.

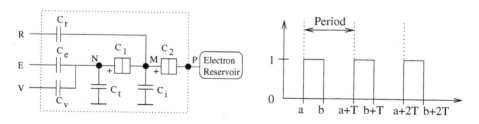

Fig. 3.1. $MVke$ block implementation   **Fig. 3.2.** Periodic Symmetric Function

A PSF block implements a Periodic Symmetric Function (PSF) F_s whose output is logic '1' within an interval from a to b, and with a period T (see Figure 3.2). Each bit s_i of a digital representation of a value X can be described as a PSF of X as $s_i = F_{s,i}(X)$, where the period is 2^{i+1}. Thus, utilizing a *PSF* block for each bit an analog to digital conversion can be performed.

An implementation of the *PSF* block is depicted in Figure 4.1 and was also proposed in [6]. The capacitor C_c and the tunnel junction C_t form an electron trap, which has a periodic transfer function. If the input voltage rises, the output voltage follows, due to capacitance division. At some point, though, the voltage over the tunnel junction exceeds the critical voltage and an electron tunnels to node T. The voltage of node T drops therefore. As the input voltage continues to rise, the voltage of node T rises again until it reaches the critical voltage. To obtain a *PSF* implementation a SET inverter [4] was added, which functions as a literal gate. As long as the input is below the threshold value, the output is '0', if the input exceeds the threshold, the output value becomes '1'.

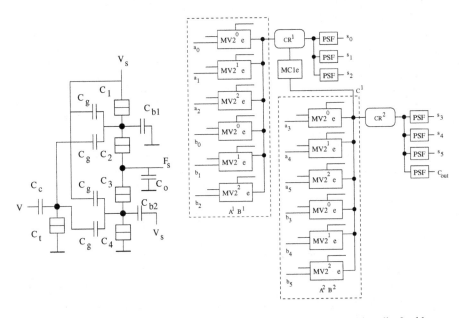

Fig. 4.1. *PSF* block implementation

Fig. 4.2. Organization of the 6-bit radix-8 adder

3.1   High Radix Strategy

In order to create a high radix EC addition scheme only small adjustments to the normal EC addition scheme are required. Figure 4.2 depicts a 6-bit radix-8 adder which operates as follows. Each 6-bit input is split into parts of three bits. The lower bits are added and stored in CR^1 using a normal 3-bit EC adder, while the higher bits are added and stored in CR^2. Consequently, charge reservoirs CR^1 and CR^2 contain the intermediate sums $IS^1 = \Sigma_{i=0}^{2}(a_i 2^i + b_i 2^i)q_e$ and $IS^2 = \Sigma_{i=3}^{5}(a_i 2^{i-3} + b_i 2^{i-3})q_e$, respectively. If the intermediate sum $IS^1 > 7q_e$, a carry signal is generated by the $MC1e$ block, adding $1q_e$ charge to CR^2, thus *conditionally* moving $1q_e$ charge. Finally, the charge values present in CR^1 and CR^2 are each converted to a binary representation by means of three and four *PSF* blocks, respectively.

3.2 Implementation

While the implementations of the *MVke* and the *PSF* block were proposed in [6] no implementation of the *MC1e* building block was previously introduced. This section presents a possible implementation of a generalized version of the *MC1e* block, i.e., the *MCke* block, that moves kq_e charge into a charge reservoir if its input value exceeds a certain value. Such a block constitutes a generalization of the *MC1e* block and it is also useful for a wider range of EC based arithmetic operations.

The *MCke* block has two Boolean inputs (enable V_e and reset V_r), one analog input V_v, and one output connected to a charge reservoir (see Figure 5). Note that the voltage V_v can be either a voltage source or the value of a charge reservoir. If $V_e = '1'$, $V_r = '0'$, and V_v exceeds a threshold ψ, then the block removes k electrons from the charge reservoir connected to the output. If $V_r = '1'$ (reset) and $V_e = '0'$ all the electrons which were previously removed from the reservoir are returned.

The functionality implemented by an *MCke* block can be thought of as consisting of two stages. The first stage detects whether V_v exceeds the threshold value ψ. If $V_v > \psi$, the Boolean output Y of the first stage is set to '1', otherwise it is set to '0'. Consequently, the operation performed by the first stage of the *MCke* block can be described as an 1-input threshold function. The SET threshold gate proposed in [9] can be utilized to realize the first stage of the *MCke* block.

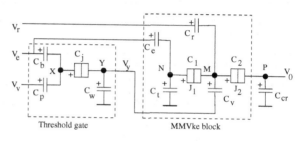

Fig. 5. *MCke* block implementation

The second stage of the *MCke* block removes k electrons from a charge reservoir when $V_r = '0'$ and $V_e = V_y = '1'$. The *MVke* block proposed in [6] performs a similar function and can be adjusted to operate as specified above. The resulting Modified Move k electrons (*MMVke*) block functions slightly different than the *MVke* block. The enable signal V_e is used to set a positive voltage over junction 2 (J2) and junction 1 (J1). Capacitance values are such that the voltage over junction 2 is close to its critical voltage while the voltage over junction 1 stays below its critical voltage. The driving input V_y is connected through a capacitor to the central node M. If $V_y = '0'$ no tunnel event can take place, but if $V_y = '1'$ the voltage over J2 exceeds its critical voltage and k electrons tunnel from node P to node N. For an extensive overview of the *MMVke* block the reader is referred to [10].

3.3 Simulation

We have verified the *MCke* implementation by means of simulation using the SET simulation package SIMON [11]. Simulation results were obtained using the following circuit parameters: logic '0'= 0mV, logic '1'= 16mV, and the capacitance of the charge reservoir is $10^{-14}F$, in correspondence with previously designed EC building blocks [6]. Assuming a threshold voltage of 12.2mV, as needed for the 6-bit radix 8 adder, we calculated the following parameters for the threshold gate: $C_w = 10aF$, $C_j = 0.5aF$, $C_p = 5aF$ and $C_b = 7.4aF$. The voltage swing on the output of the threshold gate was calculated as $15mV$. For $k = 1$ the following parameters were derived for the $MVke$ block: $C_p = 5aF$, $C_b = 5.25aF$, $C_j = 0.5aF$, $C_w = 50aF$, $C_v = 2aF$, $C_1 = 7.43aF$, $C_2 = 0.5aF$, $C_e = 200aF$, $C_t = 100aF$ and $C_r' = 5aF$. All simulations indicate that this building block functions correctly.

We also simulated the 6-bit radix 8 addition scheme as depicted in Figure 4.2. The parameters of the utilized $MVke$ and PSF building blocks are those used in the EC adder presented in [6]. As stated earlier, a carry of one electron must be generated by the $MCke$ block when the CR^1 reservoir contains eight or more electrons. Thus the threshold voltage of the $MCke$ block should be the voltage corresponding with a charge of 7.5 electrons on the capacitance of the CR^1 reservoir. Therefore, the threshold voltage V_{vth} was set to $12.2mV$, which corresponds with the threshold voltage used for the $MCke$ block in the simulation mentioned above.

The simulation results are depicted in Figure 6. The top block of two signals represent the reset

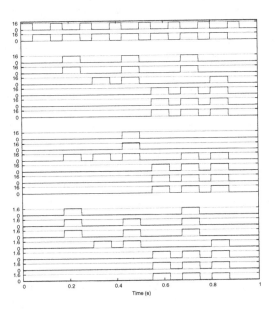

Fig. 6. Simulation results for the 6-bit radix-8 adder. From top to bottom (LSB first): reset(1), enable(1), input A(6), input B(6), sum(7)

and the enable, respectively. The second two blocks, each containing six signals, represent the input vectors A and B, respectively. The bottom block, containing seven signals represents the output vector of the adder. For each vector displayed in the graph, the top bar represents the least significant bit while the bottom bar represents the most significant bit. The test vectors A and B were chosen such that the $MCke$ block was tested for correct functionality under some extreme operating conditions. The simulation indicates that the high radix adder functions correctly. The adder requires 187 circuit elements and has a delay of $13.7\ ns$.

4   High-Radix EC Multiplier

Figure 7 depicts a basic (non high radix) multiplication scheme (first proposed in [5]), which operates as follows. Each bit of operand B is connected to an $MVke$ block, which adds $2^i q_e$ charge to the bottom charge reservoir if input b_i is logic '1'. Consequently, the charge reservoir contains the intermediate sum $IS = \Sigma_{i=0}^{1} b_i 2^i q_e$. This intermediate sum is fed into the V inputs of a next set of $MVke$ blocks. Therefore, these blocks add $IS * a_i * 2^i q_e$ charge to the top charge reservoir. Consequently, that reservoir contains the product of inputs A and B. The value in the top reservoir is analog and can be converted to the digital domain using PSF blocks as it was done in the EC addition scheme (Figure 2). The multiplication scheme contains an OpAmp which has not been designed yet, but which can potentially be implemented using a hybrid FET-SET technology [12].

4.1 High Radix Strategy

The high-radix EC multiplication scheme we propose is based on the full-tree multiplication strategy [13] often used in fast multipliers, which comprises three steps. In the first step all partial products are produced at once in parallel. When assuming binary operands this can be done by simple AND-gates and for n-bit operands, this first step produces n rows of bits. In the second step, the number of rows is reduced using one or more stages of counters. With each stage of counters, the number of rows is reduced until only two rows are left over. In the last step these two bit rows are added, often by using a fast addition scheme like carry look-ahead.

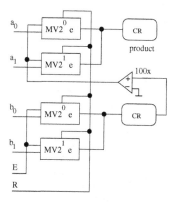

Fig. 7. 2-bit EC multiplication scheme

The strategy of the high-radix EC multiplication we propose, which is depicted in Figure 9.1 for the case of 8-bit radix 4 multiplication, comprises the same three steps with some adjustments. In the next section each step is explained in more detail.

4.2 Implementation

In the *first step*, the partial products are formed. Since we work in radix r, the operands are split into digits of $log_2 r$ bits. Assuming an operand size of n bits, this results in $\lceil \frac{n}{log_2 r} \rceil$ digits for each operand. The multiplication of these digits is performed by normal EC multipliers, of which a 2-bit instance is depicted in Figure 7.

The direct application of the EC multiplication scheme for step one requires $(\frac{n}{log_2 r})^2$ such multipliers. However, we can reduce the number of elements if we observe that each digit of B can be converted to analog once, after which this analog value is used by all multipliers in the same row (see Figure 8).

In the *second step* the number of rows is reduced by EC counters, which functionality is similar to normal population counters [14] used for binary operands. However, an EC counter assumes a number (k) of analog high-radix (r) inputs, all having the same weight, i.e., the inputs are all in the same column. The EC counter produces a number of outputs (s) in the same radix as the inputs, representing the sum of the inputs values, i.e., it produces a row. In the remainder of this paper we denote a specific instance of such an EC counter as EC ($k,r;s$) counter.

An EC counter implementation is depicted in Figure 9.2 for the case of four radix 16 inputs and operates as follows. Each analog input is buffered and amplified before

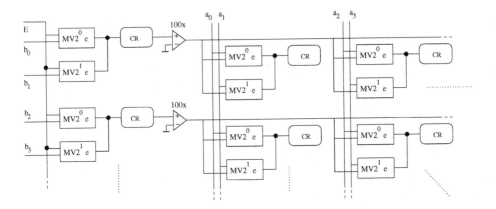

Fig. 8. Step one of high-radix EC multiplication

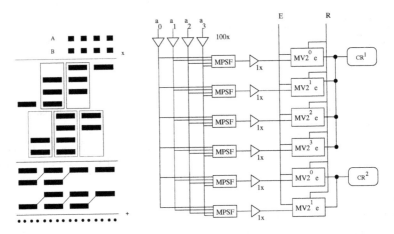

Fig. 9.1. 8-bit radix 4 EC multiplication strategy

Fig. 9.2. EC (4,16;2) counter

it is fed into the *MPSF* blocks [15] in order to eliminate feedback effects. The *MPSF* blocks, which are multiple input versions of the *PSF* block depicted in Figure 4.1, perform both the addition of the inputs and the conversion of the intermediate sum to the digital domain. Once the intermediate sum is converted to the digital domain, it is split into digits of $log_2 r$ bits, in order to guaranty that the output is in the correct radix. These digits are each converted back to the analog domain by sets of *MVke* blocks and the final result is stored in charge reservoirs.

Since in our case the maximum intermediate sum is 64, six *MPSF* blocks are required each one producing one bit. The first four of these bits are used to produce the analog sum output, which is done by four *MVke* blocks. The last two bits are used to produce the carry signal, which is done by two more *MVke* blocks.

We note here that the partial products produced by the first step do not all have the same weight. In Figure 9.1 this is graphically represented, as the partialproducts in the bottom four rows have a different alignment as the ones in the top four rows. In order to end up with equal aligned intermediate sums, an adjusted counter can be used for the partial products in the bottom rows.

In counter based binary full-tree multiplication, the number of rows is reduced to two, which subsequently is reduced to one row using a fast adder. However, as opposed to standard adders, EC adders can perform k:1 reduction (within certain limits for k) in almost the same delay as 2:1 reduction [15]. Therefore, in the high-radix EC multiplication scheme the number of rows does not have to be reduced to two, and the reduction process can be stopped earlier than in binary multiplication schemes. For example, in the 8-bit radix 4 EC multiplication in Figure 9.1 only one stage of five counters is required.

The *third step* of the high-radix EC multiplication is the final addition of a number of rows of intermediate sums. In general, this step of the multiplication is performed by some fast addition scheme like carry look-ahead, carry-skip, etc. For the EC paradigm, such a fast addition scheme is not designed yet, thus in this paper we use a ripple carry structured adder.

The addition scheme we use in here, consists of several EC addition blocks, which functions as a high radix, multiple input full adder. The addition block is implemented by an EC counter, but omitting CR^1 and the corresponding $MVke$ blocks. Thus the outputs of the first set of $MPSF$ blocks are producing the output bits. Charge reservoir CR^2 remains and contains the carry signal. To create an adder, the addition blocks are cascaded in parallel with the carry-out of block i connected to the carry-in of block $i+1$.

4.3 Simulation

To verify the high-radix multiplication scheme we simulated the 8-bit radix 4 multiplier. We used an approach of partitioning to simulate the whole multiplier, for the following reason. Although SIMON contains the OpAmp as circuit element, using it in SET circuitry causes some random effects to occur. Partitioning the circuit in parts ending with an OpAmp resolves this problem. To simulate the entire circuit, the output of each OpAmp was stored and used as an input in the next part. The simulation results indicated that the multiplier functions correctly. The multiplier requires 2372 circuit elements and has a total delay of 63.6 *ns*.

5 Conclusions

In this paper we presented a high radix EC addition scheme and a high radix EC multiplication scheme. For both arithmetic operations, first we briefly discussed the normal (non high radix) EC scheme. Second, we presented the high radix addition scheme and explained its functionality. Third, we explained the implementation of the high radix multiplication scheme in details. Finally, we presented simulation results and evaluate the schemes in terms of delay and area cost. The 6-bit radix 8 addition scheme requires 187 circuit elements and has a delay of 13.7 *ns*. The 8-bit radix 4 multiplication scheme requires 2372 circuit elements and has a total delay of 63.6 *ns*.

References

1. Waser, R., ed.: Nanoelectronics and Information Technology - Advanced Electronic Materials and Novel Devices. 1st edn. Wiley-VCH, Berlin (2003)
2. : International Technology Roadmap for Semiconductors, 2003 Edition, Executive Summary. Downloadable from website http://public.itrs.net/Home.htm (2003)
3. Likharev, K.: Single-Electron Devices and Their Applications. Proceeding of the IEEE **87** (1999) 606–632
4. Lageweg, C., Cotofana, S., Vassiliadis, S.: Static buffered set based logic gates. In: 2nd IEEE Conference on Nanotechnology (NANO). (2002) 491–494
5. Cotofana, S., Lageweg, C., Vassiliadis, S.: On computing addition related arithmetic operations via controlled transport of charge. In: proceedings of 16th IEEE Symposium on Computer Arithmetic. (2003) 245–252
6. Cotofana, S., Lageweg, C., Vassiliadis, S.: Addition Related Arithmetic Operations via Controlled Transport of Charge. IEEE Transactions of Computers **54** (2005) 243–256
7. Wasshuber, C.: About Single-Electron Devices and Circuits. PhD thesis, TU Vienna (1998)
8. Ishibashi, K., Tsuya, D., Suzuki, M., Aoyagi, Y.: Fabrication of a Single-Electron Inverter in Multiwall Carbon Nanotubes. Applied Physics Letters **82** (2001) 3307–3309
9. Lageweg, C., Cotofana, S., Vassiliadis, S.: A Linear Threshold Gate Implementation in Single Electron Technology. In: IEEE Computer Society Workshop on VLSI. (2001) 93–98
10. Meenderinck, C.: Single electron tunneling based arithmetic operations. Master's thesis, Delft University of Technology (2005)
11. (http://www.lybrary.com/simon/)
12. Likharev, K., Korotkov, A.: Ultradense Hybrid SET/FET Dynamic RAM: Feasibility of Background Charge Independent Room Temperature Single Electron Digital Circuits. In: Proceedings of the International Semiconductor Device Research Symposium, Charlottesville, Virginia (1995) 355–359
13. Parhami, B.: Computer Arithmetic. Oxford University Press (2000)
14. Dadda, L.: Some schemes for parallel multipliers. Alta Frequenza **34** (1965) 349–356
15. Meenderinck, C., Cotofana, S.D.: Computing periodic symmetric functions in single electron tunneling technology. In: Proceedings of International Semiconductor Conference (CAS). (2005) 47–50

Area, Delay, and Power Characteristics of Standard-Cell Implementations of the AES S-Box

Stefan Tillich, Martin Feldhofer, and Johann Großschädl

Graz University of Technology,
Institute for Applied Information Processing and Communications,
Inffeldgasse 16a, A–8010 Graz, Austria
{stillich,mfeldhof,jgrosz}@iaik.tugraz.at

Abstract. Cryptographic substitution boxes (S-boxes) are an integral part of modern block ciphers like the Advanced Encryption Standard (AES). There exists a rich literature devoted to the efficient implementation of cryptographic S-boxes, whereby hardware designs for FPGAs and standard cells received particular attention. In this paper we present a comprehensive study of different standard-cell implementations of the AES S-box with respect to timing (i.e. critical path), silicon area, power consumption, and combinations of these cost metrics. We examined implementations which exploit the mathematical properties of the AES S-box, constructions based on hardware look-up tables, and dedicated low-power solutions. Our results show that the timing, area, and power properties of the different S-box realizations can vary by more than an order of magnitude. In terms of area and area-delay product, the best choice are implementations which calculate the S-box output. On the other hand, the hardware look-up solutions are characterized by the shortest critical path. The dedicated low-power implementations do not only reduce power consumption by a large degree, but they also show good timing properties and offer the best power-delay and power-area product, respectively.

1 Introduction

The Internet of the 21st century will consist of billions of non-traditional computing systems like cell phones, PDAs, sensor nodes, and other mobile devices ("gadgets") with wireless networking capability. Wireless networking, along with the fact that many of these devices (e.g. sensor nodes) are easily accessible, have raised a number of security concerns. Sophisticated security protocols, in combination with well-established cryptographic primitives, can ensure privacy and integrity of communication over insecure networks. Consequently, there is an increasing demand to implement cryptographic algorithms on resource-limited embedded devices like sensor nodes, smart cards, or mobile phones. Even some extremely constrained systems like radio frequency identification (RFID) tags may require cryptographic processing.

S. Vassiliadis et al. (Eds.): SAMOS 2006, LNCS 4017, pp. 457–466, 2006.

The Advanced Encryption Standard (AES), which has been announced by the NIST in 2001, defines one of the most important symmetric ciphers for the next decades [11]. The AES algorithm is a variant of the Rijndael cipher [4] and can be implemented efficiently in both software and hardware. Common AES hardware implementations take the form of cryptographic ASICs and co-processors. In addition, hardware/software co-design techniques like instruction set extensions have also been proposed in recent years [14]. Due to the high performance of modern microprocessors, AES software implementations can reach throughput rates which are sufficient for most applications. Therefore, hardware implementations of the AES algorithm are mainly important for high-end server systems with extreme performance requirements and for low-power and low-energy environments.

Most of the published AES hardware designs focus on high speed and high throughput for implementation on FPGAs [3,12]. In addition, some ASIC implementations have been reported in the recent literature. For instance, Hodjat et al. developed a 3.84 Gbits/s coprocessor based on a 0.18-μm CMOS technology with intended usage in high-end server applications [6]. Another high-speed implementation can be found in [16]. A completely different approach is necessary for low-power and low-energy devices. Feldhofer et al. published an AES implementation suited for passively-powered devices like RFID tags [5]. It is the smallest and most power-saving implementation known so far.

Modern symmetric ciphers require non-linear functions in order to defend against linear cryptanalysis. Substitution is a popular function for introducing non-linearity. A substitution function is commonly referred to as S-box and can be defined on basis of arithmetic operations or as an arbitrary mapping. Different cipher algorithms also use different numbers of S-boxes, e.g. DES uses eight S-boxes which map six to four bits, while AES uses a single S-box which is a bijective mapping from eight to eight bits.

The AES algorithm makes use of its S-box in the SubBytes round transformation as well as in the key expansion. From a mathematical point of view, the AES S-box is defined as an *inversion* in the finite field $GF(2^8)$ with a specific reduction polynomial [7], followed by an affine transformation [4]. The inverse S-box, which is required for the InvSubBytes round transformation for decryption, is simply the inverse of the affine transformation, followed by an inversion in $GF(2^8)$. The finite field inversion is the only non-linear operation of the AES algorithm. Since there exist many design options for the S-box in hardware, it is challenging to find an optimal implementation for a particular purpose. On the one hand, the main criterion for high-speed implementations is a short critical path, which allows to reach high clock frequencies[1]. On the other hand, S-box implementations for embedded devices call for small silicon area and low power consumption. In this paper we analyze and compare silicon area, critical path delay, and power consumption characteristics of the most common standard-cell implementations of the AES S-box. We hope that our results will help system designers to find the optimal S-box for their application.

---

[1] The S-box normally lies on the critical path of AES hardware implementations.

The remainder of this paper is organized as follows. In Section 2 the different implementation strategies for the AES S-box are discussed. In Section 3 we describe the particular implementations which we have examined. In Section 4 we discuss our experimental results and we conclude in Section 5.

2   Implementation Strategies for the AES S-Box

The AES is based on rounds consisting of linear and non-linear transformations [4]. All transformations operate on a two-dimensional array of 4×4 bytes (128 bits), called the *State*. One of the strengths of the AES algorithm is its simplicity, which facilitates the implementation on a wide range of different platforms under different constraints. Various hardware designs have been reported in the literature, whereby the efficient implementation of the S-box received particular attention [1,2,8,9,10,13,15].

The SubBytes transformation substitutes all 16 bytes of the State independently using the S-box. Furthermore, the S-box is also used in the AES key expansion. In software, the S-box is typically realized in form of a look-up table since the inversion in the finite field $GF(2^8)$ can not be calculated efficiently on general-purpose processors. In hardware, on the other hand, the implementation of the S-box is directed by the desired trade-off between area, delay, and power consumption. The most obvious implementation approach for the S-box takes the form of hardware look-up tables. However, since encryption and decryption require different tables, and each table contains 2048 bits, the overall hardware cost of this approach is relatively high.

An implementation option related to standard cells is the usage of ROM compilers to produce hardware macros. For the standard-cell technology that we have used, a ROM macro of sufficient size would require a considerable amount of silicon area. The critical path delay is very similar to a hardware look-up approach, but the power consumption of generated ROMs is about 2–3 orders of magnitude higher. Therefore, we do not consider the implementation of the S-box as ROM macro in this paper

More advanced approaches calculate the S-box function in hardware using its arithmetic properties. The focus of such implementations is the efficient realization of the inversion in $GF(2^8)$, which can be achieved by decomposing the finite field into the sub-fields $GF(2^4)$ and $GF(2^2)$. An inversion in a finite field of characteristic 2 can be carried out in different ways, depending on the basis which is used to represent the field elements [7]. The two most common types of bases for $GF(2^m)$ are the *polynomial basis* and the *normal basis*. A polynomial basis is a basis of the form $\{1, \alpha, \alpha^2, \dots, \alpha^{m-1}\}$ where α is a root of an irreducible polynomial $p(t)$ of degree m with coefficients from $GF(2)$. On the other hand, a normal basis can be found by selecting a field element $\beta \in GF(2^m)$ such that the elements of the set $\{\beta, \beta^2, \beta^4, \dots, \beta^{2^{m-1}}\}$ are linearly independent.

A third approach for implementing the AES S-box was proposed by Bertoni et al. in [1]. By using an intermediate one-hot encoding of the input, arbitrary logic functions (including cryptographic S-boxes) can be realized with minimal power consumption. The main drawback of this approach is that it results in relatively large silicon area.

3   Examined Implementations

All surveyed AES S-box implementations can perform forward and inverse byte substitution for encryption and decryption respectively. We have implemented all analyzed solutions either by ourselves or have obtained them from the authors of the respective publications[2]. All implementations just consist of combinatorial logic, i.e. no pipelining stages have been inserted.

The simplest design in our comparison is a straight-forward implementation of a hardware look-up table. The synthesizer transforms the behavioral description of the look-up table into a mass of unstructured standard cells. This approach will be denoted as **hw-lut**. A modification of that approach is to use sub-tables in order to minimize switching activity in the look-up tables to reduce power consumption. We have examined such solutions with sub-tables of size 16, 32, 64, 128, and 256 bytes, but in this paper we only cite results for size 16 (**sub16-lut**).

Implementations which calculate the S-box transformation in hardware have been first proposed by Wolkerstorfer et al. [15] and Satoh et al. [13]. The first approach decomposes the elements of $GF(2^8)$ into polynomials over the sub-field $GF(2^4)$ and performs inversion there. Our implementation of this solution is denoted as **wolkerstorfer**. Satoh's solution decomposes the field elements further into polynomials over the sub-field $GF(2^2)$, where inversion is a trivial swap of the lower and higher bit of the representation. This implementation is called **satoh** in the following. Both of these approaches represent the field elements by using a polynomial basis. Canright improved the calculation of the S-box by switching the representation to a normal basis [2]. Like in Satoh's solution, the finite field element's representation is mapped to a polynomial over the sub-field $GF(2^2)$. This approach will be denoted as **canright**.

A compromise between hardware look-up and calculation has also been examined. In this implementation (denoted as **hybrid-lut**) only the inversion in $GF(2^8)$ is implemented as look-up table. As this inversion is used for both encryption and decryption, the size of the look-up table is halved in relation to the **hw-lut** approach. The affine and inverse affine transformations are done in logic just as in the calculating implementations of **wolkerstorfer**, **satoh**, and **canright**.

The low-power approach of Bertoni et al. [1] uses a decode stage to represent the 8 bits of the input byte and the control bit which selects encryption or decryption into a one-hot encoding on 512 lines. The substitution itself is just a simple rewiring of these lines. As two of the lines always map to the same 8-bit result (one for encryption and one for decryption), these line pairs are combined with a logical OR to result in a one-hot encoding of the result on 256

---

[2] We would like to thank Johannes Wolkerstorfer and David Canright for providing their HDL source code.

lines. A subsequent encoder stage transforms this result back to an 8-bit binary value. Due to this decoder-permute-encoder structure, there is only very little signal activity within the circuit at a change of the input, resulting in low power consumption. Note that the structure of Bertoni's approach makes it in principle easily possible to introduce pipeline stages. However, it may be necessary to add a large number of additional flip-flops when the pipeline stage is placed between the decoder and encoder, i.e. on the one-hot encoded signal lines. These flip-flops will increase power consumption considerably and can easily mitigate the low-power advantages of this solution. For design scenarios where both power consumption and silicon area are of minor importance, Bertoni's approach can offer the best opportunity for reaching very high clock frequencies.

We have tested two implementations of Bertoni's approach: One implementation used a decoder with four stages as proposed in the original publication for minimal power consumption (**bertoni**). The second realization, denoted as **bertoni-2stg**, used a different decoder structure with only two stages in order to reduce the critical path of the circuit.

In the remainder of this paper we will refer to **wolkerstorfer**, **satoh**, and **canright** as *calculating implementations*. We will denote **hw-lut** and **hybrid-lut** as *look-up implementations*, and **sub16-lut**, **bertoni**, and **bertoni-2stg** as *low-power implementations*.

4   Experimental Results

For our experiments we have used a 0.35 μm CMOS standard cell library from austriamicrosystems. We synthesized all implementations described in Section 3 using the Physically Knowledgeable Synthesis (PKS) tool from Cadence. For each implementation numerous synthesis runs with different target values for maximal critical path delay have been performed. Each synthesis run provided the actual critical path delay, the area of the synthesized design, and the total power consumption. However, for our evaluation we only used results where the timing constraints were met by the synthesizer.

Most of the following figures use a logarithmic scale on the Y-axis, as otherwise it would not be possible to display the results for all implementations within a single figure. Each legend cites the functions in the same top-down order as they are contained in the respective figure.

In Figure 1 the area of synthesized designs with a specific critical path delay are shown. The area is given in gate equivalents (GE), calculated as total area divided by the size of a 2-input NAND with the lowest driving strength, which is the NAND20 standard cell of the library we used.

Amongst the three calculating implementations (at the bottom of the figure), **canright** is clearly the best. It has the smallest size, but suffers from a longer critical path than the hardware look-up implementations and the low-power implementations. The calculating implementations are smaller than the other two approaches because they make use of the algebraic structure of the S-box to implement the substitution. On the other hand, this structure has a relatively

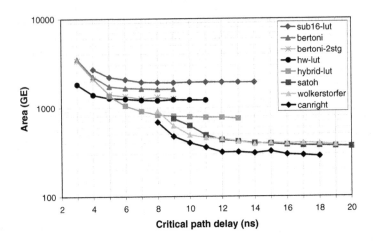

Fig. 1. Area vs. critical path delay

long critical path. The shortest critical path can be achieved with **hw-lut** but its size is 2–3 times that of **canright**. Look-up implementations neglect the algebraic structure of the S-box and just aim at a straightforward realization of the boolean equations constituted by the input-output relation. Hence, the synthesizer has a much higher degree of freedom for optimizing the circuit, which allows for a much shorter critical path at the expense of silicon area. Also good speed can be achieved with **bertoni** and **bertoni-2stg**, but they require even more silicon area.

The low-power implementations also neglect the arithmetic properties of the substitution and just implement the boolean equations of the input-output relation. However, they use a specific structure (decode-permute-encode) to reduce signal activity. Although the critical path is similarly short as for look-up implementations, the one-hot encoding requires more silicon area than the look-up implementations. The **sub16-lut** approach also has a significant area overhead introduced by the address decoding of the sub-tables, which makes it the solution requiring the most silicon area. Moreover, the address decoding logic leads to a longer critical path. As expected, the compromise between hardware look-up and calculation (**hybrid-lut**) lies roughly between **hw-lut** and the calculating implementations in regard of both critical path delay and area.

Figure 2 shows the total power consumption in relation to the critical path delay. All power figures have been normalized to the power consumption of **hw-lut** for 5.0 ns delay. The low-power implementations based on the approach by Bertoni (**bertoni, bertoni-2stg**) show the lowest power consumption. The original implementation **bertoni** has the best characteristics while the modified version **bertoni-2stg** is slightly worse. Bertoni's approach is solely directed towards low power consumption with a minimal level of signal activity in the circuit. Therefore, it is better than the **sub16-lut** approach, which tries to improve a straightforward look-up table implementation (**hw-lut**) with low-power

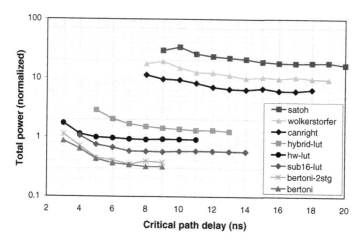

Fig. 2. Total power consumption vs. critical path delay

measures. The **sub16-lut** implementation requires almost twice as much power as **bertoni**, while **hw-lut** consumes 2–3 times more power. The **hybrid-lut** approach requires even considerable more power than **hw-lut**.

The power consumption of the calculating implementations is much higher than that of the low-power and look-up versions. The algebraic evaluation of the S-box function in calculating implementations requires re-computation of all intermediate values even if only a few number of input bits toggle. This behavior entails very high signal activity. In look-up implementations a change of a few input bits affects the calculation of all output bits separately. As some output bits will be left unchanged, the signal activity within this particular path is low and hence limits the power consumption. The most power-efficient variant among the calculating implementations is **canright**, which has 6–10 times the power consumption of **hw-lut**. The power consumption of **wolkerstorfer** is about 9–20 times higher and those of **satoh** is even 17–34 times higher.

Figure 3 shows our results in terms of the power-area product. This metric is particularly relevant for applications which require both small silicon area and low power consumption, e.g. cryptographically enhanced RFID tags or sensor nodes. Due to their high power consumption, the calculating implementations have the worst power-area products.

For relaxed critical path conditions, **hybrid-lut**, **sub16-lut**, and **hw-lut** have similar characteristics, with slight advantages for **hybrid-lut** if a longer critical path is tolerable. When further reducing the critical path, **hybrid-lut** shows rather bad properties compared to **sub16-lut**. Finally, if an extremely short critical path is desired, **hw-lut** and **bertoni** have the best power-area product, followed by **bertoni-2stg**. Among these three designs, **bertoni** and **bertoni-2stg** should be preferred over **hw-lut** if a critical path delay of more than 4 ns is acceptable. Our results show slight advantages for **bertoni-2stg** compared to **bertoni** for some critical path targets (5–7 ns).

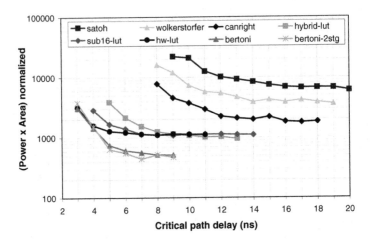

Fig. 3. Power-area product vs. critical path delay

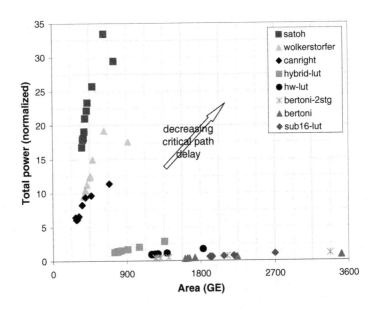

Fig. 4. Total power consumption vs. area

Figure 4 displays total power consumption in relation to required silicon area. Generally, the points farther away from the point of origin belong to synthesis results for shorter critical path delays. The figure shows that calculating implementations tend to sacrifice power efficiency to achieve higher speed. On the other hand, look-up and low-power implementations trade silicon area for a shorter critical path. To minimize the critical path delay, the synthesizer uses optimization techniques like the utilization of standard cells with higher driving strengths and duplication of logic paths, which results in a considerable higher power consumption for signal switches. Calculating implementations have an inherently high number of signal switches and therefore incur an over-proportional increase in power consumption for reduced critical path delays. Look-up and low-power implementations, on the other hand, have much lower levels of signal activity which only leads to moderate increases in power consumption for shorter critical paths.

5   Conclusions

In this paper we have examined eight AES S-box implementations which follow three different design strategies. We have analyzed and compared various cost metrics like critical path delay, silicon area, and power consumption of these implementations based on synthesis runs with a 0.35 μm CMOS standard cell library. To our knowledge this is the first comprehensive survey of all possible standard cell implementations of the AES S-box published so far. While the results for the calculating implementations only apply to the AES S-box, the insights from the other two implementation strategies (look-up except **hybrid-lut** and low-power) are also useful for other cryptographic S-boxes.

Acknowledgements

The research described in this paper has been supported by the Austrian Science Fund under grant P16952–N04 and by the FIT-IT initiative of the Austrian Federal Ministry of Transport, Innovation, and Technology (project SNAP).

The work described in this paper has been supported in part by the European Commission through the IST Programme under Contract IST-2002-507932 ECRYPT. The information in this document reflects only the author's views, is provided as is and no guarantee or warranty is given that the information is fit for any particular purpose. The user thereof uses the information at its sole risk and liability.

References

1. G. Bertoni, M. Macchetti, L. Negri, and P. Fragneto. Power-efficient ASIC Synthesis of Cryptographic Sboxes. In *Proceedings of the 14th ACM Great Lakes Symposium on VLSI (GLSVLSI 2004)*, pp. 277–281. ACM Press, 2004.
2. D. Canright. A very compact S-Box for AES. In *Cryptographic Hardware and Embedded Systems — CHES 2005*, vol. 3659 of *Lecture Notes in Computer Science*, pp. 441–455. Springer Verlag, 2005.
3. P. Chodowiec and K. Gaj. Very compact FPGA implementation of the AES algorithm. In *Cryptographic Hardware and Embedded Systems — CHES 2003*, vol. 2779 of *Lecture Notes in Computer Science*, pp. 319–333. Springer Verlag, 2003.
4. J. Daemen and V. Rijmen. *The Design of Rijndael*. Springer Verlag, 2002.

5. M. Feldhofer, J. Wolkerstorfer, and V. Rijmen. AES implementation on a grain of sand. *IEE Proceedings Information Security*, 152(1):13–20, Oct. 2005.
6. A. Hodjat, D. D. Hwang, B.-C. Lai, K. Tiri, and I. M. Verbauwhede. A 3.84 Gbits/s AES crypto coprocessor with modes of operation in a 0.18-μm CMOS technology. In *Proceedings of the 15th ACM Great Lakes Symposium on VLSI (GLSVLSI 2005)*, pp. 351–356. ACM Press, 2005.
7. R. Lidl and H. Niederreiter. *Finite Fields*. Cambridge University Press, second edition, 1996.
8. M. Macchetti and G. Bertoni. Hardware implementation of the Rijndael SBOX: A case study. *ST Journal of System Research*, 0(0):84–91, July 2003.
9. N. Mentens, L. Batina, B. Preneel, and I. M. Verbauwhede. Systematic evaluation of compact hardware implementations for the Rijndael S-box. In *Topics in Cryptology — CT-RSA 2005*, vol. 3376 of *Lecture Notes in Computer Science*, pp. 323–333. Springer Verlag, 2005.
10. S. Morioka and A. Satoh. An optimized S-Box circuit architecture for low power AES design. In *Cryptographic Hardware and Embedded Systems — CHES 2002*, vol. 2523 of *Lecture Notes in Computer Science*, pp. 172–186. Springer Verlag, 2002.
11. National Institute of Standards and Technology (NIST). Advanced Encryption Standard (AES). Federal Information Processing Standards (FIPS) Publication 197, Nov. 2001.
12. N. Pramstaller and J. Wolkerstorfer. A universal and efficient AES co-processor for field programmable logic arrays. In *Field Programmable Logic and Application — FPL 2004*, vol. 3203 of *Lecture Notes in Computer Science*, pp. 565–574. Springer Verlag, 2004.
13. A. Satoh, S. Morioka, K. Takano, and S. Munetoh. A compact Rijndael hardware architecture with S-Box optimization. In *Advances in Cryptology — ASIACRYPT 2001*, vol. 2248 of *Lecture Notes in Computer Science*, pp. 239–254. Springer Verlag, 2001.
14. S. Tillich, J. Großschädl, and A. Szekely. An Instruction Set Extension for Fast and Memory-Efficient AES Implementation. In *Communications and Multimedia Security — CMS 2005*, vol. 3677 of *Lecture Notes in Computer Science*, pp. 11–21. Springer Verlag, 2005.
15. J. Wolkerstorfer, E. Oswald, and M. Lamberger. An ASIC implementation of the AES SBoxes. In *Topics in Cryptology — CT-RSA 2002*, vol. 2271 of *Lecture Notes in Computer Science*, pp. 67–78. Springer Verlag, 2002.
16. X. Zhang and K. K. Parhi. High-speed VLSI architectures for the AES algorithm. *IEEE Transactions on Very Large Scale Integration (VLSI) Systems*, 12(9):957–967, Sept. 2004.

Integrated Microsystems in Industrial Applications

Paddy J. French

EI/EWI-DIMES, TU Delft, Mekelweg 4, 2628 CD Delft, The Netherlands
Tel.: +31-15-2784729
P.J.French@tudelft.nl

Abstract. Since the 1960s etching of silicon has been used to make three-dimensional structures. The first devices were pressure sensors using a thin silicon membrane. More recently accelerometers and gyroscopes have been developed. All of these devices can be integrated with electronics enabling the introduction of extra functions such as self-test and self-calibration. A broader look at sensors shows a wealth of integrated devices. The critical issues are reliability and packaging if these devices are to find the applications. A number of silicon sensors have shown great commercial success. This paper will give a brief overview of the technologies and some examples of applications.

Keywords: integrated sensors, packaging.

1 Introduction

Silicon is brittle, but has a high Young's modulus, which makes it an excellent mechanical material for micromechanical devices. The mechanical properties are well documented in the paper from Petersen [1]. The first examples of micromachined structures go back to the early 1960s with a membrane based pressure sensor. The mid 1960s also saw the first surface micromachined structures using a resonating gate device, although this did not perhaps receive the attention it deserved [2]. Instead the attention was concentrated on anisotropic etching using etchants such as KOH, EDP and hydrazine and later TMAH [3-4], yielding structures as shown in Fig. 1. In addition to wet etching, dry etching {reactive ion etching (RIE) and also Deep RIE (DRIE)} has become a major player in the Microsystems industry. Surface micromachining only became prominent with the publication of a number of papers using polysilicon as the mechanical layer [5-6].

Surface micromachining involves the deposition of thin films and the selective removal of one or more layers to produce free-standing structures. This is illustrated in Fig. 2.

A clear difference between the two technologies is the dimensions. With bulk micromachining the dimensions are often the full wafer thickness (about 500μm) and lateral dimensions in the mm range, whereas with surface micromachining are usually less than 5μm, with lateral in the order of 200μm-500μm.

Further issues are packaging and reliability, which in some case has prevented devices reaching the market. Furthermore, Microsystems are being applied to an

S. Vassiliadis et al. (Eds.): SAMOS 2006, LNCS 4017, pp. 467–476, 2006.

increasing number of harsh environments. Wafer-level packaging is able to offer protection of delicate structures during wafer handling and also simplified and more flexible packaging. For the future development of Microsystems, a number of issues are important, although their relative importance depends on the applications. These factors include, amongst others, low power, increased functionality, reduced size. The issue of whether or not to integrate depends on application and process complexity. The following sections will briefly give a description of the technology and the potential problems followed by a look into industrial applications.

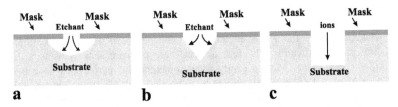

Fig. 1. Three etch structures (a) isotropic, (b) wet anisotropic and (c) deactive ion etching

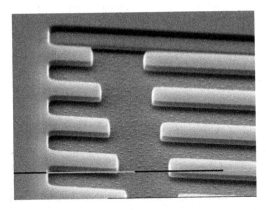

Fig. 2. Example of surface micromachined cantilevers [7]

2 Bulk Micromachining

Most of the early micromachined devices were produced using anisotropic wet etching in, for example, KOH. The advantage of this technique is that the lateral dimension are well defined in (100) wafers due to the stop on the (111) plane. The simplicity of the process lead to a number of commercial devices, such as pressure sensors and accelerometers. An important issue in fabricating devices is to define an etch-stop. The simplest is the time stop, but this is rather inaccurate. A more accurate technique is the p++ etch stop, where the etching slows down with high p-doping. This technique is simple and accurate but requires high doping which may not be desirable in terms of stress [8]. An accurate method, without high stress is the electrochemical etch-stop. Initially the p-type substrate is etched until the n-type epi is reached. At this point a current is able to flow, and the surface is passivated. The main problems with this technique is that it is difficult for batch processing and also the holder can create stress in the wafer [9-10]. An alternative to this technique is the galvanic etch-stop [11-13]. This uses a gold layer on the front side of the wafer creating a galvanic cell to achieve the same etchstop.

A further wet etching technique, which has received attention in recent years is macro-porous silicon, which is formed by electrochemical etching in HF. This simple process enables the fabrication of high aspect-ratio holes and trenches, and the nature of the process allows three-dimensional structures to be fabricated in a single step [14]. An example of a free-standing structure fabricated in this process is given in Fig. 3.

Fig. 3. Free-standing structure fabricated using a single etch step for macro-porous processing

Dry etching techniques were developed in the IC industry to improve profiles and reduce under-etching. The introduction of deep RIE using processes such as the Bosch and cryogenic processes opened many opportunities for the micromachining community.

2.1 Devices

As mentioned above, bulk micromachining has been successfully applied to pressure sensors, accelerometers and more recently gyroscopes [15-21]. Silicon pressure sensors were amongst the first micromachined sensors to find industrial applications. In many medical applications size and bio-compatibility are the critical issues. An example of a catheter pressure sensor from Lucas NovaSensor is given in Fig. 4 (left). An example of a sensor for higher pressures is also given in Fig. 4. In this case the pressure is exerted on a steel membrane, who thickness determines the pressure range. This device does not make use of micromachining, like many pressure sensors, it uses simple mechanical system to transfer the bending of the membrane to a stress on the surface of the chip. The size of the chip is in this case is 10x1 mm^2.

The market for accelerometers and gyroscopes as been greatly boosted by the automotive industry. In these applications reliability are critical and the ability to insert a self-test gave further confidence to the user. For the accelerometer the first

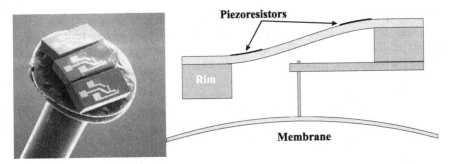

Fig. 4. (left Intercardial catheter-tip sensors for monitoring blood pressure. (Lucas NovaSensor, Fremont, CA), (right) Pressure sensor for high-pressure range using a steel membrane. This figure represents a sensor from Bell and Howell Corporation.

application was the airbag, to detect a crash and generate a signal to inflate the airbag. More recently lower range accelerometers have been applied to active suspension. Having this large market helped to bring down the price and stimulate further development and new markets. Gyroscopes, have been a more recent addition to the silicon based sensor field, for measuring rotation. Examples of a bulk micromachined accelerometer and a gyroscope can be seen in Fig. 5.

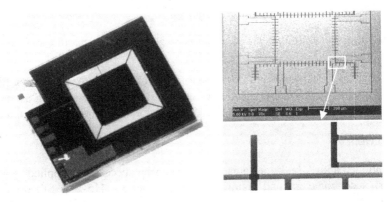

Fig. 5. (left) and example of a bulk micromachined accelerometer [17], (right) a bulk micromachined gyroscope [22]

3 Surface Micromachining

Although also a product of the 1960s, surface micromachining did not come to prominence until the 1980s. This period showed the potential of materials such as polysilicon for both sensors and actuators. Surface micromachining uses layers deposited on top of the substrate and one or more layer (sacrificial layer) is then selectively removed to yield structures such as shown in Fig. 2. A wide range of materials are available for both mechanical and sacrificial layers, as shown in table 1, where for each combination a sacrificial etchant is chosen which etches the sacrificial layer without serious damage to the mechanical layer. It should be noted that table 1 gives a few examples and is by no means a complete list.

Table 1. Examples of sacrificial and mechanical layers with the appropriate etchant

Sacrificial layer	Mechanical layer	Sacrificial etchant
Oxide (PSG, LTO etc)	Polysilicon, silicon nitride, silicon carbide	HF
Oxide (PSG, LTO etc)	Aluminium	Pad etch, HF (73%)
Polysilicon	Silicon nitride	KOH, TMAH
Polysilicon	Silicon dioxide	TMAH
Resist	Aluminium	Acetone/oxygen plasma

3.1 Devices

As with bulk micromachining a range of devices can be found. Pressure sensors can be fabricated with membrane in the range of 100μm, which can be useful for

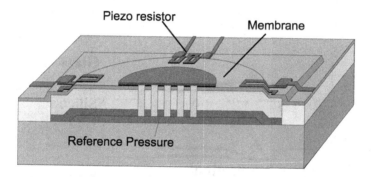

Fig. 6. Catheter pressure sensors using epi-poly [23]

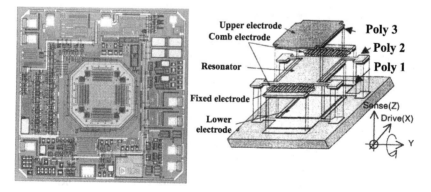

Fig. 7. The Analog Devices 2-D surface micromachined accelerometer. Reproduced with kind permission Kevin Chau, Analog Devices and (right) a polysilicon gyroscope [25].

applications such as catheters. Fig. 6 shows an example of a pressure sensor for catheter applications using epi-poly and piezoresistive output.

A surface micromachined accelerometer and a gyroscope are given in Fig. 7. The Analog Devices accelerometer is an example of a complete system, with sensor, read-out electronics, controlled power supply and self-test. With surface micro-machined accelerometers, electrostatic activation is an effective way to test the device.

4 Packaging and Reliability

Packaging and reliability are major issues in bring devices to the market, although it should not be forgotten that testing can also result in a major part of the final cost. Reliability can be divided into two categories (1) process yield and (2) reliability in operation. One of the issues of yield is related to packaging. Once etched the micromachined devices are extremely delicate until they are packaged. In many cases the devices are encapsulated in additional wafers prior to packaging using wafer-to-wafer bonding [26]. In the example given in Fig. 8, the lower glass wafer was bonded before the mass was released. This figure is a cross-sectional view of the device shown in Fig. 5 (left).

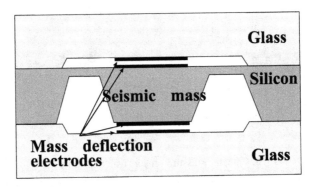

Fig. 8. Cross sectional view of an accelerometer with glass capping layers

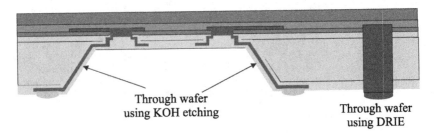

Fig. 9. Two through wafer interconnect options, using KOH and DRIE

An additional packaging option is to take the contact through the wafer. This can be done using KOH etching or DRIE. These two options are shown in **Fig. 9**. In both cases the metallisation was fabricated using electroplating of copper. In the case of the KOH option it is necessary to define metal lines from the backside to the wafer through the wafer to the frontside. This can be achieved either using a spray resist or electroplated resist. This technique can be extremely useful in cases where the bond wires on the frontside represent a problem. Although this complicates the processing, it is performed at wafer scale and thus when the wafers are diced, the packaging is simplified.

5 Microsystems in Standard IC Technologies

The devices described above have all required additional micromachining steps. However, many sensing devices can be integrated with standard electronics without use of additional steps. Simple Hall plates are a good example, since this can use diffusions already used in the transistor. A further example is given in Fig. 10. This is a thermal wind sensor. The basic principle is to heat part of the chip and measure the transfer of the heat down wind. The advantage of this system is that there are no moving parts.

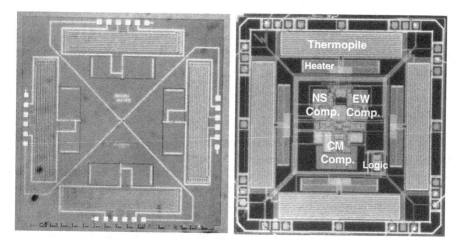

Fig. 10. (left) Thermal flow sensor and, (right) an integrated thermal flow sensor [27-28]

The new generation flow sensor (Fig. 10-right) is the same size but contains all the read-out electronics and thermal management. Furthermore, the whole device can be fabricated using standard electronics. In this case the sensor chip is more expensive but the total system is cheaper and less complicated.

The issue of testing, mentioned above, can also be tackled through electronics design. Fig. 11 shows an example of this approach. The problem in this case was

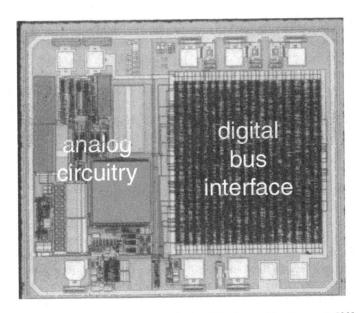

Fig. 11. Smart temperature sensor, designed for low calibration costs [29]

the lengthy calibration process, leading to high costs. Using electronic design, the calibration time could be greatly reduced, while maintaining accuracy, although the chip is more complicated. The end result was a reduction in the cost of the end product.

6 Conclusions

Silicon based sensors date back to the 1960s. In the early days they were simple membrane structures using piezoresistive output. Micromachining technologies have developed to an extend that complicated 3-D structures can be fabricated. The technologies can be divided into bulk and surface micromachining. Bulk micromachining, generally uses the full wafer thickness, whereas surface micromachining uses thin film on the surface of the wafer. The critical issues which were largely ignored in the early development are packaging and reliability. In sensor fabrication testing and packaging can easily represent more that 50% of the cost of the device. Packaging of delicate structures or structures that have to be exposed to the environment represent a number of challenges and if these are not considered at an early stage there is the risk that the device will not have commercial success.

References

1. K.E. Petersen, Silicon as a mechanical material, Proc. IEEE, 70, (1982), pp 420-457.
2. H.C. Nathanson and R.A. Wickstrom, A resonant-gate silicon surface transistor with high-Q band pass properties, Appl. Phys. Lett., 7, (1965), p 84.

3. K.E. Bean, "Anisotropic etching of silicon", IEEE Trans Electron Devices, ED-25, (1978), pp 1185-1193

4. A. Merlos, M.Acero, M.H.Bao, J.Bauselles, J.Esteve, TMAH/IPA anisotropic etching characteristics, Sensors & Actuators A 37-38 (1993) 737-743.

5. R.T. Howe and R.S. Muller, "Polycrystalline and amorphous silicon micromechanical beams: annealing and mechanical properties", Sensors and Actuators, 4, (1983), pp 447-454.

6. L-S. Fan, Y-C. Tai and R.S. Muller, "Pin joints, gears, springs, cranks and other novel micromechanical structures", Proceedings Transducers 87, Tokyo, (1987), pp 849-852.

7. M. Bartek, P.J. French and R.F. Wolffenbuttel, Planarization in surface micromachining using selective epitaxial growth. Proceedings Eurosensors 94, Toulouse, France, 26-28 September 1994, p 210.

8. E.D.Palik et al., Study of the etch-stop mechanism in silicon, J. Electrochem. Soc. 137 (1982) 2051-2059

9. B.Kloek, S.D.Colllins, N.F.de Rooij, R.L.Smith, Study of electrochemical etch-stop for high precision thickness control of silicon membranes, IEEE Electron Dev., 36 (1989) 663-669.

10. P.M.Sarro, A.W.van Herwaarden, Silicon cantilever beams fabricated by electrochemically controlled etching for sensor applications, J. Electrochem. Soc. 133 (1986) 1724-1729.

11. P.J.French, M.Nagao, M.Esashi, Electrochemical etch-stop in TMAH without externally applied bias, Sensors & Actuators A, 56 (1996) 279-280.

12. C.M.A. Ashruf, P.J.French, P.M.M.C.Bressers, P.M.Sarro, J.J.Kelly, A new contactless electrochemical etch-stop based on gold/silicon/TMAH galvanic cell, Sensors & Actuators A, 66 (1998) 284-291.

13. E.J. Connolly, S. Sakarya, P.J. French, X.H. Xia and J.J. Kelly, "A pratical galvanic etch-stop in KOH using sodium hypochlorite", Proceedings IEEE MEMS 2003, Kyoto, Japan, January 2003, pp 566-569.

14. H. Ohji, P.J. Trimp and P.J. French, "Fabrication of free standing structures using a single step electrochemical etching in hydrofluoric acid", Sensors and Actuators, A73 (1999) pp. 95-100.

15. H.V. Allen, S.C. Terry and D.W. de Bruin, "Accelerometer systems with self-testable features", Sensors and Actuators, 20, (1989), pp 153-161.

16. F. Rudolf, A. Jornod, J. Bergqvist and H. Leuthold, "Precision accelerometers with µg resolution" Sensors and Actuators, A21-23, (1990), pp 297-302

17. R.P. van Kampen, M.J. Vellekoop, P.M. Sarro and R.F. Wolffenbuttel, "Application of electrostatic feedback to critical damping of an integrated silicon capacitive accelerometer", Sensors and Actuators, A43, (1994), pp 100-106

18. Chr. Burrer and J. Esteve, "A novel resonant silicon accelerometer in bulk-micromachining technology", Sensors and Actuators, A46-47 (1995), pp 185-189.

19. O. Lüdtke, V. Biefeld, A. Buhrdorf and J. Binder, "Laterally driven accelerometer fabricated in single crystalline silicon" Sensors and Actuators, A82, (2000), pp 149-54.

20. H. Li, M. Bao, H. Yang, S. Shen and D. Lu, "A micromachined piezoresistive angular rate sensors with a composite beam structure" Sensors and Actuators, A 72, (1999), pp 217-223.

21. T. Fujita, K. Maenaka, T. Mizuno, T. Matusoka, T. Kojima, T. Oshima and M. Maeda, "Disk-shaped bulk micromachined gyroscope with vacuum sealing", Sensors and Actuators, A82, (2000), pp 198-204.

22. G. Craciun, H. Yang, M.A. Blauw, E. van der Drift and P.J. French, "Single step cryogenic SF_6/O_2 plasma etching process for the development of a novel quad beam gyroscope", Proceeding MME 02, Sinaia, Romania, October 2002, pp 55-28.

23. D. Tanase, J.F.L. Goosen, P.J. Trimp, P.J. French, "Multi-parameter sensor system with intravascular navigation for catheter/guide wire application", Sensors and Actuators A 97-98 (2002) pp116-124.

24. E. Kälvesten, L. Smith, L. Tenerz and G. Stemme, "The first micromachined pressure sensor for cardiovasular pressure measurements", Proceedings MEMS 98, Heidelberg, Germany, 25-29 January 1998, pp 574-579

25. T. Tsuchiya, Y. Kageyama, H. Funabashi and J. Sakata, "Vibrating gyroscope consisting of three layers of polysilicon thin films", Proceedings Transducers 99, Sendai, Japan, June 1999, pp 976-979.

26. R.P. van Kampen, M.J. Vellekoop, P.M. Sarro and R.F. Wolffenbuttel, "Application of electrostatic feedback to critical damping of an integrated silicon capacitive accelerometer", Sensors and Actuators, 43. (19944), pp 100-106.

27. B. van Oudheusden and J.H. Huijsing, An electronic wind meter based on a silicon flow sensor. Sens. Actuators A 21–23 (1990), pp. 420–424

28. K.A.A. Makinwa and J.H. Huijsing, "A smart wind sensor using thermal sigma-delta modulation techniques", Sensors and Actuators, 97-98, pp 15-20.

29. A. Bakker, High-accuracy CMOS smart temperature sensors", PhD thesis, TU Delft, The Netherlands, (2000), ISBN 90-901-3643-6.

A Solid-State 2-D Wind Sensor

K.A.A. Makinwa, Johan H. Huijsing, and Arend Hagedoorn

EI/EWI-DIMES, TU Delft, Mekelweg 4, 2628 CD Delft, The Netherlands
Tel.:+31-15-2786466
k.a.a.makinwa@tudelft.nl

Abstract. This paper describes the industrial realization of a solid-state wind sensor, that is, one without moving parts. The key component of the sensor is a heated silicon chip that is packaged in such a way that it is non-uniformly cooled by the wind. The resulting flow-induced temperature gradient is measured by on-chip temperature sensors. Their output is then digitized and processed by a microprocessor in order to determine both wind speed and direction. For wind speeds between 0.1 and 25m/s, the errors in the computed wind speed and direction are less than 0.5m/s (or ±3%) and ±3° respectively.

Keywords: thermal flow sensor, sensor systems.

1 Introduction

Over the centuries, many techniques have been devised to measure wind speed and direction. Probably the most well known involves the use of a cup anemometer to measure wind speed, and a wind vane to measure wind direction. While capable of giving excellent results, these instruments are mechanical devices, with moving parts which require regular maintenance, and which will eventually wear out. More elaborate techniques, such as laser and acoustic anemometry, are commercially available but are, at this moment, prohibitively expensive. This paper describes the realization of a solid-state wind sensor, i.e. a single instrument that measures both wind speed and direction, and which has no moving parts [1][2].

2 Operating Principle

The solid-state wind sensor described here makes use of the fact that airflow over a heated plate will cool it non-uniformly, as shown in Fig. 1. As a result, the heat distribution in the plate will no longer be symmetrically distributed, giving rise to a temperature gradient δT between two points straddling the centre of the plate (A and B in Fig. 1). In previous work [3], it has been shown that the magnitude of this flow-induced temperature gradient is a function of flow speed, and its direction is aligned with that of the flow. Thus, by accurately measuring this temperature gradient, both wind speed and direction may be determined.

The magnitude of the flow-induced gradient is also proportional to the temperature difference between the sensor and the airflow. To compensate for slow changes in

S. Vassiliadis et al. (Eds.): SAMOS 2006, LNCS 4017, pp. 477–484, 2006.

ambient temperature, the sensor is operated in a so-called constant-temperature-difference mode, in which it heated to a constant temperature (typically 15°C) above that of the airflow [4]. Operating in this mode also improves the speed at which the sensor responds to changes in flow velocity, since only the, much smaller, temperature gradient in the sensor changes. However, it complicates the sensor system, since it requires a separate ambient temperature sensor, which must be thermally isolated from the heated sensor, and as such cannot be co-integrated.

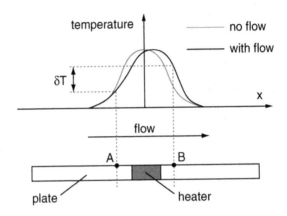

Fig. 1. Operating principle of the wind sensor

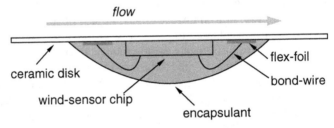

Fig. 2. Schematic cross-section of the packaged wind sensor chip

3 Sensor Packaging

The wind sensor consists of a thin ceramic disc, which is heated by resistors implemented on a square silicon chip glued to the disc, as shown in Fig. 2. The ceramic disc protects the chip from direct contact with the environment. Due to its thinness (0.25mm) and moderate thermal conductivity (20W/m•K) relative to that of silicon (150W/m•K), temperature sensors on the chip can measure the flow-induced temperature gradient in the disc.

Electrical contacts between the chip and the outside world are made via wire-bonded leads and a flex-foil. The fragile leads and the chip are then sealed by an opaque encapsulant. This method of packaging employs standard chip-on-board techniques and thus results in a robust, low-cost sensor.

4 Sensor Chip

A schematic layout of the sensor chip is shown in Fig. 3. It consists of a square silicon chip on which four heating resistors, four thermopiles and a central diode have been realized. The chip is fabricated in a standard (non-micromachined) low-cost (2 micron) bipolar process. The heaters are p^+-diffusion resistors, while the thermopiles each consist of 12 thermocouples made from p^+-diffusion resistors connected by strips of aluminium. Each thermopile has a temperature coefficient of about 6mV/K.

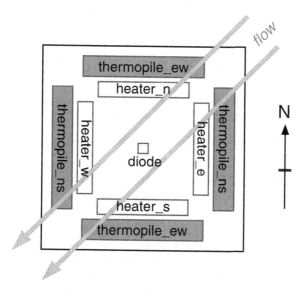

Fig. 3. Schematic layout of the sensor chip

The thermopiles measure north-south and east-west components (δT_{ns} and δT_{ew}) of the flow-induced temperature gradient. Thermopiles are ideally suited for this task because, being passive devices, they are inherently offset free. The flow-induced temperature differences are however quite small (in the milli-Kelvin range). As a result, the output of the thermopiles is quite small (in the millivolt range). Since thermopiles on opposite sides of the chip measure similar temperature differences, they are connected in series, thus doubling the sensor's output. The central diode is used to measure the chip's average temperature. When forward biased, the voltage drop across the diode has a sensitivity of approximately −2.1mV/K.

5 Interface Electronics

A block diagram of the sensor's interface electronics is shown in Fig. 4. It consists of three parts, a temperature control loop, circuitry that digitizes the thermopile outputs, and a low-cost microprocessor (PIC16C711) that uses this information to compute wind speed and direction.

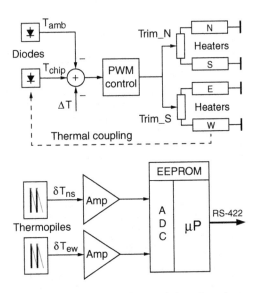

Fig. 4. Block diagram of the wind sensor's interface electronics\

The temperature control loop is a negative feedback circuit that maintains the sensor's average temperature T_{chip} at a constant temperature *difference* ΔT above that of the flow T_{amb}. The latter is measured by an external diode, which is thermally isolated from the heated chip. A pulse-width modulator drives the heaters with a constant-amplitude pulse train. The frequency of the resulting heat pulses (10kHz) is fixed and is chosen such that their harmonics are filtered out by the sensor's intrinsic thermal capacitance. Driven by the error signal of the feedback loop, the modulator varies the duty-cycle of the pulses, and thus the average heating power, such that ΔT is kept constant.

To compensate for thermal asymmetry, which may occur during the sensor's packaging, the heat distribution in the chip is centred by adjusting two potentiometers connected to the north-south and east-west heater pairs. These potentiometers are adjusted such that at zero flow, the temperature differences δT_{ns} and δT_{ew} measured by the thermopiles are nulled.

The millivolt-level output of the thermopiles is boosted by low-offset amplifiers to the 0-5V input range of the microprocessor's 8-bit ADC. To avoid degrading the sensor's performance, the effective resolution of the ADC is increased to approximately 9.5 bits by averaging eight successive 8-bit samples. Using the digitized thermopile outputs, the microprocessor computes wind speed and direction.

6   Aerodynamic Housing

As shown in Fig. 5, the packaged wind sensor chip is mounted in an aerodynamic housing, which guides horizontal wind components over the sensor in a well-defined

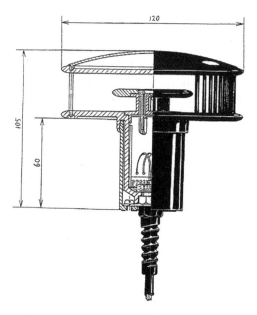

Fig. 5. Cross-sectional view of the wind sensor

Fig. 6. External view of the wind sensor

manner. The ceramic disc bearing the chip is mounted flush with the surface of a small inner disc, which in turn is located between two larger guide discs. The housing dramatically reduces the influence of vertical wind components, or sensor tilt, on the sensor's output. It also protects the sensor against direct sunshine or precipitation and houses the interface electronics.

The outer discs are joined together by struts, as shown in Fig. 6. These act as local obstructions to the wind and cause the airflow over the sensor to become turbulent. Without the struts, a discontinuity in the sensor's characteristic will be observed at high Reynolds numbers (which correspond to wind speeds of a few meters per second) at the natural transition between laminar and turbulent flow [4].

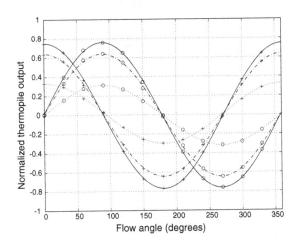

Fig. 7. Sensor output δT_{ns} (o) and δT_{ew} (+) as a function of wind speed

7 Sensor Calibration

Each sensor is calibrated in a wind tunnel at three wind speeds. At each speed, the sensor is rotated through 360 degrees to simulate variations in wind direction. As shown in Fig. 6, the north-south and east-west temperature differences δT_{ns} and δT_{ew} may be well approximated by sine and cosine functions of wind direction ϕ, which may be expressed as,

$$\delta T_{ns} = A_{ns} \sin(\phi + \varepsilon_{ns}) + a_{ns}, \tag{1}$$

$$\delta T_{ew} = A_{ew} \cos(\phi + \varepsilon_{ew}) + a_{ew}. \tag{2}$$

Where the amplitude A is a monotonic function of wind speed U, a is an offset due to residual thermal asymmetry in the sensor, and ε is a constant phase shift. The latter reflects the fact that the sensor's reference axis may not be exactly aligned with that of the measurement system.

The dependence of the amplitude and offset of the thermopile outputs on wind speed is shown in Fig. 8 for a typical sensor. By curve fitting, the amplitude is found to be proportional to U^n, where $n = 0.47$. This is very close to the value of 0.5 predicted by a theoretical analysis [5]. The temperature differences may now be expressed as,

$$\delta T_{ns} = U^n C_{ns} \sin(\phi + \varepsilon_{ns}) + a_{ns}, \tag{3}$$

$$\delta T_{ew} = U^n C_{ew} \cos(\phi + \varepsilon_{ew}) + a_{ew}, \tag{4}$$

where C is a constant sensitivity factor. Equations (3) and (4) may be inverted to obtain expressions for wind speed and direction in terms of the measured temperature differences and the offsets, [6]. Since the offsets are actually functions of wind speed, a recursive algorithm is employed in which the previously computed wind speed is used to determine the offset values used. The various constants determined during calibration are stored in a non-volatile memory (EEPROM). These are then used by the microprocessor in computing wind speed and direction.

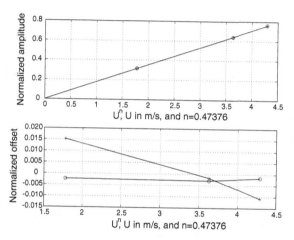

Fig. 8. Amplitude and offset of δT_{ns} (o) and δT_{ew} (+) as a function of wind speed

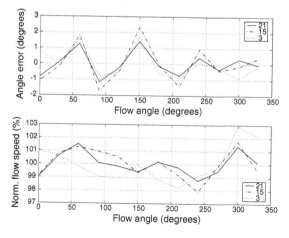

Fig. 9. Error in wind sensor output as a function of wind direction

8 Sensor Performance

The performance of a typical sensor is shown in Fig. 9. It may be seen that at the three calibration speeds, the sensor's accuracy is better than 0.5m/s (or ±3%) in wind speed and 3° in wind speed and direction respectively over the range 0.1 to 25m/s. At wind speeds below 0.2m/s, air currents generated by natural convection ultimately limit the sensor's accuracy. The sensor's response time to step changes in wind velocity is less than one second, which is fast enough for meteorological applications.

9 Conclusion

A solid-state wind sensor, i.e. one without moving parts has been successfully developed. The absence of moving parts makes for low maintenance and long life. The accuracy of the sensor is better than 0.5m/s (or ±3%) and 3° in wind speed and direction respectively over the range 0.1 to 25m/s. The sensor's small size and robust construction makes it suitable for a wide range of wind sensing applications.

References

1. Mierij Meteo B.V., "Solid state wind sensor MMW 005," http://www.mierijmeteo.nl.
2. J.H. Huijsing, A. Hagedoorn, B. W. van Oudheusden and H.J. Verhoeven, "Device for determining the direction and speed of an air flow," U.S. patent 6035711, March 2000.
3. B.W. van Oudheusden, "Integrated silicon flow sensors," Ph.D. thesis, Delft University of Technology (1989).
4. B.W. van Oudheusden and J. H. Huijsing, "An electronic wind meter based on a silicon flow sensor," Sensors and Actuators A, 21-23 (1990) pp. 420-424.
5. B. W. van Oudheusden, "The thermal modeling of a flow sensor based on differential convective heat transfer," Sensors and Actuators A, vol. 29, 1991, pp. 565-575.
6. K.A.A. Makinwa and J.H. Huijsing, "A wind sensor interface using thermal sigma-delta modulation techniques," Sensors and Actuators A, 92 (2001) pp. 280-285.

Fault-Tolerant Bus System for Airbag Sensors and Actuators

Klaas-Jan de Langen

Philips Semiconductors, Nijmegen, The Netherlands
klaas-jan.de.langen@philips.com

Abstract. In order to satisfy the increasing safety requirements for airbag deployment systems in cars, the number of airbag actuators and sensors increases steadily. It is important to keep the complexity of the system manageable, for example by replacing the current point-to-point systems by a networked system. This paper gives an overview of such a system and discusses some of the interesting implementation details.

Keywords: integrated circuits, in-vehicle networks.

1 Introduction

The older airbag systems consist of just a single crash sensor and two airbags and were relatively easy to wire. Modern airbag systems, however, are becoming more and more complex. The use of more than one airbag per passenger and the application of dual-stage airbags can bring the number of airbag actuators, also known as squibs, in a typical car to over ten. In addition, the sensing system comprises several devices such as a front crash sensor, several side-impact sensors and a roll-over sensor. Therefore, the Safe-by-Wire consortium has created a network specification for airbag sensors and actuators [1].

A brief overview of the bus specification will be given in Section 2. Subsequently, in Section 3 the implementation details are presented. Finally, conclusions are drawn.

2 Bus Specification Overview

An example of a typical Safe-by-Wire (SbW) network is shown in Figure 1. Several slaves are connected using a two-wire bus to the SbW master. The master communicates to the micro controller via an SPI interface. Although the specification allows mixing of sensor slaves and deployable squib slaves, the sensor slaves and squib slaves are preferably grouped together in a separate sensor bus and a deployment bus.

For EMC reasons, data is transmitted as a differential signal via a twisted pair. To keep costs down, no other wires are allowed and therefore the distribution of power and data has to be combined. The bus signal therefore consists of a sequence of power phases and data phases as depicted in Figure 2. During the power phase, the slaves

S. Vassiliadis et al. (Eds.): SAMOS 2006, LNCS 4017, pp. 485–489, 2006.

extract power from the bus and charge a local energy reserve capacitor that is used as a local supply for the slave. The process of switching between power and data level also results in a clock signal for the slaves, while the use of two different data levels implements a '0' or a '1'. An additional data level, S0, is used for special purposes such as interrupts and during firing commands.

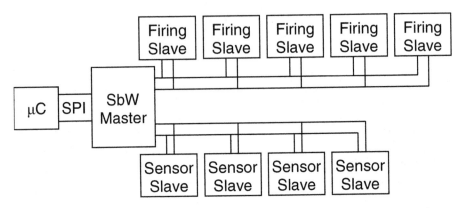

Fig. 1. Example of a SbW bus topology with a separate sensor bus and a deployment bus

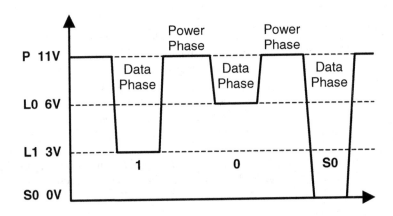

Fig. 2. Bus signal showing all voltage levels

The master creates the basic bus signal, but the '0' level is recessive and can be changed into a '1' by a slave. This way, slaves can fill in the required data. An example layout of data communication on the bus is the D-frame used for deployment devices as shown in Figure 3. The master starts with a start of frame (SOF), a power level followed by a data level at a lower frequency than the normal bus frequency.

Then, a reserved R bit is sent follow by a 4-bit command and an 8-bit slave address. Thereafter, 8 bits of data are sent by the master or the slave followed by an 8 bit CRC. The last bit, the E bit, can be set by the master in case an error was encountered during the frame transmission.

1	2	3	4	5	6	7	8	9	10	11	12	13	14	15	16	17	18	19	20	21	22	23	24	25	26	27	28	29
				transmitted by master												transmitted by master or slave												
SOF	R	4-bit command			6-bit slave address					8-bit data										8-bit CRC								E

Fig. 3. Example layout of bus communication

3 Implementation Details

A block diagram of a master with two SbW channels is depicted in Figure 4. The master consists of digital circuits such as the SPI interface and the SbW protocol controller while the circuits that implement the SbW physical layer, the floating supply and the transceiver are mainly analog.

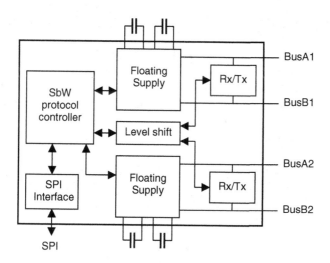

Fig. 4. Block diagram of a SbW master with two channels

A very important feature of the bus is that operation should continue even if one of the wires is shorted to ground or to the battery voltage. Shorts to ground (chassis) can easily occur, especially during a crash. This feature is implemented by the floating supply. A simplified schematic of the floating supply is presented in Figure 5. The supply voltage of the bus system is isolated from the ground-based battery voltage by using a capacitor C_1 that is charged during the data phase by closing switches S_1 and S_2 and then used to power the bus during the power phase by closing switches S_3 and S_4. This way, the bus voltages are completely floating with respect to the ground connection and shorting of one of the bus wires to any voltage is possible without impeding the bus communication. Note that the circuits are implemented in an SOI process so that handling of negative voltages is not a problem.

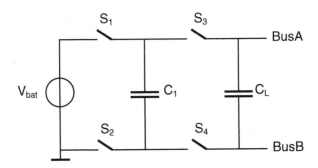

Fig. 5. Simplified schematic of floating supply

An interesting problem that remains to be solved is how to communicate between the ground-based system and the floating bus system. Shorting BusA to ground forces BusB more than 10V below ground while a short to battery forces the BusB voltage above ground. Therefore, the digital signals for the transceiver can be at any level. A very simple technique can solve this problem of level shifting between the ground-based circuit and the circuits connected to the bus [2]. As shown in Figure 6, diodes D_1 and D_2 are used to select the higher of the two supply voltage V_{sup1} and V_{sup2}. The selected voltage is then used to supply current mirror M_1, M_2 that can always mirror current I_1 into load resistor R_L. By modifying the current I_1 the voltage across R_L can be changed. This technique can be used to transfer digital as well as analog signals.

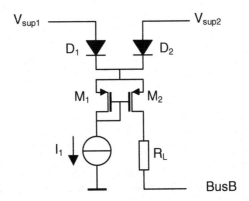

Fig. 6. Level shifting principle

As an example of a slave, the block diagram of a deployment slave is presented in Figure 7. Using the diode the voltage of the power level is stored on capacitor C_1. A charge pump creates a higher voltage of the order of 20V. This voltage is stored on C_2 and can be used to fire the squib by closing the switches. To avoid inadvertent firing of the airbag, two switches are used. Furthermore, capacitor C_2 is only charged when a number of diagnostics have been performed and the firing command should use the special data level 'S0' for the whole firing message.

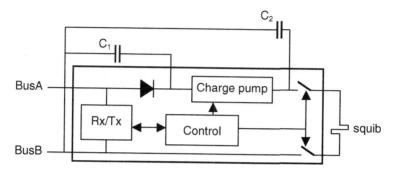

Fig. 7. Block diagram of a deployment slave

4 Conclusion

In order to reduce the complexity of modern airbag networks, the Safe-by-Wire bus standard has been created. This standard has briefly been discussed and some of the most important implementation details have been shown, these include the use of a floating power supply and the level shifting of signals between ground and the floating bus system.

References

1. "Safe-by-Wire Plus, Automotive Safety Restraints Bus Specification", Version 2.0, September 24, 2004.
2. K.J. de Langen, B. Singh, E. Toy, "Level shifting circuit between isolated systems," *U.S. patent application 20060001447*, January 5, 2006.

Author Index

Lecture Notes in Computer Science

For information about Vols. 1–3983

please contact your bookseller or Springer

Vol. 4031: M. Ali, R. Dapoigny (Eds.), Innovations in Applied Artificial Intelligence. XXIII, 1353 pages. 2006. (Sublibrary LNAI).

Vol. 4029: L. Rutkowski, R. Tadeusiewicz, L.A. Zadeh, J. Zurada (Eds.), Artificial Intelligence and Soft Computing – ICAISC 2006. XXI, 1235 pages. 2006. (Sublibrary LNAI).

Vol. 4027: H.L. Larsen, G. Pasi, D. Ortiz-Arroyo, T. Andreasen, H. Christiansen (Eds.), Flexible Query Answering Systems. XVIII, 714 pages. 2006. (Sublibrary LNAI).

Vol. 4026: P.B. Gibbons, T. Abdelzaher, J. Aspnes, R. Rao (Eds.), Distributed Computing in Sensor Systems. XIV, 566 pages. 2006.

Vol. 4025: F. Eliassen, A. Montresor (Eds.), Distributed Applications and Interoperable Systems. XI, 355 pages. 2006.

Vol. 4024: S. Donatelli, P. S. Thiagarajan (Eds.), Petri Nets and Other Models of Concurrency - ICATPN 2006. XI, 441 pages. 2006.

Vol. 4021: E. André, L. Dybkjær, W. Minker, H. Neumann, M. Weber (Eds.), Perception and Interactive Technologies. XI, 217 pages. 2006. (Sublibrary LNAI).

Vol. 4020: A. Bredenfeld, A. Jacoff, I. Noda, Y. Takahashi (Eds.), RoboCup 2005: Robot Soccer World Cup IX. XVII, 727 pages. 2006. (Sublibrary LNAI).

Vol. 4019: M. Johnson, V. Vene (Eds.), Algebraic Methodology and Software Technology. XI, 389 pages. 2006.

Vol. 4018: V. Wade, H. Ashman, B. Smyth (Eds.), Adaptive Hypermedia and Adaptive Web-Based Systems. XVI, 474 pages. 2006.

Vol. 4017: S. Vassiliadis, S. Wong, T.D. Hämäläinen (Eds.), Embedded Computer Systems: Architectures, Modeling, and Simulation. XV, 492 pages. 2006.

Vol. 4016: J.X. Yu, M. Kitsuregawa, H.V. Leong (Eds.), Advances in Web-Age Information Management. XVII, 606 pages. 2006.

Vol. 4014: T. Uustalu (Ed.), Mathematics of Program Construction. X, 455 pages. 2006.

Vol. 4013: L. Lamontagne, M. Marchand (Eds.), Advances in Artificial Intelligence. XIII, 564 pages. 2006. (Sublibrary LNAI).

Vol. 4012: T. Washio, A. Sakurai, K. Nakajima, H. Takeda, S. Tojo, M. Yokoo (Eds.), New Frontiers in Artificial Intelligence. XIII, 484 pages. 2006. (Sublibrary LNAI).

Vol. 4011: Y. Sure, J. Domingue (Eds.), The Semantic Web: Research and Applications. XIX, 726 pages. 2006.

Vol. 4010: S. Dunne, B. Stoddart (Eds.), Unifying Theories of Programming. VIII, 257 pages. 2006.

Vol. 4009: M. Lewenstein, G. Valiente (Eds.), Combinatorial Pattern Matching. XII, 414 pages. 2006.

Vol. 4008: J.C. Augusto, C.D. Nugent (Eds.), Designing Smart Homes. XI, 183 pages. 2006. (Sublibrary LNAI).

Vol. 4007: C. Àlvarez, M. Serna (Eds.), Experimental Algorithms. XI, 329 pages. 2006.

Vol. 4006: L.M. Pinho, M. González Harbour (Eds.), Reliable Software Technologies – Ada-Europe 2006. XII, 241 pages. 2006.

Vol. 4005: G. Lugosi, H.U. Simon (Eds.), Learning Theory. XI, 656 pages. 2006. (Sublibrary LNAI).

Vol. 4004: S. Vaudenay (Ed.), Advances in Cryptology - EUROCRYPT 2006. XIV, 613 pages. 2006.

Vol. 4003: Y. Koucheryavy, J. Harju, V.B. Iversen (Eds.), Next Generation Teletraffic and Wired/Wireless Advanced Networking. XVI, 582 pages. 2006.

Vol. 4001: E. Dubois, K. Pohl (Eds.), Advanced Information Systems Engineering. XVI, 560 pages. 2006.

Vol. 3999: C. Kop, G. Fliedl, H.C. Mayr, E. Métais (Eds.), Natural Language Processing and Information Systems. XIII, 227 pages. 2006.

Vol. 3998: T. Calamoneri, I. Finocchi, G.F. Italiano (Eds.), Algorithms and Complexity. XII, 394 pages. 2006.

Vol. 3997: W. Grieskamp, C. Weise (Eds.), Formal Approaches to Software Testing. XII, 219 pages. 2006.

Vol. 3996: A. Keller, J.-P. Martin-Flatin (Eds.), Self-Managed Networks, Systems, and Services. X, 185 pages. 2006.

Vol. 3995: G. Müller (Ed.), Emerging Trends in Information and Communication Security. XX, 524 pages. 2006.

Vol. 3994: V.N. Alexandrov, G.D. van Albada, P.M.A. Sloot, J. Dongarra, Computational Science – ICCS 2006, Part IV. XXXV, 1096 pages. 2006.

Vol. 3993: V.N. Alexandrov, G.D. van Albada, P.M.A. Sloot, J. Dongarra, Computational Science – ICCS 2006, Part III. XXXVI, 1136 pages. 2006.

Vol. 3992: V.N. Alexandrov, G.D. van Albada, P.M.A. Sloot, J. Dongarra, Computational Science – ICCS 2006, Part II. XXXV, 1122 pages. 2006.

Vol. 3991: V.N. Alexandrov, G.D. van Albada, P.M.A. Sloot, J. Dongarra, Computational Science – ICCS 2006, Part I. LXXXI, 1096 pages. 2006.

Vol. 3990: J. C. Beck, B.M. Smith (Eds.), Integration of AI and OR Techniques in Constraint Programming for Combinatorial Optimization Problems. X, 301 pages. 2006.

Vol. 3989: J. Zhou, M. Yung, F. Bao, Applied Cryptography and Network Security. XIV, 488 pages. 2006.

Vol. 3988: A. Beckmann, U. Berger, B. Löwe, J.V. Tucker (Eds.), Logical Approaches to Computational Barriers. XV, 608 pages. 2006.

Vol. 3987: M. Hazas, J. Krumm, T. Strang (Eds.), Location- and Context-Awareness. X, 289 pages. 2006.

Vol. 3986: K. Stølen, W.H. Winsborough, F. Martinelli, F. Massacci (Eds.), Trust Management. XIV, 474 pages. 2006.

Vol. 3984: M. Gavrilova, O. Gervasi, V. Kumar, C.J. K. Tan, D. Taniar, A. Laganà, Y. Mun, H. Choo (Eds.), Computational Science and Its Applications - ICCSA 2006, Part V. XXV, 1045 pages. 2006.